Gambling
Mapping the American Moral Landscape

Alan Wolfe
Erik C. Owens
editors

BAYLOR UNIVERSITY PRESS

Cover Design by Trudi Gershinov, Trudi Gershinov Design
Cover image © Corbis Premium RF / Alamy. Used by
permission.

Library of Congress Cataloging-in-Publication Data

Gambling : mapping the American moral landscape / Alan
Wolfe and Erik C. Owens, editors.
    p. cm.
  Includes bibliographical references and index.
  ISBN 978-1-60258-195-1 (pbk. : alk. paper)
  1. Gambling--Moral and ethical aspects--United States. I.
Wolfe, Alan, 1942- II. Owens, Erik C.

  HV6715.G2856 2009
  175--dc22

                              2009010370

Printed in the United States of America on acid-free paper
with a minimum of 30% recycled content.

Contents

Acknowledgments

Early drafts of chapters in this volume were first presented at a conference entitled "Gambling and the American Moral Landscape," held at Boston College in October 2007. After two years of planning, the conference coincidentally took place amidst a surge of public interest in the topic in Massachusetts, where the governor had recently proposed expanding the state's legal gambling options to include three resort casinos. Documentary filmmakers from London, England and Richmond, Virginia filmed portions of the conference, and local media and political leaders took the opportunity to speak with the assembled experts. The conference was hosted by the Boisi Center for Religion and American Public Life (whose director and assistant director are this book's editors), with generous financial assistance from the Smith Richardson Foundation. We therefore begin our thanks with special appreciation to Mark Steinmeyer, the foundation's senior program officer for domestic public policy, for his support of this project. (For more information about the conference, please visit http://www.bc.edu/gambling, where you can download audio recordings of the presentations, view photos, and catch up on gambling-related news. Information about the Boisi Center is available at http://www.bc.edu/boisi.)

Of course we would not have a book of this caliber without the sterling work of its contributors. We thank them for the terrific chapters they offer here and for their energetic engagement at the conference that began this project.

We are delighted to work with the talented and tireless staff at Baylor University Press, and we thank director Carey Newman, editor Casey Blaine and the rest of the editorial staff for sharing our enthusiasm about this project.

Finally, we thank the staff and research assistants at the Boisi Center for their work on various aspects of this project. Susan Richard's daily contributions have kept the Boisi Center running for the past nine years; Andrew Finstuen helped to draft the original project proposal; Suzanne Hevelone provided much-appreciated editorial assistance; Matthew Bagot, John Crowley-Buck, Hillary Thompson and Karen Teel provided important research and logistical support for the conference; Isabelle Martinez designed and maintained the conference Web site; and Joshua Darr provided extensive bibliographical support. We couldn't have done it without you.

Alan Wolfe and Erik Owens
Chestnut Hill, Massachusetts
July 2008

Introduction

Alan Wolfe and Erik C. Owens

Gambling has had an astonishingly broad impact on American life, yet the academic attention paid to it has been uneven at best. In 2005 the American Gaming Association estimated total revenue from gambling at $84.65 billion for the year—nearly ten times the amount Americans spent on movie tickets, and similarly dwarfing the revenues from sporting events, concerts, books, and newspaper publishing. That year, American Indian casinos together accounted for $22.62 billion in revenues, while state-run lotteries collected vast sums in Massachusetts ($4.4 billion), California ($3.6 billion), and Connecticut ($970 million). The numbers testify to just how ubiquitous gambling has become in American society. Yet for years sociologists ignored its impact on the family, historians (save for a precious few) were more interested in Prohibition or prostitution, and economists treated gamblers as more likely to be addicted or obsessive than motivated by considerations of rational self-interest.

The editors of this book understand that academic interest in gambling will never grow at the same rate as gambling itself. Nonetheless, we are convinced that there is an increasing interest across many academic disciplines in the phenomenon and that, as a result, academics are beginning to develop the tools to understand why gambling has become so prevalent in American culture—as well as what the consequences of that fact are likely to be. *Gambling: Mapping the American Moral Landscape* originated as a conference at Boston College that sought to bring together experts from a wide variety of backgrounds to analyze the role gambling plays in American life. Some were specialists on the topic; others were experts in fields such as theology, moral philosophy, and sociology who were intrigued by the prospect of addressing gambling from the perspective of their discipline. The conference was well attended, exciting, and newsworthy. We hope the book will be equally well received.

Not long ago, legal gambling was confined to one state, Nevada, which had developed a reputation along the way as the place to get divorced or buy sex; things forbidden everywhere else were permitted there. We usually think of taboos as deeply entrenched, separating the dirty from the clean, yet not only are Las Vegas and other Nevada cities now among the fastest growing in the United States, gambling in one form or another is now permitted in forty-eight of the fifty American states, plus the District of Columbia. (The exceptions are Utah and Hawaii.)

Gambling, moreover, has taken root in a country with a Puritan background that is to this day marked by its public religiosity. Once upon a time, religious figures were second to none in their condemnation of gambling: Billy Sunday, the prototypical right-wing revivalist, denounced it in his sermons in the early twentieth century, while Walter Rauschenbusch, the left-wing founder of the Social Gospel, called it "the vice of the savage." Yet in contemporary America, not only are religious figures unable to make much of a dent in the public's attraction to gambling, some of them have themselves been gamblers (most conspicuously *Book of Virtues* author William J. Bennett), while others (in particular Ralph Reed, former executive director of the Christian Coalition) have earned enormous paychecks for lobbying Congress on behalf of the American Indian gaming industry.

It would be easy to conclude that gambling has become so prominent in American life because we have become a hedonistic country in which anything goes. But as Father Richard McGowan, a Jesuit priest and gambling expert at Boston College, reminds us in his contribution to this volume, just thirty years ago gambling was considered a sin while smoking was fashionable, whereas today the reverse is true. We continue to be deeply puritanical in some aspects of our culture while decidedly libertarian in others. At a time when free speech activists condemn hate speech, feminists campaign against pornography, and politicians support zero tolerance for drinking or sexual misconduct, gambling is on the rise. It resonates with the permissive rather than the prohibitive side of our culture.

Far from being a simple matter in which religion has treated gambling as a sin, moreover, the relationship between faith and betting is complex and nuanced. At least four chapters in this book address those complexities. In "Grace and Gambling," theologian Kathryn Tanner updates Pascal's famous wager to demonstrate the many ways in which Christians treat faith as a good bet, even as they are and ought to be witnesses against a culture of consumption. William Stuntz and David Skeel examine in their chapter the ways in which evangelical Protestants, who once treated sin as a theological violation of the contract between people and God, began to view sin as a criminal violation of the contract between people and the state. Like other adherents of world religions, Jews have had a long history of interest in— and at least partial opposition to—gambling, as William Galston points out in "The Memory of Sin" and Dwayne Carpenter recalls in "Playing and Praying." Islamic laws traditionally forbid gambling, but resort casinos are enormously profitable—and capital intensive—enterprises that have begun to draw large investments from Muslim sovereign wealth funds bulging with oil revenues. (The chief example here is Dubai World, whose multibillion dollar investment in American casino operator MGM Mirage has financed MGM's massive new project in Las Vegas.) Gambling and religion have been both friends and enemies.

Given these complications, it should not be surprising that gambling has failed to generate substantial political opposition. Whenever people on one side of a political issue mobilize, people on the other side generally counter-mobilize; this has happened in recent years on issues ranging from abortion to gay rights. But the growth in gaming, as Alan Wolfe argues in this book, has not produced an antigambling movement. Republican conservatives who believe that we can regulate morality tend to be sympathetic toward business, and gambling is big business indeed. Democrats who distrust business not only tend to be laissez-faire with respect to moral issues, but also have ambitious plans to spend any revenues that gambling might bring in, usually for education.

Perhaps the single best explanation for the absence of a strong antigambling movement in American politics is offered in this book by Michael Nelson. In "The Politics of Sovereignty and Public Policy toward Gambling," Nelson recounts how California's Proposition 13 (a ballot initiative that slashed property taxes) spurred the national "tax revolt" of 1978. Facing aggressive opposition to higher taxes, California and other states turned to gambling revenues to fill the budget gap. Gambling revenues were a boon to Republicans who did not want to raise taxes and to Democrats who were afraid to try. Tax policy, as much as anything else, initiated the modern era of gambling in the United States. But once the gambling revenue ball got rolling, as Shep Melnick points out in "New Politics, Same Old Vice," it became hard to stop. Unlike the American prohibitionist movement, a movement to ban gambling is unlikely to gain similar approval in state legislatures or the U.S. Congress, especially considering the financial incentives that gambling offers to state governments and corporations.

Gambling is also intimately tied up with our complicated history of race. American Indians are among the most impoverished and historically oppressed minority groups in the United States, yet a 1987 U.S. Supreme Court decision (*California v. Cabazon Band of Mission Indians*) laid the groundwork for the establishment of hundreds of tribal casinos that would, by 2008, be within a short drive of nearly every American. The world's largest and most profitable casino, Foxwoods, is owned by the Mashantucket Pequot Tribal Nation and operated on its tribal lands in rural Connecticut. But as Kathryn R.L. Rand and Steven Andrew Light show in "Negotiating a Different Terrain," most tribal casinos are quite small in comparison and provide Indian nations only minimal levels of income.

Meanwhile, state lotteries remain the most lucrative gambling enterprise for state coffers (to the tune of $56 billion in revenues in 2006), even as they disproportionately draw their revenues from the poorest and least-educated sectors of society. Researchers consistently find an inverse correlation between a person's level of education and the amount she spends in the lottery, so it is no small irony that more than half the states with lotteries devote some or all of the proceeds to public education. A better-educated community should mean considerably smaller lottery revenues, yet states spent nearly a half-billion dollars in advertising last year to perpetuate the existing cycle by convincing us that the odds are not too low to gamble with our paychecks. All this adds up to a fraught moral and political context that Erik Owens examines in his chapter.

And then there is Internet gambling, which in 2005 was an almost $6 billion industry and growing. If the Internet had not existed, poker players would have found a way to invent it. Gambling has always involved a certain amount of role playing and theater—an individual can be Willy Loman at home but can be anyone he imagines himself to be in Las Vegas—but now that person does not need to travel to Nevada to assume a new identity. Nor would he even need to come face-to-face with other people: the Internet provides an around-the-clock way, largely immune from effective regulation, to try your luck at games of skill and chance. P. T. Barnum is reputed to have said that there is a sucker born every minute; in the age of the Internet, a gambler is born every millisecond.

Gambling, as a result, has now entered the nation's living rooms. As John Dombrink argues in his chapter, gambling has become "normalized"; we might be tempted to view it as pathological or deviant, but it is now part of the way we live. This should not come as a complete surprise, for as the historian Jackson Lears argues in "Beyond Pathology: The Cultural Meanings of Gambling," Americans have always been fascinated by the culture of risk. We pay a cost for gambling's ubiquity, particularly as we are "Gambling with the Family," as John P. Hoffmann puts it in his chapter. Problematic and pathological gamblers do exist, Hoffmann notes, and their families often suffer considerably. Just because something is ubiquitous does not mean it is good, and as the popularity of this way of life expands in coming years, we will surely require more studies of gambling's impact upon our social institutions.

Gambling's return to prominence has stimulated the interests of students of human behavior, especially in the fields of psychology and economics. Marc Potenza brings a neuropsychiatric perspective to the issue by documenting the ways in which our brains respond to the excitement of the wagering experience. Does this mean that people who gamble are acting in fundamentally irrational ways, especially given the fact that the odds against their winning are so considerable? Indeed in many ways it does, argue behavioral economists who, in recent years, have begun to question assumptions of rationality that are at the heart of neoclassical economics. Rachel Croson and colleagues James Sundali and Matthew Fox offer fascinating examples of the way gamblers try to deal with the odds against them in "Behavioral and Brain Measures of Risk-Taking." After observing gamblers in action, Croson and her colleagues point out that many gamblers are engaged, even obsessed, but not necessarily happy or proud.

Gamblers are much happier, of course—and gamble much more frequently—when the odds of winning are increased. Raising the "payout rate" by giving a greater percentage of revenues away as prizes is one of the key policy options available to state lottery officials. In the book's opening chapter, "The Importance of a Good Cause," Charles Clotfelter and Philip Cook, two of the country's foremost analysts of gambling policy and economics, argue that increasing the payout rate is much more effective in spurring lottery ticket sales than reminders of the good causes to which the profits are applied. Clotfelter and Cook carefully document and evaluate the revenue maximizing objectives of state lotteries, and offer key insights into the issues that will define lottery governance in the coming decades.

Gambling: Mapping the American Moral Landscape does not cover every issue raised by the rise of gambling, in part because there remain serious gaps in the way the subject is treated in the academic world. Gambling features in the works of Dickens, Trollope, Thackeray, Melville, and Twain; it is the subject of numerous films and plays; and is indispensable to Tchaikovsky's opera *The Queen of Spades* (based on Pushkin), Prokofiev's *The Gambler* (based on Dostoyevsky), Smetana's *The Bartered Bride*, and Mozart's *Così Fan Tutte*. Yet it is difficult to find scholars of literature and music writing about the subject. Law professors, philosophers, and theologians do not debate the morality of gambling the way they do the morality of abortion or euthanasia. Gambling is one industry upon which few schools of business administration focus. Although we very much wanted a paper on the subject for our conference and book, we were unable to find ethnographic treatments dealing with the popularity of gambling among the inner-city poor, people who in percentage terms gamble and lose the most. We hope that the publication of this volume will stimulate further interest in these and other subjects.

Consider this book, then, a beginning. We end this introduction by noting that we are betting on continued interest in the subject—but it really is not a bet at all. Although we try to keep our own moral views on the subject separate from our analysis, both of us find much that is problematic in the culture of gambling. Still, there is almost no prospect that Americans will return to the days when it was legal in only one state. To call for greater academic interest in the subject, in that sense, is not a gamble at all; it is simply a recognition of reality.

THE POLITICS AND POLICY
OF GAMBLING

1

The Importance of a Good Cause
Ends and Means in State Lotteries

Charles T. Clotfelter and Philip J. Cook

Lottery gambling is a problematic activity: those opposed to gambling on moral grounds object to government sponsorship of lotteries; revenues raised from them have distributional patterns similar to regressive taxes; and, like other forms of widely available commercial gambling, they create economic and personal difficulties for the small portion of the population who are problem gamblers. Nonetheless, lotteries are sponsored by forty-three U.S. states and over one hundred countries. The deal that typically has been struck in the United States is that lottery revenue will be dedicated to good public causes. This virtuous end thus serves to justify the dubious means. Almost never are state lotteries seen as a public service. The closest that proponents come to justifying lotteries in this way is the argument that people will gamble anyway, so government might as well take advantage of this predilection by making money on it.

The government's accommodation to lotteries is strikingly different from the ways that the government has dealt with other problematic activities. For example, states with monopolies over liquor distribution run that business primarily as a public service rather than as a revenue source. Furthermore, some states license certain commercial gambling operations and collect revenues without any concern for applying those collections to a virtuous purpose. Other problematic activities have generally not been legalized—among them, marijuana, prostitution, and cockfighting—although states could raise money for good causes by legalizing and heavily taxing them. What are the limits when it comes to public provision of "soft-core" vices?

In these cases, it is second nature in the utilitarian realm of normative economics to think about tradeoffs between the costs associated with legalizing and operating problematic activities and the benefits derived from the revenue their taxation would make possible. This realm is a natural setting for debating the classic ends-versus-means question, given that it arises with such force in the context of problematic activities. In the case of lotteries, the ends-and-means tension extends beyond the legalization question. Once a lottery is in place, the amount of revenue it generates depends largely on how it is marketed. Do the "ends" of more revenue justify aggressive or deceptive marketing efforts? Do they justify advertising that emphasizes the virtuous use of the funds (if indeed it can be honestly argued that the funds will be used in this way)? And why have the states—up to now—created lotteries as public agencies, rather than licensing one or more private providers? Would privatization ease the moral liability of the state government?

This chapter seeks to address these questions with particular attention to alternative theories of the public interest and the proper role of government, with an eye toward historical precedents and current methods of lottery operation, including a close examination of the themes used in advertising campaigns. Included too is some background for viewing the operation of contemporary state lotteries, as well as an examination of how good causes influence the adoption and operation of state lotteries.

Background

Arising out of the ashes of nineteenth-century disrepute and universal prohibition, state lotteries reemerged in the last third of the twentieth century to become an unremarkable fixture in the architecture of American state government. State lotteries made their twentieth-century debut in 1964, when New Hampshire introduced its game. The number of states with lotteries grew to seven by 1973, thirty-eight by 1997, and forty-three by 2007. Public acceptance, measured by successful referenda and growing sales, has increased as well. Per capita purchases of lottery tickets grew more than fourfold in inflation-adjusted dollars between 1973 and 2006, to $184.[1]

TABLE 1.1

U.S. State Lotteries: Number and Per Capita Sales, Selected Years

Year	Number of state lotteries	Per capita sales* (FY 2006 dollars)
1973	7	43
1987	23	157
1997	38	186
2006	43	184

Sources: Clotfelter et al., *State Lotteries at the Turn of the Century*, table 1; *International Gaming and Wagering Business*, April 2007, 27.
*Per capita sales utilize the total population (all ages) of residents of states with a lottery. Sales exclude video lottery terminal games.

Although remarkable for its speed, this growth is better judged when viewed in a longer historical lens and in the context of similar developments in other spheres and countries. In all of these applications, two forces can be seen to motivate the growth, while another force serves to restrain it. The first motivating force is the search for financial backing for civic needs (public goods, in the terminology of economics) and other "good causes." The second is the widespread impulse of people to gamble, which rather naturally leads to the realization that operating such games can be a remunerative undertaking. These two motivating forces for lotteries contend against a variable but ever-present base of opposition, often growing out of moral objections to gambling of all forms.

Before turning to a more formal consideration of the role of good causes in state lotteries, we briefly review the history and context of American lotteries. We draw particular attention to the uses of lotteries in financing early public projects and contemporary charitable organizations, note two kinds of European lotteries, and present a brief overview of structural aspects and policy questions applying to today's state lotteries in the United States.

American Lotteries through the Nineteenth Century

Lotteries came to America with its first European settlers. They were a fixture in the Colonial period, used to finance such prominent projects as Jamestown Settlement, the Continental Army, and buildings at Harvard, Yale, and Columbia. Lottery supporters included such revered figures as Benjamin Franklin, George Washington, and Thomas Jefferson. Before and after independence, state legislatures authorized lotteries for a host of projects, including bridges, wharfs, churches, and schools, but the early decades of the nineteenth century saw the orientation of lotteries gradually shift from civic to commercial aims and then come under the influence of increasingly shady operators. This descent into disrepute reached its nadir with the infamous Louisiana Lottery, which combined questionable commercial practices with rampant political corruption. By 1894 no state permitted lotteries, and 35 states had explicit prohibitions in their constitutions against them. Congress banned all interstate lottery commerce in 1895.

But if we return to the more noble decades of lottery operation in our early history, we can observe the forces operating both for and against the idea of lotteries as a means of raising money. In the several decades before and after independence, colonial or state legislatures typically authorized a limited number of lotteries for capital projects while strictly forbidding all other lotteries. According to the most authoritative count, the thirteen colonies authorized 164 different lotteries in the three decades between 1744 and 1774. Another 82 were authorized by states shortly after the Revolution, between 1782 and 1789.[2] Although it may seem jarring to today's sensibilities, it was quite common in the country's early years to have state legislatures authorizing lotteries to finance the building or repairing of churches and parsonages. Between 1727 and 1824, for example, almost half of all authorized lotteries in New Jersey were devoted to church projects.[3] These ecclesiastical construction projects represented the essence of the "good cause." How much so is admirably illustrated in the announcement of a lottery authorized by the

New Jersey legislature in 1758 (as published in the New-York Mercury):

> Whereas the Dutch and English of said Society, have laboured under great Difficulties, for want of a House to worship God in; and at Length have raised a Sum of Money by Way of Subscription; but is found insufficient for finishing said Church. It is therefore thought proper to raise the Sum of Fifteen Hundred Dollars, by Way of Lottery, for finishing said Church. It is therefore hoped that all Well-wishers for promoting the Gospel, will adventure largely, in order to forward said Building. The Lottery consists of 5,000 Tickets, at Two Dollars each; 1,234 of which are to be fortunate, and 15 per Cent. will be deducted from the Prizes after the Drawing is finished, for the Use above-mentioned.[4]

Consistent with the project's high-minded purposes, the organizers had chosen justices from Somerset County, New Jersey, to be inspectors for the lottery and had selected local reputable citizens to be its managers.[5]

A second example illustrates a more secular type of "good cause," one less charitable than civic, but nonetheless contributing clearly to the public good. This was one of the dozen lotteries authorized by the Connecticut legislature between 1775 and 1789, and the object was a structure still recognized today, the Long Wharf in New Haven. Owing to the advantageous features of its natural harbor, New Haven became a port of considerable importance in the late eighteenth century, but it needed a wharf to harness its natural advantages for commercial success. Beginning in the early eighteenth century, the town of New Haven had funded the construction of a wharf in the harbor, and its upkeep and improvement was sustained through fees paid by shippers to the wharf's commercial operators. By the 1760s, however, these arrangements were evidently insufficient to keep the wharf from deteriorating, so the owners appealed to the state legislature for the right to raise money through a lottery. In 1772 the legislature agreed, authorizing one or more lotteries, but setting four conditions: a minimum of 10 percent of sales had to be used for the project, excess profits had to be appropriated to Yale College, refunds had to be given in the event lottery sales could not sustain the promised prizes, and a short list of prominent citizens had to serve as approved lottery overseers.[6]

These two examples illustrate two important aspects of early American lotteries. First, in an age of rudimentary capital markets and tiny tax bases, lotteries represented one of the few fiscal institutions capable of raising the kind of money required for large capital projects such as bridges, college buildings, and wharfs. Second, as signified by their authorization by state legislatures and the routine participation of prominent and respected citizens in their management, these lotteries were infused with civic justification. The "good cause" was every bit as much at their core as the lack of alternative avenues of finance.

Two more aspects of these early lotteries are equally ever present: widespread popularity and concentrated opposition. Lotteries could not have been a viable means of finance without a robust demand for this kind of gambling. Although some lotteries failed to meet their intended sales target, that may have been more because of the excessive proliferation of lotteries than any lack of demand.[7] At the same time, lotteries inspired denunciation by a few religious traditions, most notably the Quakers. The moral objections to lotteries are well summarized in a letter to the editor of the *Connecticut Evangelical Magazine and Religious Intelligencer* in 1811. Besides being a waste of time, a diversion from worthwhile pursuits, and an inducement to covetousness, penned the letter writer, they led to the exploitation of the uninformed common people by the rich and sophisticated. Yet this particular writer displays a very modern ethical orientation and allows the ultimate desirability of the lottery to be based on a weighing of the benefits of the project against the costs of giving expression "to the corrupt propensities of the heart." In a dictum worthy of a twenty-first century school of public policy, the writer concludes that lotteries may be justified when they enable beneficial, nonrecurring expenditures:

> The result of the whole is, that the legislature is justified in granting lotteries for the attainment of objects important to the welfare of church or state, not constantly occurring, and permanent in their effects, when the state of things will not suffer them to have recourse to better means.[8]

Charity Raffles and Other Gambling

A second demonstration of the close connection between lotteries and good causes is the contemporary use of gambling to raise money for charitable organizations. The use of raffles, bazaars, and bingo for fundraising by churches and other nonprofits is commonplace, uncontroversial, and legal in most U.S. states. State laws are typically written to provide an exception for charitable organizations in their laws otherwise forbidding nongovernmental lotteries and other games of chance.[9] For example, Massachusetts law states, "No raffle or bazaar shall be promoted, operated or conducted by any person or organization, unless the same is sponsored and conducted exclusively by" any one of a number of categories of nonprofit, charitable organizations.[10] The law imposes the following extra conditions on the organization: it must have operated in the state for at least two years; the game must be operated exclusively by members of the organization, none of whom can receive remuneration by virtue of the game; and earnings from the game must be used exclusively for the organization's charitable purposes. The state requires organizations to obtain permits for such games and to pay a 5 percent tax on gross proceeds.[11] Similarly, North Carolina law states an explicit allowance for raffles operated by any recognized nonprofit organization, provided, as in the case of Massachusetts, that no one receives remuneration. In addition, the law limits organizations to two games a year, sets a maximum prize amount, and requires that 90 percent of the net revenues after prizes be used for the charitable purpose.[12]

Albeit on a much smaller relative scale than were the lotteries of early America, this charitable use of lotteries shares a similar explanation with those early examples: a worthy cause and the absence of good alternative means of financing. To be sure, churches and other nonprofits can solicit donations, but these forms of gambling have established themselves as secondary or tertiary sources of funding. To illustrate the relative magnitudes in one state, charity raffles accounted for about $20 million in ticket sales in Massachusetts in fiscal year 2005, or about $3 per capita. This total was swamped by bingo and other forms of charity games, though, which was almost five times that amount. And both of these categories of charity gaming fade into insignificance when compared to the state's lottery sales of $4.5 billion, or about $700 per capita.[13]

These days, not all of what goes under the heading of "charity" raffles appears to be intimately associated with an obvious charitable cause. A cursory search on Google.com for "charity raffles" uncovered some drawings that were explicitly linked to charitable causes and organizations and some for which any charitable link was obscure at best. In the first group was a raffle sponsored by the Child Life Activity Center for young patients in the Arizona Cancer Center and online raffles sponsored by the American Cancer Fund and Paws4people. For other raffles, no charitable purpose could easily be discerned on the Web page. A telling statistic based on one day's search revealed that, among the Web addresses of the sponsoring organizations, more ended in ".com" than ".org"[14]

European Lotteries

Lotteries have a long history in Europe and operate at the national level under the sponsorship of both charities and national governments. Under either authority, they feature good causes as a prominent part of their operation and public image. European lotteries make explicit appeal to the socially beneficial byproducts of their operation. Two good examples of the prominence of good causes are the UK National Lottery and the publicly authorized but charitably operated Dutch Postal Code Lottery.

Britain was late in adopting a national lottery, although betting was permitted in sports pools, charity sweepstakes, and racetracks before the lottery's adoption in 1993. Operated by a private company rather than by a government agency, the UK lottery pays 12 percent of its revenues to the government in the form of a tax and devotes another 28 percent to a fund, out of which are distributed numerous grants. The organizations and mechanisms established to do this distribution appear to have been designed to maximize transparency, visibility, easy participation, and wide distribution. Grants are made to organizations devoted to arts, recreation, historical preservation, education, and health; they include both large and small amounts; they touch all corners of the United Kingdom; and they are trumpeted widely. Not only does the lottery describe these grants in detail, it has created an

annual contest in which citizens vote for the most deserving beneficiaries, thus raising awareness through competition. Among
the 2006 winners in this contest were a recreational trail linking
the east and west coasts of England's Midlands, a charity offering groceries and meals to persons with HIV/AIDS, a pipe band
for a Scottish town, and an arts project for visually impaired
youth in Wales.[15]

The Dutch Postal Code Lottery offers a second example. A
charitable lottery, as distinguished from the country's official
national lottery, the postal code lottery is noteworthy on at least
two counts. First, it utilizes a unique tie-in to neighborhoods.
A person's postal code makes up part of his or her ticket number for each drawing, and the winning number in each drawing is a postal code. All those in the postal code who bought a
ticket receive a sizable prize (12,500 euros per ticket), and one
lucky player in the code wins a BMW. Thus all the winners in a
drawing occupy the same neighborhood, insuring a geographical focal point for stories about winners. The postal code lottery's second noteworthy feature is the effort to draw attention
to prominent international good causes in addition to charitable organizations within the Netherlands. Among the international organizations this charitable lottery has supported are
Oxfam, Doctors without Borders, Greenpeace, and Amnesty
International. To publicize the drawings and recipients, the lottery enlists the voluntary services of luminaries from sports and
business as well as internationally known leaders such as Nelson
Mandela and Mikhail Gorbachev.[16]

Contemporary American State Lotteries

Since New Hampshire legalized the first twentieth-century state
lottery in 1964, lotteries have been adopted by one state after
another so that now over 90 percent of the U.S. population lives in
a lottery state. By 1973 seven states (all but one in the Northeast)
had adopted lotteries, and another fifteen plus the District of
Columbia had joined in by 1987. In 2007 forty-two states in all
parts of the country plus D.C. now have lotteries. Average spending on lottery products exceeds $180 per capita (in 2006 dol-
lars) in states with lotteries.[17] Contemporary lotteries offer six
types of games, as shown in table 1.2. These games differ in

some important ways, so much so that one of them (video lottery terminals) is often not counted alongside the others. Perhaps the simplest of all lottery games is the raffle, wherein prenumbered tickets are sold, after which a drawing is held to determine the winning ticket numbers. These few elements constituted the core of the early American lotteries as well as the first modern lotteries in the 1960s. After nearly falling out of use among the games used by state lotteries, these passive games have recently made a comeback, with some of them being sold in denominations of $5 and $10 (and more). The second type of game, which is also the biggest selling one, is the instant, or scratch-off, game, accounting for almost half of total lottery sales in 2004. Usually sold for prices ranging from $1 to $5, these brightly colored tickets bear phrases and pictures depicting some theme. On them are latex coverings that, when scratched with a coin or other hard object, reveal symbols or numbers that immediately indicate whether the ticket holder is a winner.

TABLE 1.2
Lottery Sales by Type of Game (Fiscal Year 2004)

Game	Sales ($ billions)
Instant	23.0
Daily numbers	8.6
Lotto	10.5
Video lottery terminals[a]	3.2
Other[b]	2.4
Total	47.7

Sources: United States Bureau of the Census, Statistical Abstract, 302, table 446; *International Gaming and Wagering Business*, April 2007, pp. 27–28.
[a]Estimated, based on proportion of traditional sales plus net machine income from gaming device operations, for fiscal year 2006. In FY 2006, revenue for gaming devices was $14.5 billion, and net machine income was $3.7 billion.
[b]Includes break-open tickets, spiel, and Keno.

The remaining lottery games require a degree of player involvement that goes beyond the purchase and scratch. Lotto, the game of large jackpots and occasional frenzies of popular attention, is a computer-based game wherein players choose a series of numbers (typically six) out of a much larger field of possible numbers. The most distinctive aspect of this game is a winner's jackpot that grows until some player correctly picks all the numbers produced in a drawing. Drawings typically occur twice a week. The fourth game is a daily drawing closely parallel to the long-established illegal numbers game. Players pick three- or four-digit numbers and receive payouts for various types of bets on those numbers. The fifth game, Keno, is similar to lotto, except that drawings can occur as frequently as every few minutes. Developed in casinos, this game requires a setting with networked computers, such as a tavern. The last type of game, played on video lottery terminals (VLT), takes the frequency of betting to its logical maximum, allowing players to place bets as fast as they can manipulate the controls on a machine. In most respects, these games are much more akin to slot machines than to the raffles of yore. Because these VLT games offer so many opportunities per hour to place bets, the total amount bet on them (the "handle") is not very comparable with the sales of most other lottery games, and so they are often presented separately in statistical compilations. In addition, these games are considered to have a greater potential for addiction than other lottery games.

The basics of lottery finance can be discerned by examining how the revenue from a dollar of sales is spent by lottery agencies. As shown in table 1.3, the average state lottery returns 60.3 cents in prizes for every dollar of ticket purchases. Of the remainder, an average of 10.7 cents goes for commissions paid to retailers and other operating expenses, leaving 29 cents to be used by the state as public revenue. This breakdown is comparable to an excise tax of 29 cents imposed on a product that costs 71 cents, for a percentage rate of 41 percent (29. 0/71.0). Such a high percentage rate is virtually unheard of among real-world excise taxes. Furthermore, lottery prizes are considered taxable income in the United States. The high rate of implicit taxation and the use of advertising to increase sales suggest that the state lotteries are all built around the goal of generating revenue for the state. For obvious reasons, we have dubbed this model the "Revenue Lottery."[18]

TABLE 1.3

U.S. State Lotteries, FY 2006: Sales, Prizes, Operating Expenses, and Net Revenue

State	Total sales ($ millions)	Per capita ($)	Prizes (%)	Operating expenses (%)	Net revenue (%)
Arizona	468.7	76	55.3	14.8	29.9
California	3,585.0	98	53.9	11.5	34.6
Colorado	468.8	99	60.1	13.9	26.0
Connecticut	970.3	277	60.5	10.1	29.4
Delaware	124.5	146	52.1	15.1	32.8
District of Columbia	266.4	458	55.1	17.7	27.2
Florida	3,929.0	217	59.6	9.5	31.0
Georgia	3,177.6	339	64.1	10.4	25.5
Idaho	131.1	89	58.5	16.0	25.6
Illinois	1,964.3	153	59.0	10.2	30.8
Indiana	816.4	129	60.4	12.8	26.8
Iowa	218.1	73	56.1	19.7	24.3
Kansas	236.0	85	55.5	15.5	29.0
Kentucky	742.3	176	59.9	12.8	27.3
Louisiana	332.1	77	50.7	14.0	35.3
Maine	229.7	174	62.8	15.3	21.9
Maryland	1,560.9	278	57.9	10.1	32.0
Massachusetts	4,501.2	699	71.9	7.5	20.6
Michigan	2,212.4	219	58.7	11.9	29.4
Minnesota	449.7	87	59.5	14.3	26.2
Missouri	913.5	156	62.7	10.2	27.1
Montana	39.9	42	51.9	25.8	22.3
Nebraska	113.1	64	56.3	17.4	26.2
New Hampshire	262.7	200	58.0	11.8	30.2
New Jersey	2,405.9	276	57.4	9.2	33.4
New Mexico	154.6	79	57.7	18.8	23.5
New York	6,487.1	336	59.4	9.8	30.8
North Carolina	229.5	26	58.0	14.7	27.3
North Dakota	22.3	35	49.5	20.5	30.0

State	Total sales ($ millions)	Per capita ($)	Prizes (%)	Operating expenses (%)	Net revenue (%)
Ohio	2,220.9	193	59.0	11.2	29.7
Oklahoma	204.8	57	53.5	12.7	33.7
Oregon	363.1	98	65.2	16.0	18.8
Pennsylvania	3,070.3	247	58.8	10.5	30.7
Rhode Island	261.1	245	60.5	15.6	23.9
South Carolina	1,144.6	265	61.4	11.2	27.5
South Dakota	39.4	50	56.7	21.2	22.0
Tennessee	995.8	165	62.3	11.8	25.9
Texas	3,774.7	161	61.2	10.0	28.8
Vermont	104.9	168	63.4	15.1	21.5
Virginia	1,365.3	179	56.7	10.7	32.7
Washington	477.9	75	61.1	13.6	25.3
West Virginia	218.1	120	60.5	10.0	29.5
Wisconsin	509.1	92	57.7	12.7	29.6
Total	**51,763.4**	**184**	**60.3**	**10.7**	**29.0**

Source: *International Gaming and Wagering Business*, April 2007, p. 27.

Why Are Modern State Lotteries All the Same?

The modern state lotteries have revenue generation as their *raison d'etre*, and in almost every state these revenues are earmarked to specific causes. What explains this uniformity? We note that the ubiquitous emphasis on public revenue is not intrinsic to the lottery's operation. A seemingly natural alternative is for the state to orient its lottery to simply servicing or accommodating the public demand for reliable lottery products. The argument for such a lottery is simple: more than half the adult public enjoys playing the lottery. This "Consumer Lottery" would best serve this interest with a high payout rate—much higher than the 60 percent rate that is typical and closer to the 90 percent that would allow the average lottery to just cover operating costs. Of course, an alternative would be to legalize private lotteries (perhaps with some licensing scheme), but that might be harder to regulate effectively.

Note that there is a close analog here to liquor. Like the lottery, liquor is problematic in that consumption generates social costs. Rather than prohibit sales, states attempt to limit abuse through restrictions on marketing, and in the case of eighteen states, a monopoly on wholesale distribution.[19] While the states do collect taxes on liquor sales, the central reason for the states' role in this market lies not in collecting revenues but rather in servicing the consumers' demand for liquor. In the case of the lottery, this approach has received little attention in the public debate, and there have been no takers. Before speculating about this rather strange lacuna, we first develop the public interest analysis.

The Public Interest in Lottery Adoption and Design

Using the conventional framework of public finance, we can discuss the public interest in lottery design in terms of costs and benefits, both considered from the perspective of society as a whole. On the cost side of the ledger is the operating expense, of course, and also any negative societal consequences of lottery marketing and consumer participation. The benefit side of the ledger includes the net revenues going to finance public goods such as education as well as the value to consumers of having an opportunity to play. The public debate about lottery adoption and design has all but ignored this last item. For this reason, we begin by limiting our discussion to the conventional perspective and then bring in consumer value as a consideration.

The conventional public-interest analysis is summarized in figure 1.1, which requires some explanation. In this figure, the variable on the x-axis is the takeout rate (t), which is equal to one minus the payout rate. This takeout rate logically ranges from zero (in which case sales would be maximized but the lottery, since it is paying out all revenues in the form of prizes, could not cover operating costs[20]) up to 100 percent. At this latter extreme, nothing is left over for prizes, making the purchase of a lottery ticket purely a charitable donation to the state—an arrangement that would be unlikely to have many takers! Net revenues generated from the takeout go to cover operating costs and provide the government with money to finance public purposes. The relationship between the takeout rate and net revenue to the state is depicted by the hump-shaped curve (akin to the famous Laffer Curve), which rises as t rises from a breakeven point to a maximum and then declines as further increases in t depress sales toward zero. The second curve describes the social costs of the lottery (other than operating costs), which may be both fixed and variable. We do not attempt to specify these costs in any detail, since we are only attempting to provide a schematic characterization of the dilemmas associated with lottery adoption and design. Briefly, the fixed costs could stem from the deleterious consequences of the message communicated when the government first adopts a lottery, namely that the state does not view gambling as a problematic activity, at least in this form; the variable costs could stem from the family and community problems that tend to increase with gambling expenditures. Commentators have suggested a varied menu of such costs: increased selfishness; reduced commitment to frugality, investment, and work; neglect of family financial responsibilities; increased bankruptcy; and property crime associated with an upsurge in compulsive gambling.[21]

FIGURE 1.1

The Revenue and Social Costs Generated by a State Lottery

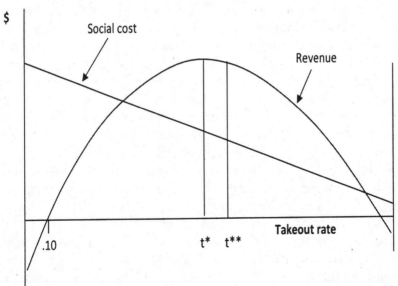

In this analysis (which ignores any benefits that might be enjoyed by players), the public interest is best served when the gap between net revenue and social cost is maximized, and in principle this would determine the takeout rate. Several cases help anchor the full list of possibilities:

- If the social costs are above net revenue for every value of t, then it would be a mistake to have a lottery—precisely the view of many critics.
- If variable social costs are negligible, the social cost curve would be a horizontal line, and the optimum value of t is that which maximizes net revenues (assuming that the fixed costs are not so high as to preclude any worthwhile lottery). In this case, the best t is t*, as shown in figure 1.1.
- If variable social costs increase with lottery expenditures (and hence are inversely related to t), then the analysis dictates a higher optimum takeout rate than would be implied by a goal of net revenue maximization alone. The optimum, as shown in the figure, is t**, where the lens between revenue and cost is widest.

Figure 1.1 does not include the value of lottery play to the consumers, of course. If we view the lottery as a commodity, then the value consumers place on the opportunity to play—the "consumers' surplus"—should be considered part of the public benefit.[22] That value diminishes as the takeout rate increases, assuming that their primary motivation is to win prizes (rather than contribute to the state treasury).[23] From the lottery players' perspective, the lower the takeout rate, the better, because a lower takeout means more money for prizes.

If we incorporate the consumers' valuation, the takeout rate that best accords with the public interest is equal to marginal costs, including both operating costs (about 10%) and social costs.[24] The case for a low takeout rate is further strengthened if consideration is given to the distribution of lottery play. Because lottery play consumes a much higher percentage of income for those at the bottom of the income and education distribution than for those at the middle or top, a reduction in the takeout rate is unambiguously pro-poor.[25] Of course, lower-income households are also most vulnerable to the financial problems created by excessive lottery play, and while it could be argued that a high takeout rate is a useful deterrent, it is very clear that the high takeout rate of contemporary state lotteries is not motivated by a desire to discourage excess play.[26] The proof is in the fact that one common feature of the Revenue Lottery is marketing—advertising and product development—intended to encourage the public to play more than they otherwise would.

The Politics of Adoption

In seeking an explanation for the universal embrace of the Revenue Lottery, it is useful to distinguish between *politics* and *marketing*. We consider these two processes from the point of view of those we might call the "lottery promoters"—individuals and interest groups who lead the effort to overcome political resistance to lottery adoption and then attempt to sustain or expand the scope of the lottery once it is in place. The list of lottery promoters includes lobbyists representing the private industry that supplies lottery products (led by Scientific Games and GTech), together with a handful of leading politicians in the state who support a lottery. Specific groups that stand to benefit from earmarked lottery revenues may also serve as important advocates.

Some lottery promoters are motivated solely by private concerns such as profit and power, but others support the lottery due to their belief that it serves the public interest. The profit motive is clear enough for the industry, which seeks to expand the market for its products by lobbying for adoption and then expansion of lotteries. Politicians may embrace this cause in a quest for support of this industry in their reelection campaigns, and for the greater personal power that may come with expansion of government. But there is no reason to believe that other higher minded motivations are absent from the mix.

The key political task for lottery promoters is to mobilize sufficient support, first for the adoption and then for the successful operation of the lottery. We begin with the adoption effort, noting that the important design decisions (including the embrace of the Revenue Lottery) have already been made at this point. To some extent, the politics of adoption are concerned with selling the lottery proposal to the public, and in most states, the adoption process has included a direct referendum. Among the politicians, advocates, and voters who will become involved in making the decision, we identify three clusters of political actors:

1. *Lottery lovers*, who simply want the chance to play and are largely indifferent to the public revenue prospect. For them, a Consumer Lottery would be better than a Revenue Lottery, but a Revenue Lottery is better than No Lottery.
2. *Lottery haters*, who strongly object to gambling or at least to state sponsorship of gambling in this form. For them, No Lottery trumps both the Revenue Lottery and the Consumer Lottery. This group represents a minority position in every state, but if well organized, they can be effective.
3. *Lottery pragmatists*, who are willing to consider a lottery only if it conveys the potential benefit of expanded government programming or reduced taxes. (They may also be influenced by a concern for competing with the illegal lotteries that flourish in the absence of a state game.) For them, a Revenue Lottery is preferable to a Consumer Lottery, and may be preferable to No Lottery, depending on the details of lottery design. These views can be summarized by the following simple table.

TABLE 1.4
Hypothetical Preferences of Political Actors in Lottery Adoption

	Consumer lottery	Revenue lottery
Lovers	Yes	Yes
Haters	No	No
Pragmatists	No	Maybe

We do not suppose that all these political actors are concerned with the public interest, but each of these views can be justified within the public-interest analysis. Lottery lovers would be those who believe the social costs of the lottery are low and that consumer sovereignty should reign. Lottery haters would be those who view the lottery's social cost as exceeding the benefit for every imaginable design. The pragmatists are a bit harder to characterize in this public-interest framework, but their position can be justified. They could believe that the social costs of lottery play outweigh the direct benefit to players, but may be willing to accept this cost for the sake of the revenue. Often the public rhetoric surrounding lottery adoption contests suggests that the revenue from the lottery is of special value in that it can be used to support vital programs that otherwise would not exist or to expand important programs by more than would be possible from the usual sources of revenues. In this view, a dollar of public spending is worth more than a dollar of private spending—a view that has been espoused most notably by John Kenneth Galbraith and that has some support in public finance theory.[27]

While it is thus logically possible for all three groups of political actors to be motivated by the public interest, a more cynical view may be warranted. For the lottery industry in particular, the goal is to sell lottery products for profit. The industry appears to be a natural ally to the majority of the public (the lottery lovers) who we suspect would favor the Consumer Lottery because it would result in the largest possible sales. Yet only the Revenue Lottery has proven politically viable in overcoming the minority opposition from the lottery haters. We know that a minority can have great power in a democracy if it is well organized around a particular issue,[28] and lottery opponents have indeed found effective political voice through faith-based organizations that advocate family values and in progressives concerned about the economic burden of gambling on poor households. The potential beneficiaries—those who would like to be able to play the lottery—have not been organized. The campaigns for adoption of state lotteries have thus focused on selling the swing group of pragmatists on the importance of this new source of state revenue. As shown in table 1.5, most states go one step further and earmark lottery revenues for specific uses, most commonly some aspect of education. Harnessing the lottery to a popular state program can mobilize concerted support by the groups that stand to benefit directly. The personal priorities of key political leaders can also influence the process.[29] The attractions of earmarking are sufficiently compelling that a number of states actually operated their lotteries initially without earmarking and then switched over, as table 1.5 shows.

TABLE 1.5

State Lotteries: Adoption Dates and Designation of Funds

State	Adoption year	Adoption method[a]	Designated use of funds
NH	1964	L	Education
NY	1967	R	K–12 education
NJ	1970	R	Public education (K–12), community colleges and four-year state colleges, state homes for disabled veterans
CT	1972	L	General fund
MA	1972	L	Cities and towns
MI	1972	R	Michigan School Aid Fund (K–12 public schools)
PA	1972	L	Senior citizens' programs
MD	1973	R	General fund
IL	1974	L	Common School Fund (K–12 public schools)[b]
ME	1974	R	General fund
OH	1974	L	Education
RI	1974	R	Distressed cities and towns, General fund
DE	1975	L	General fund
VT	1978	R	Education[b]
AZ	1981	I	Mass transit, General fund, county assistance, economic development, Heritage Fund, Local Transportation Assistance Fund
DC	1982	I	General fund
WA	1982	L	Education construction, stadium debt reduction, economic development, General fund[b]
CO	1983	I	Parks and recreation
CA	1985	I	K–12 education
IA	1985	L	General fund
OR	1985	I	Economic development, job creation, education (K–12 public schools)
MO	1986	R	Education[b]
WV	1986	R	Education, senior citizens, tourism

State	Adoption year	Adoption method[a]	Designated use of funds
KS	1987	R	Economic development (85%), prisons (15%)
MT	1987	R	General fund
SD	1987	R	General fund, Capital Construction Fund, Property Tax Reduction Fund
FL	1988	R	Educational Enhancement Trust Fund
WI	1988	R	Property tax relief
ID	1989	R	Public schools, State Permanent Building Fund
IN	1989	R	Replacement of motor vehicle tax revenue, capital projects
KY	1989	R	General fund
MN	1990	R	General fund, Environmental Trust Fund
LA	1991	R	State's Lottery Proceeds Fund (appropriated by legislature annually)
TX	1992	R	Foundation School Fund[b]
GA	1993	R	Education (HOPE Scholarship program, voluntary prekindergarten program)
NE	1993	R	Trust funds for education, the environment, compulsive gamblers' assistance
NM	1996	L	Education (60% capital improvements, 40% scholarship program)
VA	1998	R	Education[a]
SC	2002	R	Education (K–12 and college scholarships)
ND	2004	R	General fund
TN	2004	R	Education (HOPE Scholarship program)
OK	2005	R	Education
NC	2006	L	Education

Sources:[30] Adoption method and date found in Coughlin, "Geography, Economics, and Politics," 165–80; LaFleur's Lottery World, www.lafleurs.com; state lottery Web site.
[a] R = Referendum; L = Legislation; I = Initiative
[b] Original lottery legislation designated revenues for state's general fund

In the modern history of state lotteries, there has been little challenge to the existence of a lottery once it is in place. But every lottery faces a series of marketing and organizational challenges that are played out in the political arena. The key issue becomes just how far the pragmatists are willing to go in the tradeoff between increased state revenues and the possible social costs stemming from aggressive marketing practices. Thus the close link between the lottery and good causes plays a continuing political role beyond the adoption decision.

Sales

While the "good cause" appears vital to lottery promoters in the political arena, its effect on sales is a separate matter. The question is whether some consumers are moved to buy more lottery tickets because the proceeds are used to support public purposes than they would if it were a private, for-profit enterprise.

To develop this mechanism a bit, we can view a lottery ticket as a bundle of two goods—a chance to win a prize and a contribution to a good cause. Suppose that a lottery ticket costs $1 and conveys a chance (p) of winning prize J. The expected value of the prize, which is just the payout rate, is then pJ. The remainder goes to operating costs c and to the government: the expected contribution to the government is then $1 - c - pJ$.

Someone deciding on a lottery purchase will then consider the sum of benefits derived from the prize and the contribution. He or she will purchase the ticket if this sum is greater than the cost, $1:

$$U(p, J) + V(1 - c - pJ) > 1$$

Here U represents the subjective dollar value to the consumer of entering a lottery with a probability p of winning J, while V represents the subjective dollar value of making a contribution of the specified amount.[31]

In most cases of commercial gambling, we can safely assume that $V = 0$, which is to say that the player cares nothing about making a contribution to the operator's bottom line. (If the operator is an organized criminal group, then it is possible that $V < 0$.) But if the contribution goes to support an educational program or other good cause, then it is possible that $V > 0$; the overall value of the ticket is enhanced from the potential buyer's perspective, increasing the chance that the buyer will make the purchase (or choose to purchase more tickets). The result will be increased sales for a given payout rate. In short, buying a ticket to the "North Carolina Education Lottery" may be more attractive than buying a ticket to the "Walmart Winabunch Lottery."

It is also possible that this charitable motivation not only shifts demand (for given payout rate) but also reduces the elasticity of demand with respect to the payout rate. Consider the following two payout structures for a lottery where the operating costs are ten cents on the dollar:

TABLE 1.6
Hypothetical Game Designs

	Prize payout rate	Contribution to government net revenues
Game 1	.50	.40
Game 2	.60	.30

If players valued the contribution just as much as the prize payout, they would be indifferent between these two games, and the elasticity with respect to payout rate would be zero.

As far as we know there is no reliable econometric evidence on the effect of earmarking on sales.[32] On the other hand, there is considerable evidence that consumers increase their purchases in response to an increase in the expected value of the prizes.[33] It is not surprising, then, that in the face of disappointing revenues from the North Carolina lottery's first year, the governor has proposed a substantial increase in the payout rate. He and his advisors believe that more prize money would increase sales by so much that net revenues would increase despite the lower "take" per ticket.

The choices lottery agencies make (presumably based on market research) concerning how to advertise the lottery provides further evidence of the importance of a good cause in selling lottery tickets. To investigate this matter, we obtained 325 recent television ads, including all television ads entered in the Batchy Award competition in 2005 and 2006. Research assistants screened these ads and coded them according to the primary theme and also according to whether they even mentioned the public benefits created by lottery revenues. The results are shown in table 1.7. Overall, just 13 percent of the ads focused on public benefit, and a handful of others mentioned it briefly (for a total of 17% with some mention). When we divided the ads according to whether they were from states that earmark revenues or states that do not, there was some evidence that the states with earmarked revenues place greater emphasis on public benefit: 20 percent of earmark-state ads mentioned the public benefit, compared to just 6 percent of the ads from general fund states.

TABLE 1.7

Primary Themes in 325 Television Ads for U.S. State Lotteries

Primary Theme	Number of ads, by earmarking of lottery revenue			
	Earmarked	General fund[a]	All	(%)
Informational				
Direct sales appeal	82	16	98	30.2
How to play	35	3	38	11.7
Previous winners	16	3	19	5.8
Public benefits	40	3	43	13.2
Thematic				
Fun, excitement of playing	48	21	69	21.2
You could win	31	2	33	10.2
Wealth, elegance	6	0	6	1.8
Jackpot growing	13	6	19	5.8
TOTAL	**271**	**54**	**325**	**100.0**
Were public benefits mentioned?	53	3	56	17.2

Sources: Television ads were gathered from various lottery agencies and the North American Association of State and Provincial Lotteries produced in the years 2005 and 2006, including all television ads entered in the Batchy Award competition in 2005 and 2006. Ads were classified according to their primary theme and whether or not they mentioned public benefits. For more explanation of themes, see Clotfelter and Cook, *Selling Hope*, chap. 10.
[a]Lotteries whose revenues went exclusively to the state's general fund were CT, MD, ME, DE, DC, IA, MT, KY, and ND.

Ads in which the primary theme is public benefit focus on a specific use of the money. Here are several examples:

Texas: The ad shows children having fun with their parents and thanks people who help raise money for schools, especially lottery players, for helping to contribute more than $9 million to education in Texas.

Virginia: The ad shows students from across the state and the announcer speaks about how you never know when or how a student can be affected by his education. The lottery has raised $408 million for public schools. The ad ends with a picture of two crossed fingers and the announcer says, "The Virginia Lottery, helping Virginia's schools."

Washington: The ad shows various people working on construction projects, even though they are doing a poor job. The announcer then says, "Every year millions of Washington lottery players help with school construction across the state; thankfully their contribution is purely financial." Across the screen it says, "Washington Lottery. It's good to play."

West Virginia: The ad shows a home for senior citizens and then shows the couple who donated their land to the nursing home. Across the bottom of the screen it says that "the West Virginia Lottery has provided more than $300 million to Senior Citizens in WV since 1986." The ad ends by saying, "Good things happen when you play."

Arizona: The ad shows various state parks, and then the announcer mentions that, thanks to the Heritage Fund of the Arizona Lottery, "We'll be enjoying them well into the future. The Arizona Lottery. It's not just a game."

Massachusetts: The ad shows scenes from the over 350 towns and communities, and the announcer mentions that they all share the desire to make life better for their citizens. The ad then says the Massachusetts Lottery gave over $700 million to schools and communities in the last year.

Michigan: The ad shows local teachers and explains how money from the Michigan Lottery is given back to Michigan schools, paying the salaries of more than 11,000 teachers. Across the screen it says, "Play for the Fun. Play for the Future."

These messages encourage customers to play for the sake of the good cause to which the lottery is dedicated, and perhaps they have some effect. It is also possible that the lottery agencies include such ads in the mix primarily for political reasons, to sustain support for the lottery. But, as already noted, ads such as these are distinctly in the minority. The great majority of all lottery ads appeal to self-interest by emphasizing the enjoyment of the prospect of financial gain available from playing.

Conclusion

So why have all the states adopted a particular version of the lottery that focuses on generating public revenues? The first answer is that overcoming the political opposition of the "lottery haters" requires the backing of those who are not enthusiastic about a state lottery per se, but are willing to support one on the condition that it serves the purpose of financing public causes. Earmarking may further strengthen the political alliance in support of adoption and subsequent expansion of the lottery.

We are less inclined to believe that the "good cause" has much direct effect on sales once a lottery is instituted, although we may be wrong. In any event, there is no doubt that sales tend to increase in response to an increased payout rate, implying that players place lower value on dollars available for education than dollars available to increase the prize pool.

Policy Choices and the Future of State Lotteries

Like the lotteries of early America, the nearly ubiquitous state lotteries of the contemporary scene find themselves operating between two dueling force fields: on the one side are the worthy uses to which their proceeds are put, and on the other, a collection of problematic social aspects that insure a constant supply of potential critics. Although they are no longer on the leading edge in the growth of commercial gambling—that role was taken over by the casinos a decade ago—lotteries continue to evolve. With that evolution will come policy choices. We foresee six major issues.

One issue will be how much of the money states collect from ticket sales will be returned to players in the form of prizes. (This "payout rate" is the obverse of the takeout rate discussed above.) Spurred by the belief that higher payout rates will stimulate more sales and increase competition, states have gradually increased their payout rates over time. In 1989 the average rate was just 51 percent.[34] By 2006 the average rate had climbed to 60 percent, as shown in table 3. To be sure, the current rate remains far below those in many of the early American lotteries, many of which boasted payout rates of 80 to 90 percent. Although today's higher payout rates probably do stimulate sales, they can be offered to players only by reducing the rate of implicit tax. Since total revenue to the state is the product of sales and the implicit tax rate, the takeout rate that maximizes revenue is neither very low nor very high.

A second trend in addition to the rise in payout rates is the tendency of states to earmark their revenues for specific good causes if they have not already done so, as documented in the previous section. Education is the most popular beneficiary, particularly college scholarships in the mold of the Georgia HOPE Scholarship. At least four other states have followed Georgia's lead, and in Arkansas the lieutenant governor has recently proposed a lottery for his state with proceeds likewise to be used for college scholarships.[35] By earmarking funds for a new program, such an approach minimizes the danger that the impact of earmarking will be undone by future appropriations that take as a given these lottery revenues. But the use of lottery funds to finance college scholarships has its own set of problems, as noted below.

A third, more general issue is whether lotteries, because of their appeal or because of the way they are marketed, "prey upon the poor." Study after study confirms that expenditures on lotteries represent a larger share of the incomes of low-income households than those further up the income distribution, insuring that the implicit tax on lotteries is regressive. Considerable controversy has been generated by the assertion that lottery agencies direct their marketing at the poor, an assertion that generally does not hold up to scrutiny. But the regressivity charge sticks because the evidence to support it is overwhelming. One might argue that the high tax is simply the price of legalizing an activity that low-income citizens enjoy disproportionately. Yet as long as the possibility remains to raise the payout rate and thus reduce the high implicit tax rate, the regressive impact of lottery finance will be a choice, not an unavoidable feature of lotteries themselves. And the states that earmark their lottery revenues for merit scholarships will add to this regressivity by taking funds raised at the lower end of the income scale and passing them to families near the top.[36]

A fourth issue is and will continue to be what games to legalize. The starkest choice is whether to add video lotteries to the array of games. In a nod to their potential harm, states that use them typically wall them off in some way, such as by restricting them to bars and hotels. But the possibilities will surely not end there. Many states do not yet have Keno, a game with almost as much potential for habitual play as video lotteries, and there will no doubt be opportunities to bet through computers and cell phones that are as yet just ideas on the desks of electrical engineers. States will have to decide whether the good that can be derived from the use of new games will outweigh their costs.

A fifth recurring policy issue concerns advertising—how much and what kind. The fact that legislators believe that some advertising can be undesirable is implicit in the number of provisions in state lottery laws restricting the amount that can be spent on ads, the location of ads, or the content of ads. Occasionally this issue rises to the level of headlines, as when charges surfaced in Illinois that lottery ads targeted poor and minority neighborhoods, or when attacks on advertising caused Massachusetts to ban all lottery ads for a period.[37]

A final policy issue concerns who should operate a state's lottery. A recent proposal discussed in at least three states is for a private firm or investment group to purchase the right to operate a state's lottery for a number of years into the future. In return the state would receive both a lump sum payment up front and a guaranteed annual payment in future years. Such a scheme raises questions of intergenerational equity and governance. If the up-front bonanza that comes from such a sale is used to fund expenditures for the current generation, it is not hard to see how it could be made to look like robbing the kids' piggy bank. But the governance issue has more potential for mischief. If selling the rights to run the lottery means ceding control over advertising and the choice of what games to offer, the state could lose effective control of what is one of its most prominent activities. The example of the UK National Lottery, however, shows that private operation by itself does not have to lead to this kind of surrender.[38]

2

The Politics of Sovereignty and Public Policy toward Gambling

Michael Nelson

Sovereignty is commonly understood to be the ultimate authority to govern a people. A sovereign government stands apart from and independent of other governments. In unitary political systems such as France's, all sovereignty resides in the central government; other governing units live and move and have their being at its sufferance. In confederations such as the United States under the Articles of Confederation, all sovereignty resides in state governments, which jointly create, empower and, if they wish, may abolish the central government. Even in relatively straightforward examples like these, however, sovereignty is much clearer in theory than in practice. France, for example, is bound to obey certain decisions made by the European Union. The United States under the Articles exercised little sovereign authority in the Northwest Territory, where British forts remained dominant even after independence.

With the enactment of the Constitution in the late 1780s, the United States not only accepted but embraced sovereign complexity, distributing sovereignty in sometimes hard-to-specify ways between the state governments and the federal government. In a series of landmark cases in the early 1830s, the Supreme

Court recognized the existence of a third repository of sovereign authority within the nation's borders: American Indian tribes living on tribal lands. Over the years, and especially in recent times, American economic and political life increasingly has been intertwined with still another set of sovereign actors: the governments of other nations and, to some extent, of international organizations to which the United States belongs. In sum, four sets of sovereigns affect the lives of Americans: the federal government, state governments, tribal governments, and international governments.

Throughout American history, from colonial times to the present, the dominant sovereign actors shaping public policy toward gambling have been the states. In recent years, however, all the other sovereignties that affect American life—tribal, foreign, and especially federal—have become more active and influential with regard to gambling in the United States, a trend that seems likely to continue. After a brief historical introduction, this chapter chronicles the multiplication of sovereign politics and policymaking concerning four different forms of gambling: lotteries, commercial casinos, tribal casinos, and Internet betting.

Waves of Legalized Gambling

Legalized gambling is not a new phenomenon in the American experience, but it has been an episodic one.[1] Scholars refer to the recent spread of gambling legalization in the United States as gambling's "third wave," the first two having crested and then receded.

First Wave

The first wave of gambling legalization began during the colonial era. Nearly all American Indian tribes and bands had long and varied traditions of wagering. Among the colonists, racetracks flourished, especially in Virginia, Maryland, New York, and South Carolina. All thirteen colonies licensed private brokers, universities, and even churches to conduct raffle-style lotteries to raise funds for worthy causes, including the construction of buildings at Harvard and Yale, support for American troops during the revolutionary war, and, after independence was won, internal improvements such as the Erie Canal. The First

Continental Congress condemned gambling in 1774; the Second Continental Congress, faced with the challenges of funding the revolutionary army, voted two years later to sponsor four lotteries. Casinos licensed by the city of New Orleans were part of what the United States acquired in the Louisiana Purchase in 1803, and riverboat gambling subsequently flourished along the Mississippi River.

By the mid-nineteenth century, most lotteries had lost their civic purpose and become profit-making (and sometimes profit-fleecing) enterprises. Casinos degenerated in like manner. In 1835, mobs in Vicksburg, Mississippi burned the city's gambling halls and lynched five allegedly crooked professional gamblers. Eastern Puritans and Quakers and frontier evangelists had never liked gambling. Their ranks were swelled during the early nineteenth century by reformers who lumped in gambling with slavery, drinking, harsh prison conditions, and other social ills as fit objects for abolition. By 1860, legal casinos were confined to the frontier territories. Twenty-one of the twenty-four states that once allowed lotteries had outlawed them.

In banning the lotteries of the first wave, some states chose to rely not on legislation, which could easily be repealed, but on their constitutions. As a delegate argued at New York's 1821 constitutional convention, "Legislatures were always under a strong temptation to resort to lotteries as a mode of raising revenue; and from a temptation to which it was more than probable that they would yield, the constitution should preserve them."[2]

Second Wave

The second wave of gambling legalization by the states occurred during the late nineteenth century. This wave was less tidal than the first—it was a mainly southern phenomenon and was generally confined to lotteries. Bereft of most other revenue sources, some of the defeated states of the Confederacy revived the practice of chartering private companies to conduct lotteries, this time taxing the proceeds. The largest of these by far was the Louisiana Lottery Company, which received a twenty-five year charter from the state legislature in return for a $40,000 annual payment to New Orleans' Charity Hospital. The company rapidly expanded its operations to encompass the entire country.

The national network of railroads and telegraphs that recently had developed allowed the Louisiana Lottery—"the Serpent" to its critics—to market its games through the mail and in branch offices connected to headquarters by wire. About 90 percent of Louisiana Lottery tickets were sold outside Louisiana to an estimated 5 million out-of-state customers per year.

The other states, distressed by the amount of money flowing out of their borders into Louisiana, pressured the federal government to crack down on lotteries. So did antigambling reformers in the burgeoning Progressive movement who saw gambling as one of many sources of moral and political corruption infesting the nation's rapidly growing cities. In the 1890s, Congress passed its first (and only) antilottery statutes. A federal law enacted in 1890 at President Benjamin Harrison's urging forbade the postal system to deliver mail referring to lotteries. After the Supreme Court certified the constitutionality of this law in 1892, Congress further legislated in 1895 to bar all interstate transmissions of lottery materials. By 1894, not a single state permitted lotteries to operate legally. All but nine states had lottery prohibitions in their constitutions. Opposition to the lottery as a species of gambling spread to include the entire genus: by 1920 nearly all forms of gambling were illegal throughout the country. Indeed, Arizona and New Mexico, the last two of the lower forty-eight states to enter the union, were forced to outlaw casinos as a condition of statehood.

The Third Wave of Legalized Gambling: Lotteries

The third wave of legalized lottery and casino gambling began in the 1960s and, several decades later, has not abated. To be sure, a number of cash-starved states authorized and taxed pari-mutuel wagering on horse and dog racing during the Great Depression of the 1930s. But racing has waned during the third wave, even as lotteries and casinos have waxed. Indeed, many surviving racetracks exist today only because they have been allowed to become racetrack casinos, or "racinos."

The dam that the states built against legal lotteries at the end of the nineteenth century held for about seventy years. In the mid-1960s, the dam cracked when two northeastern states, New Hampshire in 1964 and New York in 1967, adopted lotteries.

During the 1970s, the dam broke: twelve states, still mostly in the Northeast, legalized lottery gambling. During the 1980s, seventeen states and the District of Columbia, representing a majority of every region of the country except the South, followed suit. Since 1990, twelve more states, seven of them southern, have created lotteries. Indeed, as of 2009 only seven generally small states remain without one: Mississippi, Alabama, Utah, Nevada, Wyoming, Hawaii, and Alaska. Together, the forty-three lottery states and the District include 96 percent of the nation's population.

Certain aspects of contemporary lotteries have remained fairly constant throughout the third wave, all of which stand in contrast to the lotteries of the first two waves. First, the lotteries created since the 1960s are owned and operated by state governments, not franchised to private firms or eleemosynary organizations. Second, voters have been directly involved in the creation of thirty-one of the forty-three lotteries through state referenda. Passage of a referendum as the final stage of the constitutional amendment process did not become a standard feature of state governance until the Progressive Era. Third, the proceeds of state lotteries have almost always been designated to meet states' ongoing revenue needs, usually for educational funding rather than to pay for one-time expenditures such as a canal or airport. Finally, southern states, for religious reasons, and smaller states, for economic ones, have embraced lottery gambling more slowly than their peers. The South has a denser concentration than the rest of the country of religious conservatives, who tend to oppose gambling as immoral. Smaller states have a hard time generating the large jackpots that stimulate active lottery participation.

In other ways, lotteries have mutated during the course of the third wave. When New Hampshire (a dramatic exception to the small state tendency) sold its first lottery ticket in 1964, it offered a single, modestly marketed, three-dollars-per-ticket, raffle-style game twice each year. Tickets were sold only at racetracks and liquor stores, and purchasers had to register their names and addresses. Within a few years, the New Jersey Lottery instituted weekly, then daily drawings in which betters, without registering, could choose their own numbers; it also advertised extensively and priced its tickets as low as fifty cents. Massachusetts soon added instant lotteries played on scratch-off cards to its menu of games. New York introduced lotto, with highly publicized prizes that sometimes reached into the millions.

Another modification of lotteries during the third wave concerns the purposes for which states conduct them. An important goal for the early-adopting states in the 1960s and 1970s, especially in the Northeast and Midwest, was to drive illegal numbers and policy games out of business by offering competing games legally. These states believed that they could, in the process, deprive organized crime of an important source of income. As numbers games continued to flourish, mostly because gamblers could play them on credit and avoid taxes on payouts, states gradually became content to focus instead on maximizing their own lottery revenues.[3]

A final modification that has occurred during the course of the current wave of lottery gambling is from one-state to multistate games. By 2006, thirty-one mostly medium-sized states belonged to the Multi-State Lottery Association, which runs the Powerball game. Twelve considerably larger states—including California, Texas, New York, and Illinois—jointly offered the Mega Millions lottery. Powerball and Mega Millions jackpots sometimes run well above $300 million, triggering long lines of frenzied ticket buyers. Such massive prizes are possible only when the betting population is larger than any individual state can muster. By banding together, states have been able to entice many people to play who otherwise would not and thus have raised more revenue than if they did not act collectively.

Explaining the Recent Spread of Lotteries

Several causes explain the proliferation of lottery gambling during the third wave. Lotteries entered their period of most rapid expansion in the late 1970s, just as anti-tax sentiment began to rise across the nation. In 1978 California voters passed Proposition 13, which placed severe restrictions on the state legislature's taxing authority and inspired other states to enact similar measures. Ronald Reagan was elected president in 1980 by promising to substantially reduce federal income taxes. Reagan not only accomplished this goal but also persuaded Congress to cut spending on grant programs to the states. To state governments, caught in a vise between widespread opposition to higher taxes and greater revenue needs, the lottery seemed an appealing way out: revenue without taxation. Meanwhile, public support for lotteries in national Gallup Polls rose from 61 percent in 1975 to 72 percent in 1982 and has remained at or near 70 percent ever since.[4]

As states considered enacting lotteries during the third wave, they were influenced by the experience of other states. In view of the corruption-riddled history of lotteries during the first two waves, state legislators needed assurance that lotteries could be run honestly. Not only were the first lotteries of the third wave perceived to be honest, but within a few years they also were generating considerable amounts of revenue from their varied menu of games. Just as the lesson spread from state to state that variety was needed to make lotteries lucrative, so did a consensus form that the key to honest lotteries was state ownership and operation.

Once it became clear that lotteries could be run honestly and profitably, the long familiar process of interstate "policy diffusion" was enhanced, even accelerated.[5] Because a state leaks revenue when its citizens cross the border to play the lotteries of neighboring states, it has a strong incentive to keep its betters at home. Examples abound of states legalizing lotteries after one or more of their neighbors did so. After Illinois created a lottery, for instance, neighboring Iowa, Indiana, and Wisconsin followed suit. As John Carlin, the former governor of Kansas, lamented, "Not having one when your neighbor has one is like tying one hand behind your back."[6] In 1998 pro-lottery South Carolina Democratic gubernatorial candidate Jim Hodges won an upset victory by running television commercials showing a convenience store clerk wearing a Georgia Bulldogs jersey. "Here in Georgia," the clerk drawled to the camera, "we appreciate you South Carolinians driving across the state line and buying our lottery tickets, over $100 million worth. Those Georgia tickets y'all buy pretty much pay for our world-class preschools."[7] Two years later South Carolina enacted a lottery.

The Federal Role

The spread of lottery gambling from no states as recently as 1963 to forty-three states in 2009 constitutes a dramatic national

trend but one in which the national government has played a
limited role. To be sure, it is not clear how far Washington's powers would extend if it decided to attack lotteries. The Louisiana
Lottery of the second wave was vulnerable to congressional
assault because it was conducted by a private firm engaged in
interstate commerce. It is less certain how far Congress' constitutional authority extends to lotteries conducted by sovereign state
governments.

Constitutional questions aside, Congress has shown little
desire to legislate concerning state lotteries. Its two most recent
pieces of lottery legislation were minor and reflect no consistent
attitude. The first, which became law in 1988, authorized the
states to advertise lottery games more freely than in the past.
It overturned a 1934 statute that had extended the 1890s ban
on printed lottery advertising to the broadcast media. In passing
the bill, Congress showed a greater level of confidence in third-
wave lotteries, owned and operated by state governments, than
it had in second-wave lotteries, owned and operated by private
organizations. The second recent law concerning lotteries was a
1992 act that prohibited all but the few states that already did so
from offering or allowing sports betting, including sports-based
lottery games.

In 1976 and 1999 national commissions created by Congress
issued reports on gambling, but they too have been only modestly important and offered offsetting conclusions. Although the
1976 report of the Commission on the Review of National Policy
toward Gambling made minor recommendations concerning lottery advertising, its main conclusions were in harmony with what
the states already were doing. "States should have the primary
responsibility for determining what forms of gambling may take
place legally within their borders," the commission argued. "The
only role of the Federal Government should be to prevent interference by one State with the gambling policies of another."[8] The
1999 report of the National Gambling Impact Study Commission
was more critical, at least in tone. It recommended "a pause of
the expansion of gambling in general," and singled out state lotteries as severely regressive devices for raising revenue because
poorer, less educated people lose much more money through
lottery wagering than wealthier, more educated people.[9] The

commission did not urge the enactment of significant federal legislation to curb lottery gambling, however, and not long after the report was issued, Tennessee, North Carolina, and Oklahoma decided to join the ranks of lottery states. The proposal before Congress starting in 2007, albeit unlikely of adoption, was to create a national lottery to help fund the federal government.

Although the federal government has played a decidedly minor role in the modern spread of lottery gambling, two national corporations have been highly influential. Gtech, which was founded in 1973, and Scientific Games, founded eight years later, have spent many millions of dollars lobbying legislators and funding referendum campaigns in states that were considering lottery legalization. Their efforts have been rewarded. Gtech operates the computer systems that run games in twenty-six lottery states. Scientific Games specializes in instant scratch-off gambling; it devises the games and prints the tickets in thirty-four states.[10]

The Third Wave of Legalized Gambling: Commercial Casinos

Nevada was one of many states to embrace legalized gambling in the 1930s as a strategy to raise revenue, but it was the only one to do so by legalizing commercial—that is, privately owned, profit-oriented—casinos. The Great Depression had increased state governments' funding needs while decreasing their traditional funding sources. Because Nevada's population was too small and spread out to make racetracks as commercially viable as in more densely populated states, the legislature authorized casino rather than pari-mutuel gambling. Organized crime, which had lost bootleg liquor as a major revenue source when Prohibition was repealed in 1933, gradually moved in to dominate the casino business. But in 1955 the state legislature, in a partially successful effort to "eliminate the undesirables in Nevada gaming," created the Gaming Control Board to oversee and license casinos. In 1969, the legislature passed the Commercial Gaming Act, which allowed publicly traded corporations to own and operate these casinos.[11] A remarkable period of expansion followed, led by entrepreneurs such as Kirk Kerkorian and Steve Wynn and by companies such as Hilton, Hyatt, Holiday Inn, and Metro-Goldwyn-Mayer. By 2005, 351 commercial casinos were operating in Nevada. Nearly half of them were in Las Vegas.

Nevada's decision to legalize commercial casino gambling in 1931 did not trigger similar efforts in other states. In contrast, New Jersey's 1976 decision to allow casinos in Atlantic City sparked multiple state legalization campaigns. For a time, however, these efforts were nearly all unsuccessful. Of seventeen casino campaigns in twelve states waged between 1978 and 1988, only one succeeded: the campaign to allow casinos in Deadwood, South Dakota, as a strategy of historic preservation.[12] Casino opponents usually prevailed by rousing fears of gambling-inspired crime more successfully than proponents were able to sell the purported economic benefits of casinos. In nearly every state that considered casino legalization, the governor and most other political, economic, and media leaders joined or even led the opposition. In some cases the existing gambling establishments in a state, usually the racetracks, spent heavily to defeat the proposed casinos. The politics of lotteries, John Dombrink and William Thompson found, could be accounted for by a "gravity model" of policymaking—that is, if most of the relevant political and economic forces in a state supported adoption, a lottery would be enacted. In contrast, they argued, a "veto model" described the politics of casino legalization. If even one of those forces was averse to a casino measure, it would fail.[13]

An additional reason that casino legalization efforts in the states were defeated during the late 1970s and 1980s is that they were voted down in referenda or never reached the ballot because legislators were certain that they would be voted down. Subsequent campaigns to expand commercial casinos focused on states whose constitutions did not ban casinos or whose constitutional amendment processes did not require approval by the voters. From 1989 to 1993, seven states legalized casino gambling, five of them by vote of the legislature without any statewide referendum: Iowa, Illinois, Mississippi, Louisiana, and Indiana.

One politically astute stratagem that marked the casino legalization campaigns in these states, as well as in Missouri, was to move the proposed casinos from land to water. In 1989 Iowa became the first state to legalize floating casinos on the Mississippi River. For reasons described below, tribal casinos were about to open in neighboring Minnesota and Wisconsin, meaning that Iowa would feel the effects of casino gambling no matter what it did. The state's farm equipment industry in Bettendorf and Davenport, two small manufacturing cities on the river, was severely depressed. The romantic lore of the ante-bellum riverboat gambler made water-based casinos seem palatable in ways that vaguely gangsterish images of the Las Vegas Strip were not. "We're selling the lore of Mark Twain," said the Iowa legislature's leading casino advocate.[14] Also contributing to the political acceptability of water-based casinos in Iowa was the requirement that gambling could only take place when the boats were actually cruising, with loss limits of $5 per bet and $200 per cruise. Ever alert to new revenue sources, Iowa taxed casinos on a steeply rising scale that peaked at 20 percent.

After Iowa's decision, casino gambling cascaded down the river in a pattern well described by the National Gambling Impact Study Commission. "Riverboat casinos seemed to be the ideal instrument for delivering the budgetary nirvana," the commission's report concluded. "When located on the border of other states, often conveniently near population centers across the river, they could be assured of drawing at least some of their revenues (and thus tax receipts) from the population of their benighted neighbors."[15] Not by accident, Iowa's casinos were located adjacent to Illinois, within striking distance of Chicago.

"Unfortunately . . . ," in the commission's opinion, "public officials in the targeted states quickly retaliated with riverboats of their own in the name of 'recapturing' the revenues of their wayward citizens." Thus did Illinois, one year after Iowa, legalize floating casinos in some of its depressed river cities, all of them closer to Chicago than were Iowa's gambling vessels—and with none of the betting limits that drove off high-stakes gamblers, the casino industry's most prized clients. Indiana, whose declining industrial city of Gary is even closer to Chicago, followed suit in 1993 with water-based casinos on Lake Michigan and the Ohio River.

In 1990 Mississippi, which is further south along the river that bears its name and has a stronger cultural claim on the riverboat mythos, legalized water-based casino gambling in its long-depressed river counties and on the Gulf Coast, which had suffered severely from natural disasters and cutbacks in federal defense spending. Hoping to lure casino companies, Mississippi kept gambling taxes low: no more than 8 percent to the state and 4 percent to the county where a casino is located. Within a few years, Mississippi trailed only Nevada and New Jersey as a center of commercial casino gambling. Louisiana legalized casinos in 1991, and Missouri moved to do so in 1992.

In other parts of the country, Colorado, inspired by South Dakota's example, legalized casino gambling in three historic mining towns in 1991 and, five years later, Michigan, responding to the daily migration of gamblers to newly opened casinos in Windsor, Ontario, authorized three casinos in downtown Detroit. Pennsylvania, which was leaking dollars to out-of-state gambling facilities across nearly all its borders, joined the ranks of commercial casino states in 2007. Kansas, bracketed by Colorado, Missouri, and Iowa, made a similar decision that same year, bringing the number of commercial casino states to thirteen. Uniquely, Kansas' casinos will be owned by the state government.

Several states also have authorized casino-style gambling at racetracks as a strategy to revive their declining horse and dog racing industries. As recently as the 1970s, pari-mutuel wagering on horse races was the most popular legal form of gambling in the United States and one of the country's leading spectator sports. But with the spread of faster and simpler forms of lottery and casino gambling, the tracks suffered. From 1990 to 1997 average daily attendance at racetracks dropped 24 percent, from 4,610 to 3,499. Although off-track and simulcast betting—both of which allow gamblers to wager on a race without being at the track— have been legalized in all but a few pari-mutuel states, the total amount of money bet on horse races shrank from $22 billion in 1975 to $14 billion in 1997. As a result, revenues to state and local governments from horse racing declined from $780 million to $422 million in the same period. Even with shortened racing seasons, racetracks continued to go out of business, including the fabled Hialeah thoroughbred track in Florida and the Roosevelt Raceway harness track in New York.[16]

In the mid-1990s, at about the time that the movement to legalize commercial casino gambling in more states was experiencing a lull, the racino was born. The owners of declining tracks in Iowa and West Virginia secured legislation from their state governments to offer casino games of various kinds, which revived the tracks' financial fortunes. Other states have since followed suit: Arkansas, Delaware, Florida, Louisiana, Maine, New Mexico, New York, Oklahoma, Pennsylvania, and Rhode Island. Still other states are actively considering doing so. In 2007, the Kentucky gubernatorial election revolved around the issue of racino legalization, which the victorious Democratic candidate favored in his bid to unseat the Republican incumbent.

Explaining the Spread of Commercial Casinos

What accounts for the recent spread of commercial casinos and their hybrid spawn, racinos? A comparison with the politics of lottery gambling in roughly this same period may be instructive.

First, as with lotteries, the anti-tax political climate fostered by Proposition 13 in the late 1970s and the Reagan presidency in the 1980s spurred states to seek other ways to raise revenue, including casino gambling. Except in Kansas, casinos, unlike modern lotteries, are state-sanctioned rather than state-owned gambling enterprises; they are private businesses allowed to operate by a state, not agencies of the state government. But the dollar a state receives from licensing a casino and taxing its corporate profits counts just as much as the dollar the lottery pays directly into the state treasury. Those arguing for racino legalization made the additional argument that for decades racetracks have been major employers and tourist attractions in their states, and should not be allowed to wither and die.

Second, again as with lotteries, the process by which public policies spread from state to state has been at work in the politics of casino legalization. Policy diffusion manifests itself in two major ways. "Ordinary" diffusion occurs when a state adopts a policy out of admiration for the approach that another state has developed to a problem that both states share. "Reactive" diffusion is the process by which a state copies a policy from another state in an effort to fend off the unwanted consequences of that state's policy.[17]

Ordinary diffusion was at work in four of the states that legalized commercial casino gambling during the third wave. New Jersey was inspired by the example of Nevada, which had recently shown that casinos operated by publicly traded corporations and regulated by the state government could generate jobs, tourism, capital investment, and substantial revenues for the state government without being dominated by organized crime. South Dakota took its cues from New Jersey's decision to use casino legalization as a strategy of economic recovery for a distressed city. Colorado, in turn, followed South Dakota's example in some of its fading mining communities. Mississippi learned the possibilities of water-based casinos from Iowa and Illinois.

The other eight states that recently have legalized commercial casinos have done so reactively, as a strategy to keep their people's gambling dollars at home instead of flowing into casinos in other jurisdictions. Iowa adopted casino gambling in the certain knowledge that tribal casinos were about to open in neighboring Minnesota and Wisconsin. Illinois legalized casinos to keep its gamblers from going to Iowa, and Indiana followed suit to protect itself against Illinois. Farther south, casino gambling in Mississippi placed Louisiana and Missouri on the defensive. Both states legalized commercial casinos shortly after Mississippi did. Michigan authorized commercial casinos in Detroit in reaction to Ontario's decision to do so in Windsor. Pennsylvania, bordered by casino or racino states New Jersey, Delaware, West Virginia, and Ohio, followed suit by awarding licenses to eleven geographically dispersed facilities, as did Kansas (four casinos), which is nestled among casino states Colorado, Iowa, and Missouri.

The Federal Role

Although the politics of commercial casinos, like the politics of lotteries, have always been states-centered, the federal government has been more actively involved in policymaking toward commercial casinos during the third wave than toward lotteries. This is not surprising: states that own and operate lotteries, unlike businesses that own and operate commercial casinos, are sovereign governments that command more deference than nonsovereign entities. In contrast, during the second wave of legalized gambling, when lotteries (like modern commercial casinos) were private organizations lacking sovereignty, the federal government did not hesitate to impede their activities severely.

More recently, the attitude of the federal government toward commercial casino gambling has changed from hostile to, at worst, neutral. One reason for the long hiatus between Nevada's decision to legalize casinos in 1931 and the flurry of successful state legalization campaigns in the 1990s and 2000s was that during the intervening decades the federal government generally treated casino gambling as a source of actual or potential criminal activity. (As discussed below, in the realm of Internet gambling, it still does.) This helps explain why casino legalization campaigns generally failed during the 1970s and 1980s while lottery gambling spread rapidly from state to state. Since the 1990s, the federal role in casino policy has been more tolerant, even on occasion supportive.

Casinos as criminal targets

Roughly once per decade from the 1950s to the 1980s, the federal government took an intense if short-lived interest in casino gambling as a hive of criminal activity, mostly outside Nevada but sometimes within it. Organized crime as a phenomenon that spanned state lines and offered a glamorous target for ambitious politicians seeking headlines helped to motivate these episodic outbreaks of federal activism. In 1950 the Special Senate Committee to Investigate Organized Crime in Interstate Commerce—popularly known as the Kefauver Committee after its chair, Senator Estes Kefauver of Tennessee—toured the country in a widely publicized effort to unmask the role of organized crime in casino gambling, both legal and illegal. Its hearings resulted in the 1951 enactment of the Johnson Act, which forbade the transportation of gambling devices from state to state.

A decade later, spurred by Attorney General Robert F. Kennedy, Congress enacted the Wire Act of 1961 to forbid the interstate transmission of wagers or wagering information by telephone, telegraph, or other communications wires. It also passed the 1962 Travel Act to prohibit people from crossing state lines to engage in illegal gambling. In 1970 Congress approved the Nixon administration–sponsored Organized Crime Control Act with its famous RICO (Racketeer-Influenced and Corrupt Organizations) provisions. One of the main purposes of the act was to prevent organized crime from channeling profits from illegal casinos into legitimate businesses; another was to make more kinds of activities subject to federal criminal prosecution. In 1986 the Money Laundering Control Act was passed, requiring

financial institutions—including casinos—to report currency
transactions of $10,000 or more to the federal government. It
was designed to prevent criminals from laundering cash proceeds
from drug sales and other illegal activities by, for example, buying chips with dirty money at casinos and then exchanging them
for checks or untainted currency.

All of these laws created new categories of federal crimes, and
together they were effective in shutting down—or in spurring
state and local campaigns to shut down—illegal casinos in previous gambling centers such as Hot Springs, Arkansas; Covington,
Kentucky; and Biloxi, Mississippi. The publicity surrounding the
laws' enactments also fostered a strong association in the public mind between casinos and crime, thus retarding for several
decades the potential spread of commercial casinos through legislative action by the states. Although support for casino legalization has risen over the years in public opinion polls, casinos
still trail state lotteries in surveys measuring the acceptability of
various forms of gambling.[18]

Washington's changing attitude

Partly because the federal government's progress in its war
against organized crime has eased public concern and partly
because, in the political realm, the commercial casino industry
has become measurably more acceptable and dramatically more
active, Washington has been less hostile to casinos in recent
years. Ironically, two federal initiatives that the casino industry
opposed played a major role in its rise to political prowess. In
1994 the Clinton administration considered imposing a 4 percent
tax on gambling revenues to help finance the president's welfare
reform initiative. Two years later, at the urging of antigambling legislators led by Representative Frank Wolf of Virginia,
Congress voted to create the National Gambling Impact Study
Commission to examine the consequences of the recent spread of
lotteries, casinos, and other forms of legalized gambling such as
video poker. Wolf urged his colleagues to create the commission
because gambling's "negative impacts on State and local economies, small businesses, and families can no longer be ignored."[19]

Clinton's "sin tax" proposal never got off the ground but it
did have one tangible effect: it provoked the casino industry—not

just commercial casino corporations but also casino equipment manufacturers, suppliers, and vendors—to form the American Gaming Association (AGA). The AGA, a Washington-based trade association headed by former Republican National Committee chair Frank Fahrenkopf of Nevada, uses both "insider" (lobbying and campaign contributions) and "outsider" (public advocacy) strategies of political influence on behalf of its members.[20] One of its first victories was to persuade Congress to limit the 1996 study commission's subpoena powers and to influence the selection of commission members to include casino supporters as well as opponents. The commission's final report, issued in 1999, was hard on some forms of gambling, notably lotteries and video poker, but it broadly absolved the commercial casino industry of its longstanding stigma of criminal involvement. It also reported the positive testimony about casinos' economic benefits that commissioners heard from local officials in new casino towns such as Bettendorf, Iowa; Elgin, Illinois; and Tunica, Mississippi.

Campaign contributions from gambling interests have skyrocketed since the AGA was formed. In 1990, 1992, and 1994, the first three federal elections for which the Center for Responsive Politics compiled data, the "Casinos/Gambling" industry ranked in the bottom half of donors among the eighty-plus industries the Center monitors. Since then, it has always ranked in the top half, with total contributions per election rising from less than a half-million dollars in 1990 to well over $10 million in recent elections. Like many astute Washington players, the highest-ranking commercial casino donors have followed the election returns: a majority of the donors gave most of their money to Democrats before the Republican sweep in the 1994 congressional elections and have given more money to Republicans ever since. (Tribal casinos have consistently contributed more to Democrats.) In light of the Democrats' success regaining Congress in 2006, it would not be surprising to see the industry revert to its pre-1994 pro-Democratic pattern in subsequent elections.[21]

Sports betting

One major gambling policy involving casinos that the federal government has tried to take control of is sports betting. For the most part, it has done so haltingly and ineffectively. In 1951, reacting to a basketball scandal in which seven players on the City College of New York championship team confessed to shaving points, Congress imposed a 10 percent tax on winnings from sports wagering, whether legal (at racetracks and Nevada casinos) or illegal (everywhere else). In the mid-1970s Congress realized that the main effect of the excise tax had been to drive gamblers from legal sports betting, on which the tax was certain, to illegal sports betting where it was, to say the least, unlikely. Congress consequently reduced the excise tax on winnings to 2 percent in 1974 and 0.25 percent in 1983.

Until the 1990s Congress did nothing to prevent states from legalizing sports betting. Few did so, however, in part because, as James Frey has pointed out, sports betting "gives the better the greatest chance of winning" of any form of gambling and thus "has the smallest retention percentage of any form of commercial gambling. It also produces the lowest net tax revenues for states of any game."[22] Except for horse and dog racing in some states and jai alai in Florida (and, sporadically, in Connecticut and Rhode Island), only three states other than Nevada—Oregon, Montana, and Delaware—have sponsored sports gambling in any form, and none of them have earned much from it. Nevada has been the exception: although sports books are little more than break-even operations for the casinos that offered them, they drew gamblers onto the casino floor where they joined the ranks of those losing at the slot machines and tables.

In 1992 Congress passed the Professional and Amateur Sports Protection Act, barring any state that had not already legalized sports betting from doing so. It acted in response to pressure from sports industry leaders such as the National Basketball Association, the National Football League, and Major League Baseball. These organizations were motivated by concerns about the actual and perceived integrity of their games, fearing that every missed shot, fumble, or called third strike would become suspect. Even one point-shaving scandal every few years, for example, could undermine basketball's widespread popularity. This lesson was underscored in 2007 when the National Basketball Association cracked down severely on referee Tim Donaghy for providing inside information to gamblers and gambling on games himself.

The 1992 act did nothing, however, to prevent the still-legal Nevada sports books from generating (and newspapers and Web sites from publishing) the point spreads used by every illegal sports gambling operation in the country. By any estimate, the vast majority of sports bets placed in the United States were illegal even before the recent explosion of sports betting on the Internet. Not surprisingly, in 2000, when the National Collegiate Athletic Association tried to persuade Congress to ban gambling on college athletics at Nevada's sports books, the effort failed. Nevada casinos, both individually and through the AGA, fought back, making the not unreasonable argument that the legal bets they took were a drop in the bucket of all the bets placed on sporting events.

The Third Wave of Legalized Gambling: Tribal Casinos

As with sports betting, the recent flourishing of casinos and other gambling facilities owned and operated by American Indian tribes marks an important departure from the largely states-centered politics of sovereignty concerning gambling. Constitutionally, sovereignty within the United States is an attribute not just of state governments and the federal government but of tribal governments as well.

Tribal sovereignty has long been a matter of great complexity.[23] As Chief Justice John Marshall ruled in the 1831 case of *Cherokee Nation v. Georgia*, the legal relationship between the federal government and the various native tribes is "unlike that of any other two people in history." On the one hand, Marshall wrote, a tribe is sovereign in the same way the federal and state governments are sovereign: it is a "distinct political society . . . capable of managing its own affairs and governing itself." On the other hand, a tribe is to the federal government as "a ward to his guardian"—that is, the relationship is one of fiduciary trust in which the federal government is empowered to make decisions for each tribe with the understanding that those decisions will be in the tribe's best interest.[24] In that sense, Marshall wrote in the related 1832 case of *Worcester v. Georgia*, tribes are "domestic dependent nations."[25]

One effect of tribal sovereignty, Marshall added in his *Worcester* ruling, is that a tribe is free from interference by the government of the state whose land surrounds it; thus, in the case at hand, "the laws of Georgia can have no force" on Cherokee land. Or, as the Supreme Court said more recently in the 1980 case of *Washington v. Confederated Colville Tribes*, unless the federal government chooses in its role as guardian to allow states to apply their laws to activities on Indian reservations, "tribal sovereignty is dependent on, and subordinate to, only the Federal Government, not the States."[26]

For many years, the federal government was an incompetent guardian at best, a venal one at worst: it did one heinous thing to American Indians after another. The government's ill treatment of tribes ranged from stripping them of their historic lands in the interests of white settlers, railroad companies, and developers to policies verging on outright extermination. The effects of this abuse continue to be felt. American Indians suffer some of the highest rates of poverty, addiction, unemployment, poor health, and incarceration of any group in the United States.[27]

Politically, however, attempts by American Indians to expand tribal influence began to bear fruit in the late 1960s and early 1970s. The activist American Indian Movement, the litigation-focused Native American Rights Fund, and other groups formed to seek a greater measure of self-determination in tribal political and economic affairs. Popular movies like *Little Big Man* (1970) and *Dances with Wolves* (1990) and bestselling books such as Vine Deloria Jr.'s *Custer Died for Your Sins* (1969) and Dee Brown's *Bury My Heart at Wounded Knee* (1970) broadened public support for American Indian causes.

Responding positively to these developments were several Republican presidents promoting a "New Federalism" that would devolve power from Washington to subnational units of government (including tribes), as well as a number of Democratic Congresses that were sympathetic to the demands of ethnic and racial minorities. In 1975, for example, the Democratic Congress passed and Republican President Gerald R. Ford signed the Indian Self-Determination and Education Assistance Act, which gave tribal governments considerable discretion concerning how federal programs would be administered on their reservations. During the 1980s, the Reagan administration concentrated its efforts on economic self-determination for American Indian tribes, partly out of concern for the Indians' well-being and partly in the expectation that flourishing reservation economies would reduce tribes' dependence on federal assistance, which the administration severely reduced in 1981.[28]

One form of enterprise by federally recognized tribes that the Reagan administration favored was gambling.[29] In the late 1970s, the Seminole Tribe in Florida had opened a bingo hall offering much higher-stakes games than the state of Florida permitted in nontribal bingo halls. When a federal appeals court rejected the state's efforts to shut down the Seminole facility in 1981,[30] tribes in Wisconsin, California, and other states opened high-stakes bingo halls of their own. Several federal agencies provided loans and other financial assistance to help tribes build gambling facilities that could attract customers from surrounding areas. By 1985, around 100 tribes were sponsoring bingo games, some with jackpots exceeding $100,000.

Several state governments, alarmed that much more extensive gambling facilities were operating within their borders than their legislatures had authorized, elected to fight these efforts. Constitutionally, however, Chief Justice Marshall's decisions from the early 1830s left them on weak ground. Although the relationship between federal and tribal sovereignty is complex, the relationship between state and tribal sovereignty is not. State governments have no intrinsic power over tribes—that is, none that the federal government does not specifically assign to them. As noted above, far from wanting to help the states stifle tribal gambling, the federal government was encouraging such enterprises.

Nonetheless, in 1980, the state of California tried to shut down two bingo parlors and a card room operated by the Cabazon and Morongo Bands of Mission Indians on their reservations near Palm Springs. California cited Public Law 280, a federal statute enacted in 1953 that empowers the states to enforce their criminal laws on tribal land. In 1987, in a six-to-three decision that crossed ideological lines (it placed conservative Chief Justice William Rehnquist alongside liberal Justice William Brennan on the tribes' side and liberal Justice John Paul Stevens with conservative Justice Antonin Scalia on the state's), the Court ruled in favor of the tribes in the case of *California v. Cabazon Band of Mission Indians*. In essence, the majority held that unless a state consistently treats gambling as either a crime or a violation of its constitution, it cannot forbid gambling on tribal lands. Because California offered a cornucopia of legal gambling—not just bingo and card rooms but also a lottery and pari-mutuel betting on horse races—the Cabazons' gambling operations stood on solid, sovereign, constitutional ground.[31]

Responding to concerns expressed by many state governments, Congress quickly passed the Indian Gaming Regulatory Act (IGRA) of 1988. IGRA was an effort to foreclose some of the more dramatic possibilities raised by *Cabazon*. To be sure, Congress did not allow state and local governments to tax, zone, or regulate tribal gambling operations on tribal land—activities that clearly would be out of keeping with the Supreme Court's oft-affirmed doctrine of tribal sovereignty. But while sounding the all clear for bingo, IGRA stated that a tribe could operate a "Class III" gambling facility (that is, a casino) against a state government's will only if its reservation was in a state whose own laws allowed Class III gambling. IGRA also stipulated that, before opening a casino, a tribe must negotiate a compact with the state government covering matters such as the terms of tribal-state criminal justice cooperation and standards for the operation of gambling facilities. Only an entire tribe could own a gambling facility, IGRA further specified, not just a group of enterprising tribal members. The only tribes IGRA authorized to do so were those that had secured federal recognition as historic tribes.[32]

These restrictions on tribal gambling initially turned out to be less imposing in practice than either Congress or the states had hoped. Consider, for example, the provision of the act stating that a federally recognized tribe can operate a casino on reservation land only in a "state that permits such gaming for any purpose by any person." The federal Second Circuit Court of Appeals interpreted the provision to mean that Connecticut, whose laws permitted charitable organizations to hold occasional "Las Vegas Night" fundraising events, had to allow tribes to own and operate casinos.[33] As a result, the Mashantucket Pequots, with their reservation situated midway between New York City and Boston, translated federal recognition in 1983 into the Foxwoods Resort Casino in 1992.[34] Foxwoods soon became the most financially successful casino in the world.[35]

To be sure, for the majority of Indian tribes, *Cabazon* was of limited practical benefit. To run a profitable gambling operation requires a nearby "feeder market"—that is, a metropolitan area, tourism center, or heavily trafficked interstate highway exit that is dense with potential customers. This leaves out nearly all the 232 federally recognized tribes whose reservations are in Alaska, where only three tribes have found it financially worthwhile to open gambling facilities. Furthermore, given the federal government's long history of driving Indians onto lands unwanted by white settlers, the right to offer high-stakes gambling was of little use to many of the tribes in the Plains and Rocky Mountain regions of the lower forty-eight states. Although large numbers of Indians live in Montana, Nevada, North Dakota, and South Dakota, their share of total tribal casino revenues is tiny.[36] For tribes that are more fortunately situated, however, *Cabazon* was a license to print money. Indeed, by 2006 the tribal casinos located in just five states—California, Connecticut, Florida, Arizona, and Oklahoma—accounted for more than 60 percent of all the money made by American Indian tribes from gambling.[37]

Even for well-situated tribes, not every negotiation with the states went smoothly. As noted above, Connecticut only accepted the inevitability of the Pequot-owned casino after the tribe sued the state for not negotiating "in good faith" and then won a judgment from a federal appeals court. The Supreme Court subsequently closed this door to other tribes that were being stonewalled by state governments. In the 1996 case of *Seminole Tribe of Florida v. Florida*, the Court voted five to four that the Eleventh Amendment's guarantee of sovereign immunity to the states protects them from lawsuits by Indian tribes.[38] In contrast to *Cabazon*, the voting on *Seminole* was strictly along ideological lines, with the conservative majority united in defense of state sovereignty.

Shorn by the Court of their legal right to force states to negotiate compacts, many tribes turned to politics. Indeed, some already had done so. The right of the Pequots and, soon after, the Mohegans to operate casinos on their lands in Connecticut initially did not include slot machines, which are by far the most lucrative games in the casino industry. As sovereign governments, tribes cannot be forced to pay state taxes. But they can elect to "contribute" to a state's treasury. The Connecticut tribes agreed, in return for the exclusive right to operate slot machines in the state, to give the government in Hartford 25 percent of their slot revenues—around $400 million annually in recent years.

At the federal level, the tribes' representation among the top twenty political donors in the Center for Responsive Politics' "Casinos/Gambling" sector rose from 10 percent in 1994 to 35 percent in 1996 (the year of the *Seminole* decision) and to 75 percent by 2006.[39] To be sure, some tribal spending in Washington was wasted on scams perpetrated by crooked lobbyist Jack Abramoff, who bilked several tribes out of millions of dollars by peddling influence he did not have. But for the most part casino tribes became effective inside-the-beltway players.

In the states, too, tribes in the post-*Seminole* era learned to play hardball politics adroitly. In California, for example, various tribes wanting to open casinos with slot machines poured more than $7 million into the state's 1998 gubernatorial and legislative campaigns, including $650,000 to the winning candidate for governor, Democrat Gray Davis. After the election, they spent more than $2 million lobbying the legislature. In 1999 Davis and a majority of legislators agreed to place a tribal casino constitutional amendment on the March 2000 ballot. Proposition 1A proposed to grant tribes the exclusive right to own and operate casinos in the state. Voters approved it by 53 percent to 47 percent.[40]

The sixty-two compacts signed by Governor Davis in 2002 allowed each tribe to operate as many as two thousand slot machines in return for contributing to funds that would be established to help non-casino tribes and local governments. In 2004 Gray's successor as governor, Arnold Schwarzenegger, negotiated new compacts with five tribes that roughly tripled the number of slot machines allowed in their casinos. The tribes promised an initial payment to the state treasury of $1 billion as well as a licensing fee for every new slot machine that was expected to net the state $150 to 275 million per year. In 2006 California tribes earned $7.7 billion, or 30 percent, of the $25.5 billion earned by all tribal casinos.[41]

In addition to cash and strategic savvy, tribal governments have other political assets to deploy in their relations with the state and federal governments. Indian casinos are major employers, mostly of nontribal members. They enjoy more support in public opinion polls than commercial casinos, in part because of the widespread belief that American Indians have been treated badly over the years and deserve some leeway in their efforts to attain economic self-reliance. In addition, many tribal casinos have management contracts with commercial casino companies to assist them in opening and operating their facilities. These contracts, or the prospect of them, have helped to neutralize what once was powerful opposition from the commercial casino industry. In 1998, the first year Californians voted to legalize tribal casinos, the commercial casino industry spent $26 million in opposition. In 2000, when Proposition 1A passed, commercial casinos generally stayed on the sideline.

Contentious issues still remain in the sovereign politics of tribal gambling. Under IGRA, all three sovereign governments—state, federal, and tribal—share responsibility for casino regulation in ways that are complex and sometimes full of conflict. The federal Bureau of Indian Affairs (BIA) is chiefly responsible for determining which new claimants to historic tribal status will receive federal recognition and thus become eligible to open casinos on their reservations.[42] State and local governments often fight these bids for recognition tooth and nail. The BIA also is responsible for deciding whether existing tribes' petitions to open casinos on nonreservation land, usually close to population centers, should be granted—another matter of sometimes fierce contention in state capitals and in Washington.

The Third Wave of Legalized Gambling: Internet Betting

Sovereign complexity in the politics of gambling is nowhere more apparent than in the domain of Internet betting: casinos, sports books, poker, and other forms of online wagering. In contrast to lottery and commercial casino gambling, in which state governments have always been the primary policy makers, and tribal casino gambling, in which the state, tribal, and federal governments have all been active participants, the federal government has been the dominant sovereign actor within the United States on matters concerning Internet gambling. That dominance has been complicated, however, by the overlapping activities of foreign sovereigns; both the governments of other nations and the World Trade Organization, a body that the United States not only joined but helped to create.

Internet gambling did not exist until 1995 or 1996, when the first online gambling Web sites were launched. By 1997 about fifty sites were open on the Internet. As low-overhead businesses operating in a rapidly growing global medium, they earned an estimated $300 to 350 million that year. In 2000 more than six hundred sites were operating, with annual revenues approaching $2 billion. By 2005 the number of sites had risen to about twenty-five hundred, with revenues close to $12 billion. After pornography, gambling was the leading generator of revenue on the Internet.[43] According to a 2006 study commissioned by the American Gaming Association, roughly 35 percent of this revenue comes from sports betting, about 25 percent from casino gambling, about 18 percent from poker, and the rest from lotteries, pari-mutuel betting, and other sources.[44]

Although Americans put up about half of the money wagered on the Internet, virtually every online casino, sports book, and poker site is located abroad, where foreign governments have made them legal and welcome. Nearly three-fourths of these sites are in Antigua and Barbuda (536); Costa Rica (474); the Kahnawake Mohawk reservation in Quebec, Canada (401); and Costa Rica (343).[45] In 2005 the British parliament made Internet gambling legal in Great Britain starting in September 2007. The clientele for online betting is small but growing (according to surveys conducted by Peter Hart and Frank Luntz, it doubled from about 2 percent of Americans in 2004 to 4 percent in 2005) and is much more weighted toward young college-educated men than are the clienteles for other forms of gambling.[46]

From the start, Washington and the states have been hostile to Internet betting, which for several years was as easy for credit card holders to engage in as shopping for books at Amazon.com. The coalition of opposition united the usual foes of legalized gambling, many of them motivated by moral concerns, with the established gambling industry: lottery-sponsoring state governments, racetracks and horse breeders and, for quite a while, commercial casinos. Several states enacted laws specifically banning Internet gambling, and in most others attorneys general or courts ruled that existing state laws already banned it. But as Anthony Cabot and Kevin Doty have observed, "regulating Internet gambling presents technical and legal problems that state governments are ill-equipped to handle," especially jurisdiction.[47] In a move that was unusual in its plea for federal rather than state action, the National Association of Attorneys General called on Washington in the mid-1990s to extend its authority over online gambling.

The federal government initially relied on the Wire Act of 1961 to justify crackdowns on Internet betting, and still does to some extent. In both the Clinton and George W. Bush administrations, the Department of Justice ordered occasional arrests of offshore Internet gambling operators when they entered the United States. Along with the attorney general of New York, the department successfully pressured major credit card companies to prohibit customers from using their cards to finance online wagers. It also leaned heavily on American media outlets to stop accepting advertising from gambling Web sites, making an example of the parent company of *The Sporting News*, which paid a $4.2 million fine and agreed to spend an additional $3 million for ads warning that online gambling is illegal. The Justice Department's expansive interpretation of the Wire Act, combined with a provision of the 2001 U.S.A. Patriot Act that forbids the electronic transmission of funds related to criminal activities, enabled it to crack down on PayPal, the leading online payment provider, which paid a $10 million fine and exited the Internet gambling business. Online gamblers unable to use their credit cards had turned to PayPal as a way of moving funds back and forth to online gambling Web sites.

Legally, the reliance on the Wire Act was problematic from the start. The act was written nearly a half-century ago to allow federal law enforcement officials to prosecute bookies for taking bets on a "sporting event or contest" by "wire communication"—that is, by landline telephones or telegraphs. The act did not contemplate wireless methods of communication and funds transmission, betting on poker or casino games, or offshore gambling sites invited into people's homes at the click of a mouse. It also left the United States wide open to the complaint that Antigua and Barbuda filed with the World Trade Organization in 2003. The complaint, which the WTO upheld in 2004 and later, on appeal, in 2005 and 2007, held that the American approach to cross-border online gambling violated the General Agreement on Trade in Services, which the United States and other member nations had created the WTO in 1995 to enforce. In responding to this ruling, the United States may be able to stare down tiny Antigua and Barbuda, but that will not be so easy if Great Britain files a WTO complaint on behalf of its new Internet gambling sites.

In 2000 Congress came close to passing a bill designed to place federal policy toward online gambling on firmer legal footing.[48] The Internet Gambling Prohibition Act, a bill sponsored by Republican Senator John Kyl, would have explicitly extended the Wire Act's ban on using "wire communication" to lay bets to cover "wire or electronic communication." A broad spectrum of Christian groups supported the bill, ranging from the liberal National Council of Churches, which regards gambling as a threat to the poor, to the conservative Southern Baptist Convention, which is concerned primarily with issues of personal morality. These groups were joined by the American Gaming Association, representing the established "brick-and-mortar" casinos, and by amateur and professional sports organizations such as the National Football League and the National College Athletic Association, which were worried about the effects of Internet sports betting on the integrity of their games.

Kyl's bill passed the Senate three times in the late 1990s, but the House version, sponsored by Republican representative Bob Goodlatte of Virginia, inspired an even more unusual set of political alliances. Goodlatte's bill differed from the Senate version by not exempting state lotteries from its coverage, a modification that roused the opposition of several state governors but won the support of the National Association of Convenience Stores, whose members did not want to lose lottery ticket sales to Internet sites. In addition, the House bill continued to permit states, under the 1978 Interstate Horseracing Act, to have subscriber-based online networks for racetrack betting, which provoked the Traditional Values Coalition to break ranks with other Christian organizations and announce its opposition. (Not barring these networks also set up the United States for defeat in the WTO case, since it could not claim that as a matter of national moral policy it forbade all online gambling.) Opponents won the support of the Clinton administration, which continued to maintain that the Wire Act gave it all the authority it wanted or needed. The House bill failed when a motion to suspend the rules and hasten it to the floor fell short of the required two-thirds majority.

Adding to the legal problems associated with the federal government's antique reliance on the Wire Act was the more serious problem that Internet gambling continued to grow by leaps and bounds from the mid-1990s to the mid-2000s, with American gamblers fueling the expansion. For more than a century, the Justice Department has declined to prosecute individual gamblers and instead has targeted illegal gambling operators, a difficult strategy to pursue successfully against offshore Internet gambling sites that are legal in their home countries. Not even Kyl's attempt to persuade Congress to update the Wire Act so that it would explicitly encompass the Internet would have made this difficult strategy much easier.

In 2006 Congress took a different approach, this one aimed at neither gamblers nor gambling operators but rather at the flow of funds between them. Borrowing a recommendation from the National Gambling Impact Study Commission's 1999 report, Republican representative Jim Leach of Iowa sponsored the Unlawful Internet Gambling Enforcement Act forbidding financial institutions to process payments from illegal gambling sites.[49] Specifically, the bill barred the use of credit card transactions, electronic funds transfers, and money-transmitting businesses for purposes of illegal gambling. Because, as David Stewart points out, "the Internet gambling industry has managed to stay one step ahead of enforcement authorities by migrating its payment schemes to new platforms as existing platforms become unavailable," the bill also authorized the Secretary of the Treasury to forbid the use of other payment systems that might arise in the future.[50] The bill's prohibitions on Internet gambling did not bar any state (or tribe within a state) from deciding to permit "intrastate transactions" relating to Internet gambling within its own borders. Nor did the bill bar Internet transactions that were already legal under the Interstate Horse Racing Act.

Leach and Senate Majority Leader Bill Frist (R-Tennessee) managed to slip the Unlawful Internet Gambling Enforcement

Act into the Security and Accountability for Every Port Act, an antiterrorism measure that Congress hastily passed, along with several other bills, on September 30, 2006, just before recessing for the midterm election campaign. President Bush signed the bill on October 13. From the start, reactions were mixed. Right after the new law took effect, the Justice Department subpoenaed records from sixteen major investment banks, including Credit Suisse and Deutsche Bank, demanding to see all records relating to their involvement with Internet gambling operations. In January 2007, the department indicted two former executives of Neteller, a British online money-transfer company and by far the largest processor of Internet gambling transactions in the world. Neteller promptly announced that it would no longer process such transactions from the United States. Other payment processing companies stepped forward to fill the void, however, just as Neteller had done when PayPal withdrew from the Internet gambling sector. Predicting that Internet gamblers and gambling operators would find a way around the new law, I. Nelson Rose and Joseph Kelly, respectively, dismissed it as "just a blip" and "just a hiccup" in the Internet casino business.[51]

Sovereign complexity continues to confound the politics of Internet gambling. The federal government has been generally ineffective at deterring online wagering by Americans because other sovereign governments have chosen to make legal an activity that the Internet makes ubiquitous. To the extent that Washington steps up its enforcement efforts against Internet gambling, it invites further retaliation by these governments through the World Trade Organization. Domestic political pressures on the federal government to step back from its aggressive approach may arise, however. The American Gaming Association recently abandoned its opposition to Internet gambling and took no position on the Unlawful Internet Gambling Enforcement Act. The AGA, which once saw Internet casinos as a threat to the brick-and-mortar casino industry, is now open to the possibility that if Internet betting is legalized, name-brand casino companies such as Harrah's Entertainment and MGM Mirage could quickly become the industry leaders. Although the AGA has not endorsed the bill introduced in 2007 by House Financial Services Committee Chair Barney Frank (D-Massachusetts) to federally license and regulate Internet gambling, it did issue a statement to "commend . . . his efforts to study the issue" and praised him as a "defender of individual freedom." The AGA also endorsed Nevada Democrat Shelley Berkley's bill to instruct the National Academy of Sciences to study the subject.

Conclusion

During most of American history, the sovereign politics of gambling has been the politics of the sovereign states. Over the course of the three waves of gambling legalization, lotteries in the United States have been legalized, then banned; re-legalized and banned again; and legalized once more (this time in state-owned rather than state-sanctioned form). This has been almost entirely because of decisions made by state governments. The same can be said of racetracks and commercial casinos.

Of the other sovereignties discussed in this chapter, the only one that mattered even a little for many years was the federal government, and it generally acted only when problems arose that states could not handle on their own. In the 1890s, responding to pressure from many states, Washington helped bring about the end of the Louisiana Lottery, whose tentacles reached through the mails, trains, and telegraph wires to every corner of the Union. During the quarter century after World War II, the federal government helped to create an unfavorable climate for commercial casino gambling through congressional hearings and other measures aimed at publicizing and then severing the link between casino gambling and national crime syndicates. In the early 1990s, Congress froze legal sports betting, declaring that no state that did not already allow gambling on sports was eligible to do so. The two commissions that Congress created to study gambling—one in 1976 and the other in 1996—were in a sense exceptions that demonstrated the rule of state supremacy: both of them placed the burden on the states to make the nation's most important decisions concerning gambling.

In recent years additional sovereign entities have staked a claim on policymaking toward gambling. During the 1980s, American Indian tribes, encouraged to some extent by the federal government, began entering the high-stakes bingo and casino business on their own, constitutionally free from undue interference by the states. More recently, foreign governments have legalized Internet gambling and, when impeded by Washington in their attempts to enter the lucrative American market, have turned to international organizations for support.

Nevertheless, the main result of the recent growth of sovereign complexity in gambling politics and policy has been the increased, albeit reluctant, involvement by the federal government. It is Washington that has been forced by state and tribal governments to make rules and then referee disputes concerning tribal gambling. It is Washington to which the states have turned in their efforts to resist the spread of foreign-based Internet gambling into the homes and workplaces of their people, often in competition with state lotteries and state-based casinos and racetracks. This intensifying of federal involvement has been fueled by the rise of Washington-based interest groups such as the American Gaming Association, as well as by ever-growing campaign contributions to federal candidates from commercial and tribal casinos and other gambling interests. In sum, the sovereign politics of gambling in America is becoming more Washington-centered because it is the federal government that lies at the intersection of state, tribal, and foreign sovereignties. One can only imagine how intense this politics would become if either conservatives or liberals overcame their reluctance, well described in Alan Wolfe's chapter in this volume, to place gambling high on their list of moral political concerns.

3

Negotiating a Different Terrain
Morality, Policymaking, and Indian Gaming

Kathryn R.L. Rand and Steven Andrew Light

The history of gambling suggests that risk-taking and faith in luck are part of the shared human experience.[1] Varying degrees of moral objection to gambling have coexisted alongside gambling throughout history and across cultures. In modern times, the tension between gambling's popularity and moral questionability has greatly influenced how governments treat gambling.

Debates over the morality of gambling are fairly predictable. Some people oppose gambling on religious principles, believing that the concept of "luck" is inconsistent with divine power or that gamblers exercise poor stewardship of godly gifts. Others contend that gambling is harmful, emphasizing that it undermines a societal work ethic, leads to crime, or creates human and economic costs related to problem and pathological gambling. Still others argue that the costs of gambling fall disproportionately on the poor. On the other side, gambling proponents have pointed out the industry's contributions to economic development, its status as "voluntary" taxation to benefit worthy causes or subsidize public treasuries, and the appropriateness of the state's role in maximizing individual freedom.

Government responses to gambling in the United States have run the gamut from enforced blanket prohibitions to nominal prohibitions, from regulation of select games to state-sponsored lotteries, and at last to full-scale casino gambling with the market as a primary constraint. Legal scholar Skolnick notes that the moral ambivalence toward gambling makes law and policy governing gambling dynamic, unpredictable, and less tethered to either consensus or evidence than are other, more conventional forms of policymaking.[2] As a morally and politically contested "normal vice,"[3] many object to gambling while many more enjoy it.

Policy Studies professor Peter Collins wryly notes that an individual's perspective on gambling policy "will depend on whether you think gambling is most relevantly similar to going to the movies, ingesting cocaine, watching soap operas, eating candy, playing golf, consuming pornography, smoking, having a massage, attending a ball game, visiting a brothel, riding a roller coaster, shopping, or having a drink."[4] All these activities result from individual choices, whether based on free will or on compulsion or addiction. All may afford pleasure, require some form of payment, result in overindulgence, or cause harm to the individual or others. The aggregate effects of each behavior affect society to varying degrees and with disparate results. Given their potential harms, some such behaviors suggest the need for stringent government regulation or even outright prohibition.

Morality policymaking, also known as social regulatory policymaking, involves the "use of authority to modify or replace social values, institutional practices, and norms of interpersonal behavior with new modes of conduct based upon legal proscriptions."[5] Gambling regulation invokes elements of social regulatory policymaking in which the state redistributes societal values, but this is not the only rationale for regulating gambling. Gambling policy also has the goal of facilitating the purposive allocation and reallocation of economic resources to different populations and economic sectors. In other words, gambling regulation involves the type of distributive and redistributive governmental outputs described in the classic formulation of political scientist Theodore Lowi.[6] The result is a distribution of regulatory policy outputs (gaming operators' licenses, for instance), or the redistribution of wealth, property, or power to different stakeholders (for example, upward, to commercial gaming conglomerates like Harrah's or MGM Mirage, or downward, to impoverished American Indian tribes). A regulatory scheme should ensure that those who benefit from the distribution and redistribution of gambling revenue and other valuable resources (jobs, political clout) are those whom the government intends to benefit.[7]

As a basis for morality policymaking, it stands to reason that moral convictions about gambling should be defended with rational argument and empirical evidence.[8] Oftentimes, however, impassioned debates over the appropriateness of state sanction for legalized gambling and the extent to which it should be regulated turn on intense personal preferences rooted in ideology, presupposition, or overgeneralization.[9]

A thorough examination of the problems and promise of morality policymaking and legalized gambling in the United States is beyond the scope of this chapter. In addition to the perspectives found in this volume, others have tackled the general morality of gambling policy and social regulation from the vantage point of law, political theory, economics, public health, public affairs, and research imperatives.[10] Relying on at least one overriding point of consensus among diverse accounts, we take it as a given that the gambling industry raises special legal and policy concerns requiring comprehensive and multilayered government regulation.

Our focus here is on Indian gaming, which in just two decades has become a $26 billion industry and is the fastest growing segment of the legalized gambling industry in the United States. Approximately 230 tribes own and operate some four hundred casinos in about twenty-eight states. Tribal gaming is transforming the quality of life on many reservations. Yet the spread of Indian gaming has given rise to contentious, polarizing debates over its policy rationale, socioeconomic impact, and morality. The morality policymaking landscape for Indian gaming is largely uncharted. In this chapter, we explore that terrain and map its contours.

While some of the literature on social regulatory policymaking and moral governance nods at the burgeoning Indian gaming industry, there has been virtually no in-depth or systematic analysis of whether regulatory and other legal and policy issues are any *different* in the context of Indian gaming, and if so, how they do or should inform policymaking.[11] Once the question is asked, whether the tribal gaming industry elicits unique concerns, the possibility arises that the answer to this question should guide how federal, tribal, and state authority over Indian gaming is allocated, how and what public policy should be developed and implemented, and how that public policy should be evaluated to determine whether it is serving its intended purposes.

In this chapter, we argue that Indian gaming requires adjustment to the models typically used to explain or guide morality or social regulatory policymaking concerning gambling. Indian gaming is in fact generally different than legalized gambling for three fundamental reasons: first, Indian gaming is an exercise of tribal sovereignty, which reflects tribes' unique status in the American political system; second, conducted by tribal governments, Indian gaming is public gaming; and third, Indian gaming is an effective means to address continuing socioeconomic deficits in many tribal communities. These differences create an imperative for policymakers at the local, state, federal, and tribal levels: regardless of the substantive policy outcomes, governments are obligated to take account of Indian gaming's distinct characteristics when engaged in the law- and policymaking process.

Several caveats are in order about what we are and are not attempting to accomplish in this account. Let us first be clear in drawing the distinction between individually held moral beliefs and moral or ethical law- and policymaking. Individual preferences are at least one step removed from government action; however, individuals do formulate opinions, make decisions, participate in public debate, and behave in accordance with public policy. We leave the exploration of significant questions related to individual morality to others, including several of the authors in this volume. We also recognize the importance of ongoing social-psychological research into addictive behaviors such as problem and pathological gambling and their attendant social costs, which may stem from legalized gambling. But gambling addiction and its mitigation or prevention, also discussed elsewhere in this book, are likewise beyond the scope of our inquiry.

Here we concern ourselves not with individual moral or ethical principles reflecting the place of gambling in society or with the linkages between legalized gambling and addictive behavior but rather with the question of how tribal, state, local, and federal governments should conduct themselves concerning Indian gaming. How should governments approach issues related to gambling? What is the ethical public policy for governments to enact in a society where individuals hold different preferences at different strengths concerning legalized gambling? And does Indian gaming present different issues that should inform policy specific to that industry? We wish to be clear that our focus is on identifying the potential differences between gambling sponsored by states or private entities and gambling sponsored by tribal governments, not on drawing moral conclusions about gambling or Indian gaming.

What Is Indian Gaming?

As defined by federal law, "Indian gaming" is gaming conducted by an "Indian tribe" on "Indian lands" in states whose public policy allows for such gaming.[12] Codified in the Indian Gaming Regulatory Act of 1988 (IGRA), these legal requirements create the outer boundaries of a regulatory framework that has facilitated exponential industry growth.[13]

Today all but two states, Utah and Hawaii, permit some form of legalized gambling, including gaming in riverboat or land-based casinos, racetrack pari-mutuel wagering, charitable gaming, and state-run lotteries. The rapid growth rate for Indian gaming mirrors or even exceeds that of the exploding legalized gambling industry in its many forms. In 2007 some four hundred gaming establishments, operated by approximately 230 tribes, earned over $26 billion in gaming revenue, nearly quintuple the $5.4 billion earned in 1995.[14] Tribes use Indian gaming revenue to provide basic government services and to fuel economic development that is fundamentally changing the quality of life for many American Indians across the United States.

Although popular media accounts tend to lump tribes together, providing a pan-Indian narrative of tribal gaming, there is considerable variation among tribes and tribal experiences with casino-style gaming.[15] Some tribes have decided not to pursue casino-style gaming or, in some cases, any form of gaming; for a few tribes, gaming is not feasible, either because their reservations are located in states that disallow any form of gambling or because isolated locales or lack of financial resources restrict their ability to open or sustain a casino.[16] For tribes with gaming operations, casinos located in or near large metropolitan areas with ready access to literally millions of customers earn more than those in rural locales. The most lucrative tribal gaming operations near population centers in California and Connecticut gross in excess of $1 billion in annual revenue. It is more typical, however, for annual revenues to amount to a fraction of this number. In 2007, less than 6 percent of tribal gaming operations earned more than $250 million, accounting for over 40 percent of the total industry revenue. On the other hand, more than half of tribal casinos earned $25 million or less. One out of every six tribal casinos earned less than $3 million, often just enough to keep the casino doors open and to provide some modest tribal government revenue.[17]

Indian gaming is subject to a complex regulatory scheme that in some ways reflects the public policy goals embodied in the regulation of legalized gambling more generally. The purpose and role of the state in regulating individual behavior and serving the public interest varies depending upon the type of gambling that is the subject of government intervention.

The Regulation of Legalized Gambling

Legalized gambling's explosion over the past few decades has engendered critical questions and ongoing controversy about the appropriate role of the state. Should governments permit or prohibit gambling? What public purpose does either stance serve? If permitted, what games should be allowed and why? How should government regulate gaming to maximize its benefits while minimizing its harms?

In its 1999 *Final Report*, the National Gambling Impact Study Commission (NGISC) outlined the policy rationales and challenges for government regulation of legalized gambling:

> In addition to . . . relatively well-defined policing functions, a broader and far more important role for government regulation is determining the scope and manifestation of gambling's presence in society and thus its impact on the general public. In this sense, regulation can be broadly defined to include the political process by which the major decisions regarding legalized gambling are arrived at, the

corresponding legislation and rules specifying the conditions of its operation, and the direction given to regulatory bodies. Through such means as specifying the number, location, and the size of gambling facilities; the types of games that can be offered; the conditions under which licensed facilities may operate; and so forth, governments have considerable control over the benefits and costs legalized gambling can bring with it. These measures can be as simple and straightforward as attempting to prevent underage gambling or as ambitious and contentious as promoting traditional social values.

If this basic responsibility is to be adequately met, government decisions regarding the introduction and regulation of legalized gambling would best be made according to a well-defined public policy, one formulated with specific goals and limits in mind. . . . Generally, what is missing in the area of gambling regulation is a well thought-out scheme of how gambling can best be utilized to advance the larger public purpose and a corresponding role for regulation. Instead, much of what exists is far more the product of incremental and disconnected decisions, often taken in reaction to pressing issues of the day, than one based on sober assessments of long-term needs, goals, and risks.[18]

In the last fifty years, three distinct regulatory models have accompanied the expansion of legalized gambling in the areas of commercial casinos, charitable gambling, state lotteries, and Indian gaming. The modern gambling industry is subject to intense government scrutiny through extensive regulations governing many aspects of gaming, including what forms of gambling are allowed, where and when games may be conducted and under what conditions, who may work for or own a gambling establishment, and who may gamble. Gambling regulations generally share two key social-control functions: ensuring the integrity of the games and preventing the infiltration of organized and common crime. Regulatory schemes also are intended to facilitate common economic development goals related to gambling enterprises, such as revitalization of local and regional economies, job creation, and government revenue generation. The three regulatory models are determined by both the scope and the purpose of the gaming.

Commercial Casinos

The model for regulating commercial casinos has its genesis in the casino industries of Nevada and New Jersey. Nevada legalized "wide-open gaming" in 1931, but the state legislature adopted the current regulatory model in the late 1950s in the wake of the Kefauver Commission's investigation of organized crime and its ties to Las Vegas casinos. The scope of essentially unlimited high-stakes casino games required aggressive government regulation, while the purpose of encouraging strong industry growth (and, indirectly, of increasing the state's "take" through taxation) further shaped Nevada's regulation of commercial casinos. Nevada's approach "seeks to maximize economic benefits of gaming, and allows the industry to meet market demands with little regulatory involvement."[19] Indeed, the state legislature's declaration of Nevada's public policy toward gambling begins, "The gaming industry is vitally important to the economy of the State and the general welfare of the inhabitants."[20] Business decisions concerning casino size and which and how many games are offered are left to the casinos themselves. Consumer demand and development of "niche" markets, rather than regulatory constraints, determine the scope of the gaming industry in Nevada.

When New Jersey became the second state to legalize commercial casinos in 1976, the regulatory model adopted by the state legislature sought foremost to minimize gambling's negative externalities, even at the expense of economic growth, by limiting the size and scope of gaming. The state's comprehensive regulatory scheme "strictly governs virtually every aspect of the business."[21] For example, New Jersey law sets limits on a casino's square footage and further restricts the space that may be allocated to slot machines or high-stakes games. As one commentator noted, the New Jersey model produced a highly controlled casino industry and paid for it through comparatively stunted revenues and economic impacts.[22]

Nevada's and New Jersey's regulatory schemes serve as somewhat divergent prototypical models for state regulation. Variants of these models govern the proliferation of most legalized gaming conducted by private industry, particularly riverboat and other commercial casinos, across the United States.[23]

Charitable Gambling and State Lotteries

Beginning in the mid-twentieth century, several states relaxed stringent bans on gambling to allow religious and civic organizations to conduct church bingo games, charity raffles, and "Las

Vegas night" fundraisers. It was a short step from gambling for a "good cause" to gambling to contribute to the public treasuries in lieu of direct taxation. In a trend started by New Hampshire's institution of a state lottery in 1964, some forty states and the District of Columbia currently operate lotteries.[24] State lotteries and charitable gambling gave rise to a second regulatory model with a more limited scope than commercial casinos in terms of the types and circumstances of permitted games, and with a focus on gaming for public or socially worthy purposes.

In contrast to commercial, for-profit gambling enterprises, charitable gambling operations typically contribute to not-for-profit organizations while state lotteries directly raise public funds (sometimes called a "voluntary tax"). Lottery revenue usually is earmarked for a particular programmatic purpose, often public education.

State lotteries and charitable gambling are the least regulated forms of legalized gambling, in large part because of the narrow scope of the games (charitable gambling, for example, generally has strict limits on jackpot and bet size, and often is limited to specific games that may be offered only occasionally). State lotteries are, of course, regulated by the state (often, the regulation is essentially "built in" to the operation of the lottery). In addition to ensuring fairness and preventing related crime, state lottery agencies also are responsible for marketing lottery products.

Indian Gaming

The third regulatory model governing modern legalized gambling was created through IGRA. Indian gaming regulation is in notable ways an outgrowth of the prior two models, with similarities to the scope of commercial casinos, the "good cause" of charitable gambling, and the public nature of state lotteries. Unlike most legalized gambling, which is authorized and regulated by state law, the Indian gaming industry is a product of federal and tribal authority. Importantly, IGRA's regulatory scheme is most markedly influenced by each tribe's status as a sovereign government.

Indian gaming's history is quite recent. In the late 1970s and early 1980s, a number of tribes opened high-stakes bingo palaces as a means of tribal economic development. Because federal Indian law generally precluded state regulation of tribes, tribal bingo operations frequently did not comply with state restrictions on jackpot amounts and use of gaming profits. In California, the Cabazon and Morongo Bands of Mission Indians operated bingo halls and a card club on their reservations. When the state threatened to shut down the tribes' gaming operations, the tribes challenged the state's enforcement of its gaming regulations on the tribes' reservations. The case culminated in the U.S. Supreme Court's landmark 1987 decision in *California v. Cabazon Band of Mission Indians.*[25]

Congress had granted California criminal and some civil authority over the tribes within its borders through a federal statute known as Public Law 280.[26] In the state's view, this authorized application of California's bingo regulations on the tribes' reservations. In an earlier case, the Supreme Court had ruled that Public Law 280's civil provision conferred only adjudicatory authority rather than general regulatory jurisdiction.[27] Accordingly, the *Cabazon* Court explained, while Public Law 280's broader grant of criminal jurisdiction would allow California to enforce state criminal prohibitions against gambling on tribal lands, the state did not have authority to enforce its civil gambling regulations against the tribes.

Relying on this "criminal/prohibitory–civil/regulatory" distinction,[28] the Court examined the state's public policy concerning gambling, noting that California operated a state lottery and permitted pari-mutuel horse-race betting, bingo, and card games. "In light of the fact that California permits a substantial amount of gambling activity, including bingo, and actually promotes gambling through its state lottery," the Court reasoned, "we must conclude that California regulates rather than prohibits gambling in general and bingo in particular."[29]

In its decision, the *Cabazon* Court noted that the relevant federal interests in the case were "traditional notions of Indian sovereignty and the congressional goal of Indian self-government, including its 'overriding goal' of encouraging tribal self-sufficiency and economic development."[30] The tribes' own interests paralleled those of the federal government:

> The Cabazon and Morongo Reservations contain no natural resources which can be exploited. The tribal games at present provide the sole source of revenues for the operation of the tribal governments and

the provision of tribal services. They are also the major sources of employment on the reservations. Self-determination and economic development are not within reach if the Tribes cannot raise revenues and provide employment for their members.[31]

In the end, *Cabazon* was a victory for the tribes, as the Court held that tribal gaming was a manifestation of tribes' governmental authority, thus preventing the states from regulating reservation gaming enterprises. Rather than resolving the issue, though, the Court's decision raised the stakes in the contest between tribal and state power and raised the hackles of the commercial gaming industry. The following year, Congress struck a compromise through IGRA.

Congress' declaration of policy in IGRA reflected its intent to create a comprehensive regulatory framework that ostensibly balanced tribal sovereignty and reservation economic development with state interests in controlling the crime assumed to be associated with high-stakes casino gambling. Thus, the congressional purposes served by IGRA were to codify the tribes' right to conduct gaming on Indian lands as a means of promoting tribal economic development, self-sufficiency, and strong tribal governments while also providing sufficient regulation to ensure legality and to protect the financial interests of the tribes.[32]

IGRA's key innovation was its categorization of three classes of gaming for regulatory purposes: Class I, or social or traditional tribal games, to which IGRA does not apply; Class II, or bingo and similar games as well as non-house-banked card games, which are regulated primarily by tribal governments with federal oversight; and Class III, or casino-style games, which require both tribal regulation and a tribal-state compact.[33] Class II and Class III gaming are legal only in states that "permit such gaming."[34] In other words, generally speaking, if a type of gambling is legal under state public policy, it is legal for a tribe as well. For Class III gaming, Congress intended the tribal-state compact requirement to encourage states and tribes to negotiate, on a government-to-government basis, issues related to the regulation of casino-style gaming on tribes' reservations.

Indian gaming, then, is regulated by three levels of government: tribal, state, and federal. Depending on state law, its scope may include full-scale casino gambling or may be limited to bingo. Like state lotteries, Indian gaming is public gaming—that is, government-operated—and tribal gaming revenues must be used for specified purposes related to the welfare of the tribe and its members. Indian gaming's primary purpose is to promote tribal economic development, self-sufficiency, and strong tribal governments. As discussed below, this purpose is the product of tribes' unique status in the American political system as well as the legacies of colonialism and tribal-federal-state conflict.

Morality Policymaking and Legalized Gambling

Morality policymaking can be examined on two levels: process and outcome. As observed by political scientists, citizen involvement in the process of morality policymaking reflects intensely held moral beliefs and policy preferences concerning the substantive outcomes. The government's response can be informed by public policy goals, as discussed in the preceding section on gambling regulatory models, as well as by principles of representation and moral governance.

Explaining the Process

Lowi's landmark insight into the policymaking process was that different types of policy generate different types of politics.[35] Although robust in its explanatory force, Lowi's breakthrough seemed to be lacking an essential policy type.[36] Lowi had accounted for the regulation of economic or market-based activity, but not necessarily for the state's regulation of individual moral behavior, or what political scientists Raymond Tatalovich and Byron Daynes labeled "social regulatory policy."[37] Hence social regulatory or morality policies came to be identified as value-based forms of social regulation undergirded by moral arguments to support a policy position.[38] Contemporary morality policy issues include abortion, capital punishment, euthanasia, gay and lesbian rights, gun control, medical marijuana, obscenity and pornography, religious free exercise, or establishment matters such as school prayer and the teaching of intelligent design, and, of course, gambling.

As the conception of morality policy was refined to encompass the state's redistribution of social values,[39] the key variable in the politics of morality policy emerged as core values, often rooted in individuals' "first principles," with strongly held or even uncompromising religious underpinnings.[40] Morality policy issues tend to be nontechnical; an individual can develop an intensely held substantive opinion without much specialized knowledge or expertise. The policy questions that give rise to the politics of social regulation generate high degrees of citizen interest and participation and interest group activity.[41] The policymaking process for morality issues therefore receives intense public scrutiny, and public officials may act according to electoral imperatives.[42] Public opinion and direct political engagement on morality issues, mediated by such factors as religious affiliation or religiosity, partisanship, and ideology, can influence the type and scope of public policy outcomes.[43]

As the product of core values concerning vice, sin, or just deserts which frequently are rooted in religious teachings or other moral and ethical worldviews that generate intense policy preferences, gambling policy is a paradigmatic example of morality policy.[44] Gambling policy is generated by political or economic variables that shape legal, regulatory, and other policy outcomes.[45] Although the contemporary policy debates over the state's appropriate role in sponsoring or promoting gambling are intense and even volatile,[46] outright prohibition seems not to be on the table. Instead, gambling in its many manifestations is subject to regulatory schemes generally designed to mitigate negative externalities, such as problem and pathological gambling, and to restrict market expansion while maximizing consumer freedom and economic benefits to the state.

Informing the Outcome

As Skolnick notes,[47] the policy outcomes on morality issues vary widely over a "normal vice" such as gambling. Because there is no clear moral consensus on gambling, the results of moral policymaking are inconsistent, unpredictable, and highly dynamic.[48] Lowi observes that "the politics of gambling is only one of the more recent morality plays" in which morality is pitted against utility in a contest "between the angels and the agents."[49]

One option to resolve such contests—or at least to stake out a position—is to retreat to unyielding principles of political theory that rest on an underlying premise that the goals of moral statecraft and moral governance are the appropriate determinants of morality law- and policymaking. Here, the moral or ethical high ground can be obtained by marrying Western political thought to empirically rooted assertions.

Collins, for example, categorizes the arguments in favor of government prohibition of gambling as grounded in enforcement of morals, paternalism or protectionism, human and social costs (particularly of problem and pathological gambling), democratic consensus or majoritarianism, and practical difficulties of effective regulation.[50] The answer to a pivotal question—"What should the law be regarding gambling?"—stems from a "combination of normative and empirical judgments" dependent upon both the "political principles and social ideals to which we subscribe" and "what we think as a matter of fact will be the likely consequences of adopting one policy rather than another."[51] Collins then sets forth why gambling should be legal and regulated based on his "value judgments" and "conception of how a morally attractive society will be governed."[52] He summarizes and responds to the case to be made based on utilitarianism (what will be the greatest good or happiness for the greatest number of people) and the moral principles of justice (retributive or just deserts versus distributive or social justice). Informed by John Stuart Mill's *On Liberty*, Collins concludes that the right to liberty (government should leave individuals alone to make their own decisions about their own lives) compels the maximization of individual freedom; however, this principle is not incompatible with subjecting legalized gambling to special regulation.[53]

When it comes to morality policymaking and legalized gambling, however, well thought-out, clearly articulated theoretical positions may not actually inform policy in the real world. As Collins notes throughout his arguments, sound application of moral principles may require better and more complete information on gambling's impacts.[54] Some observers have criticized the fact that gambling policy outcomes result from a process that privileges emotion or strongly held convictions rooted in individual moral beliefs and worldviews over soundly gathered and analyzed information and evidence. The NGISC, for example, cited the "lack of reliable information" as one of legalized gambling's defining characteristics: "On examination, much of what Americans think they know about gambling turns out to be exaggerated or taken out of context. And much of the information in circulation is inaccurate or even false, although loudly voiced by adherents."[55] The NGISC's caution is not limited to conventional wisdom, moreover, as some research is intended to promote one partisan view over another.[56] With gambling policy, as with morality policymaking generally, the quality of the information unfortunately tends to be less important than whether the information aligns with individual belief systems.

We turn now to examining the three fundamental reasons why Indian gaming is different than legalized gambling more generally: tribal sovereignty, the status of tribal gaming as public gaming, and tribal socioeconomic deficits.

The Different Terrain of Indian Gaming
Tribal Sovereignty

Tribal governments may conduct gambling on reservations not because a state or Congress has authorized them to do so but because Indian gaming is an aspect of tribal sovereignty. Tribal sovereignty—a historically rooted concept recognizing tribes' inherent rights as independent nations preexisting the United States and its Constitution—informs the primary legal and political foundation of federal Indian law and policy, thus informing Indian gaming as well. Yet tribal sovereignty is perhaps the most misunderstood aspect of Indian gaming.

The legally protected political autonomy of Indian tribes is a peculiar tenet of federal Indian law. The contemporary legal doctrine of tribal sovereignty essentially means that the United States recognizes tribes as independent sovereign nations whose location within the boundaries of a state does not subject them to the application of state law. At the same time, as "conquered" or "discovered" nations, tribes retain only the political and legal authority that Congress has not expressly abrogated under its asserted plenary power pursuant to the U.S. Constitution's Indian Commerce Clause. The federal legal doctrine of tribal sovereignty effectively means that tribes, in fact, are "semi-sovereign."[57]

Nevertheless, tribal sovereignty is the defining characteristic of tribal governments. Tribal governments and tribal members maintain deeply held convictions about the origins, meaning, and immutability of tribal sovereignty (views which, not incidentally, often are at odds with the federal legal doctrine). As one tribal leader put it, sovereignty is "the heart and soul" of American Indian peoples.[58]

Both the U.S. Supreme Court in deciding *Cabazon* and Congress in enacting IGRA recognized Indian gaming as an exercise of the tribes' inherent governmental authority. Although often erroneously identified as the source of the tribes' right to conduct gaming, IGRA actually is a set of legal, political, and regulatory limitations on that right. In particular, under IGRA, in order to exercise their sovereign right to operate gaming, tribes are required to submit to federal and, for casino-style gaming, state regulation.[59]

Debates over legalized gambling generally are internal to a state. That is, a state's own citizenry and policymakers consider whether and to what extent the state should legalize gambling. State officials in Utah, for instance, may not agree with Nevada's gaming policy, but have little if any direct influence over Nevada's policy choices. Since tribal governments are sovereign governments, the decision whether to legalize gambling under tribal law rests with tribal members and policymakers. However, under IGRA, a tribe's policy decision to conduct gaming can be implemented only in accordance with federal and state law. Thus, non-Indian governments exert control over what tribal governments do. What otherwise would be a presumptive tribal right to open a casino is limited by the real-world force of externally mediated tribal sovereignty.

Indian Gaming Is Public Gaming

The fact that Indian gaming is an aspect of tribal sovereignty gives rise to a second fundamental difference. As Indian gaming is conducted by tribal governments, it is "public gaming," making it distinct from both commercial and charitable gaming, and more (but not wholly) akin to state lotteries.

As public gaming, Congress intended Indian gaming to serve its primary policy goals of promoting tribal economic development, self-sufficiency, and strong tribal governments. Thus, government regulation of Indian gaming reflects a markedly different intent than does the regulation of commercial gaming, which primarily seeks to facilitate revenue and profit maximization

while minimizing infiltration of organized crime and other negative externalities, such as problem gambling. IGRA's legislative
history described tribal bingo operations, even those with only
modestly profitable games, as providing the foundation for tribal
self-government and self-sufficiency:

> Bingo revenues have enabled tribes, like lotteries and other games
> have done for State and local governments, to provide a wider range
> of government services to tribal citizens and reservation residents
> than would otherwise have been possible. For various reasons, not
> all tribes can engage in profitable gaming operations. However, for
> those tribes that have entered into the business of business [sic], the
> income often means the difference between an adequate govern-
> mental program and a skeletal program that is totally dependent on
> Federal funding.[60]

Congress saw Indian gaming as a tool for tribal governments,
as did the tribes themselves. As IGRA's legislative history stated,
"The Committee views tribal gaming as governmental gaming, the purpose of which is to raise tribal revenues for member
services."[61]

Generally, the success of legalized gambling is measured by
profits. Even state lotteries have raising significant revenue as
their primary goal. For Indian gaming, the public policy goals are
not limited to profitability. Indian gaming's role in strengthening
tribal governments and increasing tribal self-sufficiency and self-
determination is not necessarily reflected in a tribal casino's bottom line.[62] For tribes, the role of public gaming is less to subsidize
a single line item, such as public school funding, of an otherwise
relatively healthy treasury, and more to build the infrastructure
required by a fully functioning, "full-service" government. Thus,
job creation, provision of public services, and economic development are the bedrock economic rationales for tribal gaming.

For many tribes, gaming operations have become the primary
source of government funding. Tribes across the United States
use gaming revenue to fund law enforcement; provide fire and
emergency services; improve public infrastructure; build public
housing and retirement or assisted living facilities; provide various social programs to children, the elderly, or those in poverty;
and preserve or reinvigorate tribal cultural heritage through the
construction of museums, social activities centers, and language

retention programs.[63] Such benefits need not be seen as exclusive to a tribe; a healthy reservation community ultimately benefits both surrounding nontribal communities and the state.

Socioeconomic Deficits and Reservation Quality of Life

The public nature of Indian gaming and its specific policy goals gives rise to its third fundamental difference from legalized gambling more generally: tribal gaming's role in addressing socioeconomic adversity. Historically, reservations have exemplified some of the most difficult living conditions in the United States. As many tribes face high poverty and unemployment rates and accompanying social ills, basic quality-of-life indicators for tribal members living on reservations still lag significantly behind those of other racial or ethnic groups. Yet there have been marked improvements for many American Indian communities, largely due to gaming revenue or the opportunities it has provided to leverage economic development.[64]

In 1990, nearly one-third of American Indians lived in poverty as reservation unemployment rates often exceeded 50 percent. South Dakota's Pine Ridge Reservation, the poorest locale in the nation according to the 1990 Census, had a poverty rate in excess of 60 percent, an unemployment rate approaching 90 percent, and an average annual family income of less than $4,000.[65]

Extreme poverty is closely linked to a myriad of social problems, ranging from substance abuse to crime to domestic violence. American Indians have disproportionately high rates of infant mortality, suicide, substance abuse, obesity, and mental health problems.[66] They are more likely to be victims of violent crime than are members of any other racial group in the nation.[67] American Indians also have significantly higher mortality rates from illness such as diabetes, tuberculosis, and alcoholism.[68]

Today, there are about 2.5 million self-identified American Indians or Alaska Natives in the United States, or just under 1 percent of the population. About 40 percent of this population lives on reservations, trust lands, or rural areas bordering tribal lands. For these reasons, American Indians are sometimes called the "invisible minority," since—other than as the operators of tribal casinos—they are "overlooked and, in the minds of many, forgotten."[69] As a result, tribal governments must (and willingly do) bear responsibility for the welfare of tribal members. As Indian law scholar Robert Porter wrote, addressing the federal government on behalf of tribal nations,

> We can revitalize our sovereignty and thus ensure the survival of our future generations. In order to do so, we must find ways to generate economic opportunity for all of our people, to preserve our unique languages and cultures, and to develop vibrant tribal governments. Perhaps as never before, some of us currently have resources that might allow us to accomplish these goals and to cast off the hardship associated with the last few hundred years. While we know that much of the blame for our condition can be placed at the feet of your Nation, we fully accept that the burden of safeguarding our future rests on our own shoulders.[70]

The 2000 Census provided a subsequent statistical snapshot of American Indians and life on reservations, as well as an opportunity to assess the socioeconomic effects of Indian gaming on tribal communities. While poverty still prevails on reservations, several of the twenty-five largest tribes in the United States saw improvements in poverty and income rates from 1990 to 2000. Overall, the poverty rate for the Indian population decreased to 26 percent and the median household income increased to nearly $32,000.[71] From 1990 to 2000, both gaming and nongaming tribes experienced economic growth at a rate three times that of the U.S. economy, but American Indians living on reservations remained four times as likely to live in poverty as the average American.[72] Some commentators saw these modest improvements as indicative of a turning point in the well-being of tribes, likely reflecting the positive impacts of Indian gaming, while critics of Indian gaming saw the changes either as tracking national trends through the 1990s or simply as too small to justify tribal gaming as the foundation for economic development.

Morality Policymaking and Indian Gaming
Explaining the Process

Observations about morality policymaking become problematic when applied to Indian gaming. As discussed above, morality policy issues generate a high degree of public interest and participation. Morality policymaking does not require technical expertise to form an opinion; instead, individuals rely on their strongly held core values.

As reflections of these "first principles," differences in political culture explain inconsistent policy approaches to gambling— Utah's blanket prohibition against gambling and Nevada's "wide-open" legalization of gambling, for example, or South Dakota's authorization of limited casino gaming restricted to the town of Deadwood. Though the policy results may vary, there is nothing inherently wrong with citizens relying on deeply held convictions to guide their views and their political input on moral issues; indeed, some might argue that exactly such convictions should influence state gambling policy.

The three fundamental differences of Indian gaming complicate this view. For many Americans, tribal sovereignty is truly a foreign concept. One cannot understand Indian gaming at the level required for informed and sound policymaking without first understanding tribal sovereignty—in other words, morality policymaking decisions on Indian gaming issues do require "technical expertise" in tribal sovereignty.[73] Hence, although Indian gaming, like legalized gambling, may generate high levels of citizen participation due to its perceived nontechnical nature, federal, state, or local public officials must take care to separate and weigh their responsibility to be responsive to their electorates from the imperatives of acting in accordance with tribal sovereignty as well as federal law. Moreover, issues related to legalized gambling generally are appropriately influenced by state citizens' participation in state political processes. In the context of Indian gaming, however, the ordinary state-level democratic process should be perceived as secondary to the imperatives of intergovernmental relations. Through IGRA, Congress explicitly subjected bingo and other Class II games to tribal and federal authority, and intended states and tribes to resolve conflicts over casino-style gaming through government-to-government negotiation.

The public nature of Indian gaming and the socioeconomic realities of American Indian populations also must be taken into account. As "full-service" governments facing the challenges of extraordinary and historically rooted socioeconomic deficits, tribal governments use gaming revenue to create jobs, to provide government services, and to build strong government institutions. This in and of itself may be both necessary and sufficient to create a moral policy imperative. As the recent Evangelical Lutheran Church in America's *Gambling Study* noted, "[I]f any groups are justified in using gambling for economic development, it would be the Indian nations."[74] Despite the continued controversy over Indian gaming, American Indians remain the "invisible minority," as public perceptions of tribal gaming work to hide the continuing poverty and unemployment on many reservations and may undermine tribal governments' abilities to respond to the needs of their memberships.

Collins views legalized and regulated gambling industries as partnerships between the public and private sectors in which both share interests in profitability and a positive public image.[75] Similar conclusions could plausibly be drawn for public gaming— a state's interests in operating its lottery rest on profits and perception. Certainly, then, tribal as well as nontribal governments also share common ground concerning the policy goals and potential outcomes from Indian gaming. The stakes inarguably are higher for tribes. Yet commercial investors and management companies also may be invested in these goals, as are the vendors who sell their wares to tribes, the state's regulatory authorities, and those who increasingly rely on direct or indirect distributions of tribal gaming revenue to fund state and local public policy initiatives. Indian gaming's strong potential for partnership and cooperative policymaking is clear, but as a result of intense ambivalent or negative opinions, this potential may be overlooked.

In short, standard models of morality policymaking in the area of legalized gambling do not readily apply to Indian gaming. Further, tribal gaming's differences make the strong influence of state citizens' moral beliefs more problematic. Morality policymaking in the area of Indian gaming needs to account for these important differences as well as any shared interests among political jurisdictions or between the public and private sectors.

Informing the Outcome

These observations extend beyond the morality policymaking process. Furthermore, the principles guiding moral government action do not adequately account for Indian gaming's differences.

Here, the public policy goals related to legalized gambling serve as a starting point.

Sound and responsible policy for legalized gambling generally incorporates some balance between individual freedom of choice and the state's interests in raising funds to accomplish legitimate policy goals with attempts to minimize social and economic harms to individuals or society.[76] Gambling regulations typically share two key social control functions: ensuring the integrity of the games and preventing the infiltration of organized and common crime. Although perhaps more pressing in the context of private, for-profit gaming, these functions inform Indian gaming regulation as well. Regulatory schemes also are intended to facilitate the purpose of legalizing gambling in the first place: most often, this purpose is to promote economic development goals such as revitalization of local and regional economies, job creation, and government revenue generation. Here as well Indian gaming shares a similar objective.

As IGRA's statement of congressional intent reflects, however, the primary purpose of Indian gaming is to promote tribal economic development, self-sufficiency, and strong tribal governments.[77] This rationale is firmly grounded in Indian gaming's three fundamental differences.

For nearly all tribes with gaming operations, gaming revenue provides the base for tribal economies. In communities previously often lacking significant business enterprise beyond a local gas station, gaming is an unprecedented opportunity to build functioning tribal economies. Foremost for many tribes is the critical importance of job creation to counter staggering poverty and unemployment rates. Tribes are just beginning to diversify their economies beyond gaming and to facilitate private enterprise on reservations. Economic development on reservations is uniquely tied to tribal self-sufficiency, creating imperatives that stem both from each tribe's distinct status and history as well as the practical need to build tribal economies nearly from scratch. Thus the scope of tribal gaming's economic purpose far exceeds the relatively narrow public policy goals of commercial casinos, such as revitalizing Atlantic City's boardwalk, or state lotteries, such as subsidizing public education.

Tribal self-sufficiency is not merely economic in nature; it also is tied to the ability of tribal governments to respond to members' needs. Congress' emphasis on Indian gaming as a tool for tribal governments highlights tribal gaming's role in building culturally appropriate institutions, allowing tribes better to serve their members through increased and enhanced government institutions and services. Plainly, gaming revenue can assist tribes in building government institutions; less obvious to many is the role that tribal regulation of Indian gaming plays in institution building by making tribes responsible for the legal operation of complex business enterprises and for responding to the multitude of issues that arise from legalized gambling. Finally, strong tribal governments are necessary to meaningfully fulfill an implicit goal of IGRA: to improve tribal-state relations by encouraging cooperative policymaking between tribes and states.[78] Once again, IGRA's public policy goals give rise to a different framework for assessing the morality of policy outcomes than do the goals of legalized gambling generally.

Indian gaming's differences also complicate moral principles of government decision making grounded in political theory. For example, the principles of utilitarianism, moral principles of justice, and individual liberty, on which Collins relies in making his case for the morality of legalized gambling, operate somewhat differently in the less straightforward context of federal-tribal-state intergovernmental relations.[79] The question of whether Indian gaming does more harm than good must take into account the benefits and costs to tribal communities. It should not ignore the fact of tribal sovereignty by reducing tribal populations to a percentage of the state's electorate (usually small to negligible, and easily discounted) or by seeing them as just another minority special interest or group.

With regard to moral or ethical governance, one is reminded of preeminent federal Indian law scholar Felix Cohen's famous assertion: "Like the miner's canary, the Indian marks the shift from fresh air to poison gas in our political atmosphere; and our treatment of Indians, even more than our treatment of other minorities, reflects the rise and fall of our democratic faith."[80] Cohen was referring, of course, to the unique and complicating fact of tribal sovereignty as well as the history of federal-tribal-state relations. Against the history of the near eradication of American indigenous nations by colonizers and its continuing legacies, federal and state governments' fair and equitable treatment of both tribal governments and tribal members on issues related to Indian gaming present opportunities to leave the past behind.

Informed Morality Policymaking on Indian Gaming

Extensive and systematic inquiry could lead to the development of a principled yet pragmatic "Indian Gaming Ethic" that could guide policymaking and assist people in understanding what their government does, why it does it, and what is "right" for the government to do. The result could be a relatively uncomplicated ethic, such as "Indian gaming is in the public interest" or "legalized gambling is in the public interest, so Indian gaming is, too" (or the converse of each); alternative ethics could be considerably more complex. While not rejecting such propositions out of hand, our intent here is neither to prove nor disprove them; nor is it to tackle the development of an overarching "Indian Gaming Ethic." Rather, our project is to develop standards that others might use to develop the key normative and empirical policy questions that should—or must—be asked and answered to inform sensible law- and policymaking on Indian gaming. These standards, however, are not best implemented in a vacuum—they require sufficient evidence to back them up.

The systematic and scientific study of legalized gambling is young and has yet to reach consensus on how best to specify key questions that need answers, the appropriate research methods to provide them, and the ideal mechanisms to translate those answers into sound public policy. As the NGISC concluded, "what is very clear is that there is still a dearth of impartial, objective research" to guide informed and effective public policymaking on legalized gambling.[81] Yet as the Commission also noted, the scarcity of quality information has not stopped governments from making policy decisions, many of which likely are informed more by politics (or ideology) than by scientific research.

The NGISC's observations about the lack of scientific research on the social and economic effects of legalized gambling as well as the fact that policy decisions are made even without the requisite information remain as salient today as they were a decade ago. Indeed, they are more relevant in the area of Indian gaming than ever. Even a cursory examination of the public discourse on tribal gaming might lead one to conclude that the law and policy that govern tribal gaming are developed in more of an information vacuum, and are guided more by the politics of misinformation, than any other form of legalized gambling.

To ensure the morality of social regulatory policy concerning Indian gaming, it is time for a comprehensive and collaborative effort to harness the experiences of political jurisdictions throughout the United States to systematically collect and analyze the relevant data needed to identify emergent best practices in the ideation, development, implementation, and evaluation of tribal gaming law and policy.[82] Such a weighty mission requires collaboration and cooperation, extensive resources and objective study,[83] and understanding of and respect for tribal as well as state sovereignty.[84] Despite widespread variation in the historical, regional, cultural, and traditional experiences of tribes—as well as those of states and localities—useful generalizations can be drawn if the correct questions are asked and answered.

Morality policymaking concerning legalized gambling in essence poses the relatively straightforward question: What is the moral responsibility of governments to serve the public interest? With regard to Indian gaming and morality policymaking, however, two corollary questions arise: What is the moral responsibility of *tribal* governments to serve the public interest? and, What is the moral responsibility of *nontribal* governments to serve the public interest, including that of tribal governments and tribal members? The three fundamental differences between Indian gaming and legalized gambling that we identified should guide nontribal governments' consideration and adoption of policy that impacts Indian gaming. Sound social regulatory policymaking regarding Indian gaming cannot rely simply on moral views of gambling. Instead, Indian gaming requires specialized knowledge of its differences and the particular public policy goals it is intended to serve. The reality of tribes' unique status within and without the American political system means that nontribal governments must be cognizant of public policymaking that accounts for tribal interests, not just their own.

Conclusion

Legalized gambling always has been and most likely always will be a part of America's moral landscape and therefore of American public life. Given the unique policy rationale and regulatory framework governing Indian gaming, one might reasonably assume that it, too, is around for the long term as the industry matures and tribal governments become increasingly well equipped to provide for their members, engage in effective tribal-state intergovernmental relations, and deal with the complexities presented by any real or perceived ethical lapses by individual tribes or tribal public officials along the way.[85]

The challenge of negotiating the sometimes rocky American moral terrain on Indian gaming requires the threshold understanding that Indian gaming is different than other forms of legalized gambling. While the differences between tribal gaming and other forms of legalized gambling may or may not dictate particular substantive policy outcomes, policymakers have an obligation to take those differences into account to inform the process of developing morally sound and principled public policy on Indian gaming.

4

New Politics, Same Old Vice
Gambling in the Twenty-first Century

R. Shep Melnick

As several chapters in this volume point out, gambling politics and policy in the United States have changed dramatically over the past several decades. Forty-five years ago, not one state ran a lottery, and only one state—that perennial renegade, Nevada— allowed casinos. Indeed, from 1920 to 1964 "nearly all forms of gambling were illegal throughout the country."[1] Today, in contrast, 95 percent of Americans live in states with lotteries. While only one state had a lottery in 1964, by 1973 seven states had adopted lotteries; by 1997, the number grew to thirty-eight and today stands at forty-three. Between 1973 and 2006, per capita purchases of lottery tickets grew more than four-fold in inflation-adjusted dollars.[2] Commercial casinos have sprung up in New Jersey, Mississippi, Missouri, Louisiana, Iowa, Michigan, Illinois, Indiana, South Dakota, and Colorado. Other states are likely to jump on the casino bandwagon in coming years. On top of this, nearly four hundred Indian casinos operate in over thirty states, generating revenues of nearly $25 billion annually.[3] The South, the most religious section of the country and once the region most resistant to the contagion, has now "joined the gambling nation."[4] John Lyman Mason and Michael Nelson report that "in dollar terms, legalized gambling is bigger than movies, bigger than spectator sports, bigger than theme parks, bigger than all the books, magazines, and newspapers published in the United States put together."[5] Yet few scholars have asked why public policy on gambling has changed so significantly or what difference this makes for our politics and our citizens.

One reason for this scholarly neglect is that gambling policy is made primarily at the state level, and most political scientists and policy experts are focused on national politics. The decentralized nature of gambling policy has resulted in the slow, incremental expansion of state-sponsored and state-sanctioned lotteries and casinos that has kept gambling below the scholarly radar screen. No one much noticed when tiny, quirky New Hampshire drilled a small hole in the dike by initiating a modest lottery in 1964. Over the next decade the expansion of lotteries was modest: the big shift did not come until the Reagan years. Casinos spread even more slowly, at least until federal court decisions and federal legislation opened the door to the proliferation of Indian casinos in the late 1980s. Here, too, most of the action took place at the subnational level, with state governments negotiating agreements with American Indian tribes under rules laid down by Congress and the Supreme Court. Technology, not politics, drove the expansion of Internet gambling in the late 1990s. The federal government has adopted only halting and generally ineffective measures to regulate this vast international business. Taken individually, none of these changes is earthshaking. Taken together, they represent a profound change in public policy and citizen behavior.

Why have publicly run lotteries and publicly sanctioned casinos spread inexorably in recent decades? As Michael Nelson explains in chapter 2, a major part of the explanation is intense competitions among various units of government. We usually think of competition among states as impeding innovation. According to the conventional wisdom, federalism produces a "race to the bottom" that discourages states from imposing environmental restrictions on business or from expanding social welfare programs. With gambling, though, competition among the states— and between state governments and Indian tribes—proved to be a powerful accelerant: it produced more lotteries, more casinos, bigger jackpots, glitzier ads, and increasingly aggressive efforts to attract those hard-core players who account for the bulk of gambling revenues.

Nelson's chapter and his previous work with John Lyman Mason show that state officials first sold state-sponsored gambling to the public as a way to extract revenues from out-of-staters and then as a way to prevent neighboring states from getting rich off home-state citizens. To describe the issue more bluntly, each state has an interest both in making suckers out of the citizens of other states and in using their own suckers to fund their own programs. That is why Iowa put its casino on a riverboat and sent it upstream toward Wisconsin and Chicago. And that is why neighboring states soon authorized their own riverboat casinos. But don't blame Iowa: it was spurred into action by the threat of Indian casinos in nearby Wisconsin and Minnesota. Similarly, Mississippi passed legislation to allow riverboat casinos because they wanted to get the jump on Louisiana. When Louisiana followed suit a few years later, its governor explained, "We knew that with our two hundred mile border with Texas, we could do to Texas what Mississippi had been doing to us."[6] In South Carolina, Governor Jim Hodges convincingly portrayed the lottery as a way to prevent South Carolina dollars from subsidizing the college tuition of Georgians.[7] A few years later the governor of North Carolina turned the argument against South Carolina: "Our people are playing the lottery," Mike Easley stated in a speech touting the North Carolina Education Lottery. "We just need to decide which schools we should fund, other states' or ours."[8]

The proliferation of Indian casinos described by Rand and Light in chapter 3 intensified this competition. Proponents of casino gambling in Massachusetts point out that Bay State dollars are now flowing to the Indian casinos at Foxwood and Mohegan Sun. Before long, Indian casinos are likely to open within Massachusetts itself. Why should the gambling windfall be claimed by tiny American Indian tribes rather than used to educate Massachusetts children? For that matter, why should the United States allow the proceeds from Internet gambling flow to entrepreneurs of ill repute on small Caribbean islands? International competition can be as powerful a driver of gambling expansion as interstate competition: Michigan authorized casinos in Detroit largely to prevent American gambling dollars from escaping to Windsor, Ontario. As the cynical police sergeant Stan Jablonski used to say on Hill Street Blues, "Let's do it to them before they do it to us."

The gambling arms race does not end once states and tribes enter the "gaming" business. They engage in an unending search for faster, ever more enticing and addictive games. Games that provide instant gratification—such as Keno and video lottery terminals that provide winners every few minutes—have become more common.[9] Jackpots have grown larger and larger, as have the denominations of lottery tickets. Texas created the most recent buzz by introducing a $50 scratch-off game.[10] In states along the Mississippi, casinos were first limited to riverboats, but through a series of transparent subterfuges eventually "crawl[ed] up on the land," as one state legislator put it.[11]

One thing that political science can teach us about gambling policy is that however these state-sponsored enterprises come into being, they quickly build constituencies that make them virtually impossible to scale back. Once states become dependent on gambling revenue, it is difficult to wean them from it, particularly when these revenues are earmarked for popular programs. The best example of this is Georgia's HOPE Scholarships, which were initially billed as a mechanism for allowing children from underprivileged families to attend college but soon became "a politically invulnerable middle-class entitlement program."[12] In 2006, almost two hundred thousand retailers sold lottery tickets, earning $3.3 billion in commissions and drawing millions of customers into their stores.[13] They will not relinquish this windfall without a bruising political fight. According to the New York Times, the two companies that dominate the designing, marketing, and running of lottery games, Gtech and Scientific Games, "have spent millions of dollars lobbying legislators and bankrolling lottery referendum proposals that have led to the establishment of lotteries. . . . Often the companies have also helped draft the very language used in lottery legislation."[14] Not surprisingly, this legislative language has often helped them win lucrative contracts. To put it politely, Gtech and Scientific Games have a history of playing hardball politics.[15] Having saturated the American market, these industry giants are now focusing on exporting their product to Latin America, eastern Europe, and Asia. They are hardly alone in using their financial resources to expand gambling. Between 1994 and 1996 the gambling industry spent more than $100 million on political contributions and lobbying at the state level.[16] California Indian tribes raised $28 million to push a single 2008 initiative to expand their casino operations in that state.[17] The Jack Abramoff scandal provided a graphic illustration of how allowing hundreds of millions of dollars to ride on highly discretionary government decisions—such as the recognition of small American Indian tribes as eligible to operate lucrative casinos—can be an open invitation to political corruption.

Supporters of state lotteries have a powerful tool available to few other public policy advocates: massive advertising budgets. State lotteries now spend almost half a billion dollars on advertising annually.[18] This is used not only to market lottery tickets but to trumpet the virtues of the programs funded by lottery revenue. As Clotfelter and Cook note in chapter 1, emphasizing the good deeds financed by gambling revenue might not be a good way to sell lottery tickets. But it probably is a good way to maintain public support for government policies. At the same time that states have cracked down on advertising and marketing by tobacco companies and have required the tobacco industry to pay for ads dramatizing the hazards of smoking, they have cranked up their efforts to encourage—and in effect to normalize and sanitize—gambling. The Federal Trade Commission has exempted state lotteries from truth-in-advertising rules. Local television stations that collect advertising revenues (and build their ratings with Powerball drawings) have been less than aggressive watchdogs and consumer advocates in this corner of the policy world. Many of the ordinary rules of the game are suspended in lottery politics.

For all these reasons, once the gambling ball gets rolling, it is hard to stop. But why did it gather such momentum in the 1970s? For the previous hundred years, state-sponsored gambling had been relatively rare. Many state constitutions banned lotteries and casinos altogether. In the early Republic, cash-strapped states and the fledgling national government had often resorted to lotteries because they had so few other sources of revenue. But the reputation of lotteries was frequently tarnished by corruption. James Sterling Young reports that, in the early nineteenth century, "hopes for a great university to grace the capital faded when Congress refused financial assistance, and plans to raise private money by lottery ended with the incarceration of the lottery operator."[19] According to Clotfelter, Cook, Edell, and Moore, "Lotteries fell into disrepute after the Civil War, and, following the demise of the scandal-plagued Louisiana Lottery in 1894, they ceased to exist for the next seven decades."[20] This Louisiana Lottery, affectionately known as "the Serpent," drew most of its revenue from out-of-state customers. Those donor states responded not by joining Louisiana (the contemporary response), but by convincing Congress to prevent the lottery company from using the U.S. mail and interstate telegraph wires to market their product. The close relationship between organized crime and Nevada casinos further damaged the public image of publicly sponsored gambling. Thus, not only did state-sponsored gambling have many significant obstacles to overcome, but gambling opponents also had a ready solution to the "race to the bottom" problem.

What has driven the current spread of gambling policies, of course, has been the states' frantic search for new sources of revenue. As Nelson notes,

> Lotteries entered their period of most rapid expansion in the late 1970s, around the time that anti-tax sentiment began to rise across the nation. . . . To state governments, caught in a vise between opposition to higher taxes and greater revenue needs, the lottery seemed an appealing way out: revenue without taxation.[21]

Not coincidentally, the first state to adopt a lottery in the twentieth century, New Hampshire, is the only state in the nation with neither an income tax nor a general sales tax. It is impossible for the nominee of either party to win the governorship in New Hampshire without taking "the pledge" to veto any broad-based tax. In 1964, a Democratic governor convinced the Republican New Hampshire legislature to use a lottery to help fund education. This was a pattern that would frequently be repeated throughout the nation: entrepreneurial Democratic gubernatorial candidates using gambling revenues to appeal to independents and Democratic constituencies without incurring the wrath of anti-tax Republicans.[22]

The tax revolt that began in California in 1978 not only made it hard for states to raise new revenues, but in the Reagan years led to several rounds of federal budget cutting that reduced the flow of federal funds to the states and multiplied the cost of "unfunded mandates." Contrary to the conventional wisdom, the 1980s and 1990s were *not* a period in which the public demanded smaller government: per capita spending on health, education, and crime control skyrocketed. Both public opinion polls and election results show that voters wanted *bigger* government.[23] Voters may have demanded lower taxes, but they also wanted better education, more cops on the beat, more prisons, broader health-care coverage, and a wide variety of environmental amenities. As a result, politicians at all levels of government searched desperately for clever methods for meeting these competing demands. The most obvious was deficit spending. The federal deficit ballooned during the Reagan administration, and (except for a few years in the late 1990s) has remained high ever since. Most states, though, do not have this politically attractive option, so they joined federal lawmakers in trying to shift costs to other levels of government and to the private sector. They shortchanged pension funds. They renamed taxes "user fees" and "revenue enhancers." In the multistate tobacco settlement of 1998, state attorneys general invented a remarkable, judicially based mechanism for imposing a quarter of a *trillion* dollar tax on tobacco products.[24] In this political environment, gambling was impossible to ignore and difficult to oppose. Lotteries and casinos offer a way to make it seem fun and exciting to pay a regressive tax. A tax that people line up to pay, a tax that falls on poor people who tend not to vote anyway—how many hard-pressed politicians could resist that? Legalized gambling was just one small but nearly irresistible element of a much larger effort to cope with the conflicting demands of the electorate.

Michael Nelson points out that raising revenues through gambling is a strategy particularly popular under divided government. In the 1970s, 1980s, and 1990s, divided government became more and more common in the states.[25] One thing we know for sure about recent American politics is that it is increasingly partisan, polarized, and closely divided. Occasionally one party can exercise enough control to push through its agenda, but usually the result of partisan polarization is stalemate. A crucial feature of gambling policy is that it tends to split both parties internally. Consequently, it is one of those few issues on which it is possible to build a bipartisan coalition.

On the Republican side, gambling is fully endorsed by libertarians and anti-taxers. This is their dream revenue source. Imagine a world in which even taxes become voluntary! Gambling politics obviously raises the possibility of a split between economic conservatives on the one hand and social, religious conservatives on the other. In some states, to be sure, churches have opposed gambling. Occasionally they have succeeded, most notably in Alabama, where a number of religious organizations banded together to defeat a state lottery in 1999. (It helped that in Alabama black churches joined the opposition.) But conservative religious leaders have not made opposition to gambling a high priority. As Alan Wolfe notes in chapter 16, this is the gambling dog that has not barked. "One reason why conservative Protestants did not make gambling into a major culture war issue," he argues, is that "conservative religious leaders in the United States operate as political pragmatists unwilling to criticize positions or practices popular among their members." If conservative church leaders "were to force a choice" between gambling and religion, then "they might lose people to whom they wish their message to be addressed."[26]

The picture on the Democratic side is more complicated. To use Clotfelter and Cook's terms, one finds a combination of lottery lovers, lottery haters, and lottery pragmatists within the Democratic coalition. Support for lotteries has been especially strong among African Americans, a key part of the Democratic base. For example, in the 2000 South Carolina referendum, African American voters supported the lottery by a wide margin, 76 percent to 24 percent, while whites were much more evenly divided, voting 53 percent to 47 percent in support.[27]

Democratic "lottery haters" find the highly regressive nature of the gambling tax particularly distressing. Simply put, lotteries extract resources from society's most vulnerable sectors. Those earning less than $10,000 per year spend an average of $600 on lottery tickets, while those earning more than $50,000 spend about $250. High school dropouts spend four times as much as college graduates on lottery tickets; blacks spend five times as much as whites. In their careful study of lottery participation rates, Clotfelter, Cook, Edell, and Moore found that "males, blacks, high-school dropouts, and people in the lowest income category are heavily overrepresented among those who are in the top 20 percent of lottery players."[28] One of the paradoxes of lottery politics is that some members of the Democratic coalition are hostile to lotteries precisely because they are so popular among other members of the coalition.

The fate of gambling initiatives often rests in the hands of "lottery pragmatists" and entrepreneurs in the Democratic Party. In their study of gambling politics in the South, Nelson and Mason conclude that

> in most instances, gambling legalization was the solution arrived at by a Democratic politician seeking to balance the need to satisfy the party's core constituencies, especially public employees and minorities, with new spending programs against the competing need not to alienate increasingly Republican, middle-class, white voters with new taxes.[29]

Performing this delicate balancing act required linking gambling revenues with highly popular programs, usually education. Forced to choose between kindergartens funded by Keno and no public kindergarten at all, many Democrats swallow hard and choose the former.

The argument that the beneficial results of increased public spending outweigh the disturbing manner in which these revenues are raised underlies Rand and Light's defense of Indian casinos. As they put it, "Against the history of the near eradication of American indigenous nations by colonizers and its continuing legacies, federal and state governments' fair and equitable treatment of both tribal governments and tribal members on issues related to Indian gaming present opportunities to leave the past behind."[30] When you are on the side of the angels, what's wrong with encouraging a few bad habits? We stole their land—why shouldn't they be allowed to separate us from some cash?

A key issue left unaddressed by gambling pragmatists such as Rand and Light as well as most other advocates of Indian gambling is whether the huge windfalls bestowed on American Indian tribes ever actually trickle down to those tribal members who so desperately need better schools, health care, and economic opportunities. Most American Indian gambling revenues are generated by casinos owned by tiny tribes in the Northeast and in California. Rand and Light note that the modest casinos located on reservations in their state of North Dakota draw money primarily from locals—including, obviously, American Indians. The hundred facilities that generate 90 percent of Indian casino revenues are owned by one-fifth of the tribes engaged in the activity.[31] Almost half of the total revenue comes from a mere 6 percent of tribal gambling operations. On the other end of the spectrum, "One out of every five tribal casinos earned less than $3 million, often just enough to keep the casino doors open and to provide some modest tribal government revenue."[32] If, as Nelson reports, many of these casinos are actually managed by the big-time gambling corporations and employ mainly non-American Indians, does this really increase American Indian employment and entrepreneurship? Does running an operation such as this really promote tribal democracy, or does it create a powerful tribal oligarchy and strong incentives for political corruption? Rand and Light concede that "the lack of scientific research on the social and economic effects of legalized gambling" has meant that "the law and policy that govern tribal gaming" have been developed in "an information vacuum," guided "more by the politics of misinformation, than for any other form of legalized gambling."[33] In other words, their pragmatic defense of American Indian casinos rests on very shaky empirical foundations.

Given the pivotal role played by gambling pragmatists within the pro-gambling coalition, those who study gambling politics need to pay much more attention to the long-term distributional consequences of the packages of taxes and benefits created by state gambling laws. When one takes into account both the obviously regressive nature of the tax and the arguably progressive nature of the benefits, what is the bottom line? If, as seems to be the case with the Georgia HOPE Scholarship, revenues generated by the poor and minorities are used to fund scholarships for middle-class white families, the policy package does not seem particularly attractive. Moreover, as Clotfelter, Cook, Edell, and

Moore note, "While earmarking might be an excellent device for engendering political support for a lottery, there is reason to doubt if earmarked lottery revenues in fact have the effect of increasing funds available for the specified purpose."[34] Over the long run, legislators simply substitute gambling revenues for revenues raised through less regressive forms of taxation. Gambling money, like all other forms, is fungible.

"Lottery haters" such as the National Coalition Against Legalized Gambling and the National Coalition Against Gambling Expansion have long emphasized not only the regressive nature of this form of revenue raising, but also the multiple pathologies of problem gamblers" Other chapters in this volume take a detailed look at this important issue. It should be noted that while most people who play the lottery or visit casinos spend only a modest amount of money and do not become problem gamblers, most lottery and casino *revenues* come from a small portion of the playing public. Clotfelter, Cook, Edell, and Moore found that over half of lottery revenue comes from 5 percent of the players; the top 10 percent account for almost 70 percent of total sales. Consequently, "the median player, who might be considered 'typical,' is in fact of little interest from the revenue perspective."[35] In other words, rational, revenue-maximizing lottery and casino operators know that their success lies in their ability to target the part of the population most at risk for problem gambling.

One important question that has attracted comparatively little attention among scholars is the effect of the ubiquity of gambling, the daily barrage of advertising for lotteries and casinos, and the resulting normalization of these activities on *ordinary* citizens. The preceding chapters all demonstrate the extent to which government today is not just tolerating gambling, but actively encouraging it. State governments and Indian tribes run ad after ad telling people that gambling is not just fun and exciting, but profitable and, yes, even virtuous. This is how you can get rich right away! Buy a lottery ticket and support education! Go to a casino and atone for years of oppression of American Indians! Consider the career and financial advice offered by a happy young man in an ad for the Connecticut lottery:

> When I was younger I suppose I could have done more to plan for my
> future. But I didn't. I guess I could have put some money aside. But
> I didn't. Or I could have made some smart investments. But I didn't.
> Heck, I could have bought a one-dollar Connecticut lotto ticket, won
> a jackpot worth millions, and gotten a nice big check every year for
> twenty years. And I did! I won![36]

Are we to believe that the accumulation of these messages has no
effect on ordinary people's understanding of work, luck, reward,
and duty?

The following analysis of lottery advertising provided by
Clotfelter, Cook, Edell, and Moore goes to the heart of the
matter:

> Promoting lotteries does more than persuade the public that playing
> is a good investment. At one level, the sales job may be viewed as
> values education, teaching that gambling is a benign or even virtuous
> activity that offers a desirable escape from the dreariness of work
> and the confines of limited means. Not only does lottery advertis-
> ing endorse gambling per se, it may also endorse the dream of easy
> wealth that motivates most gambling. Many ads are unabashedly
> materialistic, with winners basking in luxury and lives transformed.
> Yet this is not the materialism of hard work and perseverance, but
> rather of genies and magic lamps, rooted in hopes, dreams and super-
> stition. And every lottery manager knows that many of his or her
> best customers base their bets on personal superstitions, astrological
> tables, self-styled seers, and venerable "dream books" that list num-
> bers corresponding to names, dates, and dreams. . . . It is probably
> not an exaggeration to say that the message of lottery advertising is a
> subversive one—that success lies in picking the right number.

What type of public education do these government-sponsored
ads provide? As Clotfelter, Cook, Edell, and Moore put it,

> Betting on a miracle is not the formula we usually teach our children.
> Indeed, one straightforward test of the acceptability of the message
> might be to imagine using lottery ads in the public school curriculum.
> Few school boards across the country would endorse teaching chil-
> dren lessons such as, "Play your hunch. You could win a bunch."[37]

The federal government and the states have banned most
forms of advertising for tobacco. They require tobacco companies to pay for public service announcements that explain in
graphic terms the dangers of smoking. They put tight limits on
advertising for hard liquor. The Food and Drug Administration

and the Federal Trade Commission require multiple disclaimers and warnings for over-the-counter and prescription drugs. Yet when it comes to lottery tickets sold by state governments or casinos that generate substantial revenues for government bodies, nearly anything goes. As noted above, state lotteries are explicitly exempted from FTC truth-in-advertising regulations. This is hardly surprising. After all, the *central purpose* of advertising for lotteries and casinos is to induce customers to ignore the odds. If we applied ordinary truth-in-advertising rules or insisted upon warnings similar to those mandated for cigarette packages, we would require boldface statements such as these: "WARNING: THE PROBABILITY OF WINNING MEGABUCKS IS SMALLER THAN THE PROBABILITY OF BEING STRUCK BY LIGHTNING ON YOUR WAY TO PICK UP YOUR WINNINGS," or "STATISTICAL RESEARCH DEMONSTRATES THAT THE MORE YOU PLAY, THE MORE YOU LOSE," or "RANDOM EVENTS ARE RANDOM—THAT MEANS YOU CAN NEVER BE ON A ROLL." When the private sector uses deceptive advertising and marketing to prey on the unwary—as with now-infamous subprime mortgages or the "payday loans" banned in many states—we expect the government to step in. When the government is the profiteer, regulation is predictably minimal.

To many liberals distressed by the extent to which state-sponsored gambling preys upon the vulnerable, such dramatic warnings or other efforts to discourage gambling may nonetheless smack of paternalism. These potential members of the antigambling coalition are wary of any position that imposes a particular understanding of correct moral behavior or that assumes that a substantial number of people are apt to make stupid decisions. Not only have they read their John Stuart Mill, but they fear that imposing moral norms will mean imposing the norms of the Moral Majority. As a result, they insist upon remaining "nonjudgmental"—unless, of course, the question relates to smoking, which we just *know* is unbelievably stupid.

Not too long ago, such nonjudgmentalism lay at the heart of liberals' position on welfare policy as well. In the 1960s and 1970s, reformers insisted that middle-class Americans should get over their hang-ups about promoting the Protestant work ethic.

If low-skill workers declined to take minimum-wage jobs or if teenage girls decided to have babies without a husband, this was their choice as autonomous individuals. Government had no business imposing or promoting middle-class morality. Welfare, liberal reformers repeatedly argued, should be based on economic need alone, not the behavior of recipients. By the 1990s many thoughtful liberals had concluded that such compassionate nonjudgmentalism had had a devastating effect on society's most vulnerable members. When norms of work and family responsibility declined, poor children were the biggest losers. This is one reason why welfare policy began to change many years before the Republicans took control of Congress.[38]

It may be time for a similar rethinking of liberal—and conservative—positions on gambling. At the end of the day, the question that we as a political community need to ask ourselves is whether this is a type of behavior and public understanding of work and risk that we wish to promote or to discourage. To put it bluntly, do we want to encourage people to believe that they will succeed through dumb luck and impulsive behavior? Or do we want to inculcate the belief that the only sure way to success is through working hard in school and at one's job, through persevering and patiently building skills?

Toward the end of *Democracy in America*, Tocqueville wrote these words:

> [In democratic times] governments must apply themselves to giving back to men this taste for the future which is no longer inspired by religion and the [democratic] social state. Without saying so, they must teach citizens practically every day that wealth, renown, and power are the prizes of work; that great successes are found at the end of long-lasting desires, and that one gets nothing lasting except that which is acquired with difficulty.[39]

What Tocqueville understood to be the *democratic* understanding of work, many academics today dismiss as bourgeois (and boring). Bourgeois values alone are probably not sufficient to sustain a republic. No doubt we also need to find ways to encourage and sustain warriors and bohemians (or at least that new version of creative yet domesticated bohemians David Brooks describes as Bobos[40]). But do we really want to teach our citizens to disdain work and worship dumb luck? Having mounted a major and partially successful effort to reconnect those who live in under-class neighborhoods with work, do we really want to take their hard-earned cash and tell them again and again that work is not the route to advancement? Is it really wise to sell our democratic souls in return for a 2 percent increase in state revenue?

Individual Behavior and Social Impact

5

Behavioral and Brain Measures
of Risk-Taking

Rachel T. A. Croson, Matthew Fox, and James Sundali

Gambling is America's favorite pastime by volume. The total amount won from gamblers in the United States in 2006 was over $57 billion. To put that number in perspective, the total sales for movie tickets and music recordings was around $20 billion, and the combined sales of McDonald's, Burger King, Wendy's, and Starbucks was about $28 billion in 2006. Furthermore, revenues from gambling are growing at an average of 10 percent each year, as shown in the bottom row of table 5.1.

As recently as 1978, casino gambling was available in just one state of the United States, but by 2001, thirty-three states allowed the practice in one form or another.[1] The growth in gambling activity is not just in the United States. In recent years, 82 percent of Canadians participated in some form of legalized gambling,[2] and the hottest destination for new casinos is the island of Macau.

To a mathematician, the popularity of casino (and lottery) gambling is puzzling. The expected value of the gambles offered to individuals is clearly negative, yet the activity is approached, experienced, and treated with such enthusiasm that one cannot help but wonder what gamblers are thinking when they undertake

TABLE 5.1
U.S. Casino Industry Gaming Revenues (in millions of dollars)

	Revenues (MIL. $)				% Change		
	2003	2004	2005	2006	2003–4	2004–5	2005–6
Nevada/Atlantic City, total	14,114	15,369	16,667	17,841	8.9	8.4	7.0
Nevada total	9,625	10,562	11,649	12,622	9.7	10.3	8.4
Las Vegas Strip	4,760	5,334	6,034	6,688	12.1	13.1	10.8
Atlantic City	4,488	4,807	5,018	5,219	7.1	4.4	4.0
Western towns, total	768	804	839	872	4.6	4.4	3.9
Deadwood, SD	70	78	84	90	10.9	7.7	6.9
Colorado	698	726	755	782	4.0	4.1	3.5
Other land-based, total	1,412	1,509	1,458	1,641	6.9	-3.4	12.6
New Orleans	282	320	229	338	13.5	-28.4	47.8
Detroit	1,130	1,189	1,229	1,303	5.2	3.3	6.1
Riverboats, total	10,232	10,626	10,636	12,065	3.9	0.1	13.4
Iowa	694	727	747	1,173	4.7	2.8	57.0
Illinois	1,710	1,717	1,799	1,924	0.4	4.8	6.9
Mississippi	2,700	2,777	2,468	2,570	2.9	-11.1	4.1
Louisiana	1,566	1,562	1,676	2,229	-0.3	7.3	33.0
Missouri	1,332	1,473	1,532	1,592	10.6	4.0	3.9
Indiana	2,230	2,370	2,414	2,577	6.3	1.9	6.7
Native American casinos	16,826	19,408	22,510	25,080	15.3	16.0	11.4
TOTAL	43,352	47,716	52,110	57,499	10.1	9.2	10.3

Source: Reprinted from Basham and Mathis, Casino and Hotel Analysts, page 1.

these risks.[3] Furthermore, individuals often simultaneously engage in risk-taking activities like gambling and risk-avoiding activities like purchasing insurance. This confluence raises the question of whether individuals understand the risks (and rewards) associated with gambling (or with insurance purchases), and the extent to which they reason rationally about them.

As a result of these puzzles, a significant amount of research has been done surrounding gamblers and the thought processes that lead them to engage in risky activities. Our goal is not to review this entire body of research, which would be the subject of a book in and of itself. Rather, we have identified a few areas of interest where a body of research exists and where behavioral regularities have been identified that speak to the question of why, and how, people gamble.

First, we discuss data from individuals participating in gambling decisions, either data collected from gamblers in the field or from laboratory studies that were described and framed as gambling decisions. Next, we review data from the lab designed to investigate the psychological processes underlying gambling decisions more generally. These studies often involve decisions in abstract settings that at first glance seem far from the gambling setting (at times, more akin to the insurance decision). Finally, we review recent advances in neuroscience and neuroeconomics in particular, which look closer at the activities occurring in the brain when risky decisions are made. This research both illuminates typical gambling decisions and sheds light on the causes.

Risk Attitudes in Gambling Settings

Why do gamblers gamble? One factor that is repeatedly identified is the gambler's attitudes toward risk. These attitudes can take a number of forms, including risk estimation (what are the probabilities?), risk perception (how risky is a given gamble?), and risk preferences (how risky a gamble do I want to take?).

Factors Influencing Risk Preferences: Social Context and Previous Wins/Losses

Some of the most interesting research involves the last question of how risky a gamble individuals choose. For example, a large number of laboratory experiments have identified a phenomenon called "the risky shift,"[4] where groups of people tend to choose more risky options than do their constituent individuals. A. D. Blank demonstrated this same effect in the gambling setting.[5] In this study, the experimenter recruited participants to bet on dice games, alone and in groups. The results indicated that isolated gamblers made more high probability bets (took less risk) than those in groups. However, when the subjects moved from an isolated environment to a game where there were many players, within a few rounds they had increased the number of low probability–higher payoff (riskier) bets placed. The results from this study were the first to demonstrate that the social context of the gambling activity has a strong impact on the risk preference observed.

Blascovich and coauthors conducted a series of studies on the risky shift in players of blackjack. Blascovich, Veach, and Ginsburg observed seventy-two male undergraduates playing blackjack in a laboratory setting[6] and found that they increased their risk-taking behavior (the size of their bets) when moved from an individual setting (playing alone) to a group setting (playing at a table with others).[7] Blascovich, Ginsburg, and Howe observed actual gamblers in Nevada casinos over the course of a single day and confirmed the existence of risky shift behavior in a natural setting.[8] Of the thirty-two male trial judges that the authors approached and observed, those playing alone tended to bet less than those playing in groups, and individuals increased their bets when others joined their table. Blascovich, Ginsburg, and Howe again observed gamblers, this time unobtrusively in a casino setting, and confirmed risky shift behavior as players moved from individual settings to group settings or were joined by additional players.[9]

In a follow-up experiment, Blascovich and Ginsburg tested the effect of having participants join groups with either higher or lower risk tolerances than those they had displayed while playing individually.[10] They discovered that players increased their level of risk when joining groups with similar or higher risk preferences but tended to decrease risk-taking behavior when added to a group with a lower risk tolerance. This last result suggests that the social impact on risk-taking is not simply a risky shift, but is driven by conformity effects. Note that the risky shift remained in this study; when participants joined groups with risk preferences similar to their own, their behavior shifted to be more risk loving. However, the paper also documented a conformity effect; individuals increased their risky behavior when joining a more risk-loving group and decreased it when joining a more risk-averse group.

Together, these studies suggest that individual preference for risk depends not only on the details of the gamble (likelihood of winning and amount won) but also on the social conditions under which the gamble is undertaken. This realization is sufficient to generate the observed difference between gambling behavior and insurance behavior mentioned above; although these decisions may have the same outcomes, they are made in very different social conditions. And, of course, this realization also suggests both opportunities and ethical dilemmas for those in the gaming industry.

A second set of studies demonstrates another factor that influences risk preferences: the history-dependence of the outcomes. Individuals tend to prefer risk when they have previously lost, but avoid risk when they are ahead (referred to as the "reflection effect" by Kahneman and Tversky[11]). Early evidence of this tendency was found by Leopard.[12] In this experiment, forty undergraduates chose one of four games that were designed to vary in either variance or skewness. Most participants chose games with greater risk when they had fallen behind and lower risk when they were winning. Leopard hypothesized that subjects were trying to lock in gains when ahead (taking fewer risks) and trying to catch up when behind (taking greater risks). This motivation will reappear in our discussion of the reflection effect in the next section.

Quandt found similar shifts in risk preferences at the racetrack.[13] He observed that the subjective probability of winning (the line set in the pari-mutuel market) exceeded the objective probability (the number of recorded wins for a horse with given odds) for longshots, whereas favorites were bet on less than their records would indicate was appropriate. Metzger reviewed data on over eleven thousand races and found that bettors' preference for longshots increased over the course of a day, as they fell further behind and sought to catch up.[14] Thus again, individuals exhibit more of a preference for risk (longshots) when they have been losing than when they have been winning.

Applying these lessons to the stock market, Shefrin and Statman show a similar reflection effect in financial markets.[15] They found evidence that participants in the stock market were quick to recognize gains (selling winners whose prices had risen, exhibiting risk aversion) and reluctant to realize losses (holding losers whose prices had fallen, exhibiting risk lovingness). They term this result the "disposition effect." They also found that these tendencies undermined investors' ability to maximize returns.

In summary, a number of studies have illustrated that an individual's risk preference is neither inherent in the individual nor based solely on the characteristics of the gamble faced. Instead, social factors and history dependence can affect how much risk individuals prefer in gambling settings.

Biases in Risk Perception: Illusion of Control and the Hot Hand

Another reason why individuals gamble is that they perceive the risk they face to be less than it actually is. A number of authors have identified behavioral factors that affect risk perception. In particular, gamblers often attribute their wins (or losses) not to random chance but to their own (or others') abilities. This error can affect risk perception, and in particular can make an individual believe that a given gamble is not as risky as it appears because they erroneously believe that they have some control over the outcome.

Oldman presents a fascinating sociological study of gamblers' risk perceptions at roulette.[16] He found that when gamblers won, they were likely to attribute those wins to their skill rather than to chance. Oldman's findings were consistent with earlier "attribution theory" showing that people tend to take credit for the good things that happen to them while blaming unpleasant events on circumstances outside their control. Because they believed they were skillful, subjects in his study perceived the risky activity of betting on roulette to be less risky than it actually was. Thus gambling activity could have been caused by an error in risk perception.

In a second field study, Henslin observed a group of St. Louis cab drivers in seventeen craps games and found that they participated in a variety of informal verbal and nonverbal actions designed to influence the outcome (e.g., throwing the dice hard for high numbers, soft for low numbers, concentrating on the number desired) and that they advised other players to engage in such activities.[17] This behavior suggests the illusion of control; that is, individuals believed their actions influenced a purely random event.

The misattribution of the reason for a win (to skill rather than to chance) is sometimes referred to as the "hot hand." Originally described in basketball,[18] the hot hand refers to a belief that an individual is causing an outcome that is instead due to random chance. They surveyed a wide variety of individuals involved in basketball and found that nearly everyone (coaches, fans, players, journalists) had hot-hand beliefs, especially about the probability of a given player making a shot after a success or failure. Table 5.2 summarizes some of the data described in this paper. As can be seen, the probability of making a shot conditional on having hit the last three shots is, if anything, lower than the probability of making a shot either unconditionally or after three misses. Looking at the average of an entire team shows no statistically significant hot-hand effect. Of course, some players are better than others; some make their shots with a higher percentage and others with a lower percentage. But the likelihood of any individual making a shot is independent of whether he has made the previous shot.

TABLE 5.2

Probability of Making a Shot Conditioned on the Outcome of Previous Shot

Player	P(Hit/3 Misses)	P(Hit)	P(Hit/3 Hits)
Julius Erving	.52	.52	.48
Andrew Toney	.52	.46	.34
Daryl Dawkins	.88	.62	.51
1982 Philadelphia 76ers Average	.56	.52	.46

Source: Reprinted from Gilovich, Vallone, and Tversky, *The Hot Hand in Basketball, On the Misperception of Random Sequences*, p. 299.

More recently, Chau and Phillips found similar evidence by examining the behavior of twelve experimental participants who played blackjack online.[19] In an unusual twist from most research, Chau and Phillips controlled the outcomes by manipulating the cards. As in Oldman, above, when asked about the role that luck played in their outcomes, players attributed a greater role to luck after a losing streak than after a series of wins. Players thus believed that their wins were caused by skill, and their losses were caused by (bad) luck.

Croson and Sundali observed individuals playing roulette in a casino.[20] They found that players acted consistently with beliefs in the hot hand. After the first spin, the average number of bets placed was 7.63. However, after having won on the previous spin, individuals placed significantly more bets (13.62), consistent with the belief that they were "hot" and thus more likely to win. The number of bets placed after a winning spin was also significantly higher than the number of bets placed after a losing spin (9.21), which was itself not significantly different than the number of bets placed on the individual's first spin.

TABLE 5.3
Number of Inside Bets Placed

	Average	*St. Dev.*	N
First Spin	7.63	6.12	139
Won Prior Spin Inside	13.62	6.60	570
Lost Prior Spin Inside	9.21	5.35	1487

Source: Reprinted from Croson and Sundali, *The Gambler's Fallacy and the Hot Hand: Empirical Data from Casinos*, p. 204.

Camerer examined sports betting markets and demonstrated that in pari-mutuel settings, bettors were responding to a belief in the hot hand, driving point spreads in favor of the team perceived to have momentum on their side (based on their previous wins) or against the team with negative momentum (based on their previous losses).[21] Brown and Sauer confirmed Camerer's conclusion that belief in the hot hand influenced bettors in the pari-mutuel market.[22]

Similar biases have been documented in risky financial settings, especially in choosing mutual funds. Research has indicated that investors direct large flows of money to funds that have previously experienced positive returns.[23] Unfortunately, mutual fund returns appear to be driven more by a random process than by a hot hand (much like basketball players). Carhart showed that past performance was predictive of future performance in only one case—where high costs induced persistently bad returns.[24]

In summary, a second reason why people gamble has to do with their risk perceptions. Studies in this section suggest that risk perceptions depend on the attributions individuals make about prior wins and losses. In particular, gamblers (and most humans) tend to attribute good outcomes to skill and bad outcomes to chance. This leads gamblers to believe that they have more control over the outcome of a given gamble than they actually do, thus making them more likely to gamble in the first place.

Errors in Risk Estimation: History Dependence

A final behavioral regularity often observed is error in risk estimation. In this section we discuss papers that have demonstrated beliefs of history dependence in serially uncorrelated gambles. For example, consider a roulette wheel. Further imagine that this wheel has produced a winning red number for the past ten spins. What is likely to happen on the next spin?

If the wheel is in fact unbiased, we expect to see a red and a black number with equal probability on the next spin. Thus the outcome is history independent and the outcomes serially uncorrelated. But a number of studies demonstrate that gamblers believe in negative serial autocorrelation, colloquially referred to as the "gambler's fallacy." If red has appeared ten times, they argue, black must be "due" and is thus more likely than red on the next spin.

Clotfelter and Cook found gambler's fallacy behavior in the Maryland state lottery.[25] They found that after a particular number had won, players were significantly less likely to play that number again. For three days after the winning numbers were drawn, the number of times those numbers were bet was always lower than on the day of the drawing or in the three days before.

Over time, the bias against the winning numbers was reduced. Play of winning numbers reached normal levels approximately three months later.

Keren and Lewis found incidences of the gambler's fallacy in roulette play.[26] They observed gamblers who would meticulously record the outcomes of spins of the wheel and make bets based on which color had not come up as often as they expected. These players appeared to believe that wheel spins were not independent and that every time a color came up it was less likely to come up again in the future.

Terrell and Farmer and Terrell also found evidence of the gambler's fallacy at the dog races.[27] When a dog in a particular post position won in one race, a different dog assigned to the same post position was significantly underbet in the subsequent race. Since the dog track used a pari-mutuel structure, where the odds are a reflection of the bets on each race, this bias generated the ability to earn excess returns; bets placed on post positions which had previously won generated significantly positive returns since these dogs were underbet relative to their true odds of winning. Similar evidence was found by Metzger.[28] Bettors were more willing to bet on favorites after a series of wins by longshots.

Croson and Sundali found evidence of gambler's fallacy betting behavior in their roulette data as well.[29] Figure 5.1 shows the proportion of bets placed on even-money "outside" bets based on the history of these outcomes in the past. After streaks of length four, five, or six, individuals are significantly more likely to bet on the other outcome. For example, after four black numbers appear in a row, individuals are more likely to bet on red than on black.

In summary, research from this section indicates that gamblers misestimate the probabilities involved in a given gamble in systematic ways. In particular, individuals exhibit gambler's fallacy beliefs in thinking that the probability of a particular outcome is significantly affected by the previous history of outcomes, even in a serially uncorrelated, random process. This error can cause individuals to gamble again as they underestimate the risk involved in a particular gamble, believing that betting on black after a series of red numbers is not a risk but a "sure thing."

FIGURE 5.1
*Proportion of Gambler's Fallacy Outside Bets after a Streak
of at Least Length N*

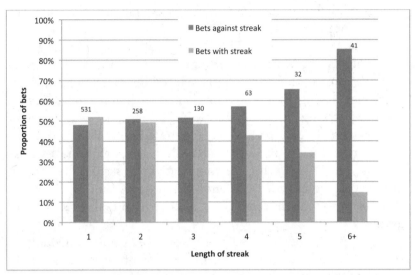

Source: Reprinted from Croson and Sundali, *The Gambler's Fallacy and the Hot
Hand: Empirical Data from Casinos*, p. 203.

Risk Attitudes in the Laboratory

Just as in the field, researchers have demonstrated a number of
these biases in the laboratory. The laboratory is a useful venue
for exploring risk attitudes, as myriad factors can be controlled
or observed that are not observable in the field. In this section we
describe a few laboratory studies which validate and more deeply
explore the biases observed in the field.

Factors Influencing Risk Preference: Social Context and Previous Wins/Losses

As in the field, lab experiments have shown that individuals are
often more likely to take gambles when they are making decisions
in groups than when they are making decisions individually. This
phenomenon, called the risky shift, has been documented in hundreds of studies.

Among the first of these studies was Wallach, Kogan, and
Bem, in which male and female undergraduates at a large state

university were asked to respond to a series of risk-based questions individually and afterwards to discuss the situations and choose actions in a group setting.[30] The results showed that the groups tended to decide upon a riskier course of action than the constituent individuals.

These types of lab studies have the advantage of being able to distinguish between competing causality in the field. It could be, for example, that individuals making decisions in groups are more risk loving than those making them alone, not because there is anything special about groups but because of the type of person who chooses to make a group decision. This is referred to as "endogeneity" in statistical analysis; the individuals whose actions you are observing are choosing which setting they are in, and it could be unobserved factors of the individual which cause them both to take more risk and to choose to make decisions in groups.

In the lab, however, we can randomly assign individuals to treatments (individual decision making or group decision making) rather than allowing them to self-select. If we see a difference between the treatments, we can confidently attribute its cause to the type of decision (individual or group), rather than something unobserved about the individual. Alternately, laboratory experiments can collect risk preference data both for the individual when deciding alone and for the same individual when deciding in a group (a within-subject design). Now we can observe a shift in the risk preference within each person as the social context changes.

The studies on risky shift have used both these methods to overcome the endogeneity problem that occurs in the field. And they have replicated the results from the field, finding a significant impact of social context on risk preferences.

A second attribute that has been observed to influence risk preference in gambling settings at the racetrack and in the stock market was the individual's financial position.[31] Gamblers tend to take more risks when they are behind, and fewer risks when they are ahead. This asymmetric risk preference is called the "reflection effect" and is one of the three key attributes of Prospect Theory.[32]

A number of laboratory experiments have demonstrated the reflection effect. For example, Payne, Laughhunn, and Crum studied the decision making of 128 managers in a laboratory setting.[33] The managers were presented a series of budget proposals with differing levels of risk and return. Of those managers, 62 percent showed risk-averse behavior when presented with a positive expected outcome, while 59 percent were risk seeking when the expected outcome was negative. Tversky and Kahneman discuss this effect in detail, suggesting that gamblers may be increasing their wagers because of a psychological need to "get back to even" that exceeds their desire to limit losses.[34] Thaler and Johnson tested this explanation directly and showed that laboratory participants would indeed take greater risks after losses when presented with the opportunity to break even, but not if the risks simply left them "less behind."[35]

The implications for gamblers' behavior are clear. When individuals are ahead, they are likely to "cash out," reducing their financial exposure and thus their risk. In contrast, when they are behind, individuals will take larger and larger risks, appearing risk seeking in an attempt to get back to even.[36] This pattern of taking larger, negative-expected-value risks when one is behind is related to problems of gambling addiction, which we will discuss below.

Biases in Risk Perception: Illusion of Control and the Hot Hand

We saw that in the gambling setting individuals misattributed their wins to their own skill rather than to pure chance,[37] and that this misattribution caused them to take more risks than they would have otherwise. Quite a lot of research from the lab on the "illusion of control" demonstrates that individuals attribute success in risky settings to their own skill, even though the outcomes are caused by chance. In many situations, people believe that they can change, or at least influence, events that are entirely beyond their control. In a series of six experiments, Langer found that subjects perceived the ability to influence the outcome of events such as lottery numbers chosen when no such control existed.[38] Furthermore, Langer found that the illusion of control can be enhanced by introducing competition, choice, familiarity, and active involvement into a chance situation.

Colloquially, this bias often appears in casino games like craps, where the players handle the randomizing device (here, the dice). Strickland, Lewicki, and Katz observed thirty-two male high school students playing craps in a laboratory setting and found that subjects decreased their bets when forced to bet after the dice had been thrown but before the results were known.[39] In contrast, they bet more before the dice had been thrown, suggesting that they believed they had control over the outcome. More generally, this research indicates that individuals believe they can control the numbers that appear and thus misperceive the riskiness of the gamble they are facing.

In the field we saw that gamblers also misperceived the probability of a given team winning (or mutual fund manager beating the market) based on its past performance. This result has been shown in the lab as well. Ayton and Fischer asked thirty-two undergraduate students at City University to participate in a modified roulette simulation as either forecasters or gamblers, making predictions about the future numbers and indicating their level of confidence.[40] When subjects experienced a history of winning or losing their bets or predictions, they tended to gain confidence that the streak would continue.

Burns and Corpus found that the illusion of control and the hot hand fallacy were related to each other.[41] They asked 195 Michigan State University students to make predictions regarding the persistence of streaks under basketball free throws and sales competitions. The authors identified hot hand beliefs for these two domains; success on a previous trial translated into expectations of success in the future. Burns and Corpus also confirmed the Strickland, Lewicki, and Katz finding that random events in the future are perceived as more controllable than those in the past.[42]

In summary, research in this section demonstrates that individuals misattribute good outcomes to their own (or others') skill rather than to random chance, as they should. This leads to a belief that people (or teams) are "hot" and thus more likely to win than chance suggests. This belief represents a misperception of the amount of risk that a given gamble entails.

Errors in Risk Estimation: History Dependence

Errors in risk estimation are the final bias we observed in the field, especially mistakes on the history-dependence of outcomes. Some of the earliest studies of perceptions of probabilities involved subjects making predictions about random sequences.

In these studies (also called probability matching experiments), subjects saw a sequence of colored lights (e.g., red, red, blue, red, blue, blue, blue, . . .), which were in fact drawn from a distribution with some probability. They were then asked to predict which color would appear next. Feldman demonstrated a negative recency effect; subjects were significantly more likely to predict the color that had not appeared recently than chance suggests.[43] This pattern is said to be caused by gambler's fallacy beliefs; since when individuals have seen three blue lights in a row, they feel that red must be due.

Kahneman and Tversky (1972) sent a questionnaire to 1,500 Israeli college preparatory high school students and asked them to look at a randomly generated sequence and judge how likely it was to have occurred.[44] For example, participants might see six flips of a coin whose outcomes were HTHTHT, or a different sequence like HHHHTT. Participants believed that the first sequence was significantly more likely than the second sequence, although in truth both were equally likely. Kahneman and Tversky conceptualized this finding as the "law of small numbers" and the "representativeness heuristic." Demonstrating the law of small numbers, respondents evaluated the probability of a sample based on the degree to which it was similar to the parent population (50% H and 50% T). Their evaluations were as though the law of large numbers should apply to small samples. Reflecting the "representativeness bias," respondents valuated the probability of a sample based on the extent to which it reflected the key features of the process by which it was generated (alternating H/T). Thus they expected samples to be representative of the random process that generated them.

In related research, Wagenaar documented numerous studies in which subjects were unable to generate random sequences.[45] This was most often as a result of negative recency;[46] the random sequences generated by participants tended to "switch too much" relative to what a truly random sample would look like. Individuals generating these sequences sought to generate sequences that "looked random" and their vision of what looked random involved both frequencies that exactly matched the underlying probability (50% H and 50% T) and which had more alternations between outcomes (H/T) than a truly random sequence would entail.

In summary, when individuals face serially uncorrelated risks (like coin flips or roulette wheel spins), they tend to incorporate the history of the outcomes into their probability beliefs, and thus to underestimate their estimates of the riskiness of a given gamble.

Neuroscience and Gambling

Neuroscience is the study of the nervous system; cognitive neuroscience focuses on how the brain interacts with the external environment to create behavior. In chapter 7, Marc Potenza describes neuroscientific studies of addicted and nonaddicted gamblers, comparing their brain activity in gambling and nongambling tasks. In this section, we focus instead on neuroeconomics, a subfield of neuroscience, focusing on the interaction between the brain and the external environment in the creation of economic behavior.[47] Advances in brain imaging techniques have significantly advanced this field in the last few years. Techniques now allow for controlled experiments with participants making risky choices while the brain is being imaged.[48] The goal of this research is to understand the underlying biological and chemical forces at work during economic decision making.

At the theoretical level, the promise of neuroeconomics is to open up the black box of the brain in order to inspire new theorizing about how economic decisions are made. On a more practical level, understanding the functioning of the brain will allow for the development of more customized products and services for consumers. For example, manufacturers of slot machines can design machines with bells and whistles tailored to the neural functioning of gaming patrons in order to increase the length of time they will play a machine and the amount of money they expect to lose.

In this section we will briefly outline some of the emerging themes from neuroeconomic experiments on decision making under risk that may be relevant to gambling researchers. We then describe a few neuroeconomic experiments on decision making under risk and offer some speculations on implications of these experiments. For recent reviews of the literature in this area we recommend to the reader Camerer, Lowenstein, and Prelec; Trepel, Fox, and Poldrack; and Lieberman.[49]

Emerging Themes in Neuroeconomics

Camerer, Lowenstein, and Prelec provide a recent review of the neuroscience literature and highlight findings that may be particularly relevant to economics.[50] The organizing schema for their literature review is shown in table 5.4.

TABLE 5.4
Systems of Decision Making

	Cognitive	*Affective*
Controlled Processes Serial Effortful Evoked deliberately Good introspective access	I Engaged when considering house refinance decision	II Used when method acting and trying to get into character
Automatic Processes Parallel Effortless Reflective No introspective access	III Controls movement of your hand as you return a tennis serve	IV Makes you jump when someone yells "Boo!"

Source: Derived from table 1 in Camerer, Loewenstein, and Prelec, "Neuroeconomics," 16.

The basic premise in table 5.4 is that the brain's organization and functioning can be explained by regional components. table 5.4 describes four regional processes of brain functioning that impact economic decision making.

The first distinction in brain functioning is between *automatic* and *controlled* processes; we can think of these as the unconscious and the conscious parts of the brain. Automatic processes involve rapid response, allow for massive multitasking, and provide tremendous power for certain functions such as visual recognition. These processes tend to be located in back (occipital), top (parietal), and side (temporal) parts of the brain. Controlled processes are described as step-by-step logic or computations that are evoked deliberately and with effort to solve a problem. These processes tend to be located in the front (orbital and prefrontal) parts of brain. Automatic processes influence behavior most of the time and controlled processes are viewed as the override or exception process.

A second distinction is made between *cognitive* and *affective* (emotional) neural functioning. Camerer, Lowenstein, and Prelec describe affective functioning as embodying emotions such as anger, fear, and jealousy, but also states such as hunger, thirst, sexual desire, and physical pain.[51] Cognitive processes, in contrast, involve logical processes and answer true/false-type questions.

Examples of decisions and behaviors that result from these four cells are given in table 5.4. The authors note that most behavior results from interaction of all four quadrants and offer the classification as an organizing schema rather than as an exclusive categorization.

From this schema, several points are relevant to the study of gambling behavior. First is the often overlooked but critical importance of affect. While our previous section described individuals facing risky decisions as flawed calculators who misperceive risk, this approach describes individuals as making decisions based on their emotions (how does this make me feel) rather than on an expected value calculation that is possibly flawed. By identifying activation in the brain that we know is related to emotional states and activation that is related to cognitive reasoning, neuroeconomics attempts to distinguish between these two models of decision making.

Second is the importance of homeostasis. Homeostasis is concerned with the monitoring and maintenance of biological equilibriums that are essential to maintaining life. For example, when the body gets too hot or cold the brain engages systems to correct the imbalance. The body may automatically begin to sweat to cool down or shiver to keep warm. In an economic setting, homeostasis appears as the desire to "get back to even" discussed in the previous section. If gamblers have lost, they will likely take action to bring the situation back into equilibrium.

A third point concerns the collaboration and competition that occurs between the brain's different regional systems. The four quadrants of table 5.4 should not be viewed as separate and distinct systems operating independently of each other. Rather, the systems both compete and collaborate to drive behavior. Again, brain scans identifying activation can help us understand which systems are engaged in facing which types of decisions.

With these organizing themes in place, we present research from several neuroeconomic experiments on decision making under risk and uncertainty and offer some speculations on implications of these experiments for gaming research. We speculate on how research from neuroeconomics might explain some of the data from the gambling industry and, conversely, how data from the industry might inform future neuroeconomic research. We conclude with some speculations on the intersection of neuroeconomics and gaming.

Neuroeconomic Experiments under Risk

Gains and losses

Smith, Dickhaut, McCabe, and Pardo examined choice under conditions of risk modeled on the classic gamble presented by Ellsberg.[52] In each condition of the experiment, subjects were given a choice of which gamble they wanted to play.

Each gamble was presented as a choice of selecting a marble from one of two containers. Inside each container was a distribution of ninety red, blue, and yellow marbles. For example, as shown in table 5.5 in the risk/gain condition, the container for gamble 1 contained thirty red marbles, thirty blue marbles, and thirty yellow marbles with payoffs of $30, $30, and $0, respectively. Gamble 2 involved a container with the same distribution of colored marbles (thirty each) but different payoffs for the colored marble ($50 red, $6 blue, $4 yellow). The gambles thus had the same expected value ($20) but there was greater spread (variance) in the payoffs for gamble 2 than gamble 1. Participants in the experiment were asked to select the gamble (container) from which they would rather draw a marble, or to indicate no preference between containers. In the risk/loss condition, the gambles were the same but the payoffs were losses rather than gains.

Subjects were presented with twenty-seven choice pairs in each experimental condition. At the conclusion of the experiment, one gain and one loss trial were selected and played out with the subject selecting a marble from a container and receiving payment based upon the marble color drawn.

This experiment was designed to elicit risk preferences in gains and losses but also to examine what portions of the brain were activated in these choices.

TABLE 5.5
Gambles Faced

Risk/Gain	Gamble 1			Gamble 2		
	Red	Blue	Yellow	Red	Blue	Yellow
Number of Marbles	30	30	30	30	30	30
Payoff if Marble Chosen	$30	$30	$0	$50	$6	$4

Risk/Loss	Gamble 1			Gamble 2		
	Red	Blue	Yellow	Red	Blue	Yellow
Number of Marbles	30	30	30	30	30	30
Payoff if Marble Chosen	$-30	$-30	$0	$-50	$-6	$-4

Source: Derived from Smith, Dickhaut, McCabe, and Pardo, "Neuronal Substrates for Choice Under Ambiguity, Risk, Certainty, Gains, and Losses," 712.

As expected, the results from this experiment were consistent with choice behavior observed in experiments reviewed above. Participants were risk avoiding in gains and risk seeking in losses, demonstrating the reflection effect.

However, the most important contribution of this study was the brain scan results. The authors showed that two separate parts of the brain were activated when these gambles were considered. One area of the brain (neocortical dorsomedial) was differentially activated when the gambles included losses but was (relatively) dormant when the gamble included only gains. This part of the brain is associated with cognition and higher processes, as opposed to affect and emotion (cell I in table 5.4 above). This suggests that gambles involving losses tend to be considered in a more calculative way, while those involving only gains or under conditions of ambiguity are reacted to more emotionally.

A second experiment by De Martino, Kumaran, Seymour, and Dolan examines the difference between describing outcomes of a gamble as a gain or a loss, sometimes referred to as "framing effects."[53] Participants were told that they had received £50. They were then instructed that they would not be able to keep the whole £50 and instead had to choose between a sure option and a gamble. In the gain condition subjects had the choice between: a) keep £20 (sure thing); or b) keep all £50 or lose all £50 (gamble). In the loss condition, subjects had the choice between: a) lose £30; or b) keep all £50 or lose all £50 (gamble). Note that these two choices are identical; keeping £20 out of £50 is the same as losing £30 out of £50. What differed is only in how they were described.

The odds of the gamble were represented by a colored pie chart and the expected value of the gamble was kept equivalent to the sure option (L20 in the gains condition and L30 in the loss condition). No feedback was given to subjects over the course of the trials. Subjects made their choices while being scanned by an fMRI machine.

The choices people made were consistent with prior experimental results and the reflection effect. When the choice was described as a gain, the majority of participants were risk averse and chose the sure thing. When the choice was described as a loss, the majority of participants were risk seeking and chose the gamble.

The authors note that individuals who were more likely to demonstrate the reflection effect had greater activation in the part of their brain typically described as dealing with emotions (the amygdala). They conclude that this reflection effect is correlated with activations in the affective regions of the brain (cells II and IV in table 5.4) and not the cognitive regions. These results again point to the finding that the decisions under risk may be significantly impacted by the emotional architecture of the brain.

Enjoying the experience

A third neuroeconomics experiment by Breiter, Aharon, Kahneman, Dale, and Shizgai was designed to investigate the neural basis of gambling experiences.[54] In this experiment, participants witnessed a game in which they won or lost money while monitored by fMRI. Unlike the previous experiment, they had no choices to make.

In the experiment, individuals saw circles divided into three segments, each with a dollar amount representing the win or loss that would occur (see figure 5.2 below). Some circles involved losses, others involved gains, and others were mixed gambles with both losses and gains. Participants watched as an arrow spun around in the circle, then stopped on a number that indicated their gain or loss.

Participants were endowed with $50 to begin the experiment and observed 152 trials in a counterbalanced design. Subjects earned an additional $78.50 from the trials.

FIGURE 5.2
Experimental Design: Loss, Mixes, and Gain Gambles

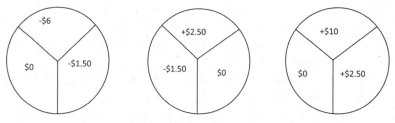

Source: Breiter et al., "Functional Imaging," 622.

One of the most interesting findings from this experiment is that activity in the dopamine fields during anticipation and experience of these gambles show intriguing similarities to prior results obtained from monkeys. The firing of dopaminergic neurons in monkeys has been shown to regulate the emotional response to both the anticipation and the experience of rewards. Specifically, the dopamine system appears to play a role in regulating the emotional pleasure received when rewards are initially anticipated, and then again when rewards are experienced and compared to expectations. In monkeys these dopamine firings accurately correlate expectations with outcomes. In this experiment, the greatest consistency in dopamine firings was found when subjects observed the good (gain) spinner and fewer dopamine firings were observed when the bad (loss) spinner was observed.

The results from this experiment suggest that the utility of gambling includes some pleasure from anticipating the outcome of the gamble, aside from the benefits that winning money might provide. While losses are indeed less pleasurable than gains, there are benefits from anticipating a possible good outcome (like $10 or $2.50 in the gain or mixed gambles) or even a less-bad outcome (like $0 in the loss gamble). This result suggests that the motivation to take a gamble is not necessarily caused by the utility received from the gamble's outcome. Utility from anticipating a possibly good outcome may be an equally strong motivator.

This result is consistent with anecdotal results from the field from gamblers and gambling addicts, who report pleasure from the act of gambling independent of the risks or even the potential rewards of the risky decision.

Loss aversion

Tom, Fox, Trepel, and Poldrack investigated how individuals acted in mixed gambles where there was both the potential to win and to lose.[55] Previous work in laboratory experiments suggested "loss aversion," that individuals dislike losing money twice as much as they like winning money.

In this experiment subjects were shown a 50/50 chance of gaining one amount of money or losing another amount. After subjects reflected on the gamble for a few seconds, they chose either to accept or reject the gamble. Similar to the previous study, the gambles were presented as colored pie displays while the subjects were being scanned by fMRI.

The gambles were not immediately resolved, but instead subjects were told that one of their decisions would be played for real money at the end of the experiment. Subjects were given $30 one week before the experiment to cover any losses they might experience.

The results were consistent with prior experimental results in that subjects valued losses twice as much as gains. That is, individuals are indifferent between taking zero for sure and a gamble which offers a 50/50 chance at a gain of $2x and a loss of $x.

The authors found two interesting results from the brain scans. First, they compared individuals in their study and found that those who exhibited more loss aversion also had greater activity in particular brain areas (the sensorimotor cortex and superior frontal cortex). This suggests a biological basis of loss aversion and that individual differences in brain activity could explain gambling choices.

The second result is that brain activation decreased over time as the experiment progressed. This result suggests that when one gambles one gets a "thrill" which wears off over time. This decreased sensitivity to gambling activity could lead individuals to take greater and greater risks in order to recapture the thrill they once experienced.

From these results, the authors conclude that there may be neural activity that corresponds to loss aversion, which reflects a primary tenet of Prospect Theory. Further, individual differences in observed loss aversion were correlated with neural activity in these areas, leading the authors to speculate that individual differences in risk-taking may be related to genetic differences in dopamine systems.

Impacts of Neuroeconomics on Gambling Trends

These initial neuroeconomic results lead us to suggest that neural gambling activity differentially takes place in regions I (controlled/cognitive) and IV (automatic/affective) as proposed by Camerer et al. in table 5.5.[56] From the reviewed experiments there is evidence that affective neural activation occurs when gamblers anticipate and experience rewards. Cognitive neural activity is likely to be more prevalent when gamblers are experiencing losses and presumably when subjects calculate odds and make decisions.

These results have important practical implications. For example, the experiment by Breiter et al., which suggested that there may be neural activity in the dopamine system before the gamble's outcome is realized, has some intriguing speculations in gaming.[57] Games that resolve "too quickly" are likely to be unpopular, as the outcomes (wins or losses) may occur before the individual has been able to enjoy the dopamine activity in anticipating the outcome. This observation can explain why even digital (computer-based) slot machines still simulate spinning reels. This simulation slows down the experience.

Tom et al., De Martino et al., and Trepel, Fox, and Poldrack all have reported results that provide neural evidence underlying some of the key tenets of Prospect Theory. Tom et al. report evidence consistent with a neural basis for loss aversion, and De Martino et al. report evidence consistent with a neural basis for framing effects. Interestingly, both these studies also suggest that there may be significant individual differences in neural architecture or dopamine systems, which may account for the individual differences in choice behavior.[58]

Support for a neural basis of Prospect Theory has contradictory implications for gambling behavior. Some elements of Prospect Theory can help explain some specific gambling behaviors; for example, individuals are more risk loving in losses, so once they start gambling they are more likely to continue the behavior (and on average they lose).

However, there are other elements of Prospect Theory that contradict gambling behavior. For example, if losses hurt twice as much as gains, then why is gambling behavior not rapidly extinguished? Experimental results that find significant individual neural differences may provide one avenue for reconciliation between the theory and this data. Along these lines, Chorvat et al. write:

> One of the most prominent findings to emerge from these studies is the heterogeneity of perception and reasoning. . . . Neuroimaging studies have shown that individuals will often use different parts of the brain for the same or similar problems and that the use of different neural mechanisms is correlated with different behavior. This indicates that what we might initially think are similar situations are likely to be perceived differently.[59]

Individual differences in neural processing can also cause another phenomenon: gambling addiction.

Gambling Addiction

Our literature review to this point has focused on how people in general and gamblers in particular make decisions with regard to risk. However, there is a subset of gamblers that bears more scrutiny—gambling addicts. While the percentage of seriously disordered gamblers in the adult population appears to be relatively low, somewhere between 2 percent and 10 percent of the gambling population, pathological gamblers respond differently on at least one major aspect of their risky behavior: the size and frequency of their wagers.[60] Thus it is worth investigating their behaviors and thought processes in more detail to better understand this small but troubling group.

The term addiction is generally used to describe destructive behaviors. Typically, addicts begin simply as casual gamblers, but their behavior quickly escalates to a point where gambling activities become more and more frequent and interfere with other aspects of their lives. Some of the neuroeconomic research may shed light on these behaviors. For example, Tom et al. found a general decreasing sensitivity over time to risky activities; the thrill of gambling wears off and individuals need more and more stimulation to achieve the same levels of pleasure.[61] Individual differences in this decreasing sensitivity might someday explain why some individuals become addicted and others do not.

One question that arises is whether people trapped in an addictive situation are capable of responding rationally to changes in the risk/reward profile of the activities. Becker and Murphy developed a model that explained how addictive behavior could be seen responding to those changes.[62] Under the Becker-Murphy model, addicts respond more strongly than nonaddicts to expected future changes in price. Mobilia applied this model to horse racing.[63] Horse tracks periodically change the takeout rate (the amount of the total bet that is allotted to the house when setting the odds on the horses in a pari-mutuel setting). This changes the "price" of gambling in a durable, predictable way. The Becker-Murphy model predicts that this change should affect all gamblers, but should affect addicted gamblers more than nonaddicted gamblers. Not only did Mobilia find a strong negative relationship between price and demand in horse racing, but the relationship was stronger among addicted gamblers than among those with nonaddictive behaviors, indicating that pathological gamblers are aware of and responsive to price changes.

Langewisch and Frisch sought to understand the interaction between gambling and other risk-taking behaviors among addicted and nonaddicted gamblers.[64] They surveyed 144 male undergraduate university students on their impulsivity and sensation-seeking activities. For the majority of their subjects, impulsivity and sensation seeking were described in similar fashion for gambling and nongambling activities. Pathological gamblers, on the other hand, did not display significant correlation between their gambling and other impulsive or sensation-seeking activities. This paper suggests that casual gamblers view gambling as one sensation-seeking activity among many, considering other activities to be close substitutes. In contrast, addicted gamblers place gambling activities in a different mental category than other risky activities, and these activities do not substitute for each other.

In summary, gambling addicts represent an important problem for casinos and other gambling hosts. Recent research has investigated behavioral dimensions along which pathological gamblers differ from casual gamblers, and future research in this area will be needed to help identify potential gambling addicts and to help them avoid or control their destructive behaviors.

Conclusion

Gambling is a puzzle. Why would a rational, self-interested individual voluntarily and consistently choose to take a gamble with a negative expected value? Economics is founded on the principle that people engage in behavior that makes them better off. Since, ex post, gambling rarely seems to make anyone better off, then, ex ante, why do people engage in the behavior?

One explanation is that gambling is an addiction, or a serious mental or chemical disorder. It is clear that this has the potential to be true for some people in some circumstances. But in a recent meta-analysis, the percentage of disordered gamblers in the population appears to be relatively low, somewhere between 2 percent and 10 percent, depending upon the sample studied and how a gambling disorder is defined.[65] Even if we assume that this estimate is significantly lower than the true problem, this still means that the vast majority of gamblers gamble without any significant disorder. So we can rephrase our question: Why would a rational individual without a gambling disorder voluntarily and consistently choose to take a gamble with a negative expected value?

A second explanation is that gambling is a mistake. Individuals attempt to calculate the costs and benefits of gambling, but they make systematic errors in risk perceptions. These errors induce individuals to take more risks than they would if they were not similarly biased. Some of the more common mistakes that individuals can (and do) make include factors influencing risk preferences (context effects, previous wins/losses), biases in risk perception (illusion of control, hot hand), and errors in risk estimation (history dependence).

A third explanation is that people make the decision about gambles in an affective rather than in a cognitive way. That is, they do not calculate the expected utility from the act (not even doing so incorrectly); instead, they make an emotional decision about whether to engage in this behavior. Evidence from neuro-economics is consistent with this, showing that parts of the brain dealing with emotions are more activated when contemplating or choosing a risky outcome than when choosing a sure outcome (especially in gains) or when exhibiting the reflection effect. But other evidence from brain scans indicates that cognitive areas of the brain are similarly activated when choosing gambles (especially in losses). Consistent with the affective decision-making framework is the existence of gambling addicts, who are perceived to make their decisions emotionally rather than cognitively.

Decision Making and Morality

The topic of this volume asks a moral question. Other chapters provide excellent discussions of important normative questions such as: Is gambling a moral activity? and, Should governments sponsor and/or participate in gambling? We conclude our chapter with a modest attempt to tie our descriptive work into these broader questions.

Economists and psychologists who study decision making are not eager to address the normative question of whether a person should gamble. Generally they are much happier to offer advice on how to gamble if one so chooses (which games have a better expected value), and how to avoid mistakes that individuals are likely to make when they gamble (avoid biases in calculating probabilities).

We believe that our line of research can best contribute to the bigger normative question by deepening our understanding of how and why people gamble and by examining the implications of this question for policy and prescriptions.

How do people gamble? The primary answer to this question is "not very well." As discussed herein, individuals are subject to a number of cognitive heuristics and biases that affect their gambling behavior. If people's decisions are biased, and they regret the decisions they make after seeing their inconsistencies and outcomes, this opens the door for regulation as a tool for social welfare maximization. Some scholars have argued that everyone in society can be better off if individuals are prohibited from engaging in actions that they will later regret.[66] Paternalistic laws (like regulations about wearing seatbelts, motorcycle helmets, and drug use) stem from this argument. In contrast, other scholars have argued that individuals are made worse off from having smaller choice sets, even when the reduction is accomplished by eliminating options that would be dominated by other available options and thus never chosen.[67]

Some research suggests that people gamble automatically. The debate on automatic versus controlled decision processes can be traced back to the work of Descartes.[68] Descartes, considered to be the first neuroscientist, proposed that behavior could be explained as purely physical interactions in physiological systems. This viewpoint suggested that human behavior was subject to the same physical laws that controlled the orbits of planets or the functioning of complex machinery. Since this line of reasoning makes it extremely difficult to provide scientific explanations for complex human behaviors and raises serious philosophical questions regarding free will, Descartes proposed a two-tiered system to explain behavior consisting of the body and the soul. Simple behaviors could be explained by the mechanistic functioning of the body while complex behaviors requiring unpredictability and volition were the subject of the soul. While neuroscience and neuroeconomics have come a long way since Descartes, the distinction drawn by Camerer et al. between automatic and controlled processes follows Descartes' basic outline from the seventeenth century and suggests we still believe that human behavior is essentially a two-tiered system.[69]

From this perspective, the stronger the mechanistic link between gambling devices and human behavior, the greater the potential for abuse by gaming manufacturers and operators. As gaming devices are further developed, possibly guided by the scientific findings in neuroscience, we should expect the devices to become more efficient at eliciting automatic neural responses in gamblers. This raises the possibility that gamblers will have less free will (or will be less likely to activate the controlled and cognitive regions of their brains) in choosing when to stop gambling and whether to gamble at all.

The recent behavior of cigarette manufacturers may be instructive on this topic. A recent study by the Massachusetts Department of Public Health reported that between 1998 and 2004 the nicotine levels in cigarettes increased by an average of 10 percent.[70] The increase of nicotine levels in cigarettes has occurred at the same time that aggressive campaigns are being conducted by governmental agencies to reduce smoking rates throughout the United States. Although cigarette manufacturers refused to comment on this study, it appears that nicotine levels are being used to maintain smoking levels. The fact that these changes in cigarette composition were not announced allows them to operate directly on the physical level (automatic processes), bypassing the cognitive system (controlled processes).

Why do people gamble? At the present time we know very little about this question. Surveys that have been done on this topic have generally been unscientific and commissioned by casinos (e.g., Harrah's in 2006[71]). However, why people gamble has important implications for the morality of gambling.

Consider two possible answers to this question and the potential implications. First, assume that the primary motivation for people to gamble is to make money. The science of probability demonstrates that over the long-term this is essentially a statistical impossibility, yet most gamblers believe it to be possible or even likely. Perhaps gamblers should be informed of the likelihood of winning in clear and understandable terms. One could imagine a warning statement parallel to that of cigarettes, stating, "The United States Government has determined that frequent gambling will result in monetary loss."

Alternatively, it might be found that the primary motivation for gambling is simply as a form of entertainment. In this scenario, gamblers are fully informed and aware of the high likelihood of monetary loss, and they accept this cost as the price of entertainment. In this case, the moral question becomes less pressing, and the case for regulation or government intervention less compelling.

One role that future research on decision making under risk and uncertainty can provide in the debate on the morality of gambling is to continue to provide relevant scientific research that can inform both the operators and regulators of gambling. In addition to the type of research that has been reviewed here, we suggest the need for additional research on the questions of how and why people gamble.

We conclude this chapter with an unsolved puzzle that remains to be answered: the role of gambling from an evolutionary perspective. Most of the "rational" explanations for gambling behavior suggest that gambling is a mistake of some sort. But gambling is not a recent phenomenon; in fact, in a recent book on the history of gambling, Schwartz reports that gambling "is simply older than history."[72] Risk-taking was an essential element in the survival of ancient societies dependent on hunting and gathering for sustenance. Evolutionarily, one might imagine that species that took risks or that learned to take better risks had a higher likelihood of survival. For example, many tribes engaged in religious ceremonies that involved the rolling of sheep hucklebones (an early precursor to dice) in order to determine the geographical direction for a hunt. Since the hucklebones were an effective randomization device, tribes that lived in areas where food and game were randomly distributed would necessarily have a higher chance of survival than tribes who used a more deterministic search strategy.

If risk-taking is indeed an evolutionarily stable strategy, then casino gambling might serve a deep-seated need in the human psyche. Alternately, casinos might be taking advantage of a hard-wired desire in an attempt to boost their own bottom line. In either case, if this evolutionary perspective is correct, it suggests that gambling and other risky activities will continue to be an important activity in human society for generations to come. Achieving a deeper and more scientific understanding of the behavioral factors and neuroeconomic causes of risk-taking behavior is itself a gamble that will certainly pay off in the future.

6

Gambling with the Family?

John P. Hoffmann

What happens in Vegas stays in Vegas . . .
> —City of Las Vegas advertisement

*Don't people who gamble realize it has an effect on the whole family;
everyone is destroyed.*
> —wife of a compulsive gambler, writing
> to a Gamblers Anonymous Web site

The end of Prohibition in 1933 moved a vice into the normative mainstream virtually overnight. The growth of legal gambling in the United States and elsewhere, although not as dramatic, has had a similar effect: Vice has transformed not into virtue, but certainly into a mainstream activity enjoyed regularly by millions of people. This is demonstrated primarily by the rise of state-supported lotteries but has also been accompanied by the growth of casinos, slot machines, and other gaming activities. The proliferation of a variety of forms of legal gambling has also generated myriad public policy arguments over their promised payoffs to state and local budgets.

Thirty years ago, thirteen states had a lottery, with only a couple of states permitting casino gambling. By the end of 2007, forty-two states and the District of Columbia sponsored lotteries (including multistate), eleven states had commercial casinos, and twenty-eight states had American Indian casinos. In fact, people within the borders of every state except for Utah and Hawaii may now place legal wagers on a variety of games. Most popular, of course, is the lottery, which has been seen as a boon for state coffers. However, other gambling activities such as legal slots, pari-mutuel betting, and even Internet gambling are also seen by state executives and legislators as cash cows, especially during a period of devolution. Recently, Thomas E. Perez, Secretary of Labor, Licensing, and Regulation for the state of Maryland, complained that citizens of his state have chosen to gamble elsewhere: "By not having slots, Maryland has already left hundreds of millions of dollars in potential general fund revenue on the table, and the tables are located in West Virginia and Delaware."[1]

Although the growth of legal gambling has been met with a broad range of reactions from the general public, elected officials, and policy experts, there is little doubt that it has had both positive and negative consequences. On the positive side, there is evidence that the revenues generated from legal gambling have increased state educational funds and generated economic growth.[2] Moreover, advocates argue that legal gambling has pushed organized crime largely out of the gambling industry because of the greater state oversight that occurs in a regulated environment. However, problems have also accompanied the rapid growth of legal gambling. For example, it is no surprise that increasing the overall number of gamblers by expanding availability may also have increased the number of people with gambling problems. For instance, the estimated prevalence of current problem gambling increased from 2.3 percent in 1974 to about 5 percent in 1999.[3] Although it is difficult to find comparable trend data, the estimated prevalence of pathological gambling—a disorder defined in the American Psychiatric Association's Diagnostic and Statistical Manual (DSM-IV)—stands at between 0.4 percent and 0.8 percent, or an estimated 900,000–1.6 million adults in the United States,[4] and has likely increased since the mid-1970s.[5] Moreover, even though it remains illegal in most jurisdictions for young people to engage in gambling, the prevalence of problem gambling is higher among adolescents than adults.[6]

Criminologists have typically placed gambling in a category known as victimless crimes.[7] Along with vices such as prostitution, pornography, and drug use, gambling was generally seen as a behavior that may have unfortunate consequences, but that affected primarily the individual. However, the term "victimless crime" is becoming more and more of an anachronism, especially as studies have adopted a broader scope and included extraindividual influences and effects. For example, family studies have shown that compulsive engagement in "victimless crimes" such as prostitution, drug use, and pornography can have substantial negative effects on marital relations, parent-child engagement, and family functioning in general.[8]

Although few rigorous studies exist at this time, a substantial body of literature provides a sense that some forms of gambling have dire consequences for families. It is clear that many people engage in legal gambling with no apparent problems, yet the practical effects of problem gambling on family functioning require not only acknowledgment, but also additional scholarly attention. Thus, the aim of this chapter is to provide a general overview of what existing studies have shown. Moreover, I examine data from two large national surveys conducted in the United States to provide a specific sense of how families might be affected by the gambling behaviors of their members. Finally, I briefly discuss research strategies that are needed to fully evaluate how problem and pathological gambling affect and are affected by individual conditions, family relationships, and other related lifestyle problems.

Some Potential Consequences of Gambling Problems

The majority of people who have gambled, whether legally or illegally, do not experience problems with this type of behavior; rather, most simply enjoy the risk or the thrill of the games, whereas a few gamble professionally. A 1998 national survey conducted by the National Opinion Research Center (NORC) for the National Gambling Impact Study Commission found, for example, that while approximately 85 percent of adults in the United States have gambled in their lifetimes, almost nine in ten had no symptoms that would indicate problem or pathological gambling.[9] According to these estimates, about 9 percent of gamblers reported some risk due to their behavior, 1.5 percent were classified as problem gamblers, and about 0.9 percent were classified as pathological gamblers. Similarly, researchers using the National Epidemiological Survey on Alcohol and Related Conditions (NESARC) estimated that about 0.42 percent of adults in the United States reported symptoms consistent with a lifetime prevalence of pathological gambling; this included 0.64 percent of men and 0.23 percent of women.[10] However, the authors did not report the overall prevalence of gamblers in the sample, so one cannot determine the proportion of gamblers with problems, even though this proportion is bound to be small.[11]

Yet considering prevalence estimates only can mask the overall negative impact that gambling presents. Whereas the prevalence of problem gambling may be relatively low, even among active participants, the number of people affected directly is still consequential. Assuming that 85 percent of adults report gambling, this translates into approximately 187 million gamblers. Thus, from the NORC national estimates, there are about 1.6 million pathological gamblers, 2.8 million problem gamblers, and 15 million at-risk gamblers among adults in the United States.[12] If the prevalence of these problems among adolescents is similar or slightly higher, there are substantially more problem and pathological gamblers in the overall population of the United States than the NORC estimates suggest.

Moreover, the attributable risk is also consequential. "Attributable risk" (AR) is a term used in epidemiology to define the difference in the rate of some disease or disorder among those who are exposed to some condition versus those who are not exposed to the condition. It gauges the excess risk of the outcome (e.g., mental health disorder) in the exposed group compared with the nonexposed group. If we consider gambling behavior as the exposure, then clearly the AR is complete if problem or pathological gambling is the outcome. However, a more useful approach is to consider the AR when problem or pathological gambling is the exposure and the outcomes are mental health problems, economic disruption, family turmoil, marital problems, or poor parent-child relationships.

Unfortunately, it is difficult to determine the AR for gambling problems and these outcomes. Consider, for example, divorce, a condition that is associated with gambling problems. One of the major problems is that we cannot determine the risk of divorce prior to the onset of gambling problems; it is conceivable that some other factor, such as impulsivity or borderline personality disorder, affects the risk of both problem gambling and divorce, thus presenting a classic confounding effect. In addition, although pathological gambling is associated with various mental health problems, such as alcohol abuse and personality disorders,[13] the sequencing of problems is not evident. It seems most likely that mental health problems affect subsequent gambling problems, but studies thus far have been only marginally successful in sorting out the temporal ordering of these conditions.[14] For example, substance use disorders may predate most gambling problems, whereas mood disorders may follow or accompany their onset. As a general alternative to the expensive prospective studies that are needed to fully establish the sequencing of disorders (many studies simply rely on respondents' memories for onset information), researchers usually compare groups of problem or pathological gamblers to gamblers with no problems or to nongamblers on the prevalence of some outcome, such as divorce, marital problems, mental health problems, or domestic abuse.[15] Thus, much of the literature reviewed in the next section is based on comparing prevalence measures (or arithmetic means from frequency scales) while statistically adjusting for the effects of potential confounding variables.

Gambling and Family Problems

The correlates of problem and pathological gambling are fairly well established. The prevalence of pathological gambling tends to be higher among adults with the following characteristics: male, African American, ages 45–64, few years of formal education, low income, living in the western United States, and divorced, separated, or never married.[16] Moreover, problem and pathological gamblers tend to share certain personality characteristics, such as a propensity for risk, impulsivity, or sensation seeking, and to experience other mental health problems such as depression, antisocial personality disorder, and drug and alcohol abuse.[17] These problems may not simply be the result of high-frequency gambling, however. For instance, Welte et al.

determined that alcohol abuse and pathological gambling are significantly associated even when holding constant the frequency of gambling.[18] Pathological gamblers also tend to suffer disproportionately from physical health problems, especially angina and liver disease.[19]

The association between problematic forms of gambling, personality characteristics, and mental health problems raises an important question when addressing family problems: Are there common sources of gambling and interpersonal problems that are made manifest by gambling behavior but do not result uniformly from this behavior? For example, as suggested earlier, the association between pathological gambling and divorce or separation may reflect a common cause, such as a tendency towards impulsivity, antisocial personality disorder, or bipolar disorder. Similarly, impulse control problems are thought to underlie much delinquent behavior among youth, and they may also lead to gambling problems among adolescents who engage in gaming activities. The association between delinquency and pathological gambling may therefore be the result of a common causal mechanism.[20]

This is not to say that gambling might not exacerbate already existing family problems or even precede particular problems. Studies have attempted to consider these possibilities by statistically adjusting for the effects of potential confounding variables when examining gambling problems and family-related outcomes. For example, in a large study of adolescents residing in Ontario, Hardoon, Gupta, and Derevensky determined that problem gambling was associated with poor perceived parental social support, drug use problems, conduct problems, and general family problems even after statistically adjusting for the effects of several potential confounding variables.[21] Similarly, several studies have found that, in general, the families of problem and pathological gamblers experience poor communication, inadequate conflict resolution, attenuated relationship quality, and ineffective parenting.[22] Unfortunately, studies have not adopted a sufficient longitudinal perspective that would be needed to determine whether a poor family environment is preceded by or the result of gambling problems.

Comprehensive literature reviews by Dickson-Swift, James, and Kippen and Kalischuk and Cardwell have also found that families with pathological gamblers experience numerous negative consequences.[23] These include a heightened risk of problem gambling among children,[24] more family financial problems, a greater degree of family conflict and arguments, harsh and critical parenting, more emotional distance between spouses, and heightened stress among all family members. Relative to other married people, spouses of problem gamblers also report more abuse, depression, anxiety, and physical problems; diminished interest in sex; and dissatisfaction with sexual relations. Moreover, a disproportionate number of spouses report that they either had left their partner or seriously considered leaving because of his or her gambling.[25]

Children are often acutely affected by their parents' gambling problems. Their parents tend to spend less time with them and are emotionally distant or preoccupied even when they are present, especially during active periods of gambling. The children often blame themselves for the family turmoil, feel abandoned, and are at heightened risk of drug and alcohol problems.[26] For instance, utilizing in-depth interviews with fifteen children and adolescents of problem gamblers in Australia, Darbyshire, Oster, and Carrig discovered that a common theme concerned pervasive loss.[27] These children experienced physical loss as their parents were absent during gambling episodes or through separation and divorce; existential loss in that they felt a diminished personal attachment to and love from parents; the sense of loss of knowing who their parents are and what they should expect out of them; the loss of trust; and the loss of tangible items, such as presents during holidays or birthdays. These loss experiences often result in a higher incidence of anxiety and depression among offspring, involvement in health-risk behaviors, and an increased probability of attempting suicide.[28]

Moreover, as mentioned earlier, children of problem and pathological gamblers are significantly more likely to gamble themselves and are at greater risk of crossing the threshold to problem and pathological gambling. This is known as an "intergenerational transmission" effect; similar processes have been found in studies of adolescent substance use and mental health disorders.[29] Although the transmission of gambling problems is due, in part, to a higher genetic risk, it also involves shared environmental influences that occur primarily within the family.[30] For example, assuming that there is a genetic-based risk of gambling problems, perhaps because of a neurological propensity toward low impulse control or impaired decision-making abilities, they likely become manifest mainly if the family environment allows or encourages gambling to occur.

It is important to consider that the link between problem or pathological gambling and family problems may not be causal but rather may result from a common set of personality, neurological, or genetic characteristics. Potenza, Kosten, and Rounsaville described several neurobiological precursors to pathological gambling, including abnormal serotonin functioning that adversely affects impulse control, decreased monoamine oxidase (MOA; an enzyme that controls neurotransmitter functioning in the human body) functionality, and deficits in decision-making capabilities that stem from impaired neurological functioning.[31] These deficits seem to result in a tendency to choose immediate rewards even when faced with punishment and may be linked to impaired frontal cortical functioning. Several of these characteristics have also been linked to delinquency, criminal behavior, low educational achievement, aggression, and mental health problems (e.g., depression, anxiety).[32] The various consequences of physiological and neurological dysfunction likely create conditions that directly affect both family problems and gambling problems. In particular, individuals with these dysfunctions are not only likely to seek out opportunities to gamble (or find other ways to satisfy their need for risk and stimulation), but accordingly have problems with gambling that may become pathological.

Nevertheless, it is also likely that gambling problems exacerbate family problems, magnifying them and, when coupled with neurological deficiencies, producing a dysfunctional environment in which aggressive interactions, impaired decision making, heightened stress, and emotional distance become more and more common. The result is that family turmoil too often culminates in family breakup or upheaval and children who suffer from acute stress, guilt, and consequent interpersonal problems.

However, another important inquiry that has rarely been pursued in research on gambling is whether family members can act as a buffer against problems or pathologies. The typical research question in this area is whether gambling problems are associated with family problems. An alternative question involves whether gambling with family members rather than alone or with friends may actually decrease the likelihood of having problems. Numerous studies have shown the important role that spouses and biological kin play in attenuating the risk of mental health disorders because they can provide social support, enhance coping strategies, and offer informal therapy.[33] Family members may thus serve a social support and coping function that operates to attenuate the risk of problematic gambling behavior. Much like the solitary drinker is thought to be ripe for alcohol problems, the solitary gambler is at risk for consequent problems. Although gambling may present problems for some individuals and their families, it seems clear that the families of most gamblers are able to function well despite variable risk in the propensity to experience problem behaviors. Yet this does not diminish the fact that a substantial number of gamblers present pathologies that negatively affect their families.

Consequences of Gambling for Family Relations and Functioning

Although there have been several studies of the effects of gambling on families, virtually all of this research has used regional samples or convenience samples of gamblers in treatment settings. In this section, I draw upon data from two extant national surveys to examine the association between gambling behavior and several family-related conditions.[34] Although data limitations do not allow consideration of a sufficient array of outcomes, information from these surveys does allow us to consider several outcomes with an eye towards understanding some important relationships among key variables. For example, one of the limitations of using standardized instruments to study gambling problems is that some of the items used in these instruments ask about family relations. Therefore, it is not possible—if researchers use standardized instruments such as the South Oaks Gambling Screen (SOGS), the National Opinion Research Center DSM-IV Screen for Gambling Problems (NODS), or the Diagnostic Interview Schedule (DIS)—to fully disentangle family problems from gambling problems. Table 6.1, for instance, lists the items that were included in the national survey portion of the National Gambling Impact and Behavior Study (NGIBS), a 1998 study conducted by the National Opinion Research Center (NORC). The items comprise the NODS, which was developed for the National Gambling Impact Study Commission. The NODS items were designed to be consistent with DSM-IV diagnostic criteria for pathological gambling.[35] Note that items 11 through 14 ask specifically about whether the respondent's gambling behavior has ever led to stealing from, lying to, or caused relationship problems with family members. Item 17 concerns asking family members for money to pay for gambling debts. Hence it is possible for respondents to be categorized as problem gamblers—gauged by affirmative responses to 3 to 4 items—if they had problems only with family members or had no problems with family members that were affected by their gambling behavior.

TABLE 6.1

DSM-IV Criteria and Matched NODS Lifetime Questions, National Gambling Impact and Behavior Study (NGIBS), 1998

	1	Have there ever been periods lasting 2 weeks or longer when you spent a lot of time thinking about your gambling experiences or planning out future gambling ventures or bets? OR
Preoccupation	2	Have there ever been periods lasting 2 weeks or longer when you spent a lot of time thinking about ways of getting money to gamble with?
Tolerance	3	Have there ever been periods when you needed to gamble with increasing amounts of money or with larger bets than before in order to get the same feeling of excitement?
	4	Have you ever tried to stop, cut down, or control your gambling?
Withdrawal	5	On one or more of the times when you tried to stop, cut down, or control your gambling, were you restless or irritable?

	6	Have you ever tried but not succeeded in stopping, cutting down, or controlling your gambling?
Loss of control	7	If so, has this happened three or more times?
	8	Have you ever gambled as a way to escape from personal problems? OR
Escape	9	Have you ever gambled to relieve uncomfortable feelings such as guilt, anxiety, helplessness, or depression?
Chasing	10	Has there ever been a period when, if you lost money gambling one day, you would return another day to get even?
	11	**Have you ever lied to family members, friends, or others about how much you gamble or how much money you lost on gambling?**
Lying	12	**If so, has this happened three or more times?**
Illegal acts	13	**Have you ever written a bad check or taken money that didn't belong to you from family members or anyone else in order to pay for your gambling?**
	14	**Has your gambling ever caused serious or repeated problems in your relationships with any of your family members or friends?** OR
	15	ASK ONLY IF R IS IN SCHOOL Has your gambling caused you any problems in school, such as missing classes or days of school or your grades dropping? OR
Risked significant relationship	16	Has your gambling ever caused you to lose a job, have trouble with your job, or miss out on an important job or career opportunity?
Bailout	17	**Have you ever needed to ask family members or anyone else to loan you money or otherwise bail you out of a desperate money situation that was largely caused by your gambling?**

Source: Gerstein et al. GIBS, 18.

Note: The NODS is composed of 17 lifetime items and 17 corresponding past-year items, compared to the 20 lifetime items and 20 past-year items that make up the SOGS, and the 20 items (19 items in the field test) that make up the Diagnostic Interview for Gambling Severity (DIGS; Winters, Specker, and Stinchfield 2002). Like the updated SOGS-R used in most of the epidemiological research on gambling since 1991, the past-year item is asked for each lifetime NODS item that receives a positive response. The maximum score on the NODS is 10, compared to 20 for the SOGS. Although there are fewer items in the NODS, and the maximum score is lower, the NODS is designed to be more demanding and restrictive in assessing problematic behaviors than the SOGS or other screens based on the DSM-IV criteria. The items that involve family-related situations and conditions are in bold font.

In order to distinguish partially between gambling problems that involve the family and other gambling problems, it may be useful to consider interrelationships among items in this instrument. Are there specific commonalities between family problems associated with gambling and other problems, or are family problems distinguishable from other problems? In order to determine some answers to this question, I examined the NODS items administered in the NORC 1998 survey using a latent class (LC) cluster analysis method.[36] In order to conduct an efficient analysis, I first included all the relevant items for which there was complete data available to estimate the models. I then examined only the items listed in table 1 that involve family issues. The results of these analyses are presented in tables 6.2 and 6.3.[37]

TABLE 6.2

Latent Class Cluster Analysis of Items from the NODS, National Gambling Impact and Behavior Study (NGIBS), 1998

Items	*Cluster 1*	*Cluster 2*	*Cluster 3*
Preoccupation with planning gambling (1)			
Yes	0.034	0.495	0.927
No	0.966	0.505	0.072
Preoccupation with money for gambling (2)			
Yes	0.011	0.327	0.746
No	0.989	0.673	0.254
Increase in tolerance (3)			
Yes	0.013	0.221	0.690
No	0.987	0.779	0.310
Tried to cut down—irritable and restless (5)			
Yes	0.009	0.274	0.778
No	0.992	0.726	0.222
Loss of control—not succeeded (6)			
Yes	0.019	0.355	0.710
No	0.981	0.645	0.290
Tried to gamble to escape personal problems (8)			
Yes	0.030	0.340	0.810
No	0.970	0.660	0.190

Items	Cluster 1	Cluster 2	Cluster 3
Chased money after a loss (10)			
Yes	0.113	0.680	0.779
No	0.887	0.320	0.221
Lied to family members or friends about gambling (11)			
Yes	0.038	0.543	0.927
No	0.962	0.457	0.070
Taken money/written bad check to pay gambling (13)			
Yes	0.001	0.017	0.362
No	0.999	0.983	0.638
Gambling caused serious relationship problems (14)			
Yes	0.005	0.152	0.946
No	0.995	0.845	0.054
Gambling caused job/occupation problems (16)			
Yes	0.000	0.029	0.234
No	0.995	0.848	0.054
Asked family members for loan/bail-out (17)			
Yes	0.011	0.187	0.689
No	0.989	0.813	0.311
Emotionally harmful arguments due to gambling[a]			
Yes	0.003	0.135	0.870
No	0.997	0.865	0.130
Cluster Size (proportion of sample)	**0.863**	**0.108**	**0.030**

Note: The questions are taken from the NORC DSM-IV Screen for Gambling Problems (NODS) and were assessed using latent class cluster analysis. The numbers in parentheses indicate the item number from table 1. The numbers in columns two through four indicate the probability that a person who falls within the particular cluster answered yes or no to the question. The sample size is 1,214.
[a]Not part of the NODS. This question was asked just after the NODS items were completed by respondents.

The key result from table 6.2 is that there are three clusters that distinguish the items in the gambling problems screening instrument.[38] Cluster 1 is the largest; it contains about 86 percent of the sample and includes mainly those who have gambled and experienced no gambling problems. Cluster 2 contains about 11 percent of the sample, and cluster 3 includes about 3 percent of the sample. Although cluster 3 is the smallest, it contains most of the reported problematic gambling behaviors. For example, respondents in cluster 3 have a 93 percent chance of reporting that they had been preoccupied with their gambling experiences, an 81 percent chance of having gambled to escape from personal problems, and a 94 percent chance that their gambling had caused serious problems in their interpersonal relationships. In fact, the only items that were answered in the affirmative by a minority of respondents involved illegal acts and having occupational problems due to gambling. Note, furthermore, that the family-related items are not distinguishable from other items in the NODS. It appears that treating several family-related gambling problem items along with other gambling problems (e.g., preoccupation, withdrawal, chasing) is reasonable.

Table 6.3 includes the results of an LC cluster analysis that included only the family-related items in the NODS. The two-cluster model fits the data best. It shows that four of the five items are consistently reported by those in cluster 2: lying to family members, relationship problems, asking for a bail-out, and emotionally harmful arguments with family members.[39] Much like the earlier analysis, the item that does not distinguish problem gamblers well involves committing illegal acts. This may be because only a small proportion of gamblers in the NORC survey answered yes to this question ($n = 16$, or 1% of gamblers). However, it may also reflect that this rather extreme behavior is not part of even many pathological gamblers' lifestyles.

Given the finding that most of the items in the NODS, and by association the DIS and the DIGS, consistently distinguish a similar set of problem-gambling symptoms, the next question is the degree to which these problems are associated with other family-related problems. One question that has already been answered involves family arguments. The question from the NORC survey is "Did you ever argue with a *family member* about your gambling to the point where it became emotionally harmful?" Given that the cluster analysis indicates that respondents in cluster 3 (see table 6.2) have an 87 percent chance of answering yes to this inquiry, it seems clear that various gambling problems predict family arguments over gambling that reach an emotionally harmful level.

TABLE 6.3

Latent Class Cluster Analysis of Items Involving the Family from the NODS, National Gambling Impact and Behavior Study (NGIBS), 1998

Indicators	Cluster 1	Cluster 2
Lied to family members or friends about gambling (11)		
Yes	0.070	0.855
No	0.930	0.145
Taken money/written bad check to pay gambling (13)		
Yes	0.002	0.183
No	0.998	0.817
Gambling caused serious relationship problems (14)		
Yes	0.005	0.692
No	0.995	0.308
Asked family members for loan/bail-out (17)		
Yes	0.018	0.625
No	0.982	0.375
Emotionally harmful arguments due to gambling[a]		
Yes	0.003	0.624
No	0.997	0.376
Cluster Size (proportion of sample)	**0.934**	**0.063**

Note: The questions are taken from the NORC DSM-IV Screen for Gambling Problems (NODS) and were assessed using a latent class cluster analysis. The numbers in parentheses indicate the item number from table 1. The numbers in columns two and three indicate the probability that a person who falls within the particular cluster answered yes or no to the question. The sample size is 1,214.

[a]Not part of the NODS. This question was asked just after the NODS items were completed by respondents.

As a subsequent step, I used the NORC NGIBS data and data from the 2001 National Epidemiological Survey of Alcohol and Related Conditions (NESARC) to construct gambling problems scales to conduct two sets of analyses.[40] The first analysis involved determining the most common symptoms of problem and pathological gambling among those who reported gambling in their lifetimes. Second, although psychiatric practice typically distinguishes pathological gamblers from other gamblers

by using five symptoms as a cutoff point, an alternative procedure that I adopted is to determine whether family problems
and gambling problems are associated in a monotonic fashion
or whether there is a clear threshold at which problems tend to
appear. I therefore categorized the battery of symptoms in two
different ways: a five-category scale and a four-category scale
drawn from Gerstein et al.[41]

Table 6.4 provides the percentage of gamblers who reported
symptoms of various lifetime gambling problems. The most frequent symptom—reported by almost 18 percent of gamblers in
the NGIBS—was whether respondents had ever tried to cut down
on their gambling. However, a similar question that was asked in
the both the NGIBS and the NESARC indicated that only about
2 percent of gamblers had been unsuccessful when attempting to
stop or decrease their gambling behavior. The second most frequent symptom reported in the NGIBS, but curiously not in the
NESARC, was chasing, or trying to regain, lost earnings. In the
NESARC, the most frequent symptom involved preoccupation
with gambling, answered affirmatively by 7 percent of lifetime
gamblers. The differences between the NGIBS and the NESARC
may result from the different criteria used to ask the questions:
to participate in the NGIBS, an individual gambler must have
reported losing $100 or more gambling in any one day, while
the NESARC required respondents to have gambled five or more
times in any one-year period during their lifetimes. Those who
did not reach or exceed these thresholds were not asked the gambling problem questions.

Among the family-related items, the most frequent symptom
reported involved lying to family members about gambling or
how much the respondent lost on gambling. It was reported by
more than 8 percent of gamblers in the NGIBS and 3 percent of
gamblers in the NESARC. On the other hand, illegal acts, some
of which may have involved family members, were reported by
few of the gamblers in these surveys. It is somewhat surprising
that only a small proportion of gamblers reported that their gambling had ever caused relationship problems (3.3% in the NGIBS;
0.3% in the NESARC).

The next analysis uses the symptom inventories to determine their associations with family-related problems and concerns. Unfortunately, the available national data sets that I have used thus far, as well as others that might have been utilized to examine problem and pathological gambling (e.g., the National Comorbidity Study;[42] the Research Institute on Addictions' 1999–2000 national telephone survey[43]), were not designed with family-relevant issues specifically in mind. The available family items are therefore sparse. The following analyses are not sufficient to provide a broad sense of the links between problem gambling and family turmoil or disruption, but, when coupled with previous studies that have focused on family issues, help to generate some general concerns and conclusions about how gambling problems negatively affect families.

Before looking at the associations among family problems and gambling problems, however, it is useful to investigate the question of how family members may serve as a protective effect. Table 6.5 uses the NGIBS data to assess reasons to gamble and with whom respondents gambled most often.[44] To provide a comparison, I also examined a question about whether respondents gambled for excitement or for the challenge of the game. The results are clear: Those who report gambling problems are more likely than others to say they gamble for excitement or for the challenge, with a step function evident. Moreover, those in the high symptoms categories are less likely than other gamblers to report that they gamble to socialize with family or friends. It is interesting to note that those who have experienced no problems are also less likely to report that socializing with family or friends is an important reason for gambling. According to an auxiliary analysis, among those with no reported problems, the most important reason was to win money (62% said this was "important" or "very important").

TABLE 6.4

Frequency of Gambling Problem Symptoms among Those Who Have Ever Gambled, NGIBS 1998 and NESARC 2001

Category	Question	NGIBS— % reporting	NESARC— % reporting
Preoccupation	Have there ever been periods lasting 2 weeks or longer when you spent a lot of time thinking about your gambling experiences or planning out future gambling ventures or bets?	9.7	7.2
	Have there ever been periods lasting 2 weeks or longer when you spent a lot of time thinking about ways of getting money to gamble with?	6.8	2.4
Tolerance	Have there ever been periods when you needed to gamble with increasing amounts of money or with larger bets than before in order to get the same feeling of excitement?	4.1	6.3
	Have you ever tried to stop, cut down, or control your gambling?	17.9	—
Withdrawal	On one or more of the times when you tried to stop, cut down, or control your gambling, were you restless or irritable?	2.0	1.0
	Have you ever tried but not succeeded in stopping, cutting down, or controlling your gambling?	2.4	2.4
Loss of control	If so, has this happened three or more times?	1.4	—
	Have you ever gambled as a way to escape from personal problems?	6.5	3.0
Escape	Have you ever gambled to relieve uncomfortable feelings such as guilt, anxiety, helplessness, or depression?	6.1	—

Category	Question		
Chasing	Has there ever been a period when, if you lost money gambling one day, you would return another day to get even?	17.4	4.4
Lying	Have you ever lied to family members, friends, or others about how much you gamble or how much money you lost on gambling?	8.6	3.2
	If so, has this happened three or more times?	2.4	—
Illegal acts	Have you ever written a bad check or taken money that didn't belong to you from family members or anyone else in order to pay for your gambling?	1.1	0.4
Risked significant relationship	Has your gambling ever caused serious or repeated problems in your relationships with any of your family members or friends?	3.3	0.3
	Has your gambling ever caused you to lose a job, have trouble with your job, or miss out on an important job or career opportunity?	0.6	0.3
Bailout	Have you ever needed to ask family members or anyone else to loan you money or otherwise bail you out of a desperate money situation that was largely caused by your gambling?	3.9	1.1
Arguments[a]	Did you ever argue with a family member about your gambling to the point where it became emotionally harmful?	2.9	—

Note: The NGIBS 1998 is the National Gambling Impact and Behavior Study conducted by the National Opinion Research Center (NORC). The NESARC 2001 is the National Epidemiological Survey of Alcohol and Related Conditions sponsored by the National Institute on Alcohol Abuse and Alcoholism (NIAAA). The NGIBS asked the problem gambling items only to those who reported losing $100 or more in any one day of gambling. The NESARC asked the problem gambling items only to those who reported they had gambled five or more times during at least one year in their lifetimes. The wording in the two surveys was slightly different; the table shows the wording used in the NGIBS. The percentages are based on weighted data. The items in bold are questions that included direct inquiries about family issues.
[a]Not part of the NODS or the items used in the NESARC. This question was asked just after the NODS items were completed by NGIBS respondents.

TABLE 6.5

Gambling Problems, Reasons to Gamble, and Gambling with Family Members, National Gambling Impact and Behavior Study (NGIBS), 1998

Problem gambling symptoms	Important or very important (%)		Who do you usually gamble with? (%)		
	Reason to gamble: To socialize with family or friends[a]	Reason to gamble: Excitement or challenge of game[a]	Alone	Spouse or other family members	Non-family members
0	24.0	34.6	36.4	33.6	29.9
1-2	41.1	62.6	30.2	24.8	44.9
3-4	40.2	83.0	37.8	29.2	33.0
5-6	29.0	80.4	21.4	24.9	53.8
7-10	27.3	90.1	15.2	14.7	70.1
Total	26.4	39.5	35.8	32.8	31.5

Note: The 1998 National Gambling Impact and Behavior Study (NGIBS) was conducted by the National Opinion Research Center (NORC). The questions that are used to gauge problem gambling symptoms are listed in table 1 and are drawn from the NODS (Gerstein et al. 1999). The percentages are based on weighted data. Fisher's exact tests were conducted to determine whether the patterns of results are statistically significant. All three tests showed a significant pattern at the p < .05 level.

[a]Percent of respondents reporting this reason for gambling as "important" or "very important." Alternative responses included "not so important" and "not at all important."

The second panel of the table suggests that those with the most gambling problems tend to gamble with friends (non-family members) rather than alone or with family members. More than half of the respondents who report five or more symptoms normally gamble with people outside their families. Of course, this does not provide convincing evidence that family members protect against gambling problems, but it does generate intriguing questions about family influences on gambling behavior. Family members may serve as anchors that mitigate problems, or perhaps gamblers who manifest problems are less likely to have family members to gamble with.

Table 6.6 explores the associations among marital status, marital history, and gambling problems. A consistent association in previous studies is that problem and pathological gamblers tend to be single or divorced. Data from both the NGIBS and the NESARC support this conclusion. Among problem and pathological gamblers, for instance, a disproportionate percentage of respondents have never married or are currently divorced. Moreover, about one-quarter of pathological gamblers have been married two or more times, with a relatively small percentage reporting only one marriage (47.4%, vs. 59.7% of gamblers reporting no symptoms). The NGIBS also included an item that asked married respondents if they were currently living with their spouses or separated. More than one in ten lifetime pathological gamblers said they were currently separated. This is more than twice the percentage relative to the remainder of the sample. Finally, the NGIBS included a question about whether their divorce was precipitated by either their or their spouse's gambling. Not surprisingly, a substantial proportion of pathological gamblers reported that this was the case. In fact, the prevalence among pathological gamblers was seven times that of the next highest group.

Table 6.7 examines relationship problems among respondents in the NGIBS and NESARC. As discussed earlier, the experience of gambling-linked relationship problems is the concern of one of the items used to gauge gambling pathology. Nonetheless, it is instructive to examine other relationship items available in these national data sets. The analysis indicates, first, that there appears to be a modest step function between symptoms of problem gambling and reports of arguments, with the highest prevalence

TABLE 6.6
Gambling Problems, Marital Status, and Marital History, NGIBS 1998 and NESARC 2001

Gambling problems	Number of marriages[a]			Current marriage[b]		Currently divorced/separated (% yes)[a]	Was gambling a factor in divorce? (% yes)[b,c]
	Never married	One	Two or more	Together	Separated		
None	18.1%	59.7%	22.2%	96.4%	3.6%	11.9	5.0
At-risk	26.9%	52.6%	20.5%	94.9%	5.1%	11.3	3.2
Problem	32.9%	49.9%	17.2%	99.8%	0.2%	15.7	3.5
Pathological	27.4%	47.4%	25.1%	88.3%	11.7%	23.9	35.0
Total	20.1%	58.1%	21.8%	96.2%	3.8%	12.2	5.5

Note: The NGIBS 1998 is the National Gambling Impact and Behavior Study conducted by the National Opinion Research Center (NORC). The NESARC 2001 is the National Epidemiological Survey of Alcohol and Related Conditions sponsored by the National Institute on Alcohol Abuse and Alcoholism (NIAAA). The questions that are used to gauge gambling problems are listed in table 1, with some variation in the NESARC instrument. The categories include no symptoms (None), 1–2 symptoms (At-risk), 3–4 symptoms (Problem), and 5 or more symptoms (Pathological), as detailed in Gerstein et al. 1999. The percentages are based on weighted data. Fisher's exact tests were conducted to determine whether the patterns of results are statistically significant. All the tests showed a significant pattern at the p < .05 level.
[a]The analysis is based on data from the NESARC 2001 data.
[b]The analysis is based on data from the NGIBS 1998 data.
[c]Among those who reported that they had ever been divorced. Two questions were used to construct this variable: (1) Whether the respondent's gambling or (2) the respondent's spouse's gambling had been a factor in the respondent's divorce.

TABLE 6.7

Relationship Problems and Gambling Problems, NGIBS 1998 and NESARC 2001

Gambling problems	Had arguments or friction with friends, family members, or others (% yes)[a]	Argued with a family member about gambling to the point where it became emotionally harmful (% yes)[b]	Household member complained about respondent's gambling (% yes)[b]
None	46.1	0.3	3.3
At-risk	52.6	1.2	4.5
Problem	53.4	20.6	12.6
Pathological	59.5	56.4	68.8
Total	**48.1**	**4.1**	**10.9**

Note: The NGIBS 1998 is the National Gambling Impact and Behavior Study conducted by the National Opinion Research Center (NORC). The NESARC 2001 is the National Epidemiological Survey of Alcohol and Related Conditions sponsored by the National Institute on Alcohol Abuse and Alcoholism (NIAAA). The questions that are used to gauge gambling problems are listed in table 1, with some variation in the NESARC instrument. The categories include no symptoms (None), 1–2 symptoms (At-risk), 3–4 symptoms (Problem), and 5 or more symptoms (Pathological), as detailed in Gerstein et al. 1999. The percentages are based on weighted data. Fisher's exact tests were conducted to determine whether the patterns of results are statistically significant. All three tests showed a significant pattern at the p < .05 level.

[a]The analysis is based on data from the NESARC 2001 data.

[b]The analysis is based on data from the NGIBS 1998 data.

(59.5%) among pathological gamblers in the NESARC. Second, arguments with family members about gambling are strongly associated with gambling problems. This was shown in tables 6.2 and 6.3 but is reiterated here. About one-fifth of problem gamblers and more than half of pathological gamblers reported arguing with family members to the point where it became "emotionally harmful." Third, a strong association exists between gambling pathology and complaints from family members. More than two-thirds of pathological gamblers reported this condition in their households, whereas only 3 percent of gamblers who had experienced no problems reported it.

The final analysis involves some associations that indirectly affect the family. Several studies have shown that gambling problems are associated with difficulties at work and high levels of debt. The NESARC survey asked respondents whether they had been fired from a job in the past year. As shown in table 6.8, the relative risk among pathological gamblers was twice that of gamblers who had experienced no problems. Moreover, the risk of having a financial crisis or reporting bankruptcy was also substantially higher among problem and pathological gamblers than among others (the risk of bankruptcy was also higher among problem and pathological gamblers in the NGIBS).[45] About 21 percent of NGIBS pathological gamblers said they had household gambling debt. As with relationship problems, being in a desperate situation over debt is one of the symptoms in the NODS and the DIS (see table 6.1, item 17), so it is no surprise that a disproportionate percentage of pathological gamblers reported gambling debts. However, it should also be clear that household gambling debts affect not only the gambler, but usually the entire family as well. For example, when this analysis was replicated using a subsample of married respondents, the same associations held.

As a last step, I used the NGIBS data to estimate how much household debt respondents reported. The modal category for pathological gamblers was $10,000–$99,999, whereas the modal category for those with no problems or for at-risk gamblers was less than $10,000. I also estimated household debt using more finely detailed categories and determined that the median debt carried by pathological gamblers was in the range of $25,000–$49,000, whereas the median debt carried by those with no problems or by at-risk gamblers was in the range of $1,000–$9,000.

TABLE 6.8

Gambling Problems, Employment Risk, Financial Problems, and Household Debt, NGIBS 1998 and NESARC 2001

Gambling problems	Been fired from a job in the past year (% yes)[a]	Major financial crisis or bankruptcy in past year (% yes)[a]	Any household gambling debt? (% yes)[b]	Current household debt (%)[b]			
				None	Less than $10,000	$10,000 to $99,999	$100,000 or more
None	6.7	11.1	0.6	15.9	35.7	35.4	13.0
At-risk	9.9	18.1	2.5	15.2	42.2	26.6	16.0
Problem	10.8	27.5	8.5	33.9	36.4	27.5	2.1
Pathological	15.8	30.2	20.9	10.1	14.4	60.0	15.5
Total	**7.5**	**13.1**	**1.7**	**16.1**	**36.2**	**34.6**	**13.1**

Note: The NGIBS 1998 is the National Gambling Impact and Behavior Study conducted by the National Opinion Research Center (NORC). The NESARC 2001 is the National Epidemiological Survey of Alcohol and Related Conditions sponsored by the National Institute on Alcohol Abuse and Alcoholism (NIAAA). The questions that are used to gauge gambling problems are listed in table 1, with some variation in the NESARC instrument. The categories include no symptoms (None), 1–2 symptoms (At-risk), 3–4 symptoms (Problem), and 5 or more symptoms (Pathological), as detailed in Gerstein et al. 1999. The percentages are based on weighted data. Fisher's exact tests were conducted to determine whether the patterns of results are statistically significant. All the tests showed a significant pattern at the p < .05 level.

[a] The analysis is based on data from the NESARC 2001 data.

[b] The analysis is based on data from the NGIBS 1998 data.

Discussion

The growth of gambling in the United States and elsewhere has been remarkable, with recent data suggesting that gambling expenditures now outstrip expenditures for many other popular forms of entertainment such as sporting events, music, and movies. Moreover, the number of gamblers has grown as the availability of gaming activities has reached almost every state and territory in the United States. This rapid expansion in what was previously a vice has included positive and negative consequences. Many policy experts, while admitting that a regulated gambling environment encourages responsible behavior and has added to state coffers (albeit through a revenue stream similar to a regressive tax), are also concerned with the potential increase in problematic forms of gambling. As with many other "vices," there is mounting acknowledgment and evidence that gambling problems affect not only the individual, but also families and communities. Nevertheless, it is important to remember that most people who gamble do not develop problems; a large majority buy lottery tickets, gamble at casinos, or bet at the track on a regular basis with no negative consequences. Rather, a small minority experience problems that cross a threshold into pathological behavior.

This chapter provides an overview of the literature on the link between problem and pathological gambling and family functioning and stability. Moreover, an analysis of data from two national surveys demonstrates some specific family-relevant correlates of problem and pathological gambling. Although these data cannot establish causality or even the sequencing of problems and outcomes, it is clear that pathological gamblers experience a relatively high prevalence of multiple marriages, separation, divorce, emotionally harmful arguments with family members, fights over gambling behavior, financial and occupational problems, and high debt. These findings complement previous studies that were designed to specifically address family problems.[46] But they also extend the scope of research by examining national-level data from the United States. In general, the results of this collection of studies suggest that there is an entire constellation of problems that accompanies pathological gambling, with many of these problems negatively affecting relations with spouses, children, and other family members.

Nevertheless, an area that has not been explored sufficiently is the role that family support may play in restraining problematic or pathological forms of gambling. Much as the mental health literature shows that cohesive families which offer social support attenuate the problems associated with mental health disorders and speed recovery, it is likely that supportive family relations may also provide a buffer against pathological forms of gambling. Although certainly not conclusive, the results in table 6.5 suggest that pathological gamblers are less likely than others to gamble with family members; rather, they are apt to gamble with friends and acquaintances who may have their own problems limiting their gambling. At the risk of overspeculation, family members may play an important role in a situation known as "natural recovery." Recent studies have shown that recovery from pathological gambling without formal treatment is common, with up to one-third of lifetime pathological gamblers no longer experiencing problems even though they had received no formal treatment.[47] Problem and pathological gambling might therefore be episodic and transitory rather than persistent. However, the term natural recovery is typically used to indicate no formal treatment or intervention, such as enrollment in Gamblers Anonymous or therapy from a mental health-care provider. What leads to this type of remission is still something of a mystery but likely includes family social support and coping skills that are enhanced by cohesive family environments. Clearly, more research should be conducted on what role family support structures play in buffering the potential for gambling problems and affecting the recovery when pathological gambling occurs.[48] This type of research requires prospective designs that would follow a group of individuals as they engage in gambling and, if they develop pathological symptoms, follow them through treatment and natural recovery. But it must also give direct and thorough attention to family relations, especially those conditions that change over time.

Although prospective studies of gambling problems and pathologies—as well as how families affect and are affected by these conditions—are valuable research models, conceptual development is also needed to better understand the course of problem gambling. We now know that pathological gambling is often comorbid with other mental health disorders such as alcohol abuse, drug abuse, depressive disorders, and antisocial personality disorder and that it negatively affects family functioning and stability, yet the mechanisms that underlie these associations are only beginning to be appreciated. There is still, moreover, substantial unobserved heterogeneity across individuals who manifest these problems. As I have argued elsewhere when examining problematic forms of drug use, certain "deviant behaviors" are related to what some have labeled "lifestyle factors" that affect not only involvement in pathological gambling and drug abuse, but also lead to diminished commitment to conventional institutions such as work, school, and families.[49] In this context, it is useful to conceptualize problem and pathological gambling as part of a constellation of factors—which may be manifest in difficulties with impulse control or self-control—that are related to a lack of investment in conventional lifestyles and activities. One of the key points of the literature on life-course transitions, for instance, is that some people, perhaps due to their particular personality compositions, neurological conditions or dysfunctions, or family and community socialization experiences, are less attached and committed to conventional institutions such as schools, legitimate employers, and families. Not only are they less likely than other people to succeed in their family or their work lives, but they are also apt to get involved in various forms of compulsive or destructive activities.[50] Continuing to conduct research that identifies this constellation of factors with greater precision is important because it will elaborate social and behavioral conditions that affect family relations, life transitions, and life-course trajectories and how they are related to problematic forms of gambling or associated disorders.

Although natural recovery may occur among a substantial proportion of pathological gamblers, a general lifestyle of problem behaviors and attenuated social relationships still exists for many of them. Without understanding the broader social, psychological, and physiological contexts within which problem and pathological gambling are embedded, we cannot begin to fully understand how to overcome their consequences for individuals, families, or communities.

7

Gambling and Morality
A Neuropsychiatric Perspective

Marc N. Potenza

Evidence of gambling can be found across cultures and throughout time. Hebraic, Egyptian, Greek, and Roman civilizations engaged in various forms of gambling, and the *Mahabharat*, a central book of Hinduism, describes a gambler who wagers and loses his kingdom and his wife.[1] The persistence of gambling for millennia suggests that the behavior may be particularly rewarding at an individual level or important in sociocultural functions. Suggestion of the former can be found in work from over a century ago in Fyodor Dostoyevsky's *The Gambler*. In this book, as well as in his personal letters of the period (Dostoyevsky himself had a gambling problem), the thrill of gambling is poignantly described as an exciting and anxious state that his nature desires.[2] The incorporation of gambling in social and cultural institutions (bingo sponsored by churches, lotteries sponsored by governments) also dates back centuries, with major institutions (e.g., Harvard University) originally founded in part with lottery proceeds. Thus, historical accounts suggest that complex reasons contribute to the societal maintenance of gambling.

Gambling and Morality

Morality has been defined as a doctrine or system of right, virtuous, or ethical conduct.[3] The term, derived from the Latin word *moralis*, initially described a consensus of manners or customs within a social group, and has been used throughout the past several centuries in efforts to identify universal principles that should guide the behaviors of humans.[4] Gambling has been described as immoral for millennia. Greek philosophers like Aristotle are reported to have grouped gamblers with thieves and robbers and denounced gambling as wrong and immoral.[5] This sentiment was voiced in other cultures throughout time. In an article on the history of gambling published in England in 1756, gamblers are described as "cheats" and "felons," and the author states that society would be better off without this group of "harpies."[6] Personal accounts of "degeneration" related to excessive involvement in gambling were described. In 1882 Mason Long described his personal struggles with excessive gambling, drinking, and tobacco smoking, culminating in his religious conversion and confession of his sins.[7] Other works from the same time period similarly describe gambling as a sin or a vice.[8] The relationship between individuals' emotional states (as described by Dostoyevsky above) and gambling appears to contribute to gambling being conceptualized as an immoral behavior. For example, when discussing in 1902 the moral qualities of gambling in *The Ethics of Gambling*, MacKenzie notes that the uncertainty about a wager "contributes largely to the gambler's pleasure, and it is around this that the emotions gather with such unnatural concentration so as to produce in some a kind of moral or spiritual inflammation which we call the gambler's craving or passion."[9] That is, the seeking of an immediate reward in an emotional or passionate manner to the extent that it might interfere with family, work, or other areas of functioning seems salient to the consideration of gambling as immoral. Over the past half century in the United States and elsewhere, individual liberties and the ability to make personal decisions about recreational and leisure activities have received high priorities. Within this context, legalized gambling has seen considerable expansion, with legalized gambling estimated to have grossed approximately $85 billion in the United States in 2005.[10] As compared to prior conceptualizations of gambling (particularly when done in excess) as a sin or a vice, one current conceptualization of gambling sees it as a personal choice of a recreational activity within a public health framework,[11] and when performed in excess, as a mental health condition.[12] Nonetheless, some of the same elements described over one hundred years ago in relationship to gambling and morality (emotion and craving and their relevance to decision making in gambling) are currently being investigated from neurobiological and medical perspectives.

Medical Model of Excessive Gambling: Pathological Gambling

The majority of adults gamble, with a minority demonstrating problems with gambling. The Gambling Impact and Behavior Study estimated that approximately two of every three adults in the United States had gambled within the past year, with less than 1 percent meeting the criteria for pathological gambling.[13] Pathological gambling is the formal diagnostic term adopted by the American Psychiatric Association to define individuals who develop substantial problems related to their gambling. The disorder was first introduced in 1980 in the third edition of the *Diagnostic and Statistical Manual of Mental Disorders* and is located in the category of "Impulse Control Disorders Not Elsewhere Classified."[14] A central defining feature of the impulse control disorders is the "failure to resist an impulse, drive, or temptation to perform an act [e.g., gambling in the case of pathological gambling] that is harmful to the person or others."[15] Typically "the individual feels an increasing sense of tension or arousal before committing the act and then experiences pleasure, gratification, or relief at the time of committing the act."[16] Guilt or regret may (or may not) be described following the act. In that the impulse control disorders as a group are characterized by a failure to resist temptation to engage in behaviors leading to immediate pleasure at the expense of other areas of life functioning, it is understandable that they could be considered immoral within a moral framework.

The diagnostic criteria for pathological gambling share similarities with those for drug dependence. Both disorders have inclusionary criteria targeting tolerance, withdrawal, interference in major aspects of life functioning, and repeated unsuccessful attempts to cut back or quit.[17] Other criteria for pathological gambling appear more specific to gambling. For example, the criteria targeting "chasing" (returning to a gambling venue in an attempt to win back money recently lost) or "bail outs" (borrowing money to escape from a desperate financial situation related to gambling losses) are relatively distinct to gambling, although similar behaviors related to drug use are often exhibited by drug-dependent individuals.[18] As such, pathological gambling has been conceptualized as a "behavioral addiction" or an "addiction without the drug."[19]

Pathological gambling has also been conceptualized as lying along an impulsive-compulsive spectrum with disorders like obsessive-compulsive disorder.[20] The relationship between impulsivity and compulsivity seems more complex than initially conceptualized.[21] In impulse control disorders and drug dependence, it is hypothesized that as use becomes compulsive in nature, brain regions involved in habit formation become increasingly involved in the psychopathology.[22] Impulsivity may predominate at early stages of the disorders and persist over time. As such, impulsivity, defined as a "predisposition toward rapid, unplanned reactions to internal or external stimuli [with diminished] regard to the negative consequences to the impulsive individual or others," is hypothesized to be a central element of pathological gambling and a broad range of psychiatric disorders that often co-occur with pathological gambling.[23] This definition highlights the complexity of impulsivity, and preliminary studies suggest that specific aspects (e.g., rapid reactivity and diminished regard to negative consequences) are not highly correlated and are differentially related to treatment outcome.[24] As such, a more complete understanding of impulsivity and its core component features as they relate to pathological gambling should not only help improve our understanding of the disorder but also generate better prevention and treatment strategies. Investigations of neurobiological aspects of impulsivity and motivated behaviors in disorders characterized by impaired impulse control are providing significant insight into neural circuits that might be disrupted in these disorders and might represent important targets for novel treatments.[25]

Brain Biology and Moral Behaviors:
The Case of Phineas Gage

Biological underpinnings for gambling were hypothesized over one hundred years ago.[26] Even earlier, a case study suggested the involvement of specific brain regions in the commission of seemingly immoral behaviors. In 1848, a railroad worker named Phineas Gage was described by his bosses as "the most efficient and capable" man whom they employed.[27] He displayed "temperate habits," had a "well balanced mind," and was "very energetic and persistent in executing all of his plans of action." In other words, Mr. Gage was a successful, hardworking, industrious young man. However, at 25 years of age, he encountered a horrible accident in which a steel tamping rod exploded through his left orbit and exited through the top of his skull. Miraculously, he survived the accident. However, he was no longer the same man: "Gage was no longer Gage." John Harlow, the physician caring for him after the accident, stated that the "equilibrium or balance, so to speak, between his intellectual faculty and animal propensities" had been damaged. Gage became "fitful, irreverent" and indulged in "the grossest profanity which was not previously his custom." He displayed "little deference" for others and was "impatient of restraint or advice when it conflicts with his desires, at times pertinaciously obstinate, yet capricious and vacillating, devising many plans of future operation, which are no sooner arranged than they are abandoned." He was described as displaying "strong animal passions" and women were advised not to be near him due to his foul language and behavior. His employers were compelled to let him go, noting that although he had the physical ability to perform his duties, his "new character" was incompatible with holding his job. After thirteen years of having difficulties holding a job, he died poor in 1861.[28]

Biology of Decision Making:
Emotions and the Ventromedial Prefrontal Cortex

The tragic case of Phineas Gage provided a unique opportunity for exploration of brain regions and circuitry contributing to moral versus immoral behaviors. That is, if one were to be able to identify the brain region(s) impacted by the tamping rod in the case of Phineas Gage, the information could generate insight into the neurobiological contributions to morality. Fortunately, the physician caring for Gage retrieved his skull and it is currently housed at the Harvard Medical School. By using the skull size and regions of skull damage to estimate the route of the tamping rod, three-dimensional images of the regions damaged in Gage's accident were generated. Consistent with accounts of Gage after the accident, brain regions responsible for motor and language function were spared. However, frontal cortical regions, including the ventromedial prefrontal cortex, are believed to have been obliterated by the tamping rod. Antonio Damasio, Hanna Damasio, Antoine Bechara, and colleagues pursued this finding further. As neurologists caring for individuals with strokes, they observed that people with stroke lesions in the ventromedial prefrontal cortex often did not fare well in real-life situations despite performing adequately on existing neurocognitive tests.[29] They developed a gambling test (the Iowa Gambling Task) to assess risk-reward decision making and found that these individuals performed disadvantageously on this task.[30] The task consists of selecting one hundred cards from four decks. When performing this task, individuals are instructed to optimize gains with the understanding that some decks are better than others. Unbeknownst to the participants, two of the decks are associated with large immediate rewards and very large intermittent losses resulting in long-term losses, and the other two are associated with small immediate rewards and small intermittent losses resulting in long-term gains. As compared to healthy control subjects, those with strokes in the ventromedial prefrontal cortex perform disadvantageously on the task (select more cards from the decks with large immediate gains and very large intermittent losses that result in long-term loss). In these studies, individuals without stroke lesions would behaviorally learn the advantageous card selection strategy prior to being able to consciously report their strategy.[31] Subsequent studies implicated additional brain regions (e.g., the amygdala) as contributing to performance on the Iowa Gambling Task.[32] These findings, in conjunction with information on the role of the prefrontal cortex and amygdala in emotional processing, led to the somatic marker hypothesis of decision making—namely, that emotional processes influence our rational decisions.[33]

Risk-Reward Decision Making: Psychiatric Implications

As risk-reward decision making enters into multiple aspects of everyday life, it is not surprising that individuals with impairments in brain regions involved in risk-reward decision making would have difficulties functioning successfully in real-life situations. Individuals with psychiatric disorders that are often characterized by immoral behaviors (e.g., substance abuse or dependence, antisocial personality disorder, pathological gambling) also frequently have problems in major areas of life functioning. Individuals with these disorders (e.g., cocaine dependence, other substance dependence, or pathological gambling) have been found to perform more disadvantageously than healthy control subjects on the Iowa Gambling Task,[34] and amongst subjects with addictions, poor performance was associated with real-life measures of poor functioning (e.g., inability to hold a job).[35]

Other cognitive tasks have been used to assess risk-reward decision making. For example, delay discounting tasks assess the extent to which individuals place value on smaller, immediate rewards as compared to larger, delayed ones. Based upon behavioral economic theories, the task assesses the extent to which one prefers specific amounts of money now or at a later time (e.g., $14 today or $25 in 19 days; $25 today or $30 in 80 days).[36] By using a range of time delays and amounts, one can generate discounting curves to examine the extent to which money loses value for individuals over time ("temporal discounting"). Individuals with pathological gambling, like those with drug dependence, tend to discount rewards rapidly; that is, immediate rewards have relatively greater saliency than do delayed ones in individuals with these disorders as compared to those without.[37] Thus, understanding the biological mechanisms underlying reward processing and the selection of immediate as compared with delayed rewards has important implications for understanding, preventing, and treating pathological gambling.

Biological Aspects of Reward Processing

Brain imaging techniques have been used to identify regions contributing to the selection of small, immediate rewards as compared to larger, delayed ones. In healthy volunteers, brain regions including the ventromedial prefrontal cortex and ventral striatum were found to activate following the selection of small immediate rewards.[38] Prior studies have identified neuronal connections between these brain regions that work together as components of the limbic system, and this neural circuit that underlies reward processing has been repeatedly implicated in addictive processes.[39] This circuitry also was impacted in Phineas Gage following his accident, as regions of the ventromedial prefrontal cortex were presumably destroyed by the tamping rod.[40] In contrast to the brain regions activated following the selection of small immediate rewards, the selection of larger delayed rewards was associated with greater activation of prefrontal cortical regions that have been previously implicated in higher order cognitive executive functioning.[41]

Independent research has investigated brain regions contributing to specific phases of the processing of small immediate rewards. Based on work performed in primates,[42] the monetary incentive delay task was designed to investigate reward processing in humans.[43] The task involves a visual cue that signifies the condition (e.g., win $1, lose $1, win $5, lose $5, win $0.20, lose $0.20, zero win/lose). Following the cue, a box appears on screen for a short period of time. Individuals are instructed to push a button while the box is on screen in order to win or avoid losing, respectively, the amount of money indicated for the condition. Shortly thereafter, participants learn of the outcome (whether or not they have won or avoided losing). In healthy adults, the anticipation of working for monetary reward was associated with activation of the ventral striatum whereas winning outcomes were associated with activation of the ventromedial prefrontal cortex.[44] Together, these data suggest that the ventral striatum and ventromedial prefrontal cortex each contribute to specific aspects of reward processing in healthy adults.

Neural Correlates of Reward Processing in Addiction

As individuals with pathological gambling and substance use disorders show behavioral differences in risk-reward decision making, an understanding brain functioning in individuals with these disorders as compared to those without has important implications. Studies of adults with alcohol dependence as compared to those without have found relatively diminished activation of the ventral striatum during the anticipation of working for monetary reward in the monetary incentive delay task.[45] This finding extends to groups of individuals at high risk for alcoholism (for example, those with a positive family history of alcoholism[46]) as well as groups with high rates of risk and addictive behaviors (e.g., adolescents as compared with adults[47]). Studies of cocaine-dependent individuals have found disruptions in orbitofrontal and prefrontal circuits contributing to reward processing in control comparison subjects.[48] Together, these findings indicate altered fronto-striatal brain function contributing to differences in reward processing in drug-addicted as compared with non-addicted individuals, and some of these functional brain differences extend to groups vulnerable to developing addictions.

Brain Imaging in Pathological Gambling: Ventromedial Prefrontal Cortex

Compared to other psychiatric disorders, relatively few brain imaging studies have been performed in subjects with pathological gambling. However, the studies that have been performed have implicated some of the same brain regions identified in studies of reward processing and drug addiction and implicated in the case of Phineas Gage. For example, in a functional magnetic resonance imaging (fMRI) study of gambling urges, subjects with pathological gambling as compared to those without showed relatively diminished activation of the ventromedial prefrontal cortex during the period of viewing the most robust gambling stimuli. This difference between the groups was not observed during the control comparison conditions (happy or sad stimuli).[49] In a separate fMRI study of cognitive control using the Stroop Color-Word Interference Task, individuals with pathological gambling as compared to those without showed relatively diminished activation of the ventromedial prefrontal cortex following the presentation of incongruent stimuli (mismatched color-word pairs).[50] A third fMRI study of simulated gambling found that individuals with pathological gambling as compared to those without showed relatively diminished activation of the ventromedial prefrontal cortex in winning versus losing contrasts.[51] Amongst the group with pathological gambling, the degree of activation within the ventromedial prefrontal cortex correlated inversely with the severity of gambling problems. In other words, the more severe the gambling problem, the less the ventromedial prefrontal cortex became activated. Taken together, these three studies suggest an important role for the ventromedial prefrontal cortex in the pathophysiology of pathological gambling.

Brain Imaging in Pathological Gambling: Ventral Striatum

As described above, the ventral striatum makes important contributions to motivated behaviors and reward processing and has been implicated repeatedly in drug addiction.[52] Individuals with pathological gambling have been found to show diminished activation of the ventral striatum during simulated gambling, and activation of this brain region correlated inversely with gambling severity amongst the subjects with pathological gambling.[53] Preliminary data suggest that gambling urges in individuals with pathological gambling and cocaine cravings in individuals with cocaine dependence are similarly characterized by relatively diminished activation of the ventral striatum and orbitofrontal cortex.[54] Further research is needed to investigate the extent to which brain activations related to other processes (e.g., reward processing) might be explained by functional differences in specific brain regions like the ventral striatum.

Neurochemical Contributions to Pathological Gambling

Although fMRI is a powerful technique for identifying functional contributions of brain regions to specific cognitive tasks, it does not allow for evaluation of the involvement of specific neurotransmitters in these processes. Other ligand-based imaging approaches (e.g., positron emission tomography or PET) permit such assessments but no ligand-based investigations involving subjects with pathological gambling have been published in peer-reviewed journals to date. Multiple neurotransmitter systems have been implicated in pathological gambling.[55] Dopamine has been hypothesized to contribute to rewarding and reinforcing behaviors, serotonin to behavioral initiation and cessation, norepinephrine to arousal and excitement, and opioids to pleasure and urges. Compared to control subjects, individuals with pathological gambling have shown differences with respect to each of these neurotransmitters. These systems will be considered with respect to some of the brain regions implicated in brain imaging studies of pathological gambling.

Serotonin in Pathological Gambling

A role for the neurotransmitter serotonin in impulse control has been described for several decades. Low levels of the serotonin metabolite 5-hydroxy-indole-acetic acid have been found in the cerebrospinal fluid samples from multiple groups of individuals characterized by impaired impulse control, including those with alcoholism, impulsive fire setting, or pathological gambling.[56] Individuals characterized by impaired impulse control also show different biochemical and behavioral responses to serotonergic drugs. For example, individuals displaying impulsive antisocial behaviors or those with alcohol dependence or pathological gambling have reported a "high" or a "buzz" to the partial serotonin agonist meta-chlorophenyl piperazine (mCPP).[57] In contrast, healthy control subjects do not report a euphorigenic response. Serotonergic drugs like mCPP and fenfluramine have been examined in conjunction with brain imaging techniques in individuals characterized by impaired impulse control, including those with alcohol dependence and impulsive aggression. In response to these drugs, relatively diminished activation or response within the ventromedial prefrontal cortex was observed in the group with impaired impulse control as compared to the control comparison group.[58] No such imaging study to date has examined the role of serotonin in ventromedial prefrontal cortical functioning in individuals with pathological gambling.

Dopamine in Pathological Gambling

The ventral striatum is a target region for dopamine neurotransmission within the mesolimbic pathway, and dopamine function within the ventral striatum contributes to reward-based learning in addiction.[59] Several lines of evidence suggest a role for dopamine in pathological gambling, although its precise role requires further investigation. For example, decreased levels of dopamine and increased levels of dopamine metabolites (suggestive of higher dopamine turnover) were reported in the cerebrospinal fluid samples of individuals with pathological gambling.[60] However, dopaminergic differences did not persist when correcting for differences in flow rate of the fluid.[61] Amphetamine, a drug with influences on dopaminergic and other biogenic aminergic systems, was found to cross-prime for gambling-related phenomena in individuals with pathological gambling, a finding suggestive of a pro-dopaminergic effect on gambling in the disorder.[62] A study from the same group found that haloperidol, a drug that blocks dopamine D2/D3 receptors, enhances the rewarding and priming effects of gambling in individuals with pathological gambling.[63] Among individuals with Parkinson's disease (which involves degeneration of dopamine systems), an association between dopamine agonist treatment and impulse control behaviors, including excessive gambling, has been reported. However, other factors (e.g., early onset of Parkinson's disease) have also been associated with the emergence or worsening of impulse control behaviors in this population, making the precise nature of the involvement of dopamine systems unclear.[64] As described above, ventral striatal function has been implicated in brain imaging studies of pathological gambling. However, no investigations to date have directly examined a possible role for ventral striatal dopamine dysfunction in pathological gambling.

Opioids in Pathological Gambling

Neurotransmitter systems and brain regions do not work in isolation but rather function in circuits in a dynamic fashion. Opioid systems influence dopamine function in the ventral striatum, and a proposed mechanism of action for drugs that block opioid receptors is through indirect modulation of mesolimbic dopamine function.[65] The opioid antagonist naltrexone is approved for the treatment of alcohol dependence and has shown efficacy in a placebo-controlled trial involving subjects with pathological gambling. As in studies of alcohol-use behaviors, the medication appeared particularly helpful for people with strong gambling urges at treatment onset.[66] A placebo-controlled, multicenter trial of the opioid antagonist nalmefene demonstrated superiority of active drug over placebo and provided further support for a role for opioid systems in pathological gambling.[67] However, preliminary results of a subsequent trial of nalmefene in pathological gambling did not generate positive findings.[68] A similar variability has been observed in studies of alcohol dependence.[69]

Variability in study outcomes might be related to individual differences amongst subjects. For example, commonly occurring variants of the gene encoding the mu-opioid receptor have been associated with differential outcomes during treatment of alcohol dependence with naltrexone.[70] The extent to which the mu-opioid receptor gene variants or other specific biological factors might be related to treatment outcome in pathological gambling warrants further investigation.

Genetics of Pathological Gambling

Technological advances have facilitated investigations into genetic factors contributing to the development of psychiatric disorders. Molecular genetic investigations have been performed in pathological gambling and have implicated genes related to multiple neurotransmitter systems including dopamine and serotonin.[71] However, many of these studies have significant methodological limitations,[72] and more conclusive studies await performance and/or publication. Large samples of twins allow for the estimation of genetic and environmental contributions to mental health disorders like pathological gambling.[73] As with other psychiatric conditions, data indicate that there exist substantial genetic contributions to pathological gambling,[74] with genetic contributions to the disorder accounting for approximately two-thirds of the variance and environmental factors for about one-third.[75] Genetic factors contributing to pathological gambling have been found to overlap with those for alcohol dependence and those for antisocial behaviors,[76] suggesting that common genetic contributions exist between excessive forms of gambling and other behaviors that have been described as immoral. These studies also identified overlaps in environmental contributions, suggesting that both heredity and life experience factors make significant contributions to these disorders and their co-occurrences.

Genetic and environmental factors have been shown to interact significantly in the development of psychiatric disorders. For example, individuals with a specific variant of the serotonin transporter allele who are exposed to early life stress are significantly more likely to experience depression than are individuals with the same allele not exposed to such stressors or individuals with a different variant irrespective of stress exposure.[77] Although stress exposure has been associated with pathological gambling (particularly among women),[78] the interaction with specific genetic factors has not been reported. Commonly occurring genetic variants also can substantially influence patterns of brain activation, including within regions related to stress responsiveness, emotional regulation, and cognition.[79] The extent to which these and other genetic variants influence moral behaviors in psychiatric and nonpsychiatric groups warrants further examination.

The identification of genetic contributions to disorders or behaviors that can be characterized as immoral suggests that certain individuals are born with a greater likelihood than others for behaving in an immoral fashion. The identification of environmental contributions to these disorders suggests that specific life events can influence the development of these disorders and the enactment of these behaviors, providing hope for prevention and treatment efforts.

Neurobiology of Ethics and Morality

Technological advances in imaging and genetics have provided exciting opportunities to investigate not only gambling, but also other behaviors and disorders with moral or ethical implications.[80] Results from these studies are relevant to multiple disciplines, including philosophy, sociology, ethics, religion, and law, among others, and investigators with expertise in different domains (neuroscience, psychology, evolutionary biology, anthropology, etc.) are contributing to an emerging field of cognitive neuroscience of human behaviors.[81]

Moral reasoning and behaviors encompass a broad range of complex behaviors influenced by cognitive, social, and emotional factors.[82] Although reasoning and cognitive processing were emphasized for decades, more recent work has examined intuitive, or emotional, and social influences on moral processes.[83] Within the emotional domain, "social" emotions such as guilt, embarrassment, pride, and jealousy are particularly relevant to moral reasoning and behaviors.[84] Moral judgments have been categorized in fashions that reflect differential contribution from cognitive, social, and emotional domains. For example, one classification defines personal and impersonal moral judgments in which the former are guided to a relatively greater extent by social and emotional contributions and the latter to a relatively greater extent by cognitive contributions.[85] However, this and similar models have been criticized in that they may not fully account for cultural influences on moral reasoning and decision making.[86] Nonetheless, existing studies suggest that moral cognitions and behaviors involve a broad range of brain regions involved in cognitive and emotional processes in a social-context-dependent fashion, with different types of moral dilemmas activating preferentially different aspects of these neural circuits.

Consistent with this hypothesis, existing data differentially implicate specific brain regions in negotiating different moral processes. Amongst the brain regions most typically implicated in imaging paradigms probing moral cognition and behavior are cortical regions (e.g., ventromedial prefrontal cortex, lateral orbitofrontal cortex, anterior prefrontal cortex, dorsolateral prefrontal cortex, anterior temporal cortex, and superior temporal sulcus) and subcortical regions (amygdala, ventromedial hypothalamus, septal area and nuclei, and basal forebrain, particularly the ventral striatum/pallidum and extended amygdala).[87] These regions include those described above in the cases of Phineas Gage and pathological gambling, and reflect the complexity of the networks underlying moral reasoning and behaviors. Moral reasoning and behaviors seem differentially determined, in part through developmental influences on these brain regions. For example, while damage to the ventromedial prefrontal cortex in adulthood has been associated with deficits in moral behaviors but not moral reasoning,[88] damage at an early age has been associated with impairments in both areas.[89] Individuals with damage to this brain region also show deficiencies in pride, embarrassment, and regret.[90] Ventromedial prefrontal and orbitofrontal cortex and amygdala are considered important contributors to social response reversal theory (commission of immoral behaviors related to difficulties in learning following negative outcomes), violent inhibition mechanism (deficiency in controlling aggressive behaviors), and somatic marker hypothesis (integration of emotional and cognitive processing in decision making) models of moral behaviors. However, these models do not necessarily account for the role of specific prefrontal cortical regions in moral reasoning and behaviors.[91] Brain regions important for conflict monitoring and cognitive control (for example, the lateral prefrontal cortex and dorsal anterior cingulate cortex[92]) also contribute to moral processing, with hypotheses positing that these cortical regions exhibit control over emotional regions in circumstances of utilitarian or impersonal moral dilemmas, and vice versa in the case of personal moral dilemmas.[93]

In contrast to theories that hypothesize a hierarchical relationship between emotions and cognition, several recent theories hypothesize an integrated model across these and other domains. For example, the event-feature-emotion complex framework posits that social, motivational, emotional, and contextual information is bound together. This model hypothesizes that information from these domains is processed and integrated with key brain regions more centrally involved in specific aspects. Specifically, structured event knowledge is supplied by prefrontal cortical subregions, social perceptual or functional features by the temporal cortex, and motivational and basic emotional states by limbic and paralimbic regions.[94] Consistent with this model, moral emotional states like compassion, embarrassment, indignation, and guilt have been associated with activations of these regions.[95] However, this and competing models require further evaluation as to how they relate to moral judgment and behaviors in clinical and community samples.

Clinical samples may provide insight into aspects of social cognition and moral processing. For example, clinical groups characterized by antisocial behavior (e.g., sociopathy[96]) or excessive prosocial engagement (e.g., Williams Syndrome[97]) show abnormalities in the amygdala. Violent behaviors have been associated with orbitofrontal cortical abnormalities in antisocial personality disorder, although other brain regions (e.g., sensorimotor cortex) have also been implicated in this and other patient groups.[98] Damage to the bilateral temporal cortices or amygdala has been associated with social and appetitive disturbances (hypersexuality, placidity, hyperorality, and pica).[99] The extent to which social and moral processing differs in individuals with pathological gambling as compared to those without warrants further investigation. Given that moral perceptions influence brain activations within reward processing regions (including the striatum) in healthy subjects, it will be important to evaluate these processes as related to gambling behaviors.

Conclusions and Future Directions

Technical advances in genetics and brain imaging are providing important insight into brain processes related to moral reasoning and behavior. These advances in neuroscience research methodologies are also generating a better understanding of brain function underlying mental health and illness. Future research should examine more closely the relationships between these domains. The acquisition of knowledge about individual brain function with respect to moral and medical states raises questions about privacy and ethics.[100] Although how best to use this information in various settings (e.g., legal, medical, and ethical venues) is currently a topic of discourse, the knowledge should help further discussion about the roots of moral and immoral thoughts and behaviors.[101] As applied to human health and disease, these advances offer hope to advance prevention and treatment strategies, diminish individual suffering, and promote societal well-being.

8

The Unproblematic Normalization of Gambling in America

John Dombrink

For the last forty years in America, the question of what society is to do with certain legally prohibited but socially desired activities like gambling, drugs, prostitution, and abortion have occupied legal scholars and reformers. Following the lead of the British Wolfenden report in 1957,[1] and leading through legal writings and arguments over the next decade or so by Schur, Packer, Kadish, Skolnick, Geis, and others, American legal scholars in the 1960s focused on the philosophical and pragmatic costs to society in enforcing laws that had, at best, divided public support.[2]

Among the several legal issues which drove these discussions—illicit drug use, abortion, prostitution, and gambling—gambling has separated itself into its own category as a result of its relatively uncontested normalization in America, as well as its enormous growth in scope and size. The growth of the legal gaming industry in the United States over that time period has been remarkable. From legal gambling revenues of $10 billion in 1982, we now find revenues of $84 billion for 2005 and legal gambling in forty-eight states.[3] We are witnessing an expanding Las Vegas with growing "RDE" (retail, dining, and entertainment) revenues and high room occupancy rates. Indian gaming has spread to over 230 tribes in twenty-eight states,[4] and hybrid forms of gaming—such as "racinos" featuring casino games at horse tracks—have proliferated.

When even William Bennett, the moralistic former education secretary, CNN political commentator, and author of the *Book of Virtues*,[5] was found to be an inveterate gambler with hundreds of thousands of dollars in losses, he explained it away as "only gambling." While many progressives cheered at Bennett's fall and his apparent hypocrisy, he also gave witness to the fact that gambling for most Americans has stepped beyond the area of contested morality and "victimless crime" considerations and has become an accepted leisure activity, like movies.

When, in September 2007, Massachusetts Governor Deval Patrick announced a plan that supported bringing as many as three casinos to that state, it was met with support from certain quarters of the state government and opposition from other well-placed leaders and organizations. In detailing the plan, the Democratic governor explained:

> I believe authorizing three resort casinos will have significant economic benefits to Massachusetts. Done the right way, destination resort casinos can play a useful part, along with other initiatives in life sciences, renewable energy and education reform, in providing our Commonwealth with sustainable, long-term economic growth.[6]

Though a relatively new governor, Patrick chose to address fiscal problems through the offset of gambling revenue, a path that many state governments have taken in various forms over the last forty years. It is not unusual for the governor of a state to champion gambling. In the expansion of legal gambling that has taken place over the last forty years in the United States, many governors of both major parties have supported the expansion of gambling, mostly for either revenue enhancement or for economic development possibilities, or a combination of the two.

Certain vocal critics in the Commonwealth of Massachusetts have eyed gambling skeptically. They have tried to counter the exhortations of those who, in considering the Massachusetts geography, support gambling expansion as an opportunity to try and "bring home" some of the gambling dollars that go over the various state borders, to New Hampshire (as in the early lottery days) or to Connecticut (in the current casino lure of the Mohegan

Sun and Foxwoods Indian casinos). Some critics immediately questioned the economic development and revenue potential of the 2007 Patrick plan.[7] Others warned of the possible deleterious effects upon vulnerable populations, such as youth.[8]

The evolving "normalization" that Patrick's proposal can be located in has also generated pockets of concern among those who point to the ill effects of the "abc" problems of legal gambling—addiction, bankruptcy, and crime. Despite the enormous growth in gambling in America over the past forty years, there still are areas in which we have held back its growth, typically for fear of its effect on vulnerable populations. Still, gambling has been increasingly normalized far beyond the status of its companion activities in the 1960s legal reform discussions, most of which remain highly contested.

But first I'll provide some context, or some caveats, especially because this volume emanates from a conference held by the Boisi Center for Religion and American Public Life. I should begin by disclosing that I have a curious history relating to religion and gambling. The two have been intertwined in my personal history. Being raised as a Catholic, I came from a cultural and religious background that not only did not consider gambling a serious sin but which actually used it for revenue raising purposes with church bingo nights.[9] I remember serving mass for a priest friend of the family one summer Sunday. The mass was held in the woods at a Lake Tahoe outdoor chapel, and the visiting churchgoers threw silver dollars and casino chips into the collection basket. This is not all that remarkable when one looks at Catholic attitudes and practices regarding gambling.

In the summer of 1969, as a recently graduated high school student from a Franciscan seminary in California, I joined a team of about a dozen recently graduated seminary students in Las Vegas assisting a priest-sociologist and his attempts to focus the Catholic diocese there on more social action programs. We worked with low-income youth in the part of town where the porters, dishwashers, and maids of the Las Vegas hotels lived, in dusty neighborhoods with few streetlamps and sidewalks.[10]

In order to make some money for college, several of us worked at various jobs in the local casinos. Some worked as busboys at a Strip hotel. I had the luck to work as a cashier at a downtown casino, where I spent three summers working for a respected Catholic casino owner. So one could consider me an apologist for the gaming industry, having grown up with its very normal presence in a decidedly unusual locale, but my views on gambling are certainly intertwined with moral grounding.

My sociological understanding of gambling expanded greatly beginning in graduate school, while I was working on Jerome Skolnick's landmark study of the regulation of Nevada casinos.[11] The autobiographical portion of this introduction is simply to signify that, to me, gambling has always been well integrated in the moral universe of my upbringing.

Doubtless, readers could see me [as an individual] as conflicted, ambivalent, inconsistent, or indecisive—which in general is a good frame to take when looking at the other law and morality issues I have written about elsewhere,[12] but I will argue here that this ambivalence is not the driving theme of American public policy and societal attitudes toward gambling, which sociologist Jerome Skolnick has called the "normal vice."[13] Instead, acceptance and relatively unproblematic normalization are the themes of gambling in recent America.

However, several chapters in this volume reflect an undercurrent of nagging concerns and critiques of the legalization of gambling. This is also an issue that Wolfe, in chapter 16, suggests has not been present in a robust public discussion and public policy debate, an argument explored later in this chapter.[14]

Problem Gambling and Skeptics of Normalization

Three of the chapters in this volume, under the heading "Individual Behavior and Social Impact," speak both to enduring issues as society has welcomed, tolerated, punished, or grown wealthy from gambling as well as to emerging issues shaped by the unique nature of today's landscape, both social and moral. As representatives of other social scientific inquiries into the conception and operation of gambling in America, these chapters are impressive in their conceptualization, research design, and operationalization of variables, as well as in their scientific rigor and scope.

"Behavioral and Brain Measures of Risk-Taking," by Rachel Croson, Matthew Fox, and James Sundali, reflects on the notion of whether gamblers are rational. Or, as the authors pose it, "How do people gamble? . . . 'not very well.'"[15] Croson and her colleagues also note that "to a mathematician, the popularity of casino (and lottery) gambling is puzzling"[16] would suggest that others who have located the lure of casino gambling in the concept of entertainment or "action" (as Croson, Fox, and Sundali consider) and the life-changing possibilities of the lottery are counterexamples. Now admittedly, not all lottery winners deal well with the reality of suddenly having life-changing wealth. Sociologist H. Roy Kaplan examined this phenomenon years ago, and a recent book puts a macabre spin on it. Still, where else can a working class person make a $5 million win? (And hence Clotfelter and Cook's findings on the regressiveness of the lottery and early theorists' talk about the safety-valve functions of such gambling for the working class.)

The differentiation and discussion of risk estimation, risk perception, and risk preferences are well articulated and helpful in any discussion of what motivates and shapes gamblers.

Like Geertz, who captured the "character proving" nature of gambling, the authors in this volume consider how preferences for risk are affected by the group context. This has significant implications, of course, for how we consider legal gambling, permit it, advertise it, or promote it.

The diffusion of legal gambling across various states is a prominent feature of legalization, as, for example, Rhode Island, Massachusetts, and Connecticut now vie for gambling tourism dollars. With Massachusetts governor Deval Patrick announcing in October 2007 that he supported the development of three casinos in the state, one could see the effects of competition between states, the diffusion of policy, and the concept of "policy contagion."

The discussion of risk is also placed in the context of the conflict between opportunities and ethical dilemmas for those in the gaming industry. This also turns up a key issue of this volume: what is the proper role of the state in legal gambling—controlling? Regulating? Promoting? Facilitating? These are very different roles, affected by how one considers the risks that individuals are willing to take. To what extent should the state countenance taking advantage of those who are willing to take enhanced risks? We expect gambling operators to maximize profit, even with the attention paid to "responsible gambling," but what do we expect of the state?

The authors discuss the "illusion of control," suggesting that we need to distinguish between games of skill and games of chance. The elaboration of the hot hand data is informative. Which risk preferences gamblers choose when "chasing" winnings to offset previous losses are a key concept. The analysis is well done that players may think that their winnings were caused by skill and that losing was caused by bad luck. Also, the concept of asymmetric risk preferences—risking more when one is behind—is a central concern, as are errors in risk estimation. Risk preferences are shown to be affected by one's reference group, in which the idea of the spread of gambling to where it is widespread, socially acceptable, and a group activity can have consequences.

Counterbalancing the ads and the come-ons from casinos is the imputed rationality promoted by books like Chris Moneymaker's memoir about how ordinary, hard-working, risk-taking poker players can win the World Series of Poker. Relevant here is the observation that, in effect, no ordinary person could expect to hit a Josh Beckett post-season pitch or sack Tom Brady, but they can see themselves in baseball cap and shades at the final table of a poker tournament.[17]

The "illusion of control" and the "hot hand fallacy" are presented as another example of the gambler's irrationality. Belief that runs of luck will advantage a gambler in other than random ways are explored and disputed.

The discussion about making decisions based on emotions rather than rationality is well developed. This ties in with Drew Westen's recent work on a different topic—political preferences, which illuminate the working of our "emotional calculator."[18]

The notion that people derive pleasure (a "strong motivator") from the anticipation of a win or reward, a possibly good outcome, is instructive. So, too, is the discussion of how problem gamblers' relation to risk changes over time and of how casual gamblers find other risk-taking activities as close substitutes, while for pathological gamblers it is only about gambling.

The discussion of gambling as a moral activity is fully developed in Hoffmann's article (it is clear that was not that article's goal), but by posing and pitting these theories against ideas that gambling is just a form of entertainment, the authors have elucidated the ongoing debate in a meaningful way with scientific precision and clarity. They have done a real intellectual and policy service.

In an examination of pathophysiology that focuses on the neural processes that accompany gambling, Potenza has elsewhere referred to gambling as "addiction without the drug."[19] Nonetheless, he also allows as to how "the majority of adults gamble, with a minority demonstrating problems with gambling."[20] The shape those problems take will be one of the subjects of the Hoffmann article.

Early in the article, Potenza nicely sketches the nature of impulsivity and compulsivity as they apply to gambling, including a discussion of the nuanced relationship they have in this sphere. Both are shown to have bearing on problem gambling.

Potenza deftly shows how gambling shares characteristics with other destructive activity: "The diagnostic behavior[s] for pathological gambling share similarities with those for drug dependence."[21] The focus on "risk-reward decision making" is a central contribution (and connects it with the Croson, Fox, and Sundali article as well).[22]

On the biological front comes Potenza's specific contribution: "The more severe the gambling problem, the less the ventromedial prefrontal cortex became activated,"[23] the opposite of the reaction for reward processing in healthy adults. Several studies suggest a role for dopamine in gambling behavior, again bringing gambling squarely into the category of those behaviors we consider physically addictive—drug use, for example. Amphetamines have similar properties. And when an anthropologist describes video poker—Bill Bennett's game—as the "crack cocaine" of gambling, we take note.

As a sociologist, I have mostly to disagree with Potenza's statement that "the identification of genetic contributions to disorders or behaviors that can be characterized as immoral suggests that certain individuals are born with a greater likelihood than others for behaving in an immoral fashion."[24] To me, morality is a much more elastic, and much more interactive and socially constructed concept, than this allows. I have the same comments about "deficiencies in pride, embarrassment, and regret."[25]

I do agree with Potenza's comments about supporting efforts to "advance prevention and treatment strategies" and "diminish individual suffering," even as the Millian conflict is always present in considering how much society should do to prevent the suffering of the few while honoring the choices of the many.

Ongoing research on various aspects of the culture wars has accentuated many instances in which the effects of changes in societal mores and accompanying legal reform on the fabric of American society are viewed as being specifically mediated through the family. The shape of these contests is often framed in their effect on the family, as reflected in the following statement by leading social conservative Dr. James Dobson of Focus on the Family, a member of the National Gambling Impact Study Commission:

> Clearly, gambling is a destroyer that ruins lives and wrecks families. A mountain of evidence presented to our Commission demonstrates a direct link between problem and pathological gambling and divorce, child abuse, domestic violence, bankruptcy, crime and suicide. More than 15.4 million adults and adolescents meet the technical criteria of those disorders. That is an enormous number—greater than the largest city in this country . . . Gambling is hazardous to your—to our—health![26]

family

It makes sense that any exploration of the "moral landscape" of gambling should consider gambling in that light. In "Gambling with the Family?" sociologist John P. Hoffmann identifies these issues as a central concern.

The Hoffmann statement that "'victimless crime' is becoming more and more of an anachronism" as studies have adopted a broader scope requires a lengthy discussion across a larger set of issues.[27] If Hoffmann's point is that empirical studies have found harms that disprove the underlying reasons for American reform and embracing of personal autonomy in these areas, then I dissent. For the purposes of this discussion, the question of harm can be redirected back to the critique of John Stuart Mill by British jurist Sir Patrick Devlin[28]—and also to the extent to which the harm to an individual extends beyond that individual to the web of society (and in this case to a more proximate entity, the family).

Hoffmann's purpose is to "examine data from two large national surveys conducted in the United States to provide a specific sense of how families might be affected by the gambling behaviors of their members."[29]

The article acknowledges the scope of the issue of problem gambling: "The majority of people who have gambled, legally or illegally, do not experience problems with this type of behavior . . . most simply enjoy the risk or the thrill of the games." Later, the article continues, "a small minority experience problems that cross a threshold into pathological behavior."

Using the 1999 report from Dean Gerstein and the National Opinion Research Center, undertaken for the NGISC, the article allows that 90 percent of those who gamble had no symptom that would indicate problem or pathological gambling.

But in pointing us to the 9 percent of adults who have some risk, the 1.5 percent who are problem gamblers, and the 0.9 percent who are pathological gamblers, the article demonstrates that there are still millions of people we should be worried about when we make policy (and a number that could change if forms and ease of gambling shift).

The propensity for risk is highlighted. The concept of attributable risk—that is, the economic disruption, family turmoil, and poor parenting that accompany problem gambling—is central. However, as Hoffmann indicates, determining sequencing and causality for these characteristics is difficult.

The vast majority of gamblers fall in the cluster with few problems. However, the data shows that for those located in the cluster(s) for problem gambling, an enormous percentage had dysfunctional family interactions.

The discussion about alcohol is instructive since alcohol consumption is a ubiquitous feature of casinos (along with no windows and no clocks) that can be aggravated when a powerful industry wants to break loose from what it perceives as stifling regulation. Atlantic City actually started out with a model in which the casinos closed after midnight, and no alcohol would be served.[30] Indeed, there is even a contemporary casino that does not serve alcohol, an anomaly to be sure.[31] (But who would have thought twenty years ago that casinos would some day be smoke-free?)

The discussion of adolescent concern is well presented, especially when the family is presented as a transmitter of gambling behavior (and of problem gambling behavior). Other critics, including many psychologists who are concerned with the prevalence of problem gambling behavior among vulnerable populations—notably youth—continue to challenge gambling's easy normalization. Psychologist Jeffrey Derevensky and colleagues, authors of numerous studies, conclude:

> With the continuous expansion of the gambling industry worldwide, more gambling opportunities and types of gambling exist today than in the past. With this increased exposure, more adolescents, already prone to risk-taking, have been tempted by the lure of excitement, entertainment, and potential financial gain associated with gambling.[32]

In the end, while focusing on the real harm to those who do experience problems with their gambling behavior, the article is mixed in its assessment of family dysfunction: "Although gambling may present problems for some individuals and their families, it seems clear that the families of most gamblers are able to function well despite variable risk in the propensity to experience problem behaviors. Yet, this does not diminish the fact that substantial numbers of gamblers present pathologies that negatively affect their families."

Gambling "Uncoupled"

One central argument of this article is that legalized gambling is the one formerly prohibited vice that has been accepted in most quarters of American society, and its route has differed greatly from any other's. It is important to understand contemporary legal gambling in the context of the stalled movement toward drug decriminalization and the gradual change—but continued contestation—of the culture war's central issues, especially abortion and gay rights.

How has gambling been normalized as these other "victimless crimes" have taken a different path, a rockier road, a series of dead ends and thwarted reforms?

Legal gambling may have had its skeptics, but little about the slot machine or lottery ticket generated the kind of excitement and antipathy that same-sex marriage did in 2004. Nor did gambling draw the ire of social and religious conservatives as when gay rights repeals were taking place in the 1980s. The lack of attention paid to gambling was probably considered a good thing by gambling operators, who desired state support but beyond that minimal intervention. One of the reasons that campaigns for the legalization of gambling did not generate a backlash is that they did not involve a critique of the establishment and did not offer up a new paradigm of gender relations (as abortion does) or sex itself (as gay rights does). They also did not offer ties to contested social movements of the day in the way, for example, that marijuana decriminalization was tied to the anti-Vietnam War protests.

Why has gambling been so unproblematic in its normalization—and in its growth and spread? Why has it been it so "uncoupled" from the paths of societal treatment of other personal morality issues?

The gaming industry has used a very different model in its growth over the past few decades. It has not relied upon opposition activists to further its growth. Instead, it has used a powerful (and traditional) corporate-political model, unique beyond other industries to the extent that the state has been even more involved in the acceptance and promotion of gambling. For scholars and policy analysts, this has often led to several central questions: What is the appropriate role of the state in promoting legal gambling? Should it be passive, merely letting something be decriminalized? Should it be a primarily regulatory presence? Should it be more of an active partner, supporting growth in various forms? Should it actually be the owner and operator of legal gambling, as in the lottery examples?

Beneath the explosive growth of legal gambling over the last forty years, some forms of gambling have not participated in this in the same manner. Casinos have not spread in a Las Vegas style, despite the prediction twenty-five years ago that they would. And they have not necessarily been slowed down by moralistic arguments, at least not those which are focused on the nature of gambling itself. Rather, there has been some concern about the effect of gaming on existing industry, such as when the Florida banking raised these and other concerns in 1978.[33]

In the cresting of what gambling law expert Nelson Rose has called the "third wave" of gambling legalization,[34] legal gambling advocates may have suffered one of their occasional setbacks, as gambling did not spread as far and as fast and in as many forms as some industry analysts had predicted. Still, neither did it generate the level of backlash that something like abortion liberalization and then legalization had created. If the 1980s backlash against liberal reforms of the 1970s was a key theme—the success of groups like the Moral Majority and the Christian Coalition—legal gambling trod lightly, as it did not offer to change deeply entrenched gender roles (as did abortion) or expand greatly minority rights and freedoms (as did gay rights).

Gambling can be distinguished in several ways from the other formerly prohibited victimless crimes because of its ubiquity and acceptance, essentially "uncoupling" it from the other morally contested activities that formed the center of the 1960s legal reform critique.

First, gambling did not challenge existing paradigms. Unlike established bureaucratic issues such as the drug war, changing gambling policies did not run directly against entrenched government entities. In fact, in the preceding era, police and prosecutors embraced de facto decriminalization. Economist Bill Eadington adds: "Gaming organizations have become mainstream in terms of objectives, management practices and corporate strategies."[35]

Also of importance was a second factor: the lack of successful opposition. Legal gambling proposals and initiatives did not mobilize waves of committed, single-issue opponents, as did other contested morality issues.

A third item was the lack of a successful antigambling "frame." In some locales and times, the issue was organized crime. In many cases, it was compulsive or problem gambling. Sometimes it would be the overpromise of economic development.

Critics of gambling expansion focus on the "abc" of legal gambling: addiction, bankruptcy, and crime. Commenting in 2007 on one state's rejection of racinos, an analyst for the social conservative group Focus on the Family Action concluded, "You can dress up gambling, spend millions on public appeal and buy favor with state officials, but you cannot hide the stench of gambling addiction, crime, bankruptcy and destroyed lives."[36]

The debate over whether this much legal gambling in the United States is a good thing has focused on several issues, as the debate has also turned in many countries. While opposition to gambling used to be centered on moralistic bases, it has increasingly turned on issues of effect on vulnerable populations, such as the low-income population, those with a psychological propensity to gamble (or to be unable to control their gambling), and youth.

Nagging problems persist with this much accepted activity. There are concerns over problem gambling, youth gambling, overblown economic development promises, and still no progress in the lucrative area of sports gambling. Focusing on the issue of regressive taxation, Clotfelter and Cook demonstrate that legal lotteries relied upon revenues from those at the lower end of the social economic structure.[37] Of course this makes sense—unlike blackjack, lotteries hold out the promise of enormous social ascension for a small investment. Critics like Goodman have argued that the expansion of legal casinos is premised on the overblown projections of economic development capacity and state tax revenue. Goodman adds:

> A state has economic problems, often due to a recession, and introduces gambling. Gambling revenues climb, then taper off, flatten out, and decline. At that point the state introduces some other form of gambling . . . the trend is always toward more "hard-core" forms of gambling. . . . Where will the states turn next? Now they are concerned about competition from offshore Internet casinos. The states may try to get in on Internet gambling.[38] *revenues*

The seeds of this ambivalence about legal gambling survive despite the significant growth in legal gambling over the last thirty years and the steady trend toward normalization of gambling in Americans' attitudes and practices.

Economist Eadington notes that, since 2006, gaming operators, gaming regulators, and the state have paid greater attention to the issue of responsible gaming than previously. To him, "this has increased from lip service to semi-commitment to full commitment." At the hotel where Eadington's most recent international gaming conference was being held (attended by gaming researchers from many countries), three brochures on responsible gambling were included in the hotel's welcome pack. This is one response by gambling operators; others include providing informed choice, implementing consumer control, instituting restrictions (like hours of operation), and placing a cap on the number and size of gaming venues.

The fourth issue has been crucial: the integral and largely positive role of the state and the importance of tax revenues and economic development to states which allow, support, promote, or partner with legal gambling operations.

In general, though, social conservatives have not found much traction with their opposition to gambling. In that way, opposition to legal gambling or gambling expansion did not become one of the leading issues in social conservative organizational growth strategies, fundraising, and profile. In becoming the "normal vice," gambling allowed the Bill Bennetts of the world to explain its normalcy, and the Ralph Reeds and other social conservative leaders to lobby for some forms of legal gambling, treating it as yet another corporate enterprise.

Meanwhile, progressives have shied away from attacking the spread of legal gambling, despite the corporate model of diffusion. Perhaps this is because the issue of gambling decriminalization at the start was tied up in a critique of the overintrusive state and allied with the autonomy-centered issues of abortion and gay rights. Groups like the Center for Responsive Politics have decried the role of gambling in lobbying at the state and federal level, but compared to older industry charges of outright bribery and corruption, the gaming industry might consider the anticorporate critique a tolerable part of the spoils of normalization.[39]

As far back as 1974, when New Jersey considered its first statewide initiative to legalize casinos in that state, research showed that there was a limit on the number of voters who would respond to a religious or moralistic challenge to gambling on its face. From that time forward, opponents may have couched their opposition in part in moral opposition, but as the normalization has taken place, more explicit moralistic opposition has not found large, receptive audiences, compared to the much more contested activities of abortion or same-sex marriage.

In 1990, at an international gambling conference in London, I suggested that the legal gaming industry was hoping to attain some of the societal consideration and protection accorded to other formerly prohibited vices such as tobacco and alcohol.[40] That position regarding tobacco seems quaint only nineteen years later, although it was clear at the time that gaming would prefer to adopt the model of alcohol regulation over that of tobacco. It is clear that gaming enjoys the advantages of that alcohol model today.

Conclusion

Even with the spread and growth of legal gambling over the past forty years, one could argue that there are limits to legal gambling, but not necessarily limitations. We do not have Las Vegas-style legal casino gambling in many states, as was predicted in the early days of gambling legalization in the 1980s (although the diffusion of Indian gaming has obscured the fact that such development has not occurred, or become less important to states).[41] Nor do states have legal sports gambling, which is a main contributor to illegal gambling revenues in the United States (at wide-ranging estimates of several billion dollars annually, a growing portion of which is accounted for by online forms). I suggest that legal gambling in America has not unleashed its full potential. In two forms—sports gambling and Internet gambling—it could grow enormously still.

A Pew Research Center report in May 2006 found a "modest backlash" on attitudes toward the legalization of gambling, suggesting that Americans feel that we have enough gambling now. But fully 70 percent of the respondents said that legalized gambling encourages people to gamble more than they can afford, suggesting a vein of ambivalence in even this normalized activity. The highest level of support for legalizing gambling as a policy option was for lotteries, with 71 percent in favor. Still, the Pew report concludes: "The negative turn in attitudes toward gambling appears to be driven by concerns that people are gambling too much rather than by any revival of the once common view that gambling is immoral."[42]

We now exist in an America with lottery numbers on television and reported in *USA Today*. The gaming industry association sponsors a "National Responsible Gambling Week," and gambling opponents position themselves as a "National Coalition Against Gambling *Expansion*."

Croson, Fox, and Sundali, and Hoffmann and Potenza bring to the forefront themes that are reflected in these following examples. The story of the spread of legal gambling and its pervasiveness, as well as its successful normalization, is the American story of the past four decades. As Edward Ugel writes: "Casinos are no longer fantasy worlds, a faraway Vegas or Atlantic City. Now, they're just down the street or the next town over."[43]

I was in a blue-collar (or "locals") Las Vegas casino last year, at a community event unrelated to gambling. I took notice of a sign demarcating: "This line only for paycheck cashing." One of the fears of the critics of gambling is that the "B" side of the critique of expanded gambling—bankruptcy—flows from the easy availability (and marketing) of legal gambling as a leisure time activity to those who are least likely to weather the economic ups and downs of wagering.

In summer 2007, most local newspapers, in their sports section, carried stories about a gambling scandal surrounding an NBA referee as well as about the dogfighting and gambling crimes of an NFL star. At the same time, many daily newspapers—not even specialty sports magazines or gambling Web pages—also now devote a quarter of a page daily to explain the composition of the betting line and to appreciate why "Team A" is favored in Sunday's game by the point spread at which Las Vegas oddsmakers have set them.

Then there is the issue of "technological creep" and its effect on gambling. Would we want those who have grown up as part of the iTunes and GameBoy generation to come to adulthood in a country with a serious debt problem and terrible trade balance, a shaky home mortgage system, and the easy availability to lose money quickly in an emerging technological manner? In the current American climate of rapid technological development, how far off is the possibility of a phone that can act as a credit card, or one that could be used to gamble on Internet sites?

It is possible to acknowledge the low prevalence of problem gambling without minimizing the effects to those so predisposed. And many people may worry about vulnerable populations, having been exposed to a large amount of legal gambling, and may even think that they have taken into account any destructive potential in gambling. But the mere consideration of technological creep (or more forms of gambling that could be unleashed), reminds us that concerns do intercede, and we choose to ignore them at own peril.

THEOLOGY, GAMBLING, AND RISK

9

The Memory of Sin
Gambling in Jewish Law and Ethics

William Galston

Public Views of Gambling

Self-reported levels of religious belief and observance are higher in the United States than in any other developed country. Given organized religion's negative stance toward gambling, one might expect a high level of public concern and disapproval, especially as gambling expands through state lotteries, casinos, and the Internet. There is some evidence to support this hypothesis. Since 1989, support for lotteries as sources of state revenue has declined from 78 percent to 71 percent and the public is modestly less likely to approve of casino gambling and off-track betting on horse races as well. Meanwhile, 70 percent of Americans now believe that legalized gambling encourages people to bet more than they can afford, up from 62 percent. And while there has been a modest decline in the percentage of people who report betting at least once during the past year, there has been a 13 percent decline in the share of gamblers who say they enjoy betting.[1]

One might infer that the spread of gambling during the past generation has triggered a latent sense of guilt among those engaging in the practice. The evidence points in the other direction, however. Only 28 percent of Americans believe that gambling is morally wrong, a bit lower than two decades ago. Even among Americans older than sixty-five, just slightly more than one-third express moral disapproval. Blacks are more likely to disapprove than are whites, and support for gambling declines among lower-income families as well. Four-fifths of secular Americans and three-quarters of Catholics and mainline Protestants report no moral qualms. Only born-again and evangelical Protestants dissent: one study found that only 27 percent of evangelicals and 45 percent of born-again Christians considered gambling to be morally acceptable.[2] Placing these results in historical context, one commentator writes that "over the past 50 years, gambling has gone from sin to vice to guilty pleasure and has come, finally, to be simply another point of interest on the entertainment map."[3] For most Americans, the sense of gambling as sin is at most a fading memory.

Religious Views of Gambling

In this context, my effort to reconstruct the treatment of gambling in Jewish law and ethics might well seem antiquarian, or of intracommunal interest only. These doubts are not without merit. Nonetheless, I want to suggest that the categories and arguments of Jewish law and ethics—indeed, of all religions—can enrich our moral understanding, whether or not we end up accepting the bottom-line judgments they render.

The classic texts and leading authorities of traditional Judaism are harshly critical of most gambling. In this regard, among others, Judaism is anything but idiosyncratic. As far as I can tell, every leading religion condemns this practice, although the grounds and arguments vary. The following brief compendium will provide a flavor.[4]

Buddhism

"There are, young householder, these six evil consequences in indulging in gambling: the winner begets hate; the loser grieves for lost wealth; loss of wealth; his word is not relied upon in a court of law; he is despised by his friends and association; [and] he is not sought after for matrimony, for people would say he is a gambler and is not fit to look after a wife."

Hinduism

"Do not take to gambling, even if you can win, for your wins will be like the baited hooks that fish swallow. . . . Spending time in the gambling hall squanders ancestral wealth and wastes personal worth. Gambling will consume a man's wealth and corrupt his honesty. It will curtail his benevolence and increase his torment. . . . The gambler's passion increases with the losses incurred."

Islam

The *Qu'ran* declares: "Satan's plan is (but) to excite enmity and hatred between you, with intoxicants and gambling, and hinder you from the remembrance of Allah and from prayer; will ye not then abstain?"[5]

Christianity

Although gambling is not expressly mentioned in the New Testament, most Christian thinkers regard it as incompatible with core biblical principles. Gambling is said to contradict the injunction to love one's neighbor, to exploit the poor, to weaken the work ethic, to exacerbate greed and covetousness, to invite deception and outright theft, to undermine the duty of stewardship, to lead oneself and others into temptation, and to betray a lack of trust in God.[6] Public sponsorship of gambling makes matters worse: rather than government fulfilling its core responsibility, to promote the welfare of citizens and discourage vice, state-sponsored gambling does just the reverse. Protestant theologians, especially Calvinists, were harshly critical of gambling. Nonetheless, in a harbinger of things to come, every Christian denomination in colonial America except the Quakers operated lotteries.[7]

Judaism: Preliminary Considerations

My hypothesis is that each religion's approach to gambling as a specific subject will reflect that religion's broader features. (If so, differences in the treatment of gambling will reflect deeper inter-religious differences.) I would characterize the basic features of traditional Judaism as follows:

- First, Judaism is *this-worldly*. While concern for one's fate in the world to come is not entirely absent, the focus is on the effect of each individual's character and deeds in this life.
- Second, Judaism is *communal*. In judging specific practices, its principal focus is on the consequences of individual actions for others, starting with the family and moving out through a series of concentric circles to include wider communities, all Jews, and finally all human beings. This communal emphasis does not mean that Judaism neglects the health of individual souls, however. Sin is regarded as a form of blindness that separates man from God: "The way of the wicked is like darkness; they know not why they stumble."[8]
- Third, Judaism (at least in its traditional form) is *totalistic*. It subjects every aspect of life to detailed scrutiny, and it regards every sphere of human conduct as within its purview of regulation and judgment. It coexists at best uneasily with the classic liberal distinction between public and private, or between the realm of law and the zone of individual liberty.
- Fourth, Judaism is *legal*. While countless Talmudic stories and rabbinical homilies express its ethical orientation, it is the halacha that gives Judaism its basic structure. Its emphasis is much more on ortho*praxy* than on ortho*doxy*. Divisions among Jews typically revolve around legal questions—what is forbidden and what is permitted—rather than conceptions of God and the afterlife. There is little in traditional Judaism that corresponds to the Catholic catechism, and even the revered Maimonides generated more controversy than agreement when he tried to distill the essence of Judaism into thirteen nonnegotiable articles of faith. Judaism has neither a Pope nor (at least since the fall of the Second Temple) a Supreme Court; multiple legal authorities ponder each question and issue an often bewildering diversity of judgments.

Given the horrors of Jewish history, Jews cannot avoid the issue of theodicy. But even here, the consequential disagreements have been about what to do rather than how to think. Zionists argued that in the face of violent anti-Jewish sentiment, Jews could find security only in a Jewish state, brought about through their own endeavor; traditionalists countered that the only security was trust in God, that only the Messiah could reestablish the Jewish state, and that human efforts to force the divine timeline amounted to impiety and blasphemy.

Legal disputation within Judaism tends to be particularistic or casuistic. The focus is on the specific features of individual cases. When general rules are put forward in the Talmud, it is almost always the prelude to lengthy discussions of cases that force interlocutors to modify or carve out exceptions to the rules.

This style of argumentation reflects a fifth key feature of Judaism—its *practicality*. Jewish legal authorities make allowance for human frailty; they are alert to the unintended consequences of even the best-intended actions; and they modify even the most sacred rules when the consequences of rigorous application are damaging in particular circumstances. (For example, nearly every command and prohibition concerning conduct on the Sabbath may be set aside when human health or life is at stake.) Nothing could be less akin to the spirit of Judaism than the ancient maxim *fiat justitia pereat mundus* (let justice rule, though the world perish); courses of conduct that jeopardize human well-being are unlikely to be considered just. In the language of moral philosophy, Jewish law and ethics is closer to consequentialism than to deontology. In the language of Max Weber, Jews are more drawn to an ethic of responsibility than to an ethic of intention.

The Jewish Critique of Gambling

Not surprisingly, the point of departure for the Jewish understanding of gambling is a legal dispute—namely, a Talmudic passage discussing categories of individuals who are ineligible to serve as witnesses in courts of law.[9] Gamblers are excluded; the issue is why. Characteristically, the rabbis debate this question. One view is that gambling is akin to robbery, because it is analogous to a contract that neither party enters in good faith. Because such a contract is not legally binding, receiving payment in accordance with its terms is a form of misappropriation, which shows that the recipient (the gambler) lacks the regard for law required of a witness. The other view is that gamblers are not concerned with the general welfare, which they reveal by engaging in an activity that does not contribute to it. This reveals an outlook incompatible with the orientation required of a witness, because someone unconcerned with the general welfare is likely to care little about the social harm that false or incomplete testimony can produce.

The argument revolves in part around details of Jewish contract law, a full exploration of which would divert us from the main theme. One point, however, merits attention. Rashi, the leading commentator on the Talmud, argues that a rabbi who advocates the general welfare explanation is distinguishing between games of pure chance and those that contain a significant element of skill. In the former case, luck rather than human agency determines the outcome; because neither party can expect to disrupt the other's initial expectations, entering the game is in effect agreeing to a contract in good faith. In skill-based games, by contrast, each party hopes to move the outcome in his direction, which is akin to entering the transaction with a mental reservation.[10]

Often the Talmud leaves such controversies unresolved, but not in this case. The passage that serves as the basis for the dispute goes on to state that only gamblers who have no other means of livelihood are unfit to serve as witnesses, but if they have other means they are eligible. This, say the rabbis, refutes the first view and affirms the second. The reason is this: A robber is still a robber, even if he also does legitimate work. So if gambling were robbery per se, the mere fact of engaging in it as part of one's portfolio would suffice to establish moral unfitness. But someone can contribute to society even if some of his or her activities are noncontributory. This criterion admits of degree, while the other does not.

This Talmudic discussion of gambling stresses the social dimension of gambling—in particular, the attitude toward the community that those engaging in the practice professionally are thought to express—rather than its intrinsic wrongness. This does not mean that the latter disappears altogether. Indeed, one can find both views—that gambling is wrong per se and only in some contexts—represented in Maimonides' synthesis of Jewish law, giving rise to perplexity among later commentators. Maimonides articulates the strict view in his discussion of laws of theft and lost objects. Not everything that is voluntary and victimless is legal; the law defines the boundary of legitimate consent. Even though gambling involves the consent of all parties, writes Maimonides, it is nonetheless theft, "since one takes the money of another for nothing."[11] But in his discussion of the laws of testimony, he endorses the more lenient view that only gamblers with no other livelihood are debarred from serving as witnesses.[12]

While the contextual view has been dominant from medieval times down to the present day, the suspicion that there is something inherently suspect about gambling has never quite disappeared from the Jewish outlook and resurfaces periodically as a subordinate motif. This motif manifests itself in the principle of "holiness": because human beings are created in the image of God, they should strive to imitate God's way to the extent that their mortal condition permits. As God is just and merciful, so should we be as well. A famous Talmudic passage declares that "any judge who issues a true verdict is considered to be a partner with God in Creation."[13] This idea is far reaching in Judaism: as God is the Creator, human beings should be creative. This leads not only to a bias toward activism ("Justice, justice you shall pursue"[14]), but also to a favorable attitude toward work of all kinds. Although work first emerges in Genesis as a curse, as a punishment for disobedience, rabbinic Judaism largely ignores this passage and redefines work, not just as a necessary source of sustenance but as an "ennobling facet of human development." Through Moses, God commands the children of Israel to "choose life," which some rabbis in the Talmud interpreted as an injunction to choose a trade or vocation. One rabbi went so far as to opine that, "Greater is one who benefits from the work of his hands than is he who stands in fear of heaven." In Judaism, then, self-sufficiency through work and spiritual growth cannot be easily separated.[15] But whatever gambling may be, it is not creative, is not work, is surely not an imitation of God. Albert Einstein's famous statement that "God does not play dice with the universe" is Jewish to the core, right down to the use of dice-playing as the synecdoche for gambling.

There is a second sense in which Judaism considers gambling to be "unholy." In the Jewish tradition, God is often described not only as active and creative, but also as studious and contemplative. God is said to "see" that his creation is good, and some stories actually describe God as studying Torah. But gambling is anything but contemplative. It offers a ceaseless whirl of activity that drives out any thought beyond narrow calculation and destroys the tranquility of contemplation in a swirl of ever-shifting emotions.

These criticisms are embedded in a larger context. In the Jewish tradition, human beings are placed on earth to work creatively, to study, and to fulfill the commandments, including the commandments of family and social life. Activities that are outside of and antithetical to these categories are worse than useless. They are diversions from our appointed purpose and represent the spiritual equivalent of what economists call "opportunity costs." Gambling is a quintessential example of this. From the Jewish standpoint, it may be a diversion, but it is anything but innocent.

There is a debate within the tradition, however, on how far to take this principle. Games not involving money often receive rabbinical approval, and some (such as chess) were objects of pride within the Jewish community. All but the strictest rabbis contented themselves with limiting chess and other game playing on the Sabbath; most recognized that a modest amount of leisure—relief from both employment and Torah study—increased the ability to sustain engagement in the serious business of life.[16] Here as elsewhere, what I have called moral realism guided the authorities. They understood that most Jews could be neither scholars nor saints, and they tried not to make the law too rigorous for average Jews to comply.

The idea of freedom is central to the Jewish understanding of human life. Good and evil are placed before us constantly, and we have the capacity to choose: "I have set before thee this day life and good, and death and evil . . . blessing and cursing: therefore choose life" (Deut 30:15, 19). The capacity to choose is embedded in a complex psychology: human beings have both a good inclination (*yetzer ha-tov*) and an evil inclination (*yetzer ha-ra*), which struggle ceaselessly for control of our wills. This duality did not lead the rabbis to an optimistic view of human nature. The forces of licentiousness were always seen as struggling to break through the restraints of norms and laws; under pressure, even minute cracks could lead to the dam's collapse. According to the Torah, gluttony and drunkenness lead to immorality that threatens the community. The Talmud suggests that uncontrolled anger is idolatry in the making.

Judaism regards gambling as an activity with a strong, perhaps unique propensity to fortify the evil inclination against the good, with the result that many gamblers lose the ability to choose the good. The phenomenon of what we now call "compulsive" gambling long preoccupied Jewish scholars and community leaders and generated ethico-legal quandaries. For example, many gamblers tried to weaken the grip of their compulsion by creating counterincentives through oaths: "If I gamble again this month, I will be obligated to contribute an additional thousand dollars in charity to the community." The rabbis regarded this practice as dubious at best: because problem gamblers could not resist the lure of the dice tables, regardless of countervailing incentives, they typically sought to evade their oaths or found themselves unable to honor them. The result was a dual violation of strictures against both gambling and dishonoring oaths. The rabbis debated the circumstances under which they should deem these oaths to be valid and enforceable, with diverse results. Some argued that man's capacity for self-control should not be overestimated and nullified all such oaths, while others took this step only under unusual circumstances.[17] The underlying ethical-psychological point was not in dispute: enforceable or not, these oaths were typically unavailing against the powerful impulse to gamble, which thus constituted a powerful threat to the capacity to choose—the core of what makes us moral agents.

So strong was this compulsion that it distorted every aspect of life. Many gamblers violated and desecrated the Sabbath. Some pawned their prayer shawls and other articles essential for religious practice. Another who had lost all his worldly goods wagered and lost his wife, who promptly deserted him for the winner. Perhaps the saddest example was the seventeenth-century

Venetian Jewish scholar Leon de Modena, the author of a brilliant youthful tract against gambling who in maturity became hopelessly addicted and squandered all his funds, including his cantorial salary.

The damage wrought by compulsive gambling rippled out from the gambler to intimate attachments and then the wider community. Within the family, this activity generated a host of problems—emotional tensions between husbands and wives, spousal abuse, drunkenness, divorce, and social disgrace. In business and commerce, gamblers often found themselves unable to honor their financial obligations, even after selling all their family's possessions. Gambling also strained communal ties—for example, the longstanding norm that no Jew in need should go without communal assistance. Some rabbis ruled that charitable funds should be closed to gamblers who lost everything. Others excommunicated habitual gamblers in the hopes that they would come to their senses, or at least inflict no more damage on the community.

Gambling challenged the rule of law itself. Beyond those suffering from compulsion, gambling enjoyed wide popularity, especially among poor individuals hoping to change their lives in a single stroke. Some communities tried to protect its impoverished members against financial ruin by limiting the amount they could wager. Others went further, enacting comprehensive antigambling statutes. These often produced strong public protests that rendered them unenforceable. Then, as now, the public alleged that censorious officials were killjoys out to suppress harmless entertainment. The Talmudic response invoked a slippery slope argument: activities that appear benign (or at least victimless) can lead step-by-step to real evils. Individuals who begin with occasional indulgence can end up in the grip of irresistible impulse. It is in these terms that the rabbis offered an ethical interpretation of the harsh treatment the Torah permits for gluttonous and alcoholic children: "It has been taught: Rabbi Jose the Galilean said, 'Did the Torah decree that the rebellious son shall be brought before the Beth Din and stoned merely because he ate a measure of meat and drank a measure of wine? But the Torah foresaw his ultimate destiny. For at the end, after dissipating his father's wealth, he will still seek to satisfy his gluttonous wants

but being unable to do so, [will] go to the crossroads and rob.'"[18]
In a similar spirit, the unfortunate Leon de Modena argued that
someone addicted to gambling can end up transgressing all of the
Ten Commandments.[19]

It would be misleading, however, to suggest that traditional
Judaism viewed all kinds of gambling as equally damaging. While
its stance toward compulsive gamblers and toward profession-
als with no other source of livelihood was unrelievedly negative,
Jewish communal and religious authorities relaxed their strictures on episodic gambling for entertainment and also during
certain holidays—especially Hanukkah and Purim, but also the
intermediary days of Passover and Sukkot. Some rabbis even suggested that gambling be permitted on fast days to distract observant Jews from their hunger pangs. In this respect, as in many
others, the practicality and moral realism of the Jewish tradition
trumped, or at least modified, doctrinal purity. (The Talmud recommends the flexibility of the reed rather than the rigidity of the
tree as the model for the exercise of authority.)

Nowhere was this flexibility more in evidence than in
Judaism's response to lotteries, which become popular in medieval times and proliferated in the eighteenth and nineteenth centuries. While some communities tried to repress the practice,
others accepted it when it could be structured so as to contribute
to Jewish life. For example, an Italian rabbi allowed a lottery for
a synagogue that otherwise would have been forced to sell off a
valuable Torah scroll to generate operating funds.[20] One rabbi
ruled, citing Talmudic authority, that anyone winning a lottery
should recite a well-known blessing giving thanks to God for
making this possible.[21]

Practices of this sort raised a broader question of whether
funds derived from gambling were appropriate sources of support
for communal activities such as synagogues and social services.
The Torah had declared that houses of worship could not accept
funds derived from prostitution or criminal activities (Deut 23:
19). The Talmud adopted a narrow interpretation of this prohibition, a stance later endorsed by the normally strict Maimonides
and codified in the famous handbook of Jewish law, the *Shulchan
Aruch*, which guided Jewish communal life for centuries. While
rabbis from medieval times down to the present worried about

synagogues becoming dependent on regular lotteries, they were (and are) allowed to make use of funds from this source.

Contemporary Jewish communities have addressed this issue in diverse ways. In the United Kingdom, numerous Jewish organizations, including Orthodox synagogues and the Jewish museum, have received grants from the Heritage Lottery, funded (as the name suggests) with proceeds from the British National Lottery. In late 2005, Akiva Adler, the founder of two Orthodox schools, went further, establishing his own "Jewish Lottery" with top monthly prizes of £10,000. The purchaser of each £1 ticket was required to designate a preferred Jewish charity, which would receive 40p, chosen from an approved list of worthy causes; a further 30p was to go to Jewish educational ventures, including the founder's own schools.[22] There is no evidence that the Chief Rabbi of the United Kingdom, a very intelligent and energetic man, raised any objection.[23] The venture soon ran aground, however; Adler was compelled to shut it down after a few months because Barclays' credit card processing company treated it as "gambling" and invoked rules against online financial transfers for this purpose. Retorted Adler, "We are not a gambling company but an initiative for the community." It would have been more accurate, and certainly more faithful to the moral and legal ambiguities of the Jewish tradition, to call Adler's Jewish Lottery a gambling company in service to the community.[24] In the United States, even Reform rabbis, ordinarily the most permissive in their interpretation of Jewish law, have expressed reservations about lotteries and other forms of gambling as sources of support for communal activities: "It is one thing to accept human frailty," they declared in an official statement, "but another to approve or encourage it through the synagogue. Although funds from dubious sources may be accepted by a synagogue, it would be wrong to make such funds a regular basis for synagogue life."[25] In Israel, leading rabbinical authorities disagree among themselves as to the propriety of individual and communal participation in the National Lottery. Those in favor cite authorities' acceptance of these practices in Europe from medieval times on, while those opposed not only cite strict authorities such as Maimonides but also the harm that participation in lotteries often inflicts on poor and desperate individuals.[26]

Conclusion
The Wider Significance of the Jewish Tradition

At the outset, I expressed the hope that readers would find this discussion to be of more than antiquarian interest. It is, of course, for those who are more or less traditional Jews—those, that is, for whom halachic interpretation remains a guide for practical life. Within the tradition, there are many areas of disagreement, but also some important fixed points and numerous cautionary notes. To take but one example, lay leaders in synagogues will hesitate to incorporate lotteries, or even games such as bingo, into their regular, ongoing fundraising efforts. For another, traditional Jews cannot blithely undertake to become professional gamblers, even if they observe the Sabbath, the laws of kashrut, and the other mitzvoth.

But what about the wider circle of readers, for whom the rabbinical tradition and perhaps even the Bible itself are not authoritative? For them, I want to suggest that important elements of the specifically Jewish approach to gambling are worthy of attention for reasons other than those that move observant Jews. Let me enumerate four.

Modern readers may find it surprising just how focused the Jewish tradition is on the risk that casual gambling can lead to life-disfiguring compulsion. Within relatively small communities, it was harder for individuals to conceal this problem than it is today. (There was no Jewish equivalent of "What happens in Vegas stays in Vegas" in Talmudic times or medieval Europe.) This means that the incidence of problem gambling is harder to assess today, not that it is lower. Politicians who advocate expanded legal gambling as an easy fix for revenue shortfalls tend to downplay, or altogether ignore, the possibility that easier access will increase compulsive gambling. But no serious moral or political evaluation of such proposals can ignore the worst-case outcomes for a minority of the population.

A second widely applicable dimension of the Jewish tradition is its psychological and moral realism. In practice, as we have seen, this outlook cuts both ways. On the one hand, it sees human beings as divided between good and bad impulses, beings for which the lure of pleasure and excitement always threatens to erode self-restraint. In this context, leaders should think twice about exposing citizens to temptation they may not be able to withstand. On the other hand, realism also means that the power of law and social norms to regulate behavior is inherently limited and that excessive rigor is likely to prove counterproductive. Efforts to reduce drunk driving are one thing; Prohibition is another. The former increases compliance, the latter, resistance. The same is true of gambling. States can prevent casino gambling if they choose; they cannot hope to wipe out office pools on the Super Bowl and should not try.

Third is the emphasis traditional Judaism places on the social consequences of gambling—for families, for faith communities, and for the rule of law, among others. This offers a useful corrective to the tendency, characteristic of some Protestant denominations, to emphasize the individual dimensions of sinful behavior. Jews are less interested in individual salvation in the afterlife and more interested in improving life for individuals and communities here on earth. Among other things, the this-worldly focus allows the debate about gambling to proceed on the basis of publicly observable facts and widely shared norms without relying on controversial theological propositions.

This does not mean that traditional Judaism ignores the individual; far from it. Which brings me to my final point. The Jewish tradition invites us to consider the human meaning of gambling in the context of a wider question—namely, how can we lead our lives in meaningful and valuable ways? Leisure, entertainment, and regulated sporting competition are legitimate aspects of our lives—and gambling can be all these things. One need not agree with traditional Judaism's account of the highest purposes of human life to acknowledge the cogency of its concern. Once we pose this question—whether one embraces Judaism, some other faith tradition, or none whatever—it is hard to argue that gambling counts as a reasonable answer.

10

Grace and Gambling

Kathryn Tanner

In today's America, state lotteries are major public funding sources, and federal policy considers commercial gambling a mostly harmless pastime. The current climate makes the familiar religious critiques of gambling in the United States from the late eighteenth through the first half of the twentieth centuries seem hopelessly anachronistic. For those religious critics, gambling was little more than personal vice. Sins of greed and sloth fueled gamblers' irresponsible and reckless chase of unearned lucre. Their passion for wealth unchecked, gamblers became thoughtless of the morrow, sacrificing their own future well-being and that of their families to the fleeting pleasures of a futile pursuit of money in games of chance. Avaricious yet unwilling to work, gamblers foolishly assumed risks that inevitably led to ruin. All those aiding and abetting gambling in order to exploit the greed and sloth of others for their own profit—casinos, racetracks, betting parlors, and the holders of lotteries—merely added a lack of concern for their fellow men—the absence of charity and concern for justice—to the usual list of vices.

Christianity includes, however, a long history of a different approach to the moral and religious evaluation of gambling, one that concentrates very little on the question of personal vice. Eschewing simple moralistic objections to gamblers' personal failings, this approach takes gambling seriously as the locus of possible cultural, moral, and religious meanings. It focuses on the human aspirations and needs behind games of chance and tries to address them by other means.

One of the most famous proponents of such an approach is the seventeenth-century Jansenist sympathizer, Blaise Pascal. According to him, the uncertainty of happiness in this life is behind the penchant to gamble: because happiness is a bad bet, one tries to gamble one's cares away. The better response to the odds against happiness, Pascal suggests, is the gamble of faith—more precisely, the gamble of the conduct appropriate to faith—for the chance of salvation or lasting happiness. In what follows, I update both Pascal's general approach and the substantive analysis he gives of gambling for a twenty-first-century American context.

Pascal's Method

What is distinctive about this general approach? In the familiar moralistic treatment of gambling, religion distances itself from gambling in order to repudiate it; gambling is sinful behavior and simply opposed, for that reason, to faith. Here, to the contrary, criticism of gambling is based on an odd sort of commonality with it. Ironically, Christianity has a critical view of gambling because of what it shares with it.

From one angle, this commonality is religious. Religious issues—serious questions about life's meaning and purpose— underlie both. Religious life and games of chance are both ways of dealing, for example, with life's precarious prospects. Gambling itself has religious overtones. Evidence of this is the way that chance events—often occasioned by human arrangement as in the drawing of lots—are the means to interpret and tap into cosmic and religious forces in a variety of religious traditions.

Christian criticism of gambling amounts in that case to criticism of its religious outlook. The objection might be, for example, that God's will is discerned in regular, lawful events rather than chance ones. And so a conflict arises between competing religious views.

But from another, more interesting angle, gambling is the commonality permitting critical engagement between the two—not religion. It is not gambling's religious dimension but Christianity's inclusion of something like ordinary gambling that provides a shared topic for disagreement. Instead of two different religious viewpoints paring off, two different understandings of gambling do. Ordinary gambling is criticized in light of an odd form of gambling in Christianity, and it is therefore the character of the gambling in games of chance and not the religious dimensions of those activities that becomes the object of critique. For example, the stakes and payout in ordinary games of chance come under fire from a religious point of view. In sum, Christianity is considered a kind of gamble in order to criticize ordinary gambling.

Thus, according to Pascal, gambling forms the common currency of Christian commitment and ordinary games of chance: both concern decision making in situations of uncertainty. Deciding whether to lead a pious life in hopes of eternal life when God's existence is uncertain is like any bet on what might turn out to be the case. More specifically, both ordinary gambling and Christian faith involve the question of when to incur a certain risk for an uncertain prospect of gain.[1] Should one risk the loss of a nickel for a 50/50 chance of winning a dime? Does it make sense to forgo certain activities—sinful activities incompatible with Christian commitment or faith—if the possible payout is eternal life? And in both cases, the appropriate process for deciding is to weigh up possible benefits and costs in the two different scenarios, win or lose, while taking the probabilities of either into account. Does it make sense, for example, to wager a great deal on a very uncertain outcome promising an enormous payout? Is the risk to one's purse outweighed by the prospect of gain, even if that gain is far from certain?

Pascal argued that the wager of faith for the prospect of eternal salvation is a consummately good bet. And he argues this despite the fact that such a bet does not merely *risk* the loss of what one stakes. The pleasures of this life are simply given up in hopes of eternal salvation, lasting happiness; and win or lose—whether or not, in other words, God exists to grant salvation to those wagering a new way of life for it—one never gets them back. Pascal argues these certain losses are more than compensated by the enormous benefit of eternal life that might come to the penitent in consequence.

The enormous, albeit uncertain, payout of salvation outweighs these certain losses not simply because all the goods of this life given up, no matter how wonderful, pale in comparison with the supreme good of salvation, but because before the infinite good all other goods are as good as nothing, as Pascal's heading for the wager fragment, "infinity-nothing," suggests. Pascal avers, moreover, that the apparent goods of this life are really valueless. They bring no genuine happiness; they give the mere appearance of happiness to a life of misery. The bet on salvation is a good one, because in the best-case scenario "one wins everything," and in the worst-case scenario one merely loses without compensation the pleasures of this life that are worth nothing anyway: "If one loses, one loses nothing."[2] If one refuses the bet of faith, one is certain to lose these pleasures in any case; their value is insubstantial and fleeting and destroyed by death. "One needs no great sublimity of soul to realize that in this life there is no true and solid satisfaction, that all our pleasures are mere vanity, that our afflictions are infinite, and finally that the death that threatens us at every moment must in a few years face us with the inescapable and appalling alternative of being annihilated or wretched throughout eternity . . . It . . . is beyond doubt that the only good thing in this life is the hope of another life."[3]

Faith is always a good bet, then, because the value of what one stakes is so low; one seems to be giving up a great deal but one really wagers next to nothing. One risks very little, indeed, for an enormous possible gain, one whose value can only be magnified by the otherwise dire straits of the player. And therefore the wager of faith is a good one no matter how long the odds of one's winning. Offered the opportunity to make a low stakes wager on a possible payout of enormous value that is one's only hope of escaping great present misfortune, even "one chance of winning . . . leaves no choice" but to bet.[4]

This low-stakes/high-payout character of the wager of faith becomes the basis of Pascal's critique of ordinary gambling. The upper-class gamblers Pascal is addressing—hangers-on of the French royal court, for example—are not in the first place inclined to low-risk gambling of this kind. These are wealthy players who gamble, not to maximize their returns, but to prove their status by the way they play.[5] They gamble to show indifference to money, to make clear that their status is a matter of landed, inherited wealth, not money. And high stakes gambling, where the risk of loss is great, is the way to do that. The wager of faith is a prudent and therefore good bet; but where gambling is about status rather than gain, risky bets have the greater appeal. One shows one has status of a non-moneyed sort by one's willingness to lose. By one's nonchalance, say, in accumulating gambling debts, one gives the impression one has the financial resources to pay them off with ease.

Gamblers also decline the wager of faith because they do not seem to see the value of the possible payout. This may be because they overvalue the pleasures of everyday life whose devaluation in comparison to salvation makes the wager of faith a good bet. They may overvalue gambling itself or, more particularly, what they stand to gain if they win. People would rather spend their days at the gaming table than lead a life of piety because they mistakenly think true happiness can be assured by their winnings. If they really believed "once they had the things they seek, they could not fail to be truly happy," then one would indeed be justified in "calling their search a vain one."[6]

The more profound reason, however, that gamblers do not appreciate the payoff of faith is that the payoff is not what appeals to them in any game of chance. They are interested in the play itself as a form of diversion, not in winning. They prefer risky games, then, because risk heightens preoccupation with the play. And if they see the appeal of games that promise attractive winnings, it is for the same reason—because the promise of those winnings makes gambling more engrossing:

> A given man lives a life free from boredom by gambling a small sum every day. Give him every morning the money he might win that day, but on condition that he does not gamble, and you will make him unhappy. It might be argued that what he wants is the entertainment of gaming and not the winnings. Make him play then for nothing; his interest will not be fired and he will become bored, so it is not just entertainment that he wants. A half-hearted entertainment without excitement will bore him. He must have excitement, he must delude

himself into imagining that he would be happy to win what he would
not want as a gift if it meant giving up gambling. He must create
some target for his passions and then arouse his desire, anger, fear,
for this object he has created, just like children taking fright at a face
they have daubed themselves.[7]

Gamblers seek happiness in the very play of games of chance,
Pascal thinks, because they recognize, deep down, what the wager
of faith itself is predicated upon: the unhappiness of life, the fact
that the search for happiness has been pursued by everyone from
time immemorial with no lasting or ultimate success.[8] Human
life makes a mockery of the pursuit of happiness by its extreme
insecurity: "We are floating in a medium of vast extent, always
drifting uncertainly, blown to and fro; whenever we think we
have a fixed point to which we can cling and make fast, it shifts
and leaves us behind; if we follow it, it eludes our grasp, slips
away."[9] The only certainty is loss and death: "Imagine a number
of men in chains, all under sentence of death, some of whom are
each day butchered in the sight of the others; those remaining see
their own condition in that of their fellows, and looking at each
other with grief and despair await their turn. This is an image
of the human condition."[10] People distract themselves from this
human condition by an all-consuming present preoccupation like
gambling that pushes such discomforting truths of human life
from their minds, as if their plight could be improved simply by
taking their minds off it. "When men are reproached for pursuing so eagerly something that could never satisfy them"—say, the
take in a crap shoot—"their proper answer, if they really thought
about it, ought to be that they simply want a violent and vigorous
occupation to take their minds off themselves" and their miserable condition.[11] In sum, gamblers have very little interest in the
wager of faith, because this wager, rather than prove diverting
or distracting, rubs one's face in what the gambler would like to
forget about for the moment.

The ultimate criticism of gambling, then, concerns the oddity
of its response to the situation of human unhappiness. The diversion of gambling is no real solution to the human predicament
but merely a futile temporary respite from life's grim realities,
and one, moreover, that simply trades on and encourages self-
deception. The promise of real happiness is lodged in salvation,

but gamblers, strangely enough—given their own deepest insights into the human condition—exhibit no interest in it. Refusing the best hope of escape from human unhappiness through the gamble of faith, they would rather get up a good card game—and in that way day-after-day inch closer to their deaths. With a kind of blindness to their own best interests, which Pascal can only consider supernatural in its inexplicability—it so goes against the grain of the human impulse to seek happiness, in other words, that its only explanation is the corruption of our faculties by sin—gamblers make a sport of their own lives.[12] They care only to distract themselves from their true predicament, as if the stakes of inattention to that plight were really not that high, and by those means continue foolishly to forgo the only genuine avenue for escaping it.

Revisions to the Method

The major problems with Pascal's approach here, in general and for an analysis of gambling in contemporary American life (we will leave his conclusions for later), are two: the approach has no interest in gambling in particular, and it ignores the historical specificity of the forms gambling takes. Pascal's analysis of gambling, in other words, has nothing specifically to do with gambling—it holds for all kinds of intensely preoccupying diversions and sees them all as responses to a universal human predicament. These limitations of method mean Pascal has only one analysis for everything, whether it is gambling in seventeenth-century France or in twenty-first-century America, whether it is gambling on fox hunting in the former or gambling on the Super Bowl in the latter. Differences among diversions and the contexts of their play can do little to alter his conclusions. If one wants a religious evaluation specific to both gambling and the contemporary U.S. context in which it occurs, Pascal's approach must therefore be modified.

One can retain the approach's basic character—which criticizes ordinary gambling from another sort of vantage point, the gamble of faith—and remedy its two deficiencies by considering gambling a form of "deep play" in the sense Clifford Geertz made famous in his article on the popular Balinese practice of gambling on cockfights.[13] What Geertz's approach to gambling has over Pascal's is that the meaning of a gambling practice is quite specific to the social and cultural context at issue and is only apparent from an analysis of its details (e.g., how much is bet, what are the odds, and so on).

Sometimes, according to Geertz, gambling is a form of "deep play"; it has a deeper meaning than mere gambling. Given the character of gambling on cockfights there, this must be the case in Bali. Especially in the center-ring cockfights, very large sums of money are wagered on 50/50 bets (ensured by pitting only evenly matched birds against each other). Wherever gambling takes a general form like this, something else must be going on besides simple gambling; some deeper meaning exists to explain the interest in it. Absent a deeper significance of that sort, such games are merely irrational ventures: one has just as much chance of winning as losing, and losing is far more harmful than winning is beneficial because the amount wagered is so high.

That deeper meaning, Geertz concludes, is that, rather than being in it for the money, Balinese are in it for what money represents or symbolizes—status. Geertz notes that "[w]here the amounts of money are great, much more is at stake than material gain: namely, esteem, honor, dignity, respect." By placing large bets, Balinese men are putting their status on the line—not because that status will be materially changed, win or lose, but because willingness to make such bets is an *exhibition* of status in a rivalry with competitors. Unlike the high-stakes gambling discussed before in connection with the landed French aristocracy, here the money does matter very much: "It is because money *does*, in this hardly unmaterialistic society, matter and matter very much that the more of it one risks, the more of a lot of other things, such as one's pride, one's poise, one's dispassion, one's masculinity, one also risks."[14] But quite like the case of high-risk gambling among the landed French aristocracy, what represents status here is again not so much money per se as the willingness to lose it: "It is in large part *because* the marginal disutility of loss is so great at the higher levels of betting that to engage in such betting is to lay one's public self, allusively and metaphorically . . . on the line."[15]

This account of when gambling is deep implies that most of the time gambling is just gambling; when one gambles simply for money—in petty games of pure chance, say, with small stakes and the primary intent of possibly picking up a little spare cash—gambling has no deeper import.[16] But there is no reason to think that Geertz's main point about deep play cannot be extended beyond the sort of high-stakes status gambling typical of Bali to any form of gambling in which there is an otherwise peculiar level of popular interest. A society's fascination with gambling, a heightened cultural interest in it—as one finds in the United States—could be accounted for in that way, explained in terms of gambling's deeper meanings, whatever the forms gambling takes. It is the widespread interest in gambling in a particular culture, in short—whether gambling is peculiarly "irrational" from the standpoint of maximizing utilities or not—that gambling's deep meanings explains.

Because it is the popularity of gambling in a particular context that is explained by way of them, these deep meanings are also quite socioculturally specific. Rather than represent some general human interest in being diverted from the hopeless prospect of happiness in this life, a penchant for gambling in a particular society suggests a deep meaning specific to that society. Betting on cockfighting would not be a prevalent pastime in Bali, for example, if status rivalry did not have the significance it does in that society. The practice of betting on cockfights is popular in Bali because of the way it spells out in compressed symbolic fashion the values of this particular society and the hopes and fears surrounding those values. The status rivalry that is so much a part of Balinese society is being played out in the form of the dueling birds with which different status groups identify in virtue of the bets they have made on them. The fact that these birds fight to the death and the heavy losses commonly sustained by participants in the high-stakes center bets typical of such contests are symbolic of the high stakes of real status rivalry among the elite in this society: "What the cockfight talks most forcibly about is status relationships, and what it says about them is that they are matters of life and death" in this society.[17]

Indeed, the ultimate appeal of cockfighting is the way it gives the Balinese a kind of safe arena—an arena of "mere play"—in which to surface the values of Balinese society in all their danger and allure, thereby gaining greater clarity about them. "That prestige is a profoundly serious business is apparent everywhere one looks in Bali. . . . The hierarchy of pride is the backbone of the society. But only in the cockfight are the sentiments upon which that hierarchy rests revealed in their natural colors . . . Without the cockfight the Balinese would have a much less certain understanding of them, which is, presumably, why they value it highly."[18] The natural colors of status rivalry are rendered quite concretely and vividly here as slaughter. Cockfighting becomes a rumination of a potentially critical sort, then, on the way this society operates: "It provides a metasocial commentary upon the whole matter of assorting human beings into fixed hierarchical ranks and then organizing the major part of collective existence around that assortment. Its function is interpretive: it is a Balinese reading of Balinese experience, a story they tell themselves about themselves."[19]

Let us assume, then—to follow the case of Bali—that gambling in American society is a way that Americans are trying to gain some clarity about the society they live in—about the tensions surrounding America's central values. The religious critique of ordinary gambling becomes, in consequence, a critique of what gambling is saying about American society and its values. If the gamble of faith is critical of ordinary gambling it is because it does not share ordinary gambling's view of American society and its values. Ordinary gambling may be expressing worries about the character of American life, but they are not the same ones the gamble of faith suggests.

The sort of gamble that faith is and the deep meaning of ordinary gambling are, in sum, both ways of commenting on American society today. The gamble of faith amounts to an indirect commentary on American society by way of what it says of a critical nature about ordinary gambling. But this commentary also takes a direct form. Expressing faith today in the language of gambling is itself a way of commenting on the symbolic resonances of gambling for the society being addressed. Religious language always makes an odd use of culturally salient categories and practices in the effort to explain better the mysteries of faith. But in doing so it offers a critical commentary on those very notions and common activities. If God is love—in a most peculiar sense, in a weirdly comprehensive and unfailing way—then that says something not just about God but about the inadequacies of love as we know it. If God makes us gamble, but in an odd way—with peculiar stakes, odds, and payouts—then that says something of a critical sort about the everyday gambles our society forces us to make.

The Deep Meanings of Gambling in Contemporary America

In contrast to societies like Bali, where status is everything and the money risked in gambling consequently becomes a mere symbol of that fact, in contemporary America money itself is everything. No matter how much money matters, in a status society it is status rather than money that counts. One has influence over others because one has status and not because one has money; people do your bidding because you are an important person, not because you have the money to pay for their services. One's status is not a product of the money one has accumulated; indeed, in the typical status society one gains status by giving wealth away in ways that make other people one's debtors. Especially in today's neoliberal America, money is, to the contrary, the object of universal desire because it has the power to determine the value of everything. One has status, for example—along with everything else, such as a comfortable place to live, health care, the opportunity of higher education, and so on—only because one has money in the bank. It is therefore unlikely that in contemporary America the practice of risking money for the uncertain chance of gaining more of it is symbolic of anything else. Gambling is instead about what it appears to be about: money, the high value placed on it in American society and the tensions that surround that fact—the life-and-death consequences of how much one has of it.

But does this really hold for all sorts of gambling and gamblers in the United States? Are there not popular forms of gambling in America in which one finds that indifference to money typical of status gambling? In earlier times, among the landed gentry in the South, it is true, one could commonly find the sort of high-stakes gambling typical of Bali and the old landed French aristocracy. The periodic practice of betting on one's horse in a race against one's neighbor's is a prime case in point.[20] Here, as in Bali, people were pitted via their animals against one another, and, as was the case among the French landed elite, one had to lose gracefully, in apparent indifference to the monetary costs, never descending so low as to show one's concern for gain by cheating or by overly methodical play. The point was to show that one's class status was not a function of money by competing with others of one's own class on that primarily non-monetary basis—by way of a competition for honor.

The class prerequisites for this sort of deep play are no longer present in American society; class is no longer primarily a function of whether one's wealth comes from land or commercial employment. But this sort of play may still persist—say, in high-stakes casino poker—and retain its character as a form of status rivalry among men, just of a more individualistic than class-based sort. Indeed, just because of the loss of its class differentiating functions, this sort of gambling can be democratized in contemporary America. Anybody can gamble in this general sort of way, whatever the nature of the game—whether or not, for example, high stakes are involved. Is that not indeed what the American premium on sporting play is all about? Whoever one is, whatever the game, one can lose gracefully, care only for the play, avoid any calculation suggestive of an inordinate interest in gain, and never be so desperate to avoid loss that one cheats.[21]

Where money means everything, as it does in contemporary America, the game is still likely, however, to be about money—even when one is not playing for the money. It is no longer possible for the deep meaning of gambling to be, "I am not in a class dependent on money in the way or to the same extent you are," since everyone is just as dependent on money as everyone else. However one makes one's money, a rather historically extreme dependence on it is now a class-spanning commonality. Rather than make a point about class, the deep meaning of sporting gambling (where one does not play to win and a premium is placed on losing gracefully) might involve, then, a more general social critique, a critique of the general importance given to money in our society as a whole. Gambling in that fashion is a way of momentarily escaping in play the otherwise overbearing importance that money has in one's own life, the net otherwise cast by money over everything and everyone.[22]

Other popular forms of gambling in contemporary America—where one really does play to win, in hopes of making money—may have deep meanings that concern not so much the importance of money as the way it is typically made nowadays. Or, deep meanings that concern the old-fashioned American ideology, at least, about the way one makes money: money comes to those who earn it, by hard work, day in and day out. Low-stakes gambling to win at casino slot machines or through the purchase of state lottery tickets, for example, has nothing against money: money is important, maybe all-important; one is gambling in order to get more of it, after all. Getting it by gambling, rather than by the usual approved means, makes a statement instead about the irrelevance of delay, discipline, and effort in the process.

The connection, first of all, between work and wealth is questioned when one plays to win. Replacing disciplined striving—all the time and effort one would have to put into gainful employment—chance now seems to be all that lies behind one's wealth. Luck, rather than merit or reward for effort expended, becomes the explanation for disparities in net worth. It is appropriate that fortune redistributes with a capricious hand in gambling what chance—rather than talent or industry—was responsible for distributing in the first place among high and low in society.[23]

One makes one's fortune as an individual when one gambles. And to that extent the gambler imitates the self-made man of American mythology—who manages to pull himself up through sheer individual effort. Here, however, it is in the end only luck—not thrift, industry, or even skill (which, depending on the game, might have had something to do with it)—that sets one apart and makes one think one owes nothing to anyone else for where one has gotten.

The promise of advancement in American society through the usual channels is illusory, gambling suggests. If one is already on the low end of the totem pole, it is better to risk the complete loss of what one stakes for the possibility of sudden gain than to face the grim predictability of one's place in an economic system far more calcified and "fixed"—in the multiple senses of that term—than the American ideology of upward mobility and opportunity for all would imply.

In the actual economy, things might be stacked against those who start with little. But in gambling—barring cheating—every player has exactly the same chance of winning; the odds are really the same for everyone. Gambling is fair in a way the present economic system is not—that, indeed, might be one of its prime attractions. Rich or poor, as they approach the gaming table, fortune makes them in fact the equals of one another.

Because in real life one's odds of success depend on where one starts, the relative standings of the various players rarely changes. Without the advantages of their betters, poor people tend to remain poor, for example, and the rich, rich. Contrary to the mobility of fortune promised by the American dream, gambling, as its widespread popularity possibly suggests, is the only real way to get ahead. Winning the lottery, say, is one's only real chance to make it big, one's only real chance to be somebody in a society that measures importance by wealth.

On this way of looking at it, the deep meaning of the popularity of gambling for money in the United States confirms American values of equality, opportunity, and upward mobility; it even shares with the American dream the acceptance of actual success as the prerogative of the few. Gambling simply insists the dream become a reality. And to the letter: not just equality of opportunity, more or less, for most people, but mathematically exact equivalent odds for all players.

In holding America to its own norms, however, gambling dares to envision a highly unusual form of wealth generation, one with potentially more radical implications for the American system. That is, by suggesting an alternative set of principles for wealth generation, gambling might be sharply critical of the fundamental principles underlying actual American methods. For example, the whole value placed on production in an industrialized economy—the need to produce something of real value in order to generate wealth—can be suspended, gambling suggests. In sharp contrast to the "real" economy of industrial production, a money bet generates payout without production of goods for the market. This is money made without, indeed, even the provision of a service to anyone else. There is no real exchange in any ordinary business sense. And therefore if one wins, the gains are total, not the "net" that comes from subtracting one's expenditures—say, the costs of rendering a service to the person who pays you for it. Money changes hands here, but because there is no real exchange in the usual economic sense between parties, loss is simply total as well. One is not even left with the trinket one paid too much for; besides the enjoyment of the game, losers receive nothing in exchange for the money they have put out. Here, as well, money immediately multiplies, replacing all slow processes of painstaking accumulation. And the drudgery and dullness of ordinary labor discipline are lifted—at least temporarily. Excitement from wild swings of fortune is the norm. And so on.

It is unlikely, however, in today's economy that the primary point of gambling is to contest any of these things—labor discipline; the need for hard work to get ahead; the patience required for slow-paced economic advancement through methodical, monotonous routine—or the premium placed on production of real goods and services, which lies behind them all. The economy just does not work this way any more. What might have been radical in the last century—when all those things were supposed to count for something—is not anymore. Rather than holding out an alternative to the way things usually work, and therefore some hope of escape from it, gambling becomes simply a metaphor for everyday life.[24]

Indeed, even in the last century, at least since the Great Depression, the U.S. economy has seen the subordination of interest in production, and of its value priorities, to that of consumption. The primary problem for capitalism at its start—getting people to be disciplined workers in the way capitalism demands—no longer seems to be capitalism's main concern. As the Great Depression made clear, capitalism's contemporary problem is not insufficient production but the inability to circulate the goods produced ever so abundantly—that is, insufficient consumption. As a result, the engines of capitalism are now stoked, it seems, only by the undisciplined indulgence by consumers of their every whim. Their infinitely expandable desires for things have become far more important than their disciplined labor power. Their spending is the point, encouraged by ubiquitous offers of credit—not their prudent calculation of self-interest or careful accumulation of funds for a rainy day.

The consumer-driven capitalism of today makes capitalists into gamblers—if they were not before. Scot Cutler Shershow has observed that "[u]nlike the frugality, prudence, and calculation that Max Weber once famously defined as its essential 'spirit' . . . entrepreneurial investment can now be envisioned as a process of reckless expenditure and ecstatic dissemination."[25] Capitalists throw everything possible onto the market in the hopes of attracting fickle, trend-conscious consumer sentiment. Who knows what they might want? Using new flexible technologies that allow for multiple product lines, capitalists try to catch such consumer sentiment in flight; accumulating little in the way of inventory, companies hope to meet demand as it happens through computer-enabled, just-in-time production techniques. What consumers will want to buy at any particular time is unpredictable, and therefore companies seem to profit or descend into bankruptcy seemingly at the consumer's whim. Jean-Joseph Goux describes the new capitalist spirit this way: "The capitalist cannot count on an assured, calculable profit from his investment. He agrees to spend money . . . in a project that is always aleatory."[26] According to the greatest apologist of this new situation, the American neoliberal economist George Gilder, because "no one knows which venture will succeed, which number will win the lottery, a society ruled by risk and freedom rather than by rational calculus, a society open to the future rather than planning it, can call forth an endless stream of invention . . . [and] enterprise."[27] In sum, "everything happens as if the traditional values of the bourgeois ethos (sobriety, calculation, foresight, etc.) were no longer those values which corresponded to the demands of contemporary capitalism"—to capitalism's demands on either producers or consumers once consumption becomes its main focus.[28]

Of course one might argue that consumption is a mere strategic element in the new capitalism; increased production is always still the ultimate end.[29] There is no consumption without production, no infinitely expandable desire for things without equally riotous production. Indeed, according to the increasingly popular supply-side view of things in America since the Reagan revolution, no expanding desires without the production of anything and everything, however superfluous and unnecessary the things might seem. A "careening acceleration of production," a "fever for any form of production," an "unprecedented multiplication of supply," is necessary since that supply itself creates demand and does not simply respond to given needs.[30]

Capitalism would, then, be all about production at bottom. Unlike gambling, where money simply changes hands by being pooled and then differently distributed, going out in order to come back (if one is lucky, with an increase), one might think that in capitalism those few who profit from the system do not get their money from a mere circulation of wealth. Ultimately, something more has to be made—something real—beyond mere cycles of circulation.

In today's economy, however, wealth generation increasingly seems to skip production altogether. Fictitious capital creation—that is, the ability to increase wealth apart from the production of real goods and services—has, until very recently, been the name of the game; big money has typically been made without the intervention of any productive investment at all. Not just among U.S. investors but worldwide, the money to be made in monetary transactions such as the selling of loans, currency speculation, and trading on the stock exchange has completely dwarfed the real economy of things made and consumed.

Indeed, in recent times there are more opportunities for fictitious capital creation than ever before in history. Limited financial regulation meant one could make money not simply by loaning it—the tried and true form of fictitious capital creation—but by selling loans themselves. Banks, for example, used the promise of future earnings on their mortgage loans as a kind of security to sell bonds, which investors either kept for the interest income or sold in secondary markets. Before the present financial crisis hit, one could turn almost any expected earnings into instant cash. The futures market was transformed; one need not contract to sell or buy some real commodity at a certain price at a certain time but could do the same for a whole host of financial instruments themselves—betting, in effect, on their price fluctuations. One can always buy stocks with the primary intention of simply benefiting from the fact that their market values go up and down. But now currencies do the same. No longer pegged to anything real like gold or to a single dominant currency such as the

U.S. dollar, they all float according to a host of economic variables suggesting something about the strength of their respective underlying economies, thereby allowing for highly lucrative bets on exchange rate fluctuations among them, especially when dealing in high volumes.

Like moneymaking through gambling, the time frame for investments in financial instruments is typically very short; one does not buy up a currency, for example, to hold it for twenty years but to sell it as soon as its value goes up relative to another. One can make a huge return, indeed, in an instant—for example, by sinking large amounts of money in currency trades. Hard work and wealth hardly seem any more tightly tethered here than in gambling, when fortunes are literally to be made overnight.[31] Like gambling too, these trades hold out the exciting prospect of wild up and down swings. They thrive on volatility; there is money to be made only if prices go up and down, and the more the better. And the potential for profit or loss from such trading is itself highly volatile in quite unpredictable ways; enormous gains often followed by total losses at a time that no one can be sure of. These financial markets are typically unregulated, and therefore money both flows freely in at the first sign of possible profit, creating bubbles of overvaluation, and rushes out all together at the slightest hint of trouble in panicked sell-offs that spell catastrophic losses for everyone who fails to get out in time.

Financial transactions of this sort are more of an exchange of services between parties than ordinary gambling is. They generally involve, that is, someone's assuming the risk from someone else in exchange for a commensurate possibility of gain. Even pure currency speculation might involve an exchange of services of this sort: "I will take all this cash whose value might go down tomorrow off your hands, and stand to profit, in return, from the difference should the value go up." But the basic similarities between economic speculation, defined as betting on changes in price, and ordinary gambling have long been noted by American commentators.[32] It used to be that the character of good business practice was established in part through the very effort to distinguish it fundamentally from gambling, but that is a far harder proposition today.

The complaint lodged by gamblers about American economic life is unlikely, moreover, to concern routine hard work or economic discipline now that economic regulation in contemporary America is no longer geared to controlling the behavior of individuals. What economic regulation there is takes place at such a broad, society-wide level that the question of individual behavior drops out altogether. Rather than being modeled on the control of individual performance on a factory line, where the question is whether each individual person is sufficiently disciplined to behave as a single part of a well-oiled machine, economic regulation focuses instead simply on large statistically significant movements of entire populations. Economic regulation occurs, for example, through tax policy, where the question is what the average person is likely to do in a particular situation. How much are people likely to cut back on their health-care spending, as the government wants them to, if they have to pay a lot more for it themselves? No one cares whether everyone does what is expected of them; the policy works simply if a statistically significant number of them do. The issue is not the individual but the aggregate, on average.

Finally, and perhaps most importantly, regular hard work at the same job can no longer be counted on to pay off. In today's America, people are more likely to have irregular than regular jobs. In an age of flexible production geared to meeting the changing whims of consumer taste, machinery can be recalibrated for a host of different product lines, and therefore what workers are expected to do at the job can shift from day to day. Company profits, moreover, seem assured preferentially today by increased use of "casual," or temporary workers, and by restructuring—the downsizing of operations through consolidation and the closing and relocating of existing facilities—by layoffs, in short. The welfare state has been downsized too, right along with the majority of the companies, and therefore the risks and anxiety attendant upon the lack of job security increase; if one loses one's job or simply loses the benefits that usually come with full-time employment, the consequences may very well be catastrophic. Employment, in short, becomes a source of historically unusual insecurity in American life, at least if the post–World War II period of "unprecedented comfort and security for a large part of the [working] population" is any benchmark.[33] As Jackson Lears eloquently sums up both the trend and what it suggests about the practice of gambling:

> The emerging business model [in the late twentieth century] demanded a contingent labor force, mobile, malleable, assemblable, and dispersable in accordance with management's ever-shifting needs—'just in time' workers to complement the 'just in time' shipments of goods that managers embraced as the key to the vaunted 'flexibility' . . . It became harder to believe that one's experience is 'more than a series of random events,' observed Richard Sennett. This change in perception may have promoted the spread of gambling, according to Robert Goodman in *The Business of Luck*. 'Legalized gambling,' he wrote, 'seizes on the public desire to get ahead through enterprises of chance in a world where work no longer seems reliable.' "[34]

At the present time, then, it is not just money, and how much is riding on it, that the deep meaning of gambling in our society is likely to focus on, but the insecurity and unpredictability in particular that surround it. It is the fact of insecurity that is being played with here, and therefore one might expect risky bets, rather than the prudent ones that Pascal recommends, to be appealing—say, bets with long odds, as in lottery mega-jackpots. It is the fact that anything can happen that is of interest, and therefore unpredictable bets might be popular—betting, say, without picks with variable odds (50/50 bets, for example, in which one outcome is just as likely as the other), the no-skill betting of slot machines, or betting where one can show one's skill (or simple luck) at getting in or out at just the right time (poker, for example, where "hold 'em" or "fold 'em" is the basis for winning or losing).

People attracted to gambling for money would be rightly recognizing the ultimate unpredictability and insecurity of their economic prospects, in contrast to people who think they can avoid such risks in today's America. Or, perhaps more accurately, they would be people for whom those risky prospects have already proven inescapable. Those whose lives seem to be at the whim of chance—agriculturalists whose fortunes are dependent on the weather, soldiers who stake their lives against unknown enemies on the battlefield, and so on—have always seen the appeal of gambling. Economic insecurity may now hold across the board in America in ways that account for gambling's general popularity, but the risk of job or income loss, and the level of threat to one's long-term job prospects and material well-being should the worst happen, are not spread evenly in our society. The wealthy in our society, those already gainfully employed in full-time work, and the highly educated can hedge their bets against risk. The highly educated, for example, have the flexible, multiskilled capacities to do a variety of things in a changing economy. The wealthy have savings or can take out more closely targeted forms of insurance policy against risk. Those with well-paying, full-time employment have the money in the bank or are creditworthy enough to retool to get a new job or pay for health-care costs when out of work. But none of that holds for the unemployed in our society, temporary workers without benefits or unemployment insurance, or people holding low-skill, low-income jobs. Gambling presents a way for them to face up to the risks they meet everyday and try to get a handle on the realities of their lives.

Unlike the everyday world where the prospects for staying above water lie out of one's hands, gambling gives one at least the illusion of being in some control of one's fate. One can pick one's own numbers, according to some system—maybe the same set of numbers every day—rub one's lucky charm or, by whatever means, try to conjure fickle fortune over to one's own side.

These may be games of chance, but it is not simply chance that is deciding one's fate; one has been singled out by fate because of who one is or what one does—because of qualities, that is, that are specific to one's person. For people who think of gambling in this way, it is not the statistical probabilities that explain one's winning; the explanation of one's winning is not the simple fact that someone eventually has to. One wins because one is fortune's favorite or an especially lucky person.

The peculiarity of the mathematical calculation of odds in gambling allows for this. The fact that the mathematical calculation of odds in gambling has very little predictive value for the individual case mirrors the paradox for individuals of the way economic regulation typically works and money is made in our society—according to statistical calculation—and becomes a kind of commentary on it. Mathematical probabilities for games of chance are accurate only over the long term for the aggregate of all, say, throws or tosses; the more one rolls the dice, the closer the results will match mathematical prediction. But those probabilities never explain what happens on the single roll, and for a gambler that is all that counts. Similarly, the paradox of economic regulation by statistical averages is that what holds on average does not hold for particular individuals—most pointedly, for the economic losers. The economy can be humming along while—maybe even because—a certain percentage of the population is unemployed and down on their luck. Good overall economic growth makes little difference to an individual if that person fails even to make the average. Even in the financial transactions so typical of wealth generation in contemporary America and so otherwise like gambling, the individual counts for little relative to the group. One makes money by betting on what one thinks everyone else will do—say, buy or sell a particular stock or currency. One just tries to do this before they do. One bets, therefore, "not as an individual, but as part of a diffuse, aggregative . . . statistical mass"; someone benefiting from price changes derives a profit "from the way his actions related to and were defined by those of all around him."[35] But when one gambles, one stands out from the crowd in a kind of pure irreducible specificity; one wins or loses alone. Particularly when gambling for the moment, and not playing the odds over the long term, the gambler is saying, in effect: "I will risk all. I may gain all, I may lose all, but I will not join the crowd and average out."[36]

Rather than provide a comforting assurance that chance might be influenced or that fortune might play favorites, gambling can also simply be a way of giving oneself over to chance, not out of resignation or despair but because risk itself is one's only hope. Putting one's fortune at risk is a bad idea if one has something to lose, but if one does not, it might simply represent the welcome hope of a new beginning, a blessed chance to start over. The possibility of economic mobility that gambling highlights is a bad thing if one can only go down but quite a good thing if one can only go up. Similarly, not being able to count on what will happen in the future is a bad thing in ordinary life, a sign of just how insecure one's prospects are and how desperate the present plight that demands one's attention: time collapses into the present when one's survival from one moment to the next is at stake. But gambling transforms this foreshortened attitude, this inability to look into the future in a life where anything can happen, into an asset. Without the ability of foresight, with a care only for the moment, one can stand to win nonetheless.

In general, if one already has something to hold on to, risk becomes simply the chance of loss; it might be reasonable in that case to flee from risk, to try to avoid it altogether or hedge against it. Why gamble with what you have if you stand a good chance of keeping it and making it grow to your further benefit? People who think they can avoid risk generally do not gamble. They do things like take out a life insurance policy instead. Making money might always involve some risk in our society, but surely the odds are better on making money some other way—especially if one already has quite a bit?

If facing high risk is one's unavoidable fate in this society and one has nothing to protect against it anyway, chance is more likely to seem one's only friend. Without anything to lose, the risks one takes in gambling hold out the prospect more of profit than of loss. Making a fortune from the lottery may be improbable, but it might well be one's only real hope of economic well-being, of freedom from worry.

The popularity of gambling among those with the least economic security in this society—among poor African Americans, for example—has its utilities as a result.[37] The small amount one bets on the lottery every week is unlikely to accumulate as savings otherwise—if one does not have enough money for a bank account, one would just end up spending that money on something else. Forgoing the little one could buy with it is no great hardship. If one plays every week for small amounts on not-so-long odds, the payout over the long term will probably be as much as one could earn by putting the same amount of money in the bank. In exchange for each bet on a mega-jackpot, moreover, one gets the prospect of a life-transforming payout. However long the odds on this, if one is uneducated, unskilled, poor, and discriminated against by the wider society, these odds are still better than the ones one has of ever getting much money by any other means. As Alex Rubner observes,

> [The] vast majority of people have no legal (and usually also no illegal) means with which to obtain command over a large lump sum of money, however hard they work, however intelligent they are,

however strenuously they strain their nerves and muscles. The only
way to procure [it] is therefore to win the lottery . . . . In a high-prize
gambling venture [one] buys the possibility of acquiring [that sum].
And at a given intensity of desire . . . the odds do not really matter.[38]

The Gamble of Grace

In contrast to Geertz, for whom gambling has a deep meaning only
when its rational utilities are nil, we have now made prudence a
good part of the deep meaning of gambling in the contemporary
United States. For people most at risk in today's society, gambling becomes a good bet. The commentary on American society
goes by way of that fact: is it unfortunate that American society
is the sort of place where that is the case, where, for example, a
large part of the populace properly deems mega-jackpots their
best bet of gaining economic security.

Notice this return to prudence makes gambling in contemporary America something like the gamble of grace that Pascal
recommends. Just like the mega-jackpot example, the risk of faith
is a prudent bet, according to Pascal, because one has nothing
to lose and everything to gain, because one risks very little for
something of very high value attainable only by these means. It
is Pascal, indeed—not just American society—who is doing his
anxiety-inducing best to assure the conditions under which the bet
will seem prudent in just this way: the situation is otherwise hopeless, one has nothing to lose, one might as well bet, even at a loss,
against long odds. For this reason, the criticism that gambling
lodges against an America that plays with the economic insecurity of its citizens extends to him as well, requiring from religious
people a revision of the usual account of the gamble of grace.

Pascal thinks everyone is already in the dire situation that
makes the bet on faith look good; the assessment of the utilities
of the wager really should not be that different whatever one's
circumstance. His primary example, indeed, is always the king—
the hardest case because, if anyone, he leads an apparently blessed
life. Into lives of apparent happiness, Pascal is trying to inject the
anxiety of insecurity and likely loss in order to equalize circumstances, in order to make clear that everyone is in the same boat.
More recent theories of probability in decision making (e.g., theories of marginal utility) would dispute the effectiveness of the

effort. "One in the hand is worth two in the bush"—and that is why people who think they already have something will not see the point of the bet. If one has nothing in hand to speak of, the assessment of relative utilities changes: one wagers nothing much and the outcome is worth much more than it would to someone who already has something. In contemporary America, such differences affecting the assessment of utilities would only come to the fore. The force of Pascal's arguments, in short, would best be seen by those in today's America already in misery or threatened by it, by those most at risk: those prone to ordinary gambling.

And that is Pascal's problem: faith for him would trade on general insecurity like a company benefiting from the job insecurities of its employees to force concessions out of them. To paraphrase Nietzsche, Pascal's account of grace first foments the disease—the unhappiness of a loss-threatened life—it offers to cure. Contrary to Christian charity, moreover, faith gains its appeal here off the backs of the least fortunate in particular. Rather than working to alleviate their condition, faith's interest is in aggravating it—even spreading it as widely as possible.

A more moral version of Pascal's gamble of faith is therefore necessary, one that might provide a better alternative both to gambling and the society it critiques. A way to make that moral improvement is to change the understanding of grace in Pascal's wager. That view of grace is not, for example, a Protestant one, nor one held by many Christians today, Protestant or Catholic. (It may not even be Pascal's own considered opinion, but a mere accommodation to the audience addressed; I leave that disputed question of scholarship open here.) In this alternative understanding of grace, there is no suggestion that trying to live differently is a condition for receiving God's grace and ultimate salvation; reception of grace and salvation do not depend on seeing the error of one's ways and making the attempt to change one's life, as Pascal's wager maintains. Indeed, Protestants in particular think that if salvation had such conditions it would not be a good bet. Sinners cannot, of their own strength, do what is required of them—face up to their predicament, reevaluate their most basic priorities, and accordingly make the effort to lead a very different sort of life. They would have to be graced by God already to have any hope of making the required changes.

Because a changed way of life is not a precondition for salvation, Christian interest in the circumstances sufficient to
motivate such a change—Christian interest, in other words, in
people living otherwise miserable lives—drops out of the wager
of faith. How happy people are—how much material prosperity
they enjoy, the security of their possession of it, and so on—is
no longer a prime factor determining the likelihood of salvation
now that having the motivation to change one's life is not either.
The morally problematic features of Pascal's wager are lessened
by making clear that undeniable misery is not a religiously privi-
leged circumstance for universal emulation.

There are clear similarities to gambling with this new version
of grace, which is the reason grace can still be talked about in
terms of it. Like a win at gambling, one has not merited what one
receives; salvation is a free gift of grace. As in gambling, when
one wins salvation, one gains with no provision of service in payment; one has done no one a good turn or service in exchange
for salvation (i.e., God). Nothing one has done makes salvation
a reward for effort expended. Divine largesse, like chance, simply replaces hard work as an explanation for the winning ticket.
Indeed, just as in gambling, what one wins here becomes one's
own by no proper title—say, by being bought, earned, or inherited. No one has any rightful claim on eternal life; eternal life is
a divine property that is ours only by grace.

Unlike, however, what one finds in ordinary gambling—and
in Pascal's gamble of faith as well—the pot of free grace is now
gained without a wager. There is no risk involved at all. This
is the least exciting wager imaginable because it is one without
stakes. In contrast to both ordinary gambling and what Pascal
suggests, the payout here just has no prior possible costs. The
gamble of faith is a consummately good one, for just this reason—it requires nothing from a person, no money down. One
gets something of utmost value—salvation—literally for nothing,
as an otherwise completely unanticipated bonanza.

Once acquired, the gift of faith does require, however, a
changed life. Saved people act differently. There might be renun-
ciations, then—costs—that come with winning. Winning means
giving up one's past life for another. Paradoxically, it is when one
wins that one risks loss.

But even here one might say that one really gives nothing up—just not for Pascal's reason. Pascal thought the costs and the reward incommensurable: what one gives up—the goods of this life—are nothing in comparison to the goods of heaven because they are of a qualitatively different sort. The new account of grace suggests, to the contrary, a greater appreciation for the goods of everyday life because of its greater apparent similarity to ordinary gambling. In both ordinary gambling and the new gamble of faith, one risks the very same sort of thing one hopes to gain more of. The goods of the life one leads now are risked in the gamble of faith for the sake of a supreme good that must include whatever genuine goods one risks. One could say, then, that one gives nothing up when winning the gamble of faith because one will simply receive back with an increase what one renounces. One suffers now, forsaking present enjoyment of the goods of life only for the sake of a life abundant that, by God's help, one will come to possess in the future along with everyone else. Or one might say one gives nothing up because even now the life one leads with faith is just the same life led better—a life of trust and security in God's love, come what may, even if outwardly everything seems the same.[39] Kierkegaard suggests both points with a profundity that escapes me: "It is great to give up one's wish, but it is greater to hold it fast after having given it up, it is great to grasp the eternal, but it is greater to hold fast to the temporal after having given it up."[40] And then, "[b]y faith I make renunciation of nothing, on the contrary, by faith I acquire everything."[41] Though I give Isaac up, I will have him back again; indeed, through faith I never lost him but have him even now in a new way, by faith, the temporal itself possessed differently in light of the eternal.

The main reason, however, that the gamble of faith is not a risky bet is that there are no losers. Payouts without prior conditions are quite naturally universally extendable—one does not even need to bet to win. How far the payout extends is of course dependent on God's free mercy. Most Christians today are willing to bet that such mercy extends universally.

God's mercy in Pascal's wager was really not all that free. God's mercy meant God's willingness to reward graciously with eternal life those who made the effort to live differently: "The proper function of mercy is to combat sloth by encouraging good works according to this passage . . . 'Let us repent, for who can tell if God will turn away from God's fierce anger?' [Jonah 3:9] . . . It is because God is merciful that we must make every effort."[42] If his wager is any indication, Pascal had no interest, indeed, in thinking the payout might be extended universally, without regard for merits. The whole wager of faith assumes the contrary: it would not make sense to give up the goods of this life in hopes of eternal life if God might very well give you that either way. The possibility not just of losing eternal salvation but of incurring an incredibly awful penalty, eternal damnation, should one refuse the wager of faith had the added benefit for Pascal, moreover, of clearly outweighing any sure bet of simply keeping what one has. And it makes the insecurity of life behind one's desire to make the right bet all the greater: the risks that attend backing the wrong horse in this case are not just death but something far worse.

Because a change of life is no longer a precondition for salvation according to the wager of faith as it is being reconceived here, conditional salvation is no longer necessary to make the wager of faith seem a good one. The possibility of universal, rather than limited, salvation is now indeed what lies behind the wager of faith instead, what gets one to bet on faith. Wager the changes to your life that are appropriate for someone who has faith because it is a good bet that you are already favored by God and therefore someone able, by grace, to lead a better sort of life. The attempt to lead a different sort of life, no matter how difficult it might be to make the change, is itself a good bet—a prudent decision—because it is likely that God wants to give everyone thereby life abundant, beginning here and now and extending to all eternity.

A major contrast, then, with both ordinary gambling and the society it complains about is that the new wager of faith envisions an unusual gambling setup in which everyone stands to benefit at once from the same gambles. If I gain from the gamble of grace because of God's free mercy, then everyone else should in principle be a winner too. And the reverse: the more other people lose, the more likely my own losing becomes and the more risky the bet that I will win begins to appear. If others are losing, God can only be less gracious and salvation more conditional than it first appeared, in ways that might very well bring harm to me. I have no interest, then, in other people's loss.

In most forms of gambling—with the possible exception of lotteries—the money pooled is not redistributed to all players, and therefore, in stark contrast to the new gamble of faith, everyone does not win at the same time. (The problem with lotteries, which everyone points out, is that the poor typically pay disproportionately for the goods they get back in public services; those least able to pay contribute the most.) Nor is widespread winning built into the new American economy. In capitalism generally, it is at least possible for everyone to win at the same time—a rising economy lifts most boats even if there is little equality of distribution across the board. But this is not the way financial markets of today work. When one bets in a mass market on the fluctuations in value of a financial instrument, the money one makes is the product of the money others have put into it—their buying that instrument is the reason, for example, that the value goes up. And when one wins they lose. The whole idea is to buy or sell before others in ways that make their purchases or sales more costly. For example, I sell all my holdings of U.S. dollars before news of an American recession becomes common knowledge and my doing so makes the dollars of everyone else worth that much less. For similar reasons, widespread winning is not even a possibility in most ordinary gambling because winners simply take what the losers have put in. In this case, indeed, the money won typically comes directly out of the losers' pockets. Because no real exchange occurs between gamblers—no "this-in-exchange-for-that"—one person's winning means someone else's simple loss. Whether one makes one's fortune at the gaming table or in a real estate bubble, one's costs for entering the game, moreover, are borne by others. The winners get back what they have risked, and more, only because other people pitch in what the winners walk away with; even if they assume those risks willingly and are betting only petty cash, one wins only by doing them harm. In short, in both ordinary gambling and in the gambling of financial-instrument trading one wins at other people's expense, and therefore one wants them to lose because that is the precondition for winning oneself. In gambling, "the desire of the one is that the other should lose"; "it is impossible that the gambler should desire his own benefit and that of his opponent at the same time."[43]

Because salvation is to be universal, in the gamble of grace there is no one-sided anticipation of profit. One does not stand, indeed, either to win or lose alone; one's destiny instead is shared with all others. Not as some fungible unit, as one indistinguishable element in the mass, but as a blessed favorite of a God who, one expects, wants to show the same personal regard for all, to shower the same loving beneficence on everyone, in ways that meet and surpass their particular needs and desires. One feels singled out by grace, basking in the limelight of one's good fortune, in much the way any winner would whose very personal lucky number has finally been drawn in the lottery. The risky play, however, which in both ordinary gambling and in everyday American life tends to isolate people from one another, has nonetheless here been transformed into certain solidarity. The salvation one would likely lose if it depended upon one's distinguishing merits has been taken out of one's hands. What one's personal merits do not allow one to count on has become, for that very reason, the prerogative of all by God's free and loving grace.

11

The Criminal Law of Gambling
A Puzzling History

David A. Skeel Jr. and William Stuntz

Beginning in the 1880s,[1] a series of moralist crusades produced federal criminal laws banning various alleged vices, or as much of the vices as the federal government was permitted to ban: polygamy in American territories (including Utah, where the then-polygamous Mormon church chiefly resided), the mailing and interstate transportation of lottery tickets, interstate movement for the purpose of engaging in illicit sex and, most famously, the manufacture and sale of alcoholic beverages. These crusades against plural marriage, gambling, prostitution, and liquor seem unsurprising to us now. Late nineteenth- and early twentieth-century politics were heavily influenced by Protestant evangelicals, the primary culture warriors of their day and ours. That constituency's political clout explains why American criminal law has traditionally been more moralist, more concerned with stamping out various forms of vice and sin, than the criminal laws of other Western nations. In the United States, theologically conservative Protestants have long been a powerful political force—much more so than elsewhere in the Western world. Moralist politics follow naturally from a moralist voting population.

Except that the voting population is not so moralist as it seems—or should not be, given its religious beliefs. Theologically conservative Protestants (a constituency to which we both belong) believe in a theology that emphasizes grace, not law; their religious convictions ought to incline them toward skepticism about the power of laws and governments to transform cultures. That was as true a century ago as it is today. Catholicism, not Protestantism, is the branch of American Christianity that seems most comfortable with legal prohibition of conduct that the church condemns but that much of the population enjoys or tolerates. The behavior of those late nineteenth- and early twentieth-century culture warriors who were quick to translate their religious convictions into criminal prohibitions was thus more surprising than it at first appears.

For over a century, Congress has played a major role in the criminal law of vice, including the law of gambling. This too should seem strange. Vice markets are traditionally local,[2] and local norms with respect to the relevant vices vary from place to place. State and (especially) local governments could handle these subjects as they have historically handled the definition and punishment of violent felonies and felony thefts. Indeed, according to most theories of federalism, morals crimes like the ones listed above are precisely the sort of thing that state and local governments *should* handle so that communities with different moral visions can live under laws consistent with those visions. To make this pattern stranger still, the federal criminal law of vice arose at a time when the federal government was much smaller and its regulatory power much weaker than today. Congress's authority to regulate interstate commerce under the Constitution—the principal source of Congressional power today, and for most of American history—was construed quite narrowly throughout the nineteenth century. The federal government regulated gambling, prostitution, and the alcohol trade in an era when it regulated little else.

The puzzles do not stop there. Roughly fifty years after the antivice crusades that gave rise to federal lottery laws began, the most important of those crusades—Prohibition—collapsed. Culture wars politics collapsed with it, or seemed to. The division between the culturally conservative Protestant countryside and more culturally liberal cities, which had defined American politics for a generation, appeared to pass from the political scene. Yet, save for the nationwide ban on alcohol, the federal vice laws that the earlier movement had spawned did *not* pass from the scene. Instead, the federal law of drugs and gambling continued to expand in the generation after Repeal,[3] even as American politics grew more culturally tolerant. Drug laws made little difference in this period, but federal gambling laws were taken seriously; the federal law enforcement bureaucracy devoted more attention to these laws in the generation after the New Deal than before. Both gambling law and associated law enforcement appeared to grow more moralist at precisely the time when they should have grown more libertarian.

This law enforcement attention did not put a dent in the market for gambling: the more federal law enforcement expanded, the more gambling seemed to grow along with it. Of course, Prohibition had failed to stamp out the liquor trade. Perhaps all efforts to criminalize popular vices are doomed to failure. But the criminal law of gambling failed in different ways than Prohibition. Prohibition's failure was political: voters wrestled with the question whether criminalizing the alcohol trade was worth the costs that attended it and changed their minds about the right answer to that question. With respect to gambling, changed minds did not lead to changed laws, or not at first—rather, the laws grew more stringent in the 1950s and 1960s and were applied more frequently, but private conduct seemed unaffected. A federal government that battled the Depression and won a world war seemed unable to contain illegal lotteries and bookmaking.

This odd history has an odd coda. Over the course of the last generation, the culture wars of the 1920s seemed to reappear; as in the earlier period, theologically conservative Protestants have been eager to support criminal prohibitions against a variety of moral wrongs. But in the midst of this resurgent moralism, the criminal law of gambling collapsed. Federal gambling prosecutions all but ceased. State lotteries multiplied, riverboat and Indian casinos proliferated, and a large and growing market in Internet gambling arose. The religious right, which hardly seemed reticent about using law to stamp out immoral conduct, appeared resigned to—and at times even uninterested in—these developments.[4]

In short, the legal battle against gambling appeared when it should not have, was nationalized when it ought to have remained local, survived even though a similar moral crusade had just been rejected by overwhelming majorities, proved ineffective notwithstanding increased enforcement resources, and collapsed just when moralist politics were reviving. What explains this strange story, and what can we learn from it?

A Surprising Story

These five puzzles—the rise of gambling prohibition, the focus on federal law, the persistence and expansion of federal gambling law after Prohibition was abandoned, the ineffectiveness of federal law enforcement, and the lower priority with the religious right of a vice that once was at the core of its political agenda—largely define the history of the criminal law of gambling. Below, we unpack these questions. In the course of the unpacking, we draw some lessons about the nature of the Christian right and its relationship to law and politics, about the role of federal law in resolving contentious moral issues, and about the ability of criminal law enforcement to shape private conduct.

The Late Nineteenth-Century Rise of Gambling Prohibition

The late nineteenth-century Protestant evangelical campaign against gambling is more than a little surprising given the Protestant conception of sin. Protestants view sin as a singular noun: a disposition, not a discrete event. One reason Protestants do not confess sins to a priest as Catholics do is the Protestant belief in the priesthood of all believers. Jesus, the one who "has made us to be a kingdom and priests," is for Protestants both necessary and sufficient to mediate between the individual and God.[5] But another reason is the Protestant belief that the individual wrongs we commit are merely symptoms. The disease is the underlying disposition—and the disease matters far more than any of its symptoms. By disposition, Protestants mean something like motivation, but it is deeper than that: it is more like *inclination*, the direction in which and the object toward which (or toward whom) one's heart inclines. After David committed adultery with Bathsheba, he begged God to "create in me a clean heart," and to "renew a right spirit within me."[6] It was his heart's inclination and disposition, not the particular sin, that most concerned him.

If sin is a disposition rather than a discrete event, legal regulation would seem to be an unlikely savior. Law deals with events—not the inclinations of human hearts, which are unknowable by human judges and juries. Plus, law is in the business of drawing lines, separating innocent from guilty, distinguishing those who must pay damages from those who escape legal liability. Yet the disposition to sin is universal. The Bible emphasizes this point by showing that even its heroes are criminals: Abraham was a coward, Jacob a liar and fraud, David an adulterer and a murderer; Moses likewise had a homicide to his account. These tendencies did not disappear after Christ came. Paul was responsible for the stoning of Stephen—the first Christian who was martyred for professing his faith—and for Christians, it is hard to imagine a worse crime. Ours is not a creed that fits naturally with the enterprise of using law to separate the virtuous from the vicious. The disease is too pervasive and runs too deep.

American law itself long reflected this sensibility, as evidenced by its treatment of two of the sins that come closest to a person's heart: disloyalty and dishonesty. Start with disloyalty. Christians worship a Savior who was betrayed by one close at hand, one who owed him fidelity. A Christianized legal system might be expected to include strong legal obligations of loyalty and severe penalties for treachery. But duties of loyalty were rare in nineteenth-century American law, and penalties for betrayal rarer still. Similarly, the Bible calls Satan "the father of lies" (John 8:44); a mostly Christian nation might be expected to criminally punish dishonesty of many different sorts. Yet until well into the twentieth century, lies told in court on the witness stand were the only significant class of falsehoods that yielded criminal penalties. Fraud—meaning, basically, stealing money through deceit—was defined so narrowly at common law that proving it was all but impossible.

If we consider the general orientation of criminal law, we find the same pattern. Motive is the legal concept that most nearly conforms to the idea of the heart's disposition or inclination. In a legal system that sought to criminalize sin, defendants' motives—the reasons why they committed their crimes—should be central to the definition of criminal offenses. Yet nineteenth-century criminal law looked to defendants' motive only as a means of *excusing* criminal defendants, not as a justification for condemning them. (The primary example of an exculpatory motive is self-preservation: the defenses of necessity, duress, and self-defense all permitted defendants to commit what would otherwise be criminal acts in order to protect themselves from harm—which hardly reflects Christian norms of self-sacrifice.) On a wide range of issues, nineteenth-century American law was decidedly libertarian, not moralist. Nor is the connection between Christians and this libertarian stance accidental: the law's libertarianism and related peculiarities were often attributed to America's Christian past.[7]

Why, then, did Protestant evangelicals become so concerned in the late nineteenth century to criminalize what appear to be low-level wrongs like gambling? Part of the answer lies in the historical moment when gambling prohibition took hold. The principal gambling prohibitions, such as the federal laws that criminalized lotteries in 1890 and 1895, arose in the generation after the Civil War and Reconstruction at a time when law and government seemed able to accomplish a great deal more than had seemed possible a few decades earlier. Like other Americans, Protestant evangelicals were optimistic about law's potential for good. This optimism was directed toward vices like gambling, prostitution, and alcohol because these vices could be defined (it was easy to identify just what the misbehavior was), because they seemed unconnected to other legitimate conduct, and because— like sin more generally—they seemed to enslave those who participated in them.

This last point is particularly important. The rhetoric of abolitionism, stressing the evils of slavery and the moral imperative to free those in bondage, ran through all the antivice movements of late nineteenth and early twentieth centuries. Gambling was no exception: prohibitions sought not so much to punish vice as to protect its victims, to save them from the dangerous scoundrels who tempted them to a life of dissipation. The late nineteenth-century crusades against gambling picked up on themes that had been sounded in literature and in moralistic prose for much of the century. In *Seven Lectures to Young Men on Various Subjects*, for example, the Reverend Henry Ward Beecher, father of Harriet Beecher Stowe and himself a well-known evangelist, had warned that gambling "destroys all domestic habits and affections" and that gamblers "will stake their property, their wives, their children, and themselves."[8] There were complicating factors, to be sure. The threats to vulnerable youth were identified with the urban Northeast, which had seen a large influx of immigrants. Most of the immigrants were Catholic, and the anti-gambling campaign was tinged at times with anti-Catholicism. But the concerns were genuine; the issue was not simply a cover for religious or ethnic bigotry. To its proponents, vice regulation would safeguard the morals of the American people and thereby keep them free.

The campaign to criminalize gambling and other vice was part of a larger vision. Nineteenth-century Protestant evangelical activism is often portrayed as having been obsessed with personal virtue but less interested in economic issues.[9] This is to project the present back upon the past. To nineteenth-century evangelicals, gambling, prostitution, and the liquor trade *were* economic issues—and economic issues, in turn, were moral issues; the division between the two is an artifact of our intellectual world, not theirs. Vice happens in markets, with buyers and sellers: or, to prohibitionists, with victims and the victimizers who tempted them. The people who made the most money from these trades seemed guilty of exploiting society's most vulnerable members: factory workers drinking or gambling away their paychecks and starving their families, young girls lured into prostitution by dire economic circumstances, and so on. To voters and politicians alike, issues like these seemed more analogous to antitrust, railroad regulation, and labor law than to the laws against homicide, assault, and theft.

This explains why so much of the political rhetoric of antivice crusades focused on the money made from the trade, not on the vices themselves—and also why so much of the political argument surrounding the Sherman Act, the Interstate Commerce Act, and other economic regulatory legislation sounds, to twenty-first-century ears, remarkably moralist. Contemporary antitrust law stresses economic efficiency and maximizing consumer choice. Those were not the goals of the early trustbusters. Rather, they sought to impose higher moral standards on those whom Theodore Roosevelt called "malefactors of great wealth." The language is not so different from the terms used to characterize those who ran illegal lotteries or the liquor industry that fought to maintain urban saloons.

In all these areas, rural populists and progressives sought to regulate the behavior of wealthy market actors in order to protect their poorer customers from exploitation. Notice again the timing of the passage of the two main federal gambling laws of this period: the law banning the sending of lottery tickets through the mails was passed in 1890, three years after the Interstate Commerce Act—the first major federal railroad rate regulation—and the same year as the Sherman Act. The law banning interstate transportation of lottery tickets was passed in 1895 by a Congress that included the largest number of Populists in that movement's history.

Each of these issues was a signature theme for William Jennings Bryan, the Populist leader, three-time Democratic presidential nominee, secretary of state, and most famous Protestant evangelical of the late nineteenth and early twentieth centuries. Bryan was a leading proponent of antivice laws; he later became a leading supporter of Prohibition because of his concerns about its effects on ordinary Americans. While "Anti-Saloon League Literature was filled with drawings of swarthy, mustachioed men luring fair-haired Americans into their lethal enterprises," as Bryan's biographer puts it, "Bryan avoided such nativist libels and kept his focus squarely on the capitalists, regardless of ethnicity, who 'impoverish the poor and multiply their sufferings' and 'increase the death rate among the children.'"[10] Bryan also campaigned against the corporate trusts that dominated many industries, complaining that they stifled individual opportunity and forced consumers to pay unconscionably high prices. "There can be no good monopoly in private hands," Bryan warned in the 1890s, "until the Almighty sends us angels to preside over the monopoly." Bryan called for aggressive regulation of the railroads for the same reasons, and for a time even advocated government ownership.[11] Bryan's career suggests that the politics of vice were more linked with the politics of business regulation than we tend to imagine.

Bryan did not figure in the debates that led to the 1890 and 1895 gambling laws, largely due to the timing of his congressional service. He served two terms in the House of Representatives in the early 1890s—just after the first lottery bill was enacted and just before the second.[12] But he spoke out against gambling and in favor of gambling prohibition in the decades that followed. In a speech to Nebraska's constitutional convention in 1920, for instance, he told the delegates that "I hope the constitution you are writing will put the seal of its condemnation upon all forms of gambling. . . . Chance should not be allowed to be substituted for honest industry; or children should know from their youth that there is at least one state in this union that makes no discrimination between kinds of gambling, high or low, large or small, but that all gambling is prohibited in Nebraska as far as law can prevent it."[13]

In theory, religious voters who were concerned with the temptations vice markets create might have advocated civil regulation of gambling (or of some forms of gambling, such as the state lotteries) rather than criminal prohibition. But from the perspective of the time, civil regulatory legislation was a strange concept. The common law—doctrines inherited from England, made by judges, and developed by American courts throughout the nineteenth century—governed disputes between private parties (what lawyers call "private law"), including large corporations. Legislators attended to the relationship between those same private parties and the government: "public law," to use the standard legal terminology. There were two chief bodies of public law in the late nineteenth century: criminal law and the law of taxation. The idea of civil government regulation, with legislatures and expert administrative agencies defining liability rules and enforcing those rules through mechanisms like corporate fines—a regulatory model that became quite common in the last two-thirds of the twentieth century—was, for the most part, foreign to this period. The few regulatory statutes that Congress did enact were anchored in the criminal law: criminal prosecutions were the Interstate Commerce Commission's chief enforcement tool, and the Sherman Act criminalized monopolization of American industries. Even as late as the 1930s, New Deal regulatory statutes invariably included criminal penalties for noncompliance.

Several of the key Supreme Court cases testing the constitutionality of New Deal statutes were criminal prosecutions.

Of course, civil lawsuits were a possibility; in addition to criminal penalties, the Sherman Act provided for suits for treble damages against would-be monopolists. But this would have been a foolhardy strategy for legislators and judges seeking to rein in vice markets. Since buyers and sellers alike were viewed, under the legal standards of the time, as voluntary participants in those markets, they assumed the risk of any harms that came their way. Plus, many judges would have held that gamblers, drinkers, customers of prostitutes, or the prostitutes themselves—the chief victims of nineteenth-century vice markets—came to the courthouse with "unclean hands" and so could not seek legal remedies for their victimization. The spouses and families of working-class gamblers and drinkers and "johns" might have argued that the relevant vice markets deprived them of life's necessities (a point that prohibitionists frequently stressed). But according to the governing legal doctrines of the nineteenth and early twentieth centuries, the sellers of the relevant products and services owed no legal duty to their customers' families. Doctrines like assumption of risk, "unclean hands," and narrow understandings of the scope of legal duty ensured that no plaintiffs could bring valid legal claims.[14]

Legislators or judges might have changed these legal doctrines. But that kind of change was nearly unimaginable in the legal world of a century ago. Before the New Deal, common-law doctrines like the ones mentioned in the preceding paragraph occupied a more exalted place in legal consciousness than they do today. Some judges believed that legislation overturning well-established common-law rules was unconstitutional because "due process of law" entitled every citizen to the full range of common-law rights and protections.[15] That and similar views tended to push legislators eager to do something about gambling and other vice markets toward criminal prohibition.

So criminal laws banning gambling and other vices arose for much the same reason that laws regulating railroads and other powerful corporations arose: partly from the belief that criminal law was the only regulatory tool available and partly from a sense that the unscrupulous rich were exploiting the vulnerable poor, tempting them into behavior harmful to themselves and to their families. The spirit of the late nineteenth-century law of vice seems to us moralistic, and it was—though no more so than was true of antitrust or railroad regulation. Likewise, the spirit of vice laws of the same period seems to us punitive, but it was not: the goal was more to protect the vulnerable than to punish those who exploited them.

Federalism and Vice

Then-Professor, now-Judge Michael McConnell famously argued for using state law, not federal law, to regulate ordinary vices:

> Assume that there are only two states, with equal populations of 100 each. Assume further that 70 percent of State A, and only 40 percent of State B, wish to outlaw smoking in public buildings. The others are opposed. If the decision is made on a national basis by a majority rule, 110 people will be pleased, and 90 displeased. If a separate decision is made by majorities in each state, 130 will be pleased, and only 70 displeased. The level of satisfaction will be still greater if some smokers in State A decide to move to State B, and some anti-smokers in State B decide to move to State A. In the absence of economies of scale in government services, significant externalities, or compelling arguments from justice, this is a powerful reason to prefer decentralized government. States are preferable governing units to the federal government, and local government to states. Modern public choice theory provides strong support for the framers' insight on this point.[16]

This argument for state power as a means of maximizing preference satisfaction is particularly strong with respect to issues about which people in different regions and jurisdictions disagree—as was the case with gambling in the late nineteenth century when Congress enacted the first federal antilottery laws. McConnell's argument was familiar to the politicians and lawyers who debated those laws (as his essay shows, the argument was equally familiar in Madison's day). In *Champion v. Ames*, Chief Justice Melville Fuller used a version of it to argue in his dissenting opinion that the federal law banning interstate transportation of lottery tickets was unconstitutional.[17]

Fuller added an argument that was common in Supreme Court decisions a century ago: that the federal government was not permitted to regulate matters that had traditionally been reserved to the states. Legal regulation of public morals, as in the federal antilottery laws, plainly fell within that category. In 1903, when Fuller pressed these arguments, the federal government regulated very little, partly because many politicians agreed with his view that the Constitution gave Congress only a small measure of power over the nation's economy (and essentially no power over anything else). It was also a time when federal judges—definitely including Supreme Court justices—were more than willing to strike down federal laws that, in the judges' view, exceeded that narrowly circumscribed constitutional authority. A few years before the decision in *Champion*, the justices had invalidated the federal income tax; a few years later, they overturned the federal government's ban on child labor.[18]

Why was federal gambling legislation enacted in this environment that seemed so unfriendly to it, and why was the legislation upheld by the courts? There are three answers. The first concerns a peculiar feature of American constitutional law: the power to regulate interstate commerce could be used to prohibit small slices—the portion that could be characterized as involving interstate commerce—of large vice markets. That is exactly what Congress did with its two lottery laws in the 1890s and again with prostitution in the Mann Act in 1910. Which leads to the second answer: A century ago, as today, the number of federal agents and prosecutors was small—far too small to tackle sizeable vice markets. Given the federal criminal justice system's small size, federal lawmakers knew that broad prohibitions would be enforced selectively, which made criminal prohibitions more politically attractive than they otherwise would have been. Federal criminal lawmaking was common in large part because it was cheap from the point of view of the politicians who defined federal crimes. The third answer concerns the character of American politics. Throughout our nation's history, contested moral issues have always moved from the state and local levels to national politics; such issues are not resolved locally, as McConnell's federalism argument suggests they should be. When resolving those issues, voters pay attention to moral principle, not just self-interest. In McConnell's example in the quoted passage above, a large fraction of the voters who want to see smoking banned would be displeased by the knowledge that some of their fellow citizens—including those in other jurisdictions—are lighting up.

Take these points in turn. Since the end of Reconstruction, the constitutional power "to regulate commerce with foreign nations, and among the several states, and with Indian tribes"[19] has been the chief source of congressional power to enact regulatory legislation. Most Progressive-Era legislation was based on the commerce power, as were the key pieces of the New Deal and the federal statutes regulating health, safety, and the environment. Antivice legislation like the federal lottery statutes and the Mann Act (which forbade interstate transportation with the intent to engage in illicit sex) fall within the same legal tradition. Politically, the most important feature of such laws may be their moralism—but legally, the crucial fact is that the vice markets they regulate are *markets*. Gambling is commerce, and some of that commerce takes place "among the several states." This simple fact made the federal law of gambling possible.

One more step was necessary to justify federal laws like the ones banning interstate lotteries and the so-called white slave traffic (the Mann Act was popularly known as the White Slave Traffic Act). When James Madison and his contemporaries wrote and ratified the Constitution, they probably intended that the commerce power would distinguish between lines of business that are and are not subject to federal power. The transportation of goods and people could be regulated; local manufacturing and mining operations could not. Pre-New Deal law drew many such lines.[20] But Madison and his colleagues did not anticipate statutes like the antilottery laws and the Mann Act. At the time those statutes were passed, the large majority of gambling transactions were local (this is less true in the age of Internet gambling). The same was and is true of the market for prostitution, the chief subject of the Mann Act. But a small slice of those markets—the transportation of lottery tickets printed in one jurisdiction and sold in another, the transportation of prostitutes or their customers from one state to another—crossed state borders. Could Congress ban that small slice—the "federal" part of the market—while leaving the rest to the states? The legally correct answer was far from obvious. In *Champion*, Fuller's dissent argued that regulatory power was indivisible: that if states had the power either to promote or to forbid lotteries (as they plainly did), the federal government could not interfere with that power by banning only a portion of the lottery market. Fuller's position was probably the conventional wisdom among lawyers of the time. But it lost: federal bans of small portions of large markets were deemed permissible in *Champion*, largely because the banned conduct was so morally problematic.[21]

This legal principle was crucial, for it permitted members of Congress to legislate in this area without preempting state legislation or local law enforcement. The federal lottery laws laid the foundation for the oddly designed federal criminal justice system. Instead of allocating some crimes to state law and others to federal law, the federal criminal code mostly covers state-law crimes with an interstate commerce element: some person or thing crossed a state border, or the crime victim ran an interstate business, or the crime itself affected interstate commerce in a significant way.[22] Robbery, extortion, fraud, racketeering, the possession or sale of illegal drugs—these are the staples of federal criminal litigation, and all are crimes under state law as well. Within the criminal justice system, the line between federal and state power is not drawn crime by crime, but case by case—usually based on the presence or absence of a tie to interstate commerce.

This feature of the system made federal criminal laws cheap from the perspective of the politicians who enacted them—the second reason gambling regulation went federal. In 1910, fifteen years after the second of the two federal lottery laws were enacted, the federal government accounted for a mere 3 percent of the nation's prison population: fewer than two thousand federal prisoners in all.[23] Federal criminal statutes like the lottery laws and the Mann Act were largely symbolic: there were few federal prosecutions, because there were few federal officials to bring them.[24] This fact made it easy to win support for federal criminal prohibitions and hard to mount opposition to them.

Which leads to the last and most important reason for the federal ban on interstate lotteries: the voters who supported the ban cared about the symbolism and the moral ideals behind the ban, not about their own material well-being. Moral principle motivated them, not personal economic interest. This is a long-standing theme in American politics. Since the rise of the slavery issue in the mid-nineteenth century, politicians seeking and holding federal office have been eager to take sides in the culture wars of the moment. A standard debate typically ensues. One side argues for tolerance and local control: live and let live; allow people in different parts of the country to resolve the relevant issue differently, according to their own preferences. The other side argues for a nationwide policy—often largely symbolic—because of the crucial nature of the moral interests at stake. Abraham Lincoln and Stephen Douglas made precisely those arguments as they battled for an Illinois Senate seat in 1858. Lincoln sought a clear national policy to put slavery on a path toward extinction; Douglas contended that North and South could have different policies, that what happened to blacks south of the Ohio River or west of the Mississippi was no business of Illinois voters. Douglas won that election, but Lincoln won the argument.

This argument has played out repeatedly over the past century and a half, usually with Lincoln's side winning the day. Slavery in the 1850s, gambling in the 1890s, prostitution in the 1910s, alcohol in the 1920s and early 1930s, abortion and gay rights in our own time—all these issues prompted large-scale disagreement; voters in different parts of the country reacted differently to them. According to the Madisonian theory of federalism, those issues ought to have been resolved locally. Douglas-style live-and-let-live arguments would maximize the number of voters living under rules they find congenial, as Judge McConnell correctly noted. But those arguments regularly lose in American politics; all the issues listed above were eventually governed, at least in part, by federal law. All were major issues in elections for federal office. Like Lincoln, many American voters—especially those who hold strong religious convictions—see such issues not as appropriate subjects for tradeoff and compromise but as matters of moral principle. One does not compromise with evil.

Ironically, the federal resolutions of these various issues usually *do* involve a large measure of compromise—but the compromise is hidden. The small number of federal agents and prosecutors means that federal bans on popular vices are rarely enforced in a consistent and systematic fashion. The vast majority of those who enjoy the relevant behavior will continue to do so without the interference of federal officials, even after a federal ban is enacted. The nature of the compromise is not severe rules in some places and lax rules in others; rather, the usual bargain on contested moral issues combines universally severe federal rules with lax federal enforcement. The federal lottery laws helped to establish that pattern.

Only twice in the last century and a half did federal politicians deviate from the pattern: during Reconstruction, when the federal government sought (briefly) to systematically enforce laws protecting the rights of ex-slaves in the South, and again during Prohibition, when federal officials tried and failed to stamp out the alcohol trade in the United States.[25] Both times, the side that sought aggressive enforcement lost—and paid a large political price for the defeat. Politicians noticed. That is why the unprincipled, under-the-table compromise between seemingly strong legal bans and weak or inconsistent enforcement survives in federal criminal law today. This compromise, in turn, makes federal criminal prohibitions all too tempting, both for politicians and for moralist voters.

The Survival of Gambling Prohibition after Alcohol Prohibition Collapsed

For the politicians and religious voters who had led the bandwagon for criminalizing vice, Repeal was the great chastening. In 1933, a mere thirteen years after its triumphant passage, Prohibition collapsed. Alcohol use was more widely tolerated than it had been before the legal ban. Criminalizing vice seemed to be a losing strategy. The passing from the scene of leading culture warriors like William Jennings Bryan served to accent the point: Bryan's death shortly after the Scopes trial in 1925 is often identified as the date when Protestant evangelicals turned away from politics.[26] Given these developments, the same political wave that ended Prohibition should have brought down the federal criminal law of gambling. Why didn't it?

One answer is that New Deal–era politics were more religious—more "Bryanite"—than they seem in retrospect. No one had replaced Bryan himself, but Populist-inflected religious themes lingered in American political discourse. In one of the most important economic speeches of his 1932 campaign, Franklin D. Roosevelt aligned himself in opposition to the "Ishmael or Insull whose hand is against every man's"—a reference that linked the bastard son of Abraham to the utility magnate Samuel Insull, whose spectacular collapse threatened the savings of ordinary investors who had bought his companies' bonds.[27] In his first inaugural address the following year, Roosevelt proclaimed that the "practices of the unscrupulous money changers stand indicted in the court of public opinion, rejected by the hearts and minds of men." Because they had "fled from their high seats in the temple of our civilization," he continued, "we may now restore that temple to the ancient truths."[28] The corporate and financial misconduct that Roosevelt denounced in such biblical terms bore an unmistakable resemblance to gambling and had long been analogized to gambling. For an administration committed to making the capital markets safe for ordinary investors by policing "corners" and other market manipulation, rolling back the federal laws against gambling would have seemed incongruous, and would have sent a contradictory message.

To put the point another way, the moralist politics that led to the federal lottery laws of the 1890s did not disappear after Repeal; rather, that politics migrated to other territory. Federal regulation of banking and the securities markets derived from the same moralist impulses, and were supported by the same voters, as the lottery bans.[29] The politics of gambling morphed for a time into the politics of financial regulation.

Something similar happened with respect to gambling itself— the kind gamblers engage in, not the kind stock traders do. The criminal law of gambling became, even more than it already was, an aspect of the law of business regulation. State laws grew more lenient: Nevada legalized casino gambling in 1931, and ten more states repealed at least some of their criminal prohibitions of the practice beginning in 1933. In a majority of the states that continued to criminalize the practice, enforcement all but ceased. This was natural: the federal government was the most aggressive regulator of business, not the states.

At the federal level, the lottery laws survived but were meaningless, either because few lottery tickets were shipped across state lines or because federal prosecutors no longer tried to find the ones that were. The chief federal gambling prohibition during the 1930s and 1940s came from the Federal Trade Commission, an agency charged with the job of regulating business in order to prevent unfair methods of competition or, as the FTC customarily calls them, unfair trade practices. During the Hoover Administration, the FTC ruled that selling goods through "games of chance" constituted such an unfair trade practice. The first case challenging that rule, *Federal Trade Comm'n v. R. F. Keppel & Bro.*,[30] involved the sale of so-called break and take candy. The packages, which sold for a penny, had less than a penny's worth of candy—but one of every thirty packages contained both candy and a penny. Other packages sometimes had prizes or tickets inside. These marketing devices were especially popular with children.

In *Keppel*, the candy manufacturer correctly noted that its marketing scheme involved no deception, and that competitors were free to adopt similar schemes in response. Consequently, the manufacturer argued, the scheme introduced no unfairness into the competitive process. The FTC did not disagree with the manufacturer's claims—rather, it defended the ban on moral grounds:[31] the banned conduct amounted to a lottery in disguise, and lotteries were contrary to public morals; worse, these lottery-like sales were often made to children. The Supreme Court upheld the ban unanimously, noting that the marketing practice in question "employs a device whereby the amount of the return [customers] receive from the expenditure of money is made to depend upon chance. Such devices have met with condemnation throughout the community."[32] The requisite "condemnation" was not economic; it was moral.

That moral condemnation was crucial to the outcome of the case. Sixteen months after *Keppel* was handed down, the Court issued another, more famous unanimous decision in *Schechter Poultry Corp. v. United States*.[33] *Schechter Poultry* invalidated the National Industrial Recovery Act, the New Deal legislation that authorized the writing of industry codes of conduct for the sale of a wide range of products bought and sold in interstate commerce. The government defended the NRA codes by relying, in part, on *Keppel*: just as the FTC had broad authority to define "unfair methods of competition," so the industry representatives who wrote the code for sale of poultry had similarly broad discretion for the same end. But the codes were very different, as the opinions in *Schechter Poultry* emphasized. The FTC banned "oppressive" or "fraudulent" or "abus[ive]" conduct (the language comes from Justice Cardozo's concurring opinion)—that is, it banned conduct that was morally wrong. The NRA codes banned morally neutral or even admirable conduct: in *Schechter Poultry*, the owners of a chicken slaughterhouse were convicted of ten misdemeanor counts for permitting buyers to select individual chickens for purchase, rather than selling the chickens in bulk as the governing NRA code required.[34]

Something similar happened in several other Court decisions invalidating New Deal legislation. The plaintiff in *Panama Refining Co. v. Ryan*[35] sued to enjoin prosecution for the "crime" of selling more oil than the relevant industry code allowed; the code was designed to limit supply and hence to prop up the price of oil. The defendant in *United States v. Butler*[36] was a cotton processor charged with a tax under the first Agricultural Adjustment Act; the real parties in interest were the cotton growers who were denied federal subsidies—in effect forcing them from the market—unless they limited the amount of cotton their farms produced. Chicken sellers were penalized for accommodating chicken buyers, sellers of oil were punished for selling too much oil, and cotton farmers for growing too much cotton: hardly the sort of immoral business practices that Populists like William Jennings Bryan and Progressives like Theodore Roosevelt had condemned. The gap between the collusive regulation of the NRA and the AAA, designed not to punish wrongdoing but to put more money in businessmen's pockets, and the moralist rhetoric used to justify that regulation had more than a little to do with the Supreme Court's initial hostility to the New Deal.[37]

No such gap appeared in the cases challenging the FTC's ban on lotteries and gambling-like marketing practices. Consequently, a federal judiciary that was eager to strike down innovative forms of business regulation found no difficulty enforcing this particular innovation. The FTC appears to have enforced its ban regularly and, so far as one can tell from the available materials, successfully. Moralist regulation of gambling survived, and survived at the federal level, both because it *was* moralist—the regulation's rationale rested on the moral condemnation of games of chance—and because it took the form of business regulation.

The Ineffectiveness of Federal Law Enforcement

Beginning in 1951, both the federal criminal law of gambling and the resources and energy devoted to enforcing it expanded. Tougher laws and tougher enforcement, taken together, sound like a recipe for law enforcement success. But the gambling laws of the 1950s and 1960s failed, and failed badly.

The core reason for the failure was indirection. Before the 1950s, the criminal law of gambling targeted gambling; after that date, the law targeted a particular class of gamblers: chiefly Mafia bosses who ran numbers rackets in cities across the country. The difference sounds small, even trivial—*of course* gambling prosecutions target gamblers; what else are prosecutors supposed to do? But this is more than semantics: there is a real and important difference between using criminal law to define crimes and using it to punish particular criminals. American criminal law began to shift its focus in the mid-twentieth century from the first purpose to the second. The consequences of this change have been enormous. The criminal law of gambling played a significant part in it.

The story starts with Estes Kefauver, one of the more interesting characters in the history of American politics. In 1950 Kefauver was in the second year of his first term in the United States Senate. He gained his seat by beating Tom Stewart, a two-term Tennessee senator who first won fame as the lead prosecutor in the Scopes trial.[38] In five terms in the House of Representatives, Kefauver's signature issue had been corporate misconduct; he sought more aggressive enforcement of the antitrust laws. But antitrust was not an issue on which to build a national political career in mid-twentieth-century America. So, early in his first term in the Senate, Kefauver persuaded the Democratic leadership to let him chair a committee investigating interstate gambling. Kefauver was given the job because it was thought that he would not make waves. Senate Republicans were eager to use the inquiry to examine corrupt urban Democratic machines; Kefauver's job was to head them off.[39]

He did not do his job. Kefauver mostly did what Republicans wanted, highlighting links between organized crime and big-city politicians and police officials, nearly all of them Democrats. But his chief focus was neither cops nor politicians. Rather, his committee hearings were America's first real look at the Mafia. Kefauver took the committee on the road, visiting fourteen cities and generating headlines wherever he went. His timing was good: television was coming into widespread use in America at that time, and the networks were scrambling to fill the airspace with programming. Kefauver's hearings were a godsend for the networks. The country watched, especially when the hearings moved to New York in March 1951. Kefauver drew more viewers than that year's World Series, and more than the Army-McCarthy hearings that brought down the Wisconsin senator three years later.[40]

The Kefauver committee drew two crucial links: one between illegal gambling and Mafia bosses like Frank Costello (head of the Genovese family in New York and the committee's star witness), and another between those Mafia bosses and the local politicians whose protection they needed and bought. Members of Congress were not eager to expand the criminal liability of fellow politicians, but they were happy to go after Mafia dons. In 1951, Congress criminalized the interstate shipment of a wide variety of gambling-related paraphernalia, including slot machines.[41] In 1961, in response to lobbying from Robert Kennedy's Justice Department, Congress added two more criminal prohibitions to the prosecutors' arsenal: a ban on gambling transactions using interstate phone lines and the Travel Act, which bars crossing a state line with the intent to violate state laws banning gambling, extortion, or blackmail.[42]

Until the 1980s—well after the passage of the Racketeer Influenced and Corrupt Organizations Act in 1970—these statutes were the chief legal means of attacking the Mafia, which became a major federal enforcement priority.[43] Since the laws in question were designed to make proof of guilt easy, nearly all federal prosecutions were successful. Yet these antigambling laws failed spectacularly: both the Mafia and illegal gambling thrived during these years.

To see why, consider the difference between the Mafia families that federal prosecutors targeted in the generation after World War II and the candy manufacturers and grocery stores the FTC targeted in the 1930s and 1940s. The latter were legitimate businesses that violated particular legal rules. The former were criminal enterprises; their very existence constituted a criminal conspiracy. Legal businesses form in order to share information and thereby reduce transaction costs. Criminal enterprises form in order to *hide* information—as a means of monitoring their members' silence and of shielding one another, and especially shielding the men at the top of the organization chart, from criminal punishment. Police and prosecutors have a limited array of tools for gathering the evidence that criminal enterprises seek to conceal. The FBI is constrained in its ability to tap phones and bug offices as it wishes. Under *Miranda* doctrine, a suspect savvy enough to use the magic words upon his arrest—"I want to see a lawyer"—cannot be questioned by the police. The upshot is that defendants, especially high-ranking ones, cannot be convicted without the testimony of other members of the organization. Punishing the men who ran major gambling enterprises required threatening their underlings not just with criminal liability (the foot soldiers who ran the numbers business were used to that), but with the kind of liability that leads to the severest possible sanctions. The law must overpunish the small fry in order to land the big fish.

This proposition became law enforcement conventional wisdom in the 1950s and 1960s and has remained so ever since. Over the course of the last half century, federal criminal law has become more and more focused on organized crime: Mafia families, drug-dealing gangs, terrorist cells. The standard approach in all these settings is the one first crafted in gambling cases: roll up the organization from the bottom. Line up the dominoes—the first one to fall fingers the next, who will turn on the one after that, and so on up the chain of command.

That strategy has three large problems. First, success is self-defeating. Even when the government manages to convict and punish mob chiefs like Costello, rivals are quick to take their positions. Criminal punishment becomes a weapon in criminals' turf wars. Second, the domino theory of criminal prosecution inevitably leads to perverse criminal punishment. Plea bargains in organized crime cases are designed not to obtain guilty pleas but to buy information: the government trades immunity or charging concessions for tips and testimony. Those who receive the most favorable bargains are those who have the most information to sell—and the greatest willingness to sell it. The reverse is also true: those members of the criminal enterprise who have little information to sell or who refuse to sell what they have, often out of loyalty to their friends and lovers (girlfriends of drug dealers regularly serve long prison terms for failing to testify against their boyfriends), receive the *least* favorable bargains. Big fish can usually hand over still bigger fish, and so escape punishment themselves. Less prominent—and less culpable—defendants have less leverage, and so may face worse punishment.

The third problem is the most serious. Over time, the domino tactic makes criminal law strategic. Lawmakers come to see criminal statutes not as legal rules but as prosecutors' tools, and prosecutors come to see those statutes solely as means of achieving desired litigation outcomes. A speech by then-Attorney General John Ashcroft captures the sensibility:

> Attorney General [Robert] Kennedy made no apologies for using all of the available resources in the law to disrupt and dismantle organized crime networks. Very often, prosecutors were aggressive, using obscure statutes to arrest and detain suspected mobsters. One racketeer and his father were indicted for lying on a federal home loan application. A former gunman for the Capone mob was brought to court on a violation of the Migratory Bird Act. Agents found 563 game birds in his freezer—a mere 539 birds over the limit. . . .
>
> Robert Kennedy's Justice Department, it is said, would arrest mobsters for "spitting on the sidewalk" if it would help in the battle against organized crime. It has been and will be the policy of this Department of Justice to use the same aggressive arrest and detention tactics in the war on terror.[44]

Ashcroft's comments did not come as news to the members of Congress who drafted the Migratory Bird Act or the ban on fraudulent loan applications. (Nor, one suspects, did Robert Kennedy's.) When federal prosecutors use criminal prohibitions strategically, members of Congress write them strategically. The consequence is more broadly defined crimes with more severe punishments attached—and greater levels of prosecutorial discretion.

These strategically defined crimes and punishments probably do more to harm deterrence than to strengthen it. As Tom Tyler's scholarship has shown, people obey legal rules (when they do so) not primarily because they fear punishment, but because they find both the rules and the system that enforces them legitimate.[45]

Justice systems seem legitimate to individuals tempted to commit crimes when those systems treat criminal defendants fairly, distinguish between more and less culpable conduct, and offer those charged with crime the opportunity to make reasonable arguments in their defense. The federal justice system that Kennedy and Ashcroft described—and helped to create—meets none of those conditions. Criminal laws designed to produce easy convictions may accomplish their goal, but only at the cost of the law's moral credibility.

This loss of credibility probably contributed to the law's failure to contain illegal gambling markets in the mid-twentieth century. But the phenomenon is broader than that. The same features that characterized gambling cases in the 1960s—strategically defined criminal prohibitions, excessive punishments attached to minor offenses, and efforts to "roll up" criminal organizations from the bottom—also characterized drug law and drug cases in the 1980s and 1990s. The chief difference is that all the relevant practices grew more extreme: drug laws are designed to make criminal convictions automatic, and the punishments attached to those laws are more draconian than even prosecutors wish to impose. (Prosecutors use those draconian laws chiefly to extract information; the worst penalties are imposed on those unfortunate defendants who refuse to bargain with the government.) The results have been no better. In the past thirty years, the drug prisoner population has grown tenfold, to nearly half a million inmates. The number of drug offenders has grown as well. Strategic lawmaking and law enforcement do not work—a lesson that might have been learned from the failed efforts to shut down Mafia-run gambling operations in the 1950s and 1960s.

The Strange Collapse of Gambling Prohibition

In the last thirty years, moralist politics and gambling regulation seem to have moved in oddly divergent directions: the former revived while the latter collapsed. After the 1930s, Protestant evangelicals put their cultural weapons down, and (mostly) retired from the moral campaigns of the past. But beginning in the 1970s, moralism returned with a vengeance, beginning with the advent of the pro-life movement and later extending to opposition to gay rights and a range of other issues. The words "religious right" entered American political discourse—and so did the words "moral majority."[46] One might have expected the resurgence in politically active evangelicalism to inject new life into the campaign against gambling and other vices.

Some of that resurgent moralism may have affected the battle against illegal drugs, which has been far more punitive than similar legal battles in the past. But the broad antivice campaigns of the late nineteenth and early twentieth centuries did not reappear in the late twentieth century. The rise of the Christian right coincided with the rise of a massive market in Internet pornography and a marked coarsening of the culture of public entertainment. Legalized gambling has become ubiquitous at the state level, and with few exceptions (really only one: Internet gambling), federal lawmakers and law enforcers have done nothing to interfere with it. Indeed, they have lent proponents a helping hand by exempting state-sponsored lotteries from federal antilottery laws.[47] Why, in an age of religion-based moralist politics, is there so little interest in stamping out gambling?

If Christian politics seems different in this "great awakening" than in the last, perhaps that is because Christian voters have different theological beliefs—which imply a different moral agenda—than the beliefs and agenda to which William Jennings Bryan's followers adhered a century ago. Bryan's version of theologically conservative Protestantism was both optimistic and paternalistic. The optimism was associated with the eschatological perspective known as postmillennialism, which holds that Christ will return at the end of a thousand-year period in which goodness abounds and the church is supreme.[48] The Civil War and Reconstruction seemed to reinforce this optimism, suggesting that the federal government could be a powerful force for cultural reform.

This last factor, the belief in the utility of law and government as agents of reform, was not limited to those who supported emancipation and radical Reconstruction. The two sides in the generation-long struggle over union, slavery, and civil rights differed about much, but they held one conviction in common: the belief that law and government mattered enormously. The Civil War was prompted by a debate about the legal status of slavery in American territories in which almost no slaves lived. Legal creeds, not practical consequences, dominated the argument. Likewise, Reconstruction was an often-murderous debate about law: about federalism and democracy, civil rights and citizenship. No generation in American history—not even the generation that survived the Articles of Confederation and wrote and ratified the Constitution—engaged so passionately in contests of legal principle. They did this because they believed in law, because they believed that it stood for large ideals and could achieve large goals.

The generation after Reconstruction saw a revolution of its own as the spread of industry and factories turned Jefferson's simple agrarian nation into a major industrial power. It was natural that, when the battle over black civil rights ended (with a victory by the side that lost the war), American Christians, like the rest of their countrymen, turned their attention to economic issues. For Bryan and for many nineteenth-century evangelicals, the goal of reform was to protect ordinary Americans from the depredations of the more powerful, from both corporate robber barons and the purveyors of vice. In Bryan's view and in the view of his millions of Protestant followers, power meant *economic* power; it was closely connected to the world of business and finance. Gambling was a natural target for these cultural warriors.

Today's warriors are different: the evangelical Protestant moralism of the late twentieth century is neither optimistic nor paternalistic. Evangelical Protestants invariably characterize their activism as defensive, as a battle to preserve traditional values in the face of cultural erosion.[49] (The "majority" in "moral majority" is ironic: the energy in religious right politics stems in large part from the belief that religious voters are an embattled *minority*.) In theological terms, today's evangelicals are more likely than their counterparts in the past to hold to the premillennial view—the view that Christ will return before the thousand-year reign of the church, at a time when society remains deeply infected by sin.[50] In addition to its cultural pessimism, the new moralism does not aim to protect ordinary Americans against exploitation—especially not against economic exploitation. Were it otherwise, opposition to state lotteries would figure much more prominently in the movement, and campaigns against gay rights less so. Instead of paternalism, the new Protestant evangelical moralism is more concerned with justice—or, from the perspective of its opponents, with judgment or judgmentalism. The abortion debate is a good illustration: while the pro-life movement has employed paternalist-sounding arguments—for example, the emphasis on protecting vulnerable unborn babies—its core objective is to stop a perceived injustice. The goal is to save lives, not to save the culture.

One mark of the difference between this version of politicized evangelicalism and the last is Christian voters' stance on economic issues. Economic exploitation plays nearly no role at all in the politics of the Christian right. Even ministries that focus on the urban poor seem more concerned with relieving individuals' distress—with saving lives—than with the larger economic forces that contribute to that distress. An administration and a Congress supported by the Christian right enacted the Bankruptcy Abuse Prevention and Consumer Protection Act of 2005, which made it harder for bankrupt debtors to have their debts discharged. The contrast with the past could not be starker. In his first run for the presidency, the core plank in William Jennings Bryan's political platform was inflation as a means of debtor relief—putting more silver currency in circulation so that indebted farmers could pay creditors cheaper dollars than they borrowed. Bryan opposed the legislation that became the Bankruptcy Act of 1898 for the same reason: he feared it might jeopardize the homes of financially precarious farmers. One reason today's evangelicals are less invested in battling gambling and state lotteries is that they are less invested in battling economic oppression more generally.

Nor is this generation of evangelicals notably optimistic about the power of law and government to effect large-scale social reform. This is one reason why Christian conservatives have found it so easy to ally themselves with libertarian free-marketeers. Legal optimism is associated with the Left; social conservatives are more inclined to embrace the legal and political pessimism of Richard John Neuhaus or Robert Bork.

This pessimism feeds the defining goal of late twentieth-century evangelicals: saving lives. The pro-life movement was born of crisis and defeat, not progress. Abortion was already becoming a common means of birth control when the Supreme Court legalized the practice in *Roe v. Wade*.[51] To those who believed that fetuses had the moral status of born children, the consequence was mass slaughter: by the late 1970s, more than one million abortions were performed each year in the United States. This was a radical change from even a single generation earlier. In this respect, the pro-life movement was quite different from the antivice movements of the late nineteenth century or the abolitionist movement that led to slavery's end. Those earlier political movements sought to right wrongs that had long existed. Participants in them believed in social progress; they assumed that society was growing morally healthier as well as more prosperous, and this assumption fueled their political movements. To pro-lifers in the post-*Roe* generation, society seemed in a state of permanent decay. Moral decline, not social betterment, seemed the norm.

A historical coincidence helped to shape this sensibility. The 1960s and 1970s—the same decades during which the abortion rate rose steeply—saw another kind of homicide rate reach record levels. The murder rate in the nation as a whole rose two-and-a-half times in those twenty years, a larger increase than in any comparable period in the past. In cities outside the South, the rise in violence was steeper still. Murders tripled in Chicago, quintupled in New York and Los Angeles, and multiplied seven times in Detroit. Nothing like that had ever happened before. To make matters worse, the 1960s and early 1970s saw not only steeply rising crime (the increases were not limited to homicide) but also steeply falling prison populations. Illinois' imprisonment rate—the number of prisoners per unit population—fell by one third; Michigan's and New York's, by 40 percent; California's, by nearly half. Nothing like *that* had ever happened before either.[52]

Nationwide, the decline in imprisonment hit its trough in 1972;[53] *Roe* was handed down in January 1973. To conservative evangelicals, it seemed that America's legal system had lost the capacity to punish even the worst crime—homicide—and no longer protected even the most basic human right: the right to live. The moralism of the pro-life movement can fairly be seen as an effort to recapture that capacity.

The tide of murderous violence that engulfed American cities also helps explain the staggeringly punitive approach to drug crime after 1970. Drug crimes were punished far more severely than similar vices were punished in earlier generations. But then, those other vices were not punished as means of punishing other, more violent crimes. Drug charges, by contrast, were—and still are—regularly used as proxies for violent crime charges that prosecutors find difficult to prove. If the drug war has been fought harder and with many more casualties than earlier vice wars, that may be because, to the lawmakers and law enforcers who have done the fighting, it has seemed more like a real war: the kind that yields body bags.[54]

Whatever its other faults, gambling produces fewer casualties than the drug war. When violent crime rates skyrocketed in the 1960s, the Mafia seemed less frightening than before: voters feared getting mugged, not dealing with the local numbers racket (which usually offered better payout rates than today's state-run lotteries). In a violent age, gambling and illegal lotteries seemed like relatively harmless vices—far less harmful than drugs, given the violence of urban drug markets.

Together, the shift in the orientation of evangelical Protestants and the growing violence of American city streets dissipated much of the energy behind gambling prohibition. At the same time, the fiscal benefits of state-sponsored gambling made legalization of casinos and lotteries politically irresistible.[55] Although the payout on state lotteries is abysmally low and the money disproportionately comes from the poor and lower middle classes, state politicians have cleverly linked the lotteries to popular middle-class initiatives such as education funding and subsidies for the elderly.[56] Protestant evangelicals are still much more likely to disapprove of gambling than other Americans, and they have led the opposition to new lotteries and casinos. But gambling no longer ranks near the top of evangelical concerns. With evangelicals having thrown up their hands, and with the declining usefulness of gambling prohibitions to federal law enforcers, gambling has become a familiar presence in nearly every state.

Lessons

Drawing lessons from history is always risky, and it is made riskier when the history is as sweeping and sketchy as are the discussions above. Nevertheless, the post–Civil War history of the criminal law of gambling seems to suggest three main lessons.

The first has to do with the link between the legal regulation of gambling and other forms of economic regulation. The tendency today is to lump vice with traditional crimes or with morally charged topics like abortion. Historically and politically, vice laws had more in common with the Sherman Act and the Pure Food and Drug Law—early Progressive-Era legislation regulating business—than with laws on those other topics. Christians believed in legal regulation of vice markets because they believed in regulating markets more generally. And both voters and politicians supported using criminal law as a regulatory tool because, in the late nineteenth and early twentieth centuries, criminal law seemed to be the most natural means for the government to regulate businesses of all sorts.

Despite their similar origins, business regulation and vice prohibition evolved in different ways—thanks in part to *civil* regulation. Lawsuits by customers or competitors of alleged antitrust violators were not the key focus of political debate when the Sherman Act was passed, but those lawsuits have proved more important—and much more frequent—than criminal antitrust prosecutions. Similar stories could be told about a range of different regulatory statutes that govern businesses. Vice laws are different. Nearly always, they consist solely of criminal prohibitions and, sometimes, government-prosecuted civil fines and forfeitures. The government's monopoly on criminal law enforcement permits the kind of enforcement tactics seen in the battles against Mafia-run gambling enterprises in the 1960s and against drug-dealing gangs in the 1980s and 1990s. These enforcement tactics, in turn, invite the strategic lawmaking that has so characterized the war on drugs. Similar developments were far less common in securities or antitrust law because those areas have been shaped more by private litigation.

The treatment of Internet gambling may be powerfully affected by this historical link between vice and criminal law—not civil regulation and litigation. Over the past decade, Internet gambling has been the target of a sustained campaign aimed at criminal prohibition. But enforcing criminal bans against Internet-based gambling seems like an impossible task since gambling Web sites can be established in countries that do not prohibit them and since such Web sites are difficult to block in legal systems that protect free speech as aggressively as ours does.[57] As one commentator wrote in a dismissive review of Congress' recent effort to stymie Internet gambling, the "temptation for good citizens to ignore a stupid law is encouraged when it is unenforceable. In this, the attempt to ban Internet gambling is exemplary."[58] A different regulatory strategy—more like the licensing used by the Food and Drug Administration than like the federal criminal prohibition of lotteries—could prove more effective at addressing the harms most often associated with Internet gambling, such as addictive behavior and the risk of fraud. If qualifying Internet gambling sites were given licenses, they could be monitored by regulators and customers could police fraud and other misconduct through private litigation. One of the chief obstacles to this approach and others like it is the ease and familiarity of criminal prohibitions. In this area, at least, Congress tends to do what it has done in the recent past. Path dependency is powerful, regulatory innovation rare. In short, vice law arose from origins similar to antitrust and securities law. But while those regulatory fields soon transcended their criminal justice origins, the law of vice never has.

The second lesson concerns the tendency of vice prohibitions to evolve in different directions than their supporters expect or intend. The politicians who enacted the antilottery laws of the 1890s would likely have found the Federal Trade Commission's ban on lottery-style marketing strategies surprising. Both those earlier politicians and FTC regulators would have found Kefauver's crusade against Mafia-run gambling astonishing. Needless to say, none of these government officials anticipated the massive punishments imposed on drug defendants during the last three decades—even though the punishments were, in large measure, the consequence of those earlier regulatory developments. The FTC's regulation seemed to follow from the merger of the late nineteenth century's moral condemnation of lotteries and the New Deal's emphasis on centralized regulation of interstate businesses. Estes Kefauver's and Robert Kennedy's focus on the Mafia seemed a natural next step in a society in which the business enterprises that ran most gambling operations were *criminal* enterprises, not legal manufacturers and chain stores. The strategic use of laws like the Travel Act to nail mobsters was likewise natural, a logical response to the difficulty of proving criminal bosses like Frank Costello guilty of ordinary crimes.[59] Once the notion of using some criminal statutes to enforce others was well established, it seemed natural to use easily proved drug offenses as a means of punishing harder-to-prove violent crimes—to punish violent drug dealers not for their own drug crimes but for the violence of their drug markets.

No one planned this progression. Politicians and prosecutors alike used the tools that seemed most readily available to respond to the challenges they faced. The character of these tools in turn depended on the nature of the choices made by the previous generation's politicians and prosecutors. The end products of these unplanned, path-dependent choices may be—and in twenty-first-century America, almost certainly are—quite different than voters or government officials would choose were they to design the relevant laws and procedures today, from scratch. Criminal justice is an evolutionary process, and in the political realm, such processes are not necessarily adaptive: progress is not the inevitable consequence of this particular form of evolution. The legal regulation of gambling needs a new design, a different path. Criminal law enforcement has failed. A more classically civil regulatory strategy akin to the regulation of *legal* drugs (perhaps backed up by controls over the payment systems that cover debts incurred on the Internet) might do better. It could hardly do worse.

The third lesson follows from the second. Moral principles do not translate neatly into effective legal prohibitions. Lotteries may be bad public policy, but criminal bans may be even worse policy. Law is a less powerful tool than Christians of past generations, and perhaps many in this generation as well, suspect. The recent history of abortion suggests as much. No one knows precisely how many illegal abortions were performed in the United States before *Roe v. Wade*, but based on conventional estimates, the number of abortions mushroomed throughout the 1960s—when abortion was a crime in all fifty states. Since 1980, the abortion rate has fallen nearly 30 percent. Abortion grew more frequent when it was criminalized, and more rare when it was constitutionally protected.

The lesson applies to more than the usual list of vices and morals offenses. The 1970s and 1980s saw criminal punishment for violent crime rise steeply—while violent crime itself continued to rise.[60] Rates of criminal violence fell after 1990 when American cities hired more police officers, not so that more offenders could be arrested and punished—arrest rates fell, and arrests of African Americans fell even more—but so would-be offenders could be persuaded to make different and better choices.[61] Softer, less coercive forms of policing have proved more effective in fighting crime than the severe criminal punishments to which Americans have become accustomed—just as crisis pregnancy centers have proved more effective means of battling abortion than pro-life legal arguments and political campaigns. Legal compulsion is a clumsier weapon than it at first appears. Often it backfires, harming the side that most wishes to use it. The pro-life movement may be better off for having lost most of its legal battles over the past thirty-five years. The great misfortune of the movement to stop gambling in the United States may be that it had too much legal success too soon.

12

Playing and Praying
What's Luck Got to Do with It?

Dwayne Eugène Carpenter

While it remains true that significant numbers of Americans—
notably conservative and evangelical Protestants—view any form
of gambling with suspicion, if not outright hostility (Seventh-
day Adventists, Mormons, and Presbyterians, for example, have
issued unequivocal condemnations of any form of gambling), for
most church and synagogue goers, gambling is a relatively harmless pastime. Some forms of play are overtly tolerated and even
sanctioned by religious bodies, as evidenced by the traditional
Catholic bingo games—a third of the existing 280 licensees in
Massachusetts are affiliated with the Catholic Church, though
even here change is in the wind.[1] On the one hand, various con-
gregations in Massachusetts worry that encroaching casinos
will siphon off already record-low revenues derived from church
bingo; on the other, risqué bingo games recently operating in
San Francisco and run by drag queens—the so-called Sisters of
Perpetual Indulgence, whose motto is "Go and sin some more"—
have given a bad name to Thursday night gaming at the local
parish. On a more encouraging note for aficionados of entertainment sponsored by religious organizations, bingo appears to have
a pedagogical future in the thirty-plus games of Catholic bingo

designed for the youth market, including "Catholic Mass Bingo," "Marian Bingo," "Stations of the Cross Bingo," "Angel Bingo," and, I'm happy to report, "L'Chaim Bingo." I happily played "Bibleopoly" on the Sabbath, which, in my mother's mind, was an effective antidote to the venom of secularism.

While gambling in the form of state lotteries is now ubiquitous, perhaps less well known is the fact that, historically, both Catholic and Jewish religious authorities actively encouraged gambling on religious holidays. As the *Libro de las Tahurerías (Treatise on Casino Legislation)*, the most important medieval legal code devoted exclusively to gambling, declares: "Christmas Eve and Christmas Day are times when people should be free to gamble, since on that night Our Lord Jesus Christ was born, and it is a holy day on which everyone should rejoice in his home."[2] For most people today, it seems more in keeping with traditional family values for everyone to gather around the Christmas tree and open presents rather than getting together for a hot game of blackjack or no-limit poker. In the Ashkenazi world, Jewish children continue to celebrate Chanukkah with endless rounds of dreidel spinning in hopes of winning chocolate gelt while their elders engage in a serious card game related to blackjack known as *kvitlech* (literally "little notes"), but also referred to by some of the Orthodox, and certainly with a sly wink, as the *klein shass* (a small Talmud) or *tehillim* (a book of Psalms). I have heard these terms in the homes of pious Jews in Brooklyn, New York. Then, as now, the rabbis were not amused. The putative origin of gambling during the eight days of Chanukkah harks back to the legend that Jews would play cards to mask their study of the Torah, which had been forbidden by the second-century-BCE Syrian-Greek monarch Antiochus IV Epiphanes.

But, as William Galston clearly indicates in chapter 9, the rabbis had graver concerns toward gambling than the use of impious nomenclature by episodic players. Issues relating to gambling, although infrequent in the Talmud, are common in medieval *takkanot*, communal ordinances, and responsa, in which authoritative rabbis provide written replies to questions of Jewish law. Nevertheless, the initial and definitive halakhic position on gambling appears in Talmudic tractate Sanhedrin 24b, which discusses those categories of men disqualified from serving as witnesses, including the *mesaheq bequbiya*, the dicer, although the term was later applied to all inveterate gamblers.[3] Notably, the Gemara and subsequent commentators distinguished between the professional and the occasional gambler, the former disqualified for his single-minded devotion to lucre, the latter allowed to testify in legal proceedings because of his merely temporary beguilement and because he has another livelihood.[4]

Jewish authorities subsequently occupied themselves with questions of playing ball on the Sabbath, with one influential rabbi, Moshe Provençal, protesting not against the profanation of the Sabbath (earlier the destruction of the Second Temple had also been attributed solely to playing ball) but against the wagering that inevitably accompanied the activity.[5] And in this regard, Italian rabbis were especially critical of Jews who bet on the outcome of chess or tennis games played on the Sabbath, even if the ostensibly pious players proposed to delay resolution of their financial affairs until after sundown.[6] Sephardic and Ashkenazi religious authorities alike inveighed against gamblers who, in a piteous effort to curb their gambling propensities, took upon themselves vows, replete with penalties, to desist from playing. One desperate soul, for instance, swore never again to eat fruits or vegetables if he returned to the gaming table, another specified that his right arm should be amputated were he to throw dice, while yet another swore to abstain from sexual relations with his wife.[7] We do not know what she thought of the vow, but in another case a man addicted to gambling actually wagered his wife, whom he promptly lost to a non-Jewish player. For her part, she was delighted with the new arrangement, even insisting on a divorce.[8] Perhaps the most colorful figure among the panoply of Jewish gamblers is the late sixteenth- and early seventeenth-century polymath, Yehudah Aryeh mi-Modena—better known as Leone da Modena—who, despite composing a treatise on the evils of gambling at the age of thirteen, was a passionate devotee of cards and dice his entire long life.[9] After one especially hapless session at the gaming table, he was led to lament that among the five catastrophes that had befallen the Jews in the Jewish month of Av, which included the destruction of both the First and Second Temples and the razing of Jerusalem, could now be added the calamity of his having lost five hundred ducats, a small fortune.[10]

Kathryn Tanner has provided us in chapter 10 with an analysis of the gamble of faith as proposed by Blaise Pascal. But Pascal was not alone in relating wagers to religion. The thirteenth-century *Cantigas de Santa Maria* (*Songs of Holy Mary*), authored by Alfonso X, the Learned, relates the story of two accomplished dice players, one possessing great wealth and the other whose only possession was an inherited church.[11] One day the two were playing a game known as *mayores*, the winner being determined by the highest roll of three dice. (Incidentally, in iconography involving gambling, including crucifixion scenes of the soldiers casting lots for Jesus' garments, there are almost always three dice portrayed.) In any event, the rich gambler wagers a large sum of money; his opponent wagers the church. The latter declares, "If it be God's will that you win the game, [then] take this church."[12] The rich man, clearly a practiced player, rolls three sixes, the maximum point value of the dice. The poor man, seeing his words apparently taken seriously, now entrusts all to the Virgin, addressing her tersely: "Win the game and take the church."[13] With trembling hand, he casts the dice on the table. Once again the three dice come up sixes, but, against all hope and defying all odds, the Virgin intervenes to cause one of the dice to split in half, revealing a one *and* a six, thus providing a winning nineteen points. Alfonso's conclusion, "In this way Holy Mary won a church for herself," implies that when the Virgin, the wizard of odds, controls the dice, the end may justify the means.[14]

Given humankind's embrace of both piety and perversion, we should not be surprised to discover that any game can be rendered sacred or profane. Perhaps the best example is chess, which, despite its secular origins and bellicose pieces, gradually became Christianized—note the presence of the bishop, which originally was an elephant. Indeed, the Spanish word today to refer to the piece we call the bishop is *alfil*, from Arabic "the elephant." Chess was also allegorized, especially in the fourteenth and fifteenth centuries, to represent different social classes and their duties. For their part, some Renaissance Jews had silver chess pieces used exclusively on Shabbat, and which acquired near-ritual value. To the inherently conflictive, and thereby divisive, nature of games—nearly all must have a winner and a loser—may be added the additional penalty of economic loss. Indeed, the transformation of gaming into gambling depends on the possibility of winning and losing some material good. Evidence for this assertion lies in the increased use of the term "casino gaming" by its proponents for what is in reality casino gambling. Nobody goes to a casino just to play games. No less an authority than the dice-splitting Virgin in the aforementioned *Songs of Holy Mary* declared gambling to be a perversion of God-given games, and she herself is said to be most displeased with revenue obtained in this fashion—unless, apparently, she does the winning.[15]

According to a number of medieval narratives, hard-core gamblers—men and women alike—hurl stones or shoot arrows at images of the Virgin and Child in disgruntled response to losses at dice. Nearly all such impudent players come to tragic ends, but it is noteworthy that it is blasphemy, not gambling, that is punished. Absent are complaints of idleness, absentee fathers, dissolute youth, squandered resources, and the like. Chapters 9, 10, and 11 have noted in various ways how concerns about gambling reflect time and place and religion. Returning for a moment to medieval Iberia, we see that gambling per se is rarely condemned; in fact, it is carefully legislated. The *Treatise on Casino Legislation*, for example, provides detailed legislation on everything from crooked dice to the legality of using human beings as pawns to the jurisdiction of clergy (the state has authority over the Church in the case of gambling priests) to the annoying problems of breaking gaming tables with your head or swallowing dice. The major moral concern, however, is with blasphemy, which is roundly criticized and severely punished by fines, lashes, or excision of the offending tongue.[16]

Skeel and Stuntz made two especially trenchant conclusions: first, that gambling regulation, and vice laws in general, are inherently linked to economic regulation; and second, that vice prohibitions tend to evolve in unpredictable directions. As we will see, what was true for twentieth-century America was also true for thirteenth-century Spain. Although not his crowning achievement, Alfonso the Learned's compilation of gambling legislation was the most significant treatise on this subject in medieval jurisprudence. But it did not appear out of nowhere, nor was it an obvious subject for its author. Alfonso is justifiably remembered for promulgating, around 1265, the monumental *Siete Partidas*, a seven-part legal code based on Roman, canonical, and customary law, in which he denounced gambling. Three years later he completely forbade gambling, but then reversed his ruling in 1272 by granting a charter of privilege to the city of Murcia for a royally regulated casino. By 1276 Alfonso had realized that games are serious business, and the new patron of the ludic arts began to take his business seriously, as evidenced by the appearance that year of the aforementioned *Treatise on Casino Legislation*.[17] Alfonso's decriminalization of gambling spanned two decades, and whatever pious concerns he may have entertained at the outset of his reign were eclipsed by the economic temptations that neither he nor subsequent politicians could resist. This radical shift in legislative posture resulting from the generation of revenue for the royal fisc is best illustrated by his decree prohibiting the creation of gambling establishments outside the royally licensed casinos. The punishment for foolhardy entrepreneurs who disregarded the royal mandate was a mind-bending, body-flaying two hundred lashes, with the lash dipped in water after each blow to increase its efficacy.[18] Alfonso, the self-styled troubadour of the Virgin Mary, was also a ruthless, monopolistic protector of his own gambling gains.

Kathryn Tanner remarked in chapter 10 how the commonality of Christianity and gambling is established by the religious nature of gambling, or at least by the implicit existential questions underlying it. Are events merely chance happenings? Does God, in fact, play dice with the universe? Is there another divine player controlling God, as Borges suggested in one of his sonnets entitled "Ajedrez II" ("Chess II")?[19] And although not moving in this direction, Tanner noted how casting lots, an exercise in putatively random selection, is an effort to obtain information from an all-too-secretive God. The Hebrew Scriptures, and to a lesser degree the New Testament, refer on dozens of occasions to this practice. Recall, for example, Jonah, who was identified by the drawing of lots as the cause of life-threatening turbulence at sea, and Matthias, who was selected by a combination of prayer and lots to replace the traitorous Judas as the new twelfth apostle. For her part, and probably not by chance, Tanner chose to focus on the wager of faith and its potentially big payoff. I do wonder, however, whether a person of unswerving belief can really be said to be taking a chance on faith. If you *know* you are going to win, do you, in fact, believe you are taking a risk?

One area of psychological-literary-religious research that remains largely unexplored by scholars but which seems to me especially suggestive is the shared praxis of credulous gamblers and faithful believers. Both groups, for example, have remarkably similar codified gestures and rituals. Think of the clasped hands and upraised eyes that characterize both the pious supplicant in church and the equally earnest petitioner in the casino. Both parties know from whence cometh their strength. And given the uncertainties, existential and otherwise, that characterize our lives and games of chance alike, these acts are repeated with single-minded devotion. Consider, as well, the ubiquitous appearance of religious articles and gambling talismans. Clasping a rosary, kissing a relic, or placing a picture of one's children on the poker table not only constitute acts of devotion but also remind the divine of our precarious situation and assuage our human fears. As one not particularly pious, but eminently pragmatic, friend of mine remarked when I asked why, whenever she entered or left her house, she always kissed the mezuzah, the container with the Hebrew text from Deuteronomy attached to the door frame: "Look, it can't hurt. If this bit of piety turns out to be nonsense, then I haven't lost anything, but if it does make a difference, then I made the right choice." Pascalian sentiments with a Jewish twist.

Of course, people who take all these precautions to ensure their safety and prosperity are understandably upset when adversity nevertheless befalls them. And just as they had earlier invoked the divine for their pious and impious requests alike, they now curse him using religious language. To the devout parishioner and gambler, pious acts followed by divinely occasioned or permitted disaster seem patently unfair, and the tongue that earlier invoked God's blessing now damns him for breach of contract. Swearing, too, is part and parcel of the player and the prayer. Finally, it is perhaps worth recalling that both religion and gambling require faith, but, as we all know, the house always wins.

GAMBLING IN AMERICAN CULTURE

13

Beyond Pathology
The Cultural Meanings of Gambling

T. J. Jackson Lears

In contemporary public discourse, idioms of morality and health often overlap and merge. Critics and clinicians who are reluctant to resort to the language of evil remain perfectly comfortable with the language of pathology. Certainly this is true of debate about gambling. In recent decades, as legalized casinos have spread, critics of gambling have resorted to the familiar rhetoric of moral decline. Walter Cronkite, for example, complains that "a nation once built on a work ethic embraces the belief that it's possible to get something for nothing."[1] But many others have turned to clinical categories of disapproval. The school of social work at my own university has recently set up a Center for Gambling Studies that (in spite of its capacious title) seems focused almost exclusively on "problem gambling."[2] Gamblers may no longer be sinners but they can still be deviants, especially if the gambler in question can be identified as an addict, a helpless slave to habit whose dependency poses a public affront to the dominant ethos of self-control and disciplined achievement. In the minds of public pathologists (whether they use the language of sickness or sin), gambling remains grouped with other vices: alcoholism, drug abuse, and prostitution.

This habit of mind obscures the larger cultural meanings of gambling; I aim to recover and explore them. Though it may be difficult to discern in the contemporary casino, gambling is enmeshed in a web of connections to ancient rituals addressing profound human needs and purposes—the casting of lots, the conjuring of luck. As the psychoanalyst Theodor Reik once said, every roll of the dice is "a question addressed to destiny."[3] There are powerful links between the gambler's dice and soothsayer's bones, between the gambler's longing for luck and the believer's longing for grace—which, as a free gift of God, has always been a kind of spiritual luck. The impulse to gamble arises from the inescapable uncertainty at the heart of human experience. It cannot be separated from our larger fascination with luck, from our desire to see chance as a possibility rather than a problem, from our longing to give up the quest to control outcomes and simply play.

Nor can it be separated from our economic life. The recognition scene that inspired me to start thinking about these matters occurred in November 1994. The Republicans had just taken over Congress under the leadership of Newt Gingrich, promising an end to welfare giveaways and a new era of personal responsibility for one's economic fate: the air was filled with calls for us all to pull ourselves up by our bootstraps, to become self-made men and women. I was standing on a subway platform in lower Manhattan amid this metaphorical din, waiting to buy a token, when I noticed an even longer line snaking around mine. It was the line for the lottery machine, filled with all colors, shapes, and sizes of people—though not, presumably, Newt Gingrich's kind of people—hard workers, maybe, but fully aware that hard work alone was not the key to success. Sometimes (these people knew) you had to get lucky, to catch a break.

I started to suspect that the lottery players were not only forking over a hope-maintenance tax to the state of New York but also paying homage to an older deity, Fortuna. I began to realize there could be a distinctive gambler's worldview, one that was at odds with what amounts to our official creed of success (whether we articulate it in religious, moral, or clinical terms)—the faith that we can master fate through force of will, and that rewards will match merits in this world as well as the next. This outlook, which has long pervaded the professional and business classes, is explicitly hostile to gambling. Consider the stance of the former *New York Times* columnist William Safire, one of the bitterest critics of legalized gambling. In the 1990s, Safire wrote numerous op-ed pieces against the spread of casinos. Gambling, he said, was based on the lie that you can get something for nothing, but "the truth is that nothing is for nothing. Hard work, talent, merit will win you something. Reliance on luck, playing the sucker, will make you a loser all your life."[4] One could hardly ask for a more predictable assertion of conventional wisdom. In contemporary American culture, no one is more contemptible than the "loser," and nothing is more terrifying than the prospect of becoming one "all your life." Winners, from Safire's view, did not leave things to chance; they set out to control outcomes, through forethought and discipline. And yet the lottery players kept lining up for tickets. I sensed that there was more to this topic than Safire could imagine.

Cultures of Chance and Control

Tracking the gambler's worldview in America led me to uncover its broader context, an American culture of chance that paralleled and occasionally overlapped the official culture of control. The culture of chance was (and is) not merely a culture of losers, at least not in Safire's sense. It is a culture more at ease with randomness and irrationality, more doubtful that diligence is the only path to success, than our dominant culture of control. The culture of chance, in short, is more willing to grant *play* the seriousness it deserves. Conflict between these two constellations of values—clustering around chance and control—illuminates two fundamentally different accounts of American character. One narrative puts the big gamble at the center of American life: from the earliest English settlements at Jamestown and Massachusetts Bay, risky ventures in real estate (and other less palpable commodities) have powered the progress of a fluid, mobile democracy. The speculative confidence man is the hero of this tale—the man (almost always he is male) with his eye on the main chance rather than the moral imperative. The other narrative exalts a different sort of hero—a disciplined, self-made man whose success comes through careful cultivation of (implicitly Protestant) virtues in cooperation with a providential plan. The first account

implies a contingent universe where luck matters and acknowledges that net worth may have nothing to do with moral worth.
The second assumes a coherent universe where earthly rewards
match ethical merits and suggests that Providence has ordered
this world as well as the next. The self-made man has been a
more influential culture hero, but the confidence man survives as
his shadowy double.

Conflict between these two cultural tendencies often exists
within the individual as well. Most of us know that we cannot
control all outcomes, that success is a mix of luck and skill. We
want to cultivate smart luck rather than dumb luck—the sort
of luck that works in poker or blackjack rather than roulette or
lotteries or slot machines. The question, of course, is when does
play turn to work? When does the apparent freedom of leaving
things to chance become a compulsion? (The people standing in
the lottery line did not look like they were having all that much
fun.) None of the cultural meanings of gambling, even the most
exalted, absolve the practice of its power to draw people into a
vortex of addiction.

Still the cultural approach does raise a serious conceptual and
definitional question: to what extent is the very notion of addictive gambling a cultural construction, a continuation in clinical
idioms of a familiar moral critique that attacks gambling as a loss
of self-control? A *New York Times* headline from the mid-1990s
revealed this rhetorical default setting: *Fervid Debate Over
Gambling: Disease or Moral Weakness?*[5] Here I raise the specter
that haunts cultural studies, the specter of sweeping, antiscien-
tific relativism. This perspective has provoked understandable
irritation among scientists themselves, such as Alan Sokal, the
physicist at New York University who parodied the pretensions
of cultural studies in the journal *Social Text* and who invited its
editors to step out the window of his twentieth-floor office, if
they believed the law of gravity was culturally constructed.

But the concept of addiction cannot be equated with the law
of gravity. Indeed, the history of narcotics control is notoriously
bound up with thoroughly unscientific fears, anxieties, and preju-
dices. The association of drug use with racial, ethnic, or cultural
minorities has made it easier to introduce draconian measures
against practices like smoking marijuana, which may not be

entirely harmless but hardly justifies imprisonment. It is possible
to use the idea that addiction is culturally constructed without
denying its biological dimension. Just as nature can be culturally
constructed, culture can be naturally constructed. Nature and
culture interact; it is time to abandon the demented dualism that
insists we have to choose one or the other as a prime mover.

As Marc Potenza demonstrates in chapter 7, neuroscientists
have developed powerful tools for investigating the biological
traces left by pathological gambling. But the gambler's worldview
is not reducible to a brain scan. Granted its biological dimension,
the concept of the addicted gambler unquestionably remains a
cultural construction. It is a product of a perspective that associ-
ates immorality with "impaired impulse control" (in Potenza's
phrase)—a product of what I am calling a culture of control.[6]
The tendency to pathologize gambling arose from the conver-
gence of liberal individualist and evangelical Protestant creeds
in the nineteenth century, with their horror of dependency and
lost self-command; it acquired new legitimacy from scientific and
managerial idioms in the twentieth century, with their emphasis
on rationality, productivity, and peak performance.

To argue that the notion of the addicted gambler is in part
a cultural construction is not to deny the destructive effects
of problem gambling. But it is to underscore the need for caution in crafting public policies that aim to regulate recreational
risk-taking. The cultural history of gambling, its deep roots in
traditions of sortilege and its long entanglement with speculative
enterprise, should remind us that attempts to keep gamblers on
the straight and narrow path are fraught with contradictions and
hemmed in by irony, as Skeel and Stuntz reveal in their illuminat-
ing account of the "war on gambling" in the post–World War II
United States in chapter 11.[7]

One of the principal ironies pervades contemporary public discourse about gambling, where one finds an odd double
standard: addicted gamblers only appear in certain contexts
historically associated with vice; they never appear in the arenas of market exchange, where gambling in the form of speculative trading has in recent decades been sanctioned and even
celebrated. Consider an icon of the 1990s bull market, the day
trader—sitting entranced at his computer, dodging bullets, riding

momentum, selling out just in time (he hoped), and feeling drawn inexorably to the frisson of danger. His solitary obsessive existence strikingly paralleled the compulsive gambler's, yet the day trader remained untainted by the language of pathology. He was engaged, however feverishly, in what previous generations might have called speculation and recent free market ideologues have redefined as investment.

For much of American history, critics of speculative capitalism likened it to gambling and capitalism's defenders denied any resemblance. The long bull market made those denials seem more plausible, despite occasional tremors that provoked renewed comparisons between stock exchanges and casinos. On the whole, as Steve Fraser demonstrates in his cultural history of Wall Street, the manipulative strategies of stock trading—once derided as diabolical by public moralists—acquired unprecedented legitimacy and luster in our era of unregulated capital markets. At least until the crash of 2008, speculation was sanitized as investment, and we never hear about anyone being addicted to investment. The gambler has often been deployed by apologists for capitalism to make the speculator look legitimate, but never more so than during the quarter century that began with the accession of Reagan.[8]

The questions surrounding gambling transcend money; they raise fundamental philosophical issues. For those who hope to conjure luck, chance is a source of knowledge and a portal of possibility—not, as in a culture of control, a demon to be denied or a problem to be solved. Of course, neither of these perspectives comes in pure form, but their fundamental assumptions are profoundly at odds, and easily recognizable even today. Despite the recent proliferation of casinos, our official values continue to be shaped profoundly by the culture of control as the custodians of national virtue promote a paradoxical blend of freedom and fate.

The paradox runs something like this: success for nations, as for individuals, has been decreed by an external force beyond their control—call it Providence or Progress, depending on whether one's taste runs to a moral or managerial idiom; our task is to cooperate with our destiny, to unite free choice and necessity. The departure from traditional Christianity is striking; in this secular formulation, our destiny is "manifest" in this world, not hidden and mysterious in God's mind. So Bill Gates, Tom Friedman, and other prophets lecture us on our responsibility to embrace the future being prepared for us by technological innovation and the globalization of capitalism. And George Bush lectures us on our redeemer nation's duty to perform its providentially scripted role as savior of the world. We must all discipline ourselves to succeed at what we have to do anyway. Despite its implicit determinism, the culture of control insists on the power of personal will and resorts frequently to a rhetoric of mastery.[9]

Evidence for the culture of chance must be located in places less exalted than the Oval Office or the op-ed pages of *The New York Times*. Yet its fetishes, rituals, beliefs, and gods are everywhere. The exotic and elaborate motifs of decoration on slot machines suggest that they have always served as fetish objects for an industrial (or postindustrial) age. The woman who buys a dream book at the grocery store checkout line consults it to interpret her unconscious life (and to learn what number to play); she is participating in an ancient tradition of divination. The man who buys a lottery ticket pays homage to Fortuna; he is trying to catch a break, acknowledging his incapacity to control fate despite public moralists' insistence he should be able to.

Even among gamblers, the desire for something for nothing is more than mere laziness and greed; it often involves a longing to transcend the realm of money worship altogether. In his *Memoir of a Gambler* (1979), the playwright Jack Richardson acknowledged that the gambler (or at least the one he knew best) was engaged in a theodicy—an effort to glimpse some coherence in the cosmos. To the "old voices" in his head demanding that he justify his life as a gambler, Richardson replied: "I want to know . . . I want finally to know . . . Whether I am to have any grace in this life."[10] The Episcopal Reverend Jeff Black of Kansas City succinctly catches the connection between the gambler's longing for luck and the believer's desire for grace: "The whole hope of a human being is that somehow, in spite of the things I've done wrong, there will be an episode when grace and fate shower down on me and an unearned blessing will come to me—that I'll be the one."[11]

Of course, this does not happen often. Losing is more common than winning. And loss, too, is a crucial component of the culture of chance. The gambler's acceptance of loss poses a fundamental challenge to conventional notions of responsibility and choice. According to the fictional female gambler in Peter Carey's novel *Oscar and Lucinda*, there was always the chance that "one could experience that lovely, lightheaded feeling of loss, the knowledge that one had abandoned one more brick from the foundation of one's fortune, that one's purse was quite, quite empty . . . and no matter what panic and remorse all this would produce on the morrow, one had in these moments of loss such an immense feeling of relief—there was no responsibility, no choice."[12] In a society such as ours, where responsibility and choice are exalted, where capital accumulation is a duty and cash a sacred cow, what could be more subversive than the readiness to reduce money to a mere counter in a game? The gambler's willingness to throw it all away with a shrug of the shoulders could embody a challenge, implicit but powerful, to the modern utopian fantasy of the systematically productive life. The idea that loss is not only inescapable but perhaps even liberating implies a rejection of the success mythology that declares (with coach Vince Lombardi): "Winning is the only thing." It also redefines success in ways that resonate powerfully with traditional notions of grace.

What is sorely missing from American public debate is a sense, historical and spiritual, of the connection between gambling and grace. Kathryn Tanner's essay in chapter 10 marks a major step toward remedying that defect.[13] This essay aims at a similar end, first with a historical overview of the national conversation about the cultural meanings of gambling and luck, then with a turn toward recent developments in American history since the 1970s. The last three decades have been characterized by the deregulation of markets in capital and labor, the decline of job security, and the rise of a contingent labor market. These developments reconfigured the cultural meanings of gambling, luck, and success. The spread of legalized lotteries and casinos suggests that gambling, like economic risk-taking in general, became more openly condoned, even encouraged. Yet at the same time, gambling continues to exude an aura of failure, frustration, and loss. Even in hard times, the paunchy slots players in Atlantic City do not measure up to the young whippets of Wall Street.

Conjurers, Gamblers, and Their Critics

The origins of the culture of chance can be traced to the dim past, to the persons who first cast stones or shells to read in their chance array the will of the cosmos—or maybe to conjure its power in their own or their clients' behalf. A vast and growing literature in history and anthropology has combed Africa, North America, and the Caribbean, documenting the connections between runes, cards, and dice and revealing the diviner, the conjurer, and the gambler to be brothers under the skin. Despite the superficial variety of counters they used, they were all playing in the same game. At ritual moments, all sorts of odd materials (glass beads, chicken feathers, graveyard dirt, seashells, dice) could acquire a sacred power: the power to decipher destiny or to conjure *mana*, or luck.[14]

In British North America, conjuring traditions arose from American Indian, Elizabethan English, and West African sources. All included the common form of divination called sortilege, the practice of casting lots to discover the will of the universe (or of God). In 1705, a Dutch trader observed that in what is now Ghana, the natives consulted their gods "by a sort of wild nuts, which they pretend to take up by guess and let fall again."[15] In contemporary Nigeria, the Yoruba throw cola nuts and cowrie shells on the ground to seek solutions to problems ranging from the cosmic to the local. The universality of such practices is enough to give warrant to some notion of a collective unconscious. Indeed, Jung himself wrote the introduction to the English translation of the *I Ching*, the ancient Chinese system of divination that postulated specific arrangements of randomly chosen coins corresponding to specific verses memorized by disciplined diviners.[16]

Even the most educated British American colonists in North America remained attached to divinatory traditions as well as a fondness of gambling. But some regions were fonder than others. Consider the regional conflict, long commemorated in literature and lore, between the New England Puritan and the Southern cavalier. Despite its formulaic quality, the opposition had an empirical basis. In eighteenth-century Tidewater Virginia, gambling and manhood were twinned. Among the planter class, legendary high rollers vindicated their masculine honor, earned the

respect of their peers, and reasserted their elite credentials by
gambling for high stakes on horse races and cockfights; the lower
sorts were legally barred from gambling (though one suspects
that prohibition was more honored in the breach than the observance). Still there was more going on here than status rivalry
and display: gambling was part of a broad and diffuse culture
of conjuring and divination, and its implications were cosmic as
well merely social. As David Hackett Fischer observes: "A gentleman's dice were like the soothsayer's bones from which they had
descended—a clue to the cosmos, and a token of each individual's place in it."[17] Dice, fighting cocks, playing cards, and fast
horses—all were instruments of luck and magical extensions of
the self. They embodied status rivalry but also carried a supernatural charge.

As the great cultural historian Johan Huizinga recognized
years ago, luck can acquire "a sacred significance: the fall of the
dice may signify and determine divine workings: by it we may
move the gods as effectively as by any other form of conquest."[18]
New England Puritans knew a rival religion when they saw one;
for them, gambling was a theological menace—not just a frivolous
waste of time but a ritual grappling with the unknowable. The
gambler sought divine favor through conjuring rather than calculating, interpreting rather than accumulating, playing rather than
working. By casting lots for mere recreation, gamblers appealed
to God's will in trivial matters, distracting him from serious concerns and flirting with nothing less than blasphemy.[19]

By the early 1800s, evangelical reformers began to attack gambling for moral rather than theological reasons. In the writings
of Mason Locke Weems, creator of the fable regarding George
Washington and the cherry tree, we have entered the recognizably
modern age. Gamblers have become wastrels rather than blas-
phemers. Weems told cautionary tales of gamblers who refused
to toil, pissed away their patrimony, courted public scorn, and
committed suicide. The fate of the gambler was (at worst) self-
murder or (at best) economic failure. Weems challenged readers
to show him "one gambler who's lived and died rich." The challenge showed the spread of new utilitarian values in the guise
of traditional Christianity. To Weems and his contemporaries,
money was becoming a measurement of moral worth.[20]

The evangelical culture of control married morality and the marketplace. Gambling was like alcohol or adultery, an enemy to the self-controlled individual and to the middle-class family. Men turned to it for relaxation but then, warned one critic, "led on as it were by an *ignis fatuus*, they soon immerse their families in distress and themselves in ruin."[21] It was a familiar argument— an apparently innocuous amusement becomes a slippery slope. But note the mystery of the gambler's motive. There is something ineffable or magical—an *ignis fatuus*—about the appeal of cards and dice.[22]

Evangelical critics of the early 1800s were the first to develop the language of addiction. They emphasized that the loss of self-control and the development of dependency were forms of slavery to one's passion. In the literature of evangelical moral reform, portraits of the gambler paralleled portraits of drunkards and masturbators. All were pathetic dreamers, idlers, anti-selves in the grip of fantasies and compulsions they could not control. Through the middle and later nineteenth century, reformers and gamblers fought pitched battles in eastern cities, southern towns and western settlements. The crusade against gambling blended with the broader evangelical movement to stamp out traditional male forms of recreation—drinking, whoring, and blood sports. In the reform imagination, gambling was simply another vice to be extirpated in the name of purifying the body politic.

But the "sporting crowd" kept surfacing on the margins of respectability. California gold fields and Mississippi riverboats created scenes that occasionally resembled Frederick Jackson Turner's all-male vision of frontier democracy. Classes—even races—forgot their social differences when they sat down to play cards. On the river, eastern and northern businessmen cast off bourgeois restraints to mix it up with vagabonds. As the English actor Joseph Cowell put it, "there [on the river] *Jack was as good as his master.*"[23] Of course it was not paradise: cheaters were omnipresent, plotting to bilk the unwary. But the true gambler insisted on the distinction between sharpers and sportsmen. The sharper was a mere greedy conniver, but the sportsman was willing to play and lose gracefully; losing, indeed, could be more important to him than winning. Like the "big man" among Southern planters (or the Mohegan chief), he affirmed his stature by displaying nobility *in extremis*—and by giving things away. Vestiges of a gift economy hovered about the edges of the gaming table.

Yet gamblers' rituals also linked them to the broader culture of capitalism. Opponents of gambling embodied the Protestant ethos of plodding self-improvement that Weber associated with rational capitalism. But rational capitalism was not the only game in town. Indeed, gamblers and their critics represented two sides of the same capitalist coin: discipline and risk. Much of the American economy's spectacular growth was financed by risk takers—boomers and plungers whose schemes acquired legitimacy only in retrospect. "When speculation proves successful, however wild it may have appeared in the beginning, it is looked upon as an excellent thing, and is commended as *enterprise*," the Jacksonian economist Richard Hildreth wrote in 1840, "it is only when unsuccessful that it furnishes occasion for ridicule and complaint, and is stigmatized as a *bubble* and a *humbug*."[24]

A few years earlier, Alexis de Tocqueville had aptly characterized American commerce as "a vast lottery." Risk-taking was obsessive; every American (man) had his eye on the main chance. "Those who live in the midst of democratic fluctuations have always before their eyes the image of chance; and they end by liking all undertakings in which chance plays a part,"[25] Tocqueville wrote. Entrepreneurs as well as gamblers could be besotted by an *ignis fatuus*. Individuals undertook business "not only for the sake of the profit it holds out to them, but for the love of the constant excitement occasioned by that pursuit." Amid constant fluctuations of fortune, Tocqueville concluded, the life of an American businessman "passed like a game of chance."[26]

It was impossible to discount luck in this roiling sea of uncertainty. Ambitious men discovered (and imagined) endless opportunities to cash in on unexpected swerves in the market value of land, wheat, cotton, oil, or other more ethereal commodities. Mere diligence was not enough to grasp the brass ring. Even Horatio Alger knew luck was as important as pluck in the ascent from rags to respectability. But other more discerning observers glimpsed an additional, crucial component of business success: the capacity to create convincing narratives that would persuade patrons, clients, and investors to join or back a shaky scheme. This reinforced the ever-present possibility of deception.

Protestant moralists celebrated sincerity, plain speech, the trust inspired by a frank and manly countenance—all (along with hard work) were essential features of self-made manhood, and all were rooted in reaction against the "universal mistrust" pervading market society. The idea of social transparency created some ontological coherence in a society swarming with imposters—the society Melville envisioned aboard a Mississippi riverboat in *The Confidence Man* (1857). Unlike most moralists, Melville found deception to be universal and nearly inescapable. But many more Americans took comfort from the ideal of the self-made man, whose frank and manly countenance exorcised the specter of the confidence man. In the desire for ontological security amid the misleading surfaces of market society, one can see the psychological roots of the culture of control. It was reassuring to believe that success was somehow produced by virtuous conduct rather than merely by the play of chance.

In this welter of contradictory impulses, the gambler became a complex cultural icon. He embodied both chance and control, both sides of capitalist success. He was the plunger, the cool risk taker but also—if he cheated—he was something else again: the confidence man or sharper who refused to *play*, who aimed to control outcomes rather than leaving things to chance as a true sportsman would. The confidence man remained the shadowy double of the self-made man in American success literature, the clever manipulator of surface effects whose favorite trick was to present himself as a hard-working, virtuous, self-made man. Benjamin Franklin was the progenitor of this trick (in his *Autobiography*); P. T. Barnum perfected it. Titling his autobiography *Struggles and Triumphs*, Barnum, a showman committed to the arts of deception, wrapped himself in the mantle of disciplined achievement. This included disdain for gambling and the faith in luck that sustained it. Barnum's *Dollars and Sense; or, How to Get On* (1890) presented as an emblem of luck a ridiculous cartoon devil surrounded by cards and dice with the caption "there is no such thing in the world as luck" (implying, of course, that there was no such thing as the devil, either).[27] The Reverend Henry Ward Beecher delivered himself of similar views in lectures reprinted throughout the second half of the nineteenth century. "I never knew an early-rising, hard-working, prudent man, careful of earnings and strictly honest, who complained of bad luck,"[28] Beecher wrote. From the perspective of the culture of control, luck had no existence apart from wistful projections of the unsuccessful.

The gambler epitomized these projections. Whether he played honestly or cheated, he was a stench in the nostrils of success mythologists. He was troubling because he was disturbingly similar to a certain type of businessman; he seemed ritually to reenact the risk-taking at the core of business enterprise—and in the process, to suggest that risk-taking capitalists had something in common with professional gamblers (as indeed they did). So nineteenth-century moralists undertook the task that their successors are still working at today: separating good gambling from bad gambling, investment from mere speculation. But by 1900, the strains in the Victorian moral synthesis were beginning to show. The economic environment was changing; new idioms and strategies of control were emerging.

Managing Chance

The growth of monopoly power represented an effort to stabilize the chaotic lurches of the laissez-faire economy. Monopoly was epitomized by John D. Rockefeller Sr., who took the risk out of a risky business (oil) and aimed to make profits predictable. This was a managerial reworking of the culture of control, but Rockefeller—a devout Baptist—displayed much of the old moralism as well. A believer in Providence, he was convinced that he was an instrument of God, a mere steward of the wealth he disbursed through systematic philanthropy. He disdained gambling, but critics thought him little more than a cheating confidence man, ruthlessly squeezing out competitors and bribing legislatures wholesale. As the journalist Ida Tarbell wrote in 1906: "Mr. Rockefeller has systematically played with loaded dice, and it is doubtful if there has been a time since 1872 when he has run a race with a competitor and started fair."[29]

Despite the dominance of monopolists like Rockefeller, in the early twentieth century it was still possible to see (as Tocqueville had done) the Great Game of Capitalism as a romantic adventure, and the pervasiveness of chance and luck as essential to that romance. In The Pit (1903), Frank Norris wrote of his protagonist

Curtis Jadwin, a daring trader in commodity futures: "In the air about him he seemed to feel an influence, a sudden new element, the presence of a new force. It was Luck, the great power, the great goddess, and all at once it had stooped from out the invisible and just over his head passed swiftly in a rush of wings."[30] The celebration of luck paralleled the celebration of regenerative risk-taking in turn-of-the-century American culture. As the economy became dominated by large corporations, opportunities for entrepreneurship contracted and more men became part of an emerging white collar salariat. The professional-managerial class idealized risk as it settled into routine.

What was equally interesting about the turn of the century years was the emergence of a new breed of reformers who called themselves "Progressives." They recognized that Luck was not only a goddess with glittering wings but also a malignant, inescapable force for ill. Luck could be bad as well as good—a simple insight, but largely absent from the literature of self-help. Progressives rejected spurious notions of natural law in the business world. They were struck instead by the pervasiveness of chance. In William Dean Howells' *The World of Chance*, the book publisher, Brandreth, says that "there are no laws of business. There is nothing but chances, and no amount of wisdom can forecast them or control them."[31]

The Progressives disliked gambling, but less because of what it did to the individual gambler than what it seemed to symbolize about American economic life: the hegemony of accident. In a chaotic laissez-faire economy, huge swaths of the population were left unprotected from flux in market conditions, not to mention the accidents of their own birth. Progressive reformers knew that chance was inescapable. They wanted to tame it, to insulate workers from suffering caused by circumstances beyond their control—the mysterious rise and fall of commodity prices, the collapse of overcapitalized companies, the unpredictable layoffs and calamitous injuries that afflicted the industrial workplace.[32]

The greatest achievement of the Progressives was that they began the movement beyond the mythology of self-made manhood and individual autonomy. In the Progressives' pursuit of what they called "the civic idea," we can see the origins of the welfare state, which began to acquire recognizable outlines during the New Deal—workmen's compensation, Aid to Families with Dependent Children, Social Security. In the emergence of the New Deal "Brains Trust," one can see the culture of control deployed for humane purposes—the creation of an (American-style) welfare state rooted both in the effort to minimize the impact of bad luck on workers' lives and also in the broader recognition that public interest could not be left entirely to the chance-ridden activities of an unregulated economy. As John Maynard Keynes put the matter in 1936: "When the capital development of a country becomes a by-product of the activities of a casino, the job is likely to be ill-done."[33] Seldom has the argument for regulating capital markets been more succinctly stated. The New Deal was a realization, in some sense, of Progressive aims—to manage economic change for humane purposes as well as for the purpose of promoting efficiency.

It is possible to see American public life during the first two-thirds of the twentieth century as the halting, uneven emergence of a managerial consensus, ultimately consolidated in the post–World War II decades. This business-government partnership moved forward under an ideology that New Left historians once derided as "corporate liberalism." (It looks a lot better these days.) In hard times, the managerial consensus promoted a collectivization of success, redefining it from singular striving to fitting in—as Dale Carnegie did in that classic Depression text, *How to Win Friends and Influence People* (1936). It also promoted a collectivization of luck—or at least of bad luck. The welfare state depended on a recognition that bad luck was universal and unavoidable, and that mutuality and community were indispensable salves for the abrasions of accident. In an increasingly organized society, it was more difficult to mobilize old maxims about individual willpower and the mastery of fate, though of course those maxims still stalked about the cultural landscape like superannuated relatives (waiting to be reanimated in the Reagan era).

The well-managed society of mid-century years had little place for luck, at least in its official values. Luck was something to be managed out of existence. Risk-taking was a relic of the 1920s bull market. Wall Street was an abode of white shoe bankers and establishment wise men, not plungers recklessly courting the glittering goddess of Luck. Even childhood was a time for caution, as the television cowboy Roy Rogers affirmed in the self-canceling advice that concluded his weekly show: "Be brave, but don't take chances."

The decades from the 1910s to the 1970s were also the period when legitimacy for casino gambling hit a low ebb. It was illegal almost everywhere except for Las Vegas. Antigambling laws were enforced more systematically and found broader public support than they had in the nineteenth century. Under the impact of Progressive reform, police departments became less pervasively and flagrantly corrupt; gambling, in the popular imagination, became one of the "rackets" operated by the suspiciously swarthy operatives of "organized crime." (Even crime was more systematic under the managerial consensus.)

Since the mid-century culture of control was more secular and managerial then moralistic, the image of the gambler changed in the prescriptive literature. An emerging clinical idiom stigmatized gambling as a syndrome rather than a sin; this was in line with the developing therapeutic orientation that defined health as "adjustment." Psychoanalysis became an adjustment psychology. The psychoanalyst Edward Bergler's *The Psychology of Gambling*, which went through several editions from 1936 to 1958, typified this transformation. The impulse to gamble, he claimed, could be traced to the desire described by Dostoevsky's fictional gambler: *"to challenge Fate."*[34] Bergler reduced this wish to its allegedly familial origins: "We have only to substitute, for fate, the child's typical picture of its parents and we have in a nutshell the gambler's psychic situation." The psychodynamics of gambling, from this view, were all too simple: "The main cog in the mechanism of gambling," according to Bergler, was "the unconscious wish to lose as a penalty for masochistically tinged aggression against parental authority."[35] The gambler was not a romantic risk taker, but a neurotic loser.

Female gamblers had an especially hard row to hoe as they became the focus for male distrust of women taking risks in public. A 1949 film, *The Lady Gambles*, revealed how conventional therapeutic wisdom could surface in mass entertainment, pathologizing gambling and equating stereotypical gender roles with notions of normality. A young couple, played by Barbara

Stanwyck and Robert Preston, is honeymooning in Las Vegas; she gambles compulsively. Divorce looms until the truth is unearthed by the husband with the help of a wise psychiatrist. The truth is that the young wife blames herself for her mother's death in childbirth. Losing at gambling is a way to expiate her guilt—a fantasy her unmarried and suspiciously mannish sister encourages. Discovering the truth allows the wife to break the cycle of self-punishment and reaffirm her domestic role. Here, as elsewhere, psychiatry defined gambling as a neurotic escape from the responsibilities of mature adulthood.

But if maturity was a euphemism for conformity, the prescription became more problematic. Gamblers' playfulness might be a refreshing alternative to an overly managed life. One finds this possibility in the fiction of Damon Runyon, who created the most enduring image of the twentieth-century gambler as a social type. Despite their wise-guy mannerisms, Runyon's gamblers displayed many traditional sporting traits. For starters, they never ratted on a friend. Like Arnold Rothstein, who survived in the hospital for two days after he was shot at the Park Central Hotel but refused to name his assassin, they "died game"—as Runyon praised Rothstein for doing.[36]

They also rarely died rich, though they may have lived well. This was usually due to their insouciant disregard for saving money. They never refused help to a tapped-out friend or passed up a bet at long odds. One of Runyon's characters, a horseplayer named Regret, was modeled on Abba Dabba Berman. Runyon was less interested in Berman's ability to rig the numbers than in his propensity to lose at the track despite occasional big wins. (Regret was the name of the Kentucky Derby winner in 1915.) Although Dutch Schulz paid him $10,000 a week for his service to the numbers racket, Berman died in possession of $87.12. Surrounded by gamblers like Berman, and given himself to losing big at the track, Runyon concluded that "All Horseplayers Die Broke."[37]

In its emphasis on circulation rather than accumulation and on the creation of authority through giving, the moral economy of the gamblers in Runyonland recalled that of the nineteenth-century sporting crowd on the Mississippi or of the eighteenth-century Virginia planters. All resembled the preindustrial gift economies described by anthropologists and cultural historians. The acceptance of chance as a source of potential beneficence, a gift from the gods, involved an implicit rejection of the linear march toward perfection enshrined by the culture of control. In a sense, Runyon's gamblers inhabited an eternal present, epitomized by his use of the historical present tense—"So I says to this guy, I says . . . "—a usage inspired by the gamblers' own, which Runyon faithfully transcribed. Runyonland was a world elsewhere, where gambling was a way of killing time.

The gambler's attraction to loss, even to self-destruction, was part of the aura of danger that made gambling sublime. But there was more than a titillating frisson at work in gambling's appeal: the figure of "the loser" became an oddly powerful specter in a society that deified winning and denied defeat. Incurably prodigal, the gambler refused to hoard money; instead he kept "throwing it away," seeking a kind of grace through what the theologian Paul Tillich (in a 1955 sermon) called "holy waste." As Tillich said, "Without the abundance of the heart nothing great can happen"—and without "accepting the waste of an uncalculated surrender" or "wasting ourselves beyond the limits of law and rationality" we forfeit that abundance of heart.[38]

The sporting crowd's ethic of fortune melded with a strain of Christianity that celebrated reckless generosity as a means of grace. Few theologians expressed that subversive version of Christianity more eloquently than an author who called himself Harlem Pete in a dream book published in Philadelphia in 1949. "If you want to be rich, Give! If you want to be poor, Grasp! If you want abundance, Scatter! If you want to be needy, Hoard!" he wrote.[39] This was a worldview profoundly at odds with the managerial culture of control. It also sounded suspiciously like the teachings of Jesus. The question was: how could that ethic of generosity be sustained (assuming it ever existed) into the dog-eat-dog years of the late twentieth century?

The Resurgence of Risk

Bull-market euphoria obscured the experience of the less affluent two-thirds of the population—the part whose income declined or stagnated during the 1980s and 1990s. By the end of the century, their lives were more vulnerable to hazard than most Americans'

had been for several decades. Secure jobs with benefits disappeared as corporations cut labor costs by turning to temporary
and part-time workers. An injury on the job, an unexpected lay-
off, a catastrophic illness—all these disasters loomed larger. As
the welfare state shrank, so did middle class.

The emerging business model demanded a contingent labor
force, one that could be moved, molded, assembled, and dispersed in accordance with managers' constantly changing priorities. Workers who could be fired at any moment through no fault
of their own could hardly be expected to cultivate the familiar
Protestant ethic of diligence in one's calling and loyalty to one's
employer. The disappearance of job security made merely staying in harness seem like a chump's game; the unpredictability of
work and the rewards associated with it made many people's lives
resemble "a series of random events," as the sociologist Richard
Sennett observed.[40] This fundamental shift in everyday experience, away from the (comparative) security of the post–World
War II decades and toward the insecurity of a deregulated economy, may well have created a population more receptive to the
allure of casino gambling—a market for the business of chance.
At the same time, the resurgence of risk in everyday life paralleled
a seismic change in public policy. Throughout the country, free
market ideologues and right-wing pseudo-populists organized an
antitax crusade, encouraging popular suspicion of government
and making it harder than ever for states and municipalities to
raise necessary revenues. Desperate for cash, political leaders
turned to state lotteries, creating regressive hope-maintenance
taxes paid primarily by the poor and working class.[41]

Legalized casinos were more complicated than the lottery.
They revealed the destructive psychological appeal of the games
themselves, the mysterious and powerful attraction that led critics to warn of addiction. Anecdotal evidence ranged from the
horrific to the ridiculous—young children left in cars in freezing
weather for ten to twelve hours while their parents posed questions to destiny, gamblers urinating in their drink cups so as not
to leave a hot slot machine. The value of the diagnosis of addiction was that it focused on the frisson—the rush of excitement,
the *ignis fatuus*—that kept gamblers coming back.

Video poker was especially seductive. "Sitting at that [video poker] machine was the only time I was happy," said Rose Hosty, a Louisiana mother of eight and owner of a Sno-cone shop, interviewed in 1998. "I didn't have to be a wife, a lover, or a mommy. It was like I went into a trance."[42] Other addicted gamblers told therapists "they feel smarter, sexier, even taller" while they're playing. Feelings of intense experience may be related to the sublime blend of pleasure and danger, or the fleeting sense of immersion in pure possibility, that gambling conveys—especially to people enmeshed in the tedium of routine work for most of the rest of their lives.

Still, gambling remains more than a titillating escape from boredom. It can still ritually enact a philosophical alternative to dominant managerial ideals of control and accumulation. It can still constitute a worldview with ethical and even religious significance. The key to that significance is the gambler's disregard of money—the sacred coin of the realm.

Contemporary gamblers, like their predecessors in the past, are well positioned to challenge the central dogma of our time—the idea that money is the fundamental gauge of human worth. As David Thompson writes: "Great gamblers have seen the grim absurdities in capital and its accumulation. They know money is merely a game (like 10,000 on the Dow), and they insist on being playful with it. There is ease and even transcendence" in this playfulness. Las Vegas, says Thomson, is "that rare thing: a city built in the spirit that knows its days are numbered. That's the eerie spirit of its profound casualness. The house itself knows it is only there by the grace of God."[43] Leaving aside the major, far-reaching problems created by gambling, it is still possible to isolate the fundamentals of the gamblers' worldview at its most exalted: an emphasis on the precariousness of wealth, the impermanence of life, and the arbitrariness of money as a measurement of worth—all this combined with the recognition that happiness is something that happens to you, not something you can pursue systematically.

Hard as it may be to see (or hear) in the contemporary casino, the longing for grace survives at the core of the culture of chance. Gambling ritualizes that yearning and underwrites its unfashionable truth. By giving up the drive for perfect mastery of fate, gamblers recognize what we so often forget: that the pursuit of happiness defies the attempt to organize it. Gamblers implicitly acknowledge that fortune is best courted obliquely rather than confronted directly and that the willingness to experience chance creates the possibility of grace—or luck, if you prefer a less-exalted idiom. That was what the great psychologist and philosopher William James recognized when he said that chance was a kind of gift, "something on which we have no effective *claim*"—something for nothing.[44]

14

Civic Values and "Education Lotteries"

The Irony of Funding Public Education with Lottery Revenues

Erik C. Owens

Americans are extraordinarily fond of their lotteries. In the last forty years the percentage of the U.S. population that lives in a state with a legally sanctioned lottery has gone from 0 to 90 percent. Accompanying this market saturation has been a certain popular satisfaction (hovering at over 70% in 2006[1]) with the large sums that lotteries provide to state coffers, with the fact that these revenues are not forcibly extracted by the state but rather volunteered by those who choose to play the lottery, and with the array of good causes to which the revenues are applied. Ten of the forty-two states with lotteries send all their lottery revenue into the state's general fund to be distributed across the full range of government programs along with most other sources of income for the state. The remaining states earmark some or all lottery revenues for specific causes and sometimes direct that money to a fund or trust (the sort of proverbial lockbox that Al Gore touted for Social Security) to protect it from the hungry stares of state legislators who need fresh revenue to satiate ongoing budget deficits.

The good causes to which lottery revenues are applied vary widely. Colorado, Minnesota, and Maine direct all or part of their lottery proceeds to natural resource conservation, parks, and outdoor programs. Kansas lottery revenues go toward economic development initiatives; in Massachusetts, local governments (i.e., cities and towns) receive the lottery proceeds; and in Wisconsin, lottery profits are spent on property tax relief. Pennsylvania stands out for dedicating its lottery revenues to various programs for senior citizens.

But far and away the most popular earmark for lottery funds is public education. Twenty-three states (of forty-two with lotteries) give at least some lottery revenues to education, and fifteen dedicate all lottery profits to education. Specific program recipients vary, with some states simply transferring the proceeds to the department of education while others fund college scholarships, prekindergarten programs, school construction, teacher training, community colleges, and other programs. Out of this common endeavor has come the expression "education lottery," which frequently finds its way into the official name of the program (as in the Tennessee Education Lottery or the Oklahoma Education Lottery Trust Fund), but is also simply used in a colloquial sense to indicate the connection between the two endeavors. The connection is so firmly established in parts of the country that some citizens believe their public schools are entirely funded by lotteries.[2]

This chapter examines the connection between state lotteries and education—a relationship fraught with a political and moral complexity often overlooked by lottery supporters and opponents alike. Among the defining aspects of this relationship is the counterintuitive fact that public schools and colleges do not necessarily receive a net financial benefit from lottery revenues, despite the enormous sums of money lotteries generate. This is primarily due to the fungibility of government funds, in which new revenues from a lottery or other sources tend to replace rather than supplement existing education funds. Most voters also have a wildly inflated sense of the percentage of education revenues that comes from the lottery, and thus are disinclined to vote for increased education funding when presented with the option.

Another crucial aspect of the relationship between education and the lottery is the fact that per capita spending on lottery tickets is inversely proportional to the level of education the buyer has attained. Simply put, the more education you have received, the less you spend on lottery tickets if you play the lottery at all. (We will review the numbers below in greater detail, but consider this teaser: high school dropouts who play the lottery spend nearly 400 percent more on tickets each year than college graduates who play the lottery.[3]) This relationship persists among the most frequent lottery players as well. About half of Americans of every demographic and socioeconomic category (including education level) play the lottery in a given year, but *how much* they play is the crucial factor for lottery managers since 5 percent of lottery players spend more than 50 percent of all lottery receipts, and 20 percent of players spend more than 80 percent of all lottery receipts.

If lottery proceeds are effective in improving and expanding education, therefore, the well-educated citizens produced by state schools and colleges will dramatically reduce the money they spend on lotteries. A decrease in revenue invariably leads lottery managers to aggressively stoke demand by increasing prize payouts and launching huge advertising campaigns that downplay the unbelievable odds against winning. ("Hey, you never know," says one New York lottery ad.) Further exacerbating an already regressive source of revenue, some of the most popular and widely admired state lottery programs dedicate most revenues to merit-based college scholarship funds primarily used by middle- and upper-class students.[4]

These (and other) facts, combined with a reckoning of the corrosive civic values implicitly and explicitly promoted by state lottery programs, make it clear that "education lottery" is something of an oxymoron. In the pages that follow I explore the irony of linking lotteries and education in three sections. First, I examine the lottery itself as an instrument of public finance and as an activity once considered a vice, closing with a reflection on the tethering of means to ends in public finance. In section two, I briefly review the history of good causes in service of which lotteries have been put, then focus upon the recent surge and future prospects of education as the most popular such cause. I close in the final section with reflections on the lottery as a form of civic education that implicitly and explicitly teaches citizens certain values, few of which, I argue, are conducive to a flourishing democratic culture.

Why Lotteries?

It makes sense to begin our examination with the lottery itself, since its capacity to generate revenue is its primary selling point for organizers (as opposed to players, who of course play for the financial and emotional benefits of risking and winning money). In this section we examine why lotteries have become such a widespread form of public finance, and how a minority with traditional perceptions of gambling as vice has led most states to promote their lottery's connection (real or perceived) with specific good causes.

A lottery is a form of gambling in which chances to share in a distribution of prizes are sold. Lotteries differ from other forms of gambling in that no player skill—and often very little activity at all—is involved.[5] As Charles Clotfelter and Philip Cook note in their chapter from this book, six types of lottery games predominate in the United States today. In a simple raffle, numbered tickets are sold and a subsequent drawing determines the winning ticket numbers. Instant or scratch-off lottery games, in which players can find winning numbers or combinations on select cards, are the most popular across the country, comprising more than 50 percent of total lottery sales. Lotto provides the most breathtaking payouts (a $390 million jackpot was split by two winning tickets in 2007) and the most impossible odds (currently about 1:146 million for Powerball) by requiring players to correctly choose a series of five or six numbers (each can range from one to fifty in most games) in any order; if no player purchased a ticket with the winning numbers, more tickets are sold and drawings continue until someone wins. The daily draw allows players to pick three or four numbers that win if certain combinations are drawn by a computer; it is a derivation of the once popular but illegal "numbers" game, which drew the winning number from public sources that promoters could not control, such as stock market volume, bank financial balances, or parimutuel totals at racetracks. Keno is a form of high-speed lotto in which drawings occur many times per hour; players choose numbers at networked terminals in bars or restaurants. Finally, video lottery terminals (VLTs) are self-contained units that provide endless, instant drawings—and the potential for addiction and financial ruin that has given many state legislatures pause when considering their adoption.[6]

Lottery games can be more or less profitable to the organizer, and the trick to maximizing revenue—this is the general goal for lotteries that do not exist purely for player satisfaction—lies in stimulating high demand while spending the least possible amount on administrative costs. Demand is primarily stimulated by increasing the percentage of lottery receipts returned to players in prize money (the "payout rate"), though advertising and product availability make important contributions as well. Profits are the remainder of revenues after prizes and administrative costs are paid. Economists use the term "takeout rate" to describe the percentage of revenues *not* paid in prize money; the payout rate plus the takeout rate equals one, or 100 percent.

Lotteries as Public Finance

Lotteries are complex and fascinating mechanisms of finance that bring together charity and greed, compulsion and voluntarism, self-interest and the common good. In colonial and early national American history, lotteries were employed to raise money for both private and public ends. Few individuals were wealthy enough to make large purchases of property (which might have included landed estates or groups of slaves), so lotteries were routinely employed in lieu of auctions. The owner (or creditor, if the property was in foreclosure) set a specific value on the property, then offered enough tickets (usually several thousand) to generate at least that amount in sales. Rather than going to the highest bidder, the property was sold for the price of the winning ticket; the ticket buyers paid a small amount for a chance to win a large estate, while the owner distributed the cost among a large population. No less a towering figure than Thomas Jefferson sought to sell his property—including Monticello—through a lottery in his waning years to climb out of deep debt and provide for his daughter after his death. The Virginia legislature authorized the lottery and appointed prominent community members to supervise it, but Jefferson died before it took place. (A posthumous lottery was initiated for his property, but not enough tickets were sold and the lottery was abandoned.[7]) Notwithstanding Jefferson's case, the effect of this sort of lottery was democratizing, and potentially disruptive, since large estates could pass quickly from the wealthy to the (formerly) poor. One notable, if unusual, example of such a transfer of wealth involved Denmark Vescey, a former slave who bought his freedom with winnings from a local lottery.[8] (This is notable not only because of a slave's rare good fortune, but because Vescey would go on to plan a massive slave rebellion in 1822 that was brutally suppressed just before it was launched.)

Most lotteries in this period paid out prize money rather than property and were used to raise money for enterprises benefiting the common good. One-time lotteries (raffles) were used by colonies (and later, states) to finance roads and outfit militias; buying a ticket was promoted as a patriotic act, just as buying war bonds was cast as a patriotic duty during World War II. The "pious use" of lotteries was approved by local governments to provide funds to construct university buildings, churches, and poorhouses, and even to pay the ransom of town citizens held hostage by American Indian tribes during periods of quiet conflict or open war. Most Americans in this period, writes gambling historian David Schwartz, "saw lotteries as sensible ways to contribute to the greater good—and get something for nothing, or next to nothing." ("Next to nothing" was truer then than now; 85 percent of revenues from these early American lotteries were usually returned as prizes, compared with 71 percent today.)[9]

Private revenue lotteries, authorized by the state but run for personal or corporate profit, flourished in the nineteenth century.[10] Corruption increased along with revenues, and by the end of the century, antigambling movements prevailed upon states to ban lotteries. Illegal lotteries persisted, though, and some suggested that states should replace them with highly regulated lotteries of their own, much as "package stores" served to enforce a state monopoly on alcohol sales.

When the modern wave of lotteries crashed onto the national shores, however, it was new revenue, not the desire to control corruption, that topped legislators' minds. New Hampshire pioneered the modern state lottery in 1963 with a semiannual drawing to benefit education. The following year it expanded the prizes and increased the frequency of drawings. New York and New Jersey soon followed, the former offering the nation's first million-dollar jackpot in 1970. The "arms race" for gambling revenue was on: states adjacent to those with a lottery fretted about border-crossing citizens depositing revenue in the next state. Seven more states followed suit in the 1970s, mostly in the northeastern and mid-Atlantic states.[11] Lotteries spread west in the 1980s, then to the last holdout region—the South—in the 1990s and 2000s. (Despite the long and colorful history of gambling in the South, conservative religious and political cultures there sustained general public opposition to gambling until the lost revenue opportunity finally seemed too high.[12]) Multistate lotteries began in 1985 with Powerball, which was soon followed by The Big Game (now called Mega Millions).

So what makes lotteries such an irresistible mechanism of public finance? The short answer is that they raise revenues without raising taxes. States are constantly on the lookout for new ways to increase revenue, particularly when economic times are tough. Raising existing taxes or establishing new ones has rarely been a popular tactic during a recession (and is considered heretical by many economists), so the prospects of cultivating a large new revenue source that is entirely voluntary is simply too good to pass up. For this reason, lotteries are frequently touted as a painless (or at least tolerably painful) tax substitute.

State lotteries also tap into a resilient demand for gambling. As David Schwartz and T. J. Jackson Lears make clear in two recent books, human beings have gambled for thousands of years, and gambling is thoroughly woven into the American ethos.[13] Luck, chance, fate, and fortune are primal motivators; stoked with enormous advertising campaigns and piles of prize money, it is no surprise that lotteries can provide strong revenue streams. Clotfelter and Cook estimate that at the national average takeout rate (which is currently 29 percent, meaning that 71 percent of revenues are returned as prizes), the government's share of lottery proceeds is the equivalent of a 41 percent excise tax on a lottery ticket—a rate "virtually unheard-of among real-world excise taxes" and more than double that of cigarettes.[14] Put another way, lottery players pay an extraordinarily high tax on the product they purchase but continue to do so without much complaint.

It is sometimes argued that modern state lotteries also flourish in part because they benefit good causes such as education, but Clotfelter and Cook debunk this argument in their chapter in this book. They found that while a good cause apparently sways enough skeptical citizens to vote for establishing a lottery, it has no measurable impact on the amount citizens spend on the lottery once it is operational.[15] More generally, though, a good cause ought not count as a reason to support lotteries per se, since (in theory anyway) any form of revenue could be tethered to any expenditure. A general sales tax increase, for example, might be more palatable to the voting public if its revenues were exclusively dedicated to college scholarships. The connection with a worthy cause says little about why lotteries are such appealing tools of public finance.

There are, of course, some downsides to the use of lotteries for public finance. First, lotteries are quite inefficient, requiring an average expenditure of 10 percent of total costs for administration, compared to 1 percent for the administration of a broad-based tax.[16] These administrative costs derive from the need to aggressively promote the lottery with marketing and advertising in order to stimulate demand (a fact that has nonfinancial downsides to be discussed below). Second, lottery revenues are not stable; they fluctuate constantly and are difficult to forecast properly.[17] Third, despite some very creative and compelling advertising, lotteries have proved capable of producing only small amounts of revenue for states relative to the overall budget. States took in $17 billion in lottery profits in 2006—a large number indeed, but it still only amounted to about 2 percent of the average state's total budget. By comparison, income and sales taxes each contributed about 25 percent of states' income.[18] One recent study estimates that a state lottery can only generate revenue equivalent to a 1 percent increase in the sales tax.[19]

The fourth and by far the most widely cited downside is the fact that lottery revenues are strongly regressive in nature. This means that lotteries draw more money from poor people (as a percentage of total income) than from rich people, a pattern that persists across the income scale. Sales taxes are regressive, too, when applied to foodstuffs and other necessities, but some studies have found the lottery to be twice as regressive as a state sales tax.[20] A look at the numbers will help to identify exactly who provides the revenues in a lottery.

A massive study of gamblers by the National Opinion Research Council (NORC) in 1999 provides the most fine-toothed dataset to date; several of the nation's leading policy economists parsed the results in an important report to the National Gaming Impact Study Commission.[21] The report's authors found that about half of Americans play the lottery, a participation rate that remains remarkably constant (between 47% and 55%) across all demographic categories and income ranges. (Only senior citizens, surprisingly, fall below this range, with a 39 percent participation rate in lotteries in 1999.) In general, lottery spending drops as income rises. Lottery players with annual household income of less than $10,000 spent on average $597 per year; those earning $25,000–$50,000 spent $382; and those earning $50,000–$100,000 spent $225.[22] As economist Earl Grinols put it, "Lotteries take money away from low-income people, or those most would agree should not be used as a tax base."[23]

Additional data on race and education highlight the lottery's core constituencies. Lottery spending is highest among African Americans, who spent $998 per capita in 1999, compared to $210 for whites and $289 for Hispanics.[24] And, as I will discuss in depth below, lottery spending drops as education rises: whereas high school dropouts spent $700 per capita in 1999, college graduates spent just $178.[25]

But while all sorts of Americans play the lottery, some do so *much* more than others. To wit: the median per capita lottery spending in 1999 was $75, but if all players had spent that amount that year, total lottery revenues would have *decreased* by 76 percent. This makes statistics about the "typical" lottery player "of little interest from the revenue perspective."[26] Data about the heaviest lottery players is hard to come by, says economist Philip Cook, since surveys "don't plumb the questions about depth of play, which the lotteries have chosen to obfuscate because they see themselves as vulnerable on this issue politically."[27] But some numbers are available on these core players. The 1999 NORC survey found that the top 5 percent of players accounted for 54 percent of nationwide lottery revenues; the top 10 percent accounted for 68 percent, and top 20 percent accounted for 82 percent of all lottery revenues. The heaviest lottery players, the top 20 percent, are much more likely to be African American, male, high school dropouts, and to have household income below $10,000, than they would in the general population.[28] Data from Texas, which requires its lottery commission to collect demographic data about its lottery players, confirms the NORC numbers. It found that African Americans spent more than three and a half times as much on lottery tickets, on average, than whites in 2006; Hispanics spent nearly two and a half times as much as whites.[29]

Upon hearing such solid evidence of the regressive nature of lotteries, many citizens simply shrug their shoulders. Indeed, too much can be made of regressivity, since buying a lottery ticket is a voluntary activity and there is no evidence that states specifically target the poor, despite claims to the contrary by some lottery opponents. This is the view expressed by the president of the North American Association of State and Provincial Lotteries, who said in a recent interview that differences in lottery spending are simply attributable to cultural preferences, not to anything inherent in income or education levels. Some people wager while playing golf, others play the lottery: "Culturally, people have experienced different ways not only to amuse themselves but to gamble," he said. "It's been that way for a long time in this country."[30]

But it is nevertheless the case that lottery states aggressively encourage behavior that tends disproportionately to harm low-income and minority citizens. We have noted the financial costs to these groups, but gambling and lotteries have historically also been associated with a moral or spiritual cost. Is this perception of gambling as a vice still a factor in public policy?

Vice or Virtue?

If lottery participation were treated by the state in the same way as other perceived vices like drinking or smoking, it would be actively discouraged by tax policy and legislation. But as Clotfelter and Cook astutely note in their chapter in this book, lotteries stand apart from other "soft-core vices" in that states never use regulated lotteries to *limit* gambling. On the contrary, gambling is actively encouraged. This notable contrast is mirrored in the survey data on Americans' views about gambling.

Only a small minority of Americans believe that gambling is a sin (and thus a vice), and even fewer believe that playing the lottery in particular is sinful. A recent Ellison Research poll found that while 87 percent of Americans said they believed in the concept of sin (defined by surveyors as "something that is almost always considered wrong, particularly from a religious or moral perspective"), only 30 percent described gambling as sinful. Even fewer (18%) identified "playing the lottery" as a sin—exactly the same percentage as reported "watching R-rated movies" to be a sin. Meanwhile, 81 percent said adultery was a sin, 47 percent claimed "gossip" was a sin, and a lonely 4 percent reported "making lots of money" to be sinful.[31] There were notable gaps in perceived sinfulness of gambling and lotteries between Protestants (50% and 31%, respectively) and Catholics (15% and 7%), and between self-identified liberals (18% of whom declared gambling "morally unacceptable") and conservatives (53% of whom said the same).[32]

Whether or not pollsters use moral or theological language in their surveys, less than a third of Americans typically express disapproval of gambling and more than two-thirds say they approve of it.[33] In fact, the Gallup Organization describes gambling as a "consensus issue" for Americans since its thirty-one-point net approval rating has remained consistent for several years.[34]

Tethering Means to Ends

Given the relatively high approval ratings of gambling as a pastime (60–70%, as noted above) and of the lottery as a source of state revenue (71%, according to a recent Pew survey), it might seem surprising that lotteries need to be attached to a good cause before citizens approve them. But a sizable minority can put up a very effective resistance movement when issues like a lottery are put to a referendum; specifying the target of new revenues not only serves to demonstrate a commitment to that cause and to transparent governance in general, but it also mobilizes the would-be beneficiaries in behalf of the lottery.[35]

It is also important to note that tethering means to ends is routine in public finance. Gasoline taxes pay for highway infrastructure funds; fishing and hunting licenses help pay for wildlife conservation; taxes on pollutants and polluting manufacturers pay for environmental cleanup efforts. In London (and New York, if Mayor Michael Bloomberg has his way), a congestion tax on cars and trucks entering the city center helps to pay for public transit improvements.[36] Some of these links are more apparent than real, since tax revenues usually flow through a general fund before distribution to earmarked programs. But other links are real and verifiable; revenues are either collected by a semiautonomous agency outside the direct reach of the state legislature or are paid immediately into a fund that cannot be raided for other purposes. These are the "lockboxes" that Al Gore promised to provide for the Social Security Trust Fund, which Congress routinely raids for current social security expenditures (rather than banking the money in trust for each person's retirement, as promised) and uses to back government bonds that finance deficit spending.

Nevertheless, the means and ends cited above have some intuitive connection to one another: gas taxes pay for the roads that cars and trucks need to drive on, and so on. But there is no natural linkage between the lottery and any core public service, let alone education, which seems especially at odds (pardon the expression) with playing the lottery. While it is true that the "education lottery" is not the most jarring disjunction between the means and ends of taxation in the United States—that award must surely go to the 2007 Texas bill proposing a tax on strip clubs to increase funds for public elementary schools[37]—it nevertheless creates substantial tensions that we will explore in the next section.

Why Education?

We have seen why lotteries emit such a powerful siren song to states facing persistent budget shortfalls and already high tax burdens (or low tolerance for taxes in the first place), and how the latent taint of vice and worries over regressivity push lottery supporters to tether their proposal to a "good cause" during the debates over lottery adoption. But why is education the most popular good cause for lotteries? Does the connection make sense? And is this relationship fixed for the foreseeable future, or is it apt to change with the political or economic winds?

The Good Cause in American Lottery History

A vast array of "good causes" have benefited from public lotteries throughout American history. During the first wave of legally

sanctioned gambling, single-drawing lotteries (raffles) were frequently employed by colonial governments in the eighteenth and
early nineteenth centuries to finance public works such as roads,
bridges, wharves, town buildings, and even the Erie Canal. The
public spirit of such projects—their contribution to the common good—was transparent and broadly accepted, and the
raffles provided an exciting means of generating extra revenues
for their completion. Lotteries in several colonies also supported
the Revolutionary War effort by helping to finance weapons and
supplies. Every colony and, later, most states, also authorized
certain churches, universities, charitable organizations, and individuals to hold lotteries to finance new buildings or relief efforts.
Harvard, Yale, and Columbia are among numerous colleges with
campus buildings financed by lotteries. The civic purpose of lotteries fell by the wayside by the mid-nineteenth century, however, in favor of profit-making enterprises for private operators,
the most illustrious of which was the Louisiana Lottery, known
insidiously as "the Serpent"; the civic causes would not return
until lotteries began to sweep the nation again in the 1960s.[38]

In recent years, education-related programs have become the
most common good cause, although many other programs benefit from lottery revenues as well. New Hampshire set the leading
example in 1964 by committing revenues from its new lottery
(the first lottery in the so-called third wave, or modern era, of
public gambling) to public education. New York and New Jersey
followed, and during the next decade, six of twelve states to
establish lotteries pegged revenues to public primary and secondary education. (Of the others, one funded programs for senior
citizens, two directed revenues to local governments, and three
declined to earmark a good cause, simply sending revenue to the
general fund.)

During the next sixteen years, from 1975 to 1991, the lottery continued to expand rapidly along with the range of causes
to which it was applied. In this sixteen-year period, twenty-one
new states established public lotteries. Education was the priority in eight of these states, but the general fund—the antithesis of
the specially promoted "good cause"—took the revenues of eight
other new state lotteries in this period.

By 1992 the South stood out as the only region not covered
with lotteries, but in the next fifteen years seven southern states
would take the plunge, almost always by earmarking lottery
revenues for education-related programs. Nine of the next ten
lotteries across the nation (North Dakota being the exception)
would make education their central theme, and several (North
Carolina, Oklahoma, and Tennessee, among others) even listed
their good cause in the name of the lottery. The modern "education lottery" was born.[39]

Surveying the current lottery landscape, we can see that
twenty-three states now dedicate some or all lottery revenues to
education, and fifteen of these give all proceeds to this worthy
cause. Notably, seventeen states (plus the District of Columbia)
have declined to designate one or more specific recipients, dump-
ing lottery revenues into a general fund. Only six states earmark
all lottery money to specific causes that do not include education:
Massachusetts (cities and towns), Pennsylvania (senior citizens),
Colorado (parks and recreation), Kansas (economic development
and prisons), Wisconsin (property tax relief), and Indiana (capital projects and motor vehicle tax relief).[40]

While first-wave raffle-style lotteries always focused on a good
cause, or at least a specific cause, modern lotteries are designed to
provide ongoing revenue streams from constant drawings. There
are dozens of different lottery games to play in most states, allowing citizens to win—and lose—nearly twenty-four hours a day.
Bigger and more ambitious causes are needed for such large-scale
lottery programs, and whatever else it is, improving education is
clearly an ambitious cause. Combined with the widespread (and
accurate) belief that public schools and colleges are underfunded,
it comes as little surprise that education would be, at first blush,
an appropriate and deserving candidate for the extra funds that
lotteries produce. But does the connection really make sense?

The Irony of Education as a Good Cause

It should be clear that, in suggesting that education is an ironic
choice of partners (i.e., a complicit good cause) for the promotion
of a lottery, I do not mean to imply that it is not a good cause
as such. To the contrary, education in the United States is woe-
fully uneven and in some areas broadly deficient. The reasons

for educational failures and inequities are structural as well as operational and have nothing to do with the lottery. Rather, the irony of funding public education with lottery revenues lies in the fact that a successful lottery requires the fruits of poor education. The lottery is sometimes called "the math tax" or, more crassly, "the stupid tax" for a reason: well-educated people may play the lottery for the excitement of a vague chance of winning, but (judging from per capita expenditures) they rarely consider it a wise investment of any sizable amount of resources.

In this section I discuss four aspects of the relationship between education and lotteries that make the concept of an "education lottery" oxymoronic: (1) lotteries depend upon the poorest and least educated segments of the population to generate most of their revenue; (2) the regressive nature of lottery revenues is exacerbated by spending them on merit-based college scholarships—a popular recent innovation in lottery financing; (3) proceeds from lotteries constitute a very small portion of overall education expenditures; and (4) education spending sometimes actually *declines* after an education lottery is put into place.

First, social scientific studies conclusively demonstrate that lotteries depend upon the poorest and least educated segments of the population to flourish. I have already summarized, in an earlier section, some of the relevant evidence demonstrating the regressive nature of lottery revenues, but the relationship of education level to lottery spending is worth highlighting here as well. Simply put, the more education one has received, the less one is likely to spend on lottery tickets, if one plays the lottery at all. This inverse correlation is dramatic. Among those who played any state lottery in 1999, college graduates spent $178 per capita on lottery tickets and those with some college education spent $210, but expenditures jumped dramatically for lottery players who did not attend college. Lottery players with (merely) high school degrees spent $409 per capita on lottery tickets, while high school dropouts spent $700 per capita. Similar inverse correlations hold for income level, and racial differences are also notable: in 1999, African Americans who played the lottery spent an *average* of $998 on lottery tickets, a vast increase over Hispanic and white players, who spent $289 and $210 per capita that year.[41]

As noted above, lottery players with low incomes, little educa-tion, and minority racial status are also strongly overrepresented among the important "core" lottery players (the top 20 percent, who together contribute more than 80 percent of lottery revenues) relative to the general population. Lottery proceeds for education are thus dependent on the players having received little educa-tion themselves, creating perverse economic incentives to cultivate more such players. It would be shocking to learn that managers of a state's "education lottery" would want to expand the ranks of the uneducated, and I am not suggesting that this is the case. But it is true that doing so would likely increase lottery revenues, a fact that itself reveals how uncomfortable the fit can be between lotteries and education. Besides, cultivating the presently under-educated lottery-playing population is much easier (if still deplor-able) than consciously undereducating future lottery players. Writes economist H. Roy Kaplan, "There is something cruelly perverse about states encouraging, even proselytizing, their poor-est and least educated citizens to gamble often for the purpose of generating funds for education."[42] There is little evidence that lottery "proselytizing" toward the poor (via marketing, advertis-ing, retail penetration, etc.) is higher than that aimed at any other demographic, but it is nevertheless troubling to see the long lines at the lottery ticket counter in the poorest areas of town.

Second, the regressive nature of lottery revenues is exacer-bated by spending them on merit-based college scholarships—a popular recent innovation in lottery financing. Georgia oper-ates a widely admired and well-run lottery that distributes rev-enues to three key programs: prekindergarten programs across the state, technology grants for computer purchases and teacher training, and the flagship HOPE (Helping Outstanding Pupils Educationally) Scholarships, which offer $3,000 grants to stu-dents with a B average in high school for use at any of Georgia's public colleges, universities, or technical schools. In its thirteen-year history, the HOPE Scholarship program has become so popular that it is seen as an untouchable benefit, largely because so many middle-class residents have received scholarships.[43] Lotteries in South Carolina and Florida, among other states, also designate the majority of lottery revenues for higher education, with hundreds of millions of dollars going toward merit-based college scholarships.[44]

These laudable programs benefit many residents of their various states, and indeed they encourage exactly the kind of higher education that the most avid lottery players tend to lack. As such they are hard to criticize, but it is nonetheless true that they continue to redistribute lottery proceeds to the middle- and upper-class students who tend to have the higher grades that qualify them for college.[45] If voters and policymakers wanted to reduce the regressive financial effects of the lottery, they would be most effective if they increased the payout rate—thereby returning money to the lower-income players who predominate—and designated the proceeds to poverty relief and economic development in impoverished areas.[46] On a generational time scale, public education *is* a form of poverty relief, perhaps the most effective kind we have; but more immediate needs could be met with enhanced social services for the hungry, unemployed, or homeless, and with business development training and loan programs.

Third, proceeds from lotteries constitute a very small portion of overall education expenditures. Despite the enormous sums of money taken out by lotteries across the country, the amounts provided to education average about 2 percent of a state's education budget—roughly enough to operate its public school system for a week. Some state lotteries contribute as much as 5 percent of total education spending, but in general the public perception of the benefit is much higher than the actual benefit. One budget analyst for the California public schools said that the state's lottery "makes it harder for us to convince people that they still need to support education. They think the lottery is taking care of education. We have to tell them we're only getting a few sprinkles; we're not even getting the icing on the cake."[47]

Fourth, and finally, total education spending sometimes actually declines after an education lottery is put into place. Several studies have found that lotteries tend to provide added per capita revenue to education for two to five years, after which the increase usually vanishes.[48] This is due in part to inflation, but also to the failure of legislators to maintain the level of education funding that existed before the lottery was introduced. Legislatures also reappropriate lottery revenues when facing budget shortfalls or emergency situations, as happened recently in Ohio, Nebraska, and in Oklahoma.[49] In fact, lottery proceeds

are considered fungible in many states even without a stated budget emergency. Policy analyst Charles Spindler argued in 1995
that this fungibility makes revenue dedication (for education
or other good causes) a budgeting shell game in many states.[50]
One Florida state representative used the same term—"a shell
game"—to describe how his peers in the state legislature moved
money back into the general fund that should have been spent
to improve education for Floridians.[51] Furthermore, lottery revenues are variable and difficult to estimate, making budgeting difficult for school systems that receive lottery funds. As Elizabeth
McAuliffe concisely puts it in her 2006 review of social scientific
data, "empirical research has discredited the claim that lotteries
help education" on the whole.

The Future of Education as a Good Cause

Despite these and other problems with tethering lotteries and education in this country, the link is likely to remain for most states.
Education is an ongoing need, and the success of college scholarship programs among the middle class is likely to guarantee
their extension well into the future. The most likely threat to the
education lottery comes from the possibility that the lottery itself
will be sold or leased. At least a dozen states are contemplating
privatizing their lotteries—a process that, if completed, would be
the biggest privatization of government enterprise in American
history. The problem, for education funding at least, comes from
the vast sums expected from such a sale. Legislators in several
states are eyeing the prospect of billions of dollars in cash and
have begun to outline allocations well outside the purview of the
current lottery revenue guidelines. Texas Governor Rick Perry
has proposed using one-third of the projected $10 to $38 billion
in proceeds from a long-term lease of the lottery to fund cancer
research, California Governor Arnold Schwarzenegger wants to
commit the $14 to $18 billion from a lease of his state's lottery to
fund health-care reform; and Illinois legislators are contemplating applying leasing fees toward the $41 billion pension liability
it currently faces.[52] In each case, the public schools in those states
face enormous opportunity costs: annual lottery revenues at a
certain level will continue to go toward education, but the benefits of increased payouts will be lost to them. As of this writing

(June 2008), no state has yet taken the plunge to privatize its lottery, but it is likely to happen soon. When it does, advocates for public education will have to fight to keep their good cause as the primary beneficiary of this revenue windfall.

Lotteries as Civic Education

Every action the government takes, every policy the government makes, conveys certain values to its citizens. The state teaches in this manner, both directly and indirectly, and we can therefore examine the laws and policies of a state—and of programs like the lottery—as forms of civic education. What do state-run lotteries teach us? What values do they convey through their administration and advertising?

It might be said that the politics and policies of education lotteries say nothing important about American values, or at least nothing interesting. From this perspective, a lottery is just another revenue stream to be maximized, and if anything, it demonstrates how clever and libertarian Americans can be when faced with the unhappy prospect of raising taxes to improve education. Like the state-run tourism industry and most other forms of advertising, lottery advertisements sell the idea of escape, fantasy, and leisure—all good things that overworked Americans could use more of.

Others might argue that the creation of education lotteries conveys the importance we collectively place on education. Certainly the revenues provided by these lotteries have done great good for millions of students across the country.

But I worry that the overall effect of the education lottery is the teaching of more deleterious values, those that are corrosive to lively civil society and a flourishing democratic culture. In the first place, the lottery itself functions as a regressive tax, which places a heavier burden on the poor to pay for public services that everyone enjoys. But more visibly, the state aggressively markets lotteries with advertising campaigns designed to separate citizens from their rational faculties, their commitment to hard work and frugality, and their general responsibility toward future generations. As one Massachusetts lottery ad proclaimed: "Work is nothing but heart-attack-inducing drudgery." "This could be your ticket out," beckons a billboard in an impoverished neighborhood in

Chicago, not far from another lottery billboard offering "How to Get from Washington Boulevard to Easy Street."[53] At this point, the government has ceased being a protector and has become a barker, a huckster, a con man trying to convince viewers that the odds of winning are in their favor.

So what should be done? Should public school officials renounce lottery revenues? Of course not—or at least not immediately. Education at all levels needs as much money as possible, but funding these programs should be a collective decision of the citizenry as a whole, not a haphazard result of the whims of a lottery-playing subsection of the public. If we are serious about funding education, we should tap the collective will of the people and their representatives to enhance education directly by making it a budgeting priority, by controlling costs, and by levying a sufficiently broad-based tax to pay for it. Dedicating the windfall profits from the lease or sale of a state lottery to education offers the possibility of a more extensive commitment to education funding, but the long-run solution lies in the collective will of the citizenry, not the vagaries of that small but intense group of core lottery players who drive lottery marketing and operations.

15

A Tale of Two "Sins"
Regulation of Gambling and Tobacco

Richard McGowan, S.J.

The year is 1964. Nearly 40 percent of the adult population in the United States smokes cigarettes and cigarette commercials account for 15 percent of network television advertising. Meanwhile, New Hampshire becomes the first state in over sixty years to conduct a lottery. The New Hampshire lottery will conduct a weekly drawing and tickets will cost $.50. There is only one state that permits casino gambling while the form of gambling that the majority of states permit is betting on the "sport" of horse racing.

Now let us move forward forty years, to 2004. Only 25 percent of the U.S. adult population smokes cigarettes and cigarette makers are not permitted to advertise in any media. North Carolina becomes the thirty-ninth state to enact a state lottery while twenty-seven states have some sort of casino gambling. Ironically, Churchill Downs, the home of U.S. horse racing, pins its survival on obtaining a license to operate slot machines.

In a forty-year period, the fortunes of these two "sin" industries changed radically. Why did this occur, and what were the rationales utilized by public policy makers as they went about their decision-making process? Is this simply the result of lack of memory of sin, which William Galston has pointed out in chapter 9?

Lawmakers love the revenue and hate the social costs from the sin industries, and therefore they are forced to carefully analyze the costs and benefits of each industry. What is the goal of introducing new forms of gaming to a state? Perhaps it is to maximize revenue, but much more likely it is the start of a process to gradually introduce more forms of gambling as neighboring states start competing for gambling revenues. Is the goal of tobacco tax policy to reduce smoking, to increase revenue, or, as in some cases, to support the very industry itself? These are not easy questions to answer for state legislators. In order to attempt to give some answers to these questions, this chapter will be divided into two parts. First, I will give a brief history of each sin industry in the United States, followed by a discussion of how two types of ethical decision making made significant contributions to how the views of public policy makers changed toward these industries over this forty-year period. Second, I will examine the relationship between revenue from a given sin industry and spending by state governments on the social cost associated with that industry. The objective is to build on the work of prior research in an attempt to develop a more comprehensive understanding of the relationships among spending on social costs across the sin industries. Hopefully the outcome of this analysis will be useful to states as they continue to make difficult policy decisions in the face of increasing budgetary pressure.

A Brief History of American Tobacco and Gambling Policy

Public policy makers have never been known for their consistency in addressing the various issues that confront them during the public policy process. In dealing with American Indian gambling, Rand and Light have shown just how conflicted states are on this issue. Some observers maintain this inconsistency merely demonstrates the highly "irrational" nature by which policy decisions are achieved. However, these inconsistencies could very well have an explanation that goes well beyond typical cost-benefit analysis that economists might utilize in what they would term a "rational" public policy decision. One area that could provide a handle on how the public policy process has evolved over the past forty years is an examination of the "ethical" reasoning that public policy makers employ as they go about the task of enacting legislation.

In order to demonstrate the importance of "ethical" reasoning in the public policy process and how ethical argumentation has changed over the past forty years, this chapter examines the changes that have occurred in two of the so-called sin industries, namely cigarettes and gambling. The very different scenarios that cigarettes and gambling industries have undergone will be chronicled. It should be noted that both of these industries depend on the "tolerance" of public policy makers for their very existence. It will be shown that the ethical thinking of public policy as it pertains to these industries has radically changed over the course of the past forty years. It is this shift that has made a profound difference in the fate of these two industries in the public policy realm.

The Cigarette Industry (1964 to the Present)

The following list offers a brief glimpse of the history of the cigarette industry in the United States. Tobacco regulation can be identified in three waves:

- First Wave (1911–1964): Making the cigarette industry competitive.
- Second Wave (1964–1985): Smoking and health.
- Third Wave (1985–present): Rights of the nonsmoker.

In 1964 the surgeon general of the United States published the now famous report concluding that "cigarette smoking is a health hazard of sufficient importance in the United States to warrant remedial action."[1] With this simple conclusion, the cigarette industry began its endless battles with government officials at all levels and branches of government.

From 1964 to 1985, the U.S. Congress passed two significant measures that it hoped would curb cigarette sales: The Cigarette Warning Label Act of 1966 and the TV and Radio Cigarette Advertising Ban of 1971.[2] Ironically, these measures did not have their intended effect. Cigarettes sales still increased throughout the period of 1964 to 1985 (although the rate of increase was less than the rate of increase prior to 1964). Why did these public policy measures not have their intended effect? The following reasons ought to give readers a moment's pause before they advocate various public policy measures to regulate the gambling industry.

First, while cigarette makers could no longer advertise, the anti-cigarette smoking groups were no longer free to play their anti-smoking advertisements. The anti-smoking advertisements had proven to be much more powerful in persuading current smokers to quit smoking than cigarette commercials had been in making cigarette smoking seem glamorous. Second, the cigarette warning label was not only largely ignored by cigarette smokers (as is the case with alcohol warning labels) but has provided cigarette makers with much legal comfort in their legal battles concerning their liability in regard to wrongful deaths of cigarette smokers.

Ironically, this period of renewed regulation of the cigarette industry resulted in higher profits due to the fact that the industry spent significantly less on advertising. Using these additional profits, cigarette firms diversified into the food industry, with Phillip Morris' purchase of Miller Beer and General Foods and RJR's purchase of Nabisco.

On December 20, 1985, Surgeon General C. Everett Koop announced the results of research on the effects of second-hand smoke, or passive smoking.[3] The most controversial finding of this report was that there was a significant increase in the rate of lung cancer among nonsmokers in households where nonsmokers were living with cigarette smokers. This report sparked off a flurry of activity in two areas: first, state legislators became extremely active in regulating where smokers could smoke, and second, the excise tax increases became much more common and pronounced. Tables 15.1 and 15.2 illustrate this renewed interest in state regulation of the cigarette industry.

TABLE 15.1

State Policy in Reaction to the Second-Hand Smoking Issue (1990)

		Excise tax level		
		Low level *(2–20/pack)*	*Mid level* *(21–49/pack)*	*High level* *(50+/pack)*
# of prohibitive laws passed	0–5	Alabama	Arkansas	Arizona
		Georgia	New Mexico	Wisconsin
		Indiana	Texas	
		Kentucky		
		Mississippi		
		North Carolina		
		Tennessee		
		West Virginia		
		Wyoming		
	6–11	Colorado	Idaho	Alaska
		South Carolina	Louisiana	District of Columbia
		Virginia	Minnesota	Hawaii
			Nebraska	Illinois
			Nevada	Maryland
			North Dakota	Massachusetts
			Ohio	Michigan
			Oklahoma	New Jersey
			Pennsylvania	Oregon
			South Dakota	Rhode Island
	12–14	Missouri	Delaware	California
		Montana	Florida	Connecticut
			Iowa	Maine
			Kansas	New Hampshire
			Vermont	New York
				Utah
				Washington

Source for tables 15.1 and 15.2: Compiled from various state Web sites as well as www.stat.com.

TABLE 15.2

State Tobacco Policies Evolving from Second-Hand Smoking (2002)

Excise tax level

# of prohibitive laws passed		Low level (2–40/pack)	Mid level (41–60/pack)	High level (61–150/pack)
	0–5	Alabama	Arizona	
		Georgia	Indiana	
		Indiana	Texas	
		Kentucky		
		Mississippi		
		New Mexico		
		North Carolina		
		Tennessee		
		West Virginia		
		Wyoming		
	6–11	Colorado	Minnesota	Alaska
		Idaho	Nebraska	District of Columbia
		Iowa	North Dakota	Hawaii
		Louisiana	Ohio	Illinois
		Oklahoma		Maryland
		Nevada		Massachusetts
		South Carolina		Michigan
		South Dakota		New Jersey
		Virginia		Oregon
				Pennsylvania
				Rhode Island
				Wisconsin
	12–14	Delaware	New Hampshire	California
		Florida		Connecticut
		Missouri		Kansas
		Montana		Maine
				New York
				Utah
				Vermont
				Washington

These two figures illustrate the passive smoking issue's powerful effect on state public policy makers. In terms of the number of smoking prohibition laws, the vast majority of states were prohibiting cigarette smoking in public places, and the only real battleground left for the cigarette industry was whether or not smokers could smoke in bars and restaurants. Even international airline flights now had banned all cigarette smoking.

Also striking are the large increases in the excise tax rates. In 1990, the state excise tax rates on cigarettes ranged from $.02/pack to a maximum of $.65/pack. By 2002, there were three states with excise tax rates of $1.50/pack! In fact, the average state excise tax rate on cigarettes increased from $.32/pack in 1990 to $.68/pack in 2002, and by 2005 had reached $1.00/pack. During the same fifteen-year period the federal excise tax rate on cigarettes doubled from $.16/pack to $.32/pack! While Congress and most state legislatures were heeding a call to lower taxes throughout the 1990s, cigarette excise tax rates seemed exempt from this trend. Even more startling was how powerless the cigarette industry was in fighting these increases. Clearly public sentiment had turned against the cigarette industry.[4]

The Gambling Industry (1964 to the Present)

Just as 1964 became a landmark year for the U.S. cigarette industry, that same year also became the year when tobacco's cousin in the sin industries, the gambling industry, began a revival that has not abated in the forty-three years that have followed. Prior to 1964, gambling was confined to two venues. In 1933, Nevada legalized casino gambling and it established Las Vegas as the "Mecca" of casino gambling. The other outlet was pari-mutuel betting on horse and dog racing that portrayed itself as a sport. But overall, gambling was considered an unacceptable social activity. The following list gives readers a brief history of gambling in the United States, documenting the five waves of U.S. gambling:

First Wave (1607–1840s): State-sanctioned lotteries.
Beneficiaries: Allowed private operators/colleges to operate lotteries in order to subsidize costs of capital improvements such as buildings or roads. Lotteries were given permission to operate only during the financing of the capital improvement. The lottery ceased operation after the completion of the project.

Second Wave (1865–1890s): National lotteries.

Beneficiaries: Southern states offered prizes through the U.S. mail in order to gather funds to reconstruct roads and railways after the Civil War. These lotteries ceased operations after numerous scandals involving the private operators.

Third Wave (1920–1964): The golden age of horse racing.

Beneficiaries: With the advent of pari-mutuel betting machines, states permitted betting on "sporting" events such as horse and dog racing. Of course, the states received a percentage of the revenue in taxes.

Fourth Wave (1964–1993): The golden age of state lotteries.

Beneficiaries: In the search for new sources of revenue, state governments began to operate their own lotteries. These lotteries differed from previous lotteries in that they were state operated and played on a continuous basis.

Fifth Wave (1993–present): The triumph of casino gambling.

Beneficiaries: As gambling became more socially acceptable, casino gambling was the logical progression in enhancing a state's ability to raise revenue. The casino industry became more concentrated as the federal government permitted American Indians to operate casinos in order to become economically self-sufficient.

In 1964 New Hampshire voters approved a state lottery. Lotteries were socially acceptable in the colonial period of U.S. history but fell out of favor following various scandals. The rationale used to "justify" the New Hampshire lottery is now a familiar one: lottery proceeds were to fund education, thereby averting the enactment of either a sales or income tax in New Hampshire. In another familiar scenario, the lottery was declared a success because most of the tickets were purchased by customers who did *not* reside in New Hampshire.

But this lesson was not lost on New Hampshire's neighboring states. In the next ten years, every state in the northeastern part of the United States approved a lottery. Then the lotteries spread to the midwestern and western United States, with the

South being the last part of the country to establish lotteries. By 1993, only Utah and Hawaii did not have some form of legalized gambling. Gambling had gained a social acceptance that it had never been able to achieve in any period of American history.

The year 1993 was a watershed for the gambling industry in another way. For the first time in U.S. history, casino revenues surpassed lottery revenues, cementing gambling's claim to be the most utilized form of entertainment in the United States.[5]

How did this expansion of casino gambling take place? There were three sources that contributed to this rapid expansion of casino gambling. First, there was the expansion of the number of what can be termed "national destination" markets for casino gambling. Throughout the 1980s and 1990s, Las Vegas transformed itself from a strictly casino operation where 90 percent of revenues came from casino operations to one where less than 50 percent of revenues were gambling related. As a result of this trend, visitors to Las Vegas stay longer (3.5 nights in 2005 compared with 2.3 nights in 1970) and the amount of money that visitors spend there on nongaming activities has increased by more than 20 percent since 1970. In 1978, casino gambling was legalized in Atlantic City, and while it is not the national destination that Las Vegas is, Atlantic City has experienced a 22 percent increase in gambling revenues as well as a 24 percent increase in visitors since the advent of casino gambling.[6]

Riverboat gambling was another form of casino gambling that exploded during the 1990s. In 1989, Iowa became the first state to permit it, soon followed by Louisiana, Illinois, Mississippi, Missouri, and Indiana. This form of casino gambling at first had a great number of restrictions placed on operators. For example, the boats actually had to cruise, patrons were limited on the amount of money they could bring aboard, and they had to leave the boats after the boats cruised. These restrictions were gradually lifted as states competed with each other for the gambling revenues. By far the most successful state in the riverboat arena is Mississippi. It is now the third largest market for casino gambling in the United States.

The final source of casino gambling revenues is American Indian casinos. In 1988, Congress passed the Indian Gaming Regulatory Act (IGRA). This legislation permitted tribes that were recognized by the federal government to develop gaming facilities.[7] As some indication of how successful Indian gaming has become, it is estimated that revenue at American Indian casinos grew to nearly $23 billion in 2005. Currently there are 420 Indian casinos in the United States that account for 310,000 full-time jobs as well as $10.5 billion in wages.[8] Hence, by any measure, American Indian casinos have been an economic success for the tribes as well as for the states where they operate, to which the tribes have contributed $6.9 billion in tax revenues since 1988.[9]

Casino gambling has clearly become the dominant force behind the virtual explosion of gambling activity in the United States. State legislators give many reasons for why they might approve the expansion of gambling: first, taxes and economic activity generated by casino gambling are useful sources of revenue and economic development; and second, if a neighboring state has casino gambling, a state risks losing all the potential tourist and tax revenue to its neighbor, thereby putting additional tax burdens on its citizens.[10]

But there also appears to be another overarching reason for gambling's increasing ubiquity besides the above economic ones, and that is the social acceptance of gambling over the past forty-three years. The public not only tolerates additional gambling opportunities but in many ways demands that a state provide them these opportunities—or they will leave the state and gamble where they are permitted. The next section of this chapter gives reasons why this fundamental change has happened, hopefully permitting readers to use these concepts as they explore the various options that legislators face as they decide on the gambling issue.

The "Ethics of Sacrifice" versus the "Ethics of Tolerance"

As previously discussed, gambling and cigarette smoking have experienced an almost complete role reversal in the public policy process. Why has cigarette smoking been condemned by the vast majority of public policy makers, whereas gambling has seemingly become the darling of legislators as a painless source of revenues for pet projects? Why have the debates over gambling and cigarette smoking evolved so differently over the past forty-three years? One way to account for this differing evolution of the two debates is to examine the manner in which the merits of a public policy issue are debated. In the United States, the conflict between the "societal good" and the "rights of the individual" has historically been the focus of the ethical controversy surrounding numerous U.S. public policy debates. Debates over controversial issues such as Prohibition were constantly appealing to either of these ethical stances in making their cases, either pro or con, about whether or not to prohibit all consumption of alcohol.[11] This conflict between the societal good and the rights of individuals is still the basis for debating the ethical merits of public policy issues ranging from gun control to environmental issues. Hence, throughout American history, public policy makers have had to deal with conflict between the common good and the individual's right to choose freely. This has resulted in what I call the "ethics of sacrifice" and the "ethics of tolerance."

Ethics of Sacrifice

When sacrifice is used as a moral concept to advance the merits of a particular public policy issue, public policy makers must be able to persuade the public that they must sacrifice some right (think of the War on Terror and the right to privacy) or benefit in order to achieve a noble goal or end. Most moral arguments that have a religious basis utilize this type of rationale (i.e., sacrifice in order to please God). The notion of sacrifice is also employed by political leaders during crises, especially times of war, such as World War II or the War on Terror. In terms of traditional ethical or moral categories, the ethics of sacrifice is teleological—that is, it is goal or end oriented. This goal is the good of society, and thus one can ascertain whether or not a public policy measure is correct by its contribution to the good of society.

In terms of public policy, the "good end" is a harmonious society. Traditionally, this ethic has been invoked by those who wish to maintain social institutions and structures that they deem desirable and think should be maintained at any cost. While some might associate this type of ethical thinking with conservative public policy makers, it actually has been employed by both liberals and conservatives to justify their stances on public policy measures. Certainly, President John F. Kennedy employed the ethics of sacrifice when he made his famous challenge to the American people, "Ask not what your country can do for you—ask what you can do for your country." It was a time when the president was asking the country to make a sacrifice in order to meet the challenges that lay ahead for the United States in the 1960s. In essence, those who utilize the ethics of sacrifice are asking the public to forgo any individual good for the good of all.

The authors of *Habits of the Heart* employ the ethics of sacrifice when they recall the work of the French social philosopher Alexis de Tocqueville. When Tocqueville analyzed American life in the 1830s, he labeled American mores as "Habits of the Heart" and demonstrated how they helped to mold our national character. Tocqueville singled out family life, religious traditions, and participation in local politics as helping to create the kind of individual who would be willing to make sacrifices in order to sustain a wider political community and maintain free institutions. It is this identification of the common good with the maintenance of societal institutions that is the hallmark of the ethics of sacrifice.[12]

In a later work, *The Good Society*, these same authors once again return to the concept of a society that needs to employ an ethics of sacrifice. In this work, they refine their analysis of the proper role of societal institutions. They define institutions as "normative patterns embedded in and enforced by laws and mores (informal customs and practices)."[13] In order to show how our understanding of institutions has an influence on the manner in which we conduct our lives, they give various examples. One of the examples has a great deal to do with the issue of gambling. It was written by A. Bartlet Giamatti, then the commissioner of Major League Baseball, on his decision to ban Pete Rose from baseball. Giamatti wrote:

> I believe baseball is an important enduring American institution. It must assert and aspire to the highest of principles —of integrity, of professionalism, of performance, of fair play within its rules It will come as no surprise that like any institution composed of human beings, this institution will not always fulfill its highest aspirations. But this one, because it is so much a part of our history as a people and because it has such a purchase on our national soul, has an obligation to the people for whom it is played—to its fans and its well-wishers—to strive for excellence in all things and to promote the highest ideals.[14]

Advocates of the ethics of sacrifice equate the preservation of institutions with the maintenance of the good life. Pete Rose's decision to gamble had to be punished severely because his gambling had damaged an institution that inspires people to act virtuously. In fact, an advocate of the ethics of sacrifice might say, gambling should be discouraged. The decision whether or not a person has the right to perform certain actions has to be measured in terms of what effect those actions will have on an institution or society at large.

At their most extreme, those who invoke the ethics of sacrifice can be accused of employing the motto, "The ends justify the means." The individual's ability to decide what is best for herself needs to be subservient to the needs of an institution such as the state, a corporation, or even the church. The good of society or an institution overrides the individual's rights and needs. This ethic is certainly the one under which the military operates. However, applied too rigorously to a society with many diverse parts, it can have many disastrous consequences. One only needs to recall America's Prohibition era to realize that one cannot impose virtue on an entire population. Yet the ethics of sacrifice calls forth what many would maintain is the noblest of human characteristics, the ability to give of oneself—even if that giving is detrimental to the individual.

Ethics of Tolerance

One of the earliest virtues that every American schoolchild is taught is tolerance. In order to escape persecution in England, the Quakers settled in Pennsylvania and are celebrated in American history texts because they permitted everyone to practice their own religious beliefs. In founding Maryland, Lord Baltimore also established religious freedom and welcomed the persecuted English Catholics, although this religious tolerance would be tested frequently throughout the colonial period. Meanwhile, the Puritans who settled Massachusetts were also trying to escape religious persecution. However, tolerance was not one of the virtues that Puritans cherished in building their New Jerusalem. Consider the case of Roger Williams. Williams questioned the long-held belief that the sons and daughters of Puritans would automatically be saved. The wrath of the Puritan elders was so intense that Williams had to flee Massachusetts and subsequently founded the colony of Rhode Island.

So while there have been differences of opinion about just how "tolerant" American society would be, in comparison to European societies, tolerance of various religious beliefs as well as other nationalities has been a hallmark of American society.

Tolerance entails that no person has to sacrifice their basic freedoms in order to achieve some goal of public welfare or to preserve some institution that promotes the societal good. When tolerance is promoted as one of the chief societal virtues, society must preserve the rights of minorities at all costs even at the expense of the majority. It also entails that American society has to tolerate the right of the individual to perform actions that might very well be destructive to that society, as long as the right to perform these activities is guaranteed by law. In traditional ethical thought, the ethics of tolerance would fall into the deontological mode of thinking—that is, the means which a person uses to achieve a goal are more important than the goal itself.

Gun control offers an example of continuous public policy controversy where the ethics of tolerance has played a part. Opponents of tougher gun control laws have utilized the ethics of tolerance as the basis for their ethical argument against tighter controls on guns. They maintain that the right to bear arms is protected in the U.S. Constitution. Therefore, even if the majority of Americans favor stricter gun restrictions, their right to bear arms has to be tolerated to uphold the rights of the minority who wish to have no limits placed on their ability to own and utilize guns.

The ethics of tolerance is based on an American ideal that founding fathers such as Adams and Jefferson insisted be part of the U.S. Constitution: that no citizen's rights can be violated to achieve an end. Government exists to protect an individual citizen's rights and must not coerce an individual to relinquish a right, even to preserve an institution that has served society well. It is a virtue and a value that in many ways has served a nation of immigrants very well. Immigrants had to be tolerated and protected by the majority in order to promote the diversity needed for a dynamic society.

But like most virtues and values, this conception of tolerance has its down side. At its worst, the ethics of tolerance promotes a rather narrow, selfish focus on the individual. The individual has to find a place in a society, and if individuals are going to live in a community some sort of hierarchy of rights must be instituted; the ethics of tolerance however provides very few clues about how to set this hierarchy. The glorification of the individual that is essential to the ethics of tolerance makes it quite difficult for a society to challenge an individual to make sacrifices that are necessary in order to preserve those institutions that, in turn, help the society to function for the common good.

Applying Ethics

So why did the cigarette industry so fall out of favor with public policy officials? Why has its "sin" cousin, gambling, flourished as it has suffered a rapid decline? In comparing the evolution of these two controversial public policy concerns, it would be instructive to analyze the roles that the ethics of sacrifice and the ethics of tolerance have played in determining how public policy makers view each issue. Let us once again examine how each type of ethical reasoning is utilized by groups that either oppose or support these activities.

Advocates of increasing gambling activities (whether lottery, casino, Internet gambling, or sport gambling) and those who wish to limit government's involvement in the cigarette industry invariably employ the ethics of tolerance as their primary moral argument as they make their case in the public policy arena. Their argument for both issues is simply that society must tolerate these activities since individuals have the right to engage in them as long as they are not harming anyone else. Of course they also point out the economic benefits that the government enjoys from these industries. While public policy makers also acknowledge that these activities might be harmful to a few individuals, they maintain that the states ought to profit from these activities, since the vast majority of smokers and gamblers will continue to smoke or gamble, whether or not the state permits these activities. So why should the state not use the profit from smoking and gambling for good causes such as education and aid to the elderly?

Meanwhile, opponents of these sin industries have generally utilized the ethics of sacrifice as their primary ethical retort in their fight against these vices. They argue that the benefits that society accrues by allowing these activities in no way justify the costs caused by engaging in these activities. Society must protect itself from these activities since they bring great harm on some segments of society. The harm done to society more than outweighs the harm done by violating an individual's right to engage in these activities. Therefore, opponents would argue that an individual ought to sacrifice the right to gamble and to smoke cigarettes for society's overall good.

So why has the cigarette industry become the endless target of public policy initiatives to restrict the use of cigarettes while the gambling industry has not only withstood attacks but has actually increased its presence throughout the United States? It is because the cigarette industry has lost its ability to utilize the ethics of tolerance to defend its right to exist while the gambling industry has effectively employed the ethics of tolerance—so much so that "a majority of U.S. adults now favor licensed casinos in their own states."[15]

Since the advent of the passive smoking debate in 1993, opponents of the cigarette industry have begun to utilize an ethics of tolerance argument that they were not able to use prior to 1993. They make the following argument: Cigarette smokers no longer have the "right" to smoke because it has been proven that nonsmokers are negatively affected by cigarette smoke. In other words, the right to smoke can no longer be tolerated since it interferes with the rights of nonsmokers to live in a smoke-free environment. Meanwhile, the vast majority of Americans seem to believe that gambling is an individual's right. Since the individual gambler is not hurting anyone else, it is generally seen as quite acceptable for the state to profit from this activity.

Next we will examine whether this shift in ethical thinking has had any impact on public policy toward treating the social costs associated with gambling and tobacco usage.

Public Policy Implications
Data Collection: Gambling

Data for state spending on gambling is not easily found. Whereas the tobacco data is aggregated and readily available, the quality of state reporting for gambling treatment varies greatly. The data for revenues from gambling and spending on problem and compulsive gambling comes from a variety of sources, depending upon the state. The last known aggregation of data like this was commissioned by the North American Association of State and Provincial Lotteries (NASPL) in 1998. Their data collection was based on a survey which was sent to state governments, local affiliates of the National Council on Problem Gambling (NCPG), lottery commissions, and casino operators. These groups self-reported contributions made to problem and compulsive gambling. The NASPL is planning on conducting another survey into state spending on problem gambling in 2008.

However, with that data unavailable, I attempted to piece together state spending on problem and compulsive gambling with public information. When looking at state revenues from gambling, I looked at five main categories: commercial casinos, racinos, Indian casinos, noncasino devices, and state lotteries. The American Gaming Association (AGA) has made publicly available all data used for commercial casinos and racinos. Indian casino revenue generally does not make its way back into state coffers unless the tribal compacts between the states and the tribes specifically allocate some monies. For instance, in Arizona, the tribes must pay a certain percentage of net casino profits to the state's general fund, part of which is allocated directly to problem gambling programs. In Connecticut, the two tribal nations that do have casinos pay an annual fee to the state, which essentially amounts to a noncompete agreement. where the state of Connecticut agrees to allow a monopoly on gaming activities to the two extant casinos. Noncasino device revenue is only included for Connecticut and Montana because each of these states publicly reported additional gaming revenue from charitable gaming and video game machines, respectively. Finally, state lottery Web sites publicly disclose the net revenue that returns to state coffers after prize payouts and administrative costs. The figures are included irrespective of how the state chooses to use the dollars, whether for general fund contributions, education, property tax relief, or otherwise. All data is from the most recent year available, usually calendar year 2004 for the nonlottery revenue and fiscal year 2005 for the lottery revenue. Due to the lack of consistency in the reporting of state data (especially given the different closing dates for state fiscal years) census figures from the U.S. Census Bureau that were used to calculate per capita numbers are from 2004. A detailed listing of state-by-state data and sources is available in the appendix at the end of this chapter.[16]

It is important to note that the revenue figures do not truly reflect the gross economic benefit (before any social costs) of gambling. The lottery revenues do not account for the federal or state income tax on winnings. They also do not count the jobs created within the lottery commissions and possibly in lottery outlets. This is even true in the case of nonlottery forms of gambling. The American Gaming Association reports gaming tax revenue in the state of Mississippi to be $333.01 million. This does not even count the 28,932 jobs that result in $1.009 billion in casino employee wages.[17] The large economic impact of casinos is one of the reasons why states have taken increasingly more positive stances towards their introduction. In summary, the economic benefit is difficult to measure, though perhaps not as difficult as the social costs.

State reporting on problem gambling spending is even more dispersed than revenue reporting. The data was culled from a variety of places—lottery Web sites, state-sponsored gambling studies newspaper articles and lottery appropriations. Data also was used from the Association of Problem Gambling Service Administrators, the North American Association of State and Provincial Lotteries, and the National Council on Problem Gambling. Once again, this data is what is most recently available, and per capita amounts of spending are calculated based on 2004 U.S. Census figures. State-by-state data and sources are available in the appendix.

It is important to note that these numbers are clearly much lower than what states actually spend on problem gambling. For instance, almost all state lotteries spend some money on running 24-hour problem gambling hotlines, which is not reported. Private contributions to problem gambling services are also not counted, unless the contribution is part of a tribal compact or a legislated agreement between the state and the commercial casinos or racinos. In most cases, state mental health spending and other medical spending for gambling addiction is not reported separately and, as a result, is not included. As in the case of the revenue figures, it is important to consider how much higher the actual social costs are than the reported spending numbers. It is probably the social costs, as hard as they are to estimate, that are the relevant costs for policy makers as they attempt to set optimal tax rates.

Data Collection: Tobacco

Data for the tobacco industry is much more readily available and is aggregated.[18] This chapter uses tobacco revenue and state funding data from the Campaign for Tobacco-Free Kids. .

Data: Summary Statistics

Gambling

Presented in table 15.3 are the summary statistics for the gambling revenue and addiction spending data in the appendix. Clearly, not many of the states spend a significant amount per capita on problem gambling treatment and prevention (median = 0.08 millions). The Pearson correlation coefficient (r), which measures the relationship between the revenue and the spending, is 0.63. Importantly, the null hypothesis that there is no relationship between revenue and spending (r = 0) can be rejected at a statistically significant level. This suggests that revenue and spending are positively related: the more revenue a state takes in from gambling, the more it usually spends on problem gambling programs. It also appears that states with casinos (such as, Iowa, Indiana, Louisiana, and Nevada) generally have good records relative to other states on their addiction spending per capita.

Tobacco

The data presented in table 15.4 are the summary statistics for the tobacco revenue and addiction spending data found in the appendix. When looking at the descriptive statistics, it is fairly clear that states spend more on tobacco problems than on gambling problems (median = $1.81 million). There is also an interesting difference in the significance of the Pearson coefficient.

TABLE 15.3
[U.S. State Gambling Revenue vs. Problem Gambling Spending]

		Top 20%	Middle 50%	Bottom 25%
Spending per Capita	Top 25%	Oregon		North Dakota
		Louisiana		Nebraska
		Iowa		
		Indiana		
		Connecticut		
		Nevada		
		Rhode Island		
		West Virginia		
		Deleware		
	Middle 50%	New Jersey	New Mexico	Arizona
		South Dakota	Tennessee	Washington
			Texas	Minnesota
			Ohio	Wisconsin
			Florida	Kansas
			South Carolina	California
			Michigan	
			Massachusetts	
			Missouri	
			Illinois	
			New York	
			Mississippi	
	Bottom 25%		Kentucky	Idaho
			Colorado	Maine
			Georgia	Vermont
			Virginia	
			New Hampshire	
			Montana	
			Pennsylvania	
			Maryland	

Note: Alabama, Alaska, Arkansas, Hawaii, North Carolina, Oklahoma, Utah, and Wyoming are not included.

TABLE 15.3 (CONT.)

Descriptive Statistics

	Revenue	Spending
25%	34.26*	0.02
Median	62.97	0.08
75%	118.42	0.38
Pearson Correlation	0.630	
Sig. (2-tailed)	0.000	

*The unit under "Descriptive Statistics" is "millions of dollars."

Though the coefficient of correlation is positive (0.185), it is not statistically significant. Therefore, unlike in the case of gambling, it cannot be said with confidence that states that take in more revenue from excise taxes on tobacco generally spend more on tobacco addiction.

Implications for Future Research

We have found that states seem to be very inconsistent with their policies towards the gambling and tobacco industries. Only in the case of gambling is addiction spending significantly and positively related to state revenues. These inconsistencies certainly arise because of how conflicted state governments are when they make policy decisions in these industries. They want people to use these industries, but not too many people. They sometimes want to discourage use, but again, not too much. It almost seems that there is a golden mean in each industry, and the lawmakers' task is to find that mean with good public policy. This task is made much more difficult because the mean changes over time due to changing state budget needs, political pressure, or social attitudes. Finally, the goal for states is not as clear as the goals for private firms. Should states maximize profits or stakeholders' interests? Even if states were to maximize profits, there is no reliable means of measuring costs and benefits. The above analysis clearly points to a trend of states harvesting revenue from the cigarette industry while placing a bet that the gambling industry will continue to flourish.

TABLE 15.4

[U.S. State Tobacco Revenue vs. Problem Addiction Spending]

		Top 20%	*Middle 50%*	*Bottom 25%*
Spending per Capita	**Top 25%**	Alaska	Arkansas	Colorado
		Delaware	Minnesota	Mississippi
		Hawaii	Montana	
		Maine	North Dakota	
		Vermont	Washington	
			Wyoming	
	Middle 50%	Massachusetts	Arizona	North Carolina
		New Jersey	California	Oklahoma
		Oregon	Illinois	Utah
		Pennsylvania	Indiana	Virginia
		Rhode Island	Iowa	
			Louisiana	
			Maryland	
			Nebraska	
			Nevada	
			New Mexico	
			New York	
			Ohio	
			South Dakota	
			West Virginia	
			Wisconsin	
	Bottom 25%	Connecticut	Florida	Alabama
		Michigan	Idaho	Georgia
		New Hampshire	Kansas	Kentucky
				Missouri
				South Carolina
				Tennessee
				Texas

TABLE 15.4 (CONT.)

Descriptive Statistics		
	Revenue	*Spending*
25%	24.25*	0.66
Median	44.77	1.81
75%	60.38	4.28
Pearson Correlation	0.185	
Sig. (2-tailed)	0.199	

*The unit under "Descriptive Statistics" is "millions of dollars."

There is much room for further research into the policy decisions of states in the sin industries. This is true especially in
the gambling industry, where information on state spending on
addiction and revenues going to state coffers is not widely available. Further research must also be done in trying to quantify
social costs in the sin industries so that states might have better
information in making policy decisions.

Finally, we need to ask the question whether or not the spread
and acceptance of gambling as a form of entertainment will
continue at its present pace. Clearly this expansion of gambling
depends on whether it can produce the revenue that the public
policy makers seek and on the continued acceptance by the public of an ethic that places an absolute premium on the expression
of the self over any claim for community or institutional need.
It is this glorification of the self that makes gambling not only
a possibility but a necessity in the near future. While the rise of
gambling has had and will continue to have many implications
for American society, as well as many other societies throughout the world, perhaps its greatest challenge to any society is the
need to establish a balance between the concerns of the ethics of
tolerance and the concerns of the ethics of sacrifice. The ability
of a society to balance these moral viewpoints is the hallmark
of a healthy and vibrant democratic system, which the world so
desperately needs in the twenty-first century.

Appendix

Table 15.A1

State Gambling Revenues and the Spending on Problem Gambling Programs

	2004 Population	Commercial Casino Revenue	Racino Revenue	Indian Casinos	Noncasino Devices	Lottery	Total Gambling Revenue	Per Capita	Problem Gambling Spending	Per Capita
AL	4.53						0	0	0.00	0.00
AK	0.66						0	0	0.00	0.00
AZ	5.74			73		116	189	33	1.61	0.28
AR	2.75						0	0	0.00	0.00
CA	34.84					1,176	1,176	33	3.09	0.09
CO	4.60	100				102	201	44	0.00	0.00
CT	3.50		0	418	7	269	693	198	1.53	0.44
DE	0.83		196			234	430	518	1.50	1.81
FL	17.39					1.133	1,133	65	1.30	0.07
GA	8.92					396	396	44	0.20	0.02
HI	1.26						0	0	0.00	0.00
ID	1.40					26	26	19	0.00	0.00
IL	12.71	802				619	1,421	112	0.90	0.07
IN	6.23	761				190	950	153	2.67	0.43

IA	2.95	253	98		51	402	136	6.54	2.21
KS	2.73				65	65	24	0.08	0.03
KY	4.14				158	158	38	0.00	0.00
LA	4.51	437	43		110	590	131	2.50	0.55
ME	1.31				42	42	32	0.00	0.00
MD	5.56		5		477	482	87	0.00	0.00
MA	6.41				661	661	103	0.65	0.10
MI	10.10	279			668	947	94	3.00	0.30
MN	5.10				106	106	21	1.90	0.37
MS	2.90	333				333	115	0.29	0.10
MO	5.76	403			218	621	108	0.45	0.08
MT	0.93			50	6	56	61	0.00	0.00
NE	1.75				22	22	13	0.75	0.43
NV	2.33	887				887	380	0.88	0.38
NH	1.30				74	74	57	0.00	0.00
NJ	8.69	471			765	1,236	142	0.60	0.07
NM	1.90		37		36	73	39	0.09	0.05
NY	19.28		137		2,063	2,200	114	1.30	0.07
NC	8.54					0	0	0.00	0.00
ND	0.64				6	6	9	0.26	0.41

TABLE 15.A1 (CONT.)

	2004 Population	Commercial Casino Revenue	Racino Revenue	Indian Casinos	Noncasino Devices	Lottery	Total Gambling Revenue	Per Capita	Problem Gambling Spending	Per Capita
OH	11.45					645	645	56	0.35	0.03
OK	3.52						0	0	0.00	0.00
OR	3.59					430	430	120	5.85	1.63
PA	12.39					852	852	69	0.00	0.00
RI	1.08		234			281	515	477	1.90	1.76
SC	4.20					278	278	66	1.00	0.24
SD	0.77	12				115	127	165	0.20	0.26
TN	5.89					234	234	40	0.20	0.03
TX	22.47					1,010	1,010	45	4.00	0.18
UT	2.42						0	0	0.00	0.00
VT	0.62					20	20	33	0.00	0.00
VA	7.48					424	424	57	0.02	0.00
WA	6.21					116	116	19	0.40	0.06
WV	1.81		328			563	891	492	1.50	0.83
WI	5.50					132	132	24	0.25	0.05
WY	0.51						0	0	0.00	0.00

Source for Table 15.A1 & 2: various statistic Web sites at www.uscensus.gov.
Correlations: Revenue vs. Spending 0.37268905; Revenue vs. Spend/Cap 0.09048353; Rev/Cap vs. Spend/Cap 0.65423831

TABLE 15.A2

State Tobacco Revenues and the Spending on Tobacco Prevention Programs

	2004 Population	Tobacco Revenue	Per Capita	Tobacco Spending	Per Capita
AL	4.53	64.2	14.19	0.325	0.07
AK	0.66	41.0	62.33	5.7	8.67
AR	5.74	274.3	47.49	23.10	4.02
AZ	2.75	128.1	46.58	17.50	6.36
CA	34.84	1021.3	28.49	79.70	2.22
CO	4.60	53.5	11.63	27.00	5.87
CT	3.50	276.2	78.94	0.04	0.01
DE	0.83	71.4	86.02	9.20	11.08
FL	17.39	421.9	24.27	1.00	0.06
GA	8.92	216.2	24.24	3.10	0.35
HI	1.26	77.5	61.40	5.80	4.60
ID	1.40	45.7	32.76	0.54	0.39
IL	12.71	728.4	57.3	11.00	0.87
IN	6.23	329.8	52.97	10.80	1.73
IA	2.95	86.9	29.43	5.60	1.90

TABLE 15.A2 (CONT.)

	2004 Population		Tobacco Revenue	Per Capita		Tobacco Spending	Per Capita
KS	2.73		120.3	44.01		1.00	0.37
KY	4.14		20.5	4.95		2.70	0.65
LA	4.51		130.3	28.91		8.00	1.78
ME	1.31		92.6	70.42		14.20	10.80
MD	5.56		264.0	47.47		9.20	1.65
MA	6.41		422.7	65.97		4.30	0.67
MI	10.10		851.0	84.22		0.00	0.00
MN	5.10		175.4	34.42		22.10	4.34
MS	2.90		42.9	14.79		20.00	6.89
MO	5.76		99.4	17.26		0.00	0.00
MT	0.93		42.2	45.53		6.80	7.34
NE	1.75		67.6	38.68		3.00	1.72
NV	2.33		122.1	52.34		4.20	1.80
NH	1.30		99.2	76.36		0.00	0.00
NJ	8.69		748.6	86.19		11.50	1.32
NM	1.90		59.6	31.32		6.00	3.15
NY	19.28		962.1	49.40		43.40	2.25

NC	8.54		39.8	4.66		15.00	1.76
ND	0.64		18.1	28.45		3.10	4.87
OH	11.45		530.7	46.35		47.20	4.12
OK	3.52		56.3	15.98		8.90	2.53
OR	3.59		240.1	66.85		3.50	0.97
PA	12.39		957.7	77.27		32.90	2.65
RI	1.08		110.9	102.69		2.10	1.94
SC	4.20		25.4	6.05		0.00	0.00
SD	0.77		26.3	34.13		0.71	0.92
TN	5.89		110.2	18.70		0.00	0.00
TX	22.47		486.5	21.65		7.00	0.31
UT	2.42		53.6	22.14		7.20	2.97
VT	0.62		49.8	80.16		4.90	7.89
VA	7.48		16.1	2.15		12.80	1.71
WA	6.21		324.3	52.25		27.20	4.38
WV	1.81		97.9	54.01		27.20	4.38
WI	5.50		291.3	52.93		10.00	1.82
WY	0.51		13.9	27.48		5.90	11.66

Correlations: Revenue vs. Spending 0.59071114; Revenue vs. Spend/Cap -0.2605155; Rev/Cap vs. Spending/Cap 0.18472558

16

The Culture War Issue That Never Was
Why the Right and Left Have Overlooked Gambling

Alan Wolfe

Gambling and Democratic Theory

An industry does not become as big as the gambling industry in the United States has become without deep and direct involvement in politics. An activity that is increasingly relied upon to fund services offered by the government cannot help but become subject to government investigation and concern. And a way of life long considered sinful by religious believers will, or so one assumes, become a prominent subject of moral debate in a society in which religion plays such a prominent role in public life. Given the particular nature of the gambling industry, it can hardly be surprising that it has become the focus of considerable public attention.

This chapter examines not whether gambling is intimately involved with politics, but how. This is more a normative than an empirical question, but in this case Americans have a well-established standard against which political practices can be normatively judged: the standard of democracy. Democratic theorists hold that the ultimate source of political authority lies with the people themselves. If a policy, political practice, or direction for a country is established with some kind of popular consent,

citizens generally approve of it procedurally, even if they disagree
with it substantively; indeed, democratic stability is premised
upon the idea that policies arrived at in legitimate fashion ought
to be accepted by all whatever their views on the policy. If, on
the other hand, citizens feel that decisions are made without public input and scrutiny—by unelected leaders, for example, or by
unrepresentative interests acting in secret—they may feel that,
lacking democratic legitimacy, such policies can be either be
ignored, disobeyed, or challenged.

Democratic theorists, as the political philosopher Hannah
Pitkin points out, can be divided between those who insist on
weak versus strong criteria of accountability.[1] Joseph Schumpeter
belongs in the first camp.[2] Rejecting any notions associated
with a Rouseauian conception of the general will, Schumpeter
famously argued that so long as elites compete for office, criteria of democratic accountability have been met. Strong theorists
of accountability, by contrast, who include John Dewey or, in
today's world, Jürgen Habermas, Amy Gutmann, and Dennis
Thompson, hold that mere competition is insufficient; there must
be arguments presented in transparent fashion to citizens who
should exercise standards of reason in judging between them.[3]
For present purposes, both approaches can be used. If gambling
is found to satisfy both weak and strong standards of accountability, it can be said to have considerable democratic legitimacy.
If it satisfies weak standards but not strong standards, we can
conclude that it has some democratic legitimacy. If it fails to satisfy either, the conclusion would follow that it has little or no
democratic legitimacy.

A second criterion of democratic performance involves some
degree of balance, competition, or power sharing. As an industry
supplying a good for which there is more than adequate demand,
gambling interests have every right to lobby legislatures in behalf
of their own interests; freedom of speech and association are generally held to be essential procedures through which processes
of democracy work. At the same time, both the Schumpeterian
emphasis on competition as well as the insights of pluralist thinkers from Tocqueville to Robert A. Dahl and Charles Lindblom
warn that democratic success is best established when the influence of any one interest group is counterbalanced by others;

freedom of association exercised in such a way that the power of any one group or side to a controversy is not checked by the others is, in this sense, insufficient for purposes of accountability.[4] A society that allowed no group to press claims on its own behalf would not be democratic. But neither, properly speaking, would be a society in which only one side of a controversy were organized.

The same idea holds for party competition. On the one hand, as theorists such as Nancy Rosenblum argue, parties are part and parcel of democratic governance.[5] At the same time, as even the weaker Schumpeterian account of responsibility holds, there must be competition between them. A party system lacking such competition would lead to a one-party state that would not generally be considered democratic, no matter how large and inclusive that party might be. To evaluate the degree to which gambling meets standards of democratic theory, it is important to consider whether the party system is sufficiently differentiated to present adequate choices and sufficiently robust to allow the public to make its preferences known.

Although gambling is a relatively recent phenomenon in the United States, it has been in existence long enough to draw some tentative conclusions about the extent to which it meets the expectations of democratic theory. I will concentrate on the two criterion just discussed. By comparing gambling to culture war issues that involve religious and moral points of view, such as prohibition, pornography, and abortion, I will examine whether the debates over gambling present citizens and voters with clearly articulated positions involving the moral tradeoffs that gambling raises. I will then look at how America's two main political parties have responded to the issue of gambling to see whether those parties have differentiated themselves sufficiently from each other on the issue such that those choices for and against gambling can be effectuated.

The Culture War That Never Was

Only a generation or so ago, gambling was legal in only one state, and that state, Nevada, had a seedy reputation because of the role played by organized crime in financing the casinos that had sprouted up in Las Vegas and other areas.[6] Not only was gambling legal in Nevada, it was also the one state in the United States where it was possible to obtain a relatively quick divorce, and it was also known as a place where sex was widely available for purchase. Gambling has been ubiquitous throughout American history: the staple of westerns, the stuff of novels, part and parcel of an expanding and vibrant commercial society.[7] But throughout the first half of the twentieth century, it was also, in most places, illegal. However much gambling Americans actually did, and surely it was always considerable, the law did not want it spread across the United States but wanted it confined to one relatively remote part of the country.

Gambling was treated as a less than wholesome activity in part due to a long-standing tradition of religious opposition to it. In the first years of the twentieth century, Walter Rauschenbusch, a left-leaning Baptist minister and the founder of the Social Gospel movement in the United States, published *Christianity and the Social Crisis*, a book that, along with denouncing capitalism's rampant inequalities, included an attack on gambling, calling it "the vice of the savage" and concluding that "true civilization ought to outgrow it, as it has outgrown tattooing and cannibalism."[8] From Rauschenbusch's perspective, gambling was evil because capitalism was evil; he saw little difference between the two. True, he wrote, risk is an inevitable part of life. But capitalist society, by making speculation an economic virtue, undermined the religious duty to care and love those to whom we are close, especially those in our families. For Rauschenbusch, greed was not good, and the instinct of a commercial society was to promote greed.

Leaders of the evangelical and fundamentalist movements that sprang up in the United States in its first two decades, such as Billy Sunday, also put gambling on their list of forbidden sins—and with far more fervor than liberal Protestants such as Rauschenbusch. As David Skeel has argued, any sympathies evangelicals may have toward libertarian economics usually disappear when gambling is the issue.[9] As late as 1997, the Southern Baptist Convention (SBC), as far to the Right on social and economic issues as Rauschenbusch was to the Left, passed a resolution, its fourteenth on the issue, asking Christians "to exercise their influence by refusing to participate in any form of gambling or its promotion" and demanding that "political leaders . . . enact laws restricting and eventually eliminating all forms of gambling and its advertisement."[10] The SBC's reasons for opposing gambling were not the same as Rauschenbusch's; criticism of capitalism has never been high on the SBC's agenda. But there were many other reasons why it made sense for Southern Baptists to view gambling as sinful. Like Rauschenbusch, SBC leaders worried about gambling's impact on the family. But they were also motivated by a concern that American society has become far too hedonistic for its own good. In their eyes, abortion and gay rights were wrong because in both cases, individuals were basking in self-indulgent behavior with no understanding of the need of sinful people to steel themselves against temptation. It is not hard to see how gambling could become part of the same critique of what, to a Southern Baptist, constituted a reign of moral decadence and value relativism.

Opposition to gambling can also be viewed as a byproduct of that Puritan strain in American culture that produced this country's first great culture war: the battle over Prohibition. Many liberal Protestants were as opposed to alcohol consumption as they were to gambling; Rauschenbusch, for example, wrote that "the Church should undertake a new temperance crusade with all the resources of advanced physiological and sociological science,"[11] a position that both underestimated the power of drink and overestimated the influence of sociology. On the Right end of the religious spectrum, support for Prohibition was even stronger; the ratification of the Eighteenth Amendment to the Constitution and the passage of the Volstead Act were both due to the power of the evangelical vote in the more rural quarters of the United States. Prohibition was an anti-immigrant and anti-urban affair, and since so many immigrant city dwellers were Catholic, it was also an anti-Catholic affair. (Even Rauschenbusch, the liberal Protestant, was decidedly anti-Catholic in his theology.) The movement to ban the manufacture and consumption of alcohol was America's version of the European *Kulturkampf*.

Prohibition is often cited as a period in which Americans were caught up in the sway of irrational passions, a "symbolic crusade," as one sociologist called it, reflective of the changing nature of American status groups at the time.[12] All that may be true, but from the standpoint of democratic theory, Prohibition offers a strong case for democratic legitimacy working at its best. When the issue was the making and consumption of alcoholic beverages, public attention was intense to the point of producing an amendment to the U.S. Constitution, the highest hurdle for any popular movement to overcome. While both the Eighteenth Amendment and the Volstead Act were routinely violated in practice, no one could argue that Prohibition, having met such high standards of accountability, was illegitimate. And the fact that an amendment to the Constitution banning drinking was repealed by yet another amendment similarly gave legitimacy to the campaign to return to the previous status quo on the issue. Debates on the issue were passionate, but they were, when all was said and done, debates. The public heard arguments on all sides of the question, made up its mind, and, when confronted with the consequences of its decision, changed its mind. From the standpoint of democratic performance, it is hard to ask for more than that.

Gambling is, in this regard, on the opposite end of the pole from Prohibition. The rate of gambling's expansion in the United States in recent years has been truly staggering. New Hampshire in 1964 became the first state to establish a lottery; now some forty-one states and the District of Columbia have them.[13] Ten states have joined Nevada to create legalized casinos. Another eleven allow racetrack casino betting. Televised poker games and Internet betting are present in more homes than can possibly be counted. Roughly one in four Americans visited a casino in 2006, and gross revenue from all gaming venues came to $32.42 billion in 2006, a 6.6 percent increase over the previous year.[14] It is hard to imagine a change in the American social fabric as dramatic as the movement of gambling from prohibited to accepted behavior in the course of one generation.

Yet in comparison to Prohibition, no large-scale national debate took place over gambling. True, conservative Protestants opposed its adoption in southern states, and usually with considerable vigor; there is no doubting the serious manner in which they took up the issue. But, with the exception of Alabama, this was without notable success; in Georgia, Tennessee, and Mississippi, either a failure to unite Christian opposition across racial lines or concerns about raising taxes overcame the efforts of conservative Christian churches to stop the spread of gambling.[15] Elsewhere in the country, moreover, religious opposition tended to be muted: Catholics were rarely as fervently opposed to gambling as were Protestants, and no opportunity existed to regret a decision to prohibit it, as had happened with Prohibition, because no attempt to prevent it was ever contemplated in the first place. For those who scorn the campaign in favor of Prohibition as the last gasp of backward forces, the lack of a similar prohibitionist movement against gambling can be taken as an indication of political maturity. Yet at the same time, the lack of any sustained debate one way or the other about gambling's virtues and vices means that gambling may never meet the high standard for political accountability associated with Prohibition.

Another major difference between the prohibition of alcohol and the lack of a sustained prohibitionist campaign against gambling is that the religious opposition to the latter exhibited at the state level never developed, as it did with respect to alcohol, into a national movement. Despite its condemnatory resolutions, the Southern Baptist Convention did not elevate gambling to the status of a major moral concern the way it did abortion and gay rights, and while other conservative Christians such as Jerry Falwell and Pat Robertson would routinely include denunciation of gambling in their sermons, their jeremiads were more like half-hearted attacks on dancing and drinking than they were akin to the full-scaled attacks on U.S. Supreme Court decisions dealing with school prayer or the right to life. The ironies here are striking. Throughout much of American history, evangelical denominations such as the Baptists were strongly committed to separation of church and state and strongly opposed to gambling. But in recent years, those positions were to some degree reversed. The SBC modified its teachings on church and state to accommodate a greater role for religion in the public sphere while downplaying the prohibitionist side of their religion that had played a dominant role in previous periods of American history.

Not only has there been less religious opposition to gambling than one might expect, but many of the best-known political activists associated with the rise of the Christian right became involved, in one way or another, with gambling itself. The most famous example was *Book of Virtues* author William Bennett, who publicly acknowledged his own gambling activities—and also made clear that, in his view, gambling was not as sinful as abortion or gay sex. Bennett, however, is Catholic, and Catholics had never viewed gambling as sinful in the way conservative Protestants had. A more serious problem for the religious right emerged when people closely associated with it found themselves intertwined with gambling interests. Ralph Reed, the very model of a Christian right political activist, had worked closely with Jack Abramoff, a well-connected Republican lobbyist, involving himself directly in efforts to deny gambling licenses to some Indian tribes while pushing for them on behalf of others. The Reverend Louis Shelton, a lesser-known but equally important Christian right political activist and fervent critic of homosexuality, also worked with Abramoff in behalf of gambling interests. Scandals involving leaders of the religious right cannot be offered as an explanation of the unwillingness of conservative Christians to make gambling a culture war issue, for these scandals occurred relatively late in the game. But they do symbolize the fact that any negative attitudes conservative Protestants may have had toward gambling were not strong enough to prevent leaders of the movement from seeking to profit from such activities.

One reason that conservative Protestants did not make gambling into a major culture war issue is that, despite their reputation as political extremists, conservative religious leaders in the United States operate as political pragmatists unwilling to criticize positions or practices popular among their members. Examples are plentiful. Although conservative Christian churches frequently forbid women from serving as clergy and call for wives to submit to their husbands, activists such as James Dobson do not directly call for women to stay home and be full-time mothers because they recognize how much women in their churches need to be in the labor force.[16] Along similar lines, conservative Protestant churches view divorce as sinful and self-indulgent, but divorce rates are so high within them that churches are more likely to offer help with the problems associated with divorce than to exclude divorced people from their membership roles.[17] Evangelicals face a dilemma when they deal with American culture.[18] They can, if they are so inclined, turn their backs upon it, as many fundamentalist churches do, but in so doing they lose an opportunity to evangelize. Or they can try to meet the culture halfway in the attempt to reach out to as many as possible, but in so doing they run the risk of being influenced by the very forces in the culture to which they object. Evangelical Protestantism has grown in the United States at least in part because most, although not all, conservative Christians opt for the latter approach.

Gambling presents another version of the same dilemma. There is no doubting gambling's popularity; if the industry lacked customers, there would be no particular reason to pay that much attention to it. Not only is gambling popular, but it also resonates with many of those among whom evangelical religion is also popular; there is no direct correlation between the popularity of gambling and the ubiquity of evangelicalism because the South, which was resistant to gambling in previous periods of American history, was relatively late in the game in the current gambling wave.[19] Still, gambling is big business in states where conservative Christianity is strong, such as Georgia and Mississippi, and the typical demographic profile of the gambler and the church-goer would appear to be similar. For this reason, gambling and religion can be viewed as competitors for the same customers; if conservative churches were to force a choice between them—and gambling establishments have no reason to insist upon such a choice—they might lose people to whom they wish their message to be addressed. Toning down language on gambling represents a necessary accommodation with American culture, the kind represented, for example, in the decision by Wheaton College, the prominent evangelical institution of higher education, to drop its long-term ban on dancing in 2003.

The religious right never developed the traction in response to gambling that they did, for example, in their response to abortion; this was in large part due to the alliances that form around and between religious denominations in the United States. Historically, evangelical Protestant denominations did not take pains to hide their hostility toward the Catholic Church; nearly everything for which Catholicism stood—a hierarchical conception of religious authority, a long tradition of theological interpretation, a celibate clergy, liturgical forms of worship, highly decorative symbols—were things conservative Protestantism opposed. In the aftermath of *Roe v. Wade*, however, conservative Protestants and conservative Catholics found common ground in their mutual opposition to abortion; as scholars such as Robert Wuthnow and James Davison Hunter have argued, the culture war transformed the conflict between religions into a form of conflict in which conservatives from all religions had more in common with each other than they did with liberals from within their own tradition.[20] Gambling, however, did not fit this scenario very well; while conservative Catholics are indeed opposed to abortion, they are not necessarily opposed to gambling. For all the efforts to bring conservatives from all faiths together around political issues, only some issues achieved that objective, and gambling was not one of them.

Finally, gambling came onto the political scene in a way quite different from abortion—or, for that matter, gay rights. In 1973 the U.S. Supreme Court issued its ruling in *Roe v. Wade. Roe*, of course, gave women the right to abortion. Whatever one's position on the merits of *Roe*, it seems fair to say that by nationalizing the issue the Supreme Court brought an end to processes at the state level seeking different policies, ranging from abortion on demand, to bans on abortion, to exceptions in particular cases such as rape or the health of the mother. For this reason, *Roe* has been strongly criticized, especially by those on the Right, for failing to meet standards of democratic accountability.[21] There was a political process underway that would have resulted in a solution widely accepted by the people because the people were involved in it, these critics maintain. All such democratic venues were shut down by a decision made by unelected judges. In some more extreme versions of this way of thinking, such as those associated with Robert Bork, we witnessed an example of judicial tyranny.[22] When the U.S. Supreme Court then overruled *Bowers v. Hardwick* to strike down state sodomy laws in Texas, thereby siding with advocates of rights for homosexuals, charges of judicial usurpation were intensified.

Yet if the Court's decision in *Roe v. Wade* preempted a search for accountability in one way, it kick-started its emergence in another. One of the unexpected legacies of *Roe* turned out to be the mobilization of the religious right; determined to reverse the Court's decision, conservative voters eventually succeeded in electing political leaders who appointed judges willing to allow restrictions on the procedure. It remains to be seen whether the U.S. Supreme Court will one day explicitly overturn the decision; if it does, it is quite possible that such a move would stimulate a counterpolitical movement from the Left. For the moment, in any case, abortion is still legal but more difficult to obtain. Legally speaking, there may not exist clear-cut guidelines about abortion. But politically, and in the most herky-jerky of ways, current policy is more or less in line with public opinion, which wants abortion regulated but also permitted.[23] A similar compromise may come to pass with respect to gay marriage, moreover, which is likely to be legal in a few states, illegal in most of the others, and subject to an interpretation of the Constitution, which would not allow a gay couple married in one state to be considered married in all of them. However such compromises are reached, they allow both sides of the controversy room to make their views known yet also produce outcomes in which both sides can claim at least partial victory. This, in its own way, is a victory for accountability.

There has been no U.S. Supreme Court decision asserting the right to gamble in a fashion comparable to the way in which *Roe* proclaimed a right to abortion. It would seem to follow, then, that compared to abortion, the legitimacy of gambling was never in question. To be sure, laws authorizing casino and racetrack gambling were often passed as a result of "stealth" campaigns without much publicity or scrutiny. Yet gambling was, after all, legalized in state after state by open votes in state legislatures and in a large number of cases was also subject to direct voter approval in the form of ballot propositions or state constitutional amendment procedures.[24] However open the process, moreover, gambling was never legalized, as the right to abortion was, by judicial decisions made by unelected judges. If one thinks gambling is a bad thing, one has to place blame on a political process that corresponds with democratic procedures.

Yet in a paradoxical way the very fact that gambling was not imposed by unelected judges on an inattentive public also meant that there was little reason to organize a countermovement against it. Lacking such a countermovement, the United States also lacked a serious and sustained debate over gambling's morality. There have been countless volumes published by political and theological thinkers debating the morality of abortion, but almost none on gambling. Religious activists have mobilized campaigns to elect candidates based on pledges to overturn *Roe v. Wade*, but no such pledges are forthcoming on matters dealing with state lotteries or casinos. U.S. Supreme Court decisions that impose restrictions on abortion are examined by law professors in great detail, but few law professors concern themselves with the ethical and moral questions raised by gambling. In other words, even though the rise of gambling was democratic in the sense that it took place through the normal political process, it has lacked the kind of sustained debate characteristic of some of the other battles fought in America's culture war.

Culture wars are not especially healthy for democracy. They encourage polarization and extremism. Political campaigns organized around them are usually negative in tone and demagogic in style. They lead antagonists on either side to demonize each other and run the risk of alienating people in the center who do not have the same strong convictions as activists on both sides do. Yet without wishing more culture wars on the United States, one can conclude that when people care passionately about an issue, it forces participants in politics to organize themselves, raise funds, make arguments, and carefully monitor the decisions of the leaders they elect. By these criteria, the fact that gambling never became part of the culture war meant that the quality of the debate over its presence in the United States suffered.

To gauge how much it has suffered, a comparison with yet another culture war issue may be instructive. One of the most interesting political alliances in recent American politics involved the seemingly unlikely joining together of conservative Christians and feminists in a campaign against pornography.[25] From the former's point of view, pornography represented a near perfect example of sexual decadence, while from the latter's, it was an expression of the exploitation of women. Although conservative Christians and feminists had usually treated each other as enemies, the fact that they could come together on an issue exposed them to views with which they would generally not have been associated, leading to crisscrossing alliances that reduced some of the tensions brought about by the culture war in the first place.

From the viewpoint of democratic accountability, this was a positive development. One of those calling for strong conceptions of accountability, James Fishkin, brings individuals together to exchange views on an issue before they are asked their opinions, and Fishkin concludes that such interchanges, by broadening people's horizons, enable them to have more strongly articulated viewpoints.[26] His experiments, however, are somewhat artificial. Surprising alliances such as the one between Christian conservatives and feminists can be viewed as a natural form of a Fishkin experiment, encouraging people from different ideological camps to overcome their stereotypes of each other.

The rise of gambling presented a similar opportunity. Had conservative Christians decided to make gambling a greater priority, they would have sought out allies in situations where state legislatures and city councils were debating the merits of casinos or lotteries. Lacking Catholic support on the issue, they might have gained support from feminists. As on many such issues, including pornography, feminists are divided about gambling. Some believe that the feminist movement ought to stand for the fact that women are just as good at gambling as men. But others point out that gambling in practice is harmful to women, especially full-time mothers dependent on their husbands' income, an income that is considerably reduced when the husband gambles. (There is also considerable reason for feminists to be concerned about issues of domestic violence and marital infidelity associated with gambling.) Yet no such alliance between conservative Christians and feminists emerged over gambling the way it did over pornography, and, as a result, a chance for different sides in the culture war to learn from each other was lost. Once again, a seemingly democratic process of quiet approval of gambling in state legislatures made it more difficult than it otherwise would have been to have a highly public debate over gambling in which participants might have come to respect each other's viewpoints.

Highly public controversies not only lead participants to learn more about their opponents; they also encourage supporters, when faced with criticism, to sharpen and on occasion change the reasons for their support. This process was on public display during the abortion controversy. *Roe* had relied on the

right to privacy as the basis for its decision. But the most prominent feminist critic of that decision, Catherine MacKinnon,
argued strongly against such reasoning;[27] the right to privacy, she
pointed out, can protect men who abuse their wives. MacKinnon
as well as other legal scholars, including Ruth Bader Ginsburg
before she assumed her seat on the U.S. Supreme Court, claimed
that the Fourteenth Amendment's commitment to equal protection of the laws offered a stronger basis for allowing abortion
than a right found only in the "penumbra" of the Constitution—
which is where William O. Douglas located the right to privacy
in *Griswold v. Connecticut*, upon which *Roe* built.[28] Had *Roe*
never fueled a countermovement, in short, the potentially weak
grounds on which it stood would never have been challenged,
even by *Roe*'s supporters. *Roe*'s opponents forced *Roe*'s supporters to develop better arguments.

No such process took place over gambling because, in the
absence of opposition from the Right, there was no need for gambling's supporters to offer any reasons for their position. As a
consequence, if there are good moral arguments in favor of gambling, one rarely hears them. About the only vocal supporters of
gambling one can find are libertarians who believe that the regulation of any private industry by government is wrong—and even
these voices tend to be relatively rare—but this is not so much
an argument in favor of gambling as it is an argument against
government intervention. One simply cannot locate thinkers in
the United States who make arguments in favor of gambling the
way that arguments have been made in favor of a woman's right
to choose or a gay couple's right to marry; there is no Ronald
Dworkin or Andrew Sullivan when it comes to betting.[29] At least
with respect to gambling's opponents, one can still hear voices
proclaiming its sinful nature, even if such voices are muted. But
when it comes to gambling's supporters, no arguments are needed
because no arguments are taking place.

From the perspective of the gaming industry, this is probably
a good thing; lack of attention is better than furious debate. But
when an activity such as gambling spreads so widely in such a
short period of time without sustained debate over its morality, it creates potential long-run problems for its legitimacy.
This could prove to be more problematic from the standpoint of

democratic accountability than the fact that abortion was a right proclaimed by judges in the absence of public input, for if gambling continues to spread to the point where increasing numbers of Americans become uncomfortable with it, there will be few arguments and positions already available to which participants will be able to turn.

Gambling's absence from the American culture war, in conclusion, is as significant as the inclusion of other issues, such as abortion, within it. As much of my previous research ought to make clear, I am not much of a fan of the culture war.[30] But democratic accountability is better served by bitter and partisan debate than it is by no debate at all. From this point of view, American political movements and, in particular, the conservative Christian movement had an opportunity to raise the quality of American moral debate by making a campaign against gambling as important as they made, say, the question of stem cell research. It is not necessary to show that gambling causes more harm than abortion, homosexuality, or any other form of activity that conservative Christians condemn; it is sufficient that it causes enough harm to matter. Earlier generations of American religious leaders, liberal and conservative, certainly thought it did. Current religious leaders evidently do not, or at least do not to a sufficient degree. I leave it for others to argue about whether gambling's popularity causes harm to individuals. But I do believe it is clear that gambling's absence from serious discussion and debate causes harm to American democracy.

Gambling and Party Competition

The idea that every interest has the right to organize itself in behalf of its goals is fundamental to democracy, especially liberal democracy. It is the essence of the First Amendment to the U.S. Constitution. It forms the basis for that kind of political activity known as lobbying. It is, normatively speaking, far preferable to a political system in which the government, acting in the fashion of a feudal patron, decides which activities will be favored and which discouraged. The rise of gambling, from this perspective, raises few problems with respect to democratic performance. Entrepreneurs saw an opportunity to create and expand an industry. Organizing themselves, they persuaded legislatures to allow them to offer something that consumers wanted. Consumers responded by purchasing the product. To this point, it is all in accord with how democracy should work.

Yet democracy also works by encouraging those who lose out when any policy is pursued to organize themselves in opposition to it. Government without opposition is really not democratic government. There is something of Newtonian physics in modern democracy; every action generates a reaction that, while not necessarily equal, at least constrains the original movement. Thus do labor unions counter the interests of business corporations, consumers the interests of farmers, racial minorities the preferences of majorities, and so on throughout the democratic process. The principle of checks and balances does not just apply to the way the government organizes itself. It also applies to those who petition government.

Political parties play a crucial role in the process by which interests organize themselves in a democracy. If there are two sides to an issue, and if one party identifies itself with one side, the way is clear for the other party to mobilize the other side. This clearly happened with respect to abortion. Although the fact is frequently forgotten, before *Roe v. Wade* it was typically Republicans, especially those living in northeastern states, who tended to be in favor of issues such as birth control and the provision of contraceptives, while heavily Catholic voters, most of whom were reliable Democrats, were against them. *Roe v. Wade*, however, altered the party landscape in a dramatic fashion. Once opposition to abortion mobilized itself, it not only became a signature issue for Republicans, but it also helped to transform the South, which had been Democratic, into the Republican column. Meanwhile the Democratic Party began to attract feminists and others supportive of movements toward privacy and personal choice, many of whom, in an earlier era, might have been Republicans. These were not "natural" alliances, since some Catholic Democrats were also critics of *Roe*. But partisan pressures to line up on one side or the other were great, reflecting the capacity of political parties to fill political vacuums and, in so doing, to channel ideological conflict into partisan competition for office.

One of the most interesting aspects of the rise of gambling is that one cannot easily find situations in which one party supports it and the other opposes it. There are, to be sure, a number of groups that represent gambling interests, including the gaming industry itself, that lobby in behalf of expanded gambling. But their approach is frequently bipartisan, searching out opportunities wherever they can find them. And because these efforts are bipartisan, they do not stimulate countermovements from opposition parties. Instead, one sees many advantages to both political parties in favor of gambling and relatively few advantages to either one in opposing it.

Republicans, for example, are increasingly identified as a party that has made tax-cutting central to its domestic political program. In theory, supply-side economics is supposed to guarantee that cutting tax revenues will stimulate economic growth and thereby provide the government with additional revenue to spend. But there is not all that much evidence that supply-side economics works as theorized, and if it does not, Republicans who cut taxes but who still want to avoid cutting services at the state level are inevitably attracted to gambling as the solution to their problem. For them, gambling serves as a kind of hidden tax whose costs are either not seen by the people who pay them or do not raise the same kind of objections associated with more explicit forms of taxation. Thus, despite opposition from the religious right in Mississippi, a Republican governor with strong ties to the national party, Harley Barbour, became an enthusiast for the state's casino interests. Not only had Barbour been a lobbyist for the industry, he was able to benefit from the financial support of casino interests in the form of campaign contributions. For southern Republicans such as Barbour, if gambling had not existed, they would have invented it, so perfectly did it mesh with the party's support for what had become the state's largest industry as well as its concern never to raise taxes.

In other states, by contrast, the major proponents of gambling have not, like Barbour, been conservative Republicans but have been liberal Democrats. Massachusetts offers in this regard an interesting contrast to Mississippi. Faced with residents of the state crossing the border in nearby Foxwoods, Massachusetts' liberal governor Deval Patrick, the first Democrat elected to the position in many years, responded with a proposal to open three casinos within the state. It is not clear whether Patrick will be able to persuade the state legislature to go ahead with such a plan, but it is fairly clear why he supports it. Patrick, like most Democrats, would like to see increased expenditures on education, particularly in urban areas. In most states, revenues from gambling are designated for educational purposes, something that no liberal Democrat can ignore. If, for Republicans, gambling seems a pain-free method of not raising taxes, for Democrats it becomes a pain-free way of increasing spending.

Once public funds are tied to education, race comes into the gambling mix in interesting ways. African Americans can be found disproportionately within conservative Protestant denominations; if religion were a unifying force, and if religious opposition to gambling was more consequential, African American leaders might have emerged as important players in an antigambling movement. But African American politicians such as Deval Patrick are clearly on the other side of the issue, and when prospects for increased spending on education are thrown into the mix, African American clergy frequently tone down any criticisms of the practice they might otherwise be tempted to utter. This was clearly evidenced in Georgia, a state that adopted a lottery rather than casino gambling. The lottery "used to be a real hot topic for us," said Timothy McDonald, a prominent black clergyman. "But once our students started to get a college education that they never would have been able to do otherwise, we do not talk about the lottery as much."[31] If Mississippi is a state in which Republicans supported gambling, and Massachusetts is one in which a Democrat took the lead, Georgia is noteworthy because the politician most responsible for the success of its lottery, Zell Miller, was a Democrat who became a Republican.

As Reverend McDonald's comment indicates, the payoff for African Americans in Georgia was a program of college scholarships funded from gambling revenues. It is certainly a legitimate decision for African American political and religious leaders to conclude that, whatever moral objections to gambling there may be, obtaining educational funding outweighs them. And in Georgia, the HOPE Scholarship program, which helped transform Zell Miller into a national figure, was a genuinely groundbreaking development offering what seemed like a more promising way of increasing African American college enrollment than more controversial attempts at affirmative action. Yet the HOPE program proved so popular that, once it began, it became impossible to target its benefits to those who needed financial help for college the most. As the model of the HOPE Scholarship was implemented across the state, the revenue transfers made available by gambling increasingly took on a regressive dimension. So long as lottery playing remained popular among inner-city residents, which it did, the poor were being taxed, albeit in a voluntary fashion, to support a program that benefited middle-class residents of the state.

The Georgia experience captures something important about the politics of gambling. One of the issues that historically has divided Democrats from Republicans is that the former call for increased governmental services while the latter insist on lower taxes. Because of the popularity of supply-side economics, clear partisan differences on these issues have been blurred, as Republicans insist that reduced revenue need not cut expenditures, and Democrats, wary of being charged as tax-and-spend liberals, respond by demanding new programs without clear guidelines for how they will be financed. Even if gambling had never developed, in other words, the parties were on their way to a situation in which clear alternatives were not being presented to the voters. Accountability became more difficult to ascertain with both parties speaking in less forthright terms. Instead, public debate became filled with claims and counterclaims backed up with statistics that no one could properly evaluate.

Gambling's popularity scrambles the picture even more. Technically speaking, gambling is not a tax; one does not have to gamble, while one most definitely has to pay taxes. But gambling does resemble recent efforts in American politics to obfuscate informed discussion about who pays how much in taxes and who receives which benefits, and in what amounts. It is not just the fact that people who gamble do not view the money they lose as a tax. This lack of information is instead because a situation in which both parties support the displacement of tax revenues by gambling revenues makes it more difficult to judge how much progressivity there is and who benefits and loses from the shift toward gambling revenues and away from tax revenues. When both parties support gambling, if for different reasons, both have an incentive not to criticize the other. As a result, Democrats rarely point out that Republicans want to use gambling revenues as a way of protecting their insistence on tax cuts while Republicans do not criticize Democrats for spending too much on public programs; if anything, as the expansion of HOPE Scholarships shows, they become invested in new public programs. In theory, voters should be choosing parties based upon differences between them. But when it comes to gambling, politics is more like one hand clapping; there are no significant disagreements capable of clarifying positions.

This lack of differences between parties would not be a problem for democratic accountability if gambling had become an issue in the larger American culture war; it was because concerned citizens viewed the parties as failing to respond to their deeply held convictions on such issues as abortion and gay rights that the culture war developed in the first place. Without a culture war, American society lacks sharply differentiated positions over gambling. Without party competition, it also lacks vehicles for expressing whatever strong convictions on the issue remain. For this reason, the missing culture war and bipartisan support combine to guarantee that gambling will continue to spread with remarkable speed through society but they do not guarantee that its spread will be met by effective public input.

Conclusion

There are times and places when the culture war can lead to violence, as has happened over the issue of abortion. Sometimes people are so angered by their alienation from the political system, their sense that politicians are pursuing what they believe to be the wrong course without sufficient scrutiny, that they take up extralegal or illegal means against them. The logical conclusion of the culture war is civil disobedience.

No such strong reaction is ever likely to emerge out of the adoption of gambling by one American state after another. Gambling is a moral issue that, for some, encourages sinful behavior that should not be encouraged by the government. But it is also an industry, one far larger than the industry that provides abortion or stands to benefit from gay marriage. Economic issues, to the dismay of the deeply religious, can easily trump moral considerations. But economic issues can also moderate extremism. Once people stand to make money—in the case of gambling, considerable money—debates about right and wrong can quickly become decisions about how to divide the pie. For this reason, whatever damage gambling may do to democratic accountability is unlikely to threaten democratic stability. Financial issues can be negotiated in ways that moral issues cannot be.

Yet we should not pass too quickly over the issues raised for democracy by the rapid spread of gambling in the United States. It is true that Americans are, in a sense, voting with their dollars; if they really believed that gambling was wrong, they would not flock to casinos or purchase lottery tickets. Yet the matter is not quite so simple. Conditions of democratic accountability are not met merely by giving people what they want. As Cass Sunstein in particular has emphasized, institutions of democratic governance are as much about informing choices as they are about making them.[32] If Americans did want gambling, their decision to endorse it would have been stronger and more legitimate if there had been extensive debate over its adoption and if the political parties had mobilized and represented effective choices. If Americans, after more reflective deliberation, had decided that they either did not want gambling or wanted it more restricted and regulated, then that, too, would have been a stronger decision, had it emerged out of a deliberative process. As I suggested at the beginning of this chapter, democratic theorists have offered both strong and weak conditions of accountability. Because of the lack of a genuine debate about it, gambling does not meet the strong criteria. Because the political parties have never presented differentiated choices, it does not meet the weaker ones either. Gambling's popularity gives it a certain amount of legitimacy. Whether it possesses sufficient legitimacy to meet any future backlash should it continue to expand remains open to question.

Notes

Chapter 1

We are grateful to David J. Fiorillo, Zachary King, Emily Loney, and Sowmya Rajan for research assistance.

1   Charles T. Clotfelter and Philip J. Cook, "On the Economics of State Lotteries," *Journal of Economic Perspectives* 4 (1990): 105–19.

2   John Samuel Ezell, *Fortune's Merry Wheel: The Lottery in America* (Cambridge, Mass.: Harvard University Press, 1960), 55–59, 71–72.

3   Not all denominations benefited from lottery finance. In particular, the Quakers, who opposed all forms of gambling, did not use this funding method. Among church lotteries in New Jersey in the eighteenth and nineteenth centuries whose beneficiary could be determined, Episcopal and Presbyterian churches were most numerous, with none recorded for Quaker meetings. The distribution of church membership in 1765, however, showed Presbyterians, Quakers, and Episcopalians, in that order, as most numerous. Harry B. Weiss and Grace M. Weiss, *The Early Lotteries of New Jersey* (Trenton, N.J.: The Past Times Press, 1966), 67.

4   *New-York Mercury*, September 25, 1758, quoted in Weiss and Weiss, *Early Lotteries*, 85.

5   Weiss and Weiss, *Early Lotteries*, 86.

6   Anisha S. Dasgupta, "Public Finance and the Fortunes of the Early American Lottery," *Quinnipiac Law Review* 24 (2006): 227.

7   Dasgupta, "Public Finance," 227.

8   Priscus, "On the Lawfulness and Expediency of Lotteries," letter to the editor, *Connecticut Evangelical Magazine and Religious Intelligencer* 4 (1811): 104.

9   Elizabeth T. Tsai, "Validity and Construction of Statute Exempting Gam-
     bling Operations Carried On by Religious, Charitable, or Other Nonprofit
     Organizations from General Prohibitions against Gambling," *American
     Law Reports 3rd* 42 (1972): 663.

10   *Massachusetts General Laws*, chap. 271: § 7A, Raffles and bazaars;
     conduct by certain organizations, http://www.gambling-law-us.com/
     Charitable-Gaming/Massachusetts/Massachusetts-Raffle.htm.

11   *Massachusetts General Laws*, chap. 271, § 7A (April 14, 2005). Available at
     http://www.gambling-law-us.com/Charitable-Gaming/Massachusetts/.

12   *North Carolina General Statutes*, § 14-309.15 (2007). Available at http://
     www.gambling-law-us.com/Charitable-Gaming/North-Carolina/.

13   Massachusetts State Lottery, *Massachusetts State Lottery Annual Report
     FY2005*, http://www.masslottery.com/pdfs/AnnualReport2005.pdf.

14   Google search on "charity raffles," August 17, 2007. In the first five pages
     of hits, there were twenty-five addresses ending in ".com," fifteen in
     ".org," and five with other endings.

15   UK National Lottery, "Lottery Funders Listing," http://www.lotteryfund
     ing.org.uk/uk/lottery-funders-uk/lottery-funders-listing.htm (accessed Aug-
     ust 31, 2007); UK National Lottery, "National Lottery for Good Causes,"
     http://www.lotterygoodcauses.org.uk/ (accessed August 31, 2007).

16   See Novamedia, "Nationale Postcode Loterij," http://www.novamedia.
     nl/web/show/id=55340; and Natuur en Milieu, "Dutch Post Code Lot-
     tery," http://www.snm.nl/page.php?extraItemID=2037 (accessed May
     11, 2007). Kapteyn et al. suggest that the structure of the postal lottery
     may accentuate the force of "regret" as a spur to purchases. (Arie Kapteyn
     et al., "Measuring Social Interactions: Results from the Dutch Post Code
     Lottery," unpublished paper, Rand and Tilburg University, April 2007.)
     "Regret" at not having made an investment or purchase is a factor thought
     to be important in motivating people to gamble, and the use of postal
     codes in this game puts a particular local imprint on regret. One strategy
     in game theory is to minimize the maximum regret, where regret is the
     difference between an actual payoff and the payoff if the correct strategy
     had been followed. (David W. Pearce, ed. *The MIT Dictionary of Modern
     Economics* [Cambridge, Mass.: MIT Press, 1992], 278–79). Another Euro-
     pean lottery that devotes proceeds to good causes is the French National
     Lottery, which devotes funds for "humanitarian and social causes,"
     including sporting causes. (World Casino Directory, *Casino and Gam-
     bling Guide*; http://74.125.45.104/search?q=cache:6bIzFFvskaQJ:www.
     worldcasinodirectory.com/france/poker+french+national+lottery+%22
     humanitarian+and+social+causes%22&hl=en&ct=clnk&cd=1&gl=us
     (accessed November 5, 2008).

17   See table 1.4 for adoption dates of U.S. lotteries.

18   Charles T. Clotfelter and Philip J. Cook, *Selling Hope: State Lotteries in
     America* (Cambridge, Mass.: Harvard University Press, 1989), 241.

19   Philip J. Cook, *Paying the Tab: The Economics of Alcohol Control Policy*
     (Princeton: Princeton University Press, 2007), 156.

20 The assumption that sales would be maximized when the takeout rate was zero is just that, an assumption. It is logically possible that consumers would spend less on a lottery with zero takeout than one with a 10 percent takeout (just as they tend to reduce expenditures in response to a reduction in price for necessities). Still, our intuition and some evidence indicate that the takeout rate is inversely related to expenditures, at least over the range of takeout rates ordinarily used.

21 John Warren Kindt, "The Economic Impacts of Legalized Gambling Activities," *Drake Law Review* 43 (1994): 73–77.

22 Clotfelter and Cook, *Selling Hope*, 219–21; Ian Walker, "The Economic Analysis of Lotteries," *Economic Policy* 13, no. 27 (1998), 358–401.

23 Some players may enjoy the process of playing the lottery and having a stake in the drawings. That value should be included in the consumers' surplus, but it will not vary much with the takeout rate.

24 That conclusion may have to be modified if at that takeout rate the fixed social costs exceed the net revenue to the state. Covering those fixed costs may require a higher takeout rate.

25 Clotfelter and Cook, *Selling Hope*, 221–27; Charles T. Clotfelter et al., *State Lotteries at the Turn of the Century: Report to the National Gambling Impact Study Commission*, April 23, 1999, available at http://govinfo.library.unt.edu/ngisc.

26 In our book *Selling Hope* (243–48), we introduce the possibility of a Sumptuary Lottery that couples a high takeout rate with low-key marketing in an effort to accommodate but not encourage play. Like the Consumer Lottery, the Sumptuary Lottery has generated little interest among policymakers.

27 John Kenneth Galbraith, *The Affluent Society* (Boston: Houghton Mifflin, 1958). Ordinarily public expenditures are financed by involuntary transfers from households to the government in the form of taxes. These transfers are not free—they cause a loss in economic efficiency by distorting incentives. For that reason, government planners should limit government programs to those where the benefit exceeds the dollar outlay at the margin by at least as much as the marginal cost of transferring dollars from private to public.

28 James Q. Wilson, *Political Organizations* (Princeton: Princeton University Press, 1995).

29 In this regard it is interesting to track the sequence of lottery bills submitted in the large state that held out the longest, North Carolina. Of the forty-four bills filed between 1989 and 2005, only a handful did not include earmark provisions. Most of these were for aspects of primary and secondary education, although several would have provided capital for infrastructure projects (harkening back to the Colonial Era), and in others the list included higher education. After 2000, the bills started including preschool education in the mix, reflecting a priority of the governor (who had been a lottery supporter). The lottery bill that was finally adopted in 2005 divided net revenues among four education-related activities.

30 *Detailed sources*: Official state lottery Web sites (accessed September 8, 2007). *Washington*: http://64.233.169.104/search?q=cache:7vn4MJwwI5MJ: www.walottery.com/sections/Education/+Use+of+lottery+revenues+Wash ington+State&hl=en&ct=clnk&cd=2&gl=us; *Missouri*: http://64.233. 169.104/search?q=cache:InLWVZkguhcJ:www.molottery.com/learn- aboutus/mediacenter/3billion.shtm+Use+of+lottery+revenues+Missouri& hl=en&ct=clnk&cd=5&gl=us; *West Virginia*: http://207.97.205.154/aspx/ faq.aspx; *Kansas*: http://www.kslottery.com/LotteryInfo/FAQ.htm; *South Dakota*: http://64.233.169.104/search?q=cache:H3Ecmdur9LgJ:www. sdlottery.org/WhereMoneyGoes.asp+Use+of+lottery+revenues+South+ Dakota&hl=en&ct=clnk&cd=2&gl=us; *Wisconsin*: http://www.wilottery .com/wiswins.asp; *Illinois*: http://www.illinoislottery.com/subsections/ news01.htm; *Oklahoma*: http://www.lottery.ok.gov/. Official state lot- tery Web sites (accessed September 11, 2007). *Vermont*: http://www .vtlottery.com/faqs/faqs.asp#q1; *Montana*: http://www.montanalottery .com/faq.xsp#faq4; *Virginia*: http://www.valottery.com/money. State laws (accessed September 8, 2007), *Indiana*: http://www.in.gov/legislative /ic/code/title4/ar30/ch17.pdf; *North Carolina*: http://www.nc-education lottery.org/uploads/fulllotterybill.pdf; Texas: TX LEGIS 107 (1993), State Lottery Act, Sec. 466.355.

31 We note that Lange, List, and Price have taken a similar approach in analyzing the effect of including a prize drawing as part of a charitable fundraising effort. They demonstrate that under some circumstances the drawing can enhance net revenues compared with a straight request for charitable donations. Andreas Lange, John A. List, and Michael K. Price, "Using Lotteries to Finance Public Goods: Theory and Experimental Evi- dence," *International Economic Review* 48, no. 3 (2007): 901–27.

32 Craig Landry and Michael Price provide an econometric estimate of this effect based on a comparison of states that changed their earmark provi- sions during the 1990s with states that did not. In particular they claim that six state lotteries that had originally directed net revenues to the gen- eral fund changed their provisions during the 1990s, earmarking revenues for education. They estimate the effect of switching to an education ear- mark as a jump in sales averaging 39 percent compared with other state lotteries. But we are dubious of this result because the authors appear to have misclassified two of the states (Montana and Oregon), and it is not clear whether other relevant changes were controlled for in this analysis. The same study found that sales were very responsive to changes in the payout rate—a one percentage point increase in the payout rate resulted in a 4 percent increase in sales by their estimate. See Craig E. Landry and Michael K. Price, "Earmarking Lottery Proceeds for Public Goods: Empirical Evidence from U.S. Lotto Expenditures," *Economics Letters* 95 (2007): 451–55.

33 Clotfelter and Cook, *Selling Hope*, chap. 6; Philip J. Cook and Charles T. Clotfelter, "The Peculiar Scale Economies of Lotto," *American Eco- nomic Review* 83, no. 3 (1993): 634–43; I. Walker, "Economic Analysis of Lotteries"; Melissa Schettini Kearney, "State Lotteries and Consumer Behavior," *Journal of Public Economics* 89 (2005): 2269–99.

34 Clotfelter and Cook, "On the Economics of State Lotteries" 107.

35 The four states are North Carolina, Tennessee, New Mexico, and South Carolina. See also Andrew DeMillo, "Arkansas Lt. Gov. Says He'll Try To Put Lottery on '08 Ballot," *Associated Press*, September 18, 2007.

36 This point has not been lost on critics of the new Arkansas proposal. One spokesman said, "You're taking money out of the pockets of the poorest people in the state [and you're] asking them to fund wealthier people going to college." DeMillo, "Arkansas Lt. Gov."

37 For a discussion of the Illinois debate, see Clotfelter and Cook, *Selling Hope*, 190; and Katie Behr, "What Advertising Strategy Should the North Carolina Education Lottery Employ?" M.P.P. project, Terry Sanford Institute of Public Policy, Duke University, 2006.

38 The UK National Lottery is operated by a for-profit company, Camelot LTD, in return for 5 percent of lottery sales. Camelot LTD, *Social Report 2005*, http://www.camelotgroup.co.uk/socialreport2005/camelot-and -national-lottery.htm.

Chapter 2

1 The historical survey of the first and second waves of legalized gambling that follows draws heavily on John Lyman Mason and Michael Nelson, *Governing Gambling: Politics and Policy in State, Tribe, and Nation* (New York: The Century Foundation, 2001), chaps. 2–3; David Schwartz, *Roll the Bones: The History of Gambling* (New York: Gotham Books, 2006); Patrick A. Pierce and Donald E. Miller, *Gambling Politics: State Governments and the Business of Betting* (Boulder, Colo.: Lynne Reiner, 2004), chap. 2; Ronald M. Pavalko, *Risky Business: America's Fascination with Gambling* (Belmont, Calif.: Wadsworth, 2000), chap. 3; and Ezell, *Fortune's Merry Wheel*.

2 John J. Dinan, *The American State Constitutional Tradition* (Lawrence: University Press of Kansas, 2006), 251.

3 Clotfelter and Cook, *Selling Hope*, 130–33.

4 Mason and Nelson, *Governing Gambling*, 13; Pew Research Center, "Gambling: As the Take Rises, So Does Public Concern" (Washington, D.C.: Pew Research Center, May 23, 2006), available at http://pewre-search.org/pubs/314/gambling-as-the-take-rises-so-does-public-concern.

5 The classic work on policy diffusion is Jack L. Walker, "The Diffusion of Innovations among the American States," *American Political Science Review* 63 (1969): 880–99. See also Michael Nelson and John Lyman Mason, *How the South Joined the Gambling Nation: The Politics of State Policy Innovation* (Baton Rouge: Louisiana State University Press, 2007); and idem, "The Politics of Gambling in the South," *Political Science Quarterly* 118 (2004): 645–70.

6 Clotfelter and Cook, *Selling Hope*, 150.

7 Nicholas Thompson, "Snake Eyes: Even Education Programs Can't Redeem State Lotteries," *Washington Monthly*, December 1999, 17.

8 Commission on the Review of the National Policy toward Gambling, *Gambling in America* (Washington, D.C.: U.S. Government Printing Office, 1976).

9   National Gambling Impact Study Commission, *National Gambling Impact Study Commission Final Report*, 1999, available at http://govinfo .library.unt.edu/ngisc/reports/fullrpt.html (hereafter cited as NGISC, *Final Report*); Clotfelter et al., *State Lotteries at the Turn of the Century*.

10   Ron Stodghill and Ron Nixon, "Divide and Conquer: Meet the Lottery Titans," *The New York Times*, October 21, 2007.

11   D. Schwartz, *Roll the Bones*, 399.

12   Casino legalization campaigns failed in Florida (1978, 1982–1984, 1986), Massachusetts (1978–1982), Connecticut (1979–1983), New York (1977–1984), New Hampshire (1979–1980), Pennsylvania (1977–1984), Michigan (1976–1981, 1988), Texas (1984), Arkansas (1984), Colorado (1982, 1984), Louisiana (1986–1988), and Ohio (1988). See John Dombrink and William N. Thompson, *The Last Resort: Success and Failure in Campaigns for Casinos* (Reno: University of Nevada Press, 1990), chaps. 3–7.

13   Dombrink and Thompson, *The Last Resort*.

14   Robert Goodman, *The Luck Business: The Devastating Consequences and Broken Promises of America's Gambling Explosion* (New York: Free Press, 1995), 97.

15   NGISC, *Final Report*.

16   Mason and Nelson, *Governing Gambling*, 30.

17   Mason and Nelson, *Governing Gambling*, chap. 3.

18   Pew Research Center, "Gambling."

19   Keith S. Whyte, "Analysis of National Gambling Impact Study Commission Act," *Journal of Gambling Studies* 14 (1998): 310.

20   Allen J. Cigler and Burdett A. Loomis, "Organized Interests and the Search for Certainty," in *Interest Group Politics*, 3rd ed., ed. Allen J. Cigler and Burdett A. Loomis (Washington, D.C.: CQ Press, 1991), 385–98.

21   Calculated by the author from data compiled by the Center for Responsive Politics, "Casinos/Gambling: Long-Term Contribution Trends" (Washington, D.C.: Center for Responsive Politics, 2006), available at http:// opensecrets.org/industries/indus.asp?Ind=N07.

22   James Frey, "Gambling on Sport: Policy Issues," *Journal of Gambling Studies* 84 (1992): 354.

23   For a fuller discussion of tribal sovereignty, see Steven Andrew Light and Kathryn R.L. Rand, *Indian Gaming and Tribal Sovereignty: The Casino Compromise* (Lawrence: University Press of Kansas, 2005).

24   *Cherokee Nation v. Georgia*, 30 U.S. (5 Pet.) 1 (1831).

25   *Worcester v. Georgia*, 30 U.S. 515 (1832).

26   *Washington v. Confederated Colville Tribes*, 447 U.S. 134 (1980).

27   Peter Katel, "American Indians," *CQ Researcher*, April 28, 2006, 363–64.

28   Samuel R. Cook, "Ronald Reagan's Indian Policy in Retrospect: Economic Crisis and Political Irony," *Policy Studies Journal* 24 (1996): 11–26.

29   For a fuller discussion of Indian gambling, see Mason and Nelson, *Governing Gambling*, chap. 4.

30   The ruling by the Fifth Circuit Court of Appeals was in the case of *Seminole Tribe of Florida v. Butterworth*, 658 F.2d 310 (1981).

31   *California v. Cabazon Band of Mission Indians*, 480 U.S. 202 (1987).

32 IGRA entitles only an "Indian tribe"—that is, a tribe that "is recognized eligible . . . for the special programs and services provided by the United States to Indians because of their status as Indians, and is recognized as possessing powers of self-government"—to operate gambling facilities. *Indian Gaming Regulatory Act of 1988*, 25 U.S.C. §§ 2703(5), 2710 (hereafter cited as IGRA).

33 Kim Isaac Eisler, *Revenge of the Pequots: How a Small Native American Tribe Created the World's Largest Casino* (New York: Simon & Schuster, 2000), 130.

34 Michael Nelson, "From Rez to Riches," *American Prospect*, May 21, 2001: 43–45.

35 Light and Rand, *Indian Gaming and Tribal Sovereignty*, 12.

36 Donald L. Bartlett and James B. Steele, "Dirty Dealing: Indian Casinos Are Making Millions for Their Investors and Providing Little to Poor," *Time*, December 8, 2002.

37 Howard Stutz, "Rate of Growth Slowed for Tribal Gaming in 2006," *Las Vegas Review-Journal*, June 28, 2007.

38 *Seminole Tribe of Florida v. Florida*, 517 U.S. 44 (1996).

39 Calculated by the author from data compiled by the Center for Responsive Politics, "Casinos/Gambling."

40 Mason and Nelson, *Governing Gambling*, chap. 4.

41 John W. Weier, *Gambling: What's at Stake?* (Detroit: Thompson/Gale, 2007), chap. 5.

42 Michael Nelson, "The Politics of Tribal Recognition: Casinos, Culture, and Controversy," in *Interest Group Politics*, 7th. ed., ed. Allen J. Cigler and Burdett A. Loomis (Washington: CQ Press, 2007), 65–85.

43 Weier, *Gambling*, 114.

44 David Stewart, "An Analysis of Internet Gambling and Its Policy Implications" (American Gaming Association, 2006), available at http://www.americangaming.org/assets/files/studies/wpaper_internet_0531.pdf.

45 Stewart, "Analysis of Internet Gambling."

46 American Gaming Association. *2006 State of States: The AGA Survey of Casino Entertainment*. Christensen Capital Advisors, 2006.

47 Anthony N. Cabot and Kevin D. Doty, "Internet Gambling: Jurisdiction Problems and the Role of Federal Law," *Gaming Law Review* 1 (1997): 22.

48 Michael Nelson, "Gambling Online," *American Prospect*, June 4, 2001, 21.

49 See also Mason and Nelson, *Governing Gambling*, 92–93.

50 Stewart, "Analysis of Internet Gambling."

51 Alice LaPlante, "Online Gambling Gone Wild: U.S. Crackdown Sparks Offshore Boom," *InformationWeek*, March 27, 2007, available at http://www.informationweek.com/shared/printableArticleSrc.jhtml?articleID=198700819.

Chapter 3

1 D. Schwartz, *Roll the Bones.*

2 Jerome H. Skolnick, "The Social Transformation of Vice," *Law and Contemporary Problems* 51 (1988): 9–30.

3   Jerome Skolnick characterizes gambling as a "normal" rather than "deviant" vice. Normal vices are those practiced widely by ordinary people, without requiring interaction with criminal organizations and, for most individuals, without experiencing impairment of lifestyle through addiction or abuse. Jerome H. Skolnick, "Regulating Vice: America's Struggle with Wicked Pleasure," in *Gambling: Who Wins? Who Loses?*, ed. Gerda Reith (Amherst, N.Y.: Prometheus Books, 2003), 313–19.

4   Peter Collins, *Gambling and the Public Interest* (Westport, Conn.: Praeger, 2003), 23.

5   Raymond Tatalovich and Byron W. Danes, "Moral Controversies and the Policymaking Process: Lowi's Framework Applied to the Abortion Issue," *Policy Studies Review* 3 (1984): 207.

6   Theodore J. Lowi, "American Business, Public Policy, Case Studies, and Political Theory," *World Politics* 16 (1964): 677–715; idem, "Four Systems of Policy, Politics and Choice," *Public Administration Review* 32 (1972): 298–310.

7   Collins, *Gambling and the Public Interest*, 11; Anthony N. Cabot, *Casino Gaming: Policy, Economics and Regulation* (Las Vegas: UNLV International Gaming Institute, 1996).

8   Collins, *Gambling and the Public Interest*, 4.

9   NGISC, *Final Report*.

10 For law, see Skolnick, "Social Transformation"; Skolnick, "Regulating Vice." For political theory, see Collins, *Gambling and the Public Interest*. For economics, see Douglas M. Walker, "Methodological Issues in the Social Cost of Gambling Studies," *Journal of Gambling Studies* 19 (2003): 149–84; William R. Eadington, "Values and Choices: The Struggle to Find Balance with Permitted Gambling in Modern Society," in Reith, *Gambling*. For public health, see Alex Blaszczynski, Robert Ladouceur, and Howard J. Shaffer, "A Science-Based Framework for Responsible Gambling: The Reno Model," *Journal of Gambling Studies* 20 (2004): 301–17. For public affairs, see Elizabeth Winslow McAuliffe, "The State-Sponsored Lottery: A Failure of Policy and Ethics," *Public Integrity* 8 (2006): 367–79. For research imperatives, see J. Borrell, "Values in Gambling Research and Implications for Public Policy," *International Journal of Mental Health & Addiction* 1, no. 1 (2003): 40–47, available at http://www.ijma-journal.com/content/full/1/1/6.

11 Elsewhere we have argued that Indian gaming is different than any other form of gambling in the U.S. and is subject to a uniquely complex regulatory scheme. Light and Rand, *Indian Gaming and Tribal Sovereignty*; Kathryn R.L. Rand and Steven Andrew Light, "How Congress Can and Should 'Fix' the Indian Gaming Regulatory Act: Recommendations for Law and Policy Reform," *Virginia Journal of Social Policy & the Law* 13 (2006): 396–473. In the latter article we also proposed specific reforms for existing Indian gaming law and policy.

12 IGRA, 25 U.S.C §§ 2703(5), 2703(4).

13 25 U.S.C. §§ 2701–21.

14 National Indian Gaming Commission, *Gaming Revenues 2006–2001*, 2007, available at http://www.nigc.gov/Default.aspx?tabid=67; Alan P.

Meister, *Indian Gaming Industry Report, 2007–2008* (Newton, Mass.: Casino City Press, 2007).

15 Light and Rand, *Indian Gaming and Tribal Sovereignty*, 9–11.

16 As discussed in the next section, under IGRA, Class II and Class III gaming are allowed only in those states that "permit . . . such gaming for any purpose by any person, organization, or entity" (25 U.S.C. §§ 2710(b)(1)(A), 2710(d)(1)(B)). In some states, Indian gaming is limited to bingo and similar games because state public policy or other laws prohibit casino-style gaming.

17 National Indian Gaming Commission, *Gaming Revenues 2006–2001*.

18 NGISC, *Final Report*, 3-1 to 3-2.

19 Cory Aronovitz, "The Regulation of Commercial Gaming," *Nevada Law Journal* 5 (2002): 190.

20 *Nevada Gaming Control Act*, Nev. Rev. Stat. § 463.0129(1).

21 Aronovitz, "Regulation of Commercial Gaming," 190.

22 Brigid Harrison, "Legislating Morality: The New Jersey Casino Control Act as 'Moral' Public Policy," *Gaming Law Review* 2 (1998): 63–69.

23 A notable exception is the racing industry, which has a regulatory model influenced heavily by pari-mutuel wagering as the dominant form of gambling as well as the need to protect the "sport" of animal racing.

24 Jeff Dense, "State Lotteries, Commercial Casinos, and Public Finance: An Uneasy Relationship Revisited," *Gaming Law Review* 11 (2007): 34–50.

25 *Cabazon*, 480 U.S. 202.

26 Act of August 15, 1953, Public Law 83-280, chap. 505, 67 Stat. 588–90 (1953), codified as amended at 18 U.S.C. § 1162, 28 U.S.C. § 1360, and other scattered sections in Titles 18 and 28, United States Code (2000). Public Law 280, enacted in 1953, gave certain states, including Florida and California, a broad grant of criminal jurisdiction and a limited grant of civil jurisdiction over tribes within their borders. In Public Law 280 states, state governments exercise some power over tribes; in non-Public Law 280 states, the state has less authority over tribes within its borders.

27 In *Bryan v. Itasca County*, 426 U.S. 373 (1976), the Court held that Public Law 280's grant of civil jurisdiction applied only to private civil litigation in state court.

28 The *Cabazon* Court's interpretation of Public Law 280 was based on its reading of congressional intent not to grant states broad regulatory authority over tribes, as that "would result in the destruction of tribal institutions and values." Thus, the Court distinguished between state laws that are "criminal/prohibitory" and "civil/regulatory":

> If the intent of a state law is generally to prohibit certain conduct, it falls within Pub. L. 280's grant of criminal jurisdiction, but if the state law generally permits the conduct at issue, subject to regulation, it must be classified as civil/regulatory and Pub. L. 280 does not authorize its enforcement on an Indian reservation. (209)

According to the *Cabazon* Court, the doctrine's "shorthand test" is whether state public policy condones the conduct. *Cabazon*, 480 U.S. at 208–9.

29 *Cabazon*, 480 U.S. at 210.

30 *Cabazon*, 480 U.S. at 216.

31 *Cabazon*, 480 U.S. at 218–219.

32 IGRA, 25 U.S.C. § 2702.

33 IGRA, 25 U.S.C. §§ 2703(6)–(8), 2710(b), (d).

34 IGRA, 25 U.S.C. §§ 2710(b)(1)(A), 2710(d)(1)(B).

35 Lowi categorized public policy as constituent, distributive, regulatory, and redistributive. See Lowi, "American Business"; and idem, "Four Systems."

36 Pierce and Miller, *Gambling Politics*.

37 Tatalovich and Danes, "Moral Controversies"; Tatalovich and Danes, *Social Regulatory Policy: Moral Controversies in American Politics* (Boulder, Colo.: Westview, 1988).

38 William T. Gormley Jr., "Regulatory Issue Networks in a Federal System," *Polity* 18 (1986): 595–620; James Davison Hunter, *Culture Wars: The Struggle to Define America* (New York: Basic Books, 1991); James Davison Hunter, *Before the Shooting Begins: Searching for Democracy in America's Culture War* (New York: Free Press, 1994); Kenneth J. Meier, *The Politics of Sin: Drugs, Alcohol and Public Policy* (Armonk, N.Y.: M. E. Sharpe, 1994); Christopher Z. Mooney and Mei-Hsien Lee, "Legislating Morality in the American States: The Case of Pre-*Roe* Abortion Regulation Reform," *American Journal of Political Science* 39 (1995): 599–627; Christopher Z. Mooney, "The Private Clash of Public Values," in *The Private Clash of Public Values*, ed. Christopher Z. Mooney (Chatham, N.J.: Chatham House, 2001), 3–20; Donald P. Haider-Markel and Kenneth J. Meier, "The Politics of Gay and Lesbian Rights: Expanding the Scope of the Conflict," *Journal of Politics* 58 (1996): 332–49; Dana Patton, "The Supreme Court and Morality Policy Adoption in the American States: The Impact of Constitutional Context," *Political Research Quarterly* 60 (2007): 468–88.

39 Meier, *The Politics of Sin*.

40 Pierce and Miller argue that Lowi's typology, into which he later attempted to "squeeze" morality policy, overlooked the essential points that individuals' core values define morality policy, and such policy generates unique costs and benefits. Pierce and Miller, *Gambling Politics*, 32.

41 Edward G. Carmines and James A. Stimson, "The Two Faces of Issue Voting," *American Political Science Review* 74 (1980): 78–91; Mooney and Lee, "Legislating Morality"; Haider-Markel and Meier, "Gay and Lesbian Rights"; Kenneth J. Meier, "Drugs, Sex, and Rock and Roll: Two Theories of Morality Politics," in Mooney, *Private Clash*; Gormley, "Regulatory Issue Networks"; Patton, "Supreme Court"; Pierce and Miller, *Gambling Politics*.

42 Mooney, "Private Clash."

43 Mooney and Lee, "Legislating Morality"; Donald P. Haider-Markel, "Morality in Congress: Legislative Voting on Gay Issues," in Mooney, *Private Clash*; Haider-Markel and Meier, "Gay and Lesbian Rights"; Kevin B. Smith, "Clean Thoughts and Dirty Minds: The Politics of Porn," in Mooney, *Private Clash*; Barbara Norrander and Clyde Wilcox, "Public

Opinion and Policymaking in the States: The Case of Post-*Roe* Abortion Policy," in Mooney, *Private Clash*; Pierce and Miller, *Gambling Politics*.

44 Pierce and Miller, *Gambling Politics*.

45 Kara L. Lindaman, "Place Your Bet on Politics: Local Governments Roll the Dice," *Politics & Policy* 35 (2007): 274–97; Meister, *Indian Gaming Industry Report*; Light and Rand, *Indian Gaming and Tribal Sovereignty*.

46 Pierce and Miller, *Gambling Politics*, 1.

47 Skolnick, "Social Transformation"; Skolnick, "Regulating Vice."

48 Eadington, "Values and Choices," 40–41.

49 Theodore J. Lowi, "Foreword," in Nelson and Mason, *Gambling Nation*, vii–viii.

50 Collins, *Gambling and the Public Interest*, 28–42.

51 Collins, *Gambling and the Public Interest*, ix, 26.

52 Collins, *Gambling and the Public Interest*, 29.

53 Collins, *Gambling and the Public Interest*, 42–51. Elizabeth Winslow McAuliffe, on the other hand, relies on similar principles to reach a dissimilar conclusion. She summarizes five moral frameworks or decision standards for ethical decision making and applies them to assess what she sees as the failure of state lotteries as moral, or morality, policy: teleology and utilitarianism (promotion of greatest happiness), deontology (means rather than consequences), virtue theory (judge acts based on character), intuitionism (internal ethics), and unified (combination). McAuliffe, "The State-Sponsored Lottery," 374–76.

54 Collins, *Gambling and the Public Interest*; Peter Collins, "The Moral Case for Legalizing Gambling," in Reith, *Gambling*.

55 NGISC, *Final Report*, 1-6.

56 Pierce and Miller, *Gambling Politics*, 160–61.

57 These underpinnings for the federal legal doctrine of tribal sovereignty are far from unproblematic, and its legal foundation as well as its application have been roundly criticized by federal Indian law scholars. See David E. Wilkins, *American Indian Sovereignty and the U.S. Supreme Court: The Masking of Justice* (Austin: University of Texas Press, 1997); Light and Rand, *Indian Gaming and Tribal Sovereignty*, 18–37.

58 Wallace Coffey and Rebecca Tsosie, "Rethinking the Tribal Sovereignty Doctrine: Cultural Sovereignty and the Collective Future of Indian Nations," *Stanford Law and Policy Review* 12 (2001): 191.

59 Light and Rand, *Indian Gaming and Tribal Sovereignty*, 36.

60 Sen. Rep. No. 446, 100th Cong., 2d sess., 1988, 2–3, reprinted in 1988 U.S.C.C.A.N. 3071, 3072 (1988).

61 Sen. Rep. No. 446, 100th Cong., 2d sess., 1988, 2–3, reprinted in 1988 U.S.C.C.A.N. 3071, 3072 (1988).

62 Light and Rand, *Indian Gaming and Tribal Sovereignty*, 137–44.

63 We detail a number of tribe-specific examples in Light and Rand, *Indian Gaming and Tribal Sovereignty*, 98–101. See also Rand and Light, "How Congress Can and Should 'Fix' the Indian Gaming Regulatory Act"; Kathryn R.L. Rand and Steven Andrew Light, *Indian Gaming Law and*

Policy (Durham, N.C.: Carolina Academic Press, 2006); Jonathan B. Taylor and Joseph P. Kalt, "*Cabazon*, the Indian Gaming Regulatory Act, and the Socioeconomic Consequences of American Indian Governmental Gaming" (Cambridge, Mass.: Harvard Project on American Indian Economic Development, 2005), available at http://www.ksg.harvard.edu/hpaied/pubs/cabazon.htm; Harvard Project on American Indian Economic Development et al., *The State of the Native Nations: Conditions Under U.S. Policies of Self-Determination* (Oxford: Oxford University Press, 2007).

64 Light and Rand, *Indian Gaming and Tribal Sovereignty*, 98–101; Taylor and Kalt, "*Cabazon*"; Harvard Project et al., *State of the Native Nations*.

65 U.S. Bureau of the Census, *Social and Economic Characteristics, American Indians and Native Alaska Areas* (Washington, D.C.: U.S. Department of Commerce, 1990), available at http://www.census.gov/prod/cen1990/cp2/cp-2.html.

66 Office of Minority Health and Health Disparities, *American Indian and Alaska Native Populations*, U.S. Center for Disease Control and Prevention, n.d., available at http://www.cdc.gov/omh/populations/AIAN/AIAN.htm.

67 Lawrence A. Greenfield and Steven K. Smith, *American Indians and Crime* (Washington, D.C.: U.S. Department of Justice, 1999), 1.

68 U.S. Commission on Civil Rights, *A Quiet Crisis: Federal Funding and Unmet Needs in Indian Country* (Washington, D.C.: U.S. Government Printing Office, 2003).

69 U.S. Commission on Civil Rights, *A Quiet Crisis*, 9.

70 Robert B. Porter, "A Proposal to the Hanodaganyas to Deçolonize Federal Indian Control Law," *University of Michigan Journal of Law Reform* 31 (1998): 899.

71 U.S. Bureau of the Census, *Social and Economic Characteristics, American Indians and Native Alaska Areas* (Washington, D.C.: U.S. Department of Commerce, 2000), available at http://factfinder.census.gov/home/aian/sf1_sf3.html.

72 Harvard Project et al., *State of the Native Nations*.

73 Light and Rand, *Indian Gaming and Tribal Sovereignty*.

74 Evangelical Lutheran Church in America, "Gambling Study," 1998, available at http://www.elca.org/socialstatements/economiclife/gambling/default.asp.

75 Collins, *Gambling and the Public Interest*, x.

76 Collins, *Gambling and the Public Interest*; Garry J. Smith and Harold J. Wynne, *A Review of the Gambling Literature in the Economic and Policy Domains* (Alberta, Canada: Alberta Gaming Research Institute, 2000), 28.

77 IGRA, 25 U.S.C. § 2702.

78 Rand and Light, "How Congress Can and Should 'Fix' the Indian Gaming Regulatory Act."

79 Collins, *Gambling and the Public Interest*; Collins, "Moral Case."

80 Frank Pommersheim, *Braid of Feathers: American Indian Law and Contemporary Tribal Life* (Berkeley: University of California Press, 1995), 51.

81 NGISC, *Final Report*, 8-1.

82 We called for such a national study in Light and Rand, *Indian Gaming and Tribal Sovereignty*. There is ample room for research on the numerous vexing policy questions surrounding Indian gaming. For instance: What are the political, economic, social, and legal variables that drive political, policy, or socioeconomic outcomes related to Indian gaming? How should the socioeconomic costs and benefits of Indian gaming be measured? How should the integrity of the gambling policy process be maintained? To what extent is Indian gaming "doing what it is supposed to do"? For an overview of similar questions that have been explored in the literature on legalized gambling generally, see Smith and Wynne, *Gambling Literature*.

83 Smith and Wynne, *Gambling Literature*, 44–45.

84 Light and Rand, *Indian Gaming and Tribal Sovereignty*.

85 The Jack Abramoff scandal presents one such example, as do recent controversies in Massachusetts over various Mashpee Wampanoag tribal officials, especially as the state considers the possibility of sanctioning casino gambling, including at least one tribal casino. On the latter, see generally the extensive daily front-page coverage by the *Boston Globe* in 2007–2008. Elsewhere we have written about the phenomenon of public discourse on the occasional well-publicized scandal related to Indian gaming and the tendency to view incidents related to a few tribes or a few tribal officials as emblematic of the behavior of all American Indians, all tribes, or all tribal governments. See Steven Andrew Light and Kathryn R.L. Rand, "The 'Tribal Loophole': Federal Campaign Finance Law and Tribal Political Participation after Jack Abramoff," *Gaming Law Review* 10 (2006): 230–39.

Chapter 4

1 Michael Nelson, "The Politics of Sovereignty and Public Policy toward Gambling," chap. 2 in this volume.

2 Charles T. Clotfelter and Philip J. Cook, "The Importance of a Good Cause: Ends and Means in State Lotteries," chap. 1 in this volume.

3 Kathryn R.L. Rand and Steven Andrew Light, "Negotiating a Different Terrain: Morality Policymaking and Indian Gaming," chap. 3 in this volume.

4 Nelson and Mason, *Gambling Nation*; Mason and Nelson, *Governing Gambling*. Nelson and Mason's two books provide by far the best analysis of gambling politics. As the reader will soon note, I rely heavily on their examination of lottery and casino politics at the state level.

5 Mason and Nelson, *Governing Gambling*, 2.

6 Quoted in Nelson and Mason, *Gambling Nation*, 193.

7 Nelson and Mason, *Gambling Nation*, chap. 3.

8 Quoted in Ron Stodghill and Ron Nixon, "For Schools, Lottery Payoffs Fall Short of Promises," *The New York Times*, October 7, 2007.

9 For example, Tennessee's "Hot Trax Champions" lottery game features a drawing every five minutes from 6 a.m. until 2 a.m. Ron Stodghill, "The Lottery Industry's Own Powerball," *The New York Times*, November 18, 2007.

10 Nelson Schwartz, "The $50 Ticket: A Lottery Boon Raises Concern," *New York Times*, December 27, 2007.

11 Quoted in Nelson and Mason, *Gambling Nation*, 37; see also p. 192 for similar developments in Louisiana.

12 Nelson and Mason, *Gambling Nation*, 63.

13 Stodghill and Nixon, "Lottery Payoffs Fall Short."

14 Stodghill and Nixon, "Divide and Conquer."

15 Stodghill and Nixon, "Divide and Conquer"; Thompson, "Snake Eyes."

16 Mason and Nelson, *Governing Gambling*, 47.

17 John Widermuth, "Expensive Ballot Fight Looms on February Vote over Indian Casinos," *San Francisco Chronicle*, December 7, 2007.

18 Stodghill and Nixon, "Lottery Payoffs Fall Short."

19 James Sterling Young, *The Washington Community, 1800–1828* (New York: Harcourt, Brace & World, 1966), 23.

20 Clotfelter et al., *State Lotteries at the Turn of the Century*.

21 Nelson, "Politics of Sovereignty."

22 Nelson and Mason, *Gambling Nation*, 11. Nelson and Mason not only provide multiple examples of this, but show that many southern Democrats self-consciously follow the lead of Zell Miller in Georgia.

23 I offer extensive evidence in support of this claim in R. Shep Melnick, "From Tax and Spend to Mandate and Sue: Liberalism after the Great Society," in Sidney Milkis and Jerome Mileur, *The Great Society and the High Tide of Liberalism* (Amherst: University of Massachusetts Press, 2005)k 387–410.

24 Martha Derthick, *Up in Smoke: From Legislation to Litigation in Tobacco Politics* (Washington, D.C.: CQ Press, 2002), chaps. 9–10.

25 Morris Fiorina, *Divided Government*, 2nd ed. (Boston: Alllyn and Bacon, 1996), chap. 2.

26 Alan Wolfe, "The Culture War Issue That Never Was: Why the Right and Left Have Overlooked Gambling," chap. 16 in this volume.

27 Nelson and Mason, *Gambling Nation*, 81.

28 Clotfelter et al., *State Lotteries at the Turn of the Century*, 13. Also see Mason and Nelson, *Governing Gambling*, 18–21.

29 Nelson and Mason, *Gambling Nation*, 221.

30 Rand and Light, "Negotiating a Different Terrain."

31 Mason and Nelson, *Governing Gambling*, 70.

32 Rand and Light, "Negotiating a Different Terrain."

33 Rand and Light, "Negotiating a Different Terrain."

34 Clotfelter et al., *State Lotteries at the Turn of the Century*, 6.

35 Clotfelter et al., *State Lotteries at the Turn of the Century*, 12.

36 Quoted in Thompson, "Snake Eyes"; and in Mason and Nelson, *Governing Gambling*, 25.

37 Clotfelter et al., *State Lotteries at the Turn of the Century*, 20–21.

38 R. Shep Melnick, *Between the Lines: Interpreting Welfare Rights* (Washington, D.C.: Brookings, 1994), chaps. 6, 13; Kent Weaver, *Ending Welfare as We Know It* (Washington, D.C.: Brookings, 2000), chap. 6; Michael Novak and John Cogan, eds., *The New Consensus on Family and Welfare* (Washington, D.C.: American Enterprise Institute, 1987); Lawrence Mead, *Government Matters: Welfare Reform in Wisconsin* (Princeton: Princeton University Press, 2004); David Ellwood, *Poor Support: Poverty in the American Family* (New York: Basic Books, 1988).

39 Alexis de Tocqueville, *Democracy in America*, trans. Harvey Mansfield and Delba Winthrop (Chicago: University of Chicago Press, 2000), 524.

40 David Brooks, *Bobos in Paradise: The New Upper Class and How They Got There* (New York: Simon & Schuster, 2000).

Chapter 5

1 Earl L. Grinols and David B. Mustard, "Management and Information Issues for Industries with Externalities: The Case for Casino Gambling," *Managerial and Decision Economics* 22, no. 1–3 (2001): 1.

2 David A. Korn and Howard J. Shaffer, "Gambling and the Health of the Public: Adopting a Public Health Perspective," *Journal of Gambling Studies* 15, no. 4 (1999): 293.

3 Note that this is not necessarily the case with poker, some types of video-poker, or other casino games of skill, where high-skill individuals may face a positive-expected value gamble.

4 K. L. Dion, R. S. Baron, and N. Miller, "Why Do Groups Make Riskier Decisions Than Individuals?" *Advances in Experimental Social Psychology* 5 (1970): 305–77; Dean G. Pruitt, "Choice Shifts in Group Discussion: An Introductory Review," *Journal of Personality and Social Psychology* 20, no. 3 (1971): 339–60; Dorwin Cartwright, "Risk Taking by Individuals and Groups: An Assessment of Research Employing Choice Dilemmas," *Journal of Personality and Social Psychology* 20, no. 3 (1971): 361–78.

5 A. D. Blank, "Effects of Group and Individual Conditions on Choice Behavior," *Journal of Personality and Social Psychology* 8, no. 3 (1968): 294–98.

6 J. Blascovich, G. P. Ginsburg, and R. C. Howe, "Blackjack and the Risky Shift, II: Monetary Stakes," *Journal of Experimental Social Psychology* 11, no. 3 (1975): 224–32.

7 Blascovich and Ginsburg observed this risky shift behavior both when participants were betting real money and when they were merely asked to behave as if they were betting real money. J. Blascovich and G. P. Ginsburg, "Emergent Norms and Choice Shifts Involving Risk," *Sociometry* 37, no. 2 (1974): 205–18.

8 Blascovich, Ginsburg, and Howe, "Blackjack and the Risky Shift, II."

9 J. Blascovich, G. P. Ginsburg, and R. C. Howe, "Blackjack, Choice Shifts in the Field," *Sociometry* 39, no. 3 (1976): 274–76.

10 Blascovich and Ginsburg, "Emergent Norms."

11   D. Kahneman and A. Tversky, "Prospect Theory: An Analysis of Decision under Risk," *Econometrica* 47, no. 2 (1979): 263–92.

12   A. Leopard, "Risk Preference in Consecutive Gambling." *Journal of Experimental Psychology: Human Perception and Performance* 4 (1978): 521–28.

13   Richard E. Quandt, "Betting and Equilibrium," *The Quarterly Journal of Economics* 101, no. 1 (1986): 201–7.

14   M. A. Metzger, "Biases in Betting: An Application of Laboratory Findings," *Psychological Reports* 56, no. 3 (1985): 883–88.

15   H. Shefrin and M. Statman, "The Disposition to Sell Winners Too Early and Ride Losers Too Long: Theory and Evidence," *Journal of Finance* 40, no. 3 (1985): 777–90.

16   D. Oldman, "Chance and Skill: A Study of Roulette," *Sociology* 8, no. 3 (1974): 407–26.

17   James M. Henslin, "Craps and Magic," *The American Journal of Sociology* 73, no. 3 (1967): 316–30.

18   T. Gilovich, R. Vallone, and A. Tversky, "The Hot Hand in Basketball: On the Misperception of Random Sequences," *Cognitive Psychology* 17 (1985): 295–314.

19   Albert Chau and James Phillips, "Effects of Perceived Control upon Wagering and Attributions in Computer Blackjack," *The Journal of General Psychology* 122 (1995): 253–69.

20   Rachel Croson and James Sundali, "The Gambler's Fallacy and the Hot Hand: Empirical Data from Casinos," *Journal of Risk and Uncertainty* 30, no. 3 (2005): 195–209.

21   Colin Camerer, "Does the Basketball Market Believe in the 'Hot Hand'?" *American Economic Review* 79, no. 5 (1989): 1257–61.

22   William Brown and Raymond Sauer, "Does the Basketball Market Believe in the 'Hot Hand'? Comment," *American Economic Review* 83, no. 5 (1993): 1377–86.

23   Erik Sirri and Peter Tufano, "Costly Search and Mutual Fund Flows," *Journal of Finance* 53, no. 5 (1998): 1589–1622.

24   Mark Carhart, "On Persistence in Mutual Fund Performance," *Journal of Finance* 52, no. 1 (1997): 57–82.

25   Clotfelter and Cook, *Selling Hope*; Charles T. Clotfelter and Philip J. Cook, "The 'Gambler's Fallacy' in Lottery Play," *Management Science* 39, no. 12 (1993): 1521–25.

26   G. Keren and C. Lewis, "The Two Fallacies of Gamblers: Type I and Type II," *Organizational Behavior and Human Decision Processes* 60, no. 1 (1994): 75–89.

27. Dek Terrell and Amy Farmer, "Optimal Betting and Efficiency in Parimutuel Betting Markets with Information Costs," *The Economic Journal* 106, no. 437 (1996): 846–68; Dek Terrell, "A Test of the Gambler's Fallacy: Evidence from Pari-Mutuel Games," *Journal of Risk and Uncertainty* 8, no. 3 (1994): 309–17.

28   Metzger, "Biases in Betting."

29   Croson and Sundali, "Gambler's Fallacy."

30 M. Wallach, N. Kogan, and D. J. Bem, "Group Influence on Individual Risk Taking," *Journal of Abnormal and Social Psychology* 65 (1962): 75–86.

31 Leopard, "Risk Preference in Consecutive Gambling"; Quandt, "Betting and Equilibrium"; Camerer, "Basketball Market"; Shefrin and Statman, "Disposition to Sell Winners."

32 Kahneman and Tversky, "Prospect Theory."

33 J. W. Payne, D. J. Laughhunn, and R. Crum, "Multiattribute Risky Choice Behavior: The Editing of Complex Prospects," *Management Science* 30, no. 11 (1984): 1355.

34 A. Tversky and D. Kahneman. "The Framing of Decisions and the Psychology of Choice," *Science* 211, no. 4481 (1981): 453–58.

35 Richard H. Thaler and E. J. Johnson, "Gambling with the House Money and Trying to Break Even: The Effects of Prior Outcomes on Risky Choice," *Management Science* 36, no. 6 (1990): 643–60.

36 Note that there is an important dimension which is left unspecified in this explanation: ahead or behind of what? The level of earnings against which individuals evaluate their current position is often referred to as the status quo point. This status quo point may be zero (breaking even) or it may be negative, as when a gambler comes to the casino willing to lose $100 in exchange for the entertainment experience of gambling. Adding more complication to the mix, the status quo point may change as the gambler wins or loses. For example, a gambler who has won $150 may decide to put $100 "in the bank" and gamble with the rest. When he loses his $50, he will consider himself even, even though he is actually $100 ahead of where he began. The study of status quo point formation and adjustment is referred to as "mental accounting," and while this question is beyond the scope of this chapter, it is nonetheless an interesting one.

37 Oldman, "Chance and Skill"; Chau and Phillips, "Effects of Perceived Control."

38 E. Langer, "The Illusion of Control," *Journal of Personality and Social Psychology* 32 (1975): 311–28.

39 L. H. Strickland, R. J. Lewicki, and A. M. Katz, "Temporal Orientation and Perceived Control as Determinants of Risk-Taking," *Journal of Experimental Social Psychology* 2 (1966): 143–51.

40 P. Ayton and I. Fischer, "The Hot Hand Fallacy and the Gambler's Fallacy: Two Faces of Subjective Randomness," *Memory and Cognition* 32, no. 8 (2004): 1369–78.

41 B. Burns and B. Corpus, "Randomness and Inductions from Streaks: 'Gambler's Fallacy' vs. 'Hot Hand.'" *Psychonomic Bulletin and Review* 11, no. 1 (2004): 179–84.

42 Strickland, Lewicki, and Katz, "Temporal Orientation."

43 J. Feldman, "On the Negative Recency Hypothesis in the Prediction of a Series of Binary Symbols," *American Journal of Psychology* 72 (1959): 597–99.

44 D. Kahneman and A. Tversky, "Subjective Probability: A Judgment of Representativeness," *Cognitive Psychology* 3, no. 3 (1972): 361–523.

45   W. A. Wagenaar, "Generation of Random Sequences by Human Subjects: A Critical Survey of the Literature," *Psychological Bulletin* 77, no. 1 (1972): 65–72.

46   Paul Bakan, "Response-Tendencies in Attempts to Generate Random Binary Series," *The American Journal of Psychology* 73, no. 1 (1960): 127–31; A. Chapanis, "Random-Number Guessing Behavior," *The American Psychologist* 8 (1953): 332; E. Mittenecker, "Die Analyse 'zufälliger' Reaktionsfolgen," *Zeitschrift für experimentelle und angewandte Psychologie* 5 (1958): 45–60; and E. Mittenecker, "Perseveration und Personlichkeit: Teil experimentelle Untersuchungen," *Zeitschrift für experimentelle und angewandte Psychologie* 1 (1953): 5–31.

47   The term *neuroeconomics* was reportedly invented by Kevin McCabe in 1996 as a term to describe a course in neurology and economics. See also T. Chorvat, K. McCabe, and V. Smith, "Law and Neuroeconomics," *Supreme Court Economic Review* 13 (2005): 44.

48   The three basic brain-imaging methods include electroencephalogram (EEG), positron emission topography (PET), and functional magnetic resonance imaging (fMRI), the newest and currently most popular technique. For purposes of this review, we do not distinguish between these competing methods.

49   Colin Camerer, George Loewenstein, and Drazen Prelec, "Neuroeconomics: How Neuroscience Can Inform Economics," *Journal of Economic Literature* 43, no. 1 (2005): 9–64; Christopher Trepel, Craig R. Fox, and Russell A. Poldrack, "Prospect Theory on the Brain? Toward a Cognitive Neuroscience of Decision under Risk," *Cognitive Brain Research* 23, no. 1 (2005): 34–50; and M. D. Lieberman, "Social Cognitive Neuroscience: A Review of Core Processes," *Annual Review of Psychology* 58, no. 1 (2007): 259–89.

50   Camerer, Lowenstein, and Prelec, "Neuroeconomics."

51   Camerer, Lowenstein, and Prelec, "Neuroeconomics."

52   K. Smith et al., "Neuronal Substrates for Choice under Ambiguity, Risk, Gains, and Losses," *Management Science* 48, no. 6 (2002): 711–18; Daniel Ellsberg, "Risk, Ambiguity, and the Savage Axioms," *The Quarterly Journal of Economics* 75, no. 4 (1961): 643–69.

53   B. De Martino et al., "Frames, Biases, and Rational Decision Making in the Human Brain," *Science* 313, no. 5787 (2006): 684–87.

54   H. C. Breiter et al., "Functional Imaging of Neural Responses to Expectancy and Experience of Monetary Gains and Losses," *Neuron* 30, no. 2 (2001): 619–39.

55   Sabrina M. Tom et al., "The Neural Basis of Loss Aversion in Decision Making under Risk," *Science* 315, no. 5811 (2007): 515–18.

56   Camerer, Loewenstein, and Prelec, "Neuroeconomics," 16.

57   Breiter et al., "Functional Imaging."

58   Tom et al., "Neural Basis"; De Martino et al., "Rational Decision Making"; Trepel, Fox, and Poldrack, "Prospect Theory on the Brain?"; Kahneman and Tversky, "Prospect Theory."

59   Chorvat, McCabe, and Smith, "Law and Neuroeconomics," 47.

60 Howard J. Shaffer, Matthew N. Hall, and Joni Vander Bilt, "Estimating the Prevalence of Disordered Gambling Behavior in the United States and Canada: A Meta-Analysis" (Harvard Medical School, Division on Addictions, 1997).

61 Tom et al., "Neural Basis."

62 Gary S. Becker and Kevin M. Murphy, "A Theory of Rational Addiction," *Journal of Political Economy* 96, no. 4 (1988): 675–700.

63 Pamela Mobilia, "Gambling as a Rational Addiction," *Journal of Gambling Studies* 9, no. 2 (1993): 121–51.

64 M. W. Langewisch and G. R. Frisch. "Classification of Pathological Gambling as an Impulse Control Disorder," *Electronic Journal of Gambling Issues* 3 (2001): 1–7.

65 Shaffer, Hall, and Bilt, "Meta-Analysis."

66 Richard H. Thaler and Cass R. Sunstein, "Libertarian Paternalism," *The American Economic Review* 93, no. 2 (2003): 175–79; Cass R. Sunstein and Richard H. Thaler, "Libertarian Paternalism Is Not an Oxymoron," *University of Chicago Law Review* 70, no. 4 (2003): 1159–1202.

67 Amartya Sen, *Rationality and Freedom* (Cambridge, Mass.: Harvard University Press, 2003).

68 P. Glimcher, *Decisions, Uncertainty, and the Brain: The Science of Neuroeconomics* (Cambridge, Mass.: MIT Press, 2003).

69 Camerer, Lowenstein, and Prelec, "Neuroeconomics."

70 S. Smith, "Cigarettes Pack More Nicotine: State Study Finds a 10 Percent Rise over Six Years," *Boston Globe*, August 30, 2006, A1.

71 Harrah's Entertainment, *Harrah's Survey: Profile of the American Casino Gambler* (Harrah's Entertainment, 2006).

72 D. Schwartz, *Roll the Bones*, 5.

Chapter 6

1 John Wagner, "O'Malley Aide Offers Case for Md. Slots; Residents' Spending In Other States Cited," *The Washington Post*, August 15, 2007, B01.

2 John Morgan, "Financing Public Goods by Means of Lotteries," *Review of Economic Studies* 67 (2000): 761–84; Terance J. Rephann et al., "Casino Gambling as an Economic Development Strategy," *Tourism Economics* 3 (1997): 161–83; Douglas M. Walker and John D. Jackson, "New Goods and Economic Growth: Evidence from Legalized Gambling," *Review of Regional Studies* 28 (1998): 47–69; Ranjana G. Madhusudhan, "Betting on Casino Revenues: Lessons from State Experiences," *National Tax Journal* 49 (1996): 401–12.

3 Nancy M. Petry and Christopher Armentano, "Prevalence, Assessment, and Treatment of Pathological Gambling: A Review," *Psychiatric Services* 50 (1999): 1022.

4 Dean R. Gerstein et al., *Gambling Impact and Behavior Study: Report to the National Gambling Impact Study Commission* (Chicago: National Opinion Research Center at the University of Chicago, 1999) (hereafter cited as Gerstein et al., GIBS), 25; Nancy M. Petry, Frederick S. Stinson,

and Bridget F. Grant, "Comorbidity of DSM-IV Pathological Gambling and Other Psychiatric Disorders: Results from the National Epidemiologic Survey on Alcohol and Related Conditions," *Journal of Clinical Psychiatry* 66 (2005): 564.

5   Howard J. Shaffer, Matthew N. Hall, and Joni Vander Bilt, "Estimating the Prevalence of Disordered Gambling Behavior in the United States and Canada: A Research Synthesis," *American Journal of Public Health* 89 (1999): 1369–76.

6   Marc N. Potenza, Thomas R. Kosten, and Bruce J. Rounsaville, "Pathological Gambling," *Journal of the American Medical Association* 286 (2007): 141; Howard J. Shaffer and David A. Korn, "Gambling and Related Mental Disorders: A Public Health Analysis," *Annual Review of Public Health* 23 (2002): 185.

7   Henry R. Lesieur and Michael Welch, "Vice Crimes: Personal Autonomy Versus Societal Dictates," in *Criminology: A Contemporary Handbook*, 3rd ed., ed. Joseph F. Sheley (Belmont, Calif.: Wadsworth, 2000), 233–63.

8   Raymond M. Bergner and Ana J. Bridges, "The Significance of Heavy Pornography Involvement for Romantic Partners: Research and Clinical Implications," *Journal of Sex and Marital Therapy* 28 (2002): 193–206; Melissa Farley, "Prostitution and the Invisibility of Harm," *Women & Therapy* 26 (2003): 247–80; John P. Hoffmann and S. Susan Su, "Parental Substance Use Disorder, Mediating Variables, and Adolescent Drug Use: A Nonrecursive Model," *Addiction* 93 (1998): 1353–66; Jill K. Manning, "The Impact of Internet Pornography on Marriage and the Family: A Review of the Research," *Sexual Addiction & Compulsivity* 13 (2006): 131–65.

9   Gerstein et al., GIBS, 25.

10   Petry, Stinson, and Grant, "Comorbidity," 568.

11   John Welte et al., "Alcohol and Gambling Pathology among U.S. Adults: Prevalence, Demographic Patterns, and Comorbidity," *Journal of Studies on Alcohol* 62 (2001): 706–12. Welte et al. conducted a national telephone survey of adults in the United States in 2000. They reported that the prevalence of current pathological gambling was 1.3 percent based on the Diagnostic Interview Schedule (DIS) (which is used to measure symptoms consistent with the DSM-IV). This is substantially higher than the other reports. Note that NESARC was based on in-person surveys, whereas the NORC study was based on a telephone survey and a casino patron survey. Although some observers claim that telephone surveys underestimate the prevalence of problem and pathological gambling because people with these problems may be hesitant to answer the telephone lest it be a debt collector (Potenza, Kosten, and Rounsaville, "Pathological Gambling"), the fact that the telephone surveys have revealed a higher prevalence of problem gambling casts doubt on this hypothesis. Rather, perhaps in-person surveys underestimate problem behaviors because of satisficing or social desirability bias (Allyson L. Holbrook, Melanie C. Green, and Jon A. Krosnick, "Telephone Versus Face-To-Face Interviewing of National Probability Samples with Long Questionnaires: Comparisons of Respondent Satisficing and Social Desirability Response Bias," *Public Opinion*

Quarterly 67 (2003): 79–125). A more reasonable explanation, though, is that sampling variability affects the results of such surveys, especially since pathological gambling is a rare condition. Perhaps if confidence intervals regularly accompanied prevalence reports, researchers could judge whether these differences are due to sampling variability, variation in measurement techniques, or some actual mechanism in the population.

12 Gerstein et al., GIBS, 25.

13 Petry, Stinson, and Grant, "Comorbidity."

14 David C. Hodgins, Nicole Peden, and Erin Cassidy, "The Association Between Comorbidity and Outcome in Pathological Gambling: A Prospective Follow-up of Recent Quitters," *Journal of Gambling Studies* 21 (2005): 255–71; Nancy M. Petry, "Gambling and Substance Use Disorders: Current Status and Future Directions," *American Journal of Addictions* 16 (2007): 1–9.

15 Yet this approach is fraught with additional problems. In particular, given the relatively low prevalence of gambling problems in general population surveys, large samples are required to gain a sufficient number of problem or pathological gamblers to conduct studies of outcomes, some of which are also relatively rare. For example, even a large study such as the NESARC (n = 43,093) yielded only 195 lifetime pathological gamblers, 79 past-year pathological gamblers, and about 400 people with a major depressive disorder. The NORC survey (n = 1,887) uncovered only 21 lifetime pathological gamblers and 3 past-year pathological gamblers, even though the NORC researchers attempted to increase the power of their study by including a survey of 530 patrons of casinos. Gerstein et al., GIBS, 22.

16 Gerstein et al., GIBS; Petry, Stinson, and Grant, "Comorbidity"; Potenza, Kosten, and Rounsaville, "Pathological Gambling"; Welte et al., "Alcohol and Gambling Pathology"; John Welte et al., "Risk Factors for Pathological Gambling," *Addictive Behaviors* 29 (2004): 323–35.

17 Karen K. Hardoon, Rina Gupta, and Jeffrey L. Derevensky, "Psychosocial Variables Associated with Adolescent Gambling," *Psychology of Addictive Behaviors* 18 (2004): 170–79; Petry, Stinson, and Grant, "Comorbidity"; Nancy M. Petry and Jeremiah Weinstock, "Internet Gambling Is Common in College Students and Associated with Poor Mental Health," *American Journal of Addictions* 16 (2007): 325–30; Shaffer, Hall, and Bilt, "Research Synthesis"; Jeffrey F. Scherrer et al., "Factors Associated with Pathological Gambling at 10-Year Follow-Up in a National Sample of Middle-Aged Men," *Addiction* 102 (2007): 970–78; Wendy S. Slutske et al., "A Twin Study of the Association between Pathological Gambling and Antisocial Personality Disorder," *Journal of Abnormal Psychology* 110 (2001): 297–308; Welte et al., "Alcohol and Gambling Pathology"; Welte et al., "Risk Factors."

18 Welte et al., "Risk Factors."

19 Benjamin J. Morasco et al., "Health Problems and Medical Utilization Associated with Gambling Disorders: Results from the National Epidemiologic Survey on Alcohol and Related Conditions," *Psychosomatic Medicine* 68 (2006): 976–84.

20 Frank Vitaro, Robert Ladouceur, and Annie Bujold, "Predictive and Con-
    current Correlates of Gambling in Early Adolescent Boys," *Journal of
    Early Adolescence* 16 (1996): 211–28.
21 Hardoon, Gupta, and Deverensky, "Psychosocial Variables."
22 Joseph Ciarrocchi and Ann A. Hohmann, "The Family Environment of
    Married Male Pathological Gamblers, Alcoholics, and Dually Addicted
    Gamblers," *Journal of Gambling Studies* 5 (1989): 283–91; David C. Hod-
    gins, N. Will Shead, and Karyn Makarchuk, "Relationship Satisfaction
    and Psychological Distress among Concerned Significant Others of Patho-
    logical Gamblers," *Journal of Nervous and Mental Disease* 195 (2007):
    65–71; Valerie C. Lorenz and Robert A. Yaffee, "Pathological Gambling,
    Psychosomatic, Emotional and Mental Differences as Reported by the
    Spouse of the Gambler," *Journal of Gambling Studies* 4 (1988): 13–26.
23 V. A. Dickson-Swift, E. L. James, and S. Kippen, "The Experience of Liv-
    ing with a Problem Gambler: Spouse and Partners Speak Out," *Journal
    of Gambling Issues* 13 (2005): 1–22; Ruth Grant Kalischuk and Kelly
    Cardwell, *Problem Gambling and Its Impact on Families: Final Report*,
    submitted to the Alberta Alcohol and Drug Abuse Commission (Alberta,
    Canada: University of Lethbridge, 2004).
24 In a concise description of this phenomenon, Kalischuk and Cardwell
    wrote,

    > Children of compulsive gamblers are four times more likely
    > to gamble themselves, often being introduced to gambling by
    > their parents (Abbott, Cramer, and Sherrets, 1995; Ladouceur
    > et al., 2001). This tendency has been described as the *"intergen-
    > erational multiplier effect"* [emphasis added] in children whose
    > parents are problem gamblers (Abbott, 2001). Hardoon, Der-
    > evensky, and Gupta (2003) reported that at risk adolescents and
    > probable pathological gamblers reported significantly more fam-
    > ily members as having gambling problems than non-gamblers
    > and social gamblers. Gambino et al. (1993) found that veterans
    > whose parents were described as problem gamblers had three
    > times the risk of scoring as probable pathological gamblers; those
    > whose grandparents were perceived as problem gamblers were
    > 12 times more likely to have gambling problems. Walters (2001)
    > found that the family history effect followed gender lines, with
    > the father's gambling raising the risk factor for a son more than
    > the mother's gambling increasing the risk factor for a daughter
    > (3–4).

    Kalischuk and Cardwell, *Problem Gambling*. See also Jennifer R. Fel-
    scher, Jeffrey L. Derevensky, and Rina Gupta, "Parental Influences and
    Social Modeling of Youth Lottery Participation," *Journal of Community
    & Applied Social Psychology* 13 (2003): 361–77.
25 See also Ronald Gaudia, "Effects of Compulsive Gambling on the Fam-
    ily," *Social Work* 32 (1987): 254–56; Lorenz and Yaffee, "Pathological
    Gambling."
26 Philip Darbyshire, Candice Oster, and Helen Carrig, "The Experience
    of Pervasive Loss: Children and Young People Living in a Family Where

Parental Gambling Is a Problem," *Journal of Gambling Studies* 17 (2001): 23–45; Philip Darbyshire, Candice Oster, and Helen Carrig, "Children of Parent(s) who have a Gambling Problem: A Review of the Literature' and Commentary on Research Approaches," *Health and Social Care in the Community* 9 (2001): 185–93; Hardoon, Gupta, and Deverensky, "Psychosocial Variables"; Durand F. Jacobs et al., "Children of Problem Gamblers," *Journal of Gambling Studies* 5 (1989): 261–68.

27 Darbyshire, Oster, and Carrig, "Experience of Pervasive Loss."

28 Jacobs et al., "Children of Problem Gamblers."

29 John P. Hoffmann, Scott A. Baldwin, and Felicia G. Cerbone, "The Onset of Major Depressive Disorders among Adolescents," *Journal of the American Academy of Child and Adolescent Psychiatry* 42 (2003): 217–24; John P. Hoffmann and Felicia G. Cerbone, "Parental Substance Use Disorder and the Risk of Adolescent Drug Abuse: An Event History Analysis," *Drug and Alcohol Dependence* 66 (2002): 255–64.

30 Seth A. Eisen et al., "Familial Influences on Gambling Behavior: An Analysis of 3359 Twin Pairs," *Addiction* 93 (1998): 1375–84. Twin studies indicate a substantial shared genetic component to problem and pathological gambling (Seth A. Eisen et al., "The Genetics of Pathological Gambling," *Seminar in Clinical Neuropsychiatry* 6 (2001): 195–204). Estimates indicate that about 35 percent of the variance in pathological gambling is due to inheritability, with about 60 percent due to shared family characteristics.

31 Potenza, Kosten, and Rounsaville, "Pathological Gambling."

32 Avshalom Caspi et al., "Role of Genotype in the Cycle of Violence in Maltreated Children," *Science* 297 (2002): 851–53; Klaus Peter Lesch and Ursula Merschdorf, "Impulsivity, Aggression, and Serotonin: A Molecular Psychobiological Perspective," *Behavioral Sciences and the Law* 18 (2000): 581–604; Terrie E. Moffitt et al., "Whole Blood Serotonin Relates to Violence in an Epidemiological Study," *Biological Psychiatry* 43 (1998): 446–57; Todd M. Moore, Angela Scarpa, and Adrian Raine, "A Meta-Analysis of Serotonin Metabolite 5-HIAA and Antisocial Behavior," *Aggressive Behavior* 28 (2002): 299–316; David D. Rowe, *Biology and Crime* (Los Angeles: Roxbury Publishing, 2002).

33 Joseph G. Grzywacz and Brenda L. Bass, "Work, Family, and Mental Health: Testing Different Models of Work-Family Fit," *Journal of Marriage and Family* 65 (2003): 248–61; Ichiro Kawachi and Lisa F. Berkman, "Social Ties and Mental Health," *Journal of Urban Health* 78 (2001): 458–67.

34 The two surveys are the National Gambling Impact and Behavior Study (NGIBS), administered by the National Opinion Research Center (NORC) for the National Gambling Impact Study Commission in 1999, and the National Epidemiological Study of Alcoholism and Related Conditions (NESARC), which was conducted under the sponsorship of the National Institute on Alcohol Abuse and Alcoholism (NIAAA). Details of these surveys and the data sets that they yielded are available in Gerstein et al., GIBS; and Bridget F. Grant et al., "Source and Accuracy Statement for Wave 1 of the 2001–2002 National Epidemiologic Survey

on Alcohol and Related Conditions" (Bethesda, Md.: National Institute
on Alcohol Abuse and Alcoholism, 2003). Briefly, the NORC study was a
telephone survey supplemented by a casino patron survey of 2,417 adults
in the United States. The NESARC was an in-person survey of 43,093
adults in the United States residing in noninstitutionalized settings. Both
surveys were designed to yield data that could be used to represent the
noninstitutionalized adult population residing in the United States. The
NGIBS also includes an adolescent survey, but I do not consider these
data.

35 Gerstein et al., GIBS, 17.

36 Jay Magidson and Jeroen K. Vermunt, "Latent Class Models," in *The
Sage Handbook of Quantitative Methodology for the Social Sciences*, ed.
David Kaplan (Newbury Park, Calif.: Sage Publications, 2004), 175–97.

37 I relied on the lifetime gambling items because there was not sufficient
variability in the past-year items to conduct the LC cluster analysis. The
following items were excluded from the model because of insufficient
data that was likely caused by the skip patterns employed in the NGIBS
survey: ever tried to cut down (item 4); loss of control happened three
or more times (item 7); ever gambled to relieve uncomfortable feelings
(item 9); lying happened three or more times (item 12); and gambling
caused school problems (item 15). Nevertheless, the analysis provides a
general picture of the pattern of responses. I replicated this analysis using
data from the NESARC. Although the specific patterns were different,
the general results were similar. In particular, the illegal activities item
did not cluster with the other items. A second item that did not fall within
the general gambling problems cluster involved a question about whether
gambling had led the respondent to break up with or nearly break up with
someone.

  Moreover, given the binary nature of the items, I also estimated a
one-parameter Rasch model to determine whether a single dimension
underlies the items in the NODS. In general, the Rasch model estimates
the probability that a respondent chooses a specific response option for an
item as

$$Ln(P_{nij}/P_{ni}(j-1)) = B_n - D_i - F_j$$

where P_{nij} is the probability of the respondent scoring in category j of item
I; $P_{ni}(j-1)$ is the probability of the respondent scoring in category $j-1$
of item I; B_n is the individual measure of the respondent n; D_i is the difficulty parameter of the item I; and F is the difficulty of category step j.
The results of this model are consistent with the cluster analysis exercise:
illegal acts and occupational problems in the NGIBS are not part of the
underlying dimension captured by the Rasch model.

38 The analyses represented in tables 6.2 and 6.3 were fit using the statistical
software Latent Gold®. The results indicated that a three cluster model
fit the data better than a one-, two-, or four-cluster model. In table 3, a
two- cluster model fit the data better than a one- or three-cluster model.
The results in the following table provide model fit information.

Latent Class Cluster Analysis Model Fit Information

	Log-likelihood	BIC	Parameters	L^2	df
Table 5.2					
1-Cluster	-3779.89	7652.05	13	2728.15	8178
2-Cluster	-2872.80	5937.22	27	913.96	8164
3-Cluster	-2782.48	5855.96	41	733.34	8150
4-Cluster	-2757.49	5905.34	55	683.35	8136
Table 5.3					
1-Cluster	-1210.17	2455.85	5	629.78	26
2-Cluster	-923.45	1924.99	11	56.32	20
3-Cluster	-906.85	1934.39	17	23.12	14

39 The item that asked about emotionally harmful arguments with family members was not part of the NODS. Nevertheless, I included it in this analysis because (1) it is clearly an important family problem that reportedly results from gambling, and (2) it maximizes the variability available to the analysis. Table 6.7 provides an additional analysis of this questionnaire item.

40 The NESARC consisted of a representative sample of noninstitutionalized adults, eighteen years and older, residing in the United States. Its sample size was 43,093. The sample frame also included the following noninstitutional group quarters and housing units: boarding houses, rooming houses, nontransient hotels and motels, shelters, facilities for housing workers, college quarters, and group homes. The purpose of the study was to estimate the prevalence of the following behaviors and associated disorders: alcohol and drug use, abuse, and dependence; mental health disorders; and pathological gambling. Grant et al., "Source and Accuracy Statement"; see also Petry, Stimson, and Grant, "Comorbidity," 566.

41 Gerstein et al., GIBS.

42 Ronald C. Kessler and Kathleen R. Merikangas, "The National Comorbidity Survey Replication (NCS-R): Background and Aims," *International Journal of Methods in Psychiatric Research* 13 (2004): 60–68.

43 Welte et al., "Alchohol and Gambling Pathology."

44 Hereafter I use the four category classification system developed by Gerstein et al., GIBS, 21. The frequency distribution of these categories is shown in the following table. Note that the percentages are different in the NGIBS and the NESARC mainly because of the different threshold criteria: the gambling problem questions were asked among all NGIBS respondents who reported lifetime gambling, whereas the NESARC limited these questions to those who reported gambling at least five times in any one year in their lifetimes.

Distribution of Lifetime Gambling Problems, NGIBS 1998 and NESARC 2001

Gambling problem category	NGIBS, 1998	NESARC, 2001
None (0 symptoms)	87.7% (86.3–89.1)	80.3% (79.2–81.3)
At-risk (1–2 symptoms)	9.1% (7.9–10.4)	13.6% (12.8–14.5)
Problem (3–4 symptoms)	1.7% (1.3–2.4)	4.5% (4.1–5.1)
Pathological (5 or more symptoms)	1.5% (1.1–1.9)	1.6% (1.3–1.9)

Note: The percentages are based on the subsample of lifetime gamblers who said they had lost $100 or more gambling in any one day in the NGIBS and those reporting lifetime gambling on five or more occasions in the NESARC. They are based on weighted data. Ninety-five percent confidence intervals appear in parentheses.

The analyses presented in tables 6.5–6.8 rely on cross-tabulations of weighted data. However, I confirmed the patterns shown in these tables with logistic and multinomial logistic regression models that included the following covariates: age, gender, years of formal education, race/ethnicity, region of the country, urban residence, and family income. Where necessary, I used multiple imputation methods to account for patterns of missing data. The multivariable models adjusted for the multistage sample design of the surveys and relied on weighted data. With few exceptions, the patterns shown in the tables were confirmed with these multivariable models.

45   Gerstein et al., GIBS, 30.
46   Darbyshire, Oster, and Carrig, "Experience of Pervasive Loss"; Darbyshire, Oster, and Carrig, "Children"; Dickson-Swift, James, and Kippen, "Living with a Problem Gambler" 2005; Hardoon, Gupta, and Derevensky, "Psychosocial Variables"; Hodgins, Shead, and Makarchuk, "Relationship Satisfaction"; Kalischuk and Cardwell, *Problem Gambling*; Lorenz and Yaffee, "Pathological Gambling."
47   Wendy S. Slutske, "Natural Recovery and Treatment Seeking in Pathological Gambling: Results from Two National Surveys," *American Journal of Psychiatry* 163 (2006): 297–302; Wendy S. Slutske, Kristina M. Jackson, and Kenneth J. Sher, "The Natural History of Problem Gambling from Ages 18 to 29," *Journal of Abnormal Psychology* 112 (2003): 263–74.
48   Linda C. Sobell, Timothy P. Ellingstad, and Mark B. Sobell, "Natural Recovery from Alcohol and Drug Problems: Methodological Review of the Research with Suggestions for Future Directions," *Addiction* 95 (2000): 749–64.
49   John P. Hoffmann, Mikaela Dufur, and Lynn Huang, "Drug Use and Job Quits: A Longitudinal Analysis," *Journal of Drug Issues* 37 (2007): 569–96.
50   Robert J. Sampson and John H. Laub, "A Life Course Theory of Cumulative Disadvantage and the Stability of Delinquency," in *Developmental Theories of Crime and Delinquency*, ed. Terence P. Thornberry (New Brunswick, N.J.: Transaction Publishers, 1997), 133–62.

Chapter 7

1   See, e.g., J. P. Quinn, *Fools of Fortune* (Chicago: The Anti-Gambling Association, 1892).

2   Fyodor Dostoyevsky, *The Gambler/Bobok/A Nasty Story* (London: Penguin Books, 1966); idem, *Complete Letters*, ed. D. A. Lowe and R. Meyer (New York: Ardis, 1998).

3   *Merriam-Webster Online Dictionary*, "Morality," http://www.m-w.com/dictionary/morality; *Merriam-Webster Online Dictionary*, "Moral," http://www.m-w.com/dictionary/moral (accessed October 2, 2007).

4   J. Moll et al., "The Neural Basis of Human Moral Cognition," *Nature Rev Neurosci* 6 (2005): 799–809.

5   Quinn, *Fools of Fortune*.

6   J. Fielding, "The History of Gambling," *The Gentleman's Magazine* December 1756, 564–67.

7   Mason Long, *The Life of Mason Long, Converted Gambler*, 5th ed. (Fort Wayne, Ind.: Mason Long, 1882).

8   Quinn, *Fools of Fortune*; R. E. Conwell, *Social Abominations* (Harrisburg, Pa.: Whitman, 1892); T. D. Talmadge, "Gambling," in *Social Dynamite; Or, the Wickedness of Modern Society* (Chicago: Standard, 1888), 144–60.

9   W. D. MacKenzie, *The Ethics of Gambling* (London: The Sunday School Union, 1902), 40.

10   American Gaming Association, *Gambling Revenue: Current Year* (Christensen Capital Advisors, 2006), http://www.americangaming.org/Industry/factsheets/statistics_detail.cfv?id=7.

11   Korn and Shaffer, "Gambling and the Health of the Public"; Howard J. Shaffer and D. A. Korn, "Gambling and Related Mental Disorders: A Public Health Analysis," *Annual Review of Public Health* 23 (2002): 171–212.

12   American Psychiatric Association, *Diagnostic and Statistical Manual of Mental Disorders*, 4th ed., test revision (Washington, D.C.: American Psychiatric Association, 2000) (hereafter cited as APA, *Manual of Mental Disorders* [2000]).

13   Gerstein et al., GIBS.

14   American Psychiatric Association, *Diagnostic and Statistical Manual of Mental Disorders*, 3rd ed. (Washington, D.C.: American Psychiatric Association, 1980).

15   APA, *Manual of Mental Disorders* (2000); J. E. Grant and Marc N. Potenza, "Impulse Control Disorders: Clinical Characteristics and Pharmacological Management," *Annals of Clinical Psychiatry* 16 (2004): 27–34; W. A. Williams and Marc N. Potenza, "The Neurobiology of Impulse Control Disorders," *Revista Brasileira Psiquiatria* 30, no. s1 (2008): 24–30.

16   APA, *Manual of Mental Disorders* (2000).

17   APA, *Manual of Mental Disorders* (2000); Marc N. Potenza, "Should Addictive Disorders Include Non-Substance-Related Conditions?" *Addiction* 101, no. s1 (2006): 142–51.

18   Potenza, "Addictive Disorders."

19   Potenza, "Addictive Disorders"; C. Holden, " 'Behavioral' Addictions: Do They Exist?" *Science* 294, no. 5544 (2001): 980–82; Nancy M. Petry, "Should the Scope of Addictive Behaviors Be Broadened to Include Pathological Gambling?" *Addiction* 101, no. s1 (2006): 152–60.

20   E. Hollander and C. M. Wong, "Obsessive-Compulsive Spectrum Disorders," *Journal of Clinical Psychiatry* 5 s4 (1995): 3–6; E. Hollander and S. D. Benzaquin, "Is There a Distinct OCD Spectrum?" *CNS Spectrums* 1, no. 1 (1996): 17–26.

21   J. E. Grant and Marc N. Potenza, "Compulsive Aspects of Impulse Control Disorders," *The Psychiatric Clinics of North America Journal* 29 (2006): 539–51; Marc N. Potenza, "To Do or Not To Do? The Complexities of Addiction, Motivations, Self-control and Impulsivity," *American Journal of Psychiatry* 164 (2007): 4–6.

22   J. A. Brewer and Marc N. Potenza, "The Neurobiology and Genetics of Impulse Control Disorders: Relationships to Drug Addictions," *Biochemical Pharmacology* 75 (2008): 63–75.

23   F. G. Moeller et al., "Psychiatric Aspects of Impulsivity," *American Journal of Psychiatry* 158 (2001): 1783–93; Nancy M. Petry, *Pathological Gambling: Etiology, Comorbidity and Treatment* (Washington, D.C.: American Psychological Association, 2005); Marc N. Potenza, "Impulse Control Disorders and Co-Occurring Disorders: Dual Diagnosis Considerations," *Journal of Dual Diagnosis* 3 (2007): 47–57.

24   S. Krishnan-Sarin et al., "Behavioral Impulsivity Predicts Treatment Outcome in a Smoking Cessation Program for Adolescent Smokers," *Drug and Alcohol Dependence* 88 (2007): 79–82.

25   Marc N. Potenza, "To Do or Not to Do? The Complexities of Addiction, Motivations, Self-Control and Impulsivity," *American Journal of Psychiatry* 164 (2007): 4–6; R. A. Chambers, J. R. Taylor, and Marc N. Potenza, "Developmental Neurocircuitry of Motivation in Adolescence: A Critical Period of Addiction Vulnerability," *American Journal of Psychiatry* 160 (2003): 1041–52; R. A. Chambers, W. K. Bickel, and Marc N. Potenza, "A Scale-Free Systems Theory of Motivation and Addiction," *Neuroscience and Biobehavioral Reviews* 31 (2007): 1017–45; M. J. Kreek et al., "Genetic Influences on Impulsivity, Risk-Taking, Stress Responsivity and Vulnerability to Drug Abuse and Addiction," *Nature Neuroscience* 8 (2005): 1450–57.

26   C. J. France, "The Gambling Impulse," *American Journal of Psychology* 13 (1902): 364–407.

27   Quotations throughout this paragraph are from A. R. Damasio, *Descartes' Error: Emotion, Reason and the Human Brain* (New York: Crosset/Putnam, 1994), 4, 8.

28   Damasio, *Descartes' Error.*

29   Damasio, *Descartes' Error.*

30   A. Bechara et al., "Insensitivity to Future Consequences Following Damage to Human Prefrontal Cortex," *Cognition* 50 (1994): 7–15; A. Bechara et al., "Dissociation of Working Memory from Decision Making within the Human Prefrontal Cortex," *Journal of Neuroscience* 18, no. 1 (1998): 428–37.

31   A. Bechara, "Deciding Advantageously before Knowing the Advantageous Strategy," *Science* 275, no. 5304 (1997): 1293–95.

32   A. Bechara, et al., "Different Contributions of the Human Amygdala and Ventromedial Prefrontal Cortex to Decision Making," *Journal of Neuroscience* 19 (1999): 5473–81.

33   Damasio, *Descartes' Error.*

34   Nancy M. Petry, "Substance Abuse, Pathological Gambling, and Impulsiveness," *Drug and Alcohol Dependence* 63 (2001): 29–38; P. Cavedini et al., "Frontal Lobe Dysfunction in Pathological Gambling," *Biological Psychiatry* 51 (2002): 334–41; A. Bechara, "Risky Business: Emotion, Decision Making, and Addiction," *Journal of Gambling Studies* 19 (2003): 23–51.

35   Bechara, "Risky Business."

36   W. K. Bickel, R. J. DeGrandpre, and S. T. Higgins, "Behavioral Economics: A Novel Experimental Approach to the Study of Drug Dependence," *Drug and Alcohol Dependence* 33, no. 2 (1993): 173–92; W. K. Bickel, A. L. Odum, and G. J. Madden, "Impulsivity and Cigarette Smoking: Delay Discounting in Current, Never, and Ex-Smokers," *Psychopharmacology* (Berlin) 146, no. 4 (1999): 447–54; K. N. Kirby, Nancy M. Petry, W. K. Bickel, "Heroin Addicts Have Higher Discount Rates for Delayed Rewards Than Non-Drug-Using Controls," *Journal of Experimental Psychology* 128 (1999): 78–87.

37   Petry, "Substance Abuse"; Nancy M. Petry and T. Casarella, "Excessive Discounting of Delayed Rewards in Substance Abusers with Gambling Problems," *Drug and Alcohol Dependence* 56 (1999): 25–32; Nancy M. Petry, "Pathological Gamblers, with and without Substance Use Disorders, Discount Delayed Rewards at High Rates," *Journal of Abnormal Psychology* 110 (2001): 482–87.

38   S. M. McClure et al., "Separate Neural Systems Value Immediate and Delayed Monetary Rewards," *Science* 306, no. 5695 (2004): 503–7.

39   Chambers, Taylor, and Potenza, "Developmental Neurocircuitry"; R. Z. Goldstein and N. D. Volkow, "Drug Addiction and Its Underlying Neurobiological Basis: Neuroimaging Evidence for the Involvement of the Frontal Cortex," *American Journal of Psychiatry* 159 (2002): 1642–52; B. Everitt and T. W. Robbins, "Neural Systems of Reinforcement for Drug Addiction: From Actions to Habits to Compulsion," *Nature Neuroscience* 8 (2005): 1481–89.

40   Damasio, *Descartes' Error.*

41   McClure et al., "Separate Neural Systems."

42   W. Schultz, L. Tremblay, and J. R. Hollerman, "Reward Processing in Primate Orbitofrontal Cortex and Basal Ganglia," *Cerebral Cortex* 10 (2000): 272–84.

43   B. Knutson et al., "fMRI Visualization of Brain Activity During a Monetary Incentive Delay Task," *Neuroimage* 12 (2000): 20–27.

44   B. Knutson et al., "Dissociation of Reward Anticipation and Outcome with Event-Related fMRI," *Neuroreport* 12 (2001): 3683–87; B. Knutson et al., "Anticipation of Increasing Monetary Reward Selectively Recruits

Nucleus Accumbens," *Journal of Neuroscience* 21 (2001): RC159 (1–5); B. Knutson et al., "A Region of Mesial Prefrontal Cortex Tracks Monetarily Rewarding Outcomes: Characterization with Rapid Event-Related fMRI," *Neuroimage* 18 (2003): 263–72.

45 D. W. Hommer, "Motivation in Alcoholism," paper presented at the International Conference on Applications of Neuroimaging to Alcoholism, New Haven, Conn., 2004.

46 Hommer, "Motivation in Alcoholism," 22A.

47 J. M. Bjork et al., "Incentive-Elicited Brain Activation in Adolescents: Similarities and Differences from Young Adults," *Journal of Neuroscience* 24 (2004): 1793–1802.

48 R. Z. Goldstein et al., "Is Decreased Prefrontal Cortical Sensitivity to Monetary Reward Associated with Impaired Motivation and Self-Control in Cocaine Addiction?" *American Journal of Psychiatry* 164 (2007): 43–51.

49 Marc N. Potenza et al., "Gambling Urges in Pathological Gamblers: An fMRI Study," *Archives of General Psychiatry* 60 (2003): 828–36.

50 Marc N. Potenza, "An fMRI Stroop Study of Ventromedial Prefrontal Cortical Function in Pathological Gamblers," *American Journal of Psychiatry* 160 (2003): 1990–94.

51 J. Reuter et al., "Pathological Gambling Is Linked to Reduced Activation of the Mesolimbic Reward System," *Nature Neuroscience* 8 (2005): 147–48.

52 Knutson et al., "Anticipation"; Knutson et al., "Dissociation"; Chambers, Taylor, and Potenza, "Developmental Neurocircuitry"; N. D. Volkow and T. Li, "Drug Addiction: The Neurobiology of Behaviour Gone Awry," *Nature Reviews Neuroscience* 5 (2004): 963–70; Chambers, Bickel, and Potenza, "Scale-Free Systems Theory."

53 Reuter et al., "Pathological Gambling."

54 Marc N. Potenza, "Should Addictions Include Non-Substance-Related Disorders?" paper presented at the European Association of Addiction Therapies, Vienna, Austria, September 12, 2007.

55 Williams and Potenza, "Impulse Control Disorders"; Brewer and Potenza, "Neurobiology and Genetics"; Marc N. Potenza and E. Hollander, "Pathological Gambling and Impulse Control Disorders," in *Neuropsychopharmacology: The 5th Generation of Progress*, ed. J. Coyle et al. (Baltimore, Md.: Lippincott Williams & Wilkens, 2002), 1725-42.

56 Potenza and Hollander, "Pathological Gambling."

57 C. M. DeCaria, T. Begaz, and E. Hollander, "Serotonergic and Noradrenergic Function in Pathological Gambling," *CNS Spectrums* 3, no. 6 (1998): 38–47.

58 D. W. Hommer et al., "Effects of M-Chlorophenylpiperazine on Regional Brain Glucose Utilization: A Positron Emission Tomographic Comparison of Alcoholic and Control Subjects," *Journal of Neuroscience* 17 (1997): 2796–2806; L. J. Siever et al., "D,L-Fenfluaramine Response in Impulsive Personality Disorder Assessed with [18f] Fluorodexyglucose Positron Emission Tomography," *Neuropsychopharmacology* 20 (1999): 413–23; A. S. New et al., "Blunted Prefrontal Cortical 18-Fluorodeoxyglucose Posi-

tron Emission Tomography Response to Meta-Chlorophenylpiperazine in Impulsive Aggression," *Archives of General Psychiatry* 59 (2002): 621–29.

59 Chambers, Taylor, and Potenza, "Developmental Neurocircuitry"; N. D. Volkow and T. Li, "Drug Addiction: The Neurobiology of Behaviour Gone Awry," *Nature Reviews Neuroscience* 5, no. 12 (2004): 963–70; E. J. Nestler, "Molecular Mechanisms of Drug Addiction," *Neuropharmacology* 47, no. 1 (2004): 24–32.

60 C. Bergh et al., "Altered Dopamine Function in Pathological Gambling," *Psychological Medicine* 27, no. 2 (1997): 473–75.

61 C. Nordin and T. Eklundh, "Tapping-Time Is Longer in Pathological Male Gamblers Than in Healthy Male Controls," *Journal of Psychiatric Research* 32 (1998): 421–22; C. Nordin and T. Eklundh, "Altered Csf 5-Hiaa Disposition in Pathologic Male Gamblers," *CNS Spectrums* 4, no. 12 (1999): 25–33.

62 M. Zack and C. X. Poulos, "Amphetamine Primes Motivation to Gamble and Gambling-Related Semantic Networks in Problem Gamblers," *Neuropsychopharmacology* 29 (2004): 195–207.

63 M. Zack and C. X. Poulos, "A D2 Antagonist Enhances the Rewarding and Priming Effects of a Gambling Episode in Pathological Gamblers," *Neuropsychopharmacology* 32 (2007): 1678–86.

64 D. Weintraub et al., "Dopamine Agonist Use Is Associated with Impulse Control Disorders in Parkinson's Disease," *Archives of Neurology* 63 (2006): 969–73; V. K. Voon et al., "Prevalence of Repetitive and Reward-Seeking Behaviors in Parkinson's Disease," *Neurology* 67 (2006): 1254–57; V. K. Voon et al., "Prospective Prevalence of Pathological Gambling and Medication Association in Parkinson's Disease," *Neurology* 66 (2006): 1750–52; V. K. Voon et al., "Factors Associated with Dopaminergic Drug-Related Pathological Gambling in Parkinson's Disease," *Archives of Neurology* 64 (2007): 212–16; Weintraub and Marc N. Potenza, "Impulse Control Disorders in Parkinson's Disease," *Current Neurology and Neuroscience Reports* 6 (2006): 302–6.

65 Williams and Potenza, "Impulse Control Disorders"; J. E. Grant, J. A. Brewer, and Marc N. Potenza, "The Neurobiology of Substance and Behavioral Addictions," *CNS Spectrums* 11 (2006): 924–30.

66 S. W. Kim et al., "Double-Blind Naltrexone and Placebo Comparison Study in the Treatment of Pathological Gambling," *Biological Psychiatry* 49 (2001): 914–21.

67 J. E. Grant et al., "Multicenter Investigation of the Opioid Antagonist Nalmefene in the Treatment of Pathological Gambling," *American Journal of Psychiatry* 163 (2006): 303–12.

68 Biotie, *Financial Report*, http://www.biotie.com/annualreports/2006/uk/ (accessed October 2, 2007).

69 J. H. Krystal et al., "Naltrexone in the Treatment of Alcohol Dependence," *New England Journal of Medicine* 345, no. 2 (2001): 1734–39.

70 D. W. Oslin et al., "A Functional Polymorphism of the Mu-Opioid Receptor Gene Is Associated with Naltrexone Response in Alcohol-Dependent Patients," *Neuropsychopharmacology* 28 (2003): 1546–52.

71 Williams and Potenza, "Impulse Control Disorders"; A. Ibanez et al., "Genetics of Pathological Gambling," *Journal of Gambling Studies* 19 (2003): 11–22.

72 Ibanez et al., "Genetics of Pathological Gambling."

73 K. R. Shah et al., "Genetic Studies of Pathological Gambling: A Review of Methodology and Analyses of Data from the Vietnam Era Twin (Vet) Registry," *Journal of Gambling Studies* 21 (2005): 177–201.

74 Eisen et al., "Familial Influences."

75 Marc N. Potenza et al., "Shared Genetic Contributions to Pathological Gambling and Major Depression in Men," *Archives of General Psychiatry* 62 (2005): 1015–21.

76 Wendy S. Slutske et al., "Common Genetic Vulnerability for Pathological Gambling and Alcohol Dependence in Men," *Archives of General Psychiatry* 57 (2000): 666–74.

77 Avshalom Caspi et al., "Influence of Life Stress on Depression: Moderation by a Polymorphism in the 5-Htt Gene," *Science* 301 (2003): 386–89.

78 Nancy M. Petry, K. L. Steinberg, and Women's Problem Gambling Research Center, "Childhood Maltreatment in Male and Female Treatment-Seeking Pathological Gamblers," *Psychology of Addictive Behaviors* 19 (2005): 226–29.

79 A. R. Hariri et al., "Serotonin Transporter Genetic Variation and the Response of the Human Amygdala," *Science* 297, no. 5580 (2002): 400–403; M. F. Egan et al., "Effect of Comt Val108/158 Met Genotype on Frontal Lobe Function and Risk for Schizophrenia," *Proceedings of the National Academy of Sciences* 98, no. 12 (2001): 6917–22.

80 M. J. Friedrich, "Neuroscience Becomes Image Conscious as Brain Scans Raise Ethical Issues," *Journal of the American Medical Association* 294 (2005): 781–83.

81 J. Moll et al., "The Neural Basis of Human Moral Cognition," *Nature Reviews Neuroscience* 6 (2005): 799-809; R. Adolphs, "Cognitive Neuroscience of Human Social Behavior," *Nature Reviews Neuroscience* 4 (2003): 165–78.

82 Moll et al., "Neural Basis"; J. D. Greene et al., "The Neural Bases of Cognitive Conflict and Control in Moral Judgment," *Neuron* 44 (2004): 389–400.

83 J. D. Greene and J. Haidt, "How (and Where) Does Moral Judgment Work?" *Trends in Cognitive Science* 6 (2002): 517–23; Greene et al., "Neural Bases."

84 Adolphs, "Cognitive Neuroscience."

85. Greene et al., "Neural Bases."

86 Moll et al., "Neural Basis."

87 Moll et al., "Neural Basis."

88 P. J. Elsinger and A. R. Damasio, "Severe Disturbance of Higher Level Cognition after Bilateral Frontal Lobe Ablation: Patient Avr.," *Neurology* 35 (1993): 1731–41.

89 S. W. Anderson et al., "Impairment of Social and Moral Behavior Related to Early Damage in Human Prefrontal Cortex," *Nature Neuroscience* 2 (1999): 1032–37.

90 J. S. Beer et al., "The Regulatory Function of Self-Conscious Emotions: Insights from Patients with Orbitofrontal Damage," *Journal of Personality and Social Psychology* 85 (2003): 594–604; N. G. Camille et al., "The Involvement of the Orbitofrontal Cortex in the Experience of Regret," *Science* 304 (2004): 1167–70.

91 Moll et al., "Neural Basis."

92 M. Botvinick et al., "Conflict Monitoring Versus Selection-for-Action in Anterior Cingulate Cortex," *Nature* 402 (1999): 179–81; M. Botvinick et al., "Conflict Monitoring and Cognitive Control," *Psychological Review* 108 (2001): 624–52.

93 Moll et al., "Neural Basis."

94 Moll et al., "Neural Basis."

95 Moll et al., "Neural Basis," Takahashi et al., "Brain Activation Associated with Evaluative Processes of Guilt and Embarassment: An fMRI Study," *Neuroimage* 23 (2004): 967–74; . Moll et al., "The Moral Affiliations of Disgust: A Functional MRI Study," *Cognitive and Behavioral Neurology* 18 (2005): 68–78; L. M. Shin et al., "Activation of Anterior Paralimbic Structures During Guilt-Related Script-Driven Imagery," *Biological Psychiatry* 48 (2000): 43–50.

96 J. R. Blair, "Neurobiological Basis of Psychopathy," *British Journal of Psychiatry* 182 (2003): 5–7.

97 M. St. George and U. Bellugi, "Preface," in "Linking Cognitive Neuroscience and Molecular Genetics: New Perspectives from Williams Syndrome," ed. M. St. George and U. Bellugi, *Journal of Cognitive Neuroscience* 12, no. s1 (2000): 1–6.

98 V. M. Narayan et al., "Regional Cortical Thinning in Subjects with Violent Antisocial Personality Disorder or Schizophrenia," *American Journal of Psychiatry* 164 (2007): 1418–27.

99 L. A. Hayman et al., "Klüver-Bucy Syndrome after Bilateral Selective Damage of Amygdala and Its Cortical Connections," *Journal of Neuropsychiatry and Clinical Neurosciences* 10 (1998): 354–58.

100 Friedrich, "Neuroscience Becomes Image Conscious."

101 Friedrich, "Neuroscience Becomes Image Conscious"; T. Buller, "What Can Neuroscience Contribute to Ethics?" *Journal of Medical Ethics* 32 (2006): 63–64; N. Eastman and C. Campbell, "Neuroscience and Legal Determination of Criminal Responsibility," *Nature Reviews Neuroscience* 7 (2006): 311–18; A. I. Leshner, "Don't Let Ideology Trump Science," *Science* 302, no. 5650 (2003): 1479.

Chapter 8

Thanks to Alan Wolfe, William Galston, and Erik Owens for their helpful comments.

1 Committee on Homosexual Offences and Prostitution, *Report of the Committee on Homosexual Offences and Prostitution* (London: Her Majesty's Stationery Office, 1957).

2 Gilbert Geis, *Not the Law's Business: An Examination of Homosexuality, Abortion, Prostitution, Narcotics, and Gambling in the United*

States (New York: Schocken Books, 1979); Sanford Kadish, "The Crisis of Overcriminalization," *Annals of the American Academy of Political and Social Science* 374 (1967): 157–70; Herbert Packer, *The Limits of the Criminal Sanction* (Stanford, Calif.: Stanford University Press, 1968); Edwin Schur, *Crimes without Victims* (Englewood Cliffs, N.J.: Prentice Hall, 1965); Jerome Skolnick, "Coercion to Virtue: The Enforcement of Morals," *Southern California Law Review* 41 (1968): 588.

3　American Gaming Association, *Gambling Revenue: Current Year.* Christensen Capital Advisors, 2006.

4　National Indian Gaming Commission, *Gaming Revenue Reports*, 2007, available at http://www.nigc.gov.

5　William J. Bennett, *The Book of Virtues: A Treasury of Great Moral Stories* (Parsippany, N.J.: Silver Burdett, 1996).

6　Commonwealth of Massachusetts, "Governor Patrick Unveils Plan For Casino Gambling In Massachusetts," Executive Department, Commonwealth of Massachusetts, September 18, 2007.

7　Ken Maguire, "Some Warn Mass. Casino Plan Brings Risk for College Students," *Boston Globe*, October 14, 2007.

8　Ken Maguire, "Patrick's Casino Revenue Doubtful, Report Says," *Newsday*, October 25, 2007.

9　This also follows a long history of the use of gambling for societally sanctioned purposes, such as public works projects and noted universities as far as back as the colonial period in America. See Cornell Law Project, *The Development of the Law of Gambling, 1776–1976* (Washington, D.C.: National Institute of Law Enforcement and Criminal Justice, 1977).

10　Annelise Orleck, *Storming Caesars Palace: How Black Mothers Fought Their Own War on Poverty* (Boston: Beacon, 2005).

11　Jerome Skolnick, *House of Cards: Legalization and Control of Casino Gambling* (Boston: Little, Brown, 1978).

12　John Dombrink and Daniel Hillyard, *Sin No More: From Abortion to Stem Cells, Understanding Crime, Law, and Morality in America* (New York: NYU Press, 2007).

13　Skolnick, "Social Transformation."

14　Alan Wolfe, "The Culture War That Never Was: Why the Right and Left Have Overlooked Gambling," paper presented at the conference "Gambling and the American Moral Landscape," Boston College, Boston, October 26, 2007.

15　Rachel Croson, Matthew Fox and James Sundali, "Behavioral and Brain Measures of Risk Taking," (paper presented at the conference "Gambling and the American Moral Landscape," Boston College, Boston, October 25, 2007), 22.

16　Croson, Fox, and Sundali, "Behavioral and Brain," 2.

17　Timothy O'Brien, "Is Poker Losing Its First Flush?" *The New York Times*, April 16, 2006.

18　Drew Westen, *The Political Brain: The Role of Emotion in Deciding the Fate of the Nation* (New York: PublicAffairs Books, 2007).

19 Marc N. Potenza, et al., "Gender-related differences in the characteristics of problem gamblers using a gambling helpline," *American Journal of Psychiatry*, Vol. 158, 2001.

20 Marc N. Potenza, "Gambling and Morality: A Neuropsychiatric Perspective," chap. 7 in this volume.

21 Potenza,"Gambling and Morality."

22 Rachel Croson, Matthew Fox and James Sundali, "Behavioral Measures of Risk-Taking," chap. 5 in this volume.

23 Potenza, "Gambling and Morality."

24 Potenza, "Gambling and Morality."

25 Potenza, "Gambling and Morality."

26 James Dobson, "Going for Broke," Focus on the Family, July 1999, available at http://www.family.org/.

27 John P. Hoffman, "Gambling with the Family," paper presented at the conference "Gambling and the American Moral Landscape." Boston College, Boston, October 25, 2007, 2.

28 Patrick Devlin, *The Enforcement of Morals* (London: Oxford University Press, 1965); John Stuart Mill, *On Liberty*, ed. Stefan Collini (Cambridge: Cambridge University Press, 1989 [1861]).

29 Hoffman, 2007, p.2.

30 Richard Lehne, *Casino Policy* (New Brunswick, N.J.: Rutgers University Press, 1986).

31 Jared Miller, "Casino Flourishes without Alcohol," *Casper Star-Tribune* (Wyo.), September 23, 2007.

32 Carmen Messerlian and Jeffrey L. Derevensky, "Youth Gambling: A Public Health Perspective," *Journal of Gambling Issues* 14 (2005): 1–20.

33 Dombrink and Thompson, *The Last Resort*.

34 I. Nelson Rose, "The Legalization and Control of Casino Gambling," *Fordham Law Review* 8 (1980): 245–300.

35 William R. Eadington, "Ten Challenges: Issues That Are Shaping the Future of Gambling and Commercial Gaming," address to the Thirteenth International Conference on Gambling and Risk-Taking, Lake Tahoe, Nevada, May 23, 2006.

36 Jennifer Mesko, "States Stand Strong against Gambling," *Citizenlink*, August 30, 2007, available at http://www.citizenlink.com/.

37 Clotfelter and Cook, *Selling Hope*.

38 Craig Lambert, "Trafficking in Chance," *Harvard Magazine*, July–August 2002, 4–5.

39 Center for Responsive Politics, "Money in Politics: Casinos/Gambling: Long-Term Contribution Trends" (Washington, D.C.: Center for Responsive Politics, 2006), available at http://www.opensecrets.org/.

40 John Dombrink, "Gambling's Status Among the Vices, 1990—A Comparative View," paper presented at the Eighth International Conference in Risk and Gambling, London, England, August 15–17, 1990.

41 Dombrink and Thompson, *The Last Resort*.

42 Pew Research Center, "Gambling."

43 Edward Ugel, *Money for Nothing: One Man's Journey Through the Dark Side of Lottery Millions* (New York: HarperCollins, 2007), xvi.

Chapter 9

1 For the figures in this paragraph, see Pew Research Center, "Gambling."
2 "Morality Continues to Decay," *The Barna Update*, November 3, 2003, available at http://www.barna.org/. Born-again Christians are those who have consciously and explicitly received Christ as their savior and are then regarded as born of God, not just of their human parents. Evangelicals are Christians committed to a Bible-centered understanding of their faith and to spreading that faith through preaching, witnessing, and conversion. These same two groups were outliers regarding a range of other morally controversial behaviors as well.
3 Jonathan Last, "Not Just for Losers Anymore," *The Wall Street Journal*, October 21, 2005.
4 The following quotes from the Buddhist, Hindu, and Islamic traditions are adapted from "Does God Play Dice? Religious Perspectives on Gambling," *Beliefnet*, available at http://www.beliefnet.com/.
5 *Al-Ma'idah, Surah* 5:90-91.
6 Ronald A. Reno, "Gambling and the Bible," *Beliefnet*, http://www.belief net.com/ (accessed September 2, 2007).
7 Don Feeny, "Is Gambling Immoral?" Minnesota Institute of Public Health, http://www.miph.org/gambling (accessed September 2, 2007).
8 Prove 4:19; quoted and discussed in Raymond L. Weiss, "The Adaptation of Philosophic Ethics to a Religious Community: Maimonides' Eight Chapters," *Proceedings of the American Academy for Jewish Research* 54 (1987): 264.
9 Babylonian Talmud, Sanhedrin 24b.
10 David Bassous and Harold Sutton, "Gambling in Jewish Law" (paper on file with the author).
11 *Mishneh Torah*, Hilchot Gezela, chap. 6, halacha 10.
12 *Mishneh Torah*, Hilchot Edut, chap. 10, halacha 4.
13 Babylonian Talmud, Shabbat 10a.
14 Deut 16:20.
15 For all this and much more, see David J. Schnall, "By the Sweat of Your Brow," Center for Business Ethics and Social Responsibility, http://www.besr.org/ (accessed September 2, 2007; link no longer available).
16 *Jewish Encyclopedia*, "Gambling," by Solomon Schechter and Julius H. Greenstone, http://www.jewishencyclopedia.com/.
17 See Leo Landman, "Jewish Attitudes toward Gambling: The Professional and Compulsive Gambler," *Jewish Quarterly Review* 57, no. 4 (1967): 302–3; and idem, "Jewish Attitudes toward Gambling II: Individual and Communal Efforts to Curb Gambling," *Jewish Quarterly Review* 58 no. 1 (1967): 34–40.
18 Babylonian Talmud, Sanhedrin 72a.
19 Yehudah Poznick, "Gambling with the Jewish Law," *Jewish Magazine*, February 2003, http://www.jewishmag.com/64mag/gambling/gambling.htm.

20 For these examples and others, see Central Conference of American Rab-
    bis, "Jewish Attitude toward Gambling," Responsum 167, Central Con-
    ference of American Rabbis, 1979.

21 Landman, "Jewish Attitudes toward Gambling," 310.

22 European Jewish Press, "Jewish Lottery launched in the UK," December
    25, 2005, http://www.ejpress.org/article/4835.

23 A search of his well-stocked Web site, chiefrabbi.org, revealed none.

24 See "Jewish Lottery Fiasco," *SomethingJewish.co.uk*, May 5, 2006, http://
    www.somethingjewish.co.uk/articles/1870_jewish_lottery_fiasc.htm.

25 Central Conference of American Rabbis, "Jewish Attitude toward
    Gambling."

26 Bassous and Sutton, "Gambling in Jewish Law," 6.

Chapter 10

1   Blaise Pascal, *Pensées*, trans. A. J. Krailsheimer (Harmondsworth, Eng-
    land: Penguin Books, 1966), 157.

2   Pascal, *Pensées*, 151.

3   Pascal, *Pensées*, 157.

4   Pascal, *Pensées*, 157.

5   Thomas M. Kavanagh, *Enlightenment and the Shadows of Chance* (Bal-
    timore, Md.: Johns Hopkins University Press, 1993), chap. 2.

6   Pascal, *Pensées*, 70.

7   Pascal, *Pensées*, 70.

8   Pascal, *Pensées*, 74.

9   Pascal, *Pensées*, 92.

10 Pascal, *Pensées*, 165.

11 Pascal, *Pensées*, 69.

12 John Tillotson, *Works* (London: Rogers, Goodwin, Nicholson & Tooke,
    1710), 30.

13 Clifford Geertz, *The Interpretation of Cultures* (New York: Basic Books,
    1973).

14 Geertz, *Interpretation*, 433; emphasis in original.

15 Geertz, *Interpretation*, 434; emphasis in original.

16 Geertz, *Interpretation*, 435. This is the sort of gambling by women and
    adolescents that surrounds the center betting in Balinese cockfights. See
    page 441 for a list of prerequisites for deep play in a Balinese gambling
    context.

17 Geertz, *Interpretation*, 448.

18 Geertz, *Interpretation*, 447.

19 Geertz, *Interpretation*, 448.

20 T. H. Breen, "Horses and Gentlemen: The Cultural Significance of Gam-
    bling among the Gentry of Virginia," *The William and Mary Quarterly*
    34, no. 2 (1977): 239–57.

21 T. J. Jackson Lears, *Something for Nothing: Luck in America* (New York:
    Viking Penguin, 2003), 156–61, 264–70.

22 Lears, *Something for Nothing*, 109, 102, 128, 151, 174, 327.

23 Lorraine Daston, *Classical Probability in the Enlightenment* (Princeton: Princeton University Press, 1988), 149.
24 Lears, *Something for Nothing*, 150.
25 Scott Cutler Shershow, *The Work and the Gift* (Chicago: University of Chicago Press, 2005), 92.
26 Jean-Joseph Goux, "General Economics and Postmodern Capitalism," *Yale French Studies* 78 (1990): 215.
27 George Gilder, *Wealth and Poverty* (New York: Basic Books, 1981), 296, quoted in Goux, "General Economics," 213.
28 Goux, "General Economics," 217.
29 Jean Baudrillard, *The Mirror of Production*, trans. Mark Poster (St. Louis, Mo.: Telos, 1975), 144–45.
30 Goux, "General Economics," 222.
31 Lears, *Something for Nothing*, 194.
32 See John A. Ryan, "The Ethics of Speculation," *International Journal of Ethics* 12, no. 3 (1902): 335–47; and Frank N. Freeman, "The Ethics of Gambling," *International Journal of Ethics* 18, no. 1 (1907): 76–91.
33 Lears, *Something for Nothing*, 19.
34 Lears, *Something for Nothing*, 325; it should be noted, however, that Lears thinks this view does not sufficiently appreciate the "vernacular culture of chance."
35. Kavanagh, *Enlightenment*, 97.
36 Pascal, *Pensées*, 66.
37 Ivan Light, "Numbers Gambling among Blacks: A Financial Institution," *American Sociological Review* 42, no. 6 (1977): 892–904; Milton Friedman and L. J. Savage, "The Utility Analysis of Choices Involving Risk," *The Journal of Political Economy* 56, no. 4 (1948): 279–304; Alex Rubner, *The Economics of Gambling* (London: Macmillan, 1966), 48–52.
38 Rubner, *Economics of Gambling*, 50.
39 Tillotson, *Works*, 22–26.
40 Søren Kierkegaard, *Fear and Trembling*, trans. Walter Lowrie (Princeton: Princeton University Press, 1941), 33.
41 Kierkegaard, *Fear and Trembling*, 59.
42 Pascal, *Pensées*, 292.
43 Freeman, *Ethics of Gambling*, 79.

Chapter 11

1   The timing roughly corresponds to the timing of what Robert William Fogel calls the Third Great Awakening. See Robert William Fogel, *The Fourth Great Awakening and the Future of Egalitarianism* (Chicago: University of Chicago Press, 2000).
2   The statement is less true of gambling markets today, given the role of the Internet in those markets. Still, the rise of the Internet is a recent phenomenon; the story we focus on here is a very old one. We return to the Internet at the end of the article.

3 The *state* criminal law of gambling contracted during the 1930s: Nevada reintroduced casino gambling in 1931, and ten states legalized gambling in the years after 1933.

4 It is important not to overstate this last point. Theologically conservative Protestants are still the principal opponents of legalized gambling. But gambling occupies a much lower priority in the evangelical political agenda than it once did.

5 Rev 1:6.

6 Ps 51:10.

7 See, e.g., Roscoe Pound, "Puritanism and the Common Law," *Proceedings of the Kansas State Bar Association*, 45 (1910). Pound attributes the late nineteenth-century hostility to legislation and emphasis on individualism to the legacy of Puritanism.

8 Henry Ward Beecher, *Seven Lectures to Young Men on Various Important Subjects* (Indianapolis: Thomas B. Cutler, 1844), 116–18. For an excellent cultural history of gambling in nineteenth-century America, see Ann Fabian, *Card Sharps and Bucket Shops: Gambling in Nineteenth-Century America* (New York: Routledge, 1999).

9 See, e.g., Gaines M. Foster, *Moral Reconstruction: Christian Lobbyists and the Federal Legislation of Morality, 1865–1920* (Chapel Hill: University of North Carolina Press, 2002).

10 Michael Kazin, *A Godly Hero: The Life of William Jennings Bryan* (New York: Alfred Knopf, 2006), 256.

11 Kazin, *A Godly Hero*, 96 (quoting Bryan on regulation of the trusts), 146 (railroads).

12 One issue that did arise during Bryan's time in Washington directly linked gambling and finance. In 1894 Congress debated legislation aimed at restricting speculation in commodity futures. Bryan strongly supported the legislation, arguing that if "gambling in these products" altered the price of a commodity, it necessarily hurt either the buyer or the seller. "By the strong arm of the law," he concluded, "we can restrain man from inflicting on his fellow-man any injury dictated by that selfishness which must ever be restrained, if man is to be fit for society and citizenship." William Jennings Bryan, *Congressional Record* 26 (June 18, 1894): 1074, 1077.

13 William Jennings Bryan, "A People's Constitution: Address Delivered Before the Constitutional Convention of Nebraska at Lincoln," January 12, 1920, William Jennings Bryan Papers, Library of Congress, Container No. 49. See also William Jennings Bryan, *The Commoner*, October 1920. In this column, Bryan argued that the baseball players who were paid by gamblers to "fix" the 1919 World Series "could not be expected to resist so great a temptation as the gamblers set before them," arguing for legal prohibition, and concluding, "Remember that the women vote now; they will use their votes to protect their boys."

14 See, e.g., G. Edward White, *Tort Law in America: An Intellectual History* (New York: Oxford University Press, 1981).

15 Roscoe Pound, who later became dean at Harvard Law School, analyzed and criticized this tendency in one of the most famous law review articles of the early twentieth century. "One cannot read the cases in detail

without feeling that the great majority of the decisions are simply wrong," he wrote, "not only in constitutional law, but from the standpoint of the common law, and even from that of a sane individualism." Roscoe Pound, "Liberty of Contract," *Yale Law Journal* 18 (1909): 1485.

16   Michael W. McConnell, "Federalism: Evaluating the Founders' Design," *University of Chicago Law Review* 54 (1987): 1484, 1494.

17   See *Champion v. Ames*, 188 U.S. 321 (1903).

18   The two cases were *Pollock v. Farmers' Loan & Trust Co.*, 158 U.S. 601 (1895); and *Hammer v. Dagenhart*, 247 U.S. 251 (1918).

19   The language is taken from Article I, Section 8 of the Constitution, which lists the permissible subjects of congressional legislation.

20   For an excellent discussion of pre-New Deal doctrine on this point, see Barry Cushman, *Rethinking the New Deal Court: The Structure of a Constitutional Revolution* (New York: Oxford University Press, 1998). The key point is that, for the most part, the law drew lines between industries—railroads were fair game; mining was not—not between different parts of the *same* industry.

21   Justice Harlan's majority opinion in *Champion*, upholding the antilottery law, refers to lotteries as a "widespread pestilence" that was "injurious to public morals," and from which ordinary citizens need "protection." *Champion* 188 U.S. at 356–57.

22   On crossing a state border, see, e.g., *Scarborough v. United States*, 431 U.S. 563 (1977). Scarborough was convicted under the federal law banning possession of firearms by felons. Federal jurisdiction existed because the guns Scarborough possessed had crossed state borders in the past. On running an interstate business, see, e.g., *United States v. Jimenez-Torres*, 435 F.3d 3 (1st Cir. 2006). The crime in *Jimenez-Torres* was robbery— a classic state-law offense. Federal courts had jurisdiction because the robbery victim owned a gas station, which closed because of the robbery. On the crime itself affecting interstate commerce, see, e.g., *Perez v. United States*, 402 U.S. 146 (1971), in which the Supreme Court found that loan-sharking sufficiently affected interstate commerce to justify federal jurisdiction.

23   Margaret Werner Cahalan, *Historical Corrections Statistics in the United States: 1850–1984* (Washington, DC: Bureau of Justice Statistics, 1987), 30, table 3-3.

24   With the federal antilottery laws, the principal objective was simply to shut down Louisiana's state lottery. See, for example, Ezell, *Fortune's Merry Wheel*. Once this effort succeeded, the laws seem to have been largely ignored.

25   On the first of those exceptions, see Lou Falkner Williams, *The Great South Carolina Ku Klux Klan Trials: 1871–1872* (Athens: University of Georgia Press, 2004). On the second, see David E. Kyvig, *Repealing National Prohibition* (Chicago: University of Chicago Press, 2000). Drug enforcement might seem a third exception to this longstanding pattern; the federal government has prosecuted drug cases aggressively, and defendants in those cases are often sentenced to long prison terms. But the pattern holds for drugs as well. Federal cases account for roughly 5 percent

of felony drug convictions nationwide. See Bureau of Justice Statistics, "Sourcebook of Criminal Justice Statistics—Online," U.S. Department of Justice, tables 5.10.2006, 5.44.2004, available at http://www.albany.edu/sourcebook/.

26 See, e.g., Mark A. Noll, *The Scandal of the Evangelical Mind* (Grand Rapids: Eerdmans, 1995), 164–65.

27 Franklin D. Roosevelt, "New Conditions Impose New Requirements upon Government and Those Who Conduct Government," in *The Public Papers and Addresses of Franklin D. Roosevelt*, ed. Samuel I. Rosenman (New York: Random House, 1938), 742, 755.

28 Franklin D. Roosevelt, "First Inaugural Address," delivered March 4, 1933, available at http://www. bartleby.com/124/pres49.html. The biblical reference is to Christ's chasing the moneychangers from the temple, as recounted in the Gospels. See, e.g., Matt 21:12.

29 One might say the same thing about the New Deal's redistributive tax and spending policies. The Second New Deal, notably more redistributive than the first—which saw the creation of the WPA, the passage of the Social Security and Wagner Acts, plus steep tax hikes on the wealthy, all of which were instituted in 1935 and 1936—was in large measure a response to Huey Long's popular Share Our Wealth program. Long's speeches supporting that program, and advocating the expropriation of large fortunes to be distributed among the poor, were riddled with biblical references to the Year of Jubilee and to God's special concern for the poor and oppressed. Both the Second New Deal and Long's program were especially popular, not in the urbanized northeast, but in the Farm Belts of the South and West—the Bible Belt jurisdictions where Bryan had won the most support.

30 *Federal Trade Comm'n v. R. F. Keppel & Bro.*, 291 U.S. 304 (1934).

31 The Court of Appeals for the Third Circuit had invalidated the FTC's rule in *R. F. Keppel & Bro. v. FTC*, 63 F.2d 81 (3d Cir. 1933). In dissent, Judge Woolley contended that the Commission's moralist stance had led to its defeat.

32 *Keppel*, 291 U.S. at 313.

33 *Schechter Poultry Corp. v. United States*, 295 U.S. 495 (1935).

34 The name by which *Schechter Poultry* was known at the time—the "sick chicken case"—was unfair to the Schechters. Only one count of a sixty-seven-count indictment (the defendants were convicted on eighteen counts) charged the sale of a sick chicken, and that count was not the reason charges were brought. The Schechters were hauled into court not because they cheated their buyers, but because they treated buyers *too well*—which made life more difficult for their competitors. Cardozo emphasized this point in his concurrence. See *Schechter Poultry*, 295 U.S. at 552–53. Chief Justice Hughes' majority opinion strikes the same note, a bit more subtly: Hughes distinguished *Keppel* by noting that the FTC's regulatory process was designed to define wrongful conduct, while the process by which NRA codes were written—for the most part, industry representatives agreed on terms of competition that would benefit the relevant industry—was designed not to stamp out immoral business practices

but to make business more convenient and profitable. See *Schechter Poultry*, 295 U.S. at 531–37.

35 *Panama Refining Co. v. Ryan*, 293 U.S. 388 (1935).

36 *United States v. Butler*, 297 U.S. 1 (1936).

37 The Court of the early- and mid-1930s included three distinct voting blocs. Four conservatives—Justices Butler, McReynolds, Sutherland, and Van Devanter, sometimes called the Four Horsemen, both at the time and in the historical literature—were fairly reliable votes to overturn any innovative or expansive regulatory scheme. Three justices on the Left—Brandeis, Cardozo, and Stone—were generally pro-New Deal, though not consistently so: note that all three of the Court's liberals found the NRA objectionable. Two centrists, Chief Justice Hughes and Justice Roberts, held the swing votes in most contested cases. Hughes and Roberts voted with the conservatives in *Butler* and *Panama Refining*; in *Schechter Poultry*, all nine justices voted to strike down the NRA.

The Court's conservatives were not particularly receptive to moralist arguments like the FTC's argument in *Keppel*. In their view, the common law's traditions formed the key limits on government power (federal and state alike); the arguments of moralist reformers were largely irrelevant. For both the Court's liberals and its moderates, these arguments were crucial. Hughes first gained prominence as an investigator exposing corruption and misconduct in the insurance industry. Brandeis won fame as an advocate for the interests of employees and consumers victimized by powerful corporations. Cardozo's pre-Court career as a state judge was marked by his eagerness to require businesses to bear responsibility for the injuries they caused, along with a willingness to ignore traditional common-law doctrines that seemed to protect dishonest or unfair business practices. Stone was the attorney general who replaced the corrupt Harry Daugherty and restored integrity to the Justice Department after the Harding administration scandals. Roberts prosecuted corrupt Harding cronies. These justices embodied the application of high moral standards to government service. Each of them formed his political and legal beliefs in the Progressive Era, which emphasized moralist arguments for regulation far more than did the New Dealers of the 1930s. It was the opposition of (some of) these justices, not the opposition of the Court's conservatives, that put the New Deal in legal jeopardy in the 1930s.

38 Stewart was endorsed by Tennessee's Democratic boss, former congressman and Memphis Mayor Ed Crump—who, until Kefauver's successful campaign, had controlled Tennessee's Senate elections for three decades. Crump accused Kefauver of being in league with Communists and of having the deceitful character of a raccoon. Kefauver made the attack a badge of honor, saying: "I may be a pet coon, but at least I'm not Boss Crump's pet coon." From then on, Kefauver wore a coonskin cap at all his campaign appearances. The campaign is recounted in Joseph Bruce Gorman, *Kefauver: A Political Biography* (New York: Oxford University Press, 1971).

39 One of the Republican senators who was most interested in the gambling inquiry was Joe McCarthy, who was up for reelection in 1952 and looking

for a campaign issue. Only after he was passed over for one of the Republican slots on Kefauver's committee did McCarthy turn his attention toward the issue that would make him famous, and infamous. For details, see Gorman, *Kefauver*, 74–80; William Haas Moore, *The Kefauver Committee and the Politics of Crime* (Columbia: University of Missouri Press, 1974). McCarthy's speech in Wheeling, West Virginia, charging the State Department with harboring dozens of known Communists, was delivered soon after Kefauver's crime hearings began.

40 Those viewers must have liked what they saw. In 1952 Kefauver knocked Harry Truman out of the presidential race, becoming the first politician to defeat a sitting president in the New Hampshire primary. He led on the first ballot of that year's Democratic convention, but lost the presidential nomination to Adlai Stevenson.

41 These prohibitions, and their origins in the Kefauver Committee hearings, are described in G. Robert Blakey and Harold A. Kurland, "The Development of the Federal Law of Gambling," *Cornell Law Review* 63 (1978): 923, 960–62.

42 Blakey and Kurland, "Development," 964–77.

43 James B. Jacobs and Lauryn P. Gouldin, "Cosa Nostra: The Final Chapter?" *Crime and Justice* 25 (1999): 148–52.

44 John Ashcroft, "Prepared Remarks for the U.S. Mayors' Conference," remarks prepared for the Mayors Emergency, Safety and Security Summit, Washington, D.C., Oct. 25, 2001, available at http://www.usdoj.gov/ag/speeches/2001/agcrisisremarks10_25.htm.

45 Tom R. Tyler, *Why People Obey the Law* (New Haven, Conn.: Yale University Press, 1990).

46 Both words in that second phrase should trouble Christians. The word "moral" seems to imply that Christians occupy a higher moral plane than unbelievers—which seems contrary to the Apostle Paul's self-description as "the worst of sinners." See 1 Tim 1:16. In this context, the word "majority" suggests that most American voters are observant Christians—which, if church attendance is any measure, was not true in the 1970s (when the phrase was coined) and is not true now.

47 See Blakey and Kurland, "Development," 950–54 (describing 1975 legislation enacted in order to exempt state lotteries from the federal prohibitions).

48 The postmillennial perspective (like the principal alternative, premillennialism) is based on, among other things, an interpretation of prophetic passages in the book of Revelation. For a brief discussion of the influence of postmillennial optimism in the late nineteenth and early twentieth centuries, see George M. Marsden, *Understanding Fundamentalism and Evangelicalism* (Grand Rapids: Eerdmans, 1991), 39, 92.

49 "Most people who comment on the evangelical movement picture it as an offensive movement," Paul Weyrich, a prominent early figure in the movement, said in the early 1990s. "It is not. It is a defensive movement. The people who got involved . . . got involved very reluctantly." Michael Cromartie, ed., *No Longer Exiles: The Religious New Right in American*

Politics (Washington, D.C.: Ethics and Public Policy Center, 1993), 25 (remarks of Paul Weyrich).

50 Premillennialism is the view that animates the popular *Left Behind* series, which portrays a coming judgment in which believers will be caught up in the Rapture while nonbelievers suffer eternal torment. Many evangelicals remain postmillennial in orientation, but premillennialist pessimism is much more pervasive than in the nineteenth century.

51 *Roe v. Wade*, 410 U.S. 113 (1973).

52 Both New York and national crime data are taken from figures assembled by the late Eric Monkkonen data and used in Eric H. Monkkonen, *Murder in New York City* (Berkeley: University of California Press, 2000); the data are available through the National Archive of Criminal Justice Data, at http://www.icpsr.umich.edu/cocoon/NACJD/STUDY/03226.xml. Crime data from other cities mentioned in this paragraph are taken from the annual volumes of Federal Bureau of Investigation, *Uniform Crime Reports,* U.S. Department of Justice, available at http://www.fbi.gov/ucr/ucr.htm. The imprisonment rates are taken from annual volumes of U.S. Bureau of the Census, *Statistical Abstract of the United States* (Washington, D.C.: U.S. Department of Commerce, 2006); and from Cahalan, *Historical Corrections Statistics,* 30, table 3-3.

53 Bureau of Justice Statistics, *Sourcebook of Criminal Justice Statistics: 1991* (Washington, D.C.: U.S. Department of Justice, 1992), 637, table 6.72.

54 This argument is developed in more detail in William J. Stuntz, "Unequal Justice," *Harvard Law Review* 121 (2008): 1969.

55 In his characteristically incisive contribution to this volume, Alan Wolfe points out that both political parties are too dependent on the revenues from gambling to seriously challenge the legalization trend; Democrats because they want to finance spending and Republicans because of their aversion to tax increases.

56 On the low payouts, see Lawrence Zelenak, "The Puzzling Case of the Revenue-Maximizing Lottery," *North Carolina Law Review* 79 (2000): 1. On the disproportionate use by those on the lower reaches of the income ladder, see Clotfelter et al., *State Lotteries at the Turn of the Century.*

57 Although the blanket ban has not passed, Congress enacted a reform prohibiting banks and credit card companies from sending payments to illegal Internet gambling cites in 2006. *Unlawful Internet Gambling Enforcement Act of 2006,* Pub. L. No. 109-374, 120 Stat. 1884. For an earlier argument that Internet gambling could and should be prohibited under existing federal criminal law, see Bruce P. Keller, "The Game's the Same: Why Gambling in Cyberspace Violated Federal Law," *Yale Law Journal* 108 (1999): 1569

58 Charles Murray, "The G.O.P.'s Bad Bet," *The New York Times,* October 19, 2006.

59 Years after Kefauver's hearings, Costello was prosecuted and convicted— of income tax evasion, the only crime federal prosecutors could prove. See *Costello v. United States,* 350 U.S. 359 (1956).

60 America's imprisonment rate stood at 96 per 100,000 in 1970, rising to 297 in 1990. Bureau of Justice Statistics, *Sourcebook of Criminal Justice Statistics: 2003* (Washington, D.C.: U.S. Department of Justice, 2005), 501, table 6.29. America's murder rate stood at 8.3 per 100,000 in 1970, rising to 9.4 in 1990. See Monkkonen, *Murder in New York City*, 9, fig. 1.1.

61 On the 1990s rise in the number of urban police officers, see the annual volumes of Federal Bureau of Investigation, *Uniform Crime Reports: Crime in the United States*, U.S. Department of Justice. On the dramatic drop in violent crime, see Franklin E. Zimring, *The Great American Crime Decline* (New York: Oxford University Press, 2006).

Chapter 12

1   Ken Maguire, "Struggling Bingo Games Brace for Casino Impact," *Boston Globe*, September 13, 2007.

2   "La vegilla de Nabidat, e el dia, que sean sueltos de jugar porque en tal noche nasçio Nuestro Sennor Iesu Cristo, e es pascua bendita e de auer cada vno alegria en su posada." Robert A. MacDonald, ed., *"Libro de las Tahurerías": A Special Code of Law, Concerning Gambling, Drawn Up by Maestro Roldán at the Command of Alfonso X of Castile*, Hispanic Seminary of Medieval Studies, Legal Series 19 (Madison, Wisc.: Hispanic Seminary of Medieval Studies, 1995), 292. My translation.

3   "And these are ineligible [to be witnesses or judges]: a gambler with dice, a usurer, a pigeon-trainer, and traders [in the produce] of the sabbatical year." Isidore Epstein, ed., *The Babylonian Talmud: Tractate Sanhedrin*, trans. Jacob Shachter (London: Soncino, 1987).

4   Leo Landman, "Jewish Attitudes toward Gambling: The Professional and Compulsive Gambler." *Jewish Quarterly Review* 57, no. 4 (1967): 298-318, at 299–301.

5   Robert W. Henderson, "Moses Provençal on Tennis," *Jewish Quarterly Review*, n.s., 26 (1935): 1-6.

6   Landman, "Jewish Attitudes toward Gambling," 308.

7   Leo Landman, "Jewish Attitudes toward Gambling II: Individual and Communal Efforts to Curb Gambling." *Jewish Quarterly Review* 58, no. 1 (1967): 34–62, at 39.

8   Landman, "Jewish Attitudes toward Gambling," 312.

9   See, in this regard, Mark R. Cohen, *The Autobiography of a Seventeenth-Century Venetian Rabbi: Leon Modena's "Life of Judah"* (Princeton: Princeton University Press, 1988).

10 Cohen, *The Autobiography*, 137.

11 The account is found in *cantiga* 214, Alfonso X, el Sabio, *Cantigas de Santa María*, ed. Walter Mettmann (Madrid: Castalia, 1988), 2:270–72.

12 "Se quer que seja / Deus que o jogo gãedes, esta ygreja levade." Alfonso X, *Cantigas de Santa María*, 2:271. All translations of this *cantiga* are mine.

13 "Venced' o jogo e a eigreja fillade." Alfonso X, *Cantigas de Santa María*, 2:271.

14　"Assi gannou a eigreja Santa Maria por sua." Alfonso X, *Cantigas de Santa María*, 2:272.

15　Ca se Deus deu aas gentes jogos pera alegria
averen, todo o tornan elas en tafuraria,
e daquesta guisa queren gāar; mais Santa Maria
non lle praz de tal gaança, mais da que é con verdade.

"Although God gave people games so they might be happy, they turn everything into gambling, and this is the way they wish to win. But Holy Mary dislikes such winning, and desires only that which is done truthfully." Alfonso X, *Cantigas de Santa María*, 2:270.

16　The catalogue of laws is conveniently summarized by MacDonald in his edition of the *Libro de las Tahurerías*, 2–5.

17　MacDonald, *Libro de las Tahurerías*, 26–28; Dwayne Eugène Carpenter, "'Alea Jacta Est': At the Gaming Table with Alfonso the Learned," *Journal of Medieval History* 24 (1998): 345.

18　*Libro de las Tahurerías*, 293 (law no. 32).

19　Jorge Luis Borges, *Obras completas: 1923–1972* (Buenos Aires: Emecé, 1974), 813.

Chapter 13

1　Walter Cronkite, "The Dice Are Loaded," Discovery Channel Special, November 12, 1994. http://news.rutgers.edu/focus/.

2　Cronkite, "The Dice Are Loaded."

3　Theodor Reik, "The Study in Dostoyevsky," in *From Thirty Years with Freud*, trans. R. Winston (New York: Farrar & Rinehart, 1940), 170. I have made the argument outlined in the rest of this paragraph at length in Lears, *Something for Nothing*.

4　William Safire, "Now: Bet While You Booze," *The New York Times*, January 11, 1993.

5　Michael Marriott, "Fervid Debate Over Gambling: Disease or Moral Weakness?" *The New York Times*, November 21, 1992.

6　Marc N. Potenza, "Gambling and Morality: A Neuropsychiatric Perspective," chap. 7 in this volume.

7　David A. Skeel and William Stuntz, "The Criminal Law of Gambling: A Puzzling History," chap. 11 in this volume.

8　Steve Fraser, *Every Man a Speculator: A History of Wall Street in American Life* (New York: HarperCollins, 2005), chaps. 15–16.

9　Bill Gates, *The Road Ahead* (New York: Penguin, 1995); Thomas Friedman, *The Lexus and the Olive Tree: Understanding Globalization* (New York: Anchor, 2000); Thomas Friedman, *The World Is Flat 3.0: A Brief History of the Twenty-first Century* (New York: Picador, 2004). Bush's views are evident in almost every one of his public utterances, but the most expansive version is his second inaugural address, reprinted in *The New York Times*, January 21, 2005.

10　Jack Richardson, *Memoir of a Gambler* (New York: Vintage, 1979), 15.

11 Ted Sickinger, "History Shows Attitudes toward Gambling Change with the Times," *Kansas City Star*, March 11, 1997.

12 Peter Carey, *Oscar and Lucinda* (New York: Vintage, 1988), 189.

13 Kathryn Tanner, "Grace and Gambling," chap. 10 in this volume.

14 The literature is immense. Some of the high points include: W. R. Halliday, *Greek Divination* (London: Macmillan, 1913); E. E. Evans-Pritchard, *Witchcraft, Oracles, and Magic Among the Azande* (Oxford: Oxford University Press, 1937); Johan Huizinga, *Homo Ludens: A Study of the Play Element in Culture* (Boston: Beacon, 1955 [1938]); Roger Caillois, *Man, Play, and Games*, trans. Meyer Barash (New York: Free Press, 1961); Clifford Geertz, "Deep Play: Notes on the Balinese Cockfight," in *The Interpretation of Cultures* (New York: Basic Books, 1973), 412–53; S. N. Tambiah, "Form and Meaning in Magical Acts: A Point of View," in *Modes of Thought: Essays on Thinking in Western and Non-Western Societies*, ed. Robin Horton and Ruth Finnegan (London: Faber & Faber, 1973), 199–229; Rosalind Shaw, "Splitting Truths from Darkness: Epistemological Aspects of Temne Divination," in *African Divination Systems: Ways of Knowing*, ed. Philip Peek (Bloomington: Indiana University Press, 1991), 141–44; Elizabeth McAlister, "A Sorcerer's Bottle: The Visual Art of Magic in Haiti," in *Sacred Arts of Haitian Vodou*, ed. Donald J. Cosentino (Los Angeles: Fowler Museum, 1995), 305–21; Peter Benes, ed., *Wonders of the Invisible World, 1600–1900: Proceedings of the Dublin Seminar for New England Folklife* (Boston: Boston University Press, 1995); Mary Nooter Roberts and Allen F. Roberts, "Memory in Motion," in *Memory: Luba Art and the Making of History*, ed. Mary Nooter Roberts and Allen F. Roberts (New York: The Museum for African Art, 1996), 177–82; Lewis Hyde, *Trickster Makes This World: Mischief, Myth, and Art* (New York: Farrar, Straus & Giroux, 1998).

15 Dutch trader quoted in William Bascom, *Ifa Divination* (Bloomington: Indiana University Press, 1969), 5.

16 Carl G. Jung, "Foreword," in *The I Ching or Book of Changes*, trans. Richard Wilhelm and Cary F. Baynes (Princeton, N.J.: Bollingen, 1967).

17 David Hackett Fischer, *Albion's Seed: Four British Folkways in America* (New York: Oxford University Press, 1989), 343. See also Bertram Wyatt-Brown, *Southern Honor: Ethics and Behavior in the Old South* (New York: Oxford University Press, 1982), 344; Breen, "Horses and Gentlemen."

18 Huizinga, *Homo Ludens*, 56.

19 On gambling as blasphemy, see John Cotton, *A Practical Commentary, or an Exposition with Observations, Reasons, and Uses Upon the First Epistle of John* (London: Thomas Parkhurst, 1656), 126–27.

20 Mason Locke Weems, *Anecdotes of Gamblers, Extracted from a Work on Gamblers* (Philadelphia: Benjamin & Thomas Kite, 1816), 2; Mason Locke Weems, *God's Revenge Against Gambling* (Philadelphia: privately printed, 1812), 34, cited in Karen A. Weyler, "'A Speculating Spirit': Trade, Speculation, and Gambling in Early American Fiction," *Early American Literature* 31 (1996): 217.

21 "Gambling," *Saturday Evening Post*, August 25, 1821, p. 8.

22 See also Timothy Flint, *The Ruinous Consequences of Gambling* (New York: American Tract Company, 1827), 6; and John Richards, *Discourse on Gambling Delivered in the Congregational Meeting House at Dartmouth College, November 7, 1852* (Hanover, N.H.: D. Kimball & Sons, 1852).

23 Joseph L. Cowell, *Thirty Years among the Players in Players in England and America* (New York: Harper, 1844), 92; emphasis in original.

24 Richard Hildreth, *Banks, Banking, and Paper Currencies, in Three Parts* (New York: Whipple & Damrell, 1840), 150.

25 Alexis de Tocqueville, *Democracy in America,* ed. and trans. Phillips Bradley (New York: Knopf, 1945 [1835]), 1:305.

26 Tocqueville, *Democracy in America*, ed. Bradley, 2:165, 2:248–49.

27 P. T. Barnum, *Dollars and Sense or How to Get On* (New York: Henry S. Allen, 1890), 67.

28 Henry Ward Beecher, *Seven Lectures to Young Men on Various Important Subjects* (Indianapolis: Thomas B. Cutler, 1844), 15.

29 Tarbell, quoted in Jean Strouse, *J. P. Morgan, American Financier* (New York: Random House, 1999), 453. See also Ron Chernow, *Titan: the Life of John D. Rockefeller* (New York: Random House, 1998).

30 Frank Norris, *The Pit* (New York: Doubleday, 1903), 86–87.

31 William Dean Howells, *The World of Chance* (New York: Harper & Brothers, 1893), 339.

32 The best overview of these developments is Daniel T. Rodgers, *Atlantic Crossings: Social Politics in a Progressive Age* (Cambridge, Mass.: Harvard University Press, 1998).

33 John Maynard Keynes, *The General Theory of Employment, Interest, and Money* (New York: Harvest Books, 1964 [1936]), 159.

34 Edmund M. Bergler, *The Psychology of Gambling* (New York: Bernard Hanison, 1958), 58; emphasis in original.

35 Bergler, *Psychology,* 64.

36 Tom Clark, *The World of Damon Runyon* (New York: Harper & Row, 1978), 192.

37. Clark, *World of Damon Runyon*, 175–79.

38 Paul Tillich, "Holy Waste," in *The New Being* (New York: Charles Scribner's Sons, 1955), 48–49.

39 *Watch Your Dreams with Harlem Pete Dream Book* (Philadelphia: privately printed 1949), 2; in Special Collections, University of Michigan Library, Ann Arbor, Michigan. I am indebted to my colleague Ann Fabian for bringing this source to my attention in her superb book, *Card Sharps, Dream Books, and Bucket Shops: Gambling in Nineteenth-Century America* (Ithaca, N.Y.: Cornell University Press, 1990).

40 Richard Sennett, *The Corrosion of Character* (New York: Norton, 1998).

41 Goodman, *The Luck Business*, 149, 154.

42 "Addiction: Are States Preying on the Vulnerable?" *Washington Post*, March 4, 1996.

43   David Thomson, *In Nevada: The Land, the People, God, and Chance* (New York: Knopf, 1999), 289, 291.
44   William James, "The Dilemma of Determinism," in *The Writings of William James,* ed. John J. McDermott (New York: Random House, 1967 [1884]), 595; emphasis in original.

Chapter 14

The author thanks Joshua Darr for helpful research assistance on this chapter.
1   Pew Research Center, "Gambling."
2   Stodghill and Nixon, "Lottery Payoffs Fall Short."
3   These numbers—$700 annual per capita spending on lottery tickets by high school dropouts versus $179 for college graduates—come from a 1999 study conducted by the National Opinion Research Center and reported in Clotfelter et al., *State Lotteries at the Turn of the Century,* table 10.
4   These sorts of programs might be said to make lotteries *triply* regressive. Elizabeth Winslow McAuliffe, among others, has argued that the lottery is doubly regressive because buying a ticket not only costs low-income players more as a percentage of their income, but low-income players also buy more tickets. McAuliffe, "The State-Sponsored Lottery."
5   H. Roy Kaplan, "The Social and Economic Impact of State Lotteries," *Annals of the American Academy of Political and Social Science,* 474 (1984): 91–106.
6   Clotfelter and Cook, "The Importance of a Good Cause," chap. 1 in this volume.
7   D. Schwartz, *Roll the Bones,* 149, and 143–52 passim.
8   D. Schwartz, *Roll the Bones,* 150.
9   D. Schwartz, *Roll the Bones,* 144.
10   One newspaper estimated in 1833 that the combined revenues of lotteries in eight states exceeded the revenues of the federal government five times over. This is a very large figure ($67 million at the time), but modulated by the fact that the federal income tax was still far away from being established. D. Schwartz, *Roll the Bones,* 149.
11   D. Schwartz, *Roll the Bones,* 387–88.
12   For a lively and thorough account of this process, see Nelson and Mason, *Gambling Nation.*
13   D. Schwartz, *Roll the Bones*; Lears, *Something for Nothing.*
14   Clotfelter and Cook, "Importance of a Good Cause."
15   Clotfelter and Cook, "Importance of a Good Cause."
16   O. Homer Erekson et al., "Fungibility of Lottery Revenues and Support of Public Education," *Journal of Education Finance* 28 (2002): 302; John Mikesell and C. Kurt Zorn, "State Lotteries as Fiscal Savior or Fiscal Fraud: A Look at the Evidence," *Public Administration Review* 46 (1986): 319.
17   Mikesell and Zorn, "State Lotteries," 319; Stodghill and Nixon, "Lottery Payoffs Fall Short."

18 Clotfelter et al., *State Lotteries at the Turn of the Century*, 7.
19 Erekson, et al., "Fungibility of Lottery Revenues," 302.
20 Mikesell and Zorn, "State Lotteries," 319; McAuliffe, "The State-Sponsored Lottery," 373.
21 Clotfelter et al., *State Lotteries at the Turn of the Century*.
22 Clotfelter et al., *State Lotteries at the Turn of the Century*, table 10.
23 Stodghill, "Powerball."
24 Clotfelter et al., *State Lotteries at the Turn of the Century*, table 9.
25 Clotfelter et al., *State Lotteries at the Turn of the Century*, table 10.
26 Clotfelter et al., *State Lotteries at the Turn of the Century*, 12.
27 Quoted in N. Schwartz, "The $50 Ticket."
28 Sixty-one percent of the heaviest lottery players are male vs. 48.5 percent of general population; 25 percent of the heaviest players are African American vs. 12 percent of general population; 20 percent of the heaviest players are high school dropouts vs. 12 percent of general population; 10 percent of the heaviest players have household income below $10,000 vs. 5 percent of general population. Clotfelter et al., *State Lotteries at the Turn of the Century*, table 12.
29 Stodghill, "Powerball."
30 N. Schwartz, "The $50 Ticket."
31 Ellison Research, "Most Americans Believe in Sin, But Differ Widely on Just What It Is," Ellison Research Poll, March 11, 2008, available at http://www.ellisonresearch.com/releases/20080311.htm.
32 Ellison Research. "Most Americans Believe in Sin."
33 In a May 2006 Pew Research Center poll, 28 percent of respondents said gambling is "immoral" (Pew Research Center, "Gambling"); 63 percent of respondents in a June 2007 Gallup poll said gambling is an "acceptable" activity (Lydia Saad, "Americans Rate the Morality of 16 Social Issues," *Gallup News Service*, June 4, 2007, 2).
34 Other consensus issues include acceptability of the death penalty (+39), divorce (+39), and embryonic stem cell research (+34); and disapproval of suicide (-62), human cloning (-75), polygamy (-82), and extramarital affairs (-85). Saad, "Morality of 16 Social Issues," 4.
35 For extended consideration of the politics of lottery adoption, see chapters in this book by Michael Nelson and by Charles Clotfelter and Philip Cook.
36 Maria Newman, "Mayor Proposes a Fee for Driving Into Manhattan," *The New York Times*, April 22, 2007.
37 This story was recounted in an article about several states' efforts to raise revenues through absurdly high fees or fines (such as a $1,000 speeding ticket in Virginia), or unusual targets of taxation like lap dancers. Paul Vitello, "The Taxman Hits, in the Guise of a Traffic Cop," *The New York Times*, July 15, 2007.
38 D. Schwartz, *Roll the Bones*, 143–49; Nelson and Mason, *Gambling Nation*, 1–5.

39 A helpful summary of state lottery adoption dates and designated uses of lottery funds can be found in table 4 of Clotfelter and Cook, "The Importance of a Good Cause: Ends and Means in State Lotteries."

40 A number of states send some lottery revenues to the general fund but also finance other specific projects ranging from mass transit (in Arizona) to property tax relief (South Dakota) to emergency relief to cities and towns (Rhode Island). (Clotfelter and Cook, "Importance of a Good Cause.") In Kansas, any proceeds in excess of $50 million are transferred to the state's general fund; in 2007, the excess totaled $20 million. See http://www .kslottery.com/WhereTheMoneyGoes/WhereTheMoneyGoes.htm

41 Clotfelter et al., *State Lotteries at the Turn of the Century*, tables 9 and 10.

42 Kaplan, "Impact of State Lotteries," 101.

43 Bruce Buchanan, "Rolling the Dice," *American School Board Journal*, May 2007, 25–27.

44 Talbot "Sandy" D'Alemberte, "Students Lose in This Shell Game," *St. Petersburg Times* (Fla.), January 11, 2008, 15A; "South Carolina's Education Lottery Shortchanges African-American College Students," *Journal of Blacks in Higher Education* 43 (2004): 51. See also the lottery Web sites of Florida (http://www.flalottery.com/inet/educationDollarTo Education.do) and South Carolina (http://www.sceducationlottery.com/ educationwins/educationwins.aspx).

45 "South Carolina's Education Lottery," 51.

46 On reduction of the payout rate as "unambiguously pro-poor," see Clotfelter and Cook, "Importance of a Good Cause."

47 Stodghill and Nixon, "Lottery Payoffs Fall Short." Another school official added in 1996: "There is a deep and widespread perception among the public that lottery revenues are being used to substantially fund education." Quoted in Michael Heberling, "State Lotteries: Advocating a Social Ill for the Social Good," *The Independent Review*, 6, no. 4 (2002): 603.

48 Donald E. Miller and Patrick A. Pierce, "Lotteries for Education: Windfall or Hoax?" *State and Local Government Review* 29, no. 1 (1997): 34–42; Buchanan, "Rolling the Dice," 25.

49. Nebraska, for example, has siphoned money from its lottery fund into the general fund in each of the past five years. Stodghill and Nixon, "Lottery Payoffs Fall Short."

50 He studied New York, New Hampshire, Ohio, Michigan, California, and Montana. See Charles Spindler, "The Lottery and Education: Robbing Peter to Pay Paul," *Public Budgeting and Finance* 15, no. 3 (1995): 54–62.

51 D'Alemberte, "Students Lose," 15A.

52 Nelson Schwartz and Ron Nixon, "Some States Consider Leasing Their Lotteries," *The New York Times*, October 14, 2007.

53 Heberling, "State Lotteries," 599.

Chapter 15

1 Surgeon General of the United States, *Report of the Surgeon General: The Health Consequences of Smoking* (Rockville, Md.: Department of Health and Human Services, 1964).

2 Jane Lang McGrew, "History of Tobacco Regulation," Schaffer Library of Drug Policy, 15–28. http://www.druglibrary.org.

3 Surgeon General of the United States, *Report of the Surgeon General: The Health Consequences of Smoking: Cancer* (Rockville, Md.: Department of Health and Human Services, 1985).

4 M. Grossman et al., "Policy Watch: Alcohol and Cigarette Taxes," *Journal of Economic Perspectives* 7 (1993): 7; Anil Markandya and David Pearce, "The Social Costs of Tobacco Smoking," *British Journal of Addiction* 84 (1989): 1139–50; W. A. Ritch and M. E. Begay, "Smoke and Mirrors: How Massachusetts Diverted Millions in Tobacco Tax Revenues," *Tobacco Control* 10 (2001): 309–316; U.S. Bureau of the Census, *State Government Tax Collections 2004* (Washington, D.C.: U.S. Department of Commerce, 2005), available at http://www.census.gov/.

5 William Eadington, "The Economics of Casino Gambling," *Journal of Economic Perspectives* 13 (1999): 173–92; Earl Grinols and J. Omorov, "Development or Dreamfield Delusions? Assessing Casino Gambling's Costs and Benefits," *Journal of Law and Commerce* 16 (1996): 49–87.

6 "Transformation of Las Vegas," *Standard and Poor's Credit Week*, June 14, 2006.

7 William Eadington, *Native American Gaming and the Law* (Reno, Nev.: Institute for the Study of Gambling and Commercial Gambling, 1990).

8 "The Economics of Native American Gambling," *Richmond Register* (Ky.), June 22, 2006.

9 National Conference of State Legislatures, "State Revenues Healthy in First Quarter of FY 2006," December 15, 2005, http://www.ncsl.org/.

10 Robert Goodman, *Legalized Gambling as a Strategy for Economic Development* (Amherst, Mass.: University of Massachusetts-Amherst, Center for Economic Development, 1994); Douglass Walker and A.H. Barnett, "The Social Cost of Gambling: An Economic Perspective," *Journal of Gambling Studies* 15 (1999): 3.

11 Jane Lang McGrew, "History of Alcohol Prohibition," National Commission on Marijuana and Drug Abuse, http://www.druglibrary.org/.

12 Robert N. Bellah, et al., *Habits of the Heart: Individualism and Commitment in American Life* (New York: Harper & Row, 1985).

13 Robert N. Bellah, et al., *The Good Society* (New York: Knopf, 1991): 146.

14 Bellah et al., *The Good Society.* 173

15 Harrah's Entertainment, *Casino Customers: An Annual Survey* (Harrah's Entertainment, 2006).

16 Angela Gonzales, "Gaming and Displacement: Winners and Losers in American Indian Casino Development," *International Social Science Journal* 55, no. 1 (2003): 123–33; U.S. Bureau of the Census, *Tax Collections 2004*; Clotfelter et al., *State Lotteries at the Turn of the Century*; Rachel A. Volberg et al., "Assessing Self-Reported Expenditures on

Gambling," *Managerial and Decision Economics* 22 (2001): 77–96; State of Maryland Department of Legislative Services, *Overview of Issues Related to Video Lottery Terminals* (Annapolis, Md.: Department of Legislative Services, January 29, 2003), http://mlis.state.md.us/Other/Video_Lottery_Briefings/Gaming_2003.pdf.

17 American Gaming Association, *Gambling Revenue: Current Year.* Christensen Capital Advisors, 2006, http://www.americangaming.org (accessed February 25, 2006).

18 F. A. Sloan, C. A. Matthews and J. G. Trogdon, "Impacts of the Master Settlement Agreement on the Tobacco Industry," *Tobacco Control* 13 (2004): 356–61.

Chapter 16

1 Hannah Pitkin, *The Concept of Representation* (Berkeley: University of California Press, 1967), 55–57.

2 Joseph Schumpeter, *Capitalism, Socialism, and Democracy,* 3rd ed. (New York: Harper Torchbooks, 1962).

3 John Dewey, *The Public and Its Problems* (New York: Henry Holt, 1927); Jürgen Habermas, *The Theory of Communicative Action,* trans. Thomas McCarthy (Boston: Beacon, 1984); Amy Gutmann and Dennis Thompson, *Why Deliberative Democracy?* (Princeton: Princeton University Press, 2004).

4 Robert A. Dahl, *On Democracy* (New Haven, Conn.: Yale University Press, 1998); Charles Lindblom, *Politics and Markets: The World's Political Economic Systems* (New York: Basic Books, 1977).

5 Nancy Rosenblum, *On the Side of Angels: An Appreciation of Parties and Partisanship* (Princeton: Princeton University Press, 2008).

6 D. Schwartz, *Roll the Bones,* 351–68.

7 Lears, *Something for Nothing.*

8 Walter Rauschenbusch, *Christianity and the Social Crisis in the 21st Century,* ed. Paul Raushenbush (San Francisco: Harper, 2007), 216.

9 David A. Skeel, "When Markets and Gambling Converge," in *Theology and the Liberal State,* ed. Charles Cohen and Len Kaplan (Madison: University of Wisconsin Press, 2006), available at http://papers.ssrn.com/sol3/papers.cfm?abstract_id=888184.

10 Southern Baptist Convention, "Issues & Answers: Gambling," 2006, http://erlc.com/article/issues-answers-gambling.

11 Rauschenbusch, *Christianity and the Social Crisis,* 305.

12 Joseph Gusfield, *Symbolic Crusade: Status Politics and the American Temperance Movement,* 2nd ed. (Urbana: University of Illinois Press, 1986).

13 Nelson and Mason, *Gambling Nation,* 2.

14 American Gaming Association, *2006 State of the States: The AGA Survey of Casino Entertainment* (Christensen Capital Advisors, 2006), http://www.americangaming.org/assets/files/2006_Survey_for_Web.pdf.

15 Nelson and Mason, *Gambling Nation,* 16, 151, 106–7, 192–93.

16 Christel J. Manning, *God Gave Us the Right: Conservative Catholic, Evangelical, and Orthodox Jewish Women Grapple with Feminism* (New Brunswick, N.J.: Rutgers University Press, 1999), 57.

17 John Bartkowski, *Remaking the Godly Marriage: Gender Negotiation in Evangelical Families* (New Brunswick, N.J.: Rutgers University Press, 2001).

18 Alan Wolfe, *The Transformation of American Religion: How We Actually Live Our Faith* (New York: Free Press, 2003).

19 Nelson and Mason, *Gambling Nation*, 5.

20 Robert Wuthnow, *The Restructuring of American Religion: Society and Faith Since World War II* (Princeton: Princeton University Press, 1988); Hunter, *Culture Wars*.

21 Mary Ann Glendon, *Abortion and Divorce in Western Law* (Cambridge, Mass.: Harvard University Press, 1987).

22 Robert Bork, *Slouching toward Gomorrah: Modern Liberalism and American Decline* (New York: ReganBooks, 1996).

23 Morris Fiorina, Samuel Abrams, and Jeremy C. Pope, *Culture Wars?: The Myth of a Polarized America* (New York: Longmans, 2004).

24 Nelson and Mason, *Gambling Nation*, 4–5; Clotfelter and Cook, *Selling Hope.*

25 Donald A. Downs, *The New Politics of Pornography* (Chicago: University of Chicago Press, 1989).

26 James Fishkin and Bruce Ackerman, *Deliberation Day* (New Haven, Conn.: Yale University Press, 2004).

27 Catharine MacKinnon, *Toward a Feminist Theory of the State* (Cambridge, Mass.: Harvard University Press, 1989).

28 Ruth Bader Ginsburg, "Some Thoughts on Autonomy and Equality in Relation to *Roe v. Wade*," *North Carolina Law Review* 63 (1985): 375–86.

29 Ronald M. Dworkin, *Life's Dominion: An Argument about Abortion, Euthanasia, and Individual Freedom* (New York: Vintage, 1994); Andrew Sullivan, *Virtually Normal: An Argument about Homosexuality* (New York: Knopf, 1996).

30 Alan Wolfe, *One Nation after All: What Middle-Class Americans Really Think about God, Country, Family, Racism, Welfare, Immigration, Homosexuality, the Right, the Left, and Each Other* (New York: Viking, 1998); James Davison Hunter and Alan Wolfe, *Is There a Culture War?: A Dialogue on Values and American Public Life* (Washington, D.C.: Brookings Institution, 2006).

31. Nelson and Mason, *Gambling Nation*, 59.

32 Cass Sunstein, *Democracy and the Problem of Free Speech* (New York: Free Press, 1993).

Bibliography

Books, Articles, and Reports

"Addiction: Are States Preying on the Vulnerable?" *Washington Post,* March 4, 1996.

Adolphs, R. "Cognitive Neuroscience of Human Social Behavior." *Nature Reviews Neuroscience* 4 (2003): 165–78.

Alfonso X, el Sabio. *Cantigas de Santa María.* 3 vols. Edited by Walter Mettmann. Madrid: Castalia, 1986-1989.

American Gaming Association. *2006 State of the States: The AGA Survey of Casino Entertainment.* Christensen Capital Advisors, 2006. http://americangaming.org/assets/file/2006_Survey_for_Web.pdf.

———. *Gambling Revenue: Current Year.* Christensen Capital Advisors, 2006. http://www.americangaming.org/Industry/factsheets/statistics_detail.cfv?id=7.

American Psychiatric Association. *Diagnostic and Statistical Manual of Mental Disorders,* 3rd ed. Washington, D.C.: American Psychiatric Association, 1980.

———. *Diagnostic and Statistical Manual of Mental Disorders.* 4th ed. Test revision. Washington, D.C.: American Psychiatric Association, 2000.

Anderson, S. W., A. Bechara, H. Damasio, D. Tranel, and A. R. Damasio. "Impairment of Social and Moral Behavior Related to

Early Damage in Human Prefrontal Cortex." *Nature Neuroscience* 2 (1999): 1032–37.

Aronovitz, Cory. "The Regulation of Commercial Gaming." *Nevada Law Journal* 5 (2002): 181–208.

Ashcroft, John. "Prepared Remarks for the U.S. Mayors' Conference." Remarks prepared for the Mayors Emergency, Safety and Security Summit, Washington, D.C., Oct. 25, 2001. Available at http://www.usdoj.gov/archive//ag/speeches/2001/agcrisisremarks10_25.htm.

Ayton, P., and I. Fischer. "The Hot Hand Fallacy and the Gambler's Fallacy: Two Faces of Subjective Randomness." *Memory and Cognition* 32, no. 8 (2004): 1369–78.

Bakan, Paul. "Response-Tendencies in Attempts to Generate Random Binary Series." *The American Journal of Psychology* 73, no. 1 (1960): 127–31.

Barnum, P. T. *Dollars and Sense or How to Get On*. New York: Henry S. Allen, 1890.

Bartkowski, John. *Remaking the Godly Marriage: Gender Negotiation in Evangelical Families*. New Brunswick, N.J.: Rutgers University Press, 2001.

Bartlett, Donald L., and James B. Steele. "Dirty Dealing: Indian Casinos Are Making Millions for Their Investors and Providing Little to Poor." *Time*, December 8, 2002.

Bascom, William. *Ifa Divination*. Bloomington: Indiana University Press, 1969.

Basham, Mark, Raymond Mathis, and Jeannine DeFoe. "Standard and Poor's Industry Survey, Lodging and Gaming." (2007): 1–30.

Bassous, David, and Harold Sutton. "Gambling in Jewish Law." Unpublished paper.

Baudrillard, Jean. *The Mirror of Production*. Translated by Mark Poster. St. Louis, Mo.: Telos, 1975.

Bechara, A. "Risky Business: Emotion, Decision Making, and Addiction." *Journal of Gambling Studies* 19 (2003): 23–51.

Bechara, A., A. R. Damasio, H. Damasio, and S. W. Anderson. "Insensitivity to Future Consequences Following Damage to Human Prefrontal Cortex." *Cognition* 50 (1994): 7–15.

Bechara, A., H. Damasio, A. R. Damasio, and G. P. Lee. "Different Contributions of the Human Amygdala and Ventromedial Prefrontal Cortex to Decision Making." *Journal of Neuroscience* 19 (1999): 5473–81.

Bechara, A., H. Damasio, D. Tranel, and S. W. Anderson. "Dissociation of Working Memory from Decision Making within the Human

Prefrontal Cortex." *Journal of Neuroscience* 18, no. 1 (1998): 428–37.

Bechara, A., H. Damasio, D. Tranel, and A. R. Damasio. "Deciding Advantageously before Knowing the Advantageous Strategy." *Science* 275, no. 5304 (1997): 1293–95.

Becker, Gary S., and Kevin M. Murphy. "A Theory of Rational Addiction." *The Journal of Political Economy* 96, no. 4 (1988): 675–700.

Beecher, Henry Ward. *Seven Lectures to Young Men on Various Important Subjects.* Indianapolis: Thomas B. Cutler, 1844. Reprinted New York, 1886.

Beer, J. S., E. A. Heerey, D. Keltner, D. Scabini, and R. T. Knight. "The Regulatory Function of Self-Conscious Emotions: Insights from Patients with Orbitofrontal Damage." *Journal of Personality and Social Psychology* 85 (2003): 594–604.

Behr, Katie. "What Advertising Strategy Should the North Carolina Education Lottery Employ?" M.P.P. project, Terry Sanford Institute of Public Policy, Duke University, 2006.

Bellah, Robert N., Richard Madsen, William M. Sullivan, Ann Swidler, and Steven M. Tipton. *Habits of the Heart: Individualism and Commitment in American Life.* New York: Harper & Row, 1985.

———. *The Good Society.* New York: Knopf, 1991.

Benes, Peter, ed. *Wonders of the Invisible World, 1600–1900: Proceedings of the Dublin Seminar for New England Folklife.* Boston: Boston University Press, 1992.

Bennett, William J. *The Book of Virtues: A Treasury of Great Moral Stories.* Parsippany, N.J.: Silver Burdett, 1996.

Bergh, C., T. Eklund, P. Sodersten, and C. Nordin. "Altered Dopamine Function in Pathological Gambling." *Psychological Medicine* 27, no. 2 (1997): 473–75.

Bergler, Edmund. *The Psychology of Gambling.* London: Bernard Hanison, 1958.

Bergner, Raymond M., and Ana J. Bridges. "The Significance of Heavy Pornography Involvement for Romantic Partners: Research and Clinical Implications." *Journal of Sex and Marital Therapy* 28 (2002): 193–206.

Bickel, W. K., R. J. DeGrandpre, and S. T. Higgins. "Behavioral Economics: A Novel Experimental Approach to the Study of Drug Dependence." *Drug and Alcohol Dependence* 33, no. 2 (1993): 173–92.

Bickel, W. K., A. L. Odum, and G. J. Madden. "Impulsivity and Cigarette Smoking: Delay Discounting in Current, Never, and Ex-Smokers." *Psychopharmacology* (Berlin) 146, no. 4 (1999): 447–54.

Biotie. *Financial Report.* http://www.biotie.com/annualreports/2006/ uk/ (accessed October 2, 2007).

Bjork, J. M., B. Knutson, G. W. Fong, D. M. Caggiano, S. M. Bennett, and D. W. Hommer. "Incentive-Elicited Brain Activation in Adolescents: Similarities and Differences from Young Adults." *Journal of Neuroscience* 24 (2004): 1793–1802.

Blair, J. R. "Neurobiological Basis of Psychopathy." *British Journal of Psychiatry* 182 (2003): 5–7.

Blakey, G. Robert, and Harold A. Kurland. "The Development of the Federal Law of Gambling." *Cornell Law Review* 63 (1978): 923.

Blank, A. D. "Effects of Group and Individual Conditions on Choice Behavior." *Journal of Personality and Social Psychology* 8, no. 3 (1968): 294–98.

Blascovich, J., and G. P. Ginsburg. "Emergent Norms and Choice Shifts Involving Risk." *Sociometry* 37, no. 2 (1974): 205–18.

Blascovich, J., G. P. Ginsburg, and R. C. Howe. "Blackjack and the Risky Shift, II: Monetary Stakes." *Journal of Experimental Social Psychology* 11, no. 3 (1975): 224–32.

———. "Blackjack, Choice Shifts in the Field." *Sociometry* 39, no. 3 (1976): 274–76.

Blascovich, J., T. L. Veach, and G. P. Ginsburg. "Blackjack and the Risky Shift, I." *Sociometry* 36, no. 1 (1973): 42–45.

Blaszczynski, Alex, Robert Ladouceur, and Howard J. Shaffer. "A Science-Based Framework for Responsible Gambling: The Reno Model." *Journal of Gambling Studies* 20 (2004): 301–17.

Borges, Jorge Luis. *Obras Completas: 1923–1972.* Buenos Aires: Emecé, 1974.

Bork, Robert. *Slouching toward Gomorrah: Modern Liberalism and American Decline.* New York: ReganBooks, 1996.

Borrell, J. "Values in Gambling Research and Implications for Public Policy." *International Journal of Mental Health & Addiction* 1, no. 1 (2003): 40–47. http://www.ijma-journal.com/content/full/1/1/6.

Botvinick, M., T. S. Braver, D. M. Barch, C. S. Carter, and J. D. Cohen. "Conflict Monitoring and Cognitive Control." *Psychological Review* 108 (2001): 624–52.

Botvinick, M., L. E. Nystrom, K. Fissell, C. S. Carter, and J. D. Cohen. "Conflict Monitoring Versus Selection-for-Action in Anterior Cingulate Cortex." *Nature* 402 (1999): 179–81.

Breen, T. H. "Horses and Gentlemen: The Cultural Significance of Gambling among the Gentry of Virginia." *William & Mary Quarterly* 34, no. 2 (1977): 239–57.

Breiter, H. C., I. Aharon, D. Kahneman, A. Dale, and P. Shizgai. "Functional Imaging of Neural Responses to Expectancy and

Experience of Monetary Gains and Losses." *Neuron* 30, no. 2 (2001): 619–39.

Brewer, J. A., and Marc N. Potenza. "The Neurobiology and Genetics of Impulse Control Disorders: Relationships to Drug Addictions." *Biochemical Pharmacology* 75, no. 1 (2008): 63–75.

Brooks, David. *Bobos in Paradise: The New Upper Class and How They Got There.* New York: Simon & Schuster, 2000.

Brown, William, and Raymond Sauer. "Does the Basketball Market Believe in the Hot Hand? Comment." *American Economic Review* 83, no. 5 (1993): 1377–86.

Bryan, William Jennings. "A People's Constitution: Address Delivered Before the Constitutional Convention of Nebraska at Lincoln." January 12, 1920. William Jennings Bryan Papers, Container No. 49, Library of Congress.

———. Column. *The Commoner*, October 1920.

———. Remarks. *Congressional Record* 26 (June 18, 1894).

Buchanan, Bruce. "Rolling the Dice." *American School Board Journal*, May 2007.

Buller, T. "What Can Neuroscience Contribute to Ethics?" *Journal of Medical Ethics* 32 (2006): 63–64.

Bureau of Justice Statistics. "Sourcebook of Criminal Justice Statistics—Online." U.S. Department of Justice. Available at http://www.albany.edu/sourcebook/.

———. *Sourcebook of Criminal Justice Statistics: 1991.* Washington, D.C.: U.S. Department of Justice, 1992.

———. *Sourcebook of Criminal Justice Statistics: 2003.* Washington, D.C.: U.S. Department of Justice, 2005.

Burns, B., and B. Corpus. "Randomness and Inductions from Streaks: 'Gambler's Fallacy' vs. 'Hot Hand.'" *Psychonomic Bulletin and Review* 11, no. 1 (2004): 179–84.

Cabot, Anthony N. *Casino Gaming: Policy, Economics and Regulation.* Las Vegas: UNLV International Gaming Institute, 1996.

Cabot, Anthony N., and Kevin D. Doty. "Internet Gambling: Jurisdiction Problems and the Role of Federal Law." *Gaming Law Review* 1 (1997): 15–29.

Cahalan, Margaret Werner. *Historical Corrections Statistics in the United States: 1850–1984.* Washington, D.C.: Bureau of Justice Statistics, 1987.

Caillois, Roger. *Man, Play, and Games.* Translated by Meyer Barash. New York: Free Press, 1961.

Camelot LTD. *Social Report 2005.* http://www.camelotgroup.co.uk/socialreport2005/camelot-and-national-lottery.htm.

Camerer, Colin. "Does the Basketball Market Believe in the 'Hot Hand'?" *American Economic Review* 79, no. 5 (1989): 1257–61.

Camerer, Colin, George Loewenstein, and Drazen Prelec. "Neuro-economics: How Neuroscience Can Inform Economics." *Journal of Economic Literature* 43, no. 1 (2005): 9–64.

Camille, N., G. Coricelli, J. Sallet, P. Pradat-Siehl, J. R. Duhamel, and A. Sirigu. "The Involvement of the Orbitofrontal Cortex in the Experience of Regret." *Science* 304 (2004): 1167–70.

Carey, Peter. *Oscar and Lucinda*. New York: Vintage, 1988.

Carhart, Mark. "On Persistence in Mutual Fund Performance." *Journal of Finance* 52, no. 1 (1997): 57–82.

Carmines, Edward G., and James A. Stimson. "The Two Faces of Issue Voting." *American Political Science Review* 74 (1980): 78–91.

Carpenter, Dwayne Eugène. "'Alea Jacta Est': At the Gaming Table with Alfonso the Learned." *Journal of Medieval History* 24 (1998): 333–45.

———. "Fickle Fortune: Gambling in Medieval Spain." *Studies in Philology* 85 (1988): 267–78.

Cartwright, Dorwin. "Risk Taking by Individuals and Groups: An Assessment of Research Employing Choice Dilemmas." *Journal of Personality and Social Psychology* 20, no. 3 (1971): 361–78.

Caspi, Avshalom, Joseph McClay, Terrie E. Moffitt, Jonathan Mill, Judy Martin, Ian W. Craig, Alan Taylor, and Richie Poulton. "Role of Genotype in the Cycle of Violence in Maltreated Children." *Science* 297 (2002): 851–53.

Caspi, Avshalom, K. Sugden, Terrie E. Moffit, Alan Taylor, Ian W. Craig, H. Harrington, Joseph McClay, et al. "Influence of Life Stress on Depression: Moderation by a Polymorphism in the 5-Htt Gene." *Science* 301 (2003): 386–89.

Cavedini, P., G. Riboldi, R. Keller, A. D'Annucci, and L. Bellodi. "Frontal Lobe Dysfunction in Pathological Gambling." *Biological Psychiatry* 51 (2002): 334–41.

Center for Responsive Politics. "Money in Politics: Casinos/Gambling: Long-Term Contribution Trends." Washington, D.C.: Center for Responsive Politics, 2006. Available at http://www.opensecrets.org/.

Central Conference of American Rabbis. "Jewish Attitude toward Gambling." Responsum 167. Central Conference of American Rabbis, 1979.

Chambers, R. A., W. K. Bickel, and Marc N. Potenza. "A Scale-Free Systems Theory of Motivation and Addiction." *Neuroscience and Biobehavioral Reviews* 31 (2007): 1017–45.

Chambers, R. A., J. R. Taylor, and Marc N. Potenza. "Developmental Neurocircuitry of Motivation in Adolescence: A Critical Period of Addiction Vulnerability." *American Journal of Psychiatry* 160 (2003): 1041–52.

Chapanis, A. "Random-Number Guessing Behavior." *The American Psychologist* 8 (1953): 332.

Chau, Albert, and James Phillips. "Effects of Perceived Control upon Wagering and Attributions in Computer Blackjack." *The Journal of General Psychology* 122 (1995): 253–69.

Chernow, Ronald. *Titan: The Life of John D. Rockefeller.* New York: Random House, 1998.

Chorvat, T., K. McCabe, and V. Smith. "Law and Neuroeconomics." *Supreme Court Economic Review* 13 (2005): 35–62.

Ciarrocchi, Joseph, and Ann A. Hohmann. "The Family Environment of Married Male Pathological Gamblers, Alcoholics, and Dually Addicted Gamblers." *Journal of Gambling Studies* 5 (1989): 283–91.

Cigler, Allen J., and Burdett A. Loomis. "Organized Interests and the Search for Certainty." In *Interest Group Politics.* 3rd ed., edited by Allen J. Cigler and Burdett A. Loomis, n.p. Washington, D.C.: CQ Press, 1991.

Clark, Tom. *The World of Damon Runyon.* New York: Harper & Row, 1978.

Clotfelter, Charles T., and Philip J. Cook. "The 'Gambler's Fallacy' in Lottery Play." *Management Science* 39, no. 12 (1993): 1521–25.

———. "On the Economics of State Lotteries." *Journal of Economic Perspectives* 4 (1990): 105–19.

———. *Selling Hope: State Lotteries in America.* Cambridge, Mass.: Harvard University Press, 1989.

Clotfelter, Charles T., Philip J. Cook, Julie Edell, and Marian Moore. *State Lotteries at the Turn of the Century: Report to the National Gambling Impact Study Commission.* April 23, 1999. Available at http://govinfo.library.unt.edu/ngisc.

Coffey, Wallace, and Rebecca Tsosie. "Rethinking the Tribal Sovereignty Doctrine: Cultural Sovereignty and the Collective Future of Indian Nations." *Stanford Law and Policy Review* 12 (2001): 191–221.

Cohen, Mark R. *The Autobiography of a Seventeenth-Century Venetian Rabbi: Leon Modena's "Life of Judah."* Princeton: Princeton University Press, 1988.

Collins, Peter. "The Moral Case for Legalizing Gambling." In Reith, *Gambling,* 322–33.

———. *Gambling and the Public Interest.* Westport, Conn.: Praeger, 2003.

Commission on the Review of the National Policy toward Gambling. *Gambling in America*. Washington, D.C.: U.S. Government Printing Office, 1976.

Committee on Homosexual Offences and Prostitution. *Report of the Committee on Homosexual Offences and Prostitution*. London: Her Majesty's Stationery Office, 1957.

Commonwealth of Massachusetts. "Governor Patrick Unveils Plan for Casino Gambling in Massachusetts." Executive Department press release, Commonwealth of Massachusetts, September 18, 2007.

Conwell, R. E. *Social Abominations*. Harrisburg, Pa.: Whitman, 1892.

Cook, Philip J. *Paying the Tab: The Economics of Alcohol Control Policy*. Princeton: Princeton University Press, 2007.

Cook, Philip J., and Charles T. Clotfelter. "The Peculiar Scale Economies of Lotto." *American Economic Review* 83, no. 3 (1993): 634–43.

Cook, Samuel R. "Ronald Reagan's Indian Policy in Retrospect: Economic Crisis and Political Irony." *Policy Studies Journal* 24 (1996): 11–26.

Cornell Law Project. *The Development of the Law of Gambling, 1776–1976*. Washington, D.C.: National Institute of Law Enforcement and Criminal Justice, 1977.

Cotton, John. *A Practical Commentary, or an Exposition with Observations, Reasons, and Uses Upon the First Epistle of John*. London: Thomas Parkhurst, 1656.

Coughlin, Cletus C. "The Geography, Economics, and Politics of Lottery Adoption," *Federal Reserve Bank of St. Louis Review* 88, no. 3 (2006): 165–80.

Cowell, Joseph L. *Thirty Years among the Players in Players in England and America*. New York, 1853.

Cromartie, Michael, ed. *No Longer Exiles: The Religious New Right in American Politics*. Washington, D.C.: Ethics and Public Policy Center, 1993.

Cronkite, Walter. "The Dice Are Loaded." Discovery Channel Special. November 12, 1994. http://news.rutgers.edu/focus/.

Croson, Rachel, and James Sundali. "The Gambler's Fallacy and the Hot Hand: Empirical Data from Casinos." *Journal of Risk and Uncertainty* 30, no. 3 (2005): 195–209.

Cushman, Barry. *Rethinking the New Deal Court: The Structure of a Constitutional Revolution*. New York: Oxford University Press, 1998.

D'Alemberte, Talbot "Sandy." "Students Lose in This Shell Game." *St. Petersburg Times* (Fla.), January 11, 2008.

Dahl, Robert A. *On Democracy*. New Haven, Conn.: Yale University Press, 1998.

Damasio, A. R. *Descartes' Error: Emotion, Reason, and the Human Brain*. New York: Crosset/Putnam, 1994.

Darbyshire, Philip, Candice Oster, and Helen Carrig. "Children of Parent(s) Who Have a Gambling Problem: A Review of the Literature and Commentary on Research Approaches." *Health and Social Care in the Community* 9 (2001): 185–93.

———. "The Experience of Pervasive Loss: Children and Young People Living in a Family Where Parental Gambling Is a Problem." *Journal of Gambling Studies* 17 (2001): 23–45.

Dasgupta, Anisha S. "Public Finance and the Fortunes of the Early American Lottery." *Quinnipiac Law Review* 24 (2006): 227.

Daston, Lorraine. *Classical Probability in the Enlightenment*. Princeton: Princeton University Press, 1988.

De Martino, B., D. Kumaran, B. Seymour, and R. J. Dolan. "Frames, Biases, and Rational Decision Making in the Human Brain." *Science* 313, no. 5787 (2006): 684–87.

DeCaria, C. M., T. Begaz, and E. Hollander. "Serotonergic and Noradrenergic Function in Pathological Gambling." *CNS Spectrums* 3, no. 6 (1998): 38–47.

DeMillo, Andrew. "Ark. Lt. Gov. Says He'll Try To Put Lottery on '08 Ballot." *Associated Press*, September 18, 2007.

Dense, Jeff. "State Lotteries, Commercial Casinos, and Public Finance: An Uneasy Relationship Revisited." *Gaming Law Review* 11 (2007): 34–50.

Derthick, Martha. *Up in Smoke: From Legislation to Litigation in Tobacco Politics*. Washington, D.C.: CQ Press, 2002.

Devlin, Patrick. *The Enforcement of Morals*. London: Oxford University Press, 1965.

Dewey, John. *The Public and Its Problems*. New York: Henry Holt, 1927.

Dickson-Swift, V. A., E. L. James, and S. Kippen. "The Experience of Living with a Problem Gambler: Spouse and Partners Speak Out." *Journal of Gambling Issues* 13 (2005): 1–22.

Dinan, John J. *The American State Constitutional Tradition*. Lawrence: University Press of Kansas, 2006.

Dion, K. L., R. S. Baron, and N. Miller. "Why Do Groups Make Riskier Decisions Than Individuals?" *Advances in Experimental Social Psychology* 5 (1970): 305–77.

Dobson, James. "Going for Broke." Focus on the Family, July 1999. http://www.family.org/.

"Does God Play Dice? Religious Perspectives on Gambling." *Beliefnet.* http://www.beliefnet.com/.

Dombrink, John. "Gambling's Status Among the Vices, 1990—A Comparative View." Paper presented at the Eighth International Conference in Risk and Gambling, London, England, August 15–17, 1990.

Dombrink, John, and Daniel Hillyard. *Sin No More: From Abortion to Stem Cells, Understanding Crime, Law, and Morality in America.* New York: New York University Press, 2007.

Dombrink, John, and William N. Thompson. *The Last Resort: Success and Failure in Campaigns for Casinos.* Reno: University of Nevada Press, 1990.

Dostoyevsky, Fyodor. *Complete Letters.* Edited by D. A. Lowe and R. Meyer. New York: Ardis, 1998.

———. *The Gambler/Bobok/A Nasty Story.* London: Penguin Books, 1966.

Downs, Donald A. *The New Politics of Pornography.* Chicago: University of Chicago Press, 1989.

Dworkin, Ronald M. *Life's Dominion: An Argument about Abortion, Euthanasia, and Individual Freedom.* New York: Vintage, 1994.

Eadington, William. "The Economics of Casino Gambling," *Journal of Economic Perspectives* 13 (1999): 173–92.

———. *Native American Gaming and the Law.* Reno, Nev.: Institute for the Study of Gambling and Commercial Gambling, 1990.

———. "Ten Challenges: Issues That Are Shaping the Future of Gambling and Commercial Gaming." Address to the Thirteenth International Conference on Gambling and Risk Taking, Lake Tahoe, Nevada, May 23, 2006.

———. "Values and Choices: The Struggle to Find Balance with Permitted Gambling in Modern Society." In Reith, *Gambling,* 31–48.

Eastman, N., and C. Campbell. "Neuroscience and Legal Determination of Criminal Responsibility." *Nature Reviews Neuroscience* 7 (2006): 311–18.

"The Economics of Native American Gambling." *Richmond Register* (Ky.), June 22, 2006.

Egan, M. F., T. E. Goldberg, B. S. Kolachana, J. H. Callicott, C. M. Mazzanti, R. E. Straub, D. Goldman, and D. R. Weinberger. "Effect of Comt Val108/158 Met Genotype on Frontal Lobe Function and Risk for Schizophrenia." *Proceedings of the National Academy of Sciences* 98, no. 12 (2001): 6917–22.

Eisen, Seth A., Nong Lin, Michael J. Lyons, Jeffrey F. Scherrer, Kristin Griffith, William R. True, Jack Goldberg, and Ming T. Tsuang. "Familial Influences on Gambling Behavior: An Analysis of 3359 Twin Pairs." *Addiction* 93 (1998): 1375–84.

Eisen, Seth A., Wendy S. Slutske, Michael J. Lyons, John Lassman, Hong Xian, Richard Toomey, S. Chantarujikapong, and Ming T. Tsuang. "The Genetics of Pathological Gambling." *Seminar in Clinical Neuropsychiatry* 6 (2001): 195–204.

Eisler, Kim Isaac. *Revenge of the Pequots: How a Small Native American Tribe Created the World's Largest Casino.* New York: Simon & Schuster, 2000.

Ellison Research. "Most Americans Believe in Sin, But Differ Widely on Just What It Is." Ellison Research Poll, March 11, 2008. Available at www.ellisonresearch.com/releases/20080311.htm.

Ellsberg, Daniel. "Risk, Ambiguity, and the Savage Axioms." *The Quarterly Journal of Economics* 75, no. 4 (1961): 643–69.

Ellwood, David. *Poor Support: Poverty in the American Family.* New York: Basic Books, 1988.

Elsinger, P. J., and A. R. Damasio. "Severe Disturbance of Higher Level Cognition after Bilateral Frontal Lobe Ablation: Patient Avr." *Neurology* 35 (1993): 1731–41.

Epstein, Isidore, ed. *The Babylonian Talmud: Tractate Sanhedrin.* Translated by Jacob Shachter. London: Soncino, 1987.

Erekson, O. Homer, Kimberly M. DeShano, Glenn Platt, and Andrea L. Ziegert. "Fungibility of Lottery Revenues and Support of Public Education." *Journal of Education Finance* 28 (2002): 302.

European Jewish Press. "Jewish Lottery Launched in the UK." December 25, 2005. http://www.ejpress.org/article/4835.

Evangelical Lutheran Church in America. "Gambling Study." 1998. http://archive.elca.org/socialstatements/economiclife/gambling/default.asp#toc.

Evans-Pritchard, E. E. *Witchcraft, Oracles, and Magic Among the Azande.* Oxford: Oxford University Press, 1937.

Everitt, B., and T. W. Robbins. "Neural Systems of Reinforcement for Drug Addiction: From Actions to Habits to Compulsion." *Nature Neuroscience* 8 (2005): 1481–89.

Ezell, John Samuel. *Fortune's Merry Wheel: The Lottery in America.* Cambridge, Mass.: Harvard University Press, 1960.

Fabian, Ann. *Card Sharps, Dream Books, and Bucket Shops: Gambling in Nineteenth-Century America.* Ithaca, N.Y.: Cornell University Press, 1990. Reprinted as *Card Sharps and Bucket Shops: Gambling in Nineteenth-Century America.* New York: Routledge, 1999.

Farley, Melissa. "Prostitution and the Invisibility of Harm." *Women & Therapy* 26 (2003): 247–80.

Federal Bureau of Investigation. *Uniform Crime Reports*. U.S. Department of Justice. Available at http://www.fbi.gov/ucr/ucr .htm.

Feeny, Don. "Is Gambling Immoral?" Minnesota Institute of Public Health. http://www.miph.org/gambling.

Feldman, J. "On the Negative Recency Hypothesis in the Prediction of a Series of Binary Symbols." *American Journal of Psychology* 72 (1959): 597–99.

Felscher, Jennifer R., Jeffrey L. Derevensky, and Rina Gupta. "Parental Influences and Social Modeling of Youth Lottery Participation." *Journal of Community & Applied Social Psychology* 13 (2003): 361–77.

Fielding, J. "The History of Gambling." *The Gentleman's Magazine*, December 1756, 564–67.

Fiorina, Morris. *Divided Government*. 2nd ed. Boston: Allyn & Bacon, 1996.

Fiorina, Morris, Samuel Abrams, and Jeremy C. Pope. *Culture Wars?: The Myth of a Polarized America*. New York: Longmans, 2004.

Fischer, David Hackett. *Albion's Seed: Four British Folkways in America*. New York: Oxford University Press, 1989.

Fishkin, James, and Bruce Ackerman. *Deliberation Day*. New Haven, Conn.: Yale University Press, 2004.

Flint, Timothy. *The Ruinous Consequences of Gambling*. New York: American Tract Society, 1828.

Fogel, Robert William. *The Fourth Great Awakening and the Future of Egalitarianism*. Chicago: University of Chicago Press, 2000.

Foster, Gaines M. *Moral Reconstruction: Christian Lobbyists and the Federal Legislation of Morality, 1865–1920*. Chapel Hill: University of North Carolina Press, 2002.

France, C. J. "The Gambling Impulse." *American Journal of Psychology* 13 (1902): 364–407.

Fraser, Steven. *Every Man a Speculator: A History of Wall Street in American Life*. New York: HarperCollins, 2005.

Freeman, Frank N. "The Ethics of Gambling." *International Journal of Ethics* 18, no. 1 (1907): 76–91.

Frey, James H. "Gambling on Sport: Policy Issues." *Journal of Gambling Studies* 84 (1992): 351–60.

Friedman, Joseph, Simon Hakim, and J. Weinblatt. "Casino Gambling as a 'Growth Pole' Strategy and Its Effect on Crime." *Journal of Regional Studies* 29 (1989): 615–23.

Friedman, Milton, and L. J. Savage. "The Utility Analysis of Choices Involving Risk." *Journal of Political Economy* 56, no. 4 (1948): 279–304.

Friedman, Thomas. *The Lexus and the Olive Tree: Understanding Globalization.* New York: Anchor, 2000.

———. *The World Is Flat 3.0: A Brief History of the Twenty-first Century.* New York: Picador, 2007.

Friedrich, M. J. "Neuroscience Becomes Image Conscious as Brain Scans Raise Ethical Issues." *Journal of the American Medical Association* 294 (2005): 781–83.

Galbraith, John Kenneth. *The Affluent Society.* Boston: Houghton Mifflin, 1958.

"Gambling." *Saturday Evening Post,* August 25, 1821.

Ganguli, K. M., ed. and trans. *Mahabharata.* Adiparva. Calcutta and Evanston: Bharata Press and American Theological Library, 1884.

Gates, Bill. *The Road Ahead.* New York: Penguin, 1995.

Gaudia, Ronald. "Effects of Compulsive Gambling on the Family." *Social Work* 32 (1987): 254–56.

Geertz, Clifford. "Deep Play: Notes on the Balinese Cockfight." In *The Interpretation of Cultures,* 412–53. New York: Basic Books, 1973.

Geertz, Clifford. *The Interpretation of Cultures.* New York: Basic Books, 1973.

Geis, Gilbert. *Not the Law's Business: An Examination of Homosexuality, Abortion, Prostitution, Narcotics, and Gambling in the United States.* New York: Schocken Books, 1979.

Gerstein, Dean R., John Hoffmann, Cindy Larison, Laszlo Engleman, Sally Murphy, Amanda Palmer, Lucian Chuchro, et al. *Gambling Impact and Behavior Study: Report to the National Gambling Impact Study Commission.* Chicago: National Opinion Research Center at the University of Chicago, April 1, 1999.

Gilovich, T., R. Vallone and A. Tversky. "The Hot Hand in Basketball: On the Misperception of Random Sequences." *Cognitive Psychology* 17 (1985): 295–314.

Ginsburg, Ruth Bader. "Some Thoughts on Autonomy and Equality in Relation to *Roe v. Wade.*" *North Carolina Law Review* 63 (1985): 375–86.

Glendon, Mary Ann. *Abortion and Divorce in Western Law.* Cambridge, Mass.: Harvard University Press, 1987.

Glimcher, P. *Decisions, Uncertainty, and the Brain: The Science of Neuroeconomics.* Cambridge, Mass.: MIT Press, 2003.

Goldstein, R. Z., N. Alia-Klein, D. Tomasi, L. Zhang, L. A. Cottone, T. Maloney, F. Telang, et al. "Is Decreased Prefrontal Cortical Sensitivity to Monetary Reward Associated with Impaired Motivation and Self-Control in Cocaine Addiction?" *American Journal of Psychiatry* 164 (2007): 43–51.

Goldstein, R. Z., and N. D. Volkow. "Drug Addiction and Its Underlying Neurobiological Basis: Neuroimaging Evidence for the Involvement of the Frontal Cortex." *American Journal of Psychiatry* 159 (2002): 1642–52.

Gonzales, Angela. "Gaming and Displacement: Winners and Losers in American Indian Casino Development." *International Social Science Journal* 55, no. 1 (2003): 123–33.

Goodman, Robert. *Legalized Gambling as a Strategy for Economic Development.* Amherst, Mass.: University of Massachusetts-Amherst, Center for Economic Development, 1994.

———. *The Luck Business: The Devastating Consequences and Broken Promises of America's Gambling Explosion.* New York: Free Press, 1995.

Gorman, Joseph Bruce. *Kefauver: A Political Biography.* New York: Oxford University Press, 1971.

Gormley, William T., Jr. "Regulatory Issue Networks in a Federal System." *Polity* 18 (1986): 595–620.

Goux, Jean-Joseph. "General Economics and Postmodern Capitalism." *Yale French Studies* 78 (1990): 206–24.

Grant, Bridget F., Karl Kaplan, Joseph Shepard, and Terry Moore. "Source and Accuracy Statement for Wave 1 of the 2001–2002 National Epidemiologic Survey on Alcohol and Related Conditions." Bethesda, Md.: National Institute on Alcohol Abuse and Alcoholism, 2003.

Grant, J. E., J. A. Brewer, and Marc N. Potenza. "The Neurobiology of Substance and Behavioral Addictions." *CNS Spectrums* 11 (2006): 924–30.

Grant, J. E., and Marc N. Potenza. "Compulsive Aspects in Impulse Control Disorders." *The Psychiatric Clinics of North America Journal* 29 (2006): 539–51.

———. "Impulse Control Disorders: Clinical Characteristics and Pharmacological Management." *Annals of Clinical Psychiatry* 16 (2004): 27–34.

Grant, J. E., Marc N. Potenza, E. Hollander, R. M. Cunningham-Williams, T. Numinen, G. Smits, and A. Kallio. "Multicenter Investigation of the Opioid Antagonist Nalmefene in the Treatment of Pathological Gambling." *American Journal of Psychiatry* 163 (2006): 303–12.

Greene, J. D., and J. Haidt. "How (and Where) Does Moral Judgment Work?" *Trends in Cognitive Science* 6 (2002): 517–23.

Greene, J. D., L. E. Nystrom, A. D. Engall, J. M. Darley, and J. D. Cohen. "The Neural Bases of Cognitive Conflict and Control in Moral Judgment." *Neuron* 44 (2004): 389–400.

Greenfield, Lawrence A., and Steven K. Smith. *American Indians and Crime*. Washington, D.C.: U.S. Department of Justice, 1999.

Grinols, Earl L., and David B. Mustard, "Management and Information Issues for Industries with Externalities: The Case for Casino Gambling," *Managerial and Decision Economics* 22 (2001): 1–3.

Grinols, Earl, and J. Omorov. "Development or Dreamfield Delusions? Assessing Casino Gambling's Costs and Benefits." *Journal of Law and Commerce* 16 (1996): 49–87.

Grossman, Michael, Frank J. Chaloupka, and Kyumin Shim. "Illegal Drug Use and Public Policy." *Health Affairs* 21 (2002): 134–45.

Grossman, Michael, J. Sindelar, J. Mullahy, and R. Anderson. "Policy Watch: Alcohol and Cigarette Taxes." *Journal of Economic Perspectives* 7 (1993): 7.

Grzywacz, Joseph G., and Brenda L. Bass. "Work, Family, and Mental Health: Testing Different Models of Work-Family Fit." *Journal of Marriage and Family* 65 (2003): 248–61.

Gusfield, Joseph. *Symbolic Crusade: Status Politics and the American Temperance Movement*. 2nd ed. Urbana: University of Illinois Press, 1986.

Gutmann, Amy, and Dennis Thompson. *Why Deliberative Democracy?* Princeton: Princeton University Press, 2004.

Habermas, Jürgen. *The Theory of Communicative Action*. Translated by Thomas McCarthy. Boston: Beacon, 1984.

Haider-Markel, Donald P. "Morality in Congress: Legislative Voting on Gay Issues." In Mooney, *Private Clash*, 115–29.

Haider-Markel, Donald P., and Kenneth J. Meier. "The Politics of Gay and Lesbian Rights: Expanding the Scope of the Conflict." *Journal of Politics* 58 (1996): 332–49.

Halliday, W. R. *Greek Divination*. London: Macmillan, 1913.

Hardoon, Karen K., Rina Gupta, and Jeffrey L. Derevensky. "Psychosocial Variables Associated with Adolescent Gambling." *Psychology of Addictive Behaviors* 18 (2004): 170–79.

Hariri, A. R., V. S. Mattay, A. Tessitore, B. Kolachana, F. Fera, D. Goldman, M. F. Egan, and D. R. Weinberger. "Serotonin" Transporter Genetic Variation and the Response of the Human Amygdala." *Science* 297, no. 5580 (2002): 400–403.

Harlem Pete. *Watch Your Dreams with Harlem Pete Dream Book*. Philadelphia: Dale Book, 1949.

Harrah's Entertainment. *Casino Customers: An Annual Survey.* Harrah's Entertainment, 2006.

———. *Harrah's Survey: Profile of the American Casino Gambler.* Harrah's Entertainment, 2006. See also http://www.harrahs.com/images/PDFs/Profile_Survey_2006.pdf.

Harrison, Brigid. "Legislating Morality: The New Jersey Casino Control Act as 'Moral' Public Policy." *Gaming Law Review* 2 (1998): 63–69.

Harvard Project on American Indian Economic Development, Eric Henson, Jonathan B. Taylor, Catherine Curtis, Stephen Cornell, Kenneth W. Grant, Miriam Jorgensen, Joseph P. Kalt, and Andrew J. Lee. *The State of the Native Nations: Conditions Under U.S. Policies of Self-Determination.* Oxford: Oxford University Press, 2007.

Hayman, L. A., J. L. Rexer, M. A. Pavol, D. Strite, and C. A. Meyer. "Klüver-Bucy Syndrome after Bilateral Selective Damage of Amygdala and Its Cortical Connections." *Journal of Neuropsychiatry and Clinical Neurosciences* 10 (1998): 354–58.

Heberling, Michael. "State Lotteries: Advocating a Social Ill for the Social Good." *The Independent Review,* 6, no. 4 (2002): 597–606.

Henderson, Robert W. "Moses Provençal on Tennis." *Jewish Quarterly Review* 26 (1935): 1–6.

Henslin, James M. "Craps and Magic." *The American Journal of Sociology* 73, no. 3 (1967): 316–30.

Hildreth, Richard. *Banks, Banking, and Paper Currencies, in Three Parts.* Boston: Whipple & Damrell, 1840.

Hodgins, David C., Nicole Peden, and Erin Cassidy. "The Association Between Comorbidity and Outcome in Pathological Gambling: A Prospective Follow-up of Recent Quitters." *Journal of Gambling Studies* 21 (2005): 255–71.

Hodgins, David C., N. Will Shead, and Karyn Makarchuk. "Relationship Satisfaction and Psychological Distress among Concerned Significant Others of Pathological Gamblers." *Journal of Nervous and Mental Disease* 195 (2007): 65–71.

Hoffmann, John P., Scott A. Baldwin, and Felicia G. Cerbone. "The Onset of Major Depressive Disorders among Adolescents." *Journal of the American Academy of Child and Adolescent Psychiatry* 42 (2003): 217–24.

Hoffmann, John P., and Felicia G. Cerbone. "Parental Substance Use Disorder and the Risk of Adolescent Drug Abuse: An Event History Analysis." *Drug and Alcohol Dependence* 66 (2002): 255–64.

Hoffmann, John P., Mikaela Dufur, and Lynn Huang. "Drug Use and Job Quits: A Longitudinal Analysis." *Journal of Drug Issues* 37 (2007): 569–96.

Hoffmann, John P., and S. Susan Su. "Parental Substance Use Disorder, Mediating Variables, and Adolescent Drug Use: A Nonrecursive Model." *Addiction* 93 (1998): 1353–66.

Holbrook, Allyson L., Melanie C. Green, and Jon A. Krosnick. "Telephone Versus Face-To-Face Interviewing of National Probability Samples with Long Questionnaires: Comparisons of Respondent Satisficing and Social Desirability Response Bias." *Public Opinion Quarterly* 67 (2003): 79–125.

Holden, C. "'Behavioral' Addictions: Do They Exist?" *Science* 294, no. 5544 (2001): 980–82.

Hollander, E., and S. D. Benzaquin. "Is There a Distinct OCD Spectrum?" *CNS Spectrums* 1, no. 1 (1996): 17–26.

Hollander, E., and C. M. Wong. "Obsessive-Compulsive Spectrum Disorders." *Journal of Clinical Psychiatry* 56, no. 4 (1995): 3–6.

Hommer, D. W. "Motivation in Alcoholism." Paper presented at the International Conference on Applications of Neuroimaging to Alcoholism, New Haven, Conn., 2004.

Hommer, D. W., P. Andreasen, D. Rio, W. Williams, U. Rettimann, R. Monenan, A. Zametkin, R. Rawlings, and M. Linnoila. "Effects of M-Chlorophenylpiperazine on Regional Brain Glucose Utilization: A Positron Emission Tomographic Comparison of Alcoholic and Control Subjects." *Journal of Neuroscience* 17 (1997): 2796–2806.

Hommer, D. W., J. M. Bjork, B. Knutson, D. Caggiano, G. Fong, and C. Danube. "Motivation in Children of Alcoholics." *Alcoholism: Clinical and Experimental Research* 28, no. 5 (2004): 22A.

Howells, William Dean. *The World of Chance.* New York: Harper & Brothers, 1893.

Huizinga, Johan. *Homo Ludens: A Study of the Play Element in Culture.* Boston: Beacon, 1955. First published in 1938.

Hunter, James Davison. *Before the Shooting Begins: Searching for Democracy in America's Culture War.* New York: Free Press, 1994.

———. *Culture Wars: The Struggle to Define America.* New York: Basic Books, 1991.

Hunter, James Davison, and Alan Wolfe. *Is There a Culture War?: A Dialogue on Values and American Public Life.* Washington, D.C.: Brookings Institution, 2006.

Hyde, Lewis. *Trickster Makes This World: Mischief, Myth, and Art.* New York: Farrar, Straus & Giroux, 1998.

Ibanez, A., C. Blanco, I. P. de Castro, J. Fernandez-Piqueras, and J. Saiz-Ruiz. "Genetics of Pathological Gambling." *Journal of Gambling Studies* 19 (2003): 11–22.

Jacobs, Durand F., Albert R. Marston, Robert D. Singer, Keith Widaman, Todd Little, and Jeannette Veizades. "Children of Problem Gamblers." *Journal of Gambling Studies* 5 (1989): 261–68.

Jacobs, James B., and Lauryn P. Gouldin. "Cosa Nostra: The Final Chapter?" *Crime and Justice* 25 (1999): 129.

James, William. "The Dilemma of Determinism." In *The Writings of William James*, edited by John J. McDermott. New York: Random House, 1967. First published 1884.

Jewish Encyclopedia. "Gambling." By Solomon Schechter and Julius H. Greenstone. http://www.jewishencyclopedia.com/.

"Jewish Lottery Fiasco." *SomethingJewish.co.uk*, May 5, 2006. http://www.somethingjewish.co.uk/articles/1870_jewish_lottery_fiasc.htm (accessed September 2, 2007).

Jung, Carl G. "Foreword." In *The I Ching or Book of Changes*, translated by Richard Wilhelm and Cary F. Baynes. Princeton, N.J.: Bollingen, 1967.

Kadish, Sanford. "The Crisis of Overcriminalization." *Annals of the American Academy of Political and Social Science* 374 (1967): 157–70.

Kahneman, D., and A. Tversky. "Prospect Theory: An Analysis of Decision under Risk." *Econometrica* 47, no. 2 (1979): 263–92.

———. "Subjective Probability: A Judgment of Representativeness." *Cognitive Psychology* 3, no. 3 (1972): 361–523.

Kalischuk, Ruth Grant, and Kelly Cardwell. *Problem Gambling and Its Impact on Families: Final Report*. Submitted to the Alberta Alcohol and Drug Abuse Commission. Alberta, Canada: University of Lethbridge, 2004.

Kaplan, H. Roy. "The Social and Economic Impact of State Lotteries." *Annals of the American Academy of Political and Social Science* 474 (1984): 91–106.

Kapteyn, Arie, Peter Kooreman, Peter Kuhn, and Adriaan R. Soetevent. "Measuring Social Interactions: Results from the Dutch Post Code Lottery." Unpublished paper, RAND and Tilburg University, April 2007.

Katel, Peter. "American Indians." *CQ Researcher*, April 28, 2006.

Kavanagh, Thomas M. *Enlightenment and the Shadows of Chance*. Baltimore, Md.: The Johns Hopkins University Press, 1993.

Kawachi, Ichiro, and Lisa F. Berkman. "Social Ties and Mental Health." *Journal of Urban Health* 78 (2001): 458–67.

Kazin, Michael. *A Godly Hero: The Life of William Jennings Bryan.* New York: Knopf, 2006.

Kearney, Melissa Schettini. "State Lotteries and Consumer Behavior." *Journal of Public Economics* 89 (2005): 2269–99.

Keller, Bruce P. "The Game's the Same: Why Gambling in Cyberspace Violated Federal Law." *Yale Law Journal* 108 (1999): 1569.

Keren, G., and C. Lewis. "The Two Fallacies of Gamblers: Type I and Type II." *Organizational Behavior and Human Decision Processes* 60, no. 1 (1994): 75–89.

Kessler, Ronald C., and Kathleen R. Merikangas. "The National Comorbidity Survey Replication (NCS-R): Background and Aims." *International Journal of Methods in Psychiatric Research* 13 (2004): 60–68.

Keynes, John Maynard. *The General Theory of Employment, Interest, and Money.* New York: Harvest Books, 1964. First published in 1936.

Kierkegaard, Søren. *Fear and Trembling.* Translated by Walter Lowrie. Princeton: Princeton University Press, 1941.

Kim, S. W., J. E. Grant , D. E. Adson, and Y. C. Shin. "Double-Blind Naltrexone and Placebo Comparison Study in the Treatment of Pathological Gambling." *Biological Psychiatry* 49 (2001): 914–21.

Kindt, John Warren. "The Economic Impacts of Legalized Gambling Activities." *Drake Law Review* 43 (1994): 73–77.

Kirby, K. N., Nancy M. Petry, and W. K. Bickel. "Heroin Addicts Have Higher Discount Rates for Delayed Rewards Than Non-Drug-Using Controls." *Journal of Experimental Psychology* 128 (1999): 78–87.

Knutson, B., C. M. Adams, G. W. Fong, and D. Hommer. "Anticipation of Increasing Monetary Reward Selectively Recruits Nucleus Accumbens." *Journal of Neuroscience* 21 (2001): RC159 (1–5).

Knutson, B., G. W. Fong, C. M. Adams, J. L. Varner, and D. Hommer. "Dissociation of Reward Anticipation and Outcome with Event-Related fMRI." *Neuroreport* 12 (2001): 3683–87.

Knutson, B., G. W. Fong, S. M. Bennett, C. M. Adams, and D. Hommer. "A Region of Mesial Prefrontal Cortex Tracks Monetarily Rewarding Outcomes: Characterization with Rapid Event-Related fMRI." *Neuroimage* 18 (2003): 263–72.

Knutson, B., A. Westdorp, E. Kaiser, and D. Hommer. "fMRI Visualization of Brain Activity During a Monetary Incentive Delay Task." *Neuroimage* 12 (2000): 20–27.

Korn, David A., and Howard J. Shaffer. "Gambling and the Health of the Public: Adopting a Public Health Perspective." *Journal of Gambling Studies* 15, no. 4 (1999): 289–365.

Kreek, M. J., D. A. Nielsen, E. R. Butelman, and K. S. LaForge. "Genetic Influences on Impulsivity, Risk-Taking, Stress Responsivity and Vulnerability to Drug Abuse and Addiction." *Nature Neuroscience* 8 (2005): 1450–57.

Krishnan-Sarin, S., B. Reynolds, A. M. Duhig, A. Smith, T. Liss, A. McFertridge, D. A. Cavallo, K. M. Carroll, and Marc N. Potenza. "Behavioral Impulsivity Predicts Treatment Outcome in a Smoking Cessation Program for Adolescent Smokers." *Drug and Alcohol Dependence* 88 (2007): 79–82.

Krystal, J. H., J. A. Cramer, W. F. Krol, and G. F. Kirk. "Naltrexone in the Treatment of Alcohol Dependence." *New England Journal of Medicine* 345, no. 2 (2001): 1734–39.

Kyvig, David E. *Repealing National Prohibition*. Chicago: University of Chicago Press, 2000.

Lambert, Craig. "Trafficking in Chance." *Harvard Magazine*, July–August, 2002.

Landman, Leo. "Jewish Attitudes toward Gambling: The Professional and Compulsive Gambler." *Jewish Quarterly Review* 57, no. 4 (1967): 298–318.

———. "Jewish Attitudes toward Gambling II: Individual and Communal Efforts to Curb Gambling." *Jewish Quarterly Review* 58, no. 1 (1967): 34–62.

Landry, Craig E., and Michael K. Price. "Earmarking Lottery Proceeds for Public Goods: Empirical Evidence from U.S. Lotto Expenditures." *Economics Letters* 95 (2007): 451–55.

Lange, Andreas, John A. List, and Michael K. Price. "Using Lotteries to Finance Public Goods: Theory and Experimental Evidence." *International Economic Review* 48, no. 3 (2007): 901–27.

Langer, E. "The Illusion of Control." *Journal of Personality and Social Psychology* 32 (1975): 311–28.

Langewisch, M. W., and G. R. Frisch. "Classification of Pathological Gambling as an Impulse Control Disorder." *Electronic Journal of Gambling Issues* 3 (2001): 1–7. http://www.camh.net/egambling/ issue3/research/research_langewisch.html.

LaPlante, Alice. "Online Gambling Gone Wild: U.S. Crackdown Sparks Offshore Boom." *InformationWeek*, March 27, 2007. Available at http://www.informationweek.com/shared/printableArticleSrc .jhtml?articleID=198700819.

Last, Jonathan. "Not Just for Losers Anymore." *The Wall Street Journal*, October 21, 2005.

Lears, T. J. Jackson. *Something for Nothing: Luck in America*. New York: Viking Penguin, 2003.

Lehne, Richard. *Casino Policy.* New Brunswick, N.J.: Rutgers University Press, 1986.

Leopard, A. "Risk Preference in Consecutive Gambling." *Journal of Experimental Psychology: Human Perception and Performance* 4 (1978): 521–28.

Lesch, Klaus Peter, and Ursula Merschdorf. "Impulsivity, Aggression, and Serotonin: A Molecular Psychobiological Perspective." *Behavioral Sciences and the Law* 18 (2000): 581–604.

Leshner, A. I. "Don't Let Ideology Trump Science." *Science* 302, no. 5650 (2003): 1479.

Lesieur, Henry R. "Costs and Treatment of Pathological Gambling." *Annals of the American Academy of Political and Social Science* 556 (1998): 153–71.

Lesieur, Henry R., and Michael Welch. "Vice Crimes: Personal Autonomy Versus Societal Dictates." In *Criminology: A Contemporary Handbook*, 3rd ed., edited by Joseph F. Sheley, 233–63. Belmont, Calif.: Wadsworth, 2000.

Lieberman, M. D. "Social Cognitive Neuroscience: A Review of Core Processes." *Annual Review of Psychology* 58, no. 1 (2007): 259–89.

Light, Ivan. "Numbers Gambling Among Blacks: A Financial Institution." *American Sociological Review* 42, no. 6 (1977): 892–904.

Light, Steven Andrew, and Kathryn R.L. Rand. *Indian Gaming and Tribal Sovereignty: The Casino Compromise.* Lawrence: University Press of Kansas, 2005.

———. "The 'Tribal Loophole': Federal Campaign Finance Law and Tribal Political Participation after Jack Abramoff." *Gaming Law Review* 10 (2006): 230–39.

Lindaman, Kara L. "Place Your Bet on Politics: Local Governments Roll the Dice." *Politics & Policy* 35 (2007): 274–97.

Lindblom, Charles. *Politics and Markets: The World's Political Economic Systems.* New York: Basic Books, 1977.

Long, Mason. *The Life of Mason Long, Converted Gambler.* 5th ed. Fort Wayne, Ind.: Mason Long, 1882.

Lorenz, Valerie C., and Robert A. Yaffee. "Pathological Gambling, Psychosomatic, Emotional, and Mental Differences as Reported by the Spouse of the Gambler." *Journal of Gambling Studies* 4 (1988): 13–26.

Lowi, Theodore J. "American Business, Public Policy, Case Studies, and Political Theory." *World Politics* 16 (1964): 677–715.

———. "Foreword." In Nelson and Mason, *Gambling Nation*, vii–viii.

———. "Four Systems of Policy, Politics, and Choice." *Public Administration Review* 32 (1972): 298–310.

MacDonald, Robert A., ed. *"Libro de las Tahurerías"*: *A Special Code of Law, Concerning Gambling, Drawn Up by Maestro Roldán at the Command of Alfonso X of Castile*. Hispanic Seminary of Medieval Studies Legal Series 19. Madison, Wisc.: Hispanic Seminary of Medieval Studies, 1995.

MacKenzie, W. D. *The Ethics of Gambling*. London: The Sunday School Union, 1902.

MacKinnon, Catharine. *Toward a Feminist Theory of the State*. Cambridge, Mass.: Harvard University Press, 1989.

Madhusudhan, Ranjana G. "Betting on Casino Revenues: Lessons from State Experiences." *National Tax Journal* 49 (1996): 401–12.

Magidson, Jay, and Jeroen K. Vermunt. "Latent Class Models." In *The Sage Handbook of Quantitative Methodology for the Social Sciences*, edited by David Kaplan, 175–97. Newbury Park, Calif.: Sage Publications, 2004.

Maguire, Ken. "Patrick's Casino Revenue Doubtful, Report Says." *Newsday*, October 25, 2007.

———. "Some Warn Mass. Casino Plan Brings Risk for College Students." *Boston Globe*, October 14, 2007.

———. "Struggling Bingo Games Brace for Casino Impact." *Boston Globe*, September 13, 2007.

Manning, Christel J. *God Gave Us the Right: Conservative Catholic, Evangelical, and Orthodox Jewish Women Grapple with Feminism*. New Brunswick, N.J.: Rutgers University Press, 1999.

Manning, Jill K. "The Impact of Internet Pornography on Marriage and the Family: A Review of the Research." *Sexual Addiction & Compulsivity* 13 (2006): 131–65.

Markandya, Anil, and David Pearce. "The Social Costs of Tobacco Smoking." *British Journal of Addiction* 84 (1989): 1139–50.

Marriott, Michael. "Fervid Debate Over Gambling: Disease or Moral Weakness?" *The New York Times*, November 21, 1992.

Marsden, George M. *Understanding Fundamentalism and Evangelicalism*. Grand Rapids: Eerdmans, 1991.

Mason, John Lyman, and Michael Nelson. *Governing Gambling: Politics and Policy in State, Tribe, and Nation*. New York: The Century Foundation, 2001.

Massachusetts State Lottery. *Massachusetts State Lottery Annual Report FY2005*. http://www.masslottery.com/pdfs/AnnualReport 2005.pdf.

McAlister, Elizabeth. "A Sorcerer's Bottle: The Visual Art of Magic in Haiti." In *Sacred Arts of Haitian Vodou*, edited by Donald J. Cosentino, 305–21. Los Angeles: Fowler Museum, 1995.

McAuliffe, Elizabeth Winslow. "The State-Sponsored Lottery: A Failure of Policy and Ethics." *Public Integrity* 8 (2006): 367–79.

McClure, S. M., D. I. Laibson, G. Loewenstein, J. D. Cohen. "Separate Neural Systems Value Immediate and Delayed Monetary Rewards." *Science* 306, no. 5695 (2004): 503–7.

McConnell, Michael W. "Federalism: Evaluating the Founders' Design." *University of Chicago Law Review* 54 (1987): 1484–1512.

McGrew, Jane Lang. "History of Alcohol Prohibition." National Commission on Marijuana and Drug Abuse. http://www.drug library.org/.

———. "History of Tobacco Regulation." Schaffer Library of Drug Policy. http://www.druglibrary.org/.

Mead, Lawrence. *Government Matters: Welfare Reform in Wisconsin*. Princeton: Princeton University Press, 2004.

Meier, Kenneth J. "Drugs, Sex, and Rock and Roll: A Theory of Morality Politics." In Mooney, *Private Clash*, 21–36.

———. *The Politics of Sin: Drugs, Alcohol and Public Policy*. Armonk, N.Y.: M. E. Sharpe, 1994.

Meister, Alan P. *Indian Gaming Industry Report, 2007–2008*. Newton, Mass.: Casino City Press, 2007.

Melnick, R. Shep. *Between the Lines: Interpreting Welfare Rights*. Washington, D.C.: Brookings, 1994.

———. "From Tax and Spend to Mandate and Sue: Liberalism after the Great Society." In *The Great Society and the High Tide of Liberalism*, edited by Sidney Milkis and Jerome Mileur, 387–410. Amherst: University of Massachusetts Press, 2005.

Merriam-Webster Online Dictionary. "Moral." http://www.m-w.com/dictionary/moral (accessed October 2, 2007).

———. "Morality." http://www.m-w.com/dictionary/morality (accessed October 2, 2007).

Mesko, Jennifer. "States Stand Strong against Gambling." *CitizenLink*, August 30, 2007. http://www.citizenlink.org/content/A000005389.cfm.

Messerlian, Carmen, and Jeffrey L. Derevensky. "Youth Gambling: A Public Health Perspective." *Journal of Gambling Issues* 14 (2005): 1–20. http://www.camh.net/egambling/issue14/jgi_14_messerlian.html.

Metzger, M. A. "Biases in Betting: An Application of Laboratory Findings." *Psychological Reports* 56, no. 3 (1985): 883–88.

Mikesell, John, and C. Kurt Zorn. "State Lotteries as Fiscal Savior or Fiscal Fraud: A Look at the Evidence." *Public Administration Review* 46 (1986): 319.

Mill, John Stewart. *On Liberty*. Edited by Stefan Collini. Cambridge: Cambridge University Press, 1989. First published in 1859.

Miller, Donald E., and Patrick A. Pierce. "Lotteries for Education: Windfall or Hoax?" *State and Local Government Review* 29, no. 1 (1997): 34–42.

Miller, Jared. "Casino Flourishes without Alcohol." *Casper Star-Tribune* (Wyo.), September 23, 2007.

Mittenecker, E. "Die Analyse 'zufälliger' Reaktionsfolgen." *Zeitschrift für experimentelle und angewandte Psychologie* 5 (1958): 45–60.

———. "Perseveration und Personlichkeit: Teil experimentelle Untersuchungen." *Zeitschrift für experimentelle und angewandte Psychologie* 1 (1953): 5–31.

Mobilia, Pamela. "Gambling as a Rational Addiction." *Journal of Gambling Studies* 9, no. 2 (1993): 121–51.

Moeller, F. G., E. S. Barratt, D. M. Dougherty, J. M. Schmitz, and A. C. Swann. "Psychiatric Aspects of Impulsivity." *American Journal of Psychiatry* 158 (2001): 1783–93.

Moffitt, Terrie E., Gary L. Brammer, Avshalom Caspi, J. Paul Fawcett, Michael Raleigh, Arthur Yuwiler, and Phil Silva. "Whole Blood Serotonin Relates to Violence in an Epidemiological Study." *Biological Psychiatry* 43 (1998): 446–57.

Moll, J., R. de Oliveira-Souza, F. T. Moll, F. A. Ignacio, I. E. Bramati, E. M. Caparelli-Daquer, and P. J. Eslinger. "The Moral Affiliations of Disgust: A Functional MRI Study." *Cognitive and Behavioral Neurology* 18 (2005): 68–78.

Moll, J., R. Zahn, R. de Oliviera-Souza, F. Krueger, and J. Grafman. "The Neural Basis of Human Moral Cognition." *Nature Reviews Neuroscience* 6 (2005): 799–809.

Monkkonen, Eric H. *Murder in New York City*. Berkeley: University of California Press, 2000.

Mooney, Christopher Z. "The Private Clash of Public Values: The Politics of Morality Policy." In Mooney, *Private Clash*, 3–20.

———, ed. *The Private Clash of Public Values*. Chatham, N.J.: Chatham House, 2001.

Mooney, Christopher Z., and Mei-Hsien Lee. "Legislating Morality in the American States: The Case of Pre-*Roe* Abortion Regulation Reform." *American Journal of Political Science* 39 (1995): 599–627.

————. "The Temporal Diffusion of Morality Policy: The Case of Death Penalty Legislation in the U.S. States." In Mooney, *Private Clash*, 170–86.

Moore, Todd M., Angela Scarpa, and Adrian Raine. "A Meta-Analysis of Serotonin Metabolite 5-HIAA and Antisocial Behavior." *Aggressive Behavior* 28 (2002): 299–316.

Moore, William Haas. *The Kefauver Committee and the Politics of Crime*. Columbia: University of Missouri Press, 1974.

"Morality Continues to Decay." *The Barna Update*, November 3, 2003. Available at http://www.barna.org/.

Morasco, Benjamin J., Robert H. Pietrzak, Carlos Blanco, Bridget F. Grant, Deborah Hasin, and Nancy M. Petry. "Health Problems and Medical Utilization Associated With Gambling Disorders: Results from the National Epidemiologic Survey on Alcohol and Related Conditions." *Psychosomatic Medicine* 68 (2006): 976–84.

Morgan, John. "Financing Public Goods by Means of Lotteries." *Review of Economic Studies* 67 (2000): 761–84.

Morse, Edward A. and Ernest P. Goss. *Governing Fortune: Casino Gambling in America*. Ann Arbor: University of Michigan Press, 2007.

Murray, Charles. "The G.O.P.'s Bad Bet." *The New York Times*, October 19, 2006.

Narayan, V. M., K. L. Narr, V. Kumari, R. P. Woods, P. M. Thompson, A. W. Toga, and T. Sharma. "Regional Cortical Thinning in Subjects with Violent Antisocial Personality Disorder or Schizophrenia." *American Journal of Psychiatry* 164 (2007): 1418–27.

National Archive of Criminal Justice Data. http://www.icpsr.umich .edu/cocoon/NACJD/STUDY/03226.xml.

National Conference of State Legislatures. "State Revenues Healthy in First Quarter of FY 2006." December 15, 2005. http://www.ncsl .org/.

National Gambling Impact Study Commission. *National Gambling Impact Study Commission Final Report*. 1999. Available at http:// govinfo.library.unt.edu/ngisc/reports/fullrpt.html.

National Indian Gaming Commission. *Gaming Revenue Reports* . 2007. Available at http://www.nigc.gov/.

————. "Gaming Revenues 2006–2001." 2007. Available at http:// www.nigc.gov/Default.aspx?tabid=67.

National Research Council. "Pathological Gambling: A Critical Review." Washington, D.C.: National Academy Press, 1999.

Natuur en Milieu. "Dutch Post Code Lottery." http://www.snm.nl/ page.php?extraItemID=2037.

Nelson, Michael. "From Rez to Riches." *American Prospect*, May 21, 2001.

———. "Gambling Online." *American Prospect*, June 4, 2001.

———. "The Politics of Tribal Recognition: Casinos, Culture, and Controversy." In *Interest Group Politics*, 7th. ed., edited by Allen J. Cigler and Burdett A. Loomis, 65–85. Washington, D.C.: CQ Press, 2007.

Nelson, Michael, and John Lyman Mason. *How the South Joined the Gambling Nation: The Politics of State Policy Innovation*. Baton Rouge: Louisiana State University Press, 2007.

———. "The Politics of Gambling in the South." *Political Science Quarterly* 118 (2004): 645–70.

Nestler, E. J. "Molecular Mechanisms of Drug Addiction." *Neuropharmacology* 47, no. 1 (2004): 24–32.

New, A. S., E. A. Hazlett, M. S. Buchsbaum, M. Goodman, D. Reynolds, V. Mitropoulou, L. Sprung Jr., et al. "Blunted Prefrontal Cortical 18-Fluorodeoxyglucose Positron Emission Tomography Response to Meta-Chlorophenylpiperazine in Impulsive Aggression." *Archives of General Psychiatry* 59 (2002): 621–29.

Newman, Maria. "Mayor Proposes a Fee for Driving Into Manhattan." *The New York Times*, April 22, 2007.

Noll, Mark A. *The Scandal of the Evangelical Mind*. Grand Rapids: Eerdmans, 1995.

Nordin, C., and T. Eklundh. "Altered Csf 5-Hiaa Disposition in Pathologic Male Gamblers." *CNS Spectrums* 4, no. 12 (1999): 25–33.

———. "Tapping-Time Is Longer in Pathological Male Gamblers Than in Healthy Male Controls." *Journal of Psychiatric Research* 32 (1998): 421–22.

Norrander, Barbara, and Clyde Wilcox. "Public Opinion and Policymaking in the States: The Case of Post-*Roe* Abortion Policy." In Mooney, *Private Clash*, 143–59.

Norris, Frank. *The Pit*. New York: Doubleday, 1903.

Novak, Michael, and John Cogan, eds. *The New Consensus on Family and Welfare*. Washington, D.C.: American Enterprise Institute, 1987.

Novamedia. "Nationale Postcode Loterij." http://www.novamedia.nl/web/show/id=55340.

O'Brien, Timothy. "Is Poker Losing Its First Flush?" *The New York Times*, April 16, 2006.

Office of Minority Health and Health Disparities. *American Indian and Alaska Native Populations*. U.S. Center for Disease Control and Prevention. http://www.cdc.gov/omhd/Populations/AIAN/ AIAN.htm.

Oldman, D. "Chance and Skill: A Study of Roulette." *Sociology* 8, no. 3 (1974): 407–26.

"An Open Letter from 200 Religious Leaders to the President and Congress on the Spread of Gambling." *Roll Call*, May 6, 2002.

Orleck, Annelise. *Storming Caesars Palace: How Black Mothers Fought Their Own War on Poverty.* Boston: Beacon, 2005.

Oslin, D. W., W. Berrettini, H. R. Kranzler, H. Pettinate, J. Gelernter, J. R. Volpicelli, and C. P. O'Brien. "A Functional Polymorphism of the Mu-Opioid Receptor Gene Is Associated with Naltrexone Response in Alcohol-Dependent Patients." *Neuropsychopharmacology* 28 (2003): 1546–52.

Packer, Herbert. *The Limits of the Criminal Sanction.* Stanford: Stanford University Press, 1968.

Pascal, Blaise. *Pensées.* Translated by A. J. Krailsheimer. Harmondsworth, England: Penguin Books, 1966.

Patton, Dana. "The Supreme Court and Morality Policy Adoption in the American States: The Impact of Constitutional Context." *Political Research Quarterly* 60 (2007): 468–88.

Pavalko, Ronald M. *Risky Business: America's Fascination with Gambling.* Belmont, Calif.: Wadsworth, 2000.

Payne, J. W., D. J. Laughhunn, and R. Crum. "Multiattribute Risky Choice Behavior: The Editing of Complex Prospects." *Management Science* 30, no. 11 (1984): 1350–61.

Pearce, David W., ed. *The MIT Dictionary of Modern Economics.* Cambridge, Mass.: MIT Press, 1992.

Petry, Nancy M. "Gambling and Substance Use Disorders: Current Status and Future Directions." *American Journal of Addictions* 16 (2007): 1–9.

———. "Pathological Gamblers, with and without Substance Use Disorders, Discount Delayed Rewards at High Rates." *Journal of Abnormal Psychology* 110 (2001): 482–87.

———. *Pathological Gambling: Etiology, Comorbidity, and Treatment.* Washington, D.C.: American Psychological Association, 2005.

———. "Should the Scope of Addictive Behaviors Be Broadened to Include Pathological Gambling?" *Addiction* 101, no. 1 (2006): 152–60.

———. "Substance Abuse, Pathological Gambling, and Impulsiveness." *Drug and Alcohol Dependence* 63 (2001): 29–38.

Petry, Nancy M., and Christopher Armentano. "Prevalence, Assessment, and Treatment of Pathological Gambling: A Review." *Psychiatric Services* 50 (1999): 1021–27.

Petry, Nancy M., and T. Casarella. "Excessive Discounting of Delayed Rewards in Substance Abusers with Gambling Problems." *Drug and Alcohol Dependence* 56 (1999): 25–32.

Petry, Nancy M., K. L. Steinberg, and Women's Problem Gambling Research Center. "Childhood Maltreatment in Male and Female Treatment-Seeking Pathological Gamblers." *Psychology of Addictive Behaviors* 19 (2005): 226–29.

Petry, Nancy M., Frederick S. Stinson, and Bridget F. Grant. "Comorbidity of DSM-IV Pathological Gambling and Other Psychiatric Disorders: Results from the National Epidemiologic Survey on Alcohol and Related Conditions." *Journal of Clinical Psychiatry* 66 (2005): 564–74.

Petry, Nancy M., and Jeremiah Weinstock. "Internet Gambling Is Common in College Students and Associated with Poor Mental Health." *American Journal of Addictions* 16 (2007): 325–30.

Pew Research Center. "Gambling: As the Take Rises, So Does Public Concern." Washington, D.C.: Pew Research Center. May 23, 2006. Available at http://pewresearch.org/pubs/314/gambling-as-the-take -rises-so-does-public-concern.

Pierce, Patrick A., and Donald E. Miller. *Gambling Politics: State Governments and the Business of Betting.* Boulder, Colo.: Lynne Reiner, 2004.

Pitkin, Hannah. *The Concept of Representation.* Berkeley: University of California Press, 1967.

Pommersheim, Frank. *Braid of Feathers: American Indian Law and Contemporary Tribal Life.* Berkeley: University of California Press, 1995.

Pontell, Henry N. and Gilbert Geis. "Religion and the Psychology of Gambling in China and the U.S." In *The Psychology of Gambling*, edited by Marco J. Esposito, 1–14. Hauppauge, N.Y.: Nova Science Publishers, 2008.

Porter, Robert B. "A Proposal to the Hanodaganyas to Decolonize Federal Indian Control Law." *University of Michigan Journal of Law Reform* 31 (1998): 899–1005.

Potenza, Marc N. "Impulse Control Disorders and Co-Occurring Disorders: Dual Diagnosis Considerations." *Journal of Dual Diagnosis* 3 (2007): 47–57.

———. "Impulsivity and Compulsivity in Pathological Gambling and Obsessive-Compulsive Disorder." *Revista Brasileira Psiquiatria* 29 (2007): 105–6.

———. "Should Addictions Include Non-Substance-Related Disorders?" Paper presented at the European Association of Addiction Therapies, Vienna, Austria, September 12, 2007.

————. "Should Addictive Disorders Include Non-Substance-Related Conditions?" *Addiction* 101, no. 1 (2006): 142–51.

————. "To Do or Not to Do? The Complexities of Addiction, Motivations, Self-Control, and Impulsivity." *American Journal of Psychiatry* 164 (2007): 4–6.

Potenza, Marc N., and E. Hollander. "Pathological Gambling and Impulse Control Disorders." In *Neuropsychopharmacology: The 5th Generation of Progress*, edited by J. Coyle, C. Nemeroff, D. Charney, and K. Davis. Baltimore, Md.: Lippincott Williams and Wilkens, 2002.

Potenza, Marc N., Thomas R. Kosten, and Bruce J. Rounsaville. "Pathological Gambling." *Journal of the American Medical Association* 286 (2007): 141–44.

Potenza, Marc N., H. C. Leung, H. P. Blumberg, B. S. Peterson, P. Skudlarski, C. Lacadie, and J. C. Gore. "An fMRI Stroop Study of Ventromedial Prefrontal Cortical Function in Pathological Gamblers." *American Journal of Psychiatry* 160 (2003): 1990–94.

Potenza, Marc N., M. A. Steinberg, P. Skudlarski, R. K. Fulbright, C. M. Lacadie, M. K. Wilber, B. J. Rounsaville, J. C. Gore, and B. E. Wexler. "Gambling Urges in Pathological Gamblers: An fMRI Study." *Archives of General Psychiatry* 60 (2003): 828–36.

Potenza, Marc N., Hong Xian, K. Shah, J. F. Scherrer, and Seth A. Eisen. "Shared Genetic Contributions to Pathological Gambling and Major Depression in Men." *Archives of General Psychiatry* 62 (2005): 1015–21.

Pound, Roscoe. "Liberty of Contract." *Yale Law Journal* 18 (1909): 1484ff.

————. "Puritanism and the Common Law." *Proceedings of the Kansas State Bar Association* 45 (1910).

Poznick, Yehudah. "Gambling with the Jewish Law." *Jewish Magazine*, February 2003. http://www.jewishmag.com/64mag/gambling/gambling.htm.

Priscus. "On the Lawfulness and Expediency of Lotteries." Letter to the editor, *Connecticut Evangelical Magazine and Religious Intelligencer* 4 (1811): 99–104.

Pruitt, Dean G. "Choice Shifts in Group Discussion: An Introductory Review." *Journal of Personality and Social Psychology* 20, no. 3 (1971): 339–60.

Quandt, Richard E. "Betting and Equilibrium." *The Quarterly Journal of Economics* 101, no. 1 (1986): 201–7.

Quinn, J. P. *Fools of Fortune*. Chicago: The Anti-Gambling Association, 1892.

Rand, Kathryn R.L., and Steven Andrew Light. "How Congress Can and Should 'Fix' the Indian Gaming Regulatory Act: Recommendations for Law and Policy Reform." *Virginia Journal of Social Policy & the Law* 13 (2006): 396–473.

———. *Indian Gaming Law and Policy.* Durham, N.C.: Carolina Academic Press, 2006.

———. *Indian Gaming Law: Cases and Materials.* Durham, N.C.: Carolina Academic Press, 2008.

Rauschenbusch, Walter. *Christianity and the Social Crisis in the 21st Century.* Edited by Paul Rauschenbusch. San Francisco: Harper, 2007.

Reik, Theodor. "The Study in Dostoyevsky." In *From Thirty Years With Freud,* translated by R. Winston, 142–58. New York: Farrar and Rinehart, 1940.

Reith, Gerda, ed. *Gambling: Who Wins? Who Loses?* Amherst, N.Y.: Prometheus Books, 2003.

Reno, Ronald A. "Gambling and the Bible." *Beliefnet.* http://www.beliefnet.com/.

Rephann, Terance J., Margaret Dalton, Anthony Stair, and Andrew Isserman. "Casino Gambling as an Economic Development Strategy." *Tourism Economics* 3 (1997): 161–83.

Reuter, J., T. Raedler, M. Rose, I. Hand, J. Glascher, and C. Buchel. "Pathological Gambling Is Linked to Reduced Activation of the Mesolimbic Reward System." *Nature Neuroscience* 8 (2005): 147–48.

Richards, John. *Discourse on Gambling Delivered in the Congregational Meeting House at Dartmouth College, November 7, 1852.* Hanover, N.H.: D. Kimball & Sons, 1852.

Richardson, Jack. *Memoir of a Gambler.* New York: Vintage, 1979.

Ritch, W. A. and M. E. Begay. "Smoke and Mirrors: How Massachusetts Diverted Millions in Tobacco Tax Revenues." *Tobacco Control* 10 (2001): 309–16.

Roberts, Mary Nooter, and Allen F. Roberts. "Memory in Motion." In *Memory: Luba Art and the Making of History,* Edited by Mary Nooter Roberts and Allen F. Roberts, 177–82. New York: The Museum for African Art, 1996.

Rodgers, Daniel T. *Atlantic Crossings: Social Politics in a Progressive Age.* Cambridge, Mass.: Harvard University Press, 1998.

Roosevelt, Franklin D. "First Inaugural Address." Delivered March 4, 1933. Available at http://www.bartleby.com/124/pres49.html.

———. "New Conditions Impose New Requirements upon Government and Those Who Conduct Government." In *The Public Papers and Addresses of Franklin D. Roosevelt,* edited by Samuel I. Rosenman. New York: Random House, 1938.

Rose, I. Nelson. "The Legalization and Control of Casino Gambling." *Fordham Law Review* 8 (1980): 245–300.

Rosenblum, Nancy. *On the Side of the Angels: An Appreciation of Parties and Partisanship.* Princeton: Princeton University Press, 2008.

Rowe, David D. *Biology and Crime.* Los Angeles: Roxbury Publishing, 2002.

Rubner, Alex. *The Economics of Gambling.* London: Macmillan, 1966.

Ryan, John A. "The Ethics of Speculation." *International Journal of Ethics* 12, no. 3 (1902): 335–47.

Rychlack, Ronald J. "Lotteries, Revenues and Social Costs: A Historical Examination of State-Sponsored Gambling." *Boston College Law Review* 34 (1992): 11.

Saad, Lydia. "Americans Rate the Morality of 16 Social Issues." *Gallup News Service,* June 4, 2007.

Safire, William. "Now: Bet While You Booze." *The New York Times,* January 11, 1993.

Sampson, Robert J., and John H. Laub. "A Life Course Theory of Cumulative Disadvantage and the Stability of Delinquency." In *Developmental Theories of Crime and Delinquency,* edited by Terence P. Thornberry, 133–62. New Brunswick, N.J.: Transaction Publishers, 1997.

Scherrer, Jeffrey F., Wendy S. Slutske, Hong Xian, Brian Waterman, Kamini R. Shah, Rachel Volberg, and Seth A. Eisen. "Factors Associated with Pathological Gambling at 10-Year Follow-Up in a National Sample of Middle-Aged Men." *Addiction* 102 (2007): 970–78.

Scherrer, Jeffrey F., Hong Xian, Julie M. Krygiel Kapp, Brian Waterman, Kamini R. Shah, Rachel Volberg, and Seth A. Eisen. "Association between Exposure to Childhood and Lifetime Traumatic Events and Lifetime Pathological Gambling in a Twin Cohort." *Journal of Nervous and Mental Disease* 195 (2007): 72–78.

Schnall, David J. "By the Sweat of Your Brow." Center for Business Ethics and Social Responsibility. http://www.besr.org/ (accessed September 2, 2007).

Schull, Natasha Dow. *Machine Life: Control and Compulsion in Las Vegas.* Princeton: Princeton University Press, 2008.

Schultz, W., Tremblay L., and Hollerman J. R. "Reward Processing in Primate Orbitofrontal Cortex and Basal Ganglia." *Cerebral Cortex* 10 (2000): 272–84.

Schumpeter, Joseph. *Capitalism, Socialism, and Democracy.* 3rd ed. New York: Harper Torchbooks, 1962.

Schur, Edwin. *Crimes without Victims.* Englewood Cliffs, N.J.: Prentice Hall, 1965.

Schwartz, David. "Casino Resort Evolution: The Four Stages, 1941–2005." UNLV Center for Gaming Research, 2005. http://gaming .unlv.edu/media/Casino_Resort_Evolution.pdf.

———. *Roll the Bones: The History of Gambling.* New York: Gotham Books, 2006.

Schwartz, Nelson. "The $50 Ticket: A Lottery Boon Raises Concern." *The New York Times,* December 27, 2007.

Schwartz, Nelson, and Ron Nixon. "Some States Consider Leasing Their Lotteries." *The New York Times,* October 14, 2007.

Sen, Amartya. *Rationality and Freedom.* Cambridge, Mass.: Harvard University Press, 2003.

Sennett, Richard. *The Corrosion of Character.* New York: Norton, 1998.

Shaffer, Howard J., Matthew N. Hall, and Joni Vander Bilt. "Estimating the Prevalence of Disordered Gambling Behavior in the United States and Canada: A Meta-Analysis." Harvard Medical School, Division on Addictions, 1997.

———. "Estimating the Prevalence of Disordered Gambling Behavior in the United States and Canada: A Research Synthesis." *American Journal of Public Health* 89 (1999): 1369–76.

Shaffer, Howard J., and D. A. Korn. "Gambling and Related Mental Disorders: A Public Health Analysis." *Annual Review of Public Health* 23 (2002): 171–212.

Shah, K .R., Seth A. Eisen, Hong Xian, and Marc N. Potenza. "Genetic Studies of Pathological Gambling: A Review of Methodology and Analyses of Data from the Vietnam Era Twin (Vet) Registry." *Journal of Gambling Studies* 21 (2005): 177–201.

Shaw, Rosalind. "Splitting Truths from Darkness: Epistemological Aspects of Temne Divination." In *African Divination Systems: Ways of Knowing,* edited by Philip Peek, 141–44. Bloomington: Indiana University Press, 1991.

Shefrin, H., and M. Statman. "The Disposition to Sell Winners Too Early and Ride Losers Too Long: Theory and Evidence." *Journal of Finance* 40, no. 3 (1985): 777–90.

Shershow, Scott Cutler. *The Work and the Gift.* Chicago: University of Chicago Press, 2005.

Shin, L. M., D. D. Dougherty, S. P. Orr, R. K. Pitman, M. Lasko, M. L. Macklin, N. M. Alpert, A. J. Fischman, and S. L. Rauch.

"Activation of Anterior Paralimbic Structures During Guilt-Related ,Script-Driven Imagery." *Biological Psychiatry* 48 (2000): 43–50.

Sickinger, Ted. "History Shows Attitudes toward Gambling Change With the Times." *Kansas City Star*, March 11, 1997.

Siever, L. J., M. S. Buchsbaum, A. S. New, J. Spiegel-Cohen, T. Wei, E. A. Hazlett, E. Sevin, M. Nunn, and V. Mitropoulou. "D,L-Fenfluaramine Response in Impulsive Personality Disorder Assessed with [18f] Fluorodexyglucose Positron Emission Tomography." *Neuropsychopharmacology* 20 (1999): 413–23.

Sirri, Erik, and Peter Tufano. "Costly Search and Mutual Fund Flows." *Journal of Finance* 53, no. 5 (1998): 1589–1622.

Skeel, David A. "When Markets and Gambling Converge." In *Theology and the Liberal State,* edited by Charles Cohen and Len Kaplan. Madison: University of Wisconsin Press, 2006. Available at http://ssrn.com/abstract=888184.

Skolnick, Jerome. "Coercion to Virtue: The Enforcement of Morals." *Southern California Law Review* 41 (1968): 588.

———. *House of Cards: Legalization and Control of Casino Gambling.* Boston: Little, Brown, 1978.

———. "Regulating Vice: America's Struggle with Wicked Pleasure." In Reith, *Gambling*, 311–21.

———. "The Social Transformation of Vice." *Law and Contemporary Problems* 51 (1988): 9–29.

Skolnick, Jerome, and John Dombrink. "The Legalization of Deviance." *Criminology* 16, no. 2 (1978): 193–208.

Sloan, F. A., C. A. Matthews, and J. G. Trogdon. "Impacts of the Master Settlement Agreement on the Tobacco Industry." *Tobacco Control* 13 (2004): 356–61.

Slutske, Wendy S. "Natural Recovery and Treatment Seeking in Pathological Gambling: Results from Two National Surveys." *American Journal of Psychiatry* 163 (2006): 297–302.

Slutske, Wendy S., Seth A. Eisen, William R. True, Michael J. Lyons, Jack Goldberg, and Ming T. Tsuang. "Common Genetic Vulnerability for Pathological Gambling and Alcohol Dependence in Men." *Archives of General Psychiatry* 57 (2000): 666–74.

Slutske, Wendy S., Seth A. Eisen, Hong Xian, William R. True, Michael J. Lyons, Jack Goldberg, and Ming T. Tsuang. "A Twin Study of the Association between Pathological Gambling and Antisocial Personality Disorder." *Journal of Abnormal Psychology* 110 (2001): 297–308.

Slutske, Wendy S., Kristina M. Jackson, and Kenneth J. Sher. "The Natural History of Problem Gambling from Ages 18 to 29." *Journal of Abnormal Psychology* 112 (2003): 263–74.

Smith, Garry J., and Harold J. Wynne. *A Review of the Gambling Literature in the Economic and Policy Domains.* Alberta, Canada: Alberta Gaming Research Institute, 2000.

Smith, K., J. Dickhaut, K. McCabe, and J.V. Pardo. "Neuronal Substrates for Choice under Ambiguity, Risk, Gains, and Losses." *Management Science* 48, no. 6 (2002): 711–18.

Smith, Kevin B. "Clean Thoughts and Dirty Minds: The Politics of Porn." In Mooney, *Private Clash,* 187–200.

Smith, S. "Cigarettes Pack More Nicotine: State Study Finds a 10 Percent Rise over Six Years." *Boston Globe,* August 30, 2006.

Sobell, Linda C., Timothy P. Ellingstad, Mark B. Sobell. "Natural Recovery from Alcohol and Drug Problems: Methodological Review of the Research with Suggestions for Future Directions." *Addiction* 95 (2000): 749–64.

"South Carolina's Education Lottery Shortchanges African-American College Students." *Journal of Blacks in Higher Education* 43 (2004): 51.

Southern Baptist Convention. "Issues & Answers: Gambling." 2006. Available at http://erlc.com/article/issues-answers-gambling.

Spindler, Charles. "The Lottery and Education: Robbing Peter to Pay Paul." *Public Budgeting and Finance* 15, no. 3 (1995): 54–62.

St. George, M., and U. Bellugi. "Preface." In "Linking Cognitive Neuroscience and Molecular Genetics: New Perspectives from Williams Syndrome," edited by M. St. George and U. Bellugi. *Journal of Cognitive Neuroscience* 12, no. 1 (2000): 1–6.

"Standard and Poor's Credit Week: Gambling Industry." *Standard and Poor's Credit Week.* http://www.standardandpoors.com/ (accessed June 14, 2006).

State of Maryland Department of Legislative Services. *Overview of Issues Related to Video Lottery Terminals.* Annapolis, Md.: Department of Legislative Services, January 29, 2003. http://mlis .state.md.us/Other/Video_Lottery_Briefings/Gaming_2003.pdf.

Stewart, David. "An Analysis of Internet Gambling and Its Policy Implications." American Gaming Association, 2006. Available at http://www.americangaming.org/assets/files/studies/wpaper_ internet_0531.pdf.

Stodghill, Ron. "The Lottery Industry's Own Powerball." *The New York Times,* November 18, 2007.

Stodghill, Ron, and Ron Nixon. "Divide and Conquer: Meet the Lottery Titans." *The New York Times,* October 21, 2007.

———. "For Schools, Lottery Payoffs Fall Short of Promises." *The New York Times,* October 7, 2007.

Strickland, L. H., R. J. Lewicki, and A. M. Katz. "Temporal Orientation and Perceived Control as Determinants of Risk-Taking." *Journal of Experimental Social Psychology* 2 (1966): 143–51.

Strouse, Jean. *J. P. Morgan, American Financier.* New York: Random House, 1999.

Stuntz, William J. "Unequal Justice." *Harvard Law Review* 121 (2008): 1969.

Stutz, Howard. "Rate of Growth Slowed for Tribal Gaming in 2006." *Las Vegas Review-Journal* June 28, 2007.

Sullivan, Andrew. *Virtually Normal: An Argument about Homosexuality.* New York: Knopf, 1996.

Sunstein, Cass R., and Richard H. Thaler. "Libertarian Paternalism Is Not an Oxymoron." *University of Chicago Law Review* 70, no. 4 (2003): 1159–1202.

Sunstein, Cass. *Democracy and the Problem of Free Speech.* New York: Free Press, 1993.

Surgeon General of the United States. *Smoking and Health: Report of the Advisory Committee to the Surgeon General of the Public Health Service.* Rockville, Md.: Public Health Service, 1964.

Surgeon General of the United States. *The Health Consequences of Smoking: Cancer and Chronic Lung Disease in the Workplace.* Rockville, Md.: Public Health Service, 1985.

Takahashi, H., N. Yahata, M. Koeda, T. Matsuda, K. Asai, and Y. Okubo. "Brain Activation Associated with Evaluative Processes of Guilt and Embarrassment: An fMRI Study." *Neuroimage* 23 (2004): 967–74.

Talmadge, T. D. "Gambling." In *Social Dynamite; Or, the Wickedness of Modern Society.* Chicago: Standard, 1888.

Tambiah, S. N. "Form and Meaning in Magical Acts: A Point of View." In *Modes of Thought: Essays on Thinking in Western and Non-Western Societies,* edited by Robin Horton and Ruth Finnegan, 199–229. London: Faber & Faber, 1973.

Tatalovich, Raymond, and Byron W. Danes. "Moral Controversies and the Policymaking Process: Lowi's Framework Applied to the Abortion Issue." *Policy Studies Review* 3 (1984): 207–22.

———. *Social Regulatory Policy: Moral Controversies in American Politics.* Boulder, Colo.: Westview, 1988.

Taylor, Jonathan B., and Joseph P. Kalt. "*Cabazon,* the Indian Gaming Regulatory Act, and the Socioeconomic Consequences of American Indian Governmental Gaming." Cambridge, Mass.: Harvard Project on American Indian Economic Development, 2005. Available at http://www.ksg.harvard.edu/hpaied/pubs/cabazon.htm.

Terrell, Dek. "A Test of the Gambler's Fallacy: Evidence from Pari-Mutuel Games." *Journal of Risk and Uncertainty* 8, no. 3 (1994): 309–17.

Terrell, Dek, and Amy Farmer. "Optimal Betting and Efficiency in Parimutuel Betting Markets with Information Costs." *The Economic Journal* 106, no. 437 (1996): 846–68.

Thaler, Richard H., and E. J. Johnson. "Gambling with the House Money and Trying to Break Even: The Effects of Prior Outcomes on Risky Choice." *Management Science* 36, no. 6 (1990): 643–60.

Thaler, Richard H., and Cass R. Sunstein. "Libertarian Paternalism." *The American Economic Review* 93, no. 2 (2003): 175–79.

"Thirteen Ways of Looking at a State Lottery." *North Carolina Insight* 19, no. 1–2 (2000): 2–57.

Thompson, Nicholas. "Snake Eyes: Even Education Programs Can't Redeem State Lotteries." *Washington Monthly*, December 1999.

Thomson, David. *In Nevada: The Land, the People, God, and Chance.* New York: Knopf, 1999.

Tillich, Paul. "Holy Waste." In *The New Being*, 15–25. New York: Charles Scribner's Sons, 1955.

Tillotson, John. *Works.* London: Rogers, Goodwin, Nicholson and Tooke, 1710.

Tocqueville, Alexis de. *Democracy in America.* Edited by Phillips Bradley. 2 vols. New York: Knopf, 1945.

———. *Democracy in America.* Translated by Harvey Mansfield and Delba Winthrop. Chicago: University of Chicago Press, 2000.

Tom, Sabrina M., Craig R. Fox, Christopher Trepel, and Russell A. Poldrack. "The Neural Basis of Loss Aversion in Decision Making under Risk." *Science* 315, no. 5811 (2007): 515–18.

"Transformation of Las Vegas." *Standard and Poor's Credit Week,* June 14, 2006.

Trepel, Christopher, Craig R. Fox, and Russell A. Poldrack. "Prospect Theory on the Brain? Toward a Cognitive Neuroscience of Decision under Risk." *Cognitive Brain Research* 23, no. 1 (2005): 34–50.

Tsai, Elizabeth T. "Validity and Construction of Statute Exempting Gambling Operations Carried On by Religious, Charitable, or Other Nonprofit Organizations from General Prohibitions against Gambling." *American Law Reports 3rd* 42 (1972): 663.

Tversky, A., and D. Kahneman. "The Framing of Decisions and the Psychology of Choice." *Science* 211, no. 4481 (1981): 453–58.

Tyler, Tom R. *Why People Obey the Law.* New Haven, Conn.: Yale University Press, 1990.

Ugel, Edward. *Money for Nothing: One Man's Journey Through the Dark Side of Lottery Millions.* New York: HarperCollins, 2007.

UK National Lottery. "Lottery Funders Listing." http://www.lottery funding.org.uk/uk/lottery-funders-uk/lottery-funders-listing.htm (accessed August 31, 2007).

———. "National Lottery for Good Causes." http://www.lotterygood-causes.org.uk/.

U.S. Bureau of the Census. *Social and Economic Characteristics, American Indians and Native Alaska Areas.* Washington, D.C.: U.S. Department of Commerce, 1990. Available at http://www .census.gov/prod/cen1990/cp2/cp-2.html.

———. *Social and Economic Characteristics, American Indians and Native Alaska Areas.* Washington, D.C.: U.S. Department of Commerce, 2000. Available at http://factfinder.census.gov/home/ aian/sf1_sf3.html.

———. *State Government Tax Collections 2004.* Washington, D.C.: U.S. Department of Commerce, 2005. Available at http://www. census.gov/govs/www/statetax04.html.

———. *Statistical Abstract of the United States: 2006.* Washington, D.C.: U.S. Department of Commerce.

U.S. Commission on Civil Rights. *A Quiet Crisis: Federal Funding and Unmet Needs in Indian Country.* Washington, D.C.: U.S. Government Printing Office, 2003.

Vitaro, Frank, Robert Ladouceur, and Annie Bujold. "Predictive and Concurrent Correlates of Gambling in Early Adolescent Boys." *Journal of Early Adolescence* 16 (1996): 211–28.

Vitello, Paul. "The Taxman Hits, in the Guise of a Traffic Cop." *New York Times,* July 15, 2007.

Volberg, Rachel A., Dean R. Gerstein, Eugene Christiansen, and John Baldridge. "Assessing Self-Reported Expenditures on Gambling." *Managerial and Decision Economics* 22 (2001): 77–96.

Volberg, Rachel A., Kari L. Nysee-Carris, and Dean R. Gerstein. *California Problem Gambling Prevalence Survey: Final Report.* Chicago: National Opinion Research Center, 2006.

Volkow, N. D., and T. Li. "Drug Addiction: The Neurobiology of Behaviour Gone Awry." *Nature Reviews Neuroscience* 5, no. 12 (2004): 963–70.

Voon, V., K. Hassan, M. Zurowski, M. de Souza, T. Thomsen, S. Fox, A. E. Lang, and J. Miyasaki. "Prevalence of Repetitive and Reward-Seeking Behaviors in Parkinson's Disease." *Neurology* 67 (2006): 1254–57.

Voon, V., K. Hassan, M. Zurowski, S. Duff-Canning, M. de Souza, S. Fox, and A. E. Lang. "Prospective Prevalence of Pathological Gambling and Medication Association in Parkinson's Disease." *Neurology* 66 (2006): 1750–52.

Voon, V., T. Thomsen, J. M. Miyasaki, M. de Souza, A. Shafro, S. H. Fox, S. Duff-Canning, A. E. Lang, and M. Zurowski. "Factors Associated with Dopaminergic Drug-Related Pathological Gambling in Parkinson's Disease." *Archives of Neurology* 64 (2007): 212–16.

Wagenaar, W. A. "Generation of Random Sequences by Human Subjects: A Critical Survey of the Literature." *Psychological Bulletin* 77, no. 1 (1972): 65–72.

Wagner, John. "O'Malley Aide Offers Case for Md. Slots; Residents' Spending In Other States Cited." *Washington Post*, August 15, 2007.

Walker, Douglas M. "Challenges that Confront Researchers on Estimating the Social Costs of Gambling." American Gaming Association, January 3, 2008. Available at http://americangaming .org/.

———. "Methodological Issues in the Social Cost of Gambling Studies." *Journal of Gambling Studies* 19 (2003): 149–84.

Walker, Douglas M., and A. H. Barnett. "The Social Cost of Gambling: An Economic Perspective." *Journal of Gambling Studies* 15 (1999): 3.

Walker, Douglas M., and John D. Jackson. "New Goods and Economic Growth: Evidence from Legalized Gambling." *Review of Regional Studies* 28 (1998): 47–69.

Walker, Ian. "The Economic Analysis of Lotteries." *Economic Policy* 13, no. 27 (1998), 358–401.

Walker, Jack L. "The Diffusion of Innovations among the American States." *American Political Science Review* 63 (1969): 880–99.

Wallach, M. A., N. Kogan, and D. J. Bem. "Group Influence on Individual Risk Taking." *Journal of Abnormal and Social Psychology* 65 (1962): 75–86.

Weaver, Kent. *Ending Welfare as We Know It*. Washington, D.C.: Brookings, 2000.

Weems, Mason Locke. *Anecdotes of Gamblers, Extracted from a Work on Gamblers*. Philadelphia: Benjamin & Thomas Kite, 1816.

———. *God's revenge against gambling exemplified in the miserable lives and untimely deaths of a number of persons from both sexes, who had sacrificed their health, wealth, and honor at the gambling tables*. Philadelphia: n.p., 1812.

Weier, John W. *Gambling: What's at Stake?* Detroit: Thompson/Gale, 2007.

Weintraub, D., and Marc N. Potenza. "Impulse Control Disorders in Parkinson's Disease." *Current Neurology and Neuroscience Reports* 6 (2006): 302–6.

Weintraub, D., A. D. Siderow, Marc N. Potenza, J. Goveas, K. H. Morales, J. E. Duda, P. J. Moberg, and M. B. Stern. "Dopamine Agonist Use Is Associated with Impulse Control Disorders in Parkinson's Disease." *Archives of Neurology* 63 (2006): 969–73.

Weiss, Harry B., and Grace M. Weiss. *The Early Lotteries of New Jersey*. Trenton, N.J.: The Past Times Press, 1966.

Weiss, Raymond L. "The Adaptation of Philosophic Ethics to a Religious Community: Maimonides' Eight Chapters." *Proceedings of the American Academy for Jewish Research* 54 (1987): 261–87.

Weitzer, Ronald. "The Moral Crusade Against Prostitution." *Society* 43 (2006): 33–38.

Welte, J. W., G. M. Barnes, W. F. Wieczorek, M. Tidwell, and J. Parker. "Alcohol and Gambling Pathology among U.S. Adults: Prevalence, Demographic Patterns, and Comorbidity." *Journal of Studies on Alcohol* 62 (2001): 706–12.

———. "Risk Factors for Pathological Gambling." *Addictive Behaviors* 29 (2004): 323–35.

Westen, Drew. *The Political Brain: The Role of Emotion in Deciding the Fate of the Nation*. New York: PublicAffairs Books, 2007.

Weyler, Karen A. "'A Speculating Spirit': Trade, Speculation, and Gambling in Early American Fiction." *Early American Literature* 31 (1996): 207–42.

White, G. Edward. *Tort Law in America: An Intellectual History*. New York: Oxford University Press, 1981.

Whyte, Keith S. "Analysis of National Gambling Impact Study Commission Act." *Journal of Gambling Studies* 14 (1998): 309–18.

Widermuth, John. "Expensive Ballot Fight Looms on February Vote over Indian Casinos." *San Francisco Chronicle*, December 7, 2007.

Wilkins, David E. *American Indian Sovereignty and the U.S. Supreme Court: The Masking of Justice*. Austin: University of Texas Press, 1997.

Williams, Lou Falkner. *The Great South Carolina Ku Klux Klan Trials: 1871–1872*. Athens: University of Georgia Press, 2004.

Williams, W. A., and Marc N. Potenza. "The Neurobiology of Impulse Control Disorders." *Revista Brasileira Psiquiatria* 30, no. 1 (2008): 24–30.

Wilson, James Q. *Political Organizations*. Princeton: Princeton University Press, 1995.

Winters, Ken C., Steven M. Specker, and Ronald D. Stinchfield. "Measuring Pathological Gambling with the Diagnostic Interview for Gambling Severity (DIGS)." In *The Down-side: Problem and Pathological Gambling*, edited by Jeffrey J. Marotta, Judy A.

Cornelius, and William R. Eadington. Reno: Institute for the Study of Gambling and Commercial Gaming, University of Nevada, 2002.

Wolfe, Alan. *One Nation after All: What Middle-Class Americans Really Think about God, Country, Family, Racism, Welfare, Immigration, Homosexuality, the Right, the Left, and Each Other.* New York: Viking, 1998.

———. *The Transformation of American Religion: How We Actually Live Our Faith.* New York: Free Press, 2003.

———. "What We Don't Know about Gambling, but Should." *Chronicle of Higher Education,* October 12, 2007.

Wuthnow, Robert. *The Restructuring of American Religion: Society and Faith Since World War II.* Princeton: Princeton University Press, 1988.

Wyatt-Brown, Bertram. *Southern Honor: Ethics and Behavior in the Old South.* New York: Oxford University Press, 1982.

Young, James Sterling. *The Washington Community, 1800–1828.* New York: Harcourt, Brace & World, 1966.

Zack, M., and C. X. Poulos. "A D2 Antagonist Enhances the Rewarding and Priming Effects of a Gambling Episode in Pathological Gamblers." *Neuropsychopharmacology* 32 (2007): 1678–86.

———. "Amphetamine Primes Motivation to Gamble and Gambling-Related Semantic Networks in Problem Gamblers." *Neuropsychopharmacology* 29 (2004): 195–207.

Zelenak, Lawrence. "The Puzzling Case of the Revenue-Maximizing Lottery." *North Carolina Law Review* 79 (2000): 1–43.

Zimring, Franklin E. *The Great American Crime Decline.* New York: Oxford University Press, 2006.

Cases and Public Laws

Act of August 15, 1953. Public Law 83-280, chap. 505, 67 Stat. 588–590 (1953). Codified as amended at 18 U.S.C. § 1162, 28 U.S.C. § 1360, and other scattered sections in Titles 18 and 28, United States Code (2000).

Bryan v. Itasca County, 426 U.S. 373 (1976).

California v. Cabazon Band of Mission Indians, 480 U.S. 202 (1987).

Champion v. Ames, 188 U.S. 321 (1903).

Cherokee Nation v. Georgia, 30 U.S. (5 Pet.) 1 (1831).

Costello v. United States, 350 U.S. 359 (1956).

Federal Trade Comm'n v. R. F. Keppel & Bro., 291 U.S. 304 (1934).

Hammer v. Dagenhart, 247 U.S. 251 (1918).

Indian Gaming Regulatory Act of 1988. 25 U.S.C. §§ 2701–21.

Massachusetts General Laws, chap. 271, § 7A (April 14, 2005). Available at http://www.mass.gov/legis/laws/mgl/.

Nevada Gaming Control Act, Nev. Rev. Stat. § 463.0129(1).

North Carolina General Statutes, § 14-309.15 (2007). Available at http://www.nega.state.nc.us/gascripts/Statures/Statutes.asp.

Panama Refining Co. v. Ryan, 293 U.S. 388 (1935).

Perez v. United States, 402 U.S. 146 (1971).

Pollock v. Farmers' Loan & Trust Co., 158 U.S. 601 (1895).

R. F. Keppel & Bro. v. FTC, 63 F.2d 81 (3d Cir. 1933).

Roe v. Wade, 410 U.S. 113 (1973).

Scarborough v. United States, 431 U.S. 563 (1977).

Schechter Poultry Corp. v. United States, 295 U.S. 495 (1935).

Seminole Tribe of Florida v. Butterworth, 658 F.2d 310 (1981).

Seminole Tribe of Florida v. Florida, 517 U.S. 44 (1996).

Sen. Rep. No. 446. 100th Cong., 2d sess., 1988. Reprinted in 1988 U.S.C.C.A.N. 3071 (1988).

United States v. Butler, 297 U.S. 1 (1936).

United States v. Jimenez-Torres, 435 F.3d 3 (1st Cir. 2006).

Unlawful Internet Gambling Enforcement Act of 2006. Pub. L. No. 109-374, 120 Stat. 1884.

Washington v. Confederated Colville Tribes, 447 U.S. 134 (1980).

Worcester v. Georgia, 30 U.S. 515 (1832).

List of Contributors

Dwayne Eugène Carpenter is professor of Hispanic studies, chair of the Department of Romance Languages and Literatures, and codirector of the Jewish Studies Program at Boston College. The author of several books on medieval religious and intellectual history, he has a special interest in the historical role of gambling in society. Among his gambling-related articles are "Fickle Fortune: Gambling in Medieval Spain" (*Studies in Philology*, 1988) and "'Alea jacta est': At the Gaming Table with Alfonso the Learned" (*Journal of Medieval History*, 1998). Carpenter holds a Ph.D. in Romance languages and literatures from the University of California, Berkeley, as well as a Ph.D. in medieval historical studies from the Graduate Theological Union, Berkeley.

Charles T. Clotfelter is Z. Smith Reynolds Professor of Public Policy Studies, professor of economics and law, and director of the Center for the Study of Philanthropy and Voluntarism of the Terry Sanford Institute of Public Policy at Duke University. He received his Ph.D. in economics from Harvard University. His research interests are the economics of education, the nonprofit sector, public finance, and tax policy. He is the author of *After Brown: The Rise and Retreat of School Desegregation* (Princeton, 2004); *Buying the Best: Cost Escalation in Elite Higher Education* (Princeton, 1996); and *Federal Tax Policy and Charitable Giving* (Chicago, 1985). He has also coauthored *Economic*

Challenges in Higher Education (with R. Ehrenberg, M. Getz, and J. Siegried, Chicago, 1991) and *Selling Hope: State Lotteries in America* (with P. Cook, Harvard, 1989).

Philip J. Cook is ITT/Terry Sanford Distinguished Professor of Public Policy Studies, professor of economics, professor of sociology, and associate director of the Terry Sanford Institute of Public Policy at Duke University. He received his Ph.D. in economics from the University of California, Berkeley. He has served as consultant to the U.S. Department of Justice (Criminal Division) and the U.S. Department of Treasury (Enforcement Division). He has also served in a variety of capacities with the National Academy of Sciences, including membership on expert panels dealing with alcohol abuse prevention, violence, and school shootings. Cook is a member of the Division Committee for the Behavioral and Social Sciences and Education. His books include *Gun Violence: The Real Costs* (with J. Ludwig, Oxford, 2000); *The Winner-Take-All Society* (with R. H. Frank, Free Press, 1995); and *Selling Hope: State Lotteries in America* (with C. Clotfelter, Harvard, 1989).

Rachel T. A. Croson holds a joint appointment as professor of economics in the School of Economic, Political and Policy Sciences and as professor of organizations, strategy, and international management in the School of Management, both at the University of Texas at Dallas. She holds a Ph.D. and an A.M. in economics from Harvard University and a B.A. from the University of Pennsylvania. The author of dozens of scholarly articles and book chapters, including several on the "gambler's fallacy," Croson brings the insights of behavioral economics to bear upon decision-making practices. Her research involves the experimental and empirical study of how individuals make strategic decisions, especially those concerning negotiation/bargaining and contributions to public goods. She is a member of numerous scholarly editorial boards and foundation advisory boards.

John Dombrink is a professor in the Department of Criminology, Law, and Society at the University of California, Irvine. He received his Ph.D. in sociology from the University of California, Berkeley, where he was a research assistant on Jerome Skolnick's landmark *House of Cards: Legalization and Control of Casino Gambling* (Little, Brown, 1978). He is the author of several articles on gambling in America and coauthor of a book about gambling legalization, *The Last Resort: Success and Failure in Campaigns for Casinos* (with W. N. Thompson, Nevada, 1990). With Daniel Hillyard, he is the author of *Dying Right:*

The Death with Dignity Movement (Routledge, 2001), a study of the legal reform of physician-assisted suicide. With Daniel Hillyard, he is also the author of *Sin No More: From Abortion to Stem Cells—Crime, Law, and Morality in America* (NYU, 2007), in which the authors examine current "morality contests" in American culture, assess the status of American laws and attitudes toward the sphere of personal morality, and address the issues of the "values voters," polarization, religion, ambivalence, and framing strategies.

Matthew Fox is an Ph.D. student at Duke University and received his BA from Colorado College. He is a founding director of Animal House Rescue and Elko County Habitat for Humanity. His research interests include organizational behavior, nonprofit management, corporate social responsibility, and, more broadly, how organizations make and implement decisions where profit is not the deciding factor.

William Galston is Senior Fellow in Governance Studies at the Brookings Institution and College Park Professor at the University of Maryland School of Public Policy. He holds a Ph.D. and an M.A. from the University of Chicago and a B.A. from Cornell University. He is a political theorist who both studies and participates in American politics and domestic policy. Galston was deputy assistant to the president for domestic policy during the first Clinton Administration and executive director of the National Commission on Civic Renewal, which was chaired by Sam Nunn and William Bennett. His books include *Public Matters: Essays on Politics, Policy, and Religion* (Rowman & Littlefield, 2005); *The Practice of Liberal Pluralism* (Cambridge, 2004); and *Liberal Pluralism: The Implications of Value Pluralism for Political Theory and Practice* (Cambridge, 2002).

John P. Hoffmann is professor of sociology at Brigham Young University. He earned a B.S. from James Madison University, an M.S. from American University, a Ph.D. from the State University of New York at Albany, and an M.P.H. from Emory University. His research interests include adolescent health behaviors, the causes and consequences of drug use, and the intersection of norms, attitudes, and religion. Selected publications include *Japanese Saints* (Lexington, 2007); "Drug Use and Job Quits: A Longitudinal Analysis" (*Journal of Drug Issues*, 2007); "Extracurricular Activities, Athletic Participation, and Adolescent Alcohol Use" (*Journal of Health and Social Behavior*, 2006); and "Religion and Problem Gambling in the United States" (*Review of Religious Research*, 2000). He is currently working on a book on empathy and social values.

T. J. Jackson Lears is Board of Governors Professor of History at Rutgers University and editor-in-chief of the *Raritan Quarterly Review*. He earned a B.A. from the University of Virginia, an M.A. from the University of North Carolina at Chapel Hill, and a Ph.D. from Yale. His research interests include U.S. cultural and intellectual history, comparative religious history, literature and the visual arts, folklore, and folk beliefs. Selected publications include *Something for Nothing: Luck in America* (Viking Penguin, 2003); *Fables of Abundance: A Cultural History of Advertising in America* (Basic Books, 1994); and *No Place of Grace: Antimodernism and the Transformation of American Culture, 1880–1920* (Pantheon, 1981; reissued by Chicago, 1994; Japanese translation by Shohakusha Publishing, forthcoming).

Steven Andrew Light is associate professor of political science and public administration and codirector of the Institute for the Study of Tribal Gaming Law and Policy at the University of North Dakota. He received a B.A. from Yale University and a Ph.D. in political science from Northwestern University. He has published widely on Indian gaming as well as policy implementation, affirmative action, environmental racism, and voting rights. He is coauthor of three books: *Indian Gaming and Tribal Sovereignty: The Casino Compromise* (Kansas, 2005); *Indian Gaming Law and Policy* (Carolina Academic, 2006); and *Indian Gaming Law: Cases and Materials* (Carolina Academic, 2008); and is writing *"The Law is Good": The Voting Rights Act, Redistricting, and Black Regime Politics* (Carolina Academic). He has testified on Indian gaming regulation before the U.S. Senate Committee on Indian Affairs and was featured on C-SPAN's *Book TV*. He is a member of the International Masters of Gaming Law and is a frequent media commentator on tribal gaming.

Richard McGowan, S.J., is associate professor of operations and strategic management at Boston College and research associate at the Harvard Medical School Division on Addictions. He received a D.B.A. in 1988 from Boston University. His research focuses on the interaction of business and public policy processes, especially as they relate to the gambling, tobacco, and alcohol industries. He has published six books: *State Lotteries and Legalized Gambling: Painless Revenue or Painful Mirage* (Quorum, 1994); *Business, Politics, and Cigarettes: Multiple Levels, Multiple Agendas* (Greenwood Press, 1995); *Industry as a Player in the Social and Political Arenas* (Quorum, 1996); *The Search for Revenue and the Common Good: An Analysis of Government Regulation of the Alcohol Industry* (Prager, 1997); *Government and the Transformation of the Gaming Industry* (Edward Elgar, 2001);

and *The Gambling Debate* (Greenwood Press, 2008). He is currently working on a book on the interaction of government with the accounting industry with Gregory Trompeter of Boston College's Accounting Department.

R. Shep Melnick is Thomas P. O'Neill Jr. Professor of American Politics at Boston College. His research and writing focuses on the intersection of law and politics. His first book, *Regulation and the Courts* (Brookings, 1983), examined judicial influence on the development of environmental policy. His second, *Between the Lines* (Brookings, 1994), investigated the ways in which statutory interpretation has shaped a variety of entitlement programs. His current research project looks at how the Rehnquist Court reshaped our governing institutions. Melnick is co-chair of the Harvard Program on Constitutional Government and a past president of the New England Political Science Department. Before coming to Boston College in 1997, he taught at Harvard and Brandeis, where he served as chair of the Politics Department.

Michael Nelson is Fulmer Professor of Political Science at Rhodes College in Memphis. He earned a B.A. from the College of William and Mary and an M.A. and Ph.D. from Johns Hopkins University. He teaches courses on U.S. politics, the American presidency, Southern politics, and the constitutional convention. He also teaches the college's humanities course, The Search for Values in the Light of Western History and Religion, and coauthored a book about the course, *Celebrating the Humanities: A Half Century of the Search Course at Rhodes College* (Vanderbilt, 1996). Nelson has published twenty-one books, the most recent of which are *How the South Joined the Gambling Nation: The Politics of State Policy Innovation* (with J. M. Mason, LSU, 2007; winner of the V.O. Key Book Award from the Southern Political Science Association), *The Elections of 2008* (CQ Press, 2009), *The American Presidency: Origins and Development, 1776–2007* (with S. M. Milkis, CQ Press, 2007); *The Presidency and the Political System*, 8th ed. (CQ Press, 2006); and *Governing Gambling: Politics and Policy in State, Tribe, and Nation* (with J. M. Mason, Century Foundation, 2000).

Erik C. Owens is assistant director of the Boisi Center for Religion and American Public Life and adjunct assistant professor of theology at Boston College. His research explores a variety of intersections between religion and public life, with particular attention to the challenge of fostering the common good of a religiously diverse society. His scholarship is fundamentally interdisciplinary, bridging the fields of theological ethics, political philosophy, law, education, and public policy. At work on a book about civic education and religious freedom in American public schools, he is the author of several scholarly articles and coeditor of two books: *Religion and the Death Penalty: A Call for Reckoning* (Eerdmans, 2004) and *The Sacred and the Sovereign: Religion and International Politics* (Georgetown, 2003). He holds a Ph.D. in religious ethics from the University of Chicago, an M.T.S. from Harvard Divinity School, and a B.A. from Duke University.

Marc N. Potenza is associate professor of psychiatry (Division of Substance Abuse), director of the Problem Gambling Clinic, director of neuroimaging for the VA MIRECC, and director of the Women and Addictive Disorders Core of Women's Health Research at Yale University. He holds a Ph.D. in cell biology and an M.D. from Yale University. Potenza investigates the relationship between behavioral addictions and drug addictions with particular focus on the etiology and treatment of pathological gambling and the relationship between pathological gambling and drug use disorders. His research group uses a variety of investigative approaches—fMRI neuroimaging, molecular genetic, clinical treatment trials, and epidemiological analyses—to investigate these areas. He is the coeditor of *Pathological Gambling: A Clinical Guide to Treatment* (American Psychiatric, 2004), and the author of many articles on pathological gambling, including "Should Addictive Disorders Include Non-Substance-Related Conditions?" (*Addiction*, 2006); "Shared Genetic Contributions to Major Depression and Pathological Gambling" (with Hong Xian et al., *Archives of General Psychiatry*, 2005); and "Pathological Gambling" (with T. R. Kosten and B. J. Rounsaville, *Journal of the American Medical Association*, 2001).

Kathryn R.L. Rand is dean and Floyd B. Sperry Professor of Law at the University of North Dakota School of Law, and is codirector of the Institute for the Study of Tribal Gaming Law and Policy. She received a B.A. from the University of North Dakota and a J.D. from the University of Michigan School of Law. She has published widely on Indian gaming as well as sex equality, affirmative action, and environmental racism. She is coauthor of three books: *Indian Gaming and Tribal Sovereignty: The Casino Compromise* (Kansas, 2005); *Indian Gaming Law and Policy* (Carolina Academic, 2006); and *Indian Gaming Law: Cases and Materials* (Carolina Academic, 2008). She has testified on Indian gaming regulation before the U.S. Senate Committee on Indian Affairs and was featured on C-SPAN's *Book TV*. She is a member of the International Masters of Gaming Law and the Editorial Board of the *Gaming Law Review*, and is a frequent media commentator on tribal gaming.

David A. Skeel Jr. is S. Samuel Arsht Professor of Corporate Law at the University of Pennsylvania. He writes on corporate law, bankruptcy, Christianity and law and other topics. He is the author of *Icarus in the Boardroom: The Fundamental Flaws in Corporate America and Where They Came From* (Oxford, 2005) and *Debt's Dominion: A History of Bankruptcy Law in America* (Princeton, 2001), as well as numerous articles. His most recent articles include "Governance in the Ruins" (*Harvard Law Review*, 2008) and "The Unbearable Lightness of Christian Legal Scholarship," (*Emory Law Journal*, 2008). He holds a J.D. from the University of Virginia and a B.A. from the University of North Carolina.

William Stuntz is Henry J. Friendly Professor of Law and vice dean for intellectual life at Harvard Law School. He received a B.A. from the College of William and Mary and a J.D. from the University of Virginia School of Law. His research interests are Christianity and legal theory, crime policy, and criminal law and procedure. Recent publications include "Christian Legal Theory" (*Harvard Law Review*, 2003); "Local Policing After the Terror" (*Yale Law Journal*, 2002); and *Comprehensive Criminal Procedure* (with R. J. Allen, J. L. Hoffman, and D. A. Livingston, (*Aspen Law & Business*, 2001).

James Sundali is an associate professor of managerial sciences at the University of Nevada, Reno. He holds a B.S. and an M.B.A. from California Polytechnic State University as well as a Ph.D. from the University of Arizona. His research interests include judgment and decision making, game theory, experimental economics, and behavioral finance. With Rachel Croson, he is the author of "Biases in Casino Betting: The Hot Hand and the Gambler's Fallacy" (*Judgment and Decision Making*, 2006) and "The Gambler's Fallacy and the Hot Hand: Empirical Data from Casinos" (*Journal of Risk and Uncertainty*, 2005).

Kathryn Tanner is Dorothy Grant Maclear Professor of Theology at the University of Chicago Divinity School. She holds a B.A., M.A., and Ph.D. from Yale University. Tanner is a Christian theologian in the Protestant tradition; she addresses contemporary challenges to belief through the creative use of the history of Christian thought and interdisciplinary methods such as critical, social, and feminist theory. Her books *God and Creation in Christian Theology* (Fortress, 2004) and *The Politics of God* (Fortress, 1992) discuss the coherence and practical force of Christian beliefs about God's relation to the world. *Theories of Culture: A New Agenda for Theology* (Fortress, 1997) explores the relevance of cultural studies for rethinking theological method. Her brief systematic theology, *Jesus, Humanity, and the Trinity* (Fortress, 2001), centers on the incarnation. Her latest book, *Economy of Grace* (Fortress, 2005), explores the intersections between theology and economics.

Alan Wolfe is professor of political science and director of the Boisi Center for Religion and American Public Life at Boston College. He earned a B.A. from Temple University and a Ph.D. in political science from the University of Pennsylvania. He currently chairs a task force of the American Political Science Association on Religion and Democracy in the United States. He serves on the advisory boards of Humanity in Action and the Future of American Democracy Foundation and on the president's advisory board of the Massachusetts Foundation for the Humanities. He is also a senior fellow with the World Policy Institute at the New School University in New York. He is the author, most recently, of *The Future of Liberalism* (Knopf, 2009); *Does American Democracy Still Work?* (Yale, 2006); *Return to Greatness: How America Lost Its Sense of Purpose and What it Needs to Do to Recover It* (Princeton, 2005); and *The Transformation of American Religion: How We Actually Practice Our Faith* (Free Press, 2003).

Index